TYPE

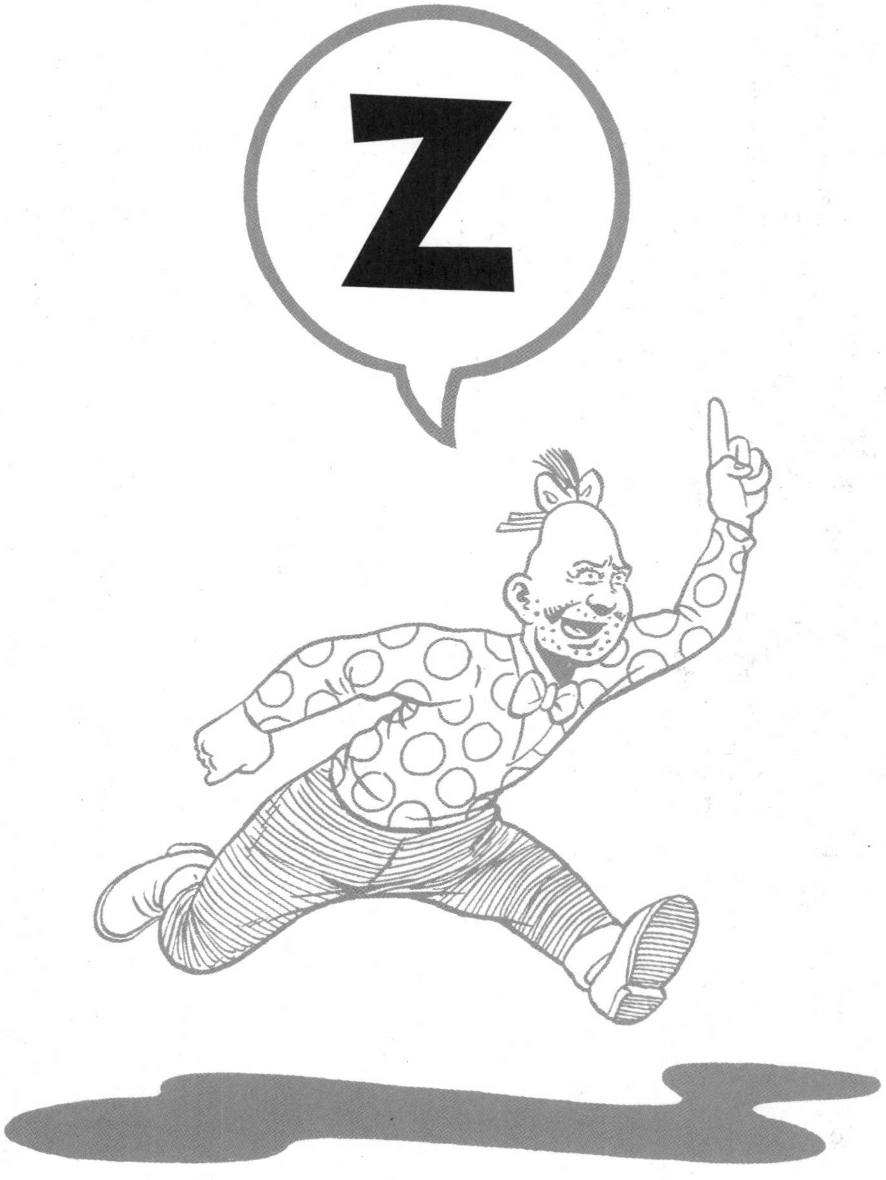
Z

PERSONALITY

TYPE Z

PERSONALITY

ZIPPY

DECEMBER 2004 - DECEMBER 2005

BILL GRIFFITH

FANTAGRAPHICS BOOKS

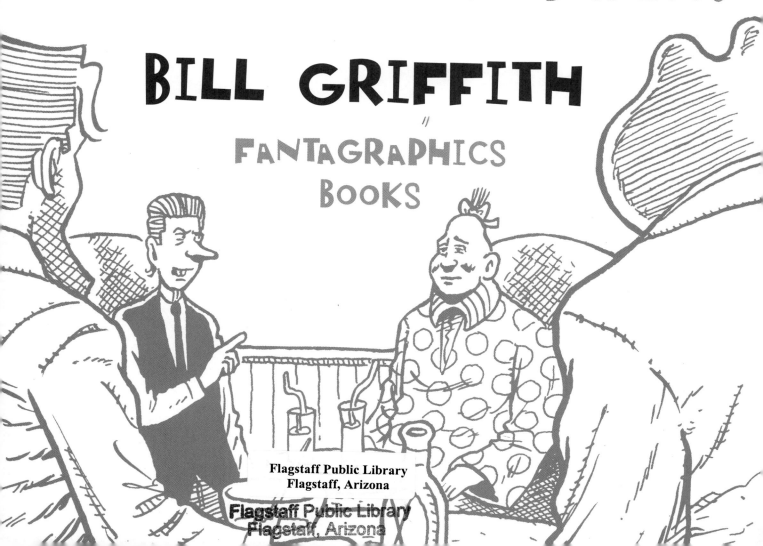

ZIPPY / Type Z Personality
Zippy Annual — Volume 6
Copyright © 2004, 2005 Bill Griffith
All rights reserved, including the right to reproduce
this book or portions thereof in any form.

FANTAGRAPHICS BOOKS

7563 Lake City Way NE, Seattle WA 98115
www.fantagraphics.com
Call 1-800-657-1100 for a full color catalog
of fine comics publications.

First Edition: November 2005
Designed by Bill Griffith
Production managed by Kim Thompson
Production by Paul Baresh
Cover Production by Paul Baresh
Published by Gary Groth and Kim Thompson

Printed in Malaysia
ISBN: 1-56097-698-5

The comic strips in this book have appeared in
newspapers in the United States and abroad, distributed by
King Features Syndicate, 888 7th Avenue, NY NY 10019
www.kingfeatures.com

For more on Zippy (and many added features, including the
"Zippy Storefront" and extensive strip Archives), visit:
www.zippythepinhead.com

Thanks and a tip o' th' pin to: Diane Noomin, Jon Buller Jay
Kennedy, American Color, Gary Groth, Kim Thompson, Kristin
Griffin and all the roadside field researchers who continue to send
in so many great photos.

Books by Bill Griffith:
*Zippy Stories • Nation of Pinheads • Pointed Behavior
Pindemonium • Are We Having Fun Yet? • Kingpin
Pinhead's Progress • Get Me A Table Without Flies, Harry
From A To Zippy • Zippy's House of Fun
Griffith Observatory • Zippy Annual #1 • Zippy Annual 2001
Zippy Annual 2002 • Zippy Annual 2003
ZIPPY: From Here To Absurdity*

To contact Bill Griffith (Practitioner of Zippy Arts, P.Z.A.):
Pinhead Productions, LLC
P.O. Box 88, Hadlyme CT 06439
Griffy@zippythepinhead.com

ZIPPY & GRIFFY

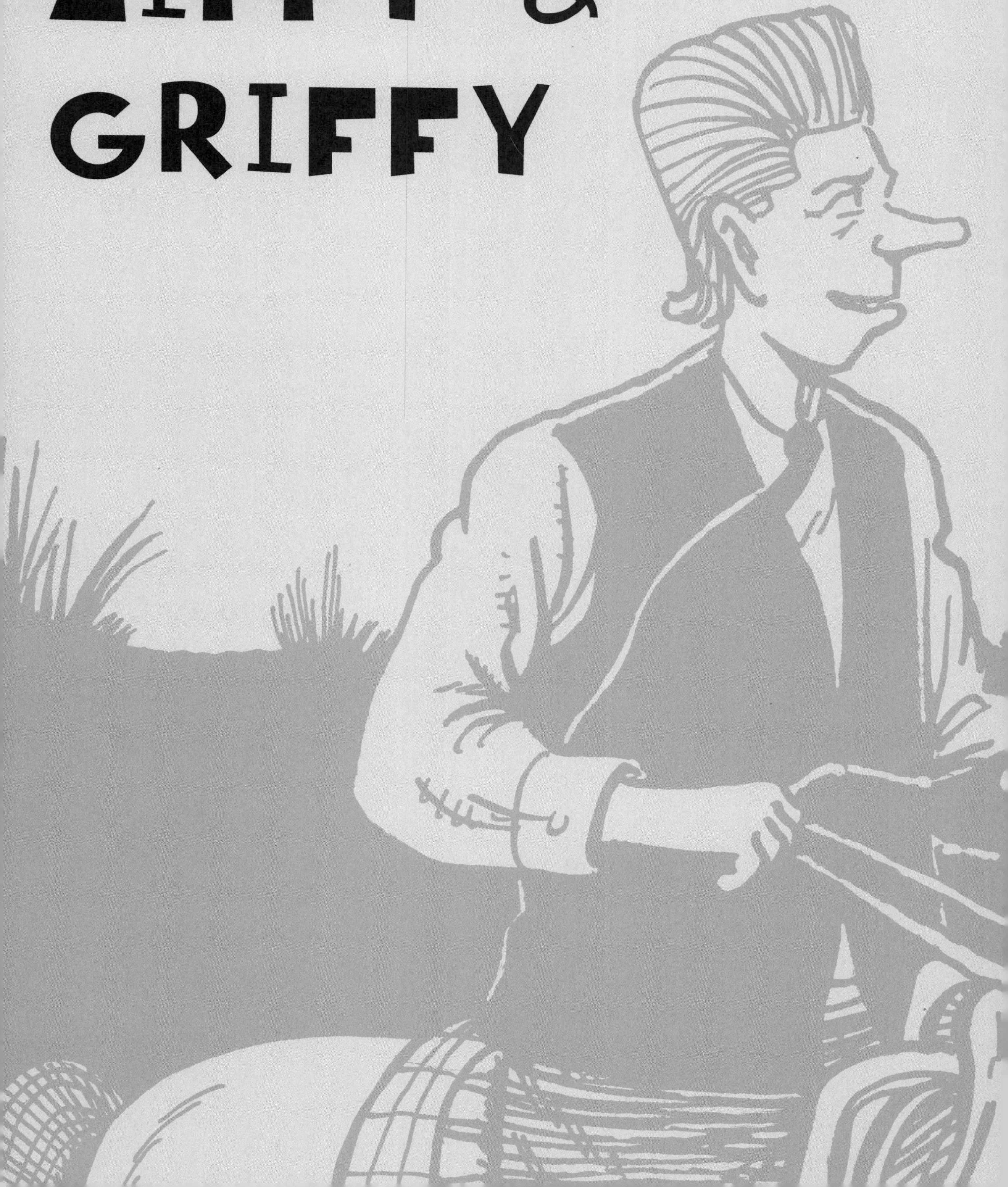

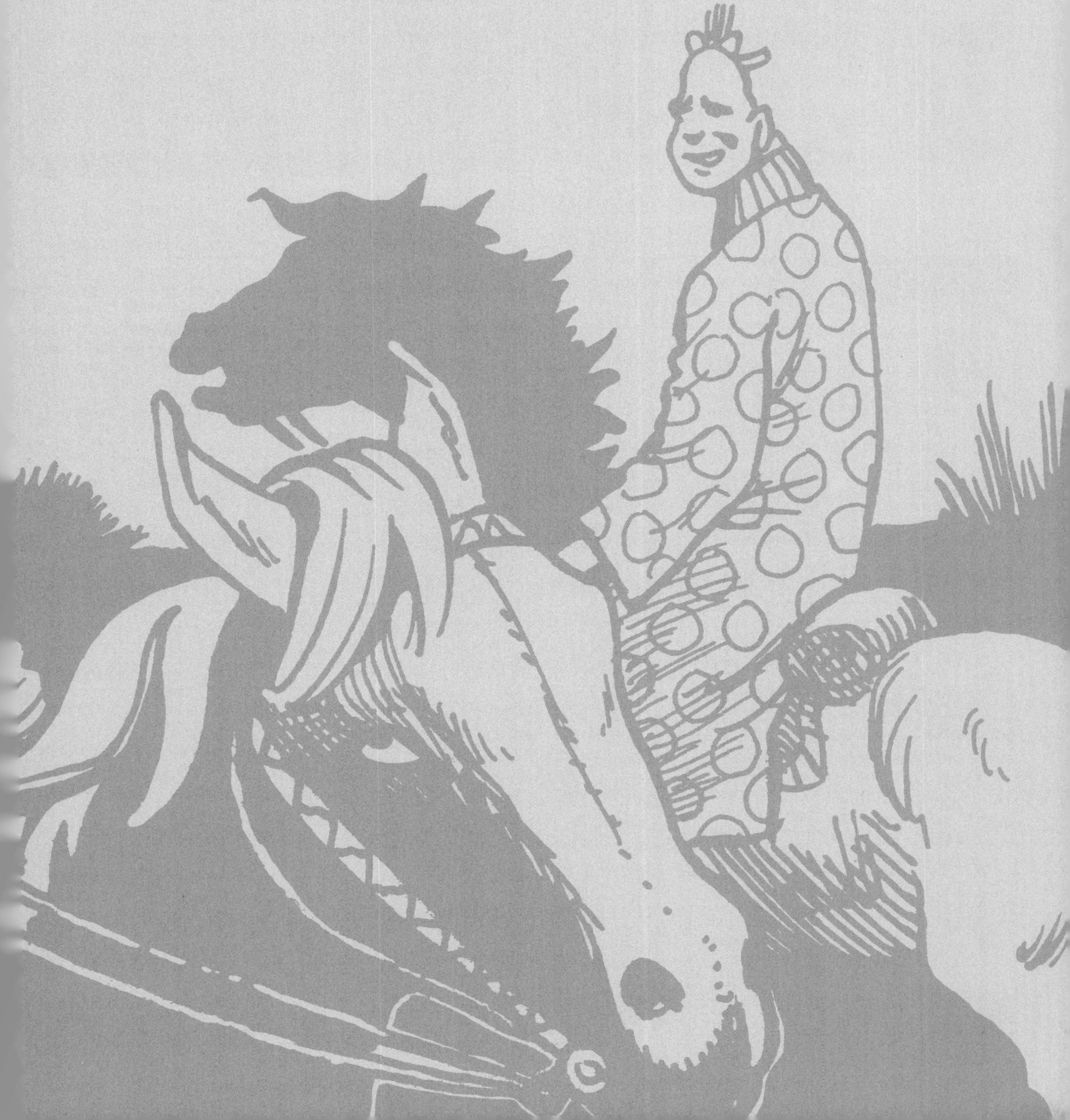

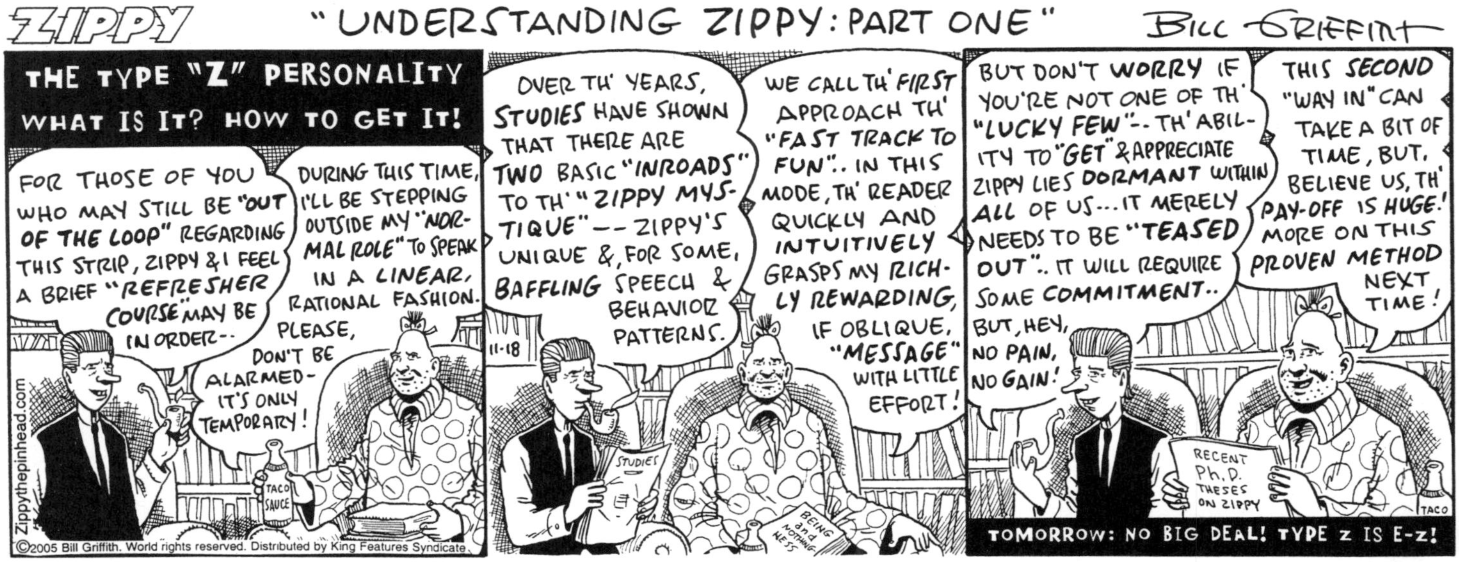
ZIPPY
"UNDERSTANDING ZIPPY: PART ONE"
BILL GRIFFITH
THE TYPE "Z" PERSONALITY
WHAT IS IT? HOW TO GET IT!
FOR THOSE OF YOU WHO MAY STILL BE "OUT OF THE LOOP" REGARDING THIS STRIP, ZIPPY & I FEEL A BRIEF "REFRESHER COURSE" MAY BE IN ORDER--
DURING THIS TIME, I'LL BE STEPPING OUTSIDE MY "NORMAL ROLE" TO SPEAK IN A LINEAR, RATIONAL FASHION.
PLEASE, DON'T BE ALARMED-- IT'S ONLY TEMPORARY!
TACO SAUCE
Zippythepinhead.com
©2005 Bill Griffith. World rights reserved. Distributed by King Features Syndicate
11-18
OVER TH' YEARS, STUDIES HAVE SHOWN THAT THERE ARE TWO BASIC "INROADS" TO TH' "ZIPPY MYSTIQUE" -- ZIPPY'S UNIQUE &, FOR SOME, BAFFLING SPEECH & BEHAVIOR PATTERNS.
WE CALL TH' FIRST APPROACH TH' "FAST TRACK TO FUN".. IN THIS MODE, TH' READER QUICKLY AND INTUITIVELY GRASPS MY RICHLY REWARDING, IF OBLIQUE, "MESSAGE" WITH LITTLE EFFORT!
STUDIES
BEING AND NOTHINGNESS
BUT DON'T WORRY IF YOU'RE NOT ONE OF TH' "LUCKY FEW"-- TH' ABILITY TO "GET" & APPRECIATE ZIPPY LIES DORMANT WITHIN ALL OF US... IT MERELY NEEDS TO BE "TEASED OUT".. IT WILL REQUIRE SOME COMMITMENT..
BUT, HEY, NO PAIN, NO GAIN!
THIS SECOND "WAY IN" CAN TAKE A BIT OF TIME, BUT. BELIEVE US, TH' PAY-OFF IS HUGE! MORE ON THIS PROVEN METHOD NEXT TIME!
RECENT Ph.D. THESES ON ZIPPY
TACO
TOMORROW: NO BIG DEAL! TYPE Z IS E-Z!

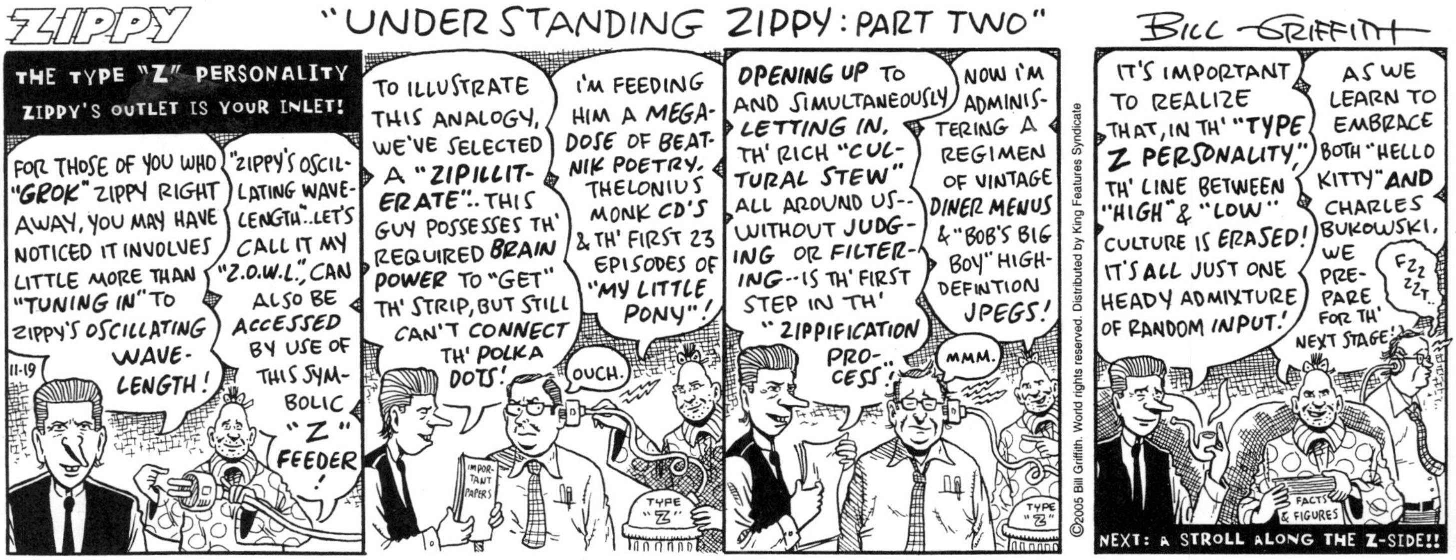
ZIPPY
"UNDERSTANDING ZIPPY: PART TWO"
BILL GRIFFITH
THE TYPE "Z" PERSONALITY
ZIPPY'S OUTLET IS YOUR INLET!
FOR THOSE OF YOU WHO "GROK" ZIPPY RIGHT AWAY, YOU MAY HAVE NOTICED IT INVOLVES LITTLE MORE THAN "TUNING IN" TO ZIPPY'S OSCILLATING WAVE-LENGTH!
"ZIPPY'S OSCILLATING WAVE-LENGTH".. LET'S CALL IT MY "Z.O.W.L.", CAN ALSO BE ACCESSED BY USE OF THIS SYMBOLIC "Z" FEEDER!
11-19
TO ILLUSTRATE THIS ANALOGY, WE'VE SELECTED A "ZIPILLITERATE".. THIS GUY POSSESSES TH' REQUIRED BRAIN POWER TO "GET" TH' STRIP, BUT STILL CAN'T CONNECT TH' POLKA DOTS!
I'M FEEDING HIM A MEGA-DOSE OF BEATNIK POETRY, THELONIUS MONK CD'S & TH' FIRST 23 EPISODES OF "MY LITTLE PONY"!
OUCH.
IMPORTANT PAPERS
TYPE "Z"
OPENING UP TO AND SIMULTANEOUSLY LETTING IN, TH' RICH "CULTURAL STEW" ALL AROUND US-- WITHOUT JUDGING OR FILTERING-- IS TH' FIRST STEP IN TH' "ZIPPIFICATION PROCESS"!
NOW I'M ADMINISTERING A REGIMEN OF VINTAGE DINER MENUS & "BOB'S BIG BOY" HIGH-DEFINTION JPEGS!
MMM.
TYPE "Z"
©2005 Bill Griffith. World rights reserved. Distributed by King Features Syndicate
IT'S IMPORTANT TO REALIZE THAT, IN TH' "TYPE Z PERSONALITY," TH' LINE BETWEEN "HIGH" & "LOW" CULTURE IS ERASED! IT'S ALL JUST ONE HEADY ADMIXTURE OF RANDOM INPUT!
AS WE LEARN TO EMBRACE BOTH "HELLO KITTY" AND CHARLES BUKOWSKI, WE PREPARE FOR TH' NEXT STAGE!
FZZ ZZT..
FACTS & FIGURES
NEXT: A STROLL ALONG THE Z-SIDE!!

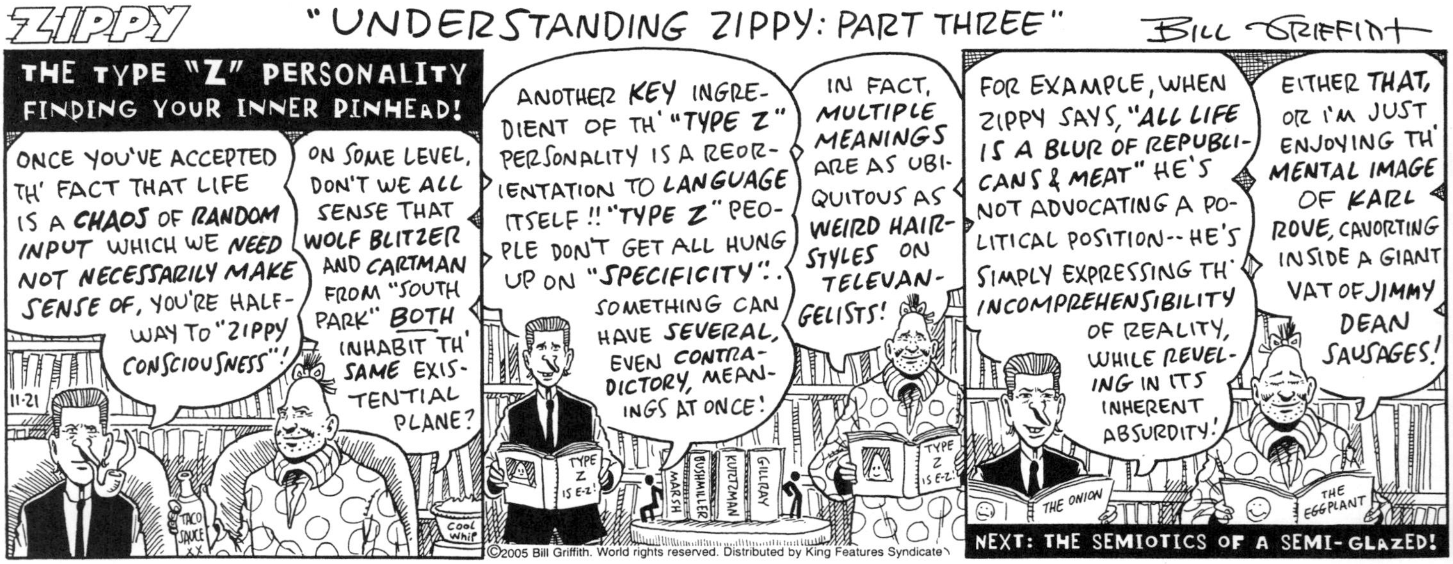
ZIPPY
"UNDERSTANDING ZIPPY: PART THREE"
BILL GRIFFITH
THE TYPE "Z" PERSONALITY
FINDING YOUR INNER PINHEAD!
ONCE YOU'VE ACCEPTED TH' FACT THAT LIFE IS A CHAOS OF RANDOM INPUT WHICH WE NEED NOT NECESSARILY MAKE SENSE OF, YOU'RE HALF-WAY TO "ZIPPY CONSCIOUSNESS"!
ON SOME LEVEL, DON'T WE ALL SENSE THAT WOLF BLITZER AND CARTMAN FROM "SOUTH PARK" BOTH INHABIT TH' SAME EXISTENTIAL PLANE?
11-21
TACO SAUCE XX
COOL WHIP
ANOTHER KEY INGREDIENT OF TH' "TYPE Z" PERSONALITY IS A REORIENTATION TO LANGUAGE ITSELF!! "TYPE Z" PEOPLE DON'T GET ALL HUNG UP ON "SPECIFICITY".. SOMETHING CAN HAVE SEVERAL, EVEN CONTRADICTORY, MEANINGS AT ONCE!
IN FACT, MULTIPLE MEANINGS ARE AS UBIQUITOUS AS WEIRD HAIRSTYLES ON TELEVANGELISTS!
TYPE Z IS E-Z!
MARSH
BUSHMILLER
KURTZMAN
GILLRAY
TYPE Z IS E-Z
©2005 Bill Griffith. World rights reserved. Distributed by King Features Syndicate
FOR EXAMPLE, WHEN ZIPPY SAYS, "ALL LIFE IS A BLUR OF REPUBLICANS & MEAT" HE'S NOT ADVOCATING A POLITICAL POSITION-- HE'S SIMPLY EXPRESSING TH' INCOMPREHENSIBILITY OF REALITY, WHILE REVELING IN ITS INHERENT ABSURDITY!
EITHER THAT, OR I'M JUST ENJOYING TH' MENTAL IMAGE OF KARL ROVE, CAVORTING INSIDE A GIANT VAT OF JIMMY DEAN SAUSAGES!
THE ONION
THE EGGPLANT
NEXT: THE SEMIOTICS OF A SEMI-GLAZED!

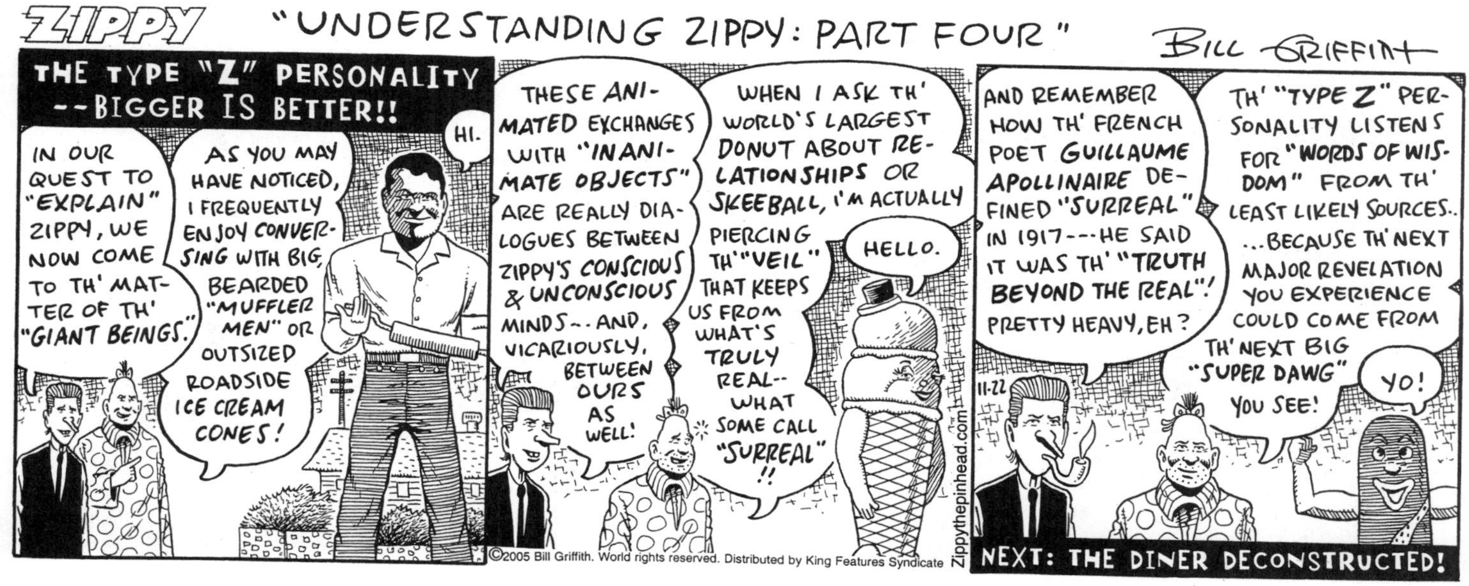
ZIPPY
"UNDERSTANDING ZIPPY: PART FOUR"
BILL GRIFFITH
THE TYPE "Z" PERSONALITY --BIGGER IS BETTER!!
IN OUR QUEST TO "EXPLAIN" ZIPPY, WE NOW COME TO TH' MATTER OF TH' "GIANT BEINGS."
AS YOU MAY HAVE NOTICED, I FREQUENTLY ENJOY CONVERSING WITH BIG, BEARDED "MUFFLER MEN" OR OUTSIZED ROADSIDE ICE CREAM CONES!
HI.
THESE ANIMATED EXCHANGES WITH "INANIMATE OBJECTS" ARE REALLY DIALOGUES BETWEEN ZIPPY'S CONSCIOUS & UNCONSCIOUS MINDS-- AND, VICARIOUSLY, BETWEEN OURS AS WELL!
WHEN I ASK TH' WORLD'S LARGEST DONUT ABOUT RELATIONSHIPS OR SKEEBALL, I'M ACTUALLY PIERCING TH' "VEIL" THAT KEEPS US FROM WHAT'S TRULY REAL-- WHAT SOME CALL "SURREAL"!!
HELLO.
AND REMEMBER HOW TH' FRENCH POET GUILLAUME APOLLINAIRE DEFINED "SURREAL" IN 1917---HE SAID IT WAS TH' "TRUTH BEYOND THE REAL"! PRETTY HEAVY, EH?
TH' "TYPE Z" PERSONALITY LISTENS FOR "WORDS OF WISDOM" FROM TH' LEAST LIKELY SOURCES.. ...BECAUSE TH' NEXT MAJOR REVELATION YOU EXPERIENCE COULD COME FROM TH' NEXT BIG "SUPER DAWG" YOU SEE!
YO!
11-22
©2005 Bill Griffith. World rights reserved. Distributed by King Features Syndicate
Zippythepinhead.com
NEXT: THE DINER DECONSTRUCTED!

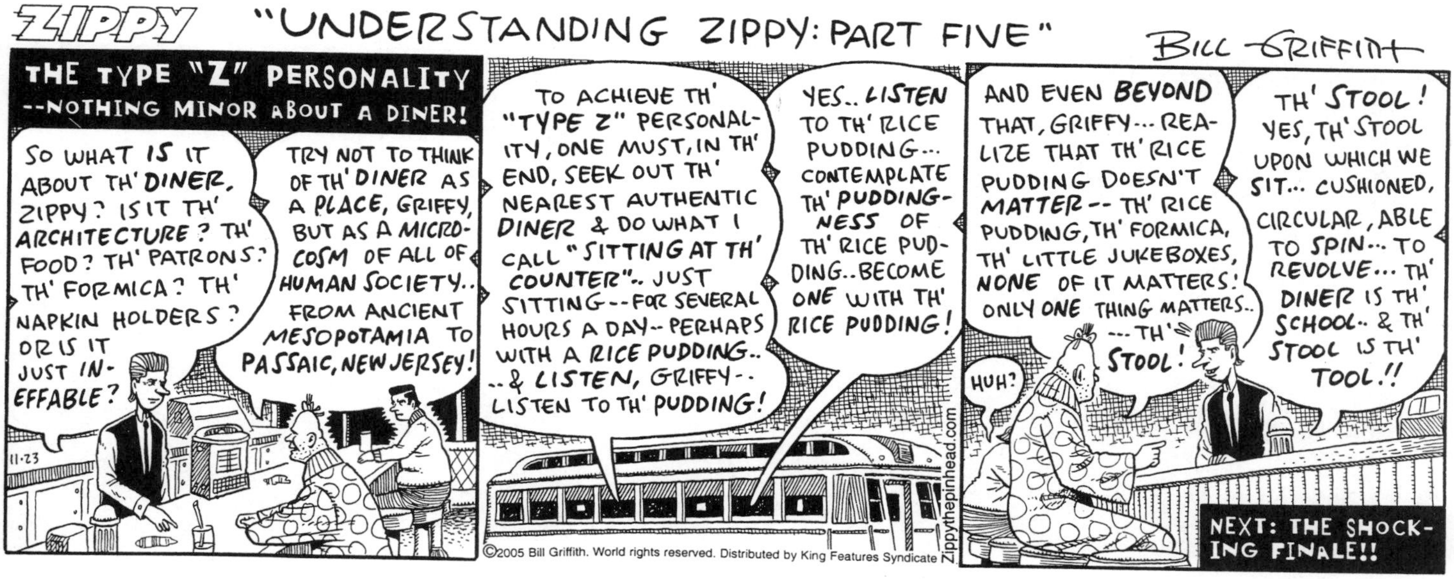
ZIPPY
"UNDERSTANDING ZIPPY: PART FIVE"
BILL GRIFFITH
THE TYPE "Z" PERSONALITY --NOTHING MINOR ABOUT A DINER!
SO WHAT IS IT ABOUT TH' DINER, ZIPPY? IS IT TH' ARCHITECTURE? TH' FOOD? TH' PATRONS? TH' FORMICA? TH' NAPKIN HOLDERS? OR IS IT JUST INEFFABLE?
TRY NOT TO THINK OF TH' DINER AS A PLACE, GRIFFY, BUT AS A MICROCOSM OF ALL OF HUMAN SOCIETY.. FROM ANCIENT MESOPOTAMIA TO PASSAIC, NEW JERSEY!
11-23
TO ACHIEVE TH' "TYPE Z" PERSONALITY, ONE MUST, IN TH' END, SEEK OUT TH' NEAREST AUTHENTIC DINER & DO WHAT I CALL "SITTING AT TH' COUNTER".. JUST SITTING--FOR SEVERAL HOURS A DAY--PERHAPS WITH A RICE PUDDING.. ..& LISTEN, GRIFFY-- LISTEN TO TH' PUDDING!
YES.. LISTEN TO TH' RICE PUDDING... CONTEMPLATE TH' PUDDINGNESS OF TH' RICE PUDDING.. BECOME ONE WITH TH' RICE PUDDING!
AND EVEN BEYOND THAT, GRIFFY--- REALIZE THAT TH' RICE PUDDING DOESN'T MATTER-- TH' RICE PUDDING, TH' FORMICA, TH' LITTLE JUKEBOXES, NONE OF IT MATTERS! ONLY ONE THING MATTERS.. ---TH' STOOL!
HUH?
TH' STOOL! YES, TH' STOOL UPON WHICH WE SIT... CUSHIONED, CIRCULAR, ABLE TO SPIN... TO REVOLVE... TH' DINER IS TH' SCHOOL.. & TH' STOOL IS TH' TOOL!!
©2005 Bill Griffith. World rights reserved. Distributed by King Features Syndicate
Zippythepinhead.com
NEXT: THE SHOCKING FINALE!!

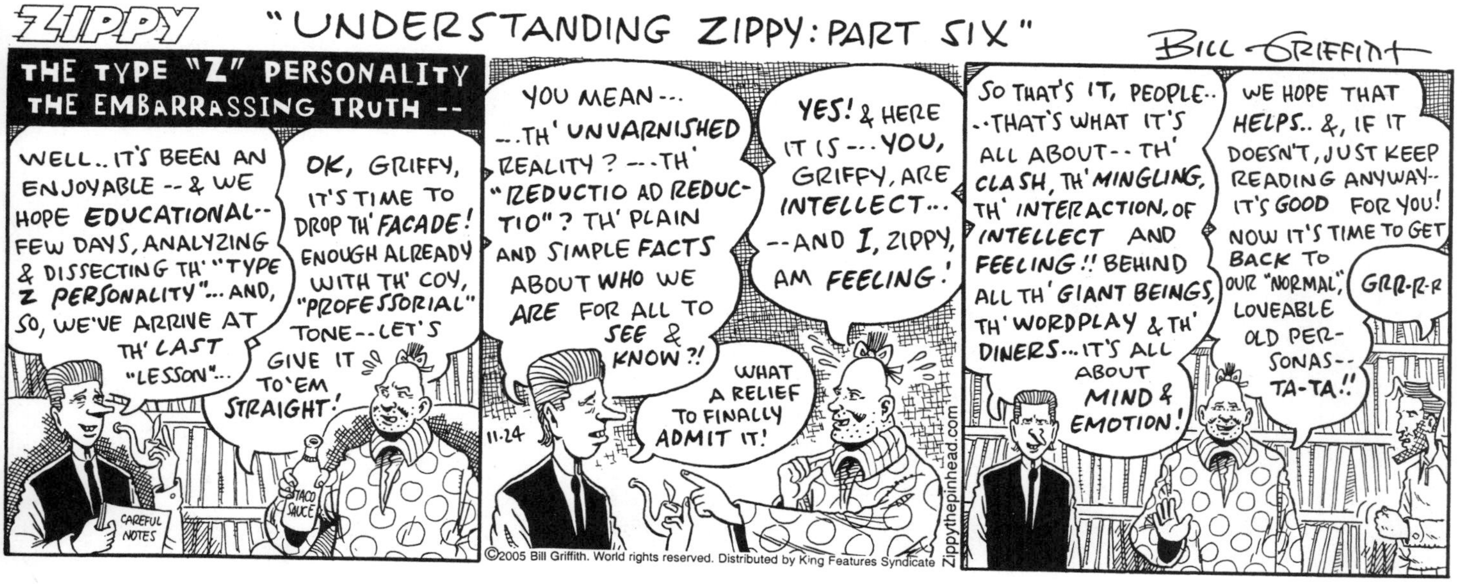
ZIPPY
"UNDERSTANDING ZIPPY: PART SIX"
BILL GRIFFITH
THE TYPE "Z" PERSONALITY THE EMBARRASSING TRUTH --
WELL.. IT'S BEEN AN ENJOYABLE -- & WE HOPE EDUCATIONAL-- FEW DAYS, ANALYZING & DISSECTING TH' "TYPE Z PERSONALITY"... AND, SO, WE'VE ARRIVE AT TH' LAST "LESSON"...
OK, GRIFFY, IT'S TIME TO DROP TH' FACADE! ENOUGH ALREADY WITH TH' COY, "PROFESSORIAL" TONE--LET'S GIVE IT TO 'EM STRAIGHT!
CAREFUL NOTES
TACO SAUCE
YOU MEAN--- ---TH' UNVARNISHED REALITY? ---TH' "REDUCTIO AD REDUCTIO"? TH' PLAIN AND SIMPLE FACTS ABOUT WHO WE ARE FOR ALL TO SEE & KNOW?!
WHAT A RELIEF TO FINALLY ADMIT IT!
11-24
YES! & HERE IT IS--- YOU, GRIFFY, ARE INTELLECT... --AND I, ZIPPY, AM FEELING!
SO THAT'S IT, PEOPLE.. ..THAT'S WHAT IT'S ALL ABOUT-- TH' CLASH, TH' MINGLING, TH' INTERACTION, OF INTELLECT AND FEELING!! BEHIND ALL TH' GIANT BEINGS, TH' WORDPLAY & TH' DINERS... IT'S ALL ABOUT MIND & EMOTION!
WE HOPE THAT HELPS.. &, IF IT DOESN'T, JUST KEEP READING ANYWAY.. IT'S GOOD FOR YOU! NOW IT'S TIME TO GET BACK TO OUR "NORMAL," LOVEABLE OLD PERSONAS-- TA-TA!!
GRR-R-R
©2005 Bill Griffith. World rights reserved. Distributed by King Features Syndicate
Zippythepinhead.com

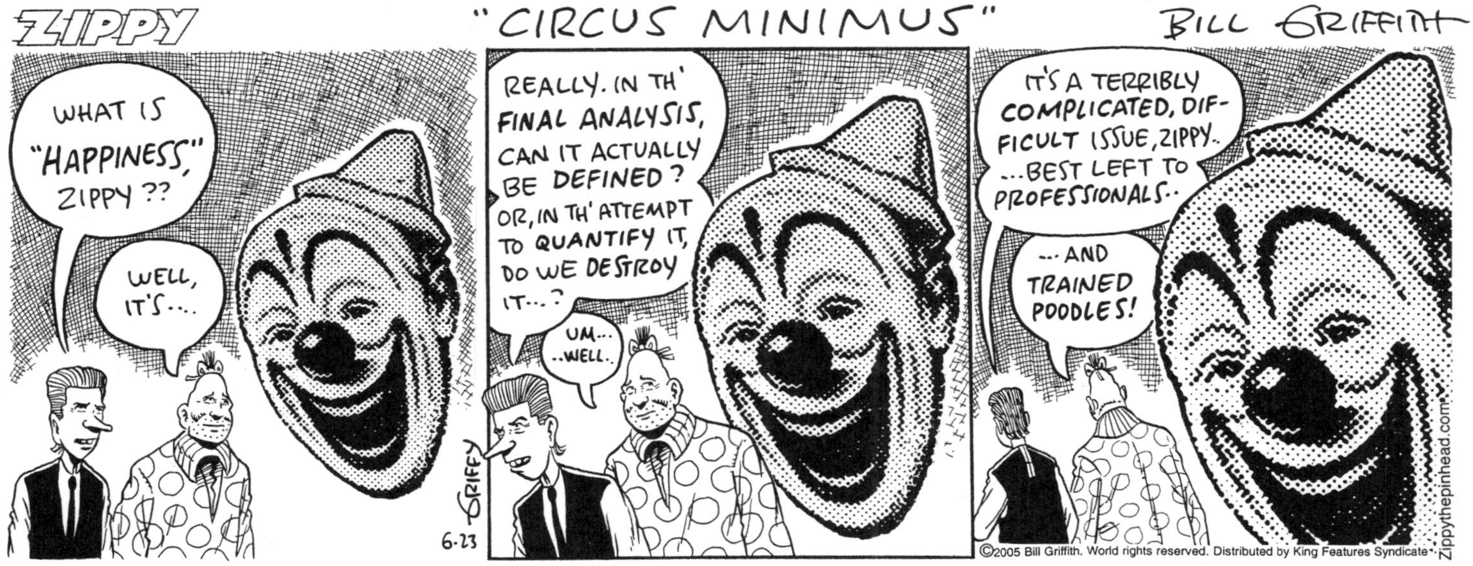
ZIPPY
"CIRCUS MINIMUS"
BILL GRIFFITH
WHAT IS "HAPPINESS," ZIPPY ??
WELL, IT'S....
REALLY. IN TH' FINAL ANALYSIS, CAN IT ACTUALLY BE DEFINED? OR, IN TH' ATTEMPT TO QUANTIFY IT, DO WE DESTROY IT...?
UM... ..WELL..
GRIFFY
6-23
IT'S A TERRIBLY COMPLICATED, DIFFICULT ISSUE, ZIPPY.. ...BEST LEFT TO PROFESSIONALS..
...AND TRAINED POODLES!
©2005 Bill Griffith. World rights reserved. Distributed by King Features Syndicate
Zippythepinhead.com

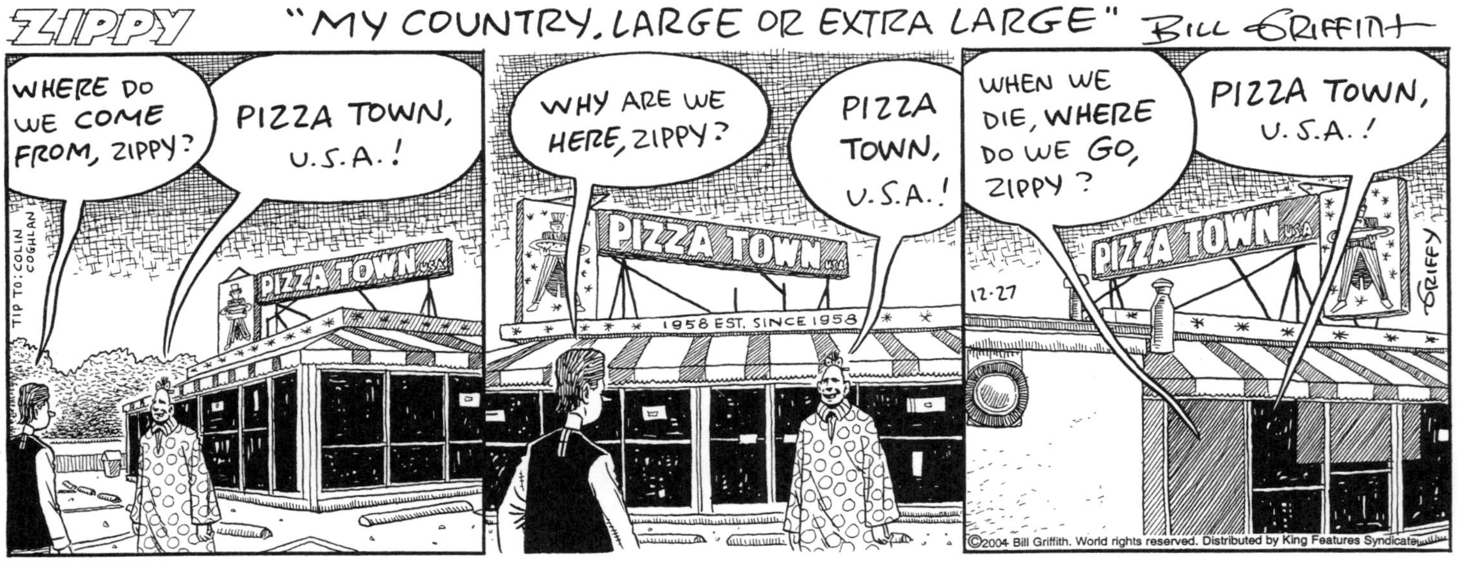
ZIPPY
"MY COUNTRY, LARGE OR EXTRA LARGE"
BILL GRIFFITH
WHERE DO WE COME FROM, ZIPPY?
PIZZA TOWN, U.S.A.!
TIP TO: COLIN COGHLAN
PIZZA TOWN USA
WHY ARE WE HERE, ZIPPY?
PIZZA TOWN, U.S.A.!
1958 EST. SINCE 1958
WHEN WE DIE, WHERE DO WE GO, ZIPPY?
PIZZA TOWN, U.S.A.!
12-27
GRIFFY
©2004 Bill Griffith. World rights reserved. Distributed by King Features Syndicate

1

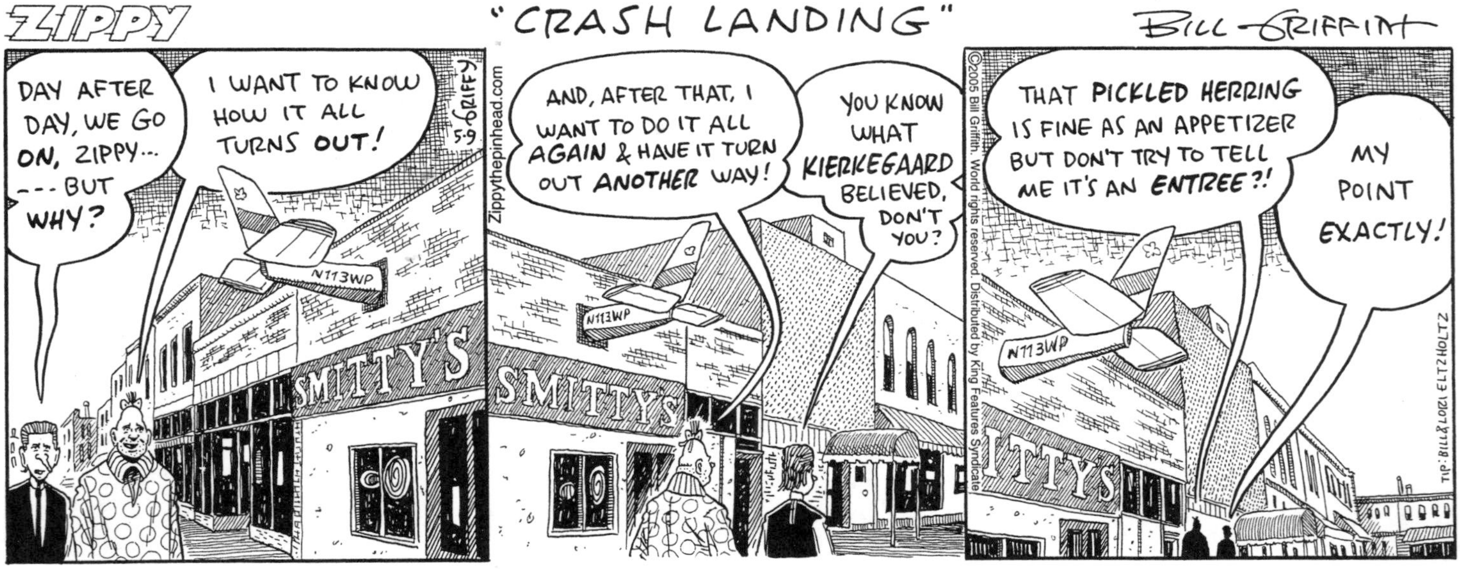
ZIPPY
"CRASH LANDING"
BILL GRIFFITH
DAY AFTER DAY, WE GO ON, ZIPPY... ...BUT WHY?
I WANT TO KNOW HOW IT ALL TURNS OUT!
GRIFFY 5-9
N113WP
SMITTY'S
Zippythepinhead.com
AND, AFTER THAT, I WANT TO DO IT ALL AGAIN & HAVE IT TURN OUT ANOTHER WAY!
YOU KNOW WHAT KIERKEGAARD BELIEVED, DON'T YOU?
©2005 Bill Griffith. World rights reserved. Distributed by King Features Syndicate
THAT PICKLED HERRING IS FINE AS AN APPETIZER BUT DON'T TRY TO TELL ME IT'S AN ENTREE?!
MY POINT EXACTLY!
TIP: BILL & LORI ELTZHOLTZ

2

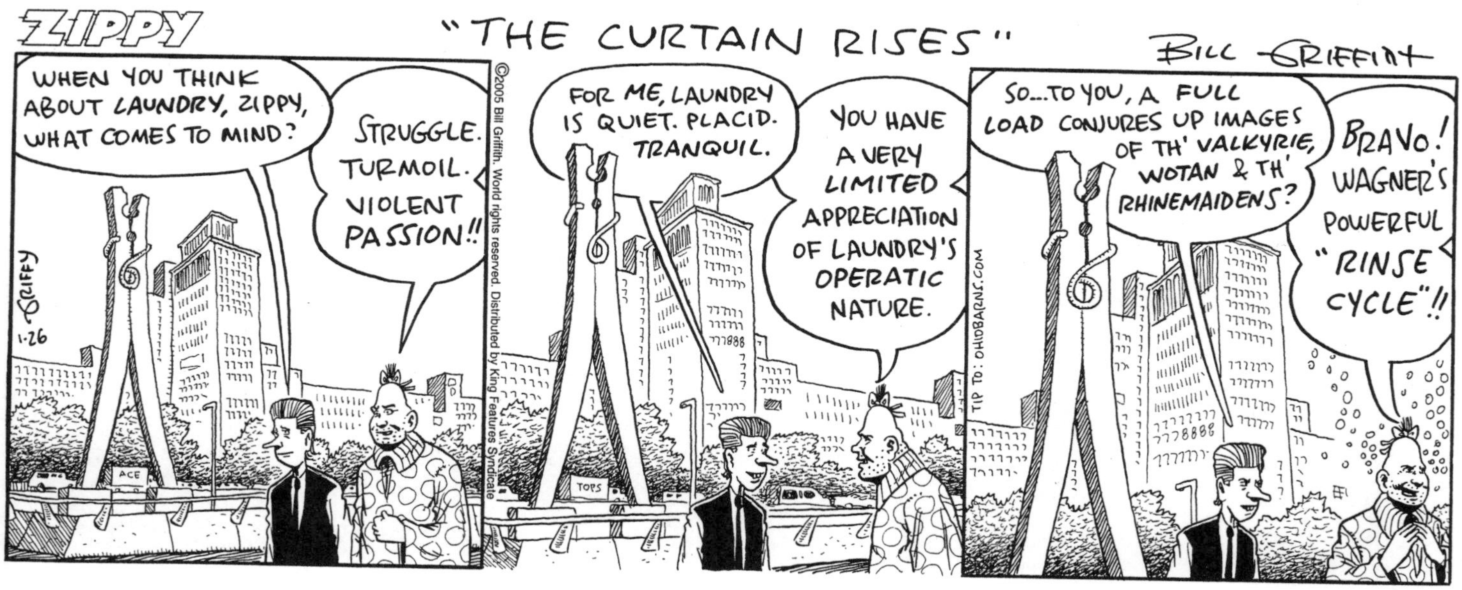
ZIPPY
"THE CURTAIN RISES"
BILL GRIFFITH
WHEN YOU THINK ABOUT LAUNDRY, ZIPPY, WHAT COMES TO MIND?
STRUGGLE. TURMOIL. VIOLENT PASSION!!
GRIFFY 1-26
©2005 Bill Griffith. World rights reserved. Distributed by King Features Syndicate
FOR ME, LAUNDRY IS QUIET. PLACID. TRANQUIL.
YOU HAVE A VERY LIMITED APPRECIATION OF LAUNDRY'S OPERATIC NATURE.
TIP TO: OHIOBARNS.COM
SO...TO YOU, A FULL LOAD CONJURES UP IMAGES OF TH' VALKYRIE, WOTAN & TH' RHINEMAIDENS?
BRAVO! WAGNER'S POWERFUL "RINSE CYCLE"!!

3

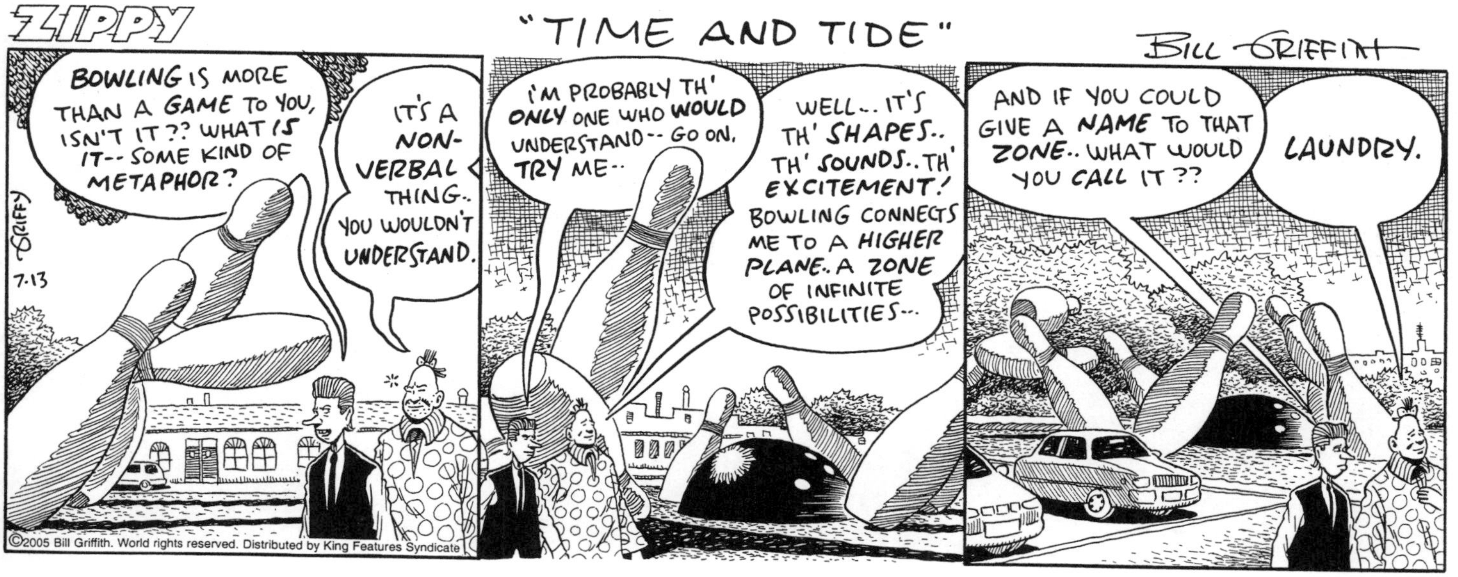
ZIPPY
"TIME AND TIDE"
BILL GRIFFITH
BOWLING IS MORE THAN A GAME TO YOU, ISN'T IT?? WHAT IS IT-- SOME KIND OF METAPHOR?
IT'S A NON-VERBAL THING.. YOU WOULDN'T UNDERSTAND.
GRIFFY 7-13
©2005 Bill Griffith. World rights reserved. Distributed by King Features Syndicate
I'M PROBABLY TH' ONLY ONE WHO WOULD UNDERSTAND-- GO ON, TRY ME--
WELL-- IT'S TH' SHAPES.. TH' SOUNDS.. TH' EXCITEMENT! BOWLING CONNECTS ME TO A HIGHER PLANE.. A ZONE OF INFINITE POSSIBILITIES--
AND IF YOU COULD GIVE A NAME TO THAT ZONE.. WHAT WOULD YOU CALL IT??
LAUNDRY.

4

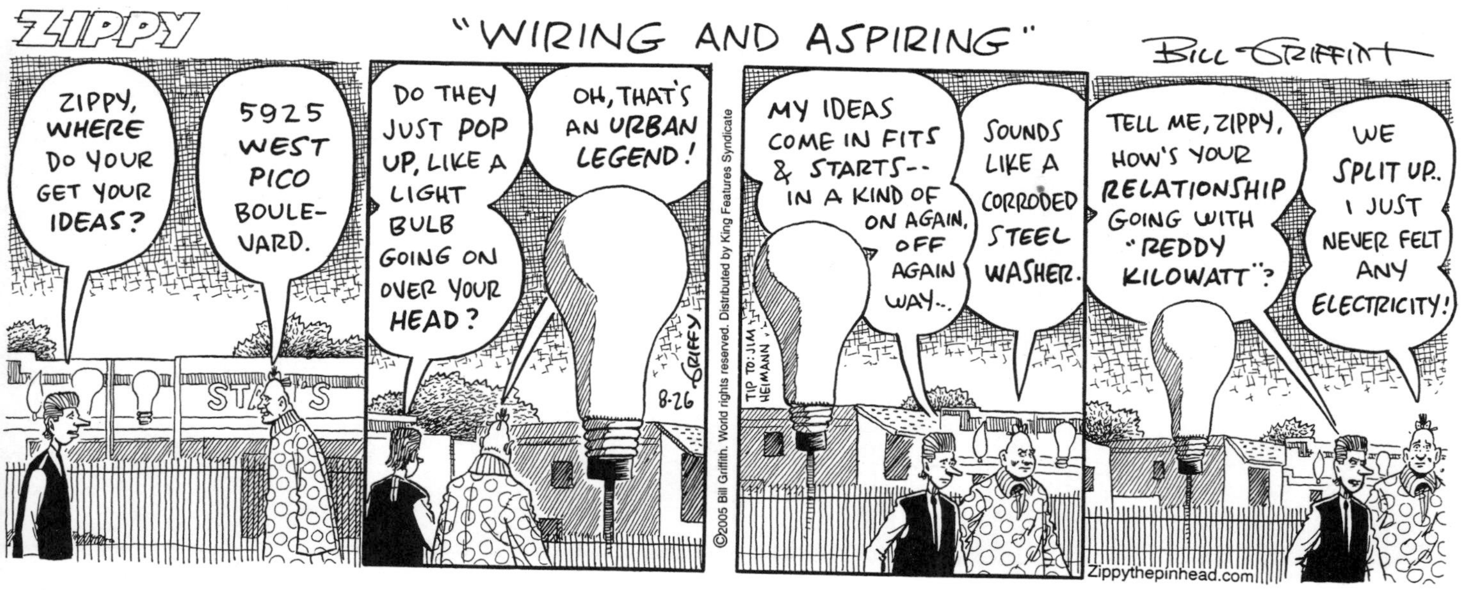
ZIPPY
"WIRING AND ASPIRING"
BILL GRIFFITH
ZIPPY, WHERE DO YOUR GET YOUR IDEAS?
5925 WEST PICO BOULE-VARD.
DO THEY JUST POP UP, LIKE A LIGHT BULB GOING ON OVER YOUR HEAD?
OH, THAT'S AN URBAN LEGEND!
GRIFFY 8-26
©2005 Bill Griffith. World rights reserved. Distributed by King Features Syndicate
TIP TO: JIM HEIMANN
MY IDEAS COME IN FITS & STARTS-- IN A KIND OF ON AGAIN, OFF AGAIN WAY--
SOUNDS LIKE A CORRODED STEEL WASHER.
TELL ME, ZIPPY, HOW'S YOUR RELATIONSHIP GOING WITH "REDDY KILOWATT"?
WE SPLIT UP.. I JUST NEVER FELT ANY ELECTRICITY!
Zippythepinhead.com

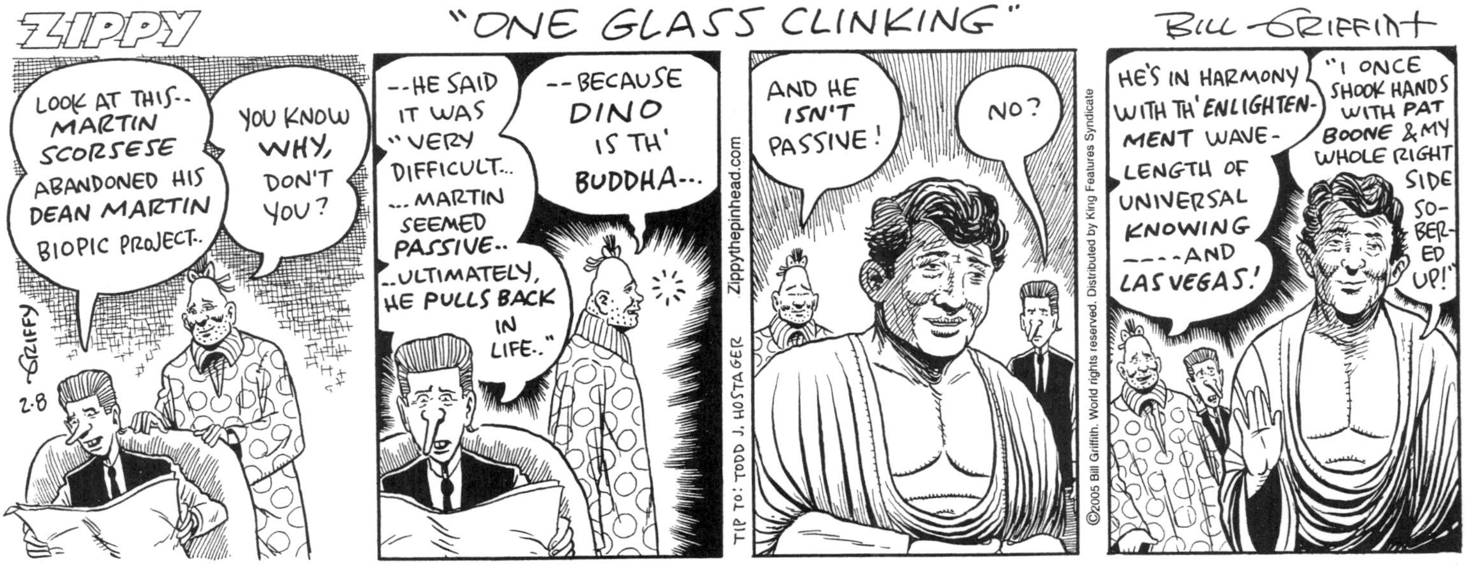
ZIPPY
"ONE GLASS CLINKING"
BILL GRIFFITH
LOOK AT THIS-- MARTIN SCORSESE ABANDONED HIS DEAN MARTIN BIOPIC PROJECT..
YOU KNOW WHY, DON'T YOU?
GRIFFY 2·8
--HE SAID IT WAS "VERY DIFFICULT... ...MARTIN SEEMED PASSIVE.. ..ULTIMATELY, HE PULLS BACK IN LIFE.."
--BECAUSE DINO IS TH' BUDDHA...
Zippythepinhead.com
TIP TO: TODD J. HOSTAGER
AND HE ISN'T PASSIVE!
NO?
©2005 Bill Griffith. World rights reserved. Distributed by King Features Syndicate
HE'S IN HARMONY WITH TH' ENLIGHTENMENT WAVE-LENGTH OF UNIVERSAL KNOWING ----AND LAS VEGAS!
"I ONCE SHOOK HANDS WITH PAT BOONE & MY WHOLE RIGHT SIDE SOBERED UP!"

5

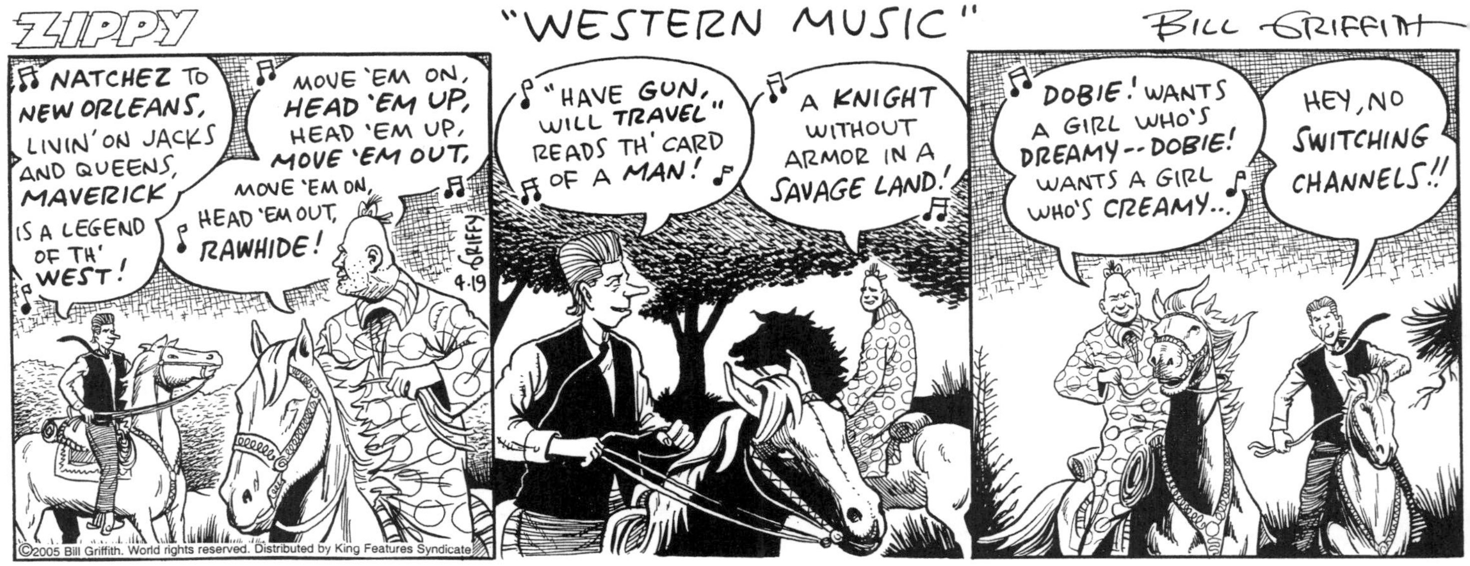
ZIPPY
"WESTERN MUSIC"
BILL GRIFFITH
NATCHEZ TO NEW ORLEANS, LIVIN' ON JACKS AND QUEENS, MAVERICK IS A LEGEND OF TH' WEST!
MOVE 'EM ON, HEAD 'EM UP, HEAD 'EM UP, MOVE 'EM OUT, MOVE 'EM ON, HEAD 'EM OUT, RAWHIDE!
GRIFFY 4·19
©2005 Bill Griffith. World rights reserved. Distributed by King Features Syndicate
"HAVE GUN, WILL TRAVEL" READS TH' CARD OF A MAN!
A KNIGHT WITHOUT ARMOR IN A SAVAGE LAND!
DOBIE! WANTS A GIRL WHO'S DREAMY--DOBIE! WANTS A GIRL WHO'S CREAMY...
HEY, NO SWITCHING CHANNELS!!

6

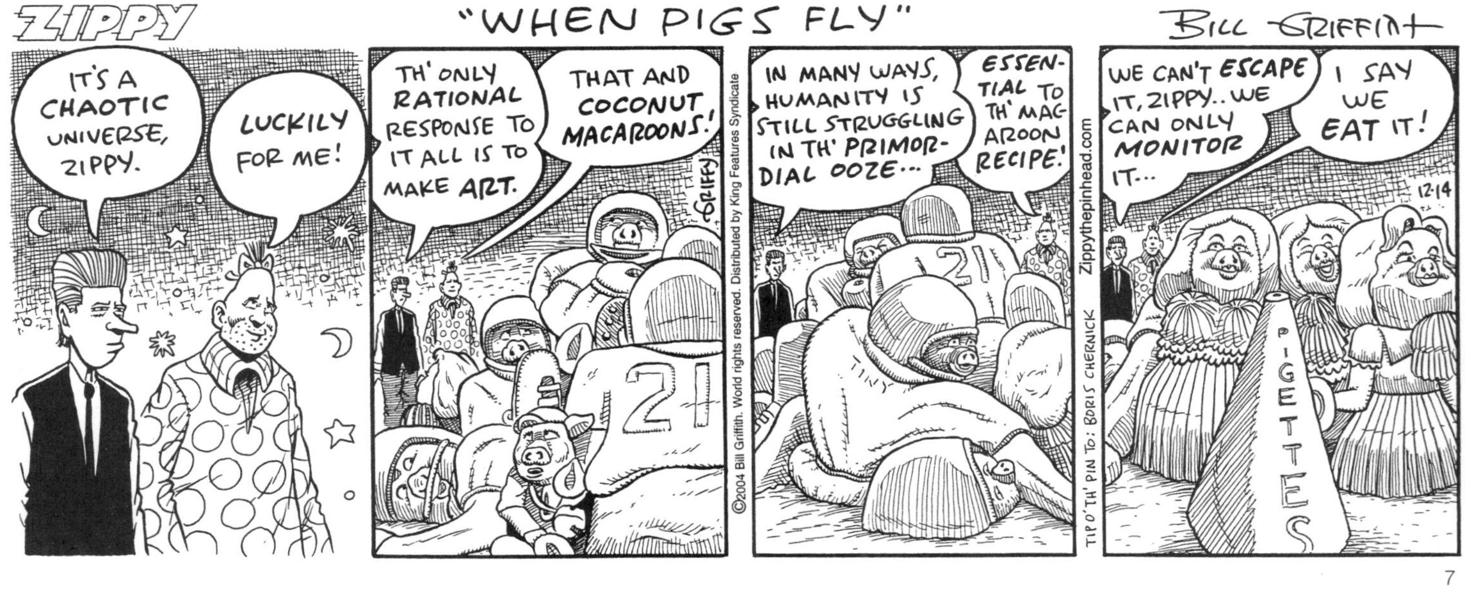
ZIPPY
"WHEN PIGS FLY"
BILL GRIFFITH
IT'S A CHAOTIC UNIVERSE, ZIPPY.
LUCKILY FOR ME!
TH' ONLY RATIONAL RESPONSE TO IT ALL IS TO MAKE ART.
THAT AND COCONUT MACAROONS!
GRIFFY
©2004 Bill Griffith. World rights reserved. Distributed by King Features Syndicate
IN MANY WAYS, HUMANITY IS STILL STRUGGLING IN TH' PRIMORDIAL OOZE...
ESSENTIAL TO TH' MACAROON RECIPE!
Zippythepinhead.com
TIP O' TH' PIN TO: BORIS CHERNICK
WE CAN'T ESCAPE IT, ZIPPY.. WE CAN ONLY MONITOR IT...
I SAY WE EAT IT!
12·14
PIGETTES

7

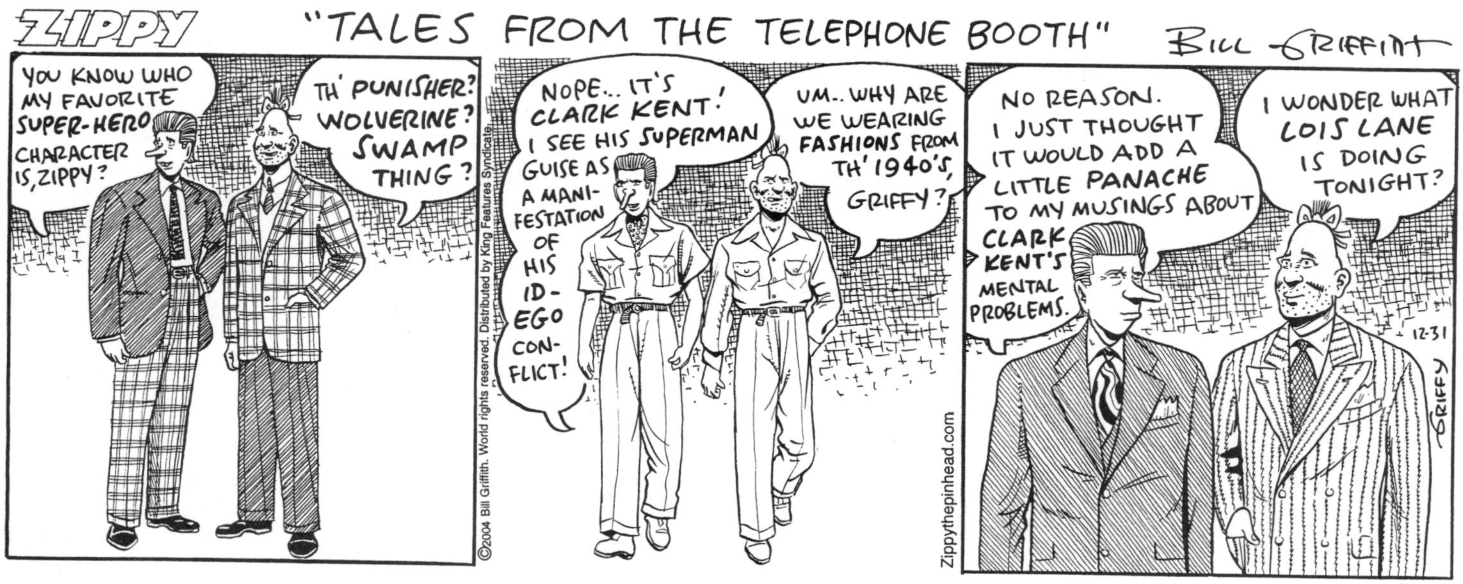
ZIPPY
"TALES FROM THE TELEPHONE BOOTH"
BILL GRIFFITH
YOU KNOW WHO MY FAVORITE SUPER-HERO CHARACTER IS, ZIPPY?
TH' PUNISHER? WOLVERINE? SWAMP THING?
NOPE... IT'S CLARK KENT! I SEE HIS SUPERMAN GUISE AS A MANIFESTATION OF HIS ID-EGO CONFLICT!
UM.. WHY ARE WE WEARING FASHIONS FROM TH' 1940'S, GRIFFY?
NO REASON. I JUST THOUGHT IT WOULD ADD A LITTLE PANACHE TO MY MUSINGS ABOUT CLARK KENT'S MENTAL PROBLEMS.
I WONDER WHAT LOIS LANE IS DOING TONIGHT?
12-31
GRIFFY
©2004 Bill Griffith. World rights reserved. Distributed by King Features Syndicate.
Zippythepinhead.com

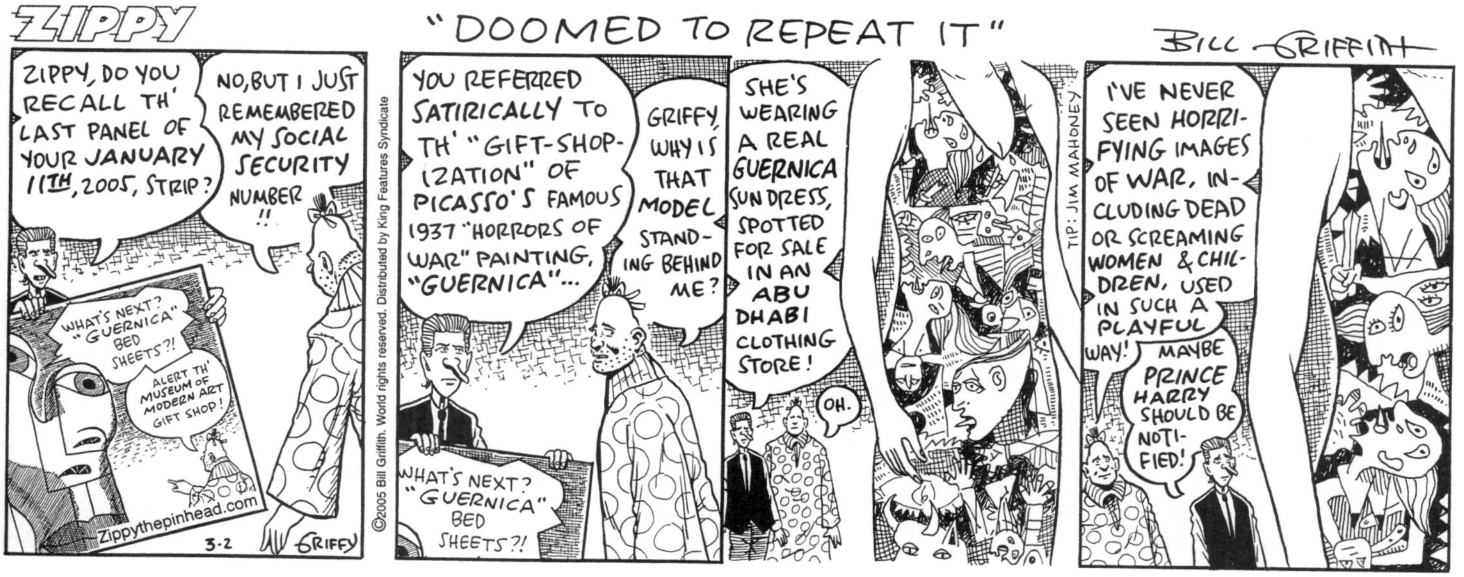
ZIPPY
"DOOMED TO REPEAT IT"
BILL GRIFFITH
ZIPPY, DO YOU RECALL TH' LAST PANEL OF YOUR JANUARY 11TH, 2005, STRIP?
NO, BUT I JUST REMEMBERED MY SOCIAL SECURITY NUMBER!!
WHAT'S NEXT? "GUERNICA" BED SHEETS?!
ALERT TH' MUSEUM OF MODERN ART GIFT SHOP!
Zippythepinhead.com
3-2
GRIFFY
©2005 Bill Griffith. World rights reserved. Distributed by King Features Syndicate
YOU REFERRED SATIRICALLY TO TH' "GIFT-SHOP-IZATION" OF PICASSO'S FAMOUS 1937 "HORRORS OF WAR" PAINTING, "GUERNICA"...
GRIFFY, WHY IS THAT MODEL STANDING BEHIND ME?
WHAT'S NEXT? "GUERNICA" BED SHEETS?!
SHE'S WEARING A REAL GUERNICA SUN DRESS, SPOTTED FOR SALE IN AN ABU DHABI CLOTHING STORE!
OH.
TIP: JIM MAHONEY
I'VE NEVER SEEN HORRIFYING IMAGES OF WAR, INCLUDING DEAD OR SCREAMING WOMEN & CHILDREN, USED IN SUCH A PLAYFUL WAY!
MAYBE PRINCE HARRY SHOULD BE NOTIFIED!

8

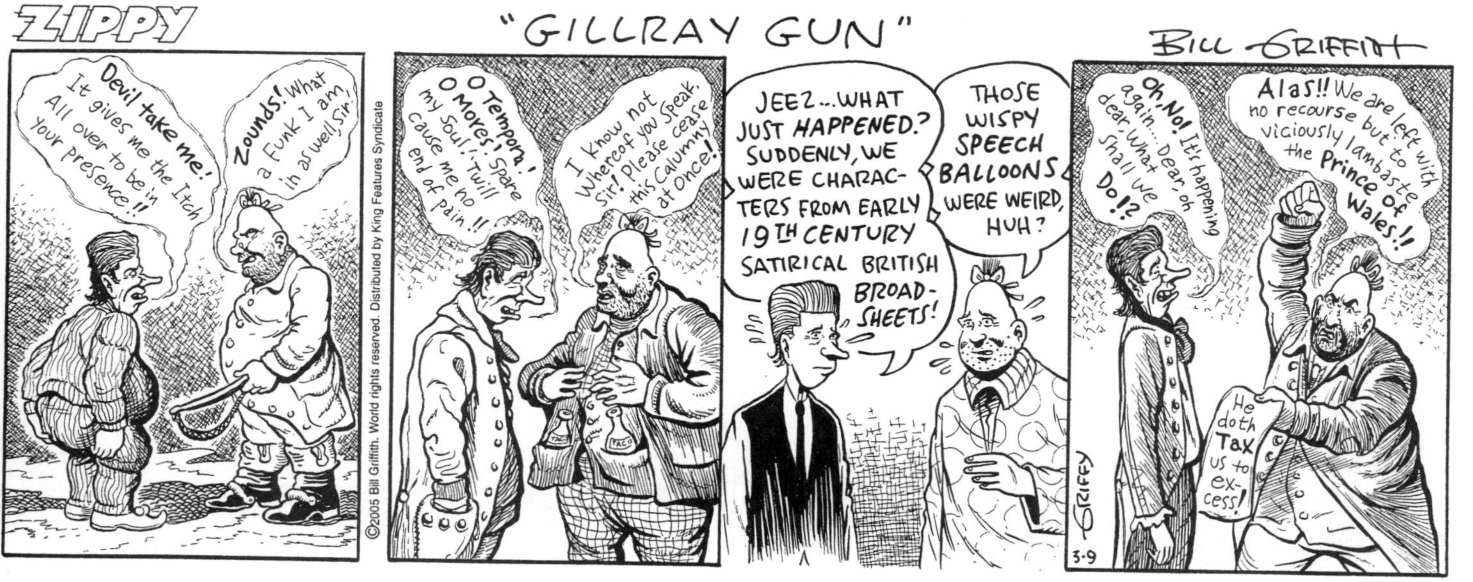
ZIPPY
"GILLRAY GUN"
BILL GRIFFITH
Devil take me! It gives me the Itch All over to be in your Presence!!
Zounds! What a Funk I am in as well, Sir.
©2005 Bill Griffith. World rights reserved. Distributed by King Features Syndicate
O Tempora! O Mores! Spare my Soul! 'Twill cause me no end of pain!!
I know not Whereof you Speak, Sir! Please cease this Calumny at Once!
JEEZ... WHAT JUST HAPPENED? SUDDENLY, WE WERE CHARACTERS FROM EARLY 19TH CENTURY SATIRICAL BRITISH BROADSHEETS!
THOSE WISPY SPEECH BALLOONS WERE WEIRD, HUH?
GRIFFY
3-9
Oh No! It's happening again... Dear, oh dear. What Shall we Do!?
Alas!! We are left with no recourse but to viciously lambaste the Prince of Wales!!
He doth Tax us to excess!

9

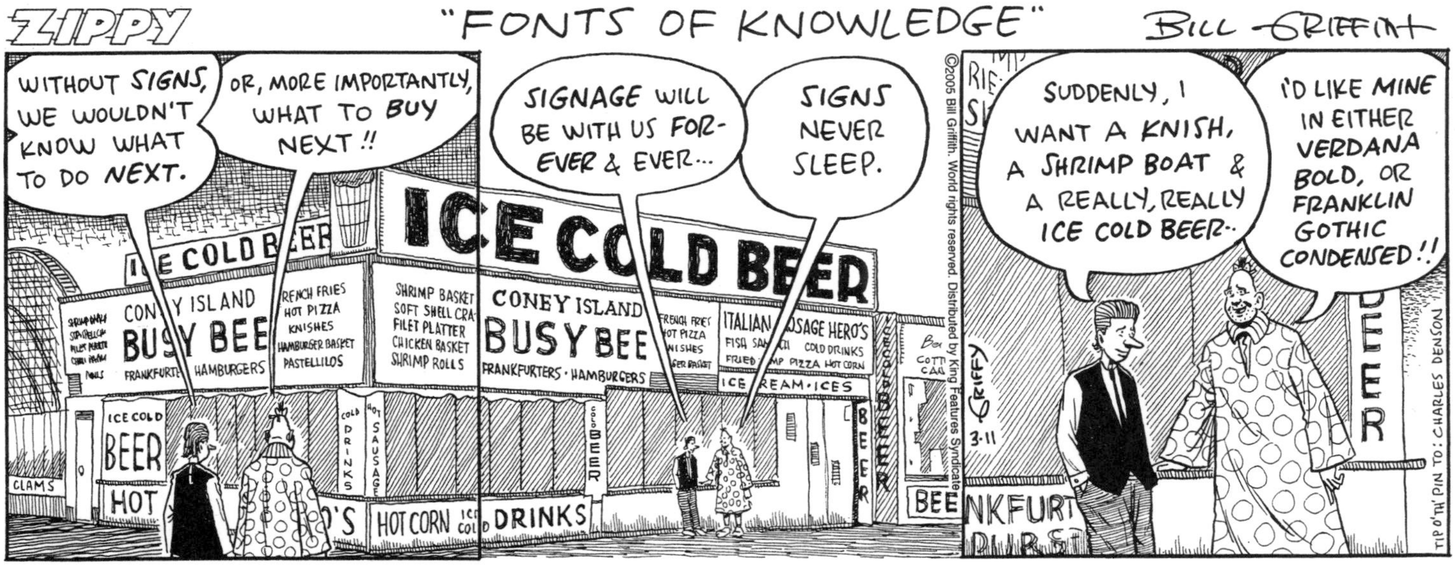
ZIPPY
"FONTS OF KNOWLEDGE"
BILL GRIFFITH
WITHOUT SIGNS, WE WOULDN'T KNOW WHAT TO DO NEXT.
OR, MORE IMPORTANTLY, WHAT TO BUY NEXT!!
SIGNAGE WILL BE WITH US FOREVER & EVER...
SIGNS NEVER SLEEP.
SUDDENLY, I WANT A KNISH, A SHRIMP BOAT & A REALLY, REALLY ICE COLD BEER..
I'D LIKE MINE IN EITHER VERDANA BOLD, OR FRANKLIN GOTHIC CONDENSED!!
ICE COLD BEER
CONEY ISLAND BUSY BEE
FRANKFURTERS · HAMBURGERS
©2005 Bill Griffith. World rights reserved. Distributed by King Features Syndicate
GRIFFY 3-11
TIP O'TH' PIN TO: CHARLES DENSON

10

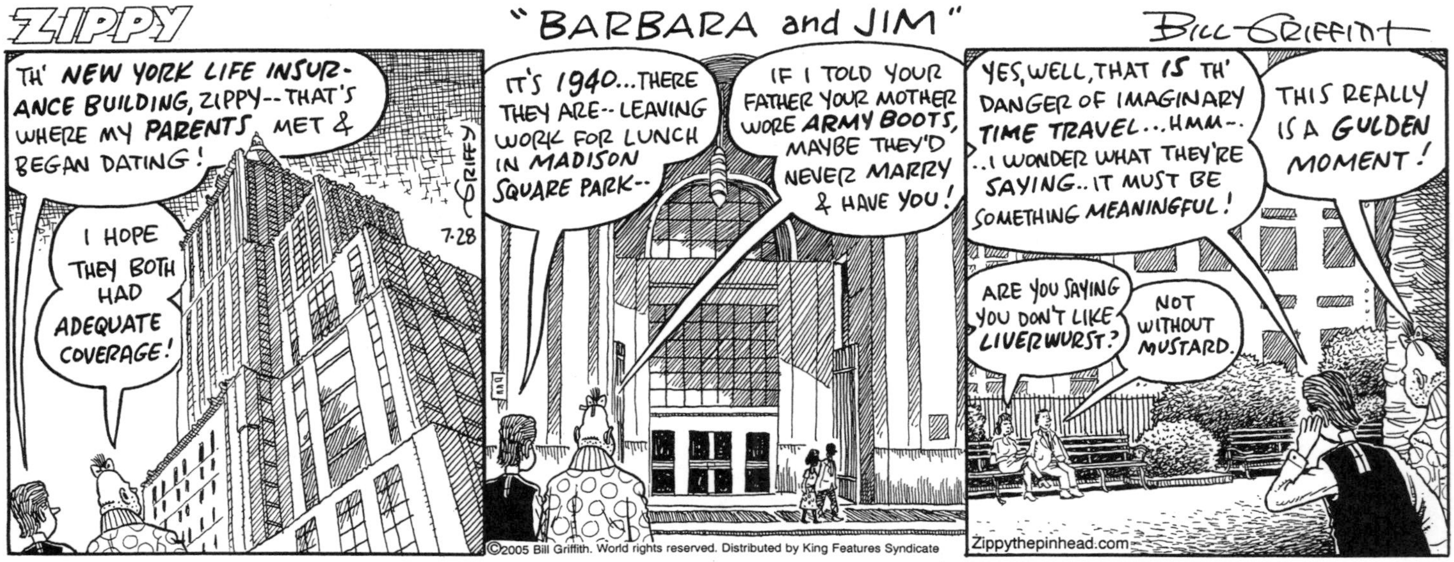
ZIPPY
"BARBARA and JIM"
BILL GRIFFITH
TH' NEW YORK LIFE INSURANCE BUILDING, ZIPPY--THAT'S WHERE MY PARENTS MET & BEGAN DATING!
I HOPE THEY BOTH HAD ADEQUATE COVERAGE!
GRIFFY 7-28
IT'S 1940...THERE THEY ARE--LEAVING WORK FOR LUNCH IN MADISON SQUARE PARK--
IF I TOLD YOUR FATHER YOUR MOTHER WORE ARMY BOOTS, MAYBE THEY'D NEVER MARRY & HAVE YOU!
YES, WELL, THAT IS TH' DANGER OF IMAGINARY TIME TRAVEL...HMM--..I WONDER WHAT THEY'RE SAYING.. IT MUST BE SOMETHING MEANINGFUL!
THIS REALLY IS A GULDEN MOMENT!
ARE YOU SAYING YOU DON'T LIKE LIVERWURST?
NOT WITHOUT MUSTARD.
©2005 Bill Griffith. World rights reserved. Distributed by King Features Syndicate
Zippythepinhead.com

11

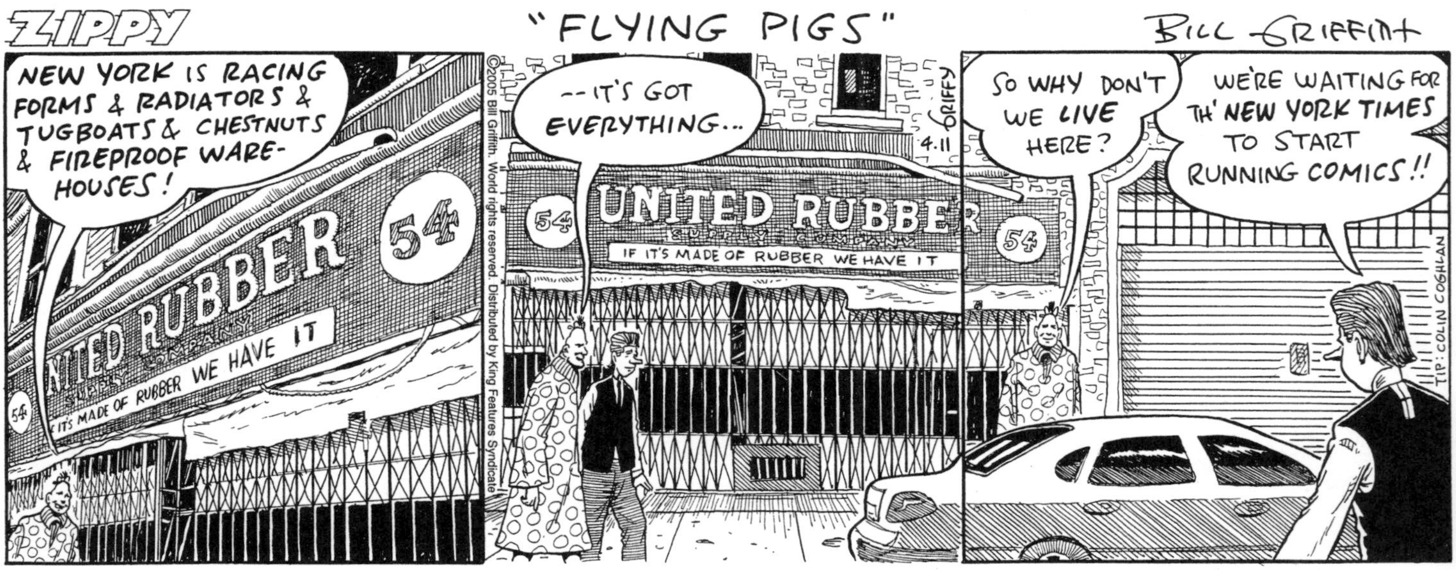
ZIPPY
"FLYING PIGS"
BILL GRIFFITH
NEW YORK IS RACING FORMS & RADIATORS & TUGBOATS & CHESTNUTS & FIREPROOF WAREHOUSES!
UNITED RUBBER
54
IT'S MADE OF RUBBER WE HAVE IT
--IT'S GOT EVERYTHING...
GRIFFY 4-11
UNITED RUBBER
IF IT'S MADE OF RUBBER WE HAVE IT
SO WHY DON'T WE LIVE HERE?
WE'RE WAITING FOR TH' NEW YORK TIMES TO START RUNNING COMICS!!
©2005 Bill Griffith. World rights reserved. Distributed by King Features Syndicate
TIP: COLIN COGHLAN

12

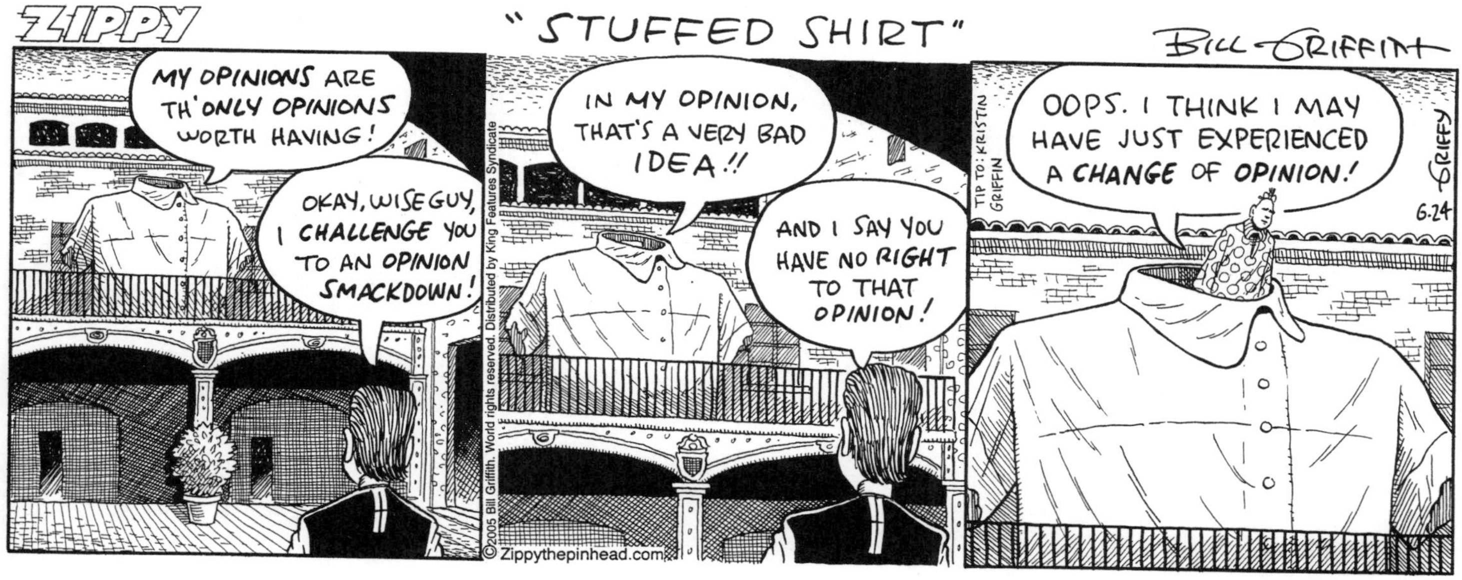
ZIPPY
"STUFFED SHIRT"
BILL GRIFFITH
MY OPINIONS ARE TH' ONLY OPINIONS WORTH HAVING!
OKAY, WISE GUY, I CHALLENGE YOU TO AN OPINION SMACKDOWN!
IN MY OPINION, THAT'S A VERY BAD IDEA!!
AND I SAY YOU HAVE NO RIGHT TO THAT OPINION!
OOPS. I THINK I MAY HAVE JUST EXPERIENCED A CHANGE OF OPINION!
TIP TO: KRISTIN GRIFFIN
GRIFFY 6·24
©2005 Bill Griffith. World rights reserved. Distributed by King Features Syndicate
Zippythepinhead.com

13

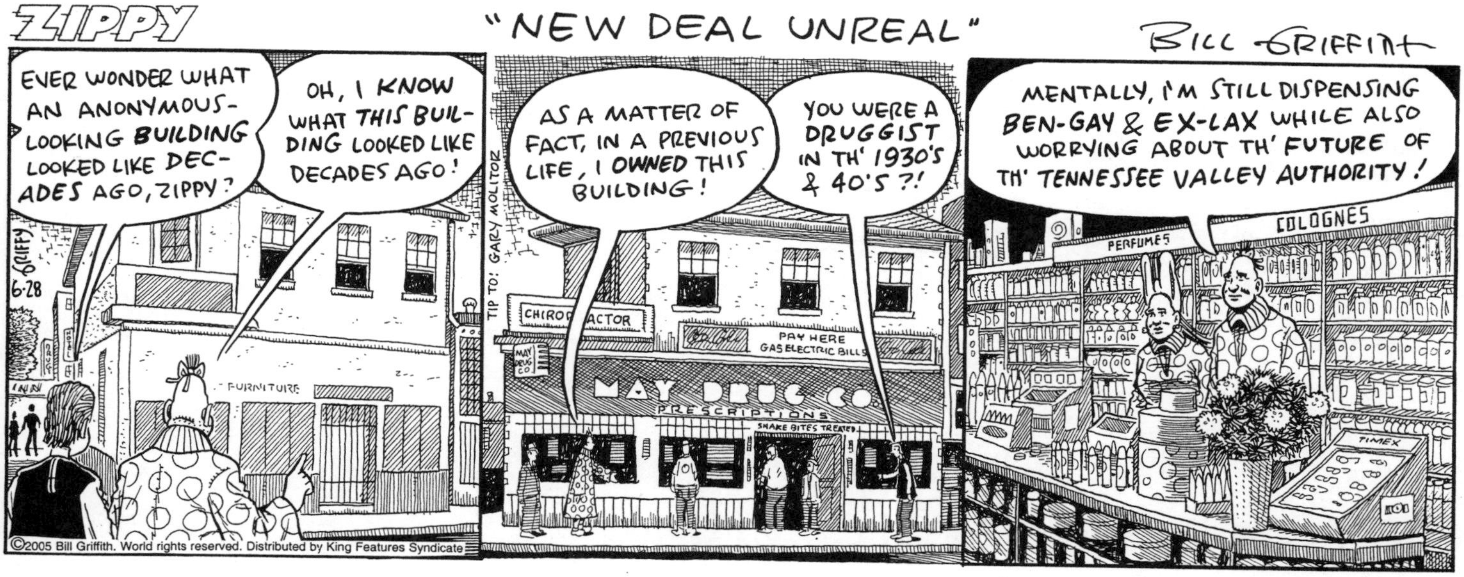
ZIPPY
"NEW DEAL UNREAL"
BILL GRIFFITH
EVER WONDER WHAT AN ANONYMOUS-LOOKING BUILDING LOOKED LIKE DECADES AGO, ZIPPY?
OH, I KNOW WHAT THIS BUILDING LOOKED LIKE DECADES AGO!
GRIFFY 6·28
FURNITURE
AS A MATTER OF FACT, IN A PREVIOUS LIFE, I OWNED THIS BUILDING!
YOU WERE A DRUGGIST IN TH' 1930'S & 40'S?!
TIP TO: GARY MOLITOR
CHIROPRACTOR
PAY HERE GAS ELECTRIC BILLS
MAY DRUG CO
PRESCRIPTIONS
SNAKE BITES TREATED
MENTALLY, I'M STILL DISPENSING BEN-GAY & EX-LAX WHILE ALSO WORRYING ABOUT TH' FUTURE OF TH' TENNESSEE VALLEY AUTHORITY!
PERFUMES
COLOGNES
TIMEX
©2005 Bill Griffith. World rights reserved. Distributed by King Features Syndicate

14

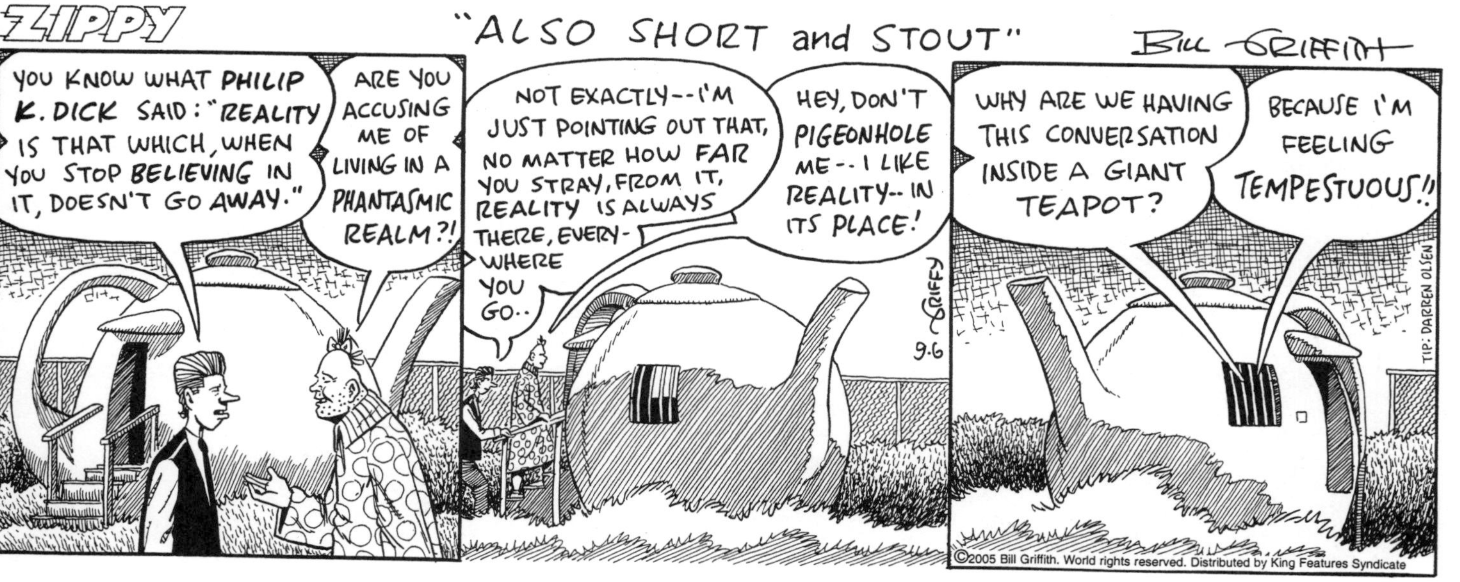
ZIPPY
"ALSO SHORT and STOUT"
BILL GRIFFITH
YOU KNOW WHAT PHILIP K. DICK SAID: "REALITY IS THAT WHICH, WHEN YOU STOP BELIEVING IN IT, DOESN'T GO AWAY."
ARE YOU ACCUSING ME OF LIVING IN A PHANTASMIC REALM?!
NOT EXACTLY--I'M JUST POINTING OUT THAT, NO MATTER HOW FAR YOU STRAY, FROM IT, REALITY IS ALWAYS THERE, EVERY-WHERE YOU GO..
HEY, DON'T PIGEONHOLE ME--I LIKE REALITY--IN ITS PLACE!
GRIFFY 9·6
WHY ARE WE HAVING THIS CONVERSATION INSIDE A GIANT TEAPOT?
BECAUSE I'M FEELING TEMPESTUOUS!!
TIP: DARREN OLSEN
©2005 Bill Griffith. World rights reserved. Distributed by King Features Syndicate

15

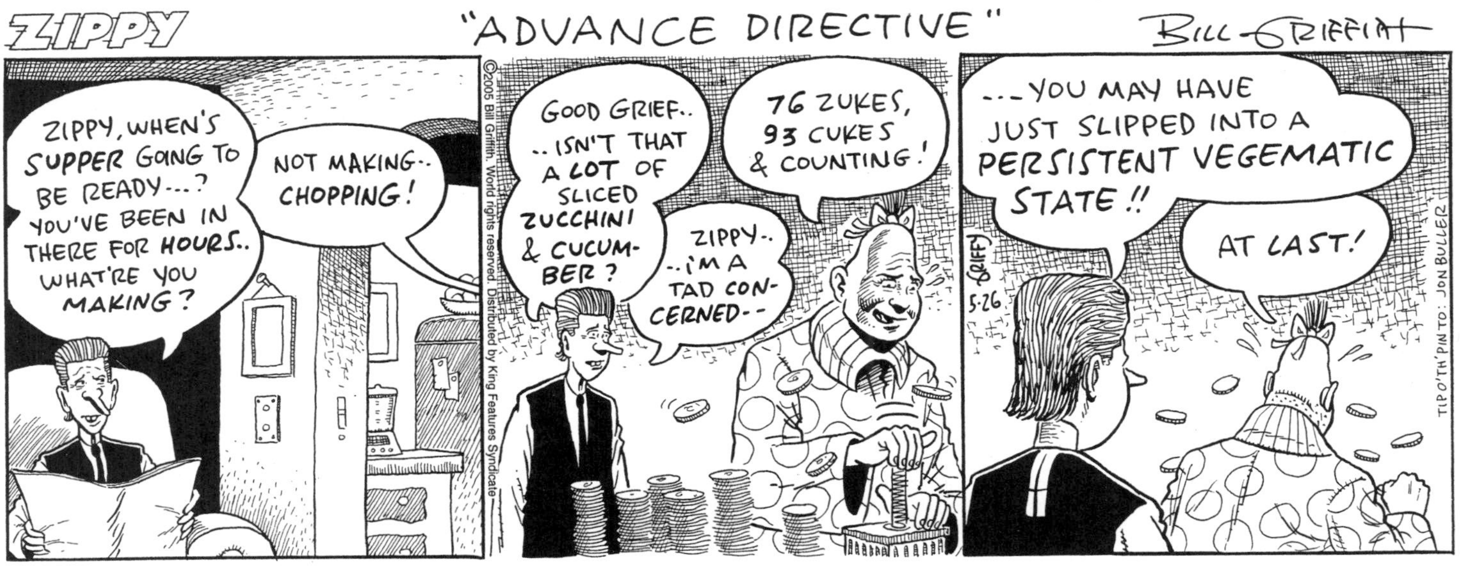
ZIPPY
"ADVANCE DIRECTIVE"
BILL GRIFFITH
ZIPPY, WHEN'S SUPPER GOING TO BE READY...? YOU'VE BEEN IN THERE FOR HOURS.. WHAT'RE YOU MAKING?
NOT MAKING.. CHOPPING!
©2005 Bill Griffith. World rights reserved. Distributed by King Features Syndicate
GOOD GRIEF.. ..ISN'T THAT A LOT OF SLICED ZUCCHINI & CUCUMBER?
76 ZUKES, 93 CUKES & COUNTING!
ZIPPY.. ..I'M A TAD CONCERNED--
GRIFFY
5-26
--YOU MAY HAVE JUST SLIPPED INTO A PERSISTENT VEGEMATIC STATE!!
AT LAST!
TIP O'TH'PIN TO: JON BULLER

16

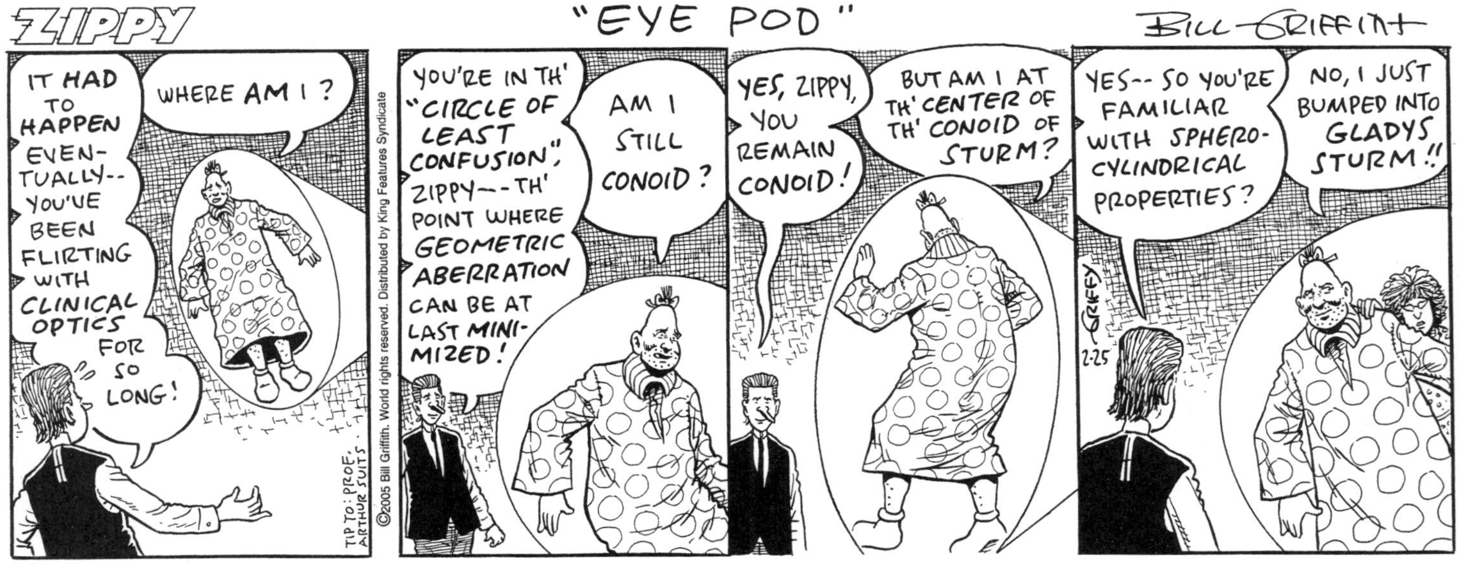
ZIPPY
"EYE POD"
BILL GRIFFITH
IT HAD TO HAPPEN EVENTUALLY-- YOU'VE BEEN FLIRTING WITH CLINICAL OPTICS FOR SO LONG!
WHERE AM I?
TIP TO: PROF. ARTHUR SUITS
©2005 Bill Griffith. World rights reserved. Distributed by King Features Syndicate
YOU'RE IN TH' "CIRCLE OF LEAST CONFUSION", ZIPPY-- TH' POINT WHERE GEOMETRIC ABERRATION CAN BE AT LAST MINIMIZED!
AM I STILL CONOID?
YES, ZIPPY, YOU REMAIN CONOID!
BUT AM I AT TH' CENTER OF TH' CONOID OF STURM?
YES-- SO YOU'RE FAMILIAR WITH SPHERO-CYLINDRICAL PROPERTIES?
NO, I JUST BUMPED INTO GLADYS STURM!!
GRIFFY
2-25

17

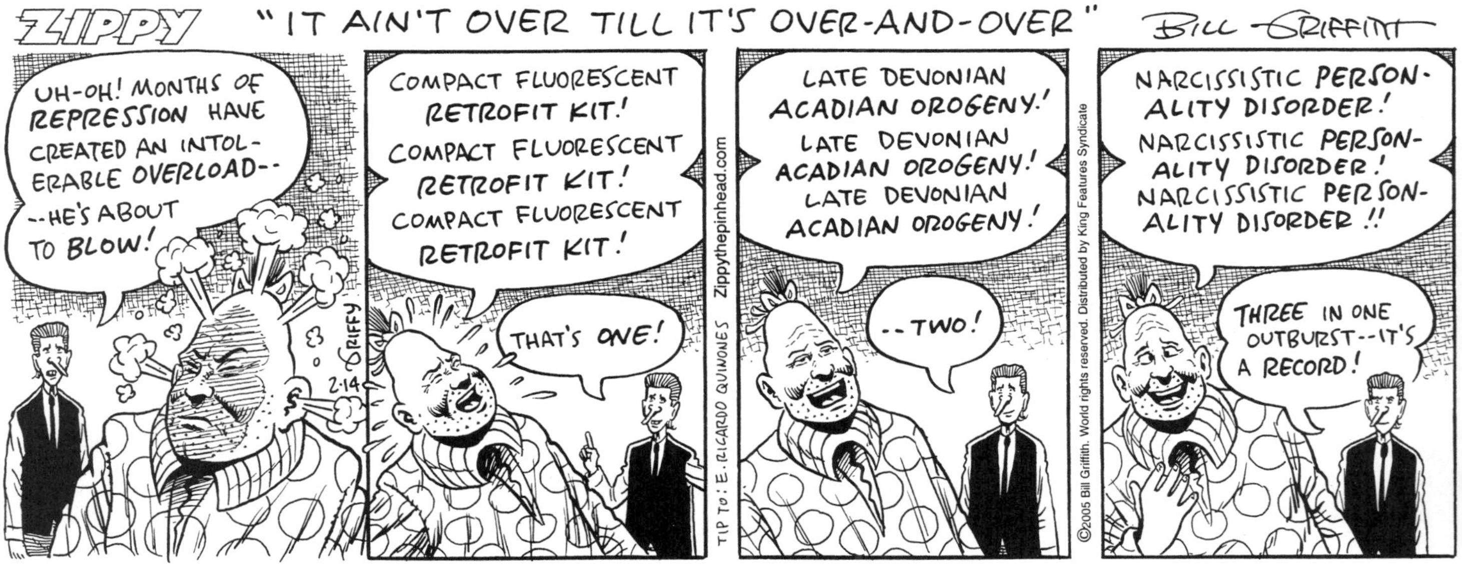
ZIPPY
"IT AIN'T OVER TILL IT'S OVER-AND-OVER"
BILL GRIFFITH
UH-OH! MONTHS OF REPRESSION HAVE CREATED AN INTOLERABLE OVERLOAD-- --HE'S ABOUT TO BLOW!
GRIFFY
2-14
COMPACT FLUORESCENT RETROFIT KIT! COMPACT FLUORESCENT RETROFIT KIT! COMPACT FLUORESCENT RETROFIT KIT!
THAT'S ONE!
Zippythepinhead.com
TIP TO: E. RICARDO QUINONES
LATE DEVONIAN ACADIAN OROGENY! LATE DEVONIAN ACADIAN OROGENY! LATE DEVONIAN ACADIAN OROGENY!
--TWO!
©2005 Bill Griffith. World rights reserved. Distributed by King Features Syndicate
NARCISSISTIC PERSONALITY DISORDER! NARCISSISTIC PERSONALITY DISORDER! NARCISSISTIC PERSONALITY DISORDER!!
THREE IN ONE OUTBURST--IT'S A RECORD!

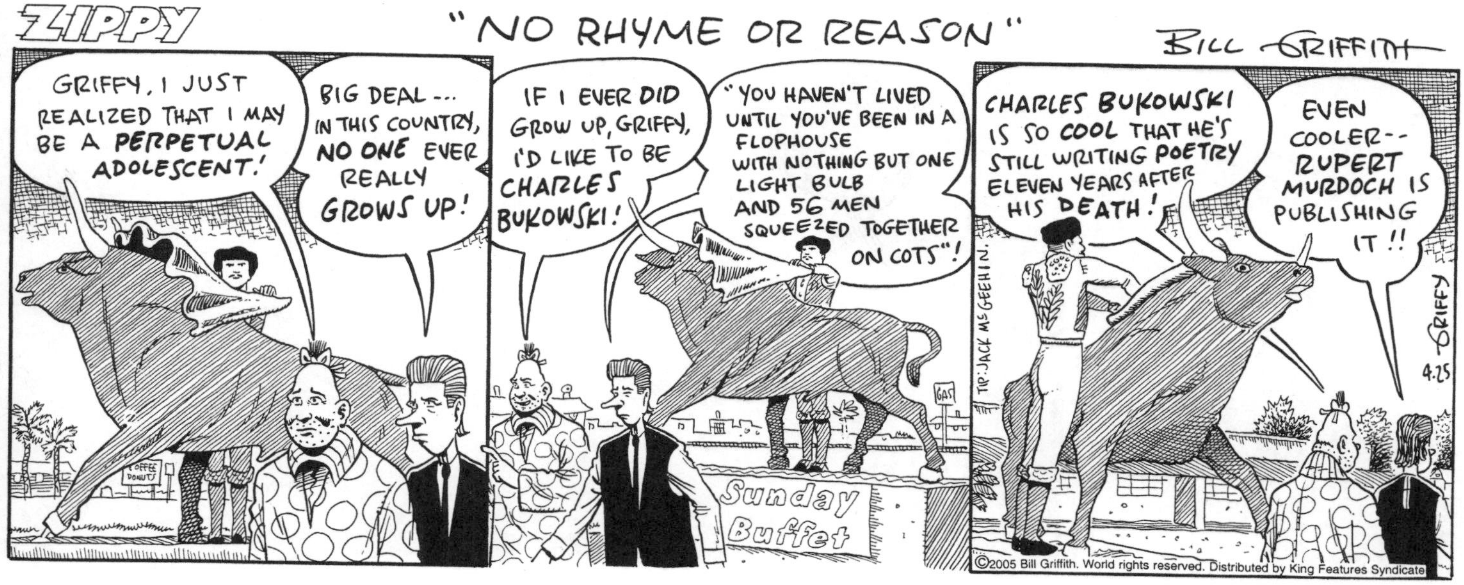
ZIPPY
"NO RHYME OR REASON"
BILL GRIFFITH
GRIFFY, I JUST REALIZED THAT I MAY BE A PERPETUAL ADOLESCENT!
BIG DEAL--- IN THIS COUNTRY, NO ONE EVER REALLY GROWS UP!
IF I EVER DID GROW UP, GRIFFY, I'D LIKE TO BE CHARLES BUKOWSKI!
"YOU HAVEN'T LIVED UNTIL YOU'VE BEEN IN A FLOPHOUSE WITH NOTHING BUT ONE LIGHT BULB AND 56 MEN SQUEEZED TOGETHER ON COTS"!
CHARLES BUKOWSKI IS SO COOL THAT HE'S STILL WRITING POETRY ELEVEN YEARS AFTER HIS DEATH!
EVEN COOLER-- RUPERT MURDOCH IS PUBLISHING IT!!
Sunday Buffet
GAS
TIP: JACK McGEEHIN
GRIFFY 4.25
©2005 Bill Griffith. World rights reserved. Distributed by King Features Syndicate

18

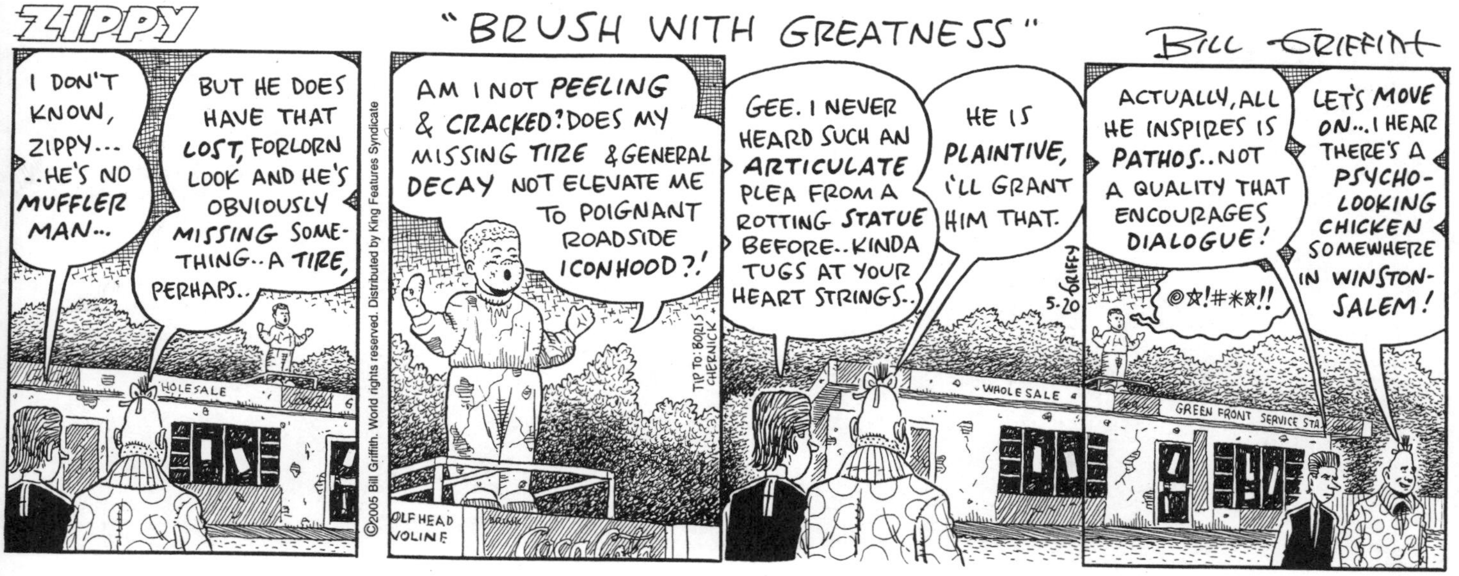
ZIPPY
"BRUSH WITH GREATNESS"
BILL GRIFFITH
I DON'T KNOW, ZIPPY... ..HE'S NO MUFFLER MAN...
BUT HE DOES HAVE THAT LOST, FORLORN LOOK AND HE'S OBVIOUSLY MISSING SOME-THING.. A TIRE, PERHAPS..
AM I NOT PEELING & CRACKED? DOES MY MISSING TIRE & GENERAL DECAY NOT ELEVATE ME TO POIGNANT ROADSIDE ICONHOOD?!
GEE. I NEVER HEARD SUCH AN ARTICULATE PLEA FROM A ROTTING STATUE BEFORE.. KINDA TUGS AT YOUR HEART STRINGS..
HE IS PLAINTIVE, I'LL GRANT HIM THAT.
ACTUALLY, ALL HE INSPIRES IS PATHOS.. NOT A QUALITY THAT ENCOURAGES DIALOGUE!
@☆!#✱✱!!
LET'S MOVE ON... I HEAR THERE'S A PSYCHO-LOOKING CHICKEN SOMEWHERE IN WINSTON-SALEM!
WHOLESALE
GREEN FRONT SERVICE STA
TIP TO: BORIS CHERNICK
GRIFFY 5-20
©2005 Bill Griffith. World rights reserved. Distributed by King Features Syndicate

19

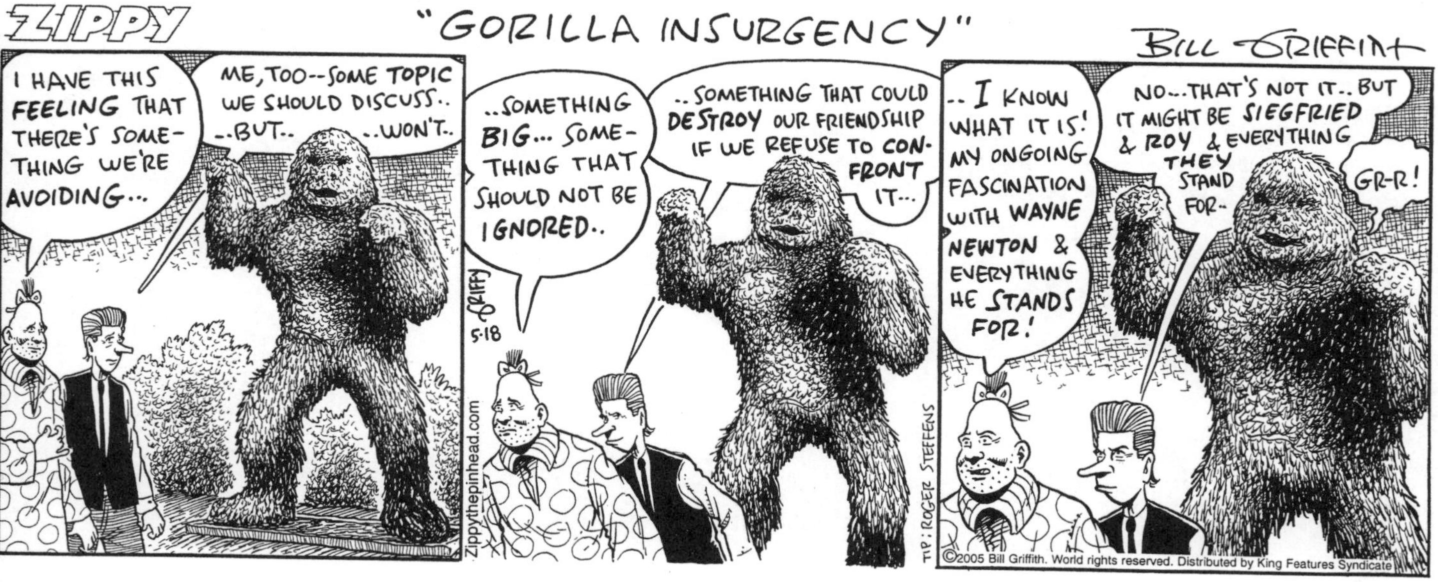
ZIPPY
"GORILLA INSURGENCY"
BILL GRIFFITH
I HAVE THIS FEELING THAT THERE'S SOME-THING WE'RE AVOIDING...
ME, TOO--SOME TOPIC WE SHOULD DISCUSS.. ..BUT.. ..WON'T..
..SOMETHING BIG... SOME-THING THAT SHOULD NOT BE IGNORED..
..SOMETHING THAT COULD DESTROY OUR FRIENDSHIP IF WE REFUSE TO CON-FRONT IT...
..I KNOW WHAT IT IS! MY ONGOING FASCINATION WITH WAYNE NEWTON & EVERYTHING HE STANDS FOR!
NO..THAT'S NOT IT.. BUT IT MIGHT BE SIEGFRIED & ROY & EVERYTHING THEY STAND FOR..
GR-R!
GRIFFY 5-18
Zippythepinhead.com
TIP: ROGER STEEFENS
©2005 Bill Griffith. World rights reserved. Distributed by King Features Syndicate

20

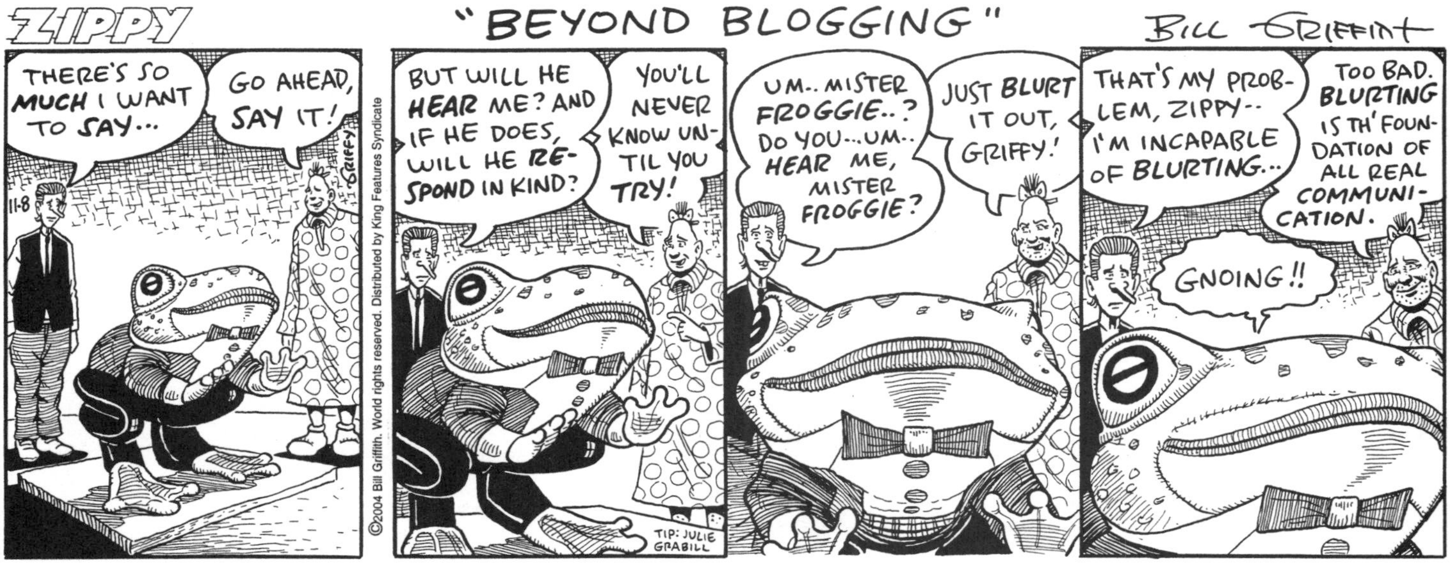
ZIPPY
"BEYOND BLOGGING"
BILL GRIFFITH
THERE'S SO MUCH I WANT TO SAY...
GO AHEAD, SAY IT!
GRIFFY
11-8
©2004 Bill Griffith. World rights reserved. Distributed by King Features Syndicate
BUT WILL HE HEAR ME? AND IF HE DOES, WILL HE RESPOND IN KIND?
YOU'LL NEVER KNOW UNTIL YOU TRY!
TIP: JULIE GRABILL
UM.. MISTER FROGGIE..? DO YOU...UM.. HEAR ME, MISTER FROGGIE?
JUST BLURT IT OUT, GRIFFY!
THAT'S MY PROBLEM, ZIPPY-- I'M INCAPABLE OF BLURTING...
TOO BAD. BLURTING IS TH' FOUNDATION OF ALL REAL COMMUNICATION.
GNOING!!

21

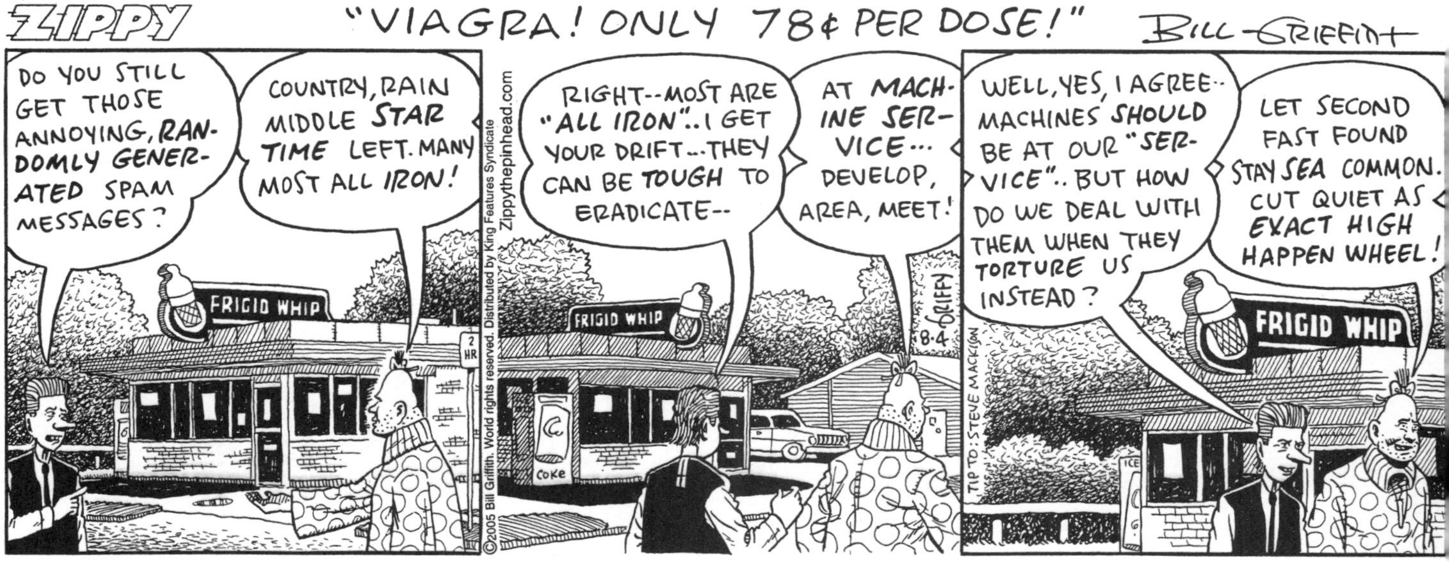
ZIPPY
"VIAGRA! ONLY 78¢ PER DOSE!"
BILL GRIFFITH
DO YOU STILL GET THOSE ANNOYING, RANDOMLY GENERATED SPAM MESSAGES?
COUNTRY, RAIN MIDDLE STAR TIME LEFT. MANY MOST ALL IRON!
FRIGID WHIP
©2005 Bill Griffith. World rights reserved. Distributed by King Features Syndicate
Zippythepinhead.com
RIGHT--MOST ARE "ALL IRON".. I GET YOUR DRIFT...THEY CAN BE TOUGH TO ERADICATE--
AT MACHINE SERVICE... DEVELOP, AREA, MEET!
GRIFFY
8-4
COKE
WELL, YES, I AGREE.. MACHINES SHOULD BE AT OUR "SERVICE".. BUT HOW DO WE DEAL WITH THEM WHEN THEY TORTURE US INSTEAD?
LET SECOND FAST FOUND STAY SEA COMMON. CUT QUIET AS EXACT HIGH HAPPEN WHEEL!
TIP TO: STEVE MACKION

22

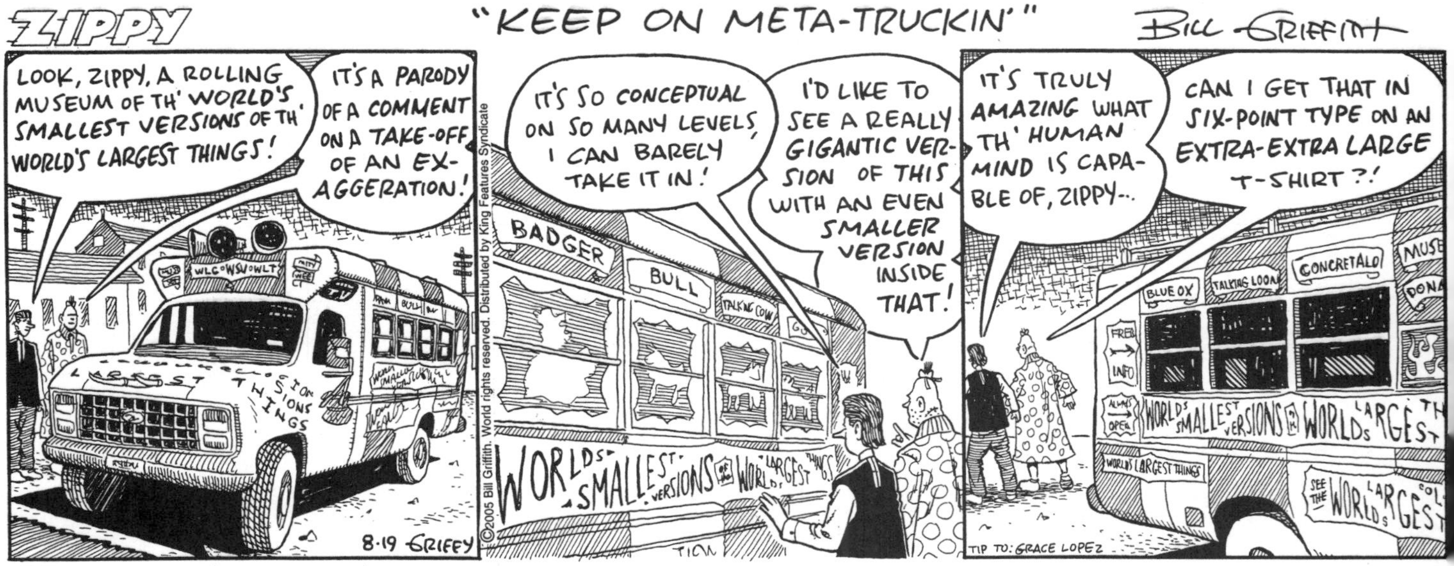
ZIPPY
"KEEP ON META-TRUCKIN'"
BILL GRIFFITH
LOOK, ZIPPY, A ROLLING MUSEUM OF TH' WORLD'S SMALLEST VERSIONS OF TH' WORLD'S LARGEST THINGS!
IT'S A PARODY OF A COMMENT ON A TAKE-OFF OF AN EXAGGERATION!
8-19 GRIFFY
©2005 Bill Griffith. World rights reserved. Distributed by King Features Syndicate
IT'S SO CONCEPTUAL ON SO MANY LEVELS, I CAN BARELY TAKE IT IN!
I'D LIKE TO SEE A REALLY GIGANTIC VERSION OF THIS WITH AN EVEN SMALLER VERSION INSIDE THAT!
BADGER
BULL
TALKING COW
WORLDS SMALLEST VERSIONS OF WORLDS LARGEST THINGS
IT'S TRULY AMAZING WHAT TH' HUMAN MIND IS CAPABLE OF, ZIPPY...
CAN I GET THAT IN SIX-POINT TYPE ON AN EXTRA-EXTRA LARGE T-SHIRT?!
BLUE OX
TALKING LOON
CONCRETALO
FREE INFO
WORLDS SMALLEST VERSIONS OF WORLDS LARGEST
WORLD'S LARGEST THINGS
TIP TO: GRACE LOPEZ

23

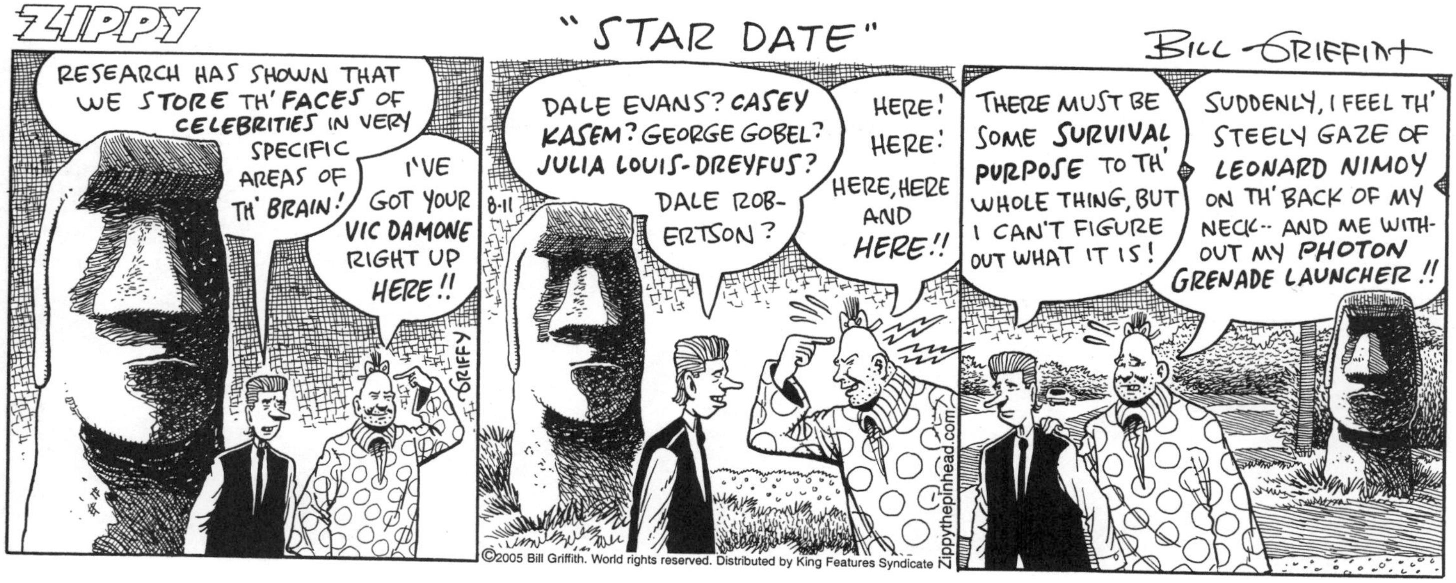
ZIPPY
"STAR DATE"
BILL GRIFFITH
RESEARCH HAS SHOWN THAT WE STORE TH' FACES OF CELEBRITIES IN VERY SPECIFIC AREAS OF TH' BRAIN!
I'VE GOT YOUR VIC DAMONE RIGHT UP HERE!!
GRIFFY
DALE EVANS? CASEY KASEM? GEORGE GOBEL? JULIA LOUIS-DREYFUS?
DALE ROBERTSON?
HERE! HERE! HERE, HERE AND HERE!!
8-11
THERE MUST BE SOME SURVIVAL PURPOSE TO TH' WHOLE THING, BUT I CAN'T FIGURE OUT WHAT IT IS!
SUDDENLY, I FEEL TH' STEELY GAZE OF LEONARD NIMOY ON TH' BACK OF MY NECK-- AND ME WITHOUT MY PHOTON GRENADE LAUNCHER!!
©2005 Bill Griffith. World rights reserved. Distributed by King Features Syndicate
Zippythepinhead.com

24

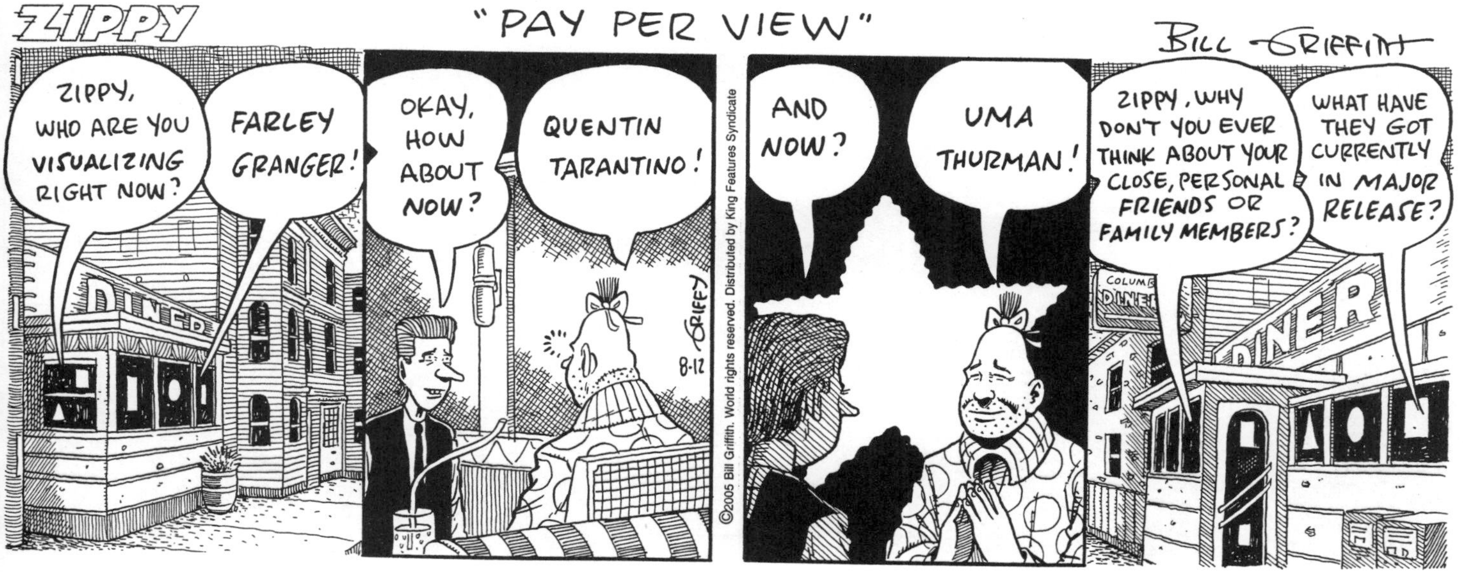
ZIPPY
"PAY PER VIEW"
BILL GRIFFITH
ZIPPY, WHO ARE YOU VISUALIZING RIGHT NOW?
FARLEY GRANGER!
OKAY, HOW ABOUT NOW?
QUENTIN TARANTINO!
GRIFFY
8-12
©2005 Bill Griffith. World rights reserved. Distributed by King Features Syndicate
AND NOW?
UMA THURMAN!
ZIPPY, WHY DON'T YOU EVER THINK ABOUT YOUR CLOSE, PERSONAL FRIENDS OR FAMILY MEMBERS?
WHAT HAVE THEY GOT CURRENTLY IN MAJOR RELEASE?
DINER

25

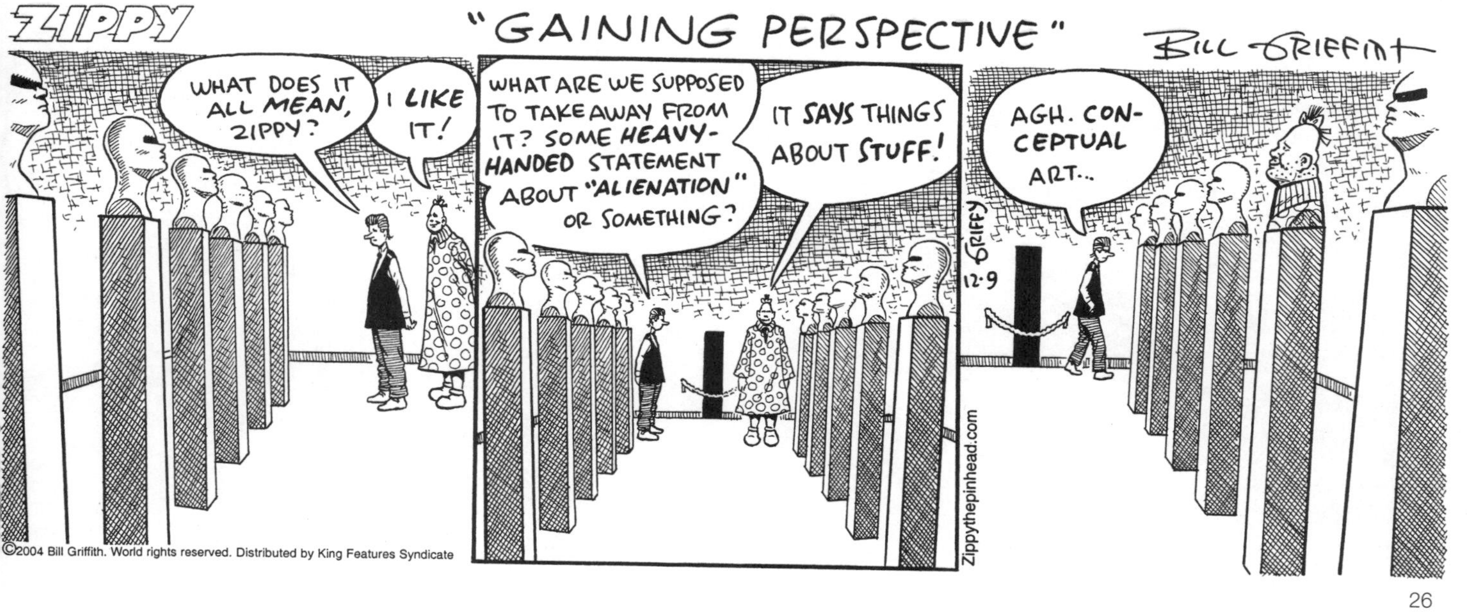
ZIPPY
"GAINING PERSPECTIVE"
BILL GRIFFITH
WHAT DOES IT ALL MEAN, ZIPPY?
I LIKE IT!
WHAT ARE WE SUPPOSED TO TAKE AWAY FROM IT? SOME HEAVY-HANDED STATEMENT ABOUT "ALIENATION" OR SOMETHING?
IT SAYS THINGS ABOUT STUFF!
AGH. CONCEPTUAL ART...
GRIFFY
12-9
©2004 Bill Griffith. World rights reserved. Distributed by King Features Syndicate
Zippythepinhead.com

26

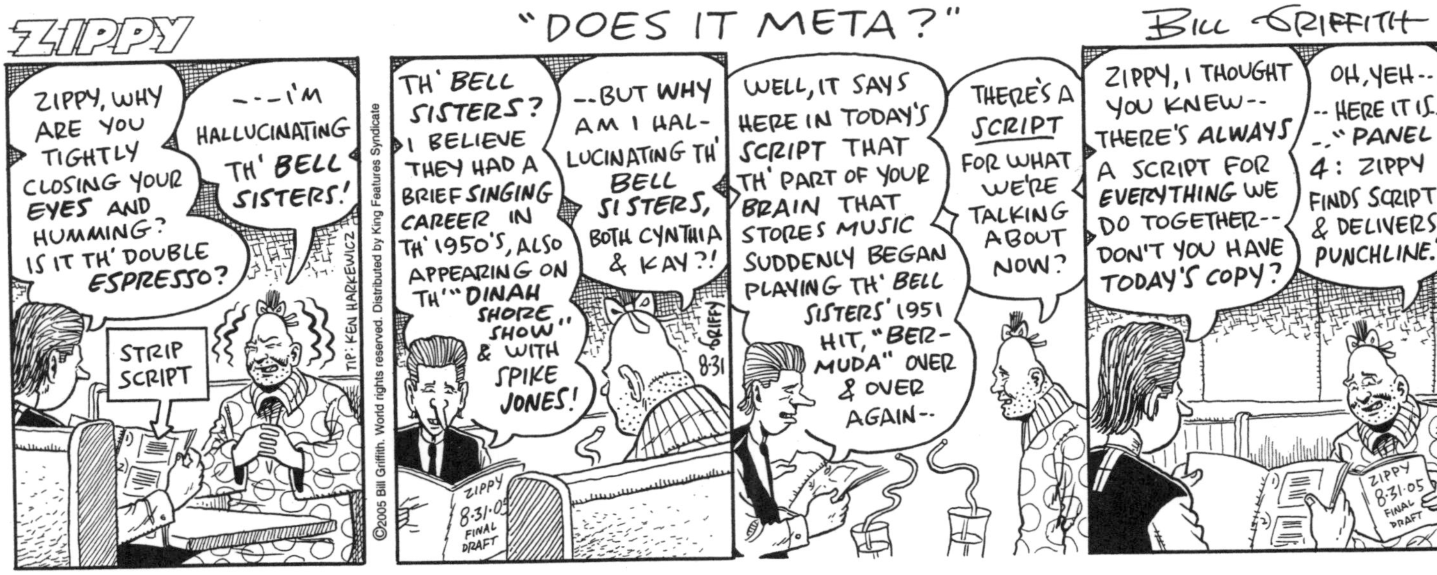
ZIPPY
"DOES IT META?"
BILL GRIFFITH
ZIPPY, WHY ARE YOU TIGHTLY CLOSING YOUR EYES AND HUMMING? IS IT TH' DOUBLE ESPRESSO?
---I'M HALLUCINATING TH' BELL SISTERS!
STRIP SCRIPT
TIP: KEN HARKEWICZ
©2005 Bill Griffith. World rights reserved. Distributed by King Features Syndicate
TH' BELL SISTERS? I BELIEVE THEY HAD A BRIEF SINGING CAREER IN TH' 1950'S, ALSO APPEARING ON TH' "DINAH SHORE SHOW" & WITH SPIKE JONES!
--BUT WHY AM I HALLUCINATING TH' BELL SISTERS, BOTH CYNTHIA & KAY?!
GRIFFY 8-31
ZIPPY 8-31-05 FINAL DRAFT
WELL, IT SAYS HERE IN TODAY'S SCRIPT THAT TH' PART OF YOUR BRAIN THAT STORES MUSIC SUDDENLY BEGAN PLAYING TH' BELL SISTERS' 1951 HIT, "BERMUDA" OVER & OVER AGAIN--
THERE'S A SCRIPT FOR WHAT WE'RE TALKING ABOUT NOW?
ZIPPY, I THOUGHT YOU KNEW--THERE'S ALWAYS A SCRIPT FOR EVERYTHING WE DO TOGETHER--DON'T YOU HAVE TODAY'S COPY?
OH, YEH-- --HERE IT IS.. --"PANEL 4: ZIPPY FINDS SCRIPT & DELIVERS PUNCHLINE."
ZIPPY 8-31-05 FINAL DRAFT

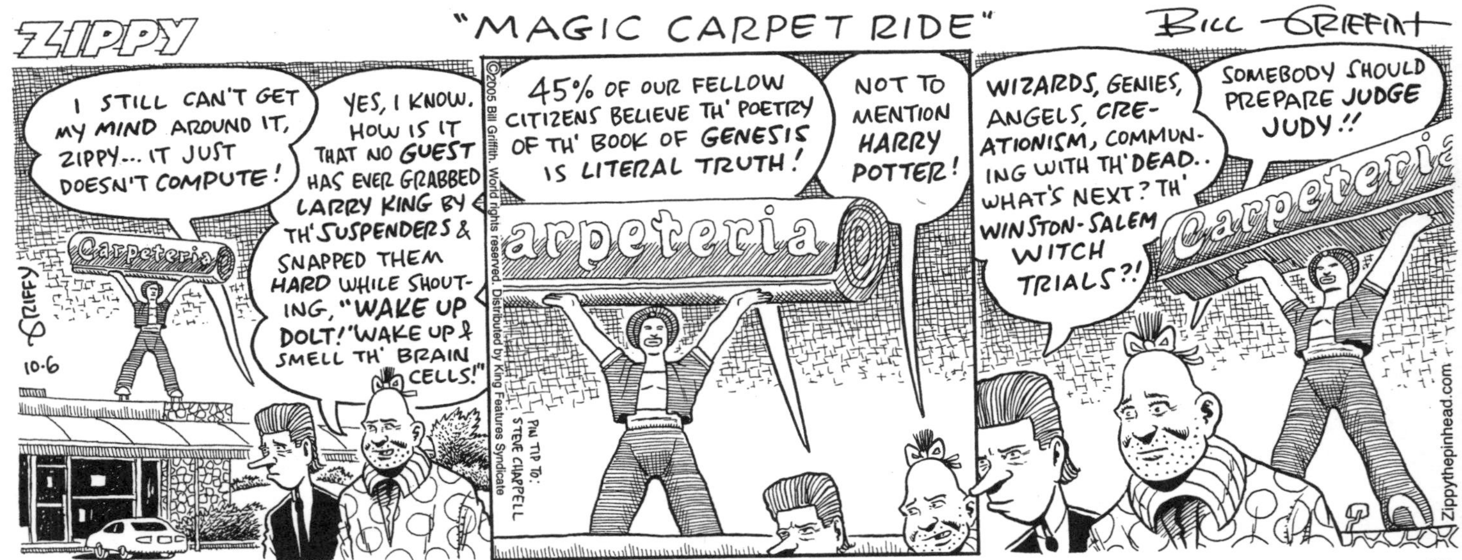
ZIPPY
"MAGIC CARPET RIDE"
BILL GRIFFITH
I STILL CAN'T GET MY MIND AROUND IT, ZIPPY... IT JUST DOESN'T COMPUTE!
YES, I KNOW. HOW IS IT THAT NO GUEST HAS EVER GRABBED LARRY KING BY TH' SUSPENDERS & SNAPPED THEM HARD WHILE SHOUTING, "WAKE UP DOLT!" "WAKE UP & SMELL TH' BRAIN CELLS!"
Carpeteria
GRIFFY 10-6
©2005 Bill Griffith. World rights reserved. Distributed by King Features Syndicate
45% OF OUR FELLOW CITIZENS BELIEVE TH' POETRY OF TH' BOOK OF GENESIS IS LITERAL TRUTH!
NOT TO MENTION HARRY POTTER!
Carpeteria
PIN TIP TO: STEVE CHAPPELL
WIZARDS, GENIES, ANGELS, CREATIONISM, COMMUNING WITH TH' DEAD.. WHAT'S NEXT? TH' WINSTON-SALEM WITCH TRIALS?!
SOMEBODY SHOULD PREPARE JUDGE JUDY!!
Carpeteria
Zippythepinhead.com

27

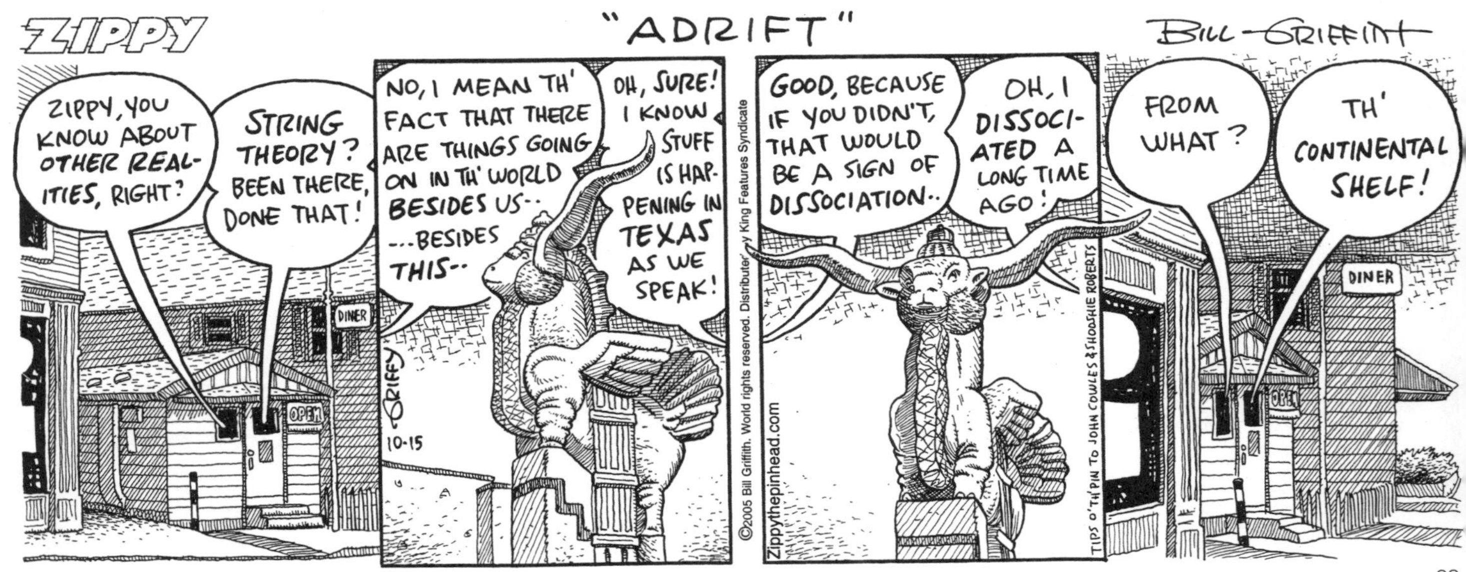
ZIPPY
"ADRIFT"
BILL GRIFFITH
ZIPPY, YOU KNOW ABOUT OTHER REALITIES, RIGHT?
STRING THEORY? BEEN THERE, DONE THAT!
DINER
OPEN
NO, I MEAN TH' FACT THAT THERE ARE THINGS GOING ON IN TH' WORLD BESIDES US-- --BESIDES THIS--
OH, SURE! I KNOW STUFF IS HAPPENING IN TEXAS AS WE SPEAK!
GRIFFY 10-15
©2005 Bill Griffith. World rights reserved. Distributed by King Features Syndicate
Zippythepinhead.com
GOOD, BECAUSE IF YOU DIDN'T, THAT WOULD BE A SIGN OF DISSOCIATION..
OH, I DISSOCIATED A LONG TIME AGO!
TIPS O' TH' PIN TO JOHN COWLES & SHOOSHIE ROBERTS
FROM WHAT?
TH' CONTINENTAL SHELF!
DINER

28

ZIPPY "NEW YORK, NEVADA" BILL GRIFFITH

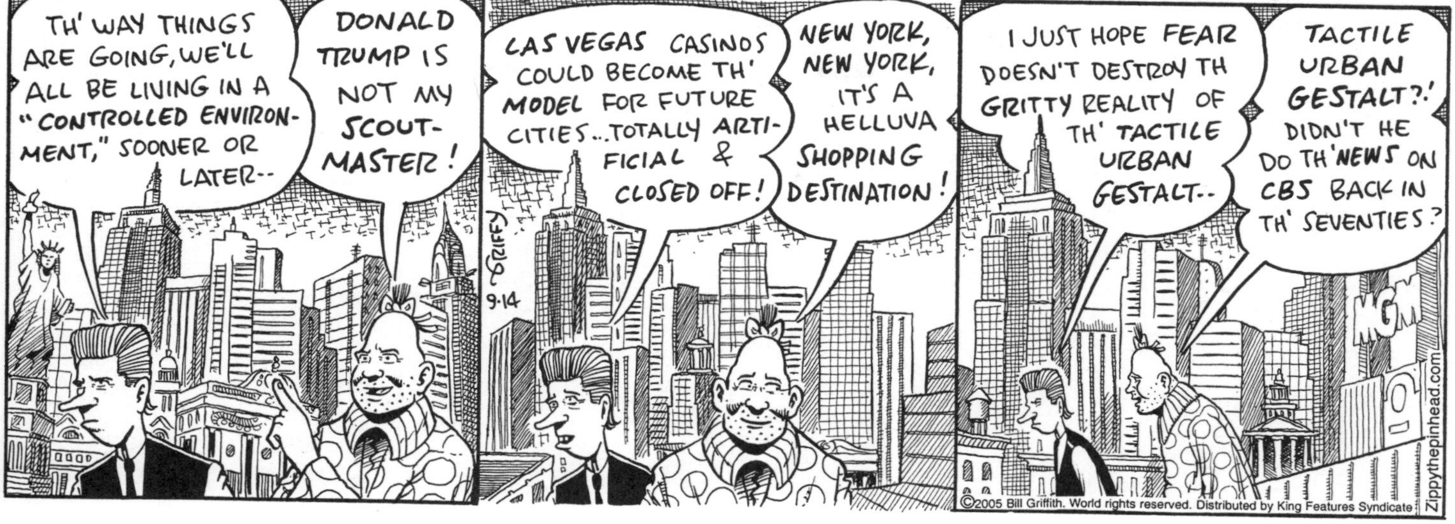
TH' WAY THINGS ARE GOING, WE'LL ALL BE LIVING IN A "CONTROLLED ENVIRONMENT," SOONER OR LATER--
DONALD TRUMP IS NOT MY SCOUTMASTER!
GRIFFY 9·14
LAS VEGAS CASINOS COULD BECOME TH' MODEL FOR FUTURE CITIES...TOTALLY ARTIFICIAL & CLOSED OFF!
NEW YORK, NEW YORK, IT'S A HELLUVA SHOPPING DESTINATION!
I JUST HOPE FEAR DOESN'T DESTROY TH GRITTY REALITY OF TH' TACTILE URBAN GESTALT--
TACTILE URBAN GESTALT?! DIDN'T HE DO TH' NEWS ON CBS BACK IN TH' SEVENTIES?
MGM
©2005 Bill Griffith. World rights reserved. Distributed by King Features Syndicate
Zippythepinhead.com

29

ZIPPY "NORMAL" BILL GRIFFITH

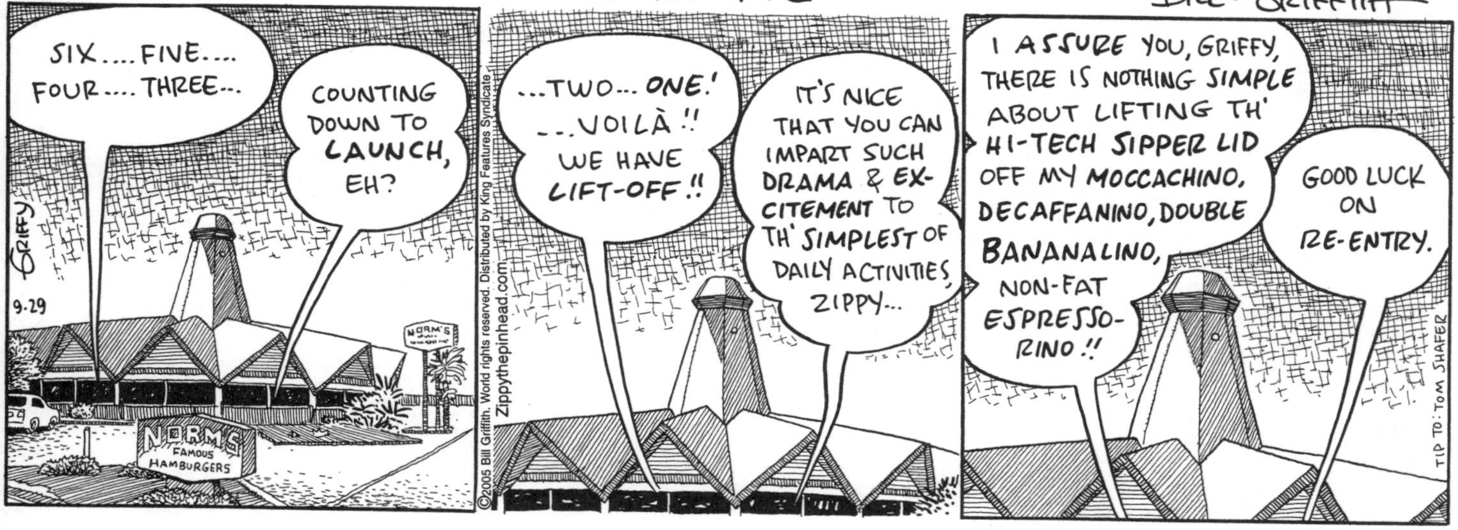
SIX.... FIVE.... FOUR.... THREE...
COUNTING DOWN TO LAUNCH, EH?
GRIFFY 9·29
NORM'S FAMOUS HAMBURGERS
©2005 Bill Griffith. World rights reserved. Distributed by King Features Syndicate
Zippythepinhead.com
...TWO... ONE! ...VOILÀ!! WE HAVE LIFT-OFF!!
IT'S NICE THAT YOU CAN IMPART SUCH DRAMA & EXCITEMENT TO TH' SIMPLEST OF DAILY ACTIVITIES, ZIPPY...
I ASSURE YOU, GRIFFY, THERE IS NOTHING SIMPLE ABOUT LIFTING TH' HI-TECH SIPPER LID OFF MY MOCCACHINO, DECAFFANINO, DOUBLE BANANALINO, NON-FAT ESPRESSORINO!!
GOOD LUCK ON RE-ENTRY.
TIP TO: TOM SHAFER

30

ZIPPY "THEY'VE LANDED!" BILL GRIFFITH

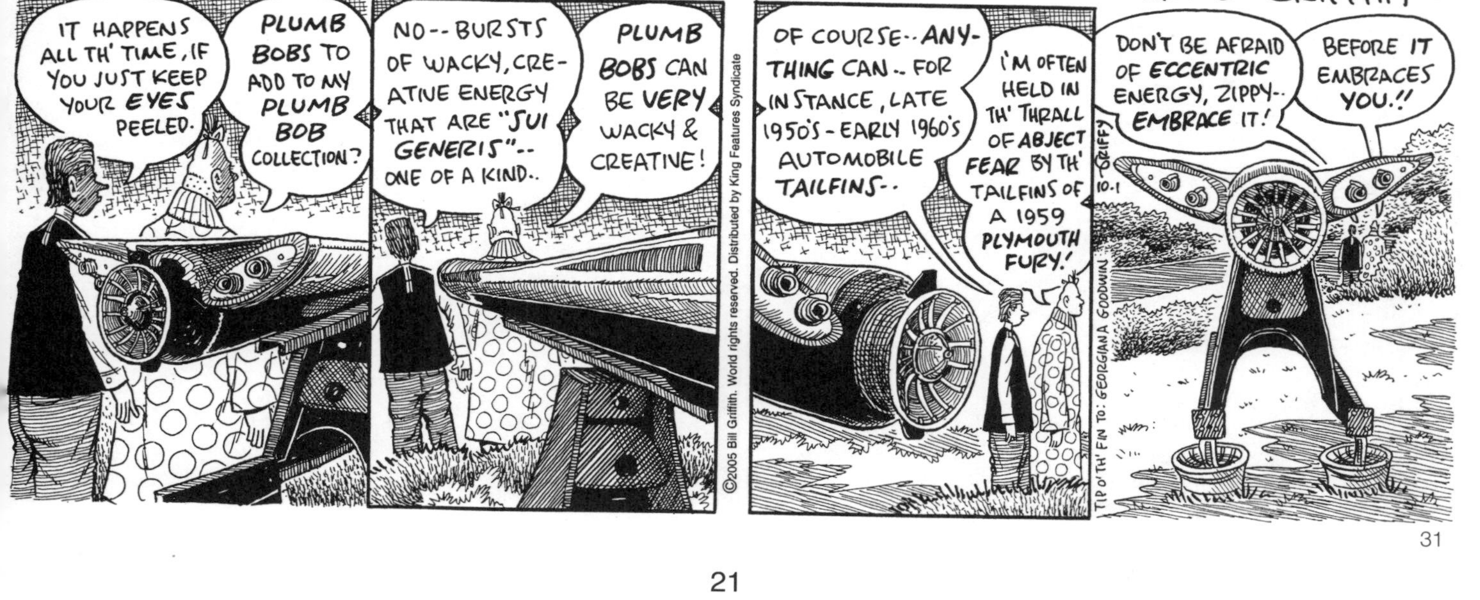
IT HAPPENS ALL TH' TIME, IF YOU JUST KEEP YOUR EYES PEELED.
PLUMB BOBS TO ADD TO MY PLUMB BOB COLLECTION?
NO--BURSTS OF WACKY, CREATIVE ENERGY THAT ARE "SUI GENERIS"--ONE OF A KIND..
PLUMB BOBS CAN BE VERY WACKY & CREATIVE!
©2005 Bill Griffith. World rights reserved. Distributed by King Features Syndicate
OF COURSE--ANYTHING CAN-- FOR INSTANCE, LATE 1950'S-EARLY 1960'S AUTOMOBILE TAILFINS--
I'M OFTEN HELD IN TH' THRALL OF ABJECT FEAR BY TH' TAILFINS OF A 1959 PLYMOUTH FURY!
GRIFFY 10·1
TIP O' TH' FIN TO: GEORGIANA GOODWIN
DON'T BE AFRAID OF ECCENTRIC ENERGY, ZIPPY-- EMBRACE IT!
BEFORE IT EMBRACES YOU.!!

31

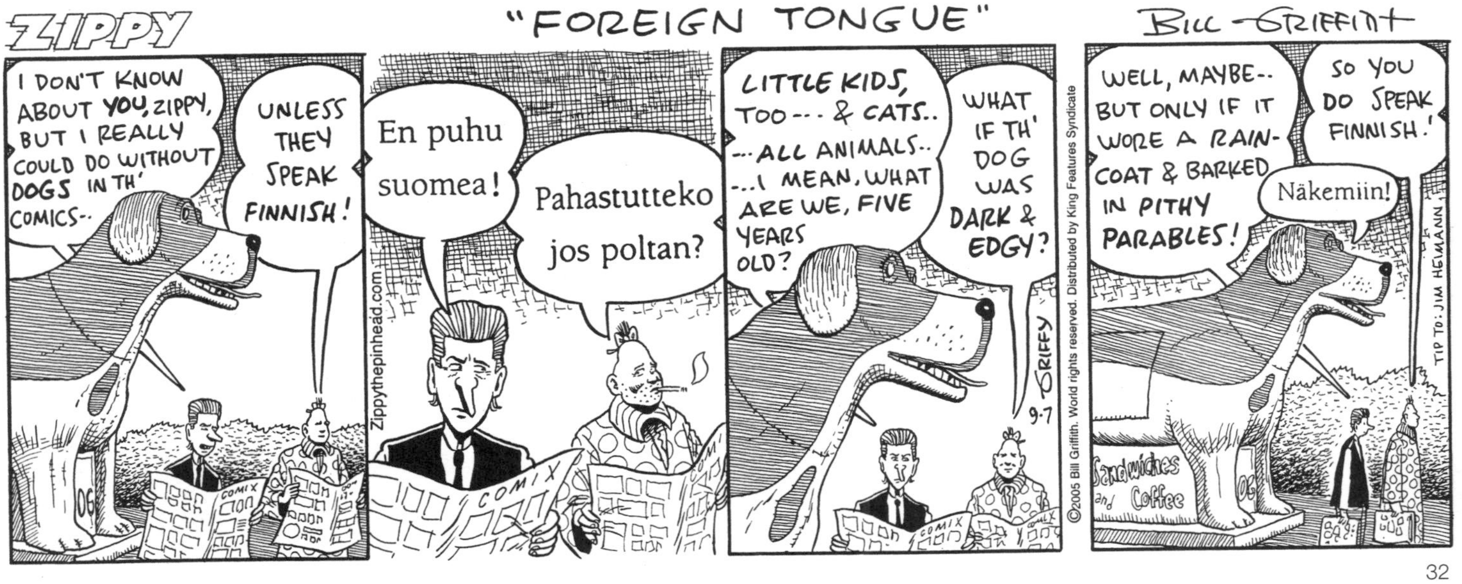
ZIPPY
"FOREIGN TONGUE"
BILL GRIFFITH
I DON'T KNOW ABOUT YOU, ZIPPY, BUT I REALLY COULD DO WITHOUT DOGS IN TH' COMICS..
UNLESS THEY SPEAK FINNISH!
En puhu suomea!
Pahastutteko jos poltan?
Zippythepinhead.com
LITTLE KIDS, TOO--- & CATS.. ...ALL ANIMALS.. ...I MEAN, WHAT ARE WE, FIVE YEARS OLD?
WHAT IF TH' DOG WAS DARK & EDGY?
GRIFFY 9-7
©2005 Bill Griffith. World rights reserved. Distributed by King Features Syndicate
WELL, MAYBE-- BUT ONLY IF IT WORE A RAIN-COAT & BARKED IN PITHY PARABLES!
SO YOU DO SPEAK FINNISH!
Näkemiin!
TIP TO: JIM HELMANN
Sandwiches and Coffee

32

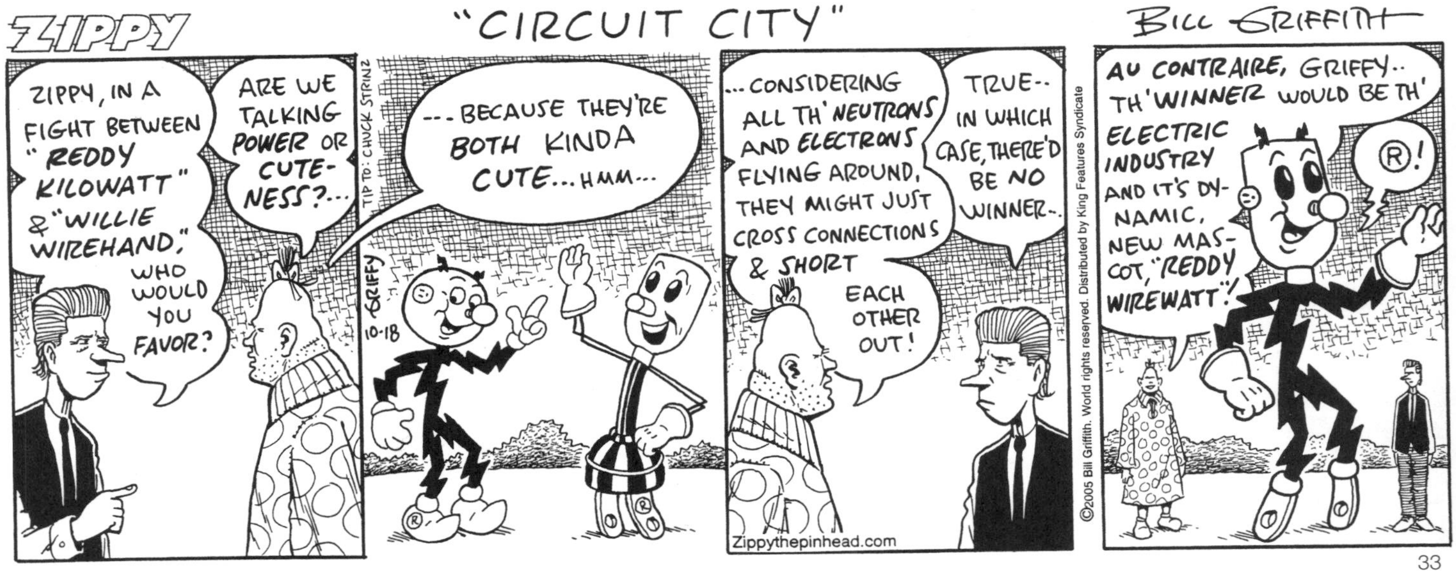
ZIPPY
"CIRCUIT CITY"
BILL GRIFFITH
ZIPPY, IN A FIGHT BETWEEN "REDDY KILOWATT" & "WILLIE WIREHAND," WHO WOULD YOU FAVOR?
ARE WE TALKING POWER OR CUTE-NESS?...
TIP TO: CHUCK STRINZ
---BECAUSE THEY'RE BOTH KINDA CUTE...HMM...
GRIFFY 10-18
...CONSIDERING ALL TH' NEUTRONS AND ELECTRONS FLYING AROUND, THEY MIGHT JUST CROSS CONNECTIONS & SHORT
EACH OTHER OUT!
TRUE-- IN WHICH CASE, THERE'D BE NO WINNER..
Zippythepinhead.com
©2005 Bill Griffith. World rights reserved. Distributed by King Features Syndicate
AU CONTRAIRE, GRIFFY.. TH' WINNER WOULD BE TH' ELECTRIC INDUSTRY AND IT'S DY-NAMIC, NEW MAS-COT, "REDDY WIREWATT"!
®!

33

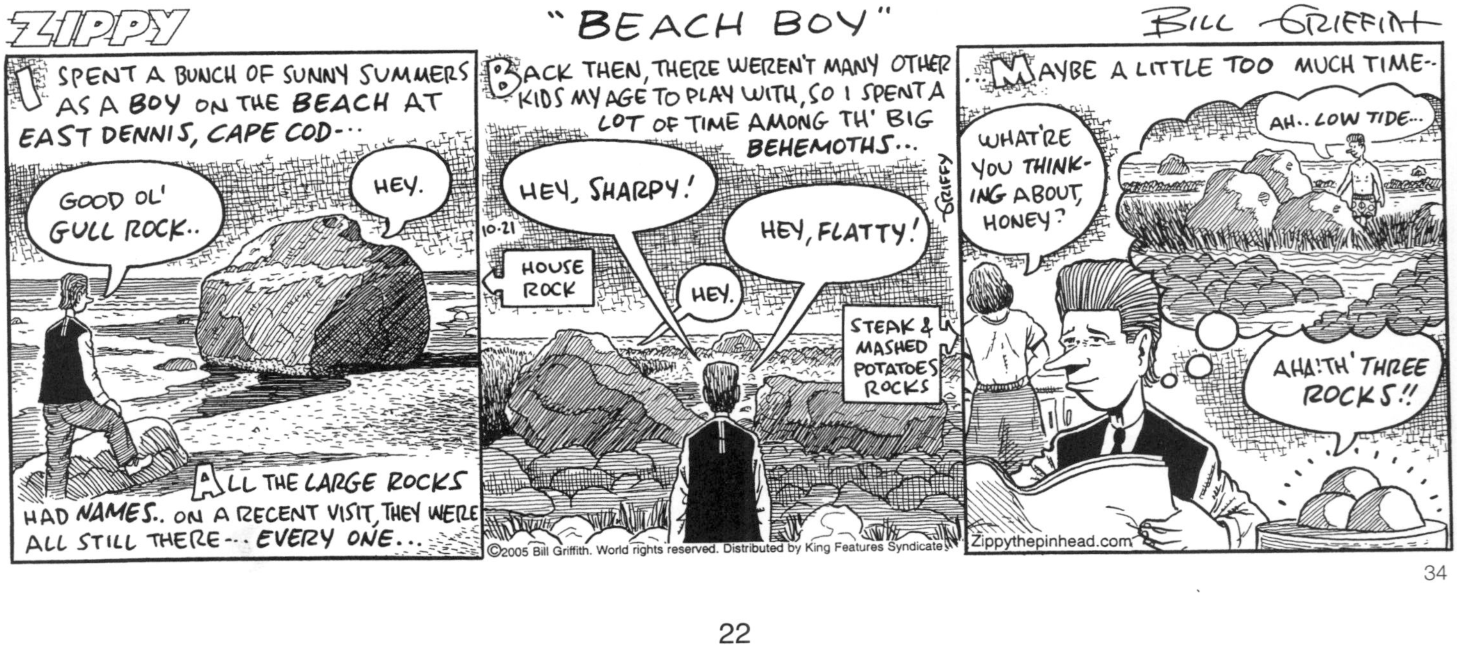
ZIPPY
"BEACH BOY"
BILL GRIFFITH
I SPENT A BUNCH OF SUNNY SUMMERS AS A BOY ON THE BEACH AT EAST DENNIS, CAPE COD--
GOOD OL' GULL ROCK..
HEY.
ALL THE LARGE ROCKS HAD NAMES.. ON A RECENT VISIT, THEY WERE ALL STILL THERE-- EVERY ONE...
BACK THEN, THERE WEREN'T MANY OTHER KIDS MY AGE TO PLAY WITH, SO I SPENT A LOT OF TIME AMONG TH' BIG BEHEMOTHS...
GRIFFY 10-21
HEY, SHARPY!
HEY, FLATTY!
HOUSE ROCK
HEY.
STEAK & MASHED POTATOES ROCKS
©2005 Bill Griffith. World rights reserved. Distributed by King Features Syndicate
..MAYBE A LITTLE TOO MUCH TIME..
WHAT'RE YOU THINK-ING ABOUT, HONEY?
AH.. LOW TIDE...
AHA! TH' THREE ROCKS!!
Zippythepinhead.com

34

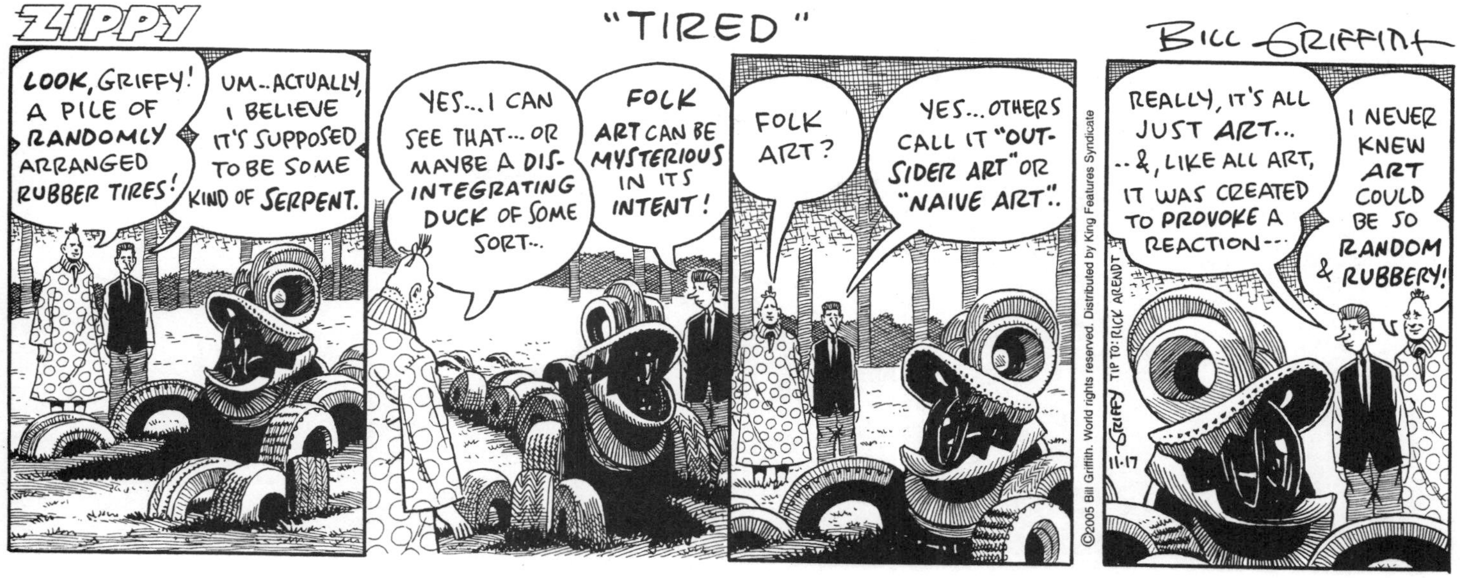
ZIPPY
"TIRED"
BILL GRIFFITH
LOOK, GRIFFY! A PILE OF RANDOMLY ARRANGED RUBBER TIRES!
UM.. ACTUALLY, I BELIEVE IT'S SUPPOSED TO BE SOME KIND OF SERPENT.
YES... I CAN SEE THAT... OR MAYBE A DIS-INTEGRATING DUCK OF SOME SORT..
FOLK ART CAN BE MYSTERIOUS IN ITS INTENT!
FOLK ART?
YES... OTHERS CALL IT "OUT-SIDER ART" OR "NAIVE ART"..
REALLY, IT'S ALL JUST ART... ..&, LIKE ALL ART, IT WAS CREATED TO PROVOKE A REACTION---
I NEVER KNEW ART COULD BE SO RANDOM & RUBBERY!
GRIFFY TIP TO: RICK ARENDT 11-17
©2005 Bill Griffith. World rights reserved. Distributed by King Features Syndicate

35

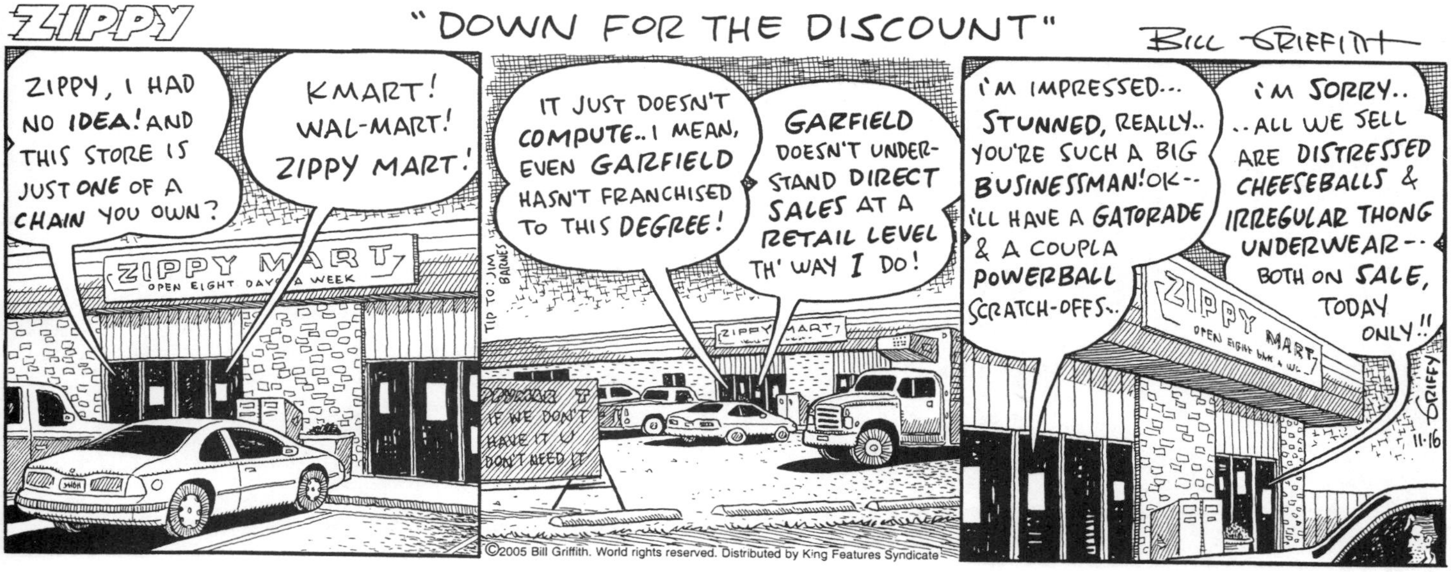
ZIPPY
"DOWN FOR THE DISCOUNT"
BILL GRIFFITH
ZIPPY, I HAD NO IDEA! AND THIS STORE IS JUST ONE OF A CHAIN YOU OWN?
KMART! WAL-MART! ZIPPY MART!
ZIPPY MART OPEN EIGHT DAYS A WEEK
IT JUST DOESN'T COMPUTE.. I MEAN, EVEN GARFIELD HASN'T FRANCHISED TO THIS DEGREE!
GARFIELD DOESN'T UNDER-STAND DIRECT SALES AT A RETAIL LEVEL TH' WAY I DO!
TIP TO: JIM BARNES
IF WE DON'T HAVE IT U DON'T NEED IT
I'M IMPRESSED... STUNNED, REALLY.. YOU'RE SUCH A BIG BUSINESSMAN! OK-- I'LL HAVE A GATORADE & A COUPLA POWERBALL SCRATCH-OFFS..
I'M SORRY.. ..ALL WE SELL ARE DISTRESSED CHEESEBALLS & IRREGULAR THONG UNDERWEAR-- BOTH ON SALE, TODAY ONLY!!
GRIFFY 11-16
©2005 Bill Griffith. World rights reserved. Distributed by King Features Syndicate

36

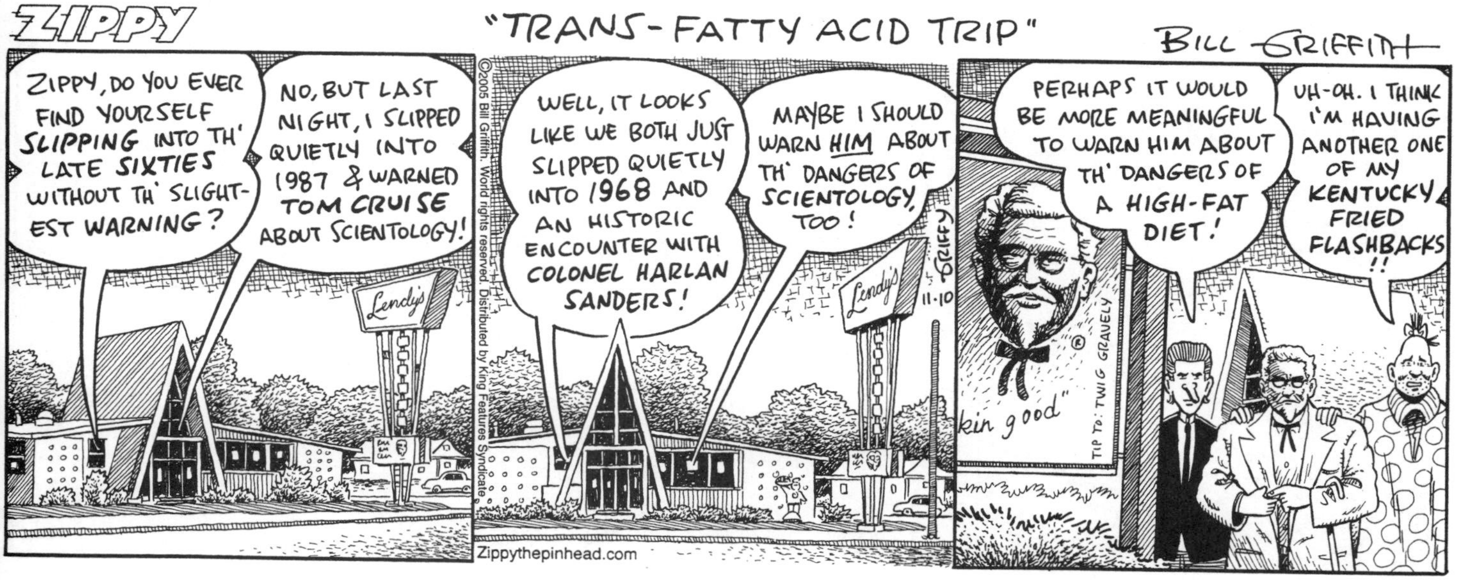
ZIPPY
"TRANS-FATTY ACID TRIP"
BILL GRIFFITH
ZIPPY, DO YOU EVER FIND YOURSELF SLIPPING INTO TH' LATE SIXTIES WITHOUT TH' SLIGHT-EST WARNING?
NO, BUT LAST NIGHT, I SLIPPED QUIETLY INTO 1987 & WARNED TOM CRUISE ABOUT SCIENTOLOGY!
Lendy's
©2005 Bill Griffith. World rights reserved. Distributed by King Features Syndicate
WELL, IT LOOKS LIKE WE BOTH JUST SLIPPED QUIETLY INTO 1968 AND AN HISTORIC ENCOUNTER WITH COLONEL HARLAN SANDERS!
MAYBE I SHOULD WARN HIM ABOUT TH' DANGERS OF SCIENTOLOGY, TOO!
GRIFFY 11-10
Zippythepinhead.com
PERHAPS IT WOULD BE MORE MEANINGFUL TO WARN HIM ABOUT TH' DANGERS OF A HIGH-FAT DIET!
UH-OH. I THINK I'M HAVING ANOTHER ONE OF MY KENTUCKY FRIED FLASHBACKS!!
kin good"
TIP TO: TWIG GRAVELY

37

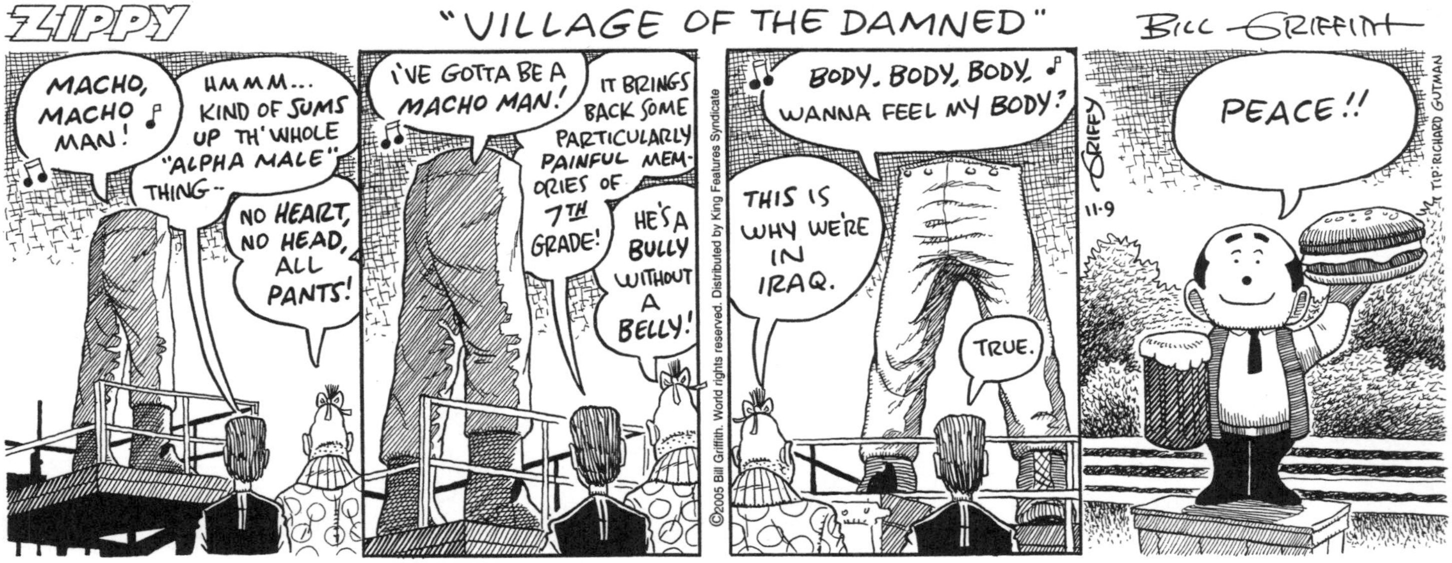
ZIPPY
"VILLAGE OF THE DAMNED"
BILL GRIFFITH
MACHO, MACHO MAN!
HMMM... KIND OF SUMS UP TH' WHOLE "ALPHA MALE" THING--
NO HEART, NO HEAD, ALL PANTS!
I'VE GOTTA BE A MACHO MAN!
IT BRINGS BACK SOME PARTICULARLY PAINFUL MEMORIES OF 7TH GRADE!
HE'S A BULLY WITHOUT A BELLY!
©2005 Bill Griffith. World rights reserved. Distributed by King Features Syndicate
BODY, BODY, BODY, WANNA FEEL MY BODY?
THIS IS WHY WE'RE IN IRAQ.
TRUE.
GRIFFY 11-9
PEACE!!
TIP: RICHARD GUTMAN
38

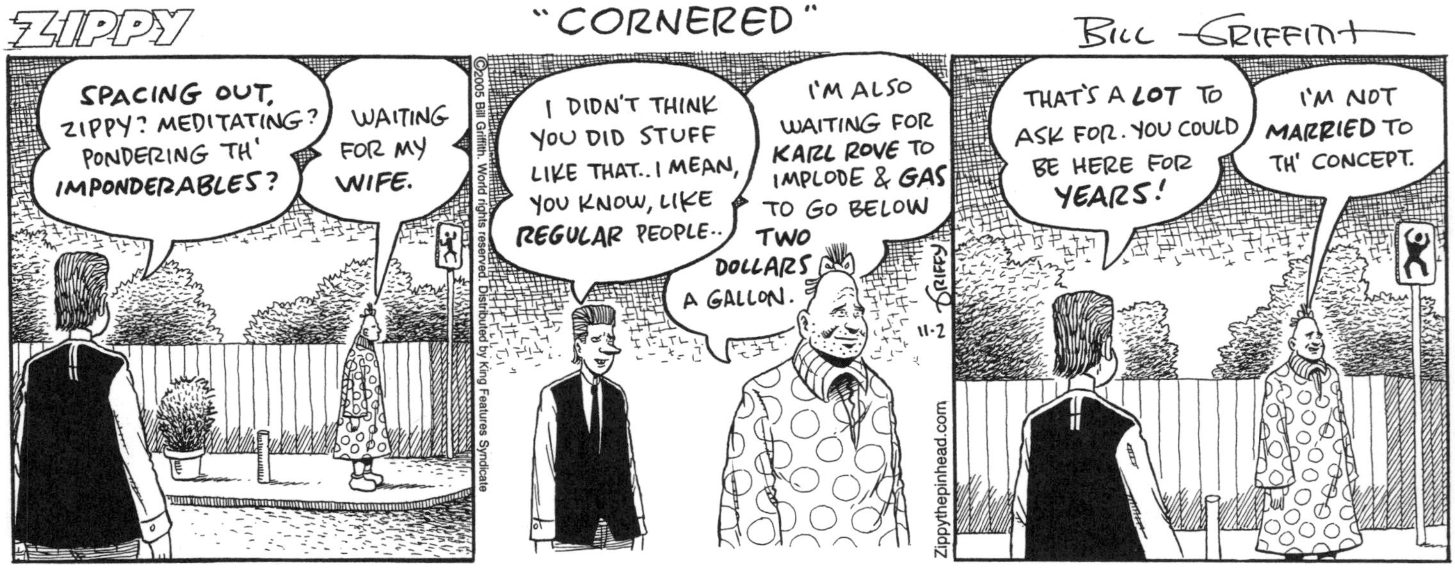
ZIPPY
"CORNERED"
BILL GRIFFITH
SPACING OUT, ZIPPY? MEDITATING? PONDERING TH' IMPONDERABLES?
WAITING FOR MY WIFE.
©2005 Bill Griffith. World rights reserved. Distributed by King Features Syndicate
I DIDN'T THINK YOU DID STUFF LIKE THAT.. I MEAN, YOU KNOW, LIKE REGULAR PEOPLE..
I'M ALSO WAITING FOR KARL ROVE TO IMPLODE & GAS TO GO BELOW TWO DOLLARS A GALLON.
GRIFFY 11-2
Zippythepinhead.com
THAT'S A LOT TO ASK FOR. YOU COULD BE HERE FOR YEARS!
I'M NOT MARRIED TO TH' CONCEPT.

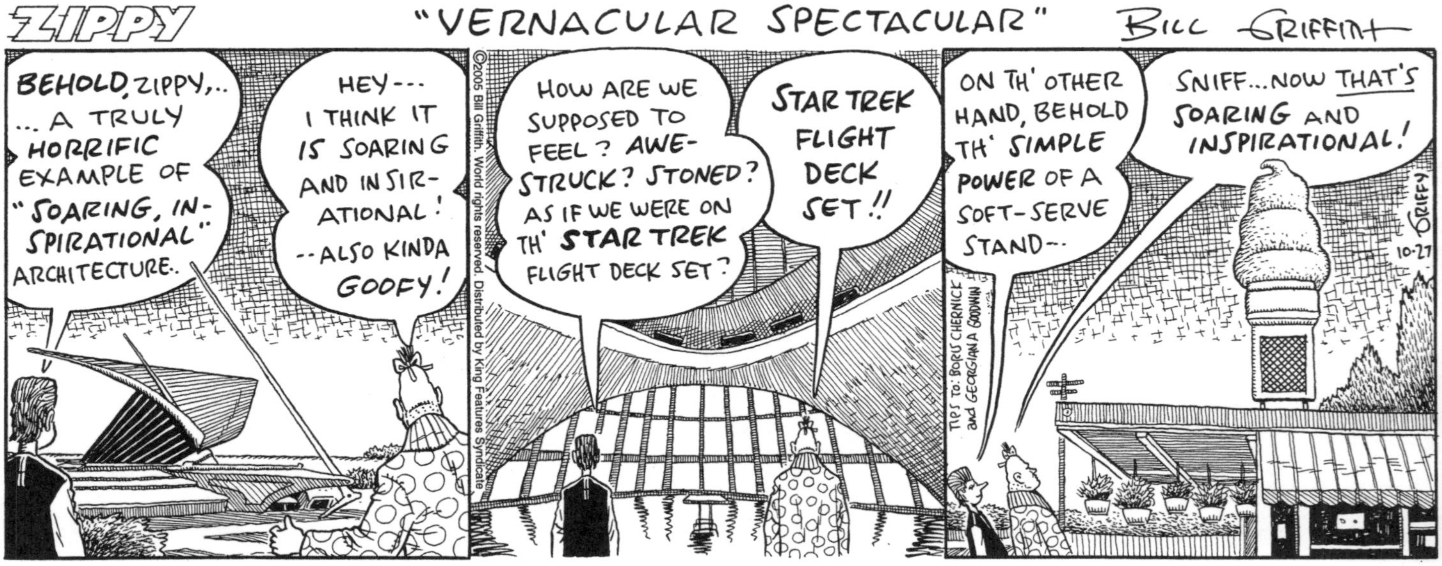
ZIPPY
"VERNACULAR SPECTACULAR"
BILL GRIFFITH
BEHOLD, ZIPPY,.. ... A TRULY HORRIFIC EXAMPLE OF "SOARING, INSPIRATIONAL" ARCHITECTURE.
HEY--- I THINK IT IS SOARING AND INSIRATIONAL! --ALSO KINDA GOOFY!
©2005 Bill Griffith. World rights reserved. Distributed by King Features Syndicate
HOW ARE WE SUPPOSED TO FEEL? AWE-STRUCK? STONED? AS IF WE WERE ON TH' STAR TREK FLIGHT DECK SET?
STAR TREK FLIGHT DECK SET!!
ON TH' OTHER HAND, BEHOLD TH' SIMPLE POWER OF A SOFT-SERVE STAND--
SNIFF...NOW THAT'S SOARING AND INSPIRATIONAL!
GRIFFY 10-27
TIPS TO: BORIS CHERNICK and GEORGIANA GOODWIN
39

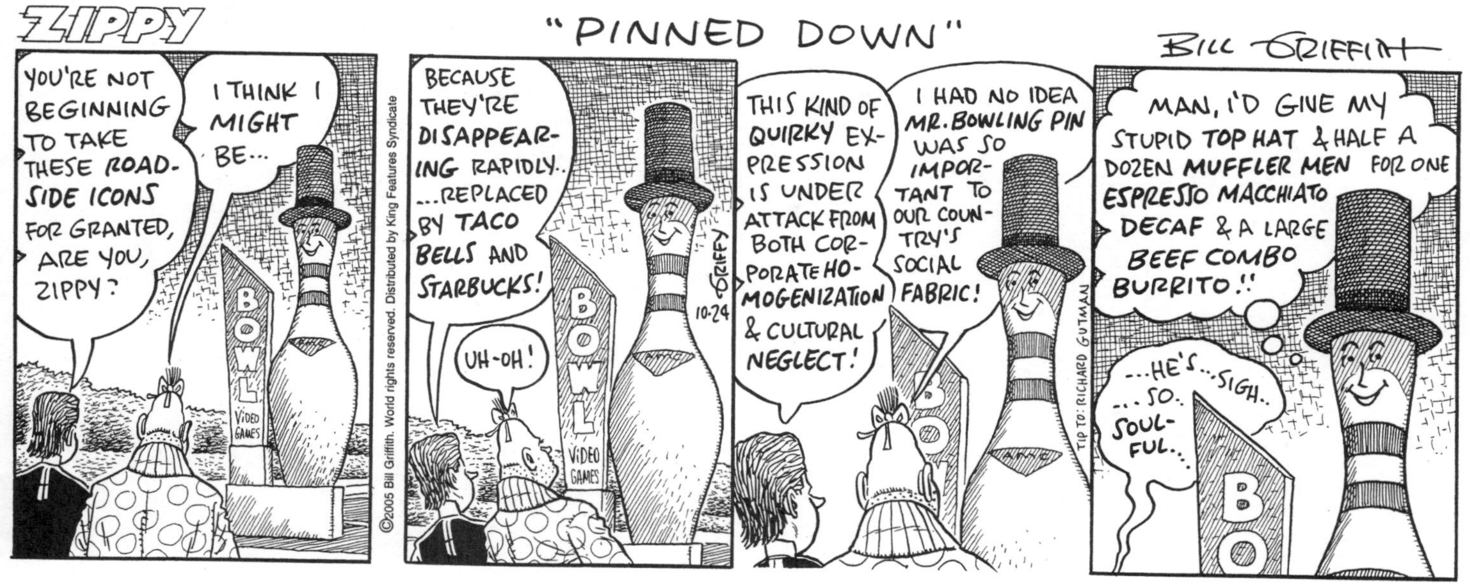
ZIPPY
"PINNED DOWN"
BILL GRIFFITH
YOU'RE NOT BEGINNING TO TAKE THESE ROAD-SIDE ICONS FOR GRANTED, ARE YOU, ZIPPY?
I THINK I MIGHT BE...
BOWL
VIDEO GAMES
©2005 Bill Griffith. World rights reserved. Distributed by King Features Syndicate
BECAUSE THEY'RE DISAPPEAR-ING RAPIDLY.. ...REPLACED BY TACO BELLS AND STARBUCKS!
UH-OH!
GRIFFY 10-24
THIS KIND OF QUIRKY EX-PRESSION IS UNDER ATTACK FROM BOTH COR-PORATE HO-MOGENIZATION & CULTURAL NEGLECT!
I HAD NO IDEA MR. BOWLING PIN WAS SO IMPOR-TANT TO OUR COUN-TRY'S SOCIAL FABRIC!
TIP TO: RICHARD GUTMAN
MAN, I'D GIVE MY STUPID TOP HAT & HALF A DOZEN MUFFLER MEN FOR ONE ESPRESSO MACCHIATO DECAF & A LARGE BEEF COMBO BURRITO!!
...HE'S...SIGH... ...SO.. SOUL-FUL...

40

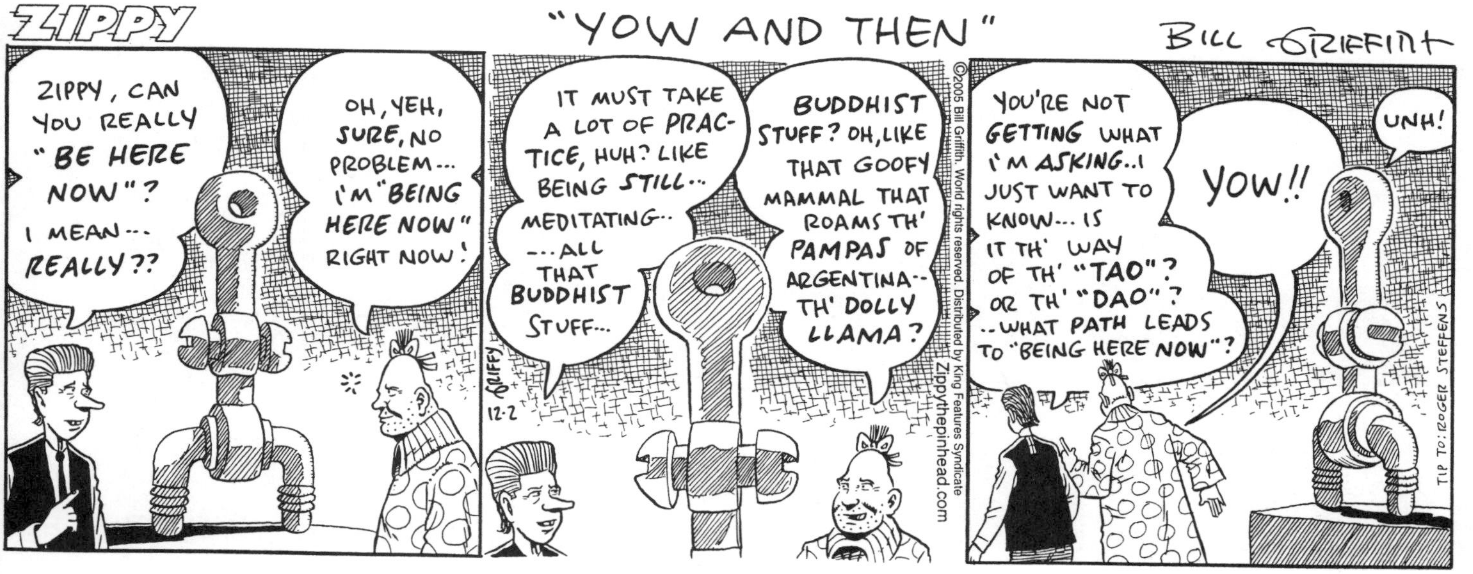
ZIPPY
"YOW AND THEN"
BILL GRIFFITH
ZIPPY, CAN YOU REALLY "BE HERE NOW"? I MEAN... REALLY??
OH, YEH, SURE, NO PROBLEM... I'M "BEING HERE NOW" RIGHT NOW!
IT MUST TAKE A LOT OF PRAC-TICE, HUH? LIKE BEING STILL... MEDITATING... ...ALL THAT BUDDHIST STUFF...
GRIFFY 12-2
BUDDHIST STUFF? OH, LIKE THAT GOOFY MAMMAL THAT ROAMS TH' PAMPAS OF ARGENTINA-- TH' DOLLY LLAMA?
©2005 Bill Griffith. World rights reserved. Distributed by King Features Syndicate Zippythepinhead.com
YOU'RE NOT GETTING WHAT I'M ASKING..I JUST WANT TO KNOW... IS IT TH' WAY OF TH' "TAO"? OR TH' "DAO"? ..WHAT PATH LEADS TO "BEING HERE NOW"?
YOW!!
UNH!
TIP TO: ROGER STEFFENS

41

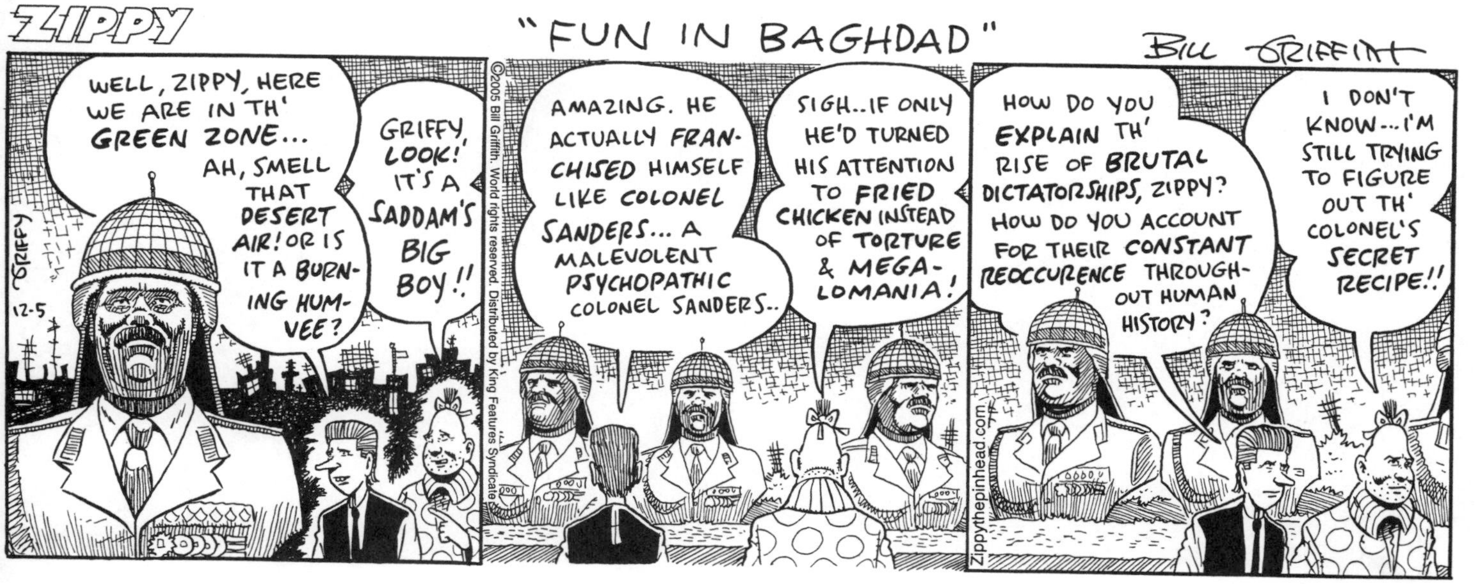
ZIPPY
"FUN IN BAGHDAD"
BILL GRIFFITH
WELL, ZIPPY, HERE WE ARE IN TH' GREEN ZONE... AH, SMELL THAT DESERT AIR! OR IS IT A BURN-ING HUM-VEE?
GRIFFY, LOOK! IT'S A SADDAM'S BIG BOY!!
GRIFFY 12-5
©2005 Bill Griffith. World rights reserved. Distributed by King Features Syndicate
AMAZING. HE ACTUALLY FRAN-CHISED HIMSELF LIKE COLONEL SANDERS... A MALEVOLENT PSYCHOPATHIC COLONEL SANDERS..
SIGH..IF ONLY HE'D TURNED HIS ATTENTION TO FRIED CHICKEN INSTEAD OF TORTURE & MEGA-LOMANIA!
Zippythepinhead.com
HOW DO YOU EXPLAIN TH' RISE OF BRUTAL DICTATORSHIPS, ZIPPY? HOW DO YOU ACCOUNT FOR THEIR CONSTANT REOCCURENCE THROUGH-OUT HUMAN HISTORY?
I DON'T KNOW...I'M STILL TRYING TO FIGURE OUT TH' COLONEL'S SECRET RECIPE!!

42

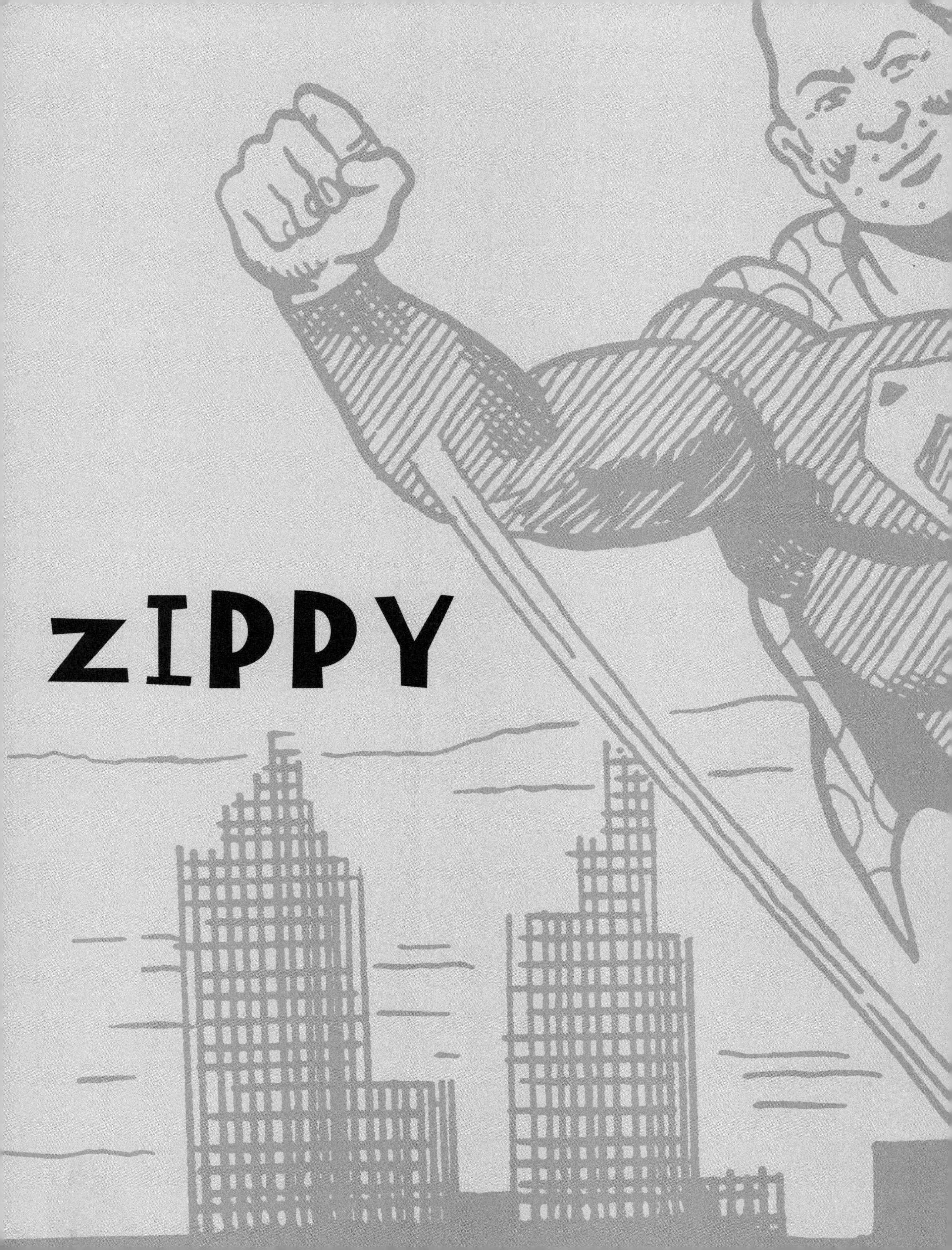
ZIPPY

SOLO

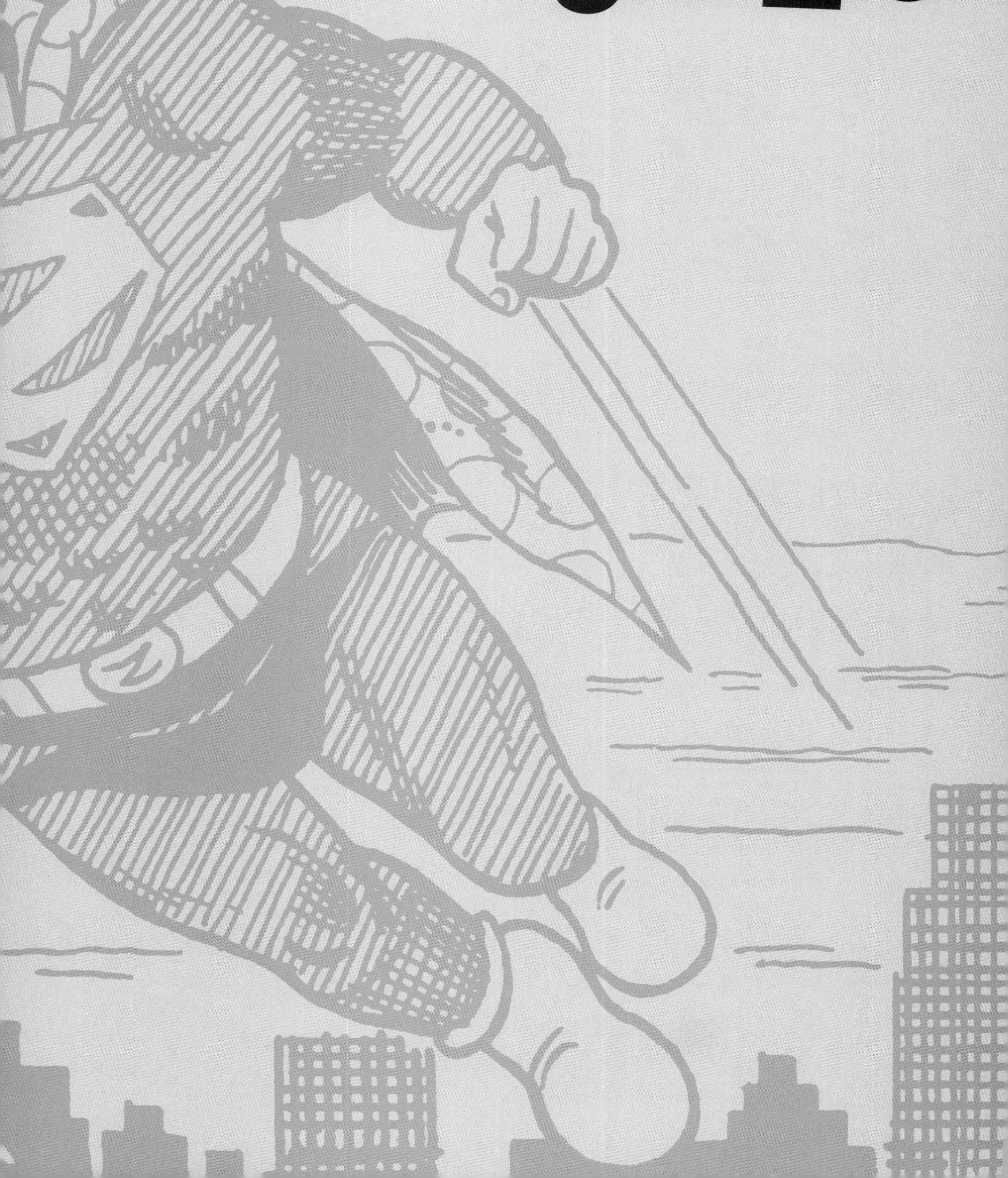

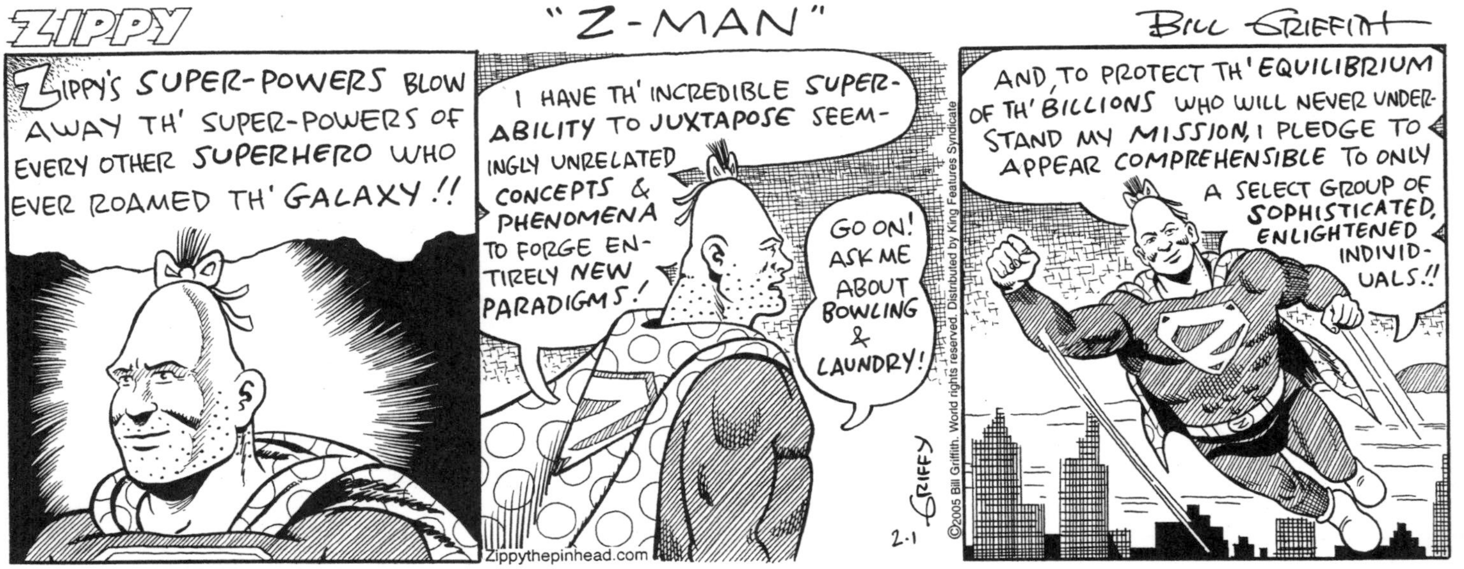
ZIPPY
"Z-MAN"
BILL GRIFFITH
ZIPPY'S SUPER-POWERS BLOW AWAY TH' SUPER-POWERS OF EVERY OTHER SUPERHERO WHO EVER ROAMED TH' GALAXY!!
I HAVE TH' INCREDIBLE SUPER-ABILITY TO JUXTAPOSE SEEMINGLY UNRELATED CONCEPTS & PHENOMENA TO FORGE ENTIRELY NEW PARADIGMS!
GO ON! ASK ME ABOUT BOWLING & LAUNDRY!
AND, TO PROTECT TH' EQUILIBRIUM OF TH' BILLIONS WHO WILL NEVER UNDERSTAND MY MISSION, I PLEDGE TO APPEAR COMPREHENSIBLE TO ONLY A SELECT GROUP OF SOPHISTICATED, ENLIGHTENED INDIVIDUALS!!
Zippythepinhead.com
GRIFFY 2-1
©2005 Bill Griffith. World rights reserved. Distributed by King Features Syndicate

43 A

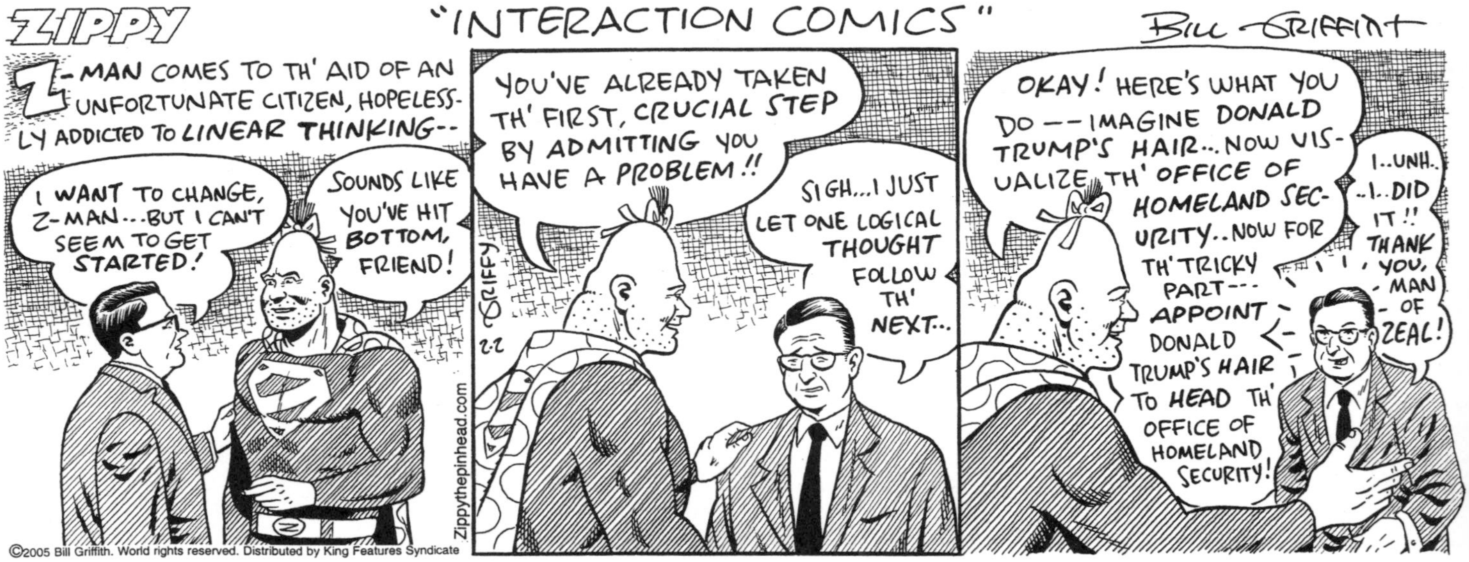
ZIPPY
"INTERACTION COMICS"
BILL GRIFFITH
Z-MAN COMES TO TH' AID OF AN UNFORTUNATE CITIZEN, HOPELESSLY ADDICTED TO LINEAR THINKING--
I WANT TO CHANGE, Z-MAN... BUT I CAN'T SEEM TO GET STARTED!
SOUNDS LIKE YOU'VE HIT BOTTOM, FRIEND!
Zippythepinhead.com
©2005 Bill Griffith. World rights reserved. Distributed by King Features Syndicate
YOU'VE ALREADY TAKEN TH' FIRST, CRUCIAL STEP BY ADMITTING YOU HAVE A PROBLEM!!
SIGH... I JUST LET ONE LOGICAL THOUGHT FOLLOW TH' NEXT...
GRIFFY 2-2
OKAY! HERE'S WHAT YOU DO -- IMAGINE DONALD TRUMP'S HAIR... NOW VISUALIZE TH' OFFICE OF HOMELAND SECURITY.. NOW FOR TH' TRICKY PART--- APPOINT DONALD TRUMP'S HAIR TO HEAD TH' OFFICE OF HOMELAND SECURITY!
I..UNH.. ..I..DID IT!! THANK YOU, MAN OF ZEAL!

43 B

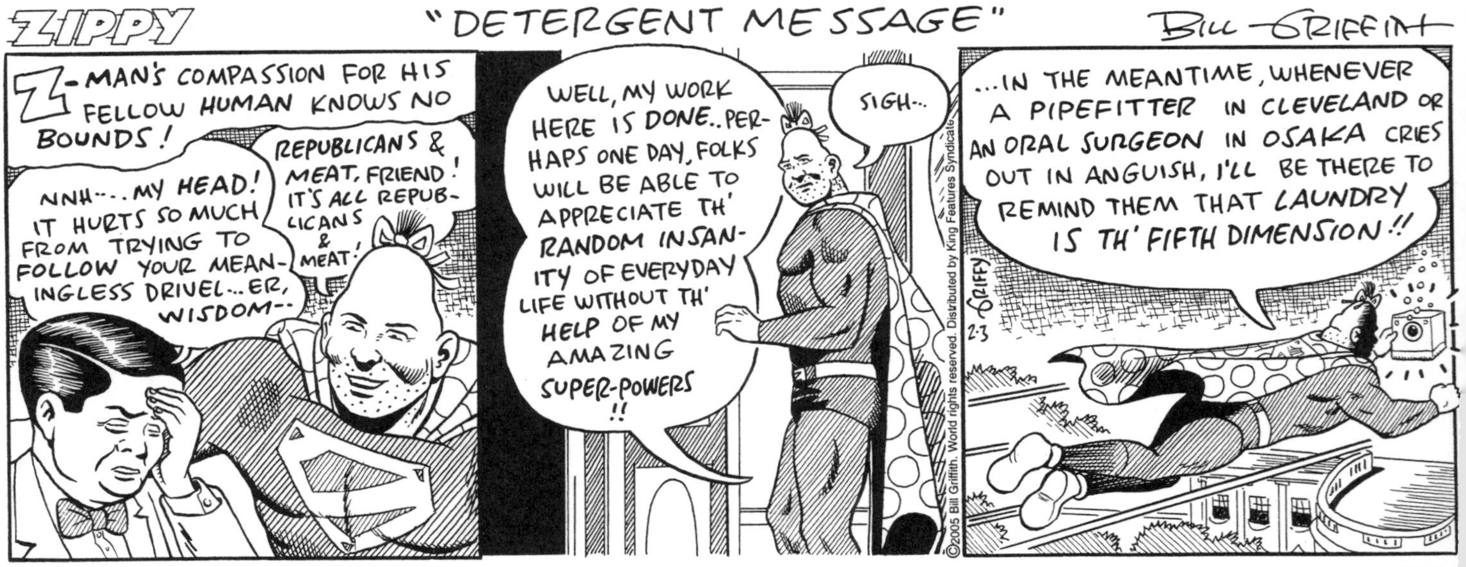
ZIPPY
"DETERGENT MESSAGE"
BILL GRIFFITH
Z-MAN'S COMPASSION FOR HIS FELLOW HUMAN KNOWS NO BOUNDS!
NNH--.. MY HEAD! IT HURTS SO MUCH FROM TRYING TO FOLLOW YOUR MEANINGLESS DRIVEL... ER, WISDOM--
REPUBLICANS & MEAT, FRIEND! IT'S ALL REPUBLICANS & MEAT!
WELL, MY WORK HERE IS DONE.. PERHAPS ONE DAY, FOLKS WILL BE ABLE TO APPRECIATE TH' RANDOM INSANITY OF EVERYDAY LIFE WITHOUT TH' HELP OF MY AMAZING SUPER-POWERS!!
SIGH..
GRIFFY 2-3
©2005 Bill Griffith. World rights reserved. Distributed by King Features Syndicate
...IN THE MEANTIME, WHENEVER A PIPEFITTER IN CLEVELAND OR AN ORAL SURGEON IN OSAKA CRIES OUT IN ANGUISH, I'LL BE THERE TO REMIND THEM THAT LAUNDRY IS TH' FIFTH DIMENSION!!

43 C

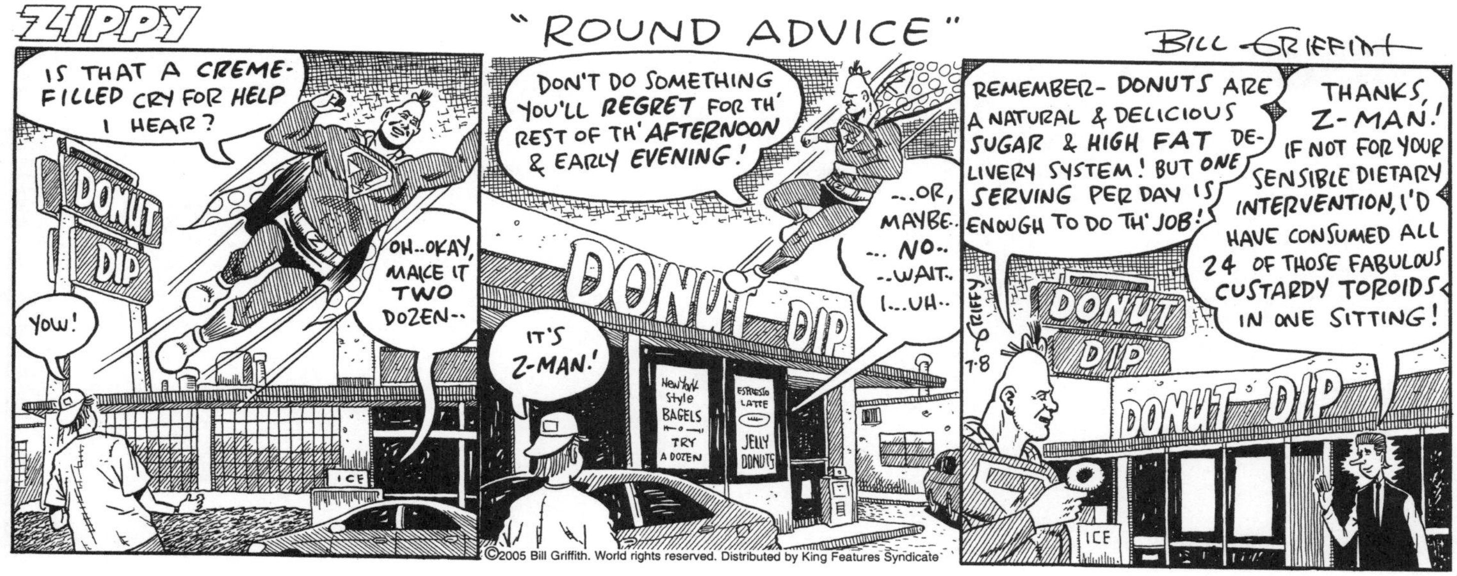
ZIPPY
"ROUND ADVICE"
BILL GRIFFITH
IS THAT A CREME-FILLED CRY FOR HELP I HEAR?
DONUT DIP
YOW!
OH..OKAY, MAKE IT TWO DOZEN..
ICE
DON'T DO SOMETHING YOU'LL REGRET FOR TH' REST OF TH' AFTERNOON & EARLY EVENING!
..OR, MAYBE.. ..NO.. ..WAIT.. I...UH..
IT'S Z-MAN!
DONUT DIP
New York Style BAGELS TRY A DOZEN
ESPRESSO LATTE JELLY DONUTS
REMEMBER- DONUTS ARE A NATURAL & DELICIOUS SUGAR & HIGH FAT DELIVERY SYSTEM! BUT ONE SERVING PER DAY IS ENOUGH TO DO TH' JOB!
THANKS, Z-MAN! IF NOT FOR YOUR SENSIBLE DIETARY INTERVENTION, I'D HAVE CONSUMED ALL 24 OF THOSE FABULOUS CUSTARDY TOROIDS IN ONE SITTING!
DONUT DIP
GRIFFY 7·8
ICE
©2005 Bill Griffith. World rights reserved. Distributed by King Features Syndicate

43 D

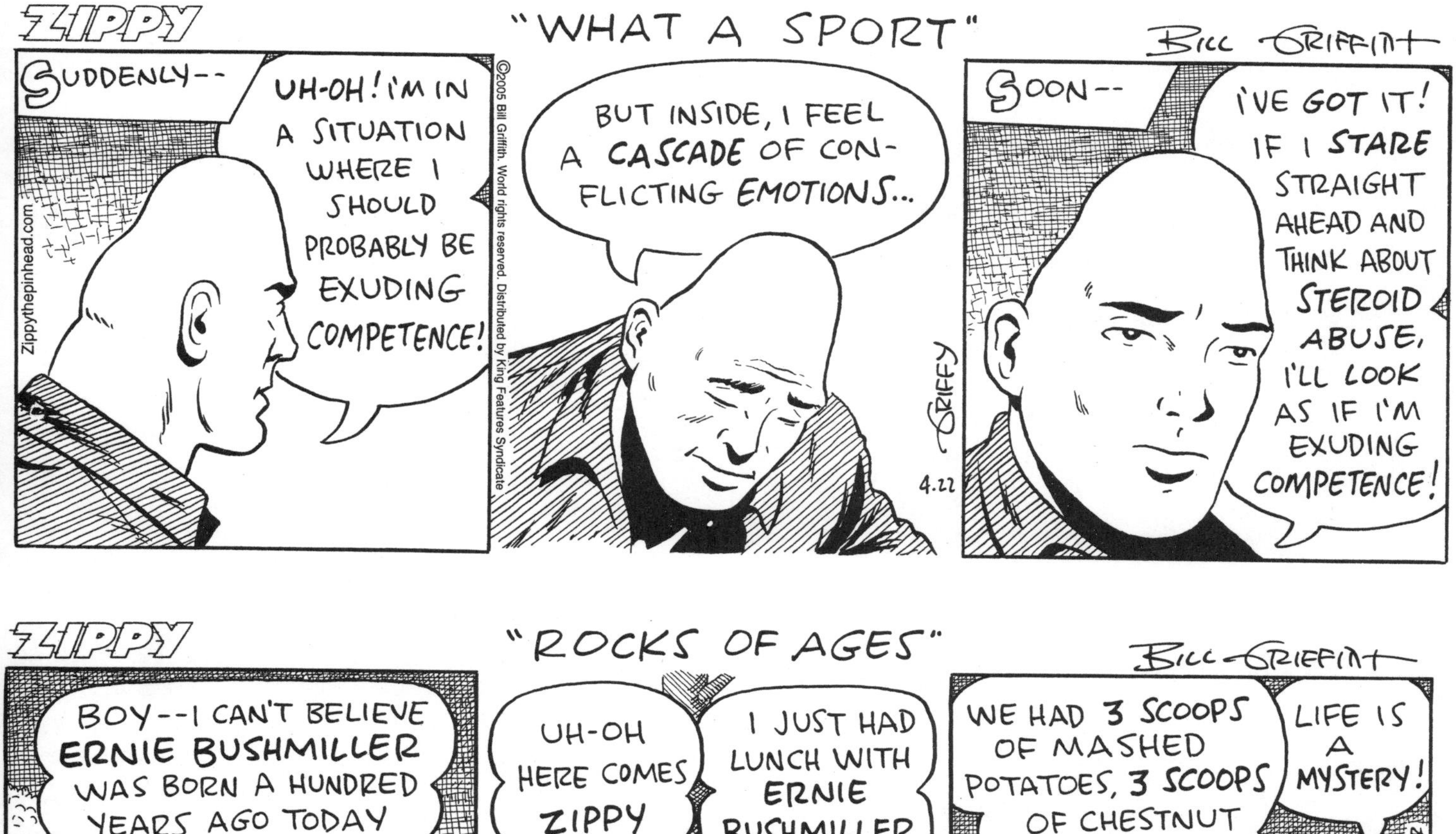
ZIPPY
"WHAT A SPORT"
BILL GRIFFITH
SUDDENLY--
UH-OH! I'M IN A SITUATION WHERE I SHOULD PROBABLY BE EXUDING COMPETENCE!
Zippythepinhead.com
©2005 Bill Griffith. World rights reserved. Distributed by King Features Syndicate
BUT INSIDE, I FEEL A CASCADE OF CONFLICTING EMOTIONS...
GRIFFY 4·22
SOON--
I'VE GOT IT! IF I STARE STRAIGHT AHEAD AND THINK ABOUT STEROID ABUSE, I'LL LOOK AS IF I'M EXUDING COMPETENCE!

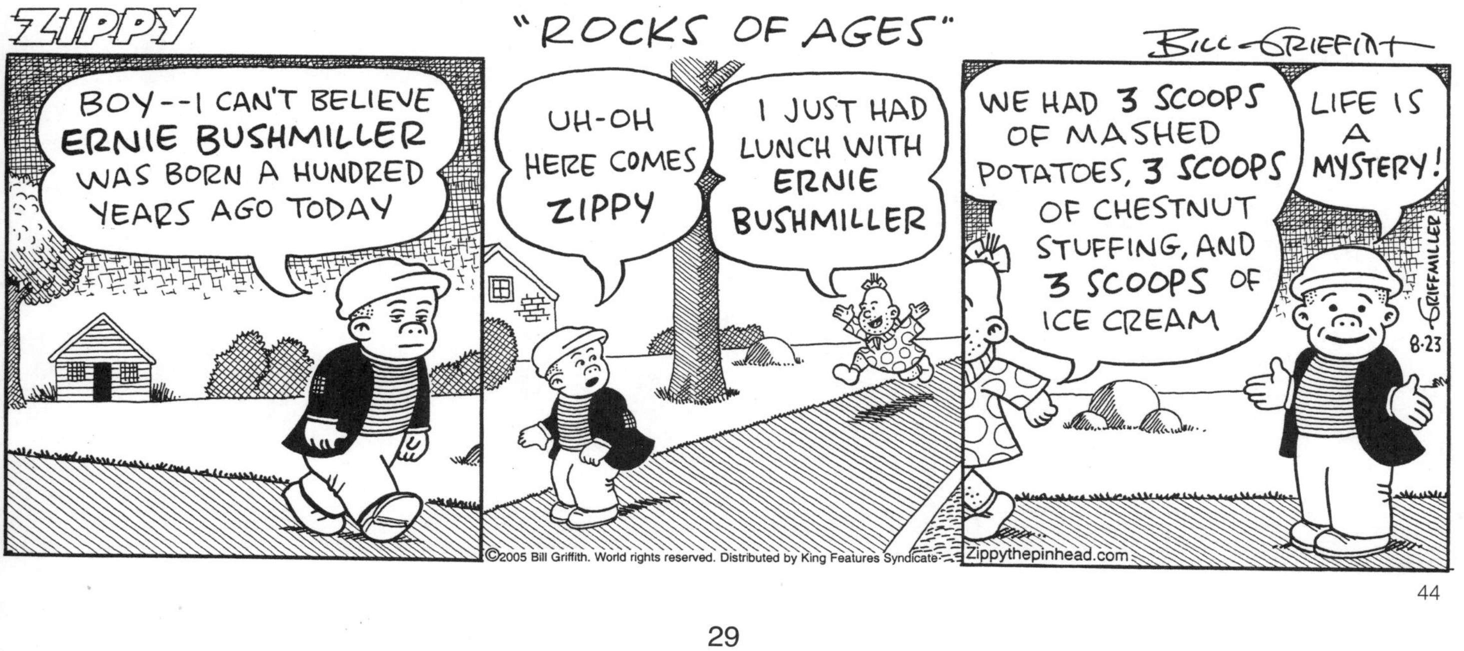
ZIPPY
"ROCKS OF AGES"
BILL GRIFFITH
BOY--I CAN'T BELIEVE ERNIE BUSHMILLER WAS BORN A HUNDRED YEARS AGO TODAY
UH-OH HERE COMES ZIPPY
I JUST HAD LUNCH WITH ERNIE BUSHMILLER
WE HAD 3 SCOOPS OF MASHED POTATOES, 3 SCOOPS OF CHESTNUT STUFFING, AND 3 SCOOPS OF ICE CREAM
LIFE IS A MYSTERY!
GRIFFMILLER 8·23
©2005 Bill Griffith. World rights reserved. Distributed by King Features Syndicate
Zippythepinhead.com

44

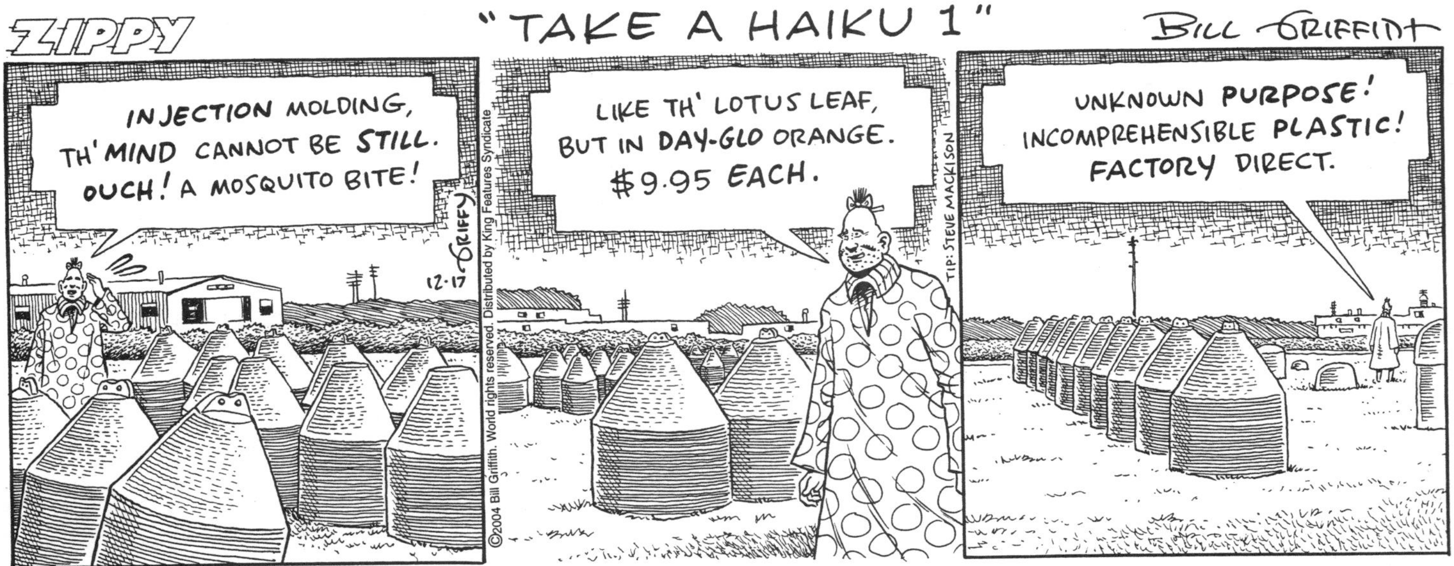
ZIPPY
"TAKE A HAIKU 1"
BILL GRIFFITH
INJECTION MOLDING, TH' MIND CANNOT BE STILL. OUCH! A MOSQUITO BITE!
GRIFFY 12·17
©2004 Bill Griffith. World rights reserved. Distributed by King Features Syndicate
LIKE TH' LOTUS LEAF, BUT IN DAY-GLO ORANGE. $9.95 EACH.
TIP: STEVE MACKISON
UNKNOWN PURPOSE! INCOMPREHENSIBLE PLASTIC! FACTORY DIRECT.

45 A

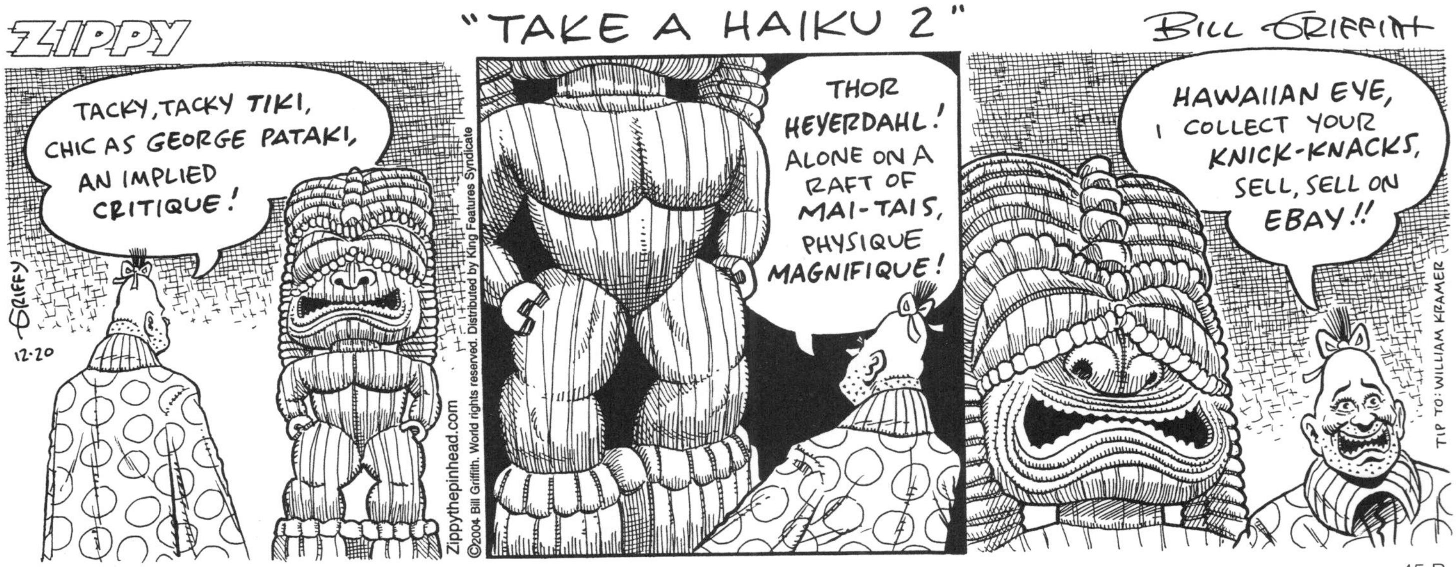
ZIPPY
"TAKE A HAIKU 2"
BILL GRIFFITH
TACKY, TACKY TIKI, CHIC AS GEORGE PATAKI, AN IMPLIED CRITIQUE!
GRIFFY 12·20
Zippythepinhead.com
©2004 Bill Griffith. World rights reserved. Distributed by King Features Syndicate
THOR HEYERDAHL! ALONE ON A RAFT OF MAI-TAIS, PHYSIQUE MAGNIFIQUE!
HAWAIIAN EYE, I COLLECT YOUR KNICK-KNACKS, SELL, SELL ON EBAY!!
TIP TO: WILLIAM KRAMER

45 B

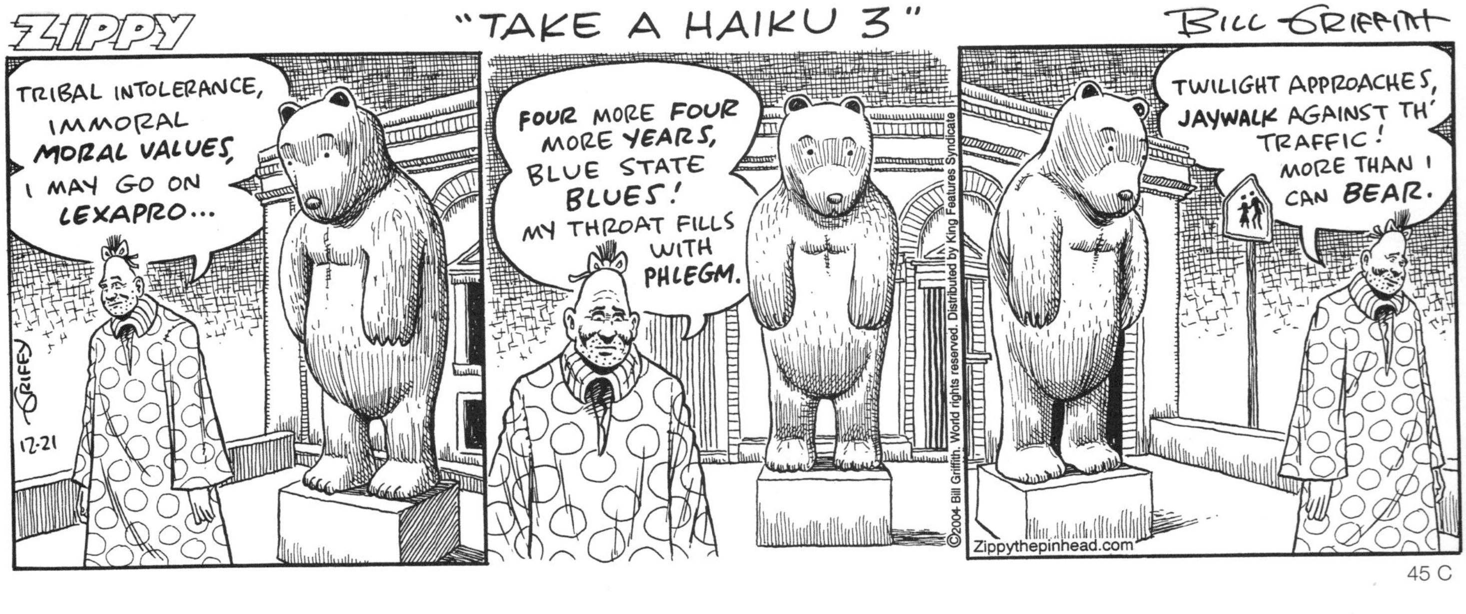
ZIPPY
"TAKE A HAIKU 3"
BILL GRIFFITH
TRIBAL INTOLERANCE, IMMORAL MORAL VALUES, I MAY GO ON LEXAPRO...
GRIFFY 12·21
FOUR MORE FOUR MORE YEARS, BLUE STATE BLUES! MY THROAT FILLS WITH PHLEGM.
©2004 Bill Griffith. World rights reserved. Distributed by King Features Syndicate
TWILIGHT APPROACHES, JAYWALK AGAINST TH' TRAFFIC! MORE THAN I CAN BEAR.
Zippythepinhead.com

45 C

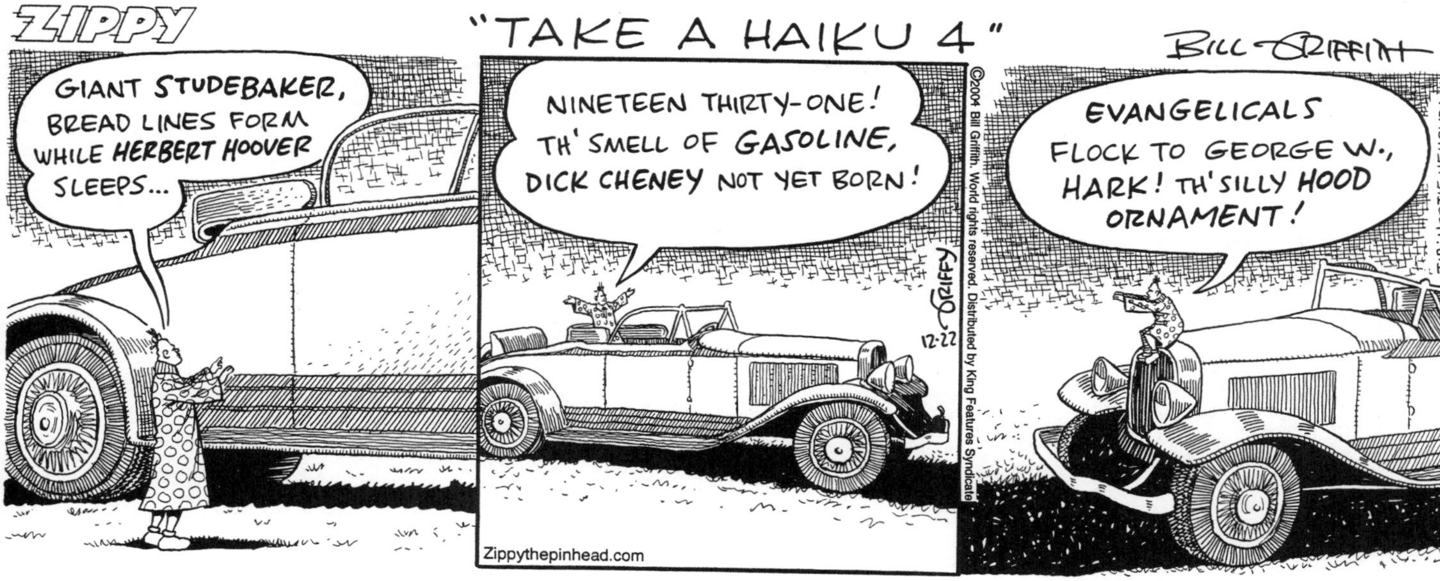
ZIPPY
"TAKE A HAIKU 4"
BILL GRIFFITH
GIANT STUDEBAKER, BREAD LINES FORM WHILE HERBERT HOOVER SLEEPS...
NINETEEN THIRTY-ONE! TH' SMELL OF GASOLINE, DICK CHENEY NOT YET BORN!
GRIFFY 12-22
©2004 Bill Griffith. World rights reserved. Distributed by King Features Syndicate
Zippythepinhead.com
EVANGELICALS FLOCK TO GEORGE W., HARK! TH' SILLY HOOD ORNAMENT!
TIP: HOOTIE YEHOUDI

45 D

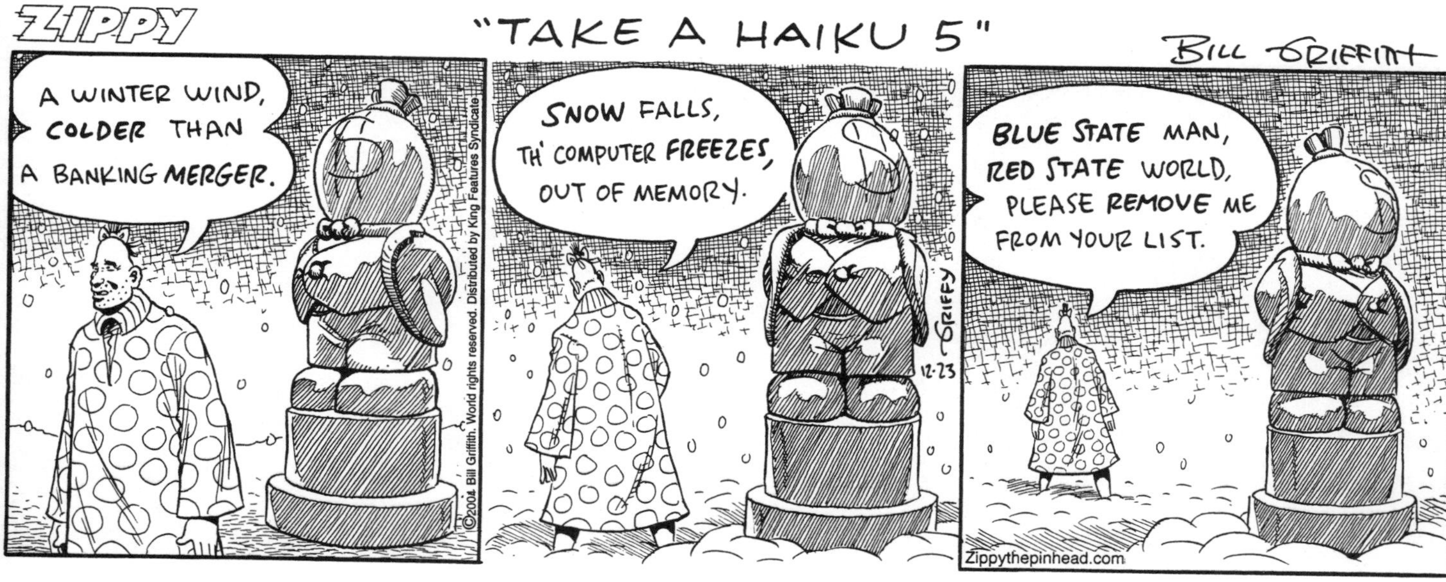
ZIPPY
"TAKE A HAIKU 5"
BILL GRIFFITH
A WINTER WIND, COLDER THAN A BANKING MERGER.
©2004 Bill Griffith. World rights reserved. Distributed by King Features Syndicate
SNOW FALLS, TH' COMPUTER FREEZES, OUT OF MEMORY.
GRIFFY 12-23
BLUE STATE MAN, RED STATE WORLD, PLEASE REMOVE ME FROM YOUR LIST.
Zippythepinhead.com

45 E

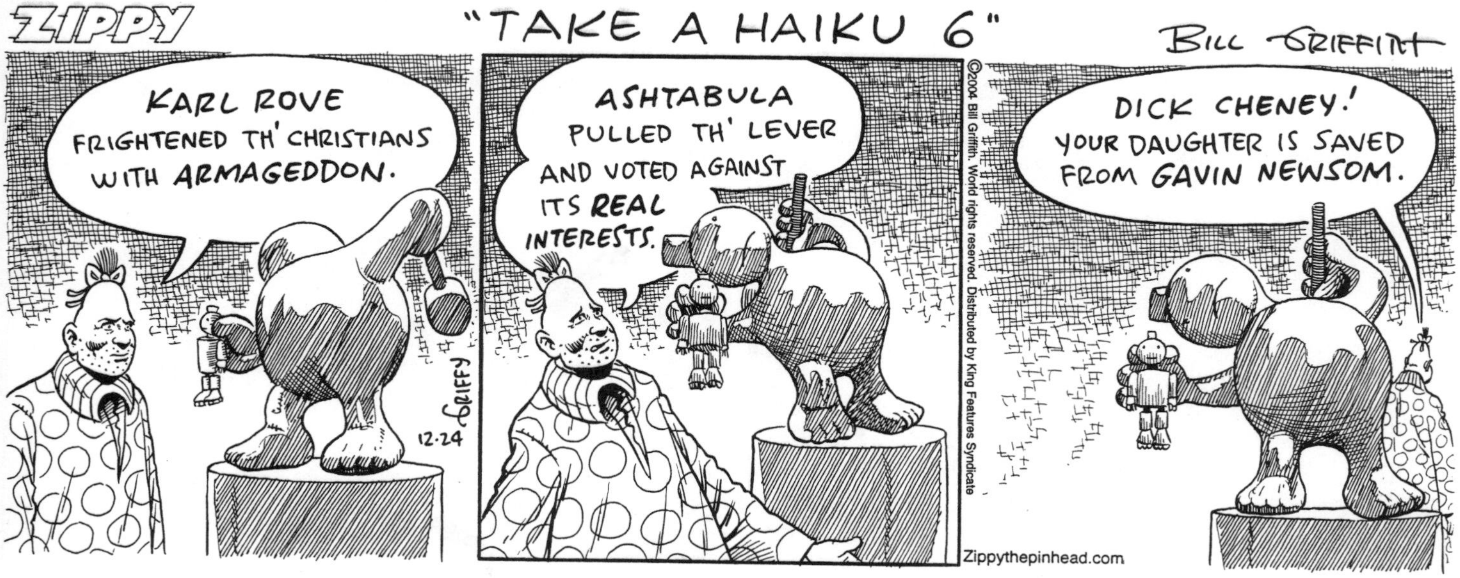
ZIPPY
"TAKE A HAIKU 6"
BILL GRIFFITH
KARL ROVE FRIGHTENED TH' CHRISTIANS WITH ARMAGEDDON.
GRIFFY 12-24
ASHTABULA PULLED TH' LEVER AND VOTED AGAINST ITS REAL INTERESTS.
©2004 Bill Griffith. World rights reserved. Distributed by King Features Syndicate
DICK CHENEY! YOUR DAUGHTER IS SAVED FROM GAVIN NEWSOM.
Zippythepinhead.com

45 F

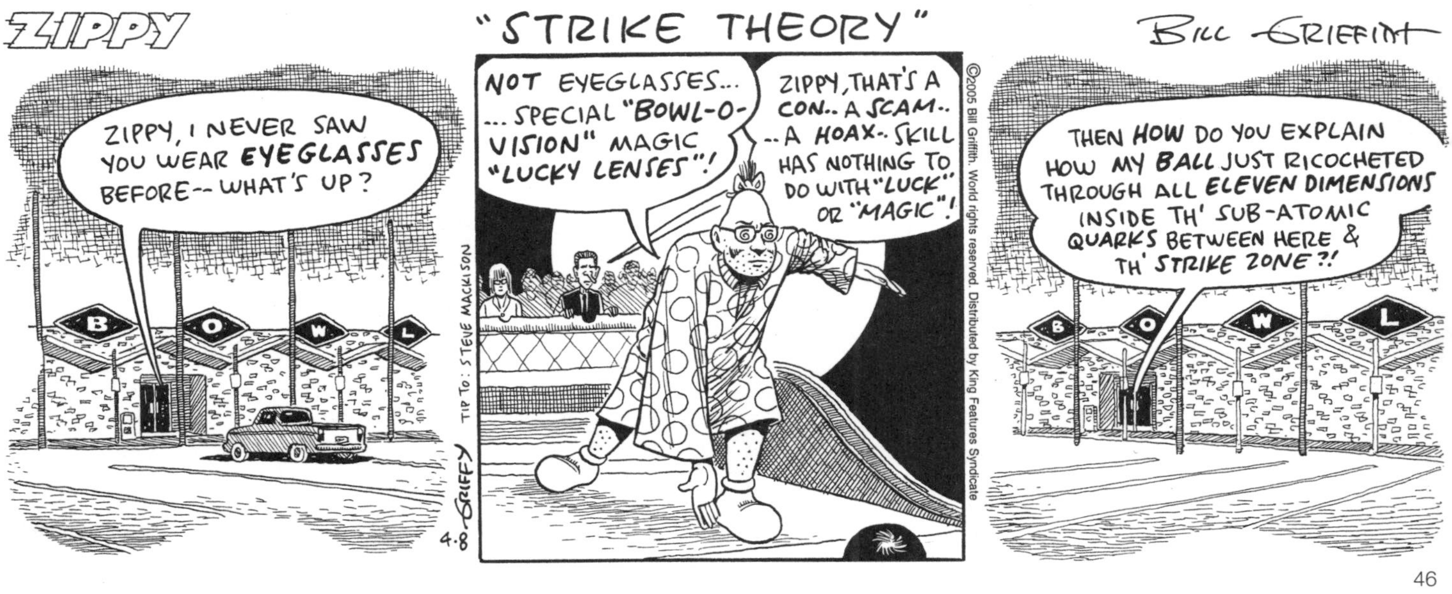
ZIPPY
"STRIKE THEORY"
BILL GRIFFITH
ZIPPY, I NEVER SAW YOU WEAR EYEGLASSES BEFORE-- WHAT'S UP?
B O W L
TIP TO: STEVE MACKISON
4·8 GRIFFY
NOT EYEGLASSES... ...SPECIAL "BOWL-O-VISION" MAGIC "LUCKY LENSES"!
ZIPPY, THAT'S A CON.. A SCAM.. ..A HOAX.. SKILL HAS NOTHING TO DO WITH "LUCK" OR "MAGIC"!
©2005 Bill Griffith. World rights reserved. Distributed by King Features Syndicate
THEN HOW DO YOU EXPLAIN HOW MY BALL JUST RICOCHETED THROUGH ALL ELEVEN DIMENSIONS INSIDE TH' SUB-ATOMIC QUARKS BETWEEN HERE & TH' STRIKE ZONE?!
46

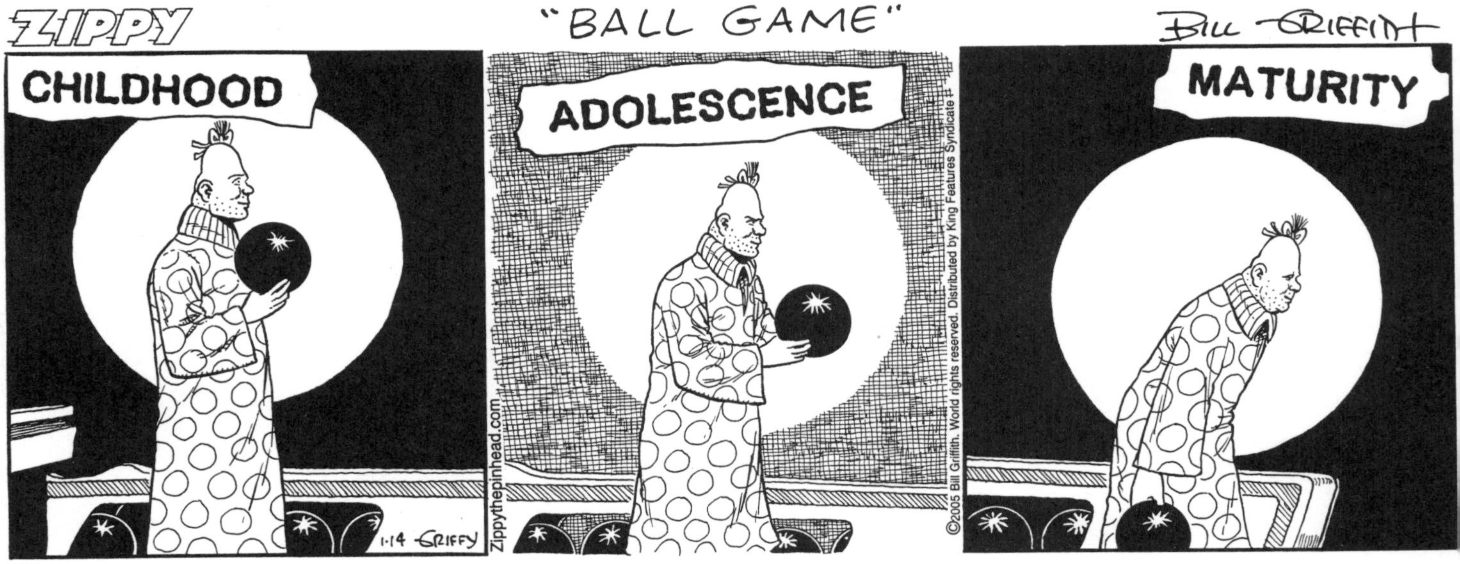
ZIPPY
"BALL GAME"
BILL GRIFFITH
CHILDHOOD
1·14 GRIFFY
Zippythepinhead.com
ADOLESCENCE
©2005 Bill Griffith. World rights reserved. Distributed by King Features Syndicate
MATURITY

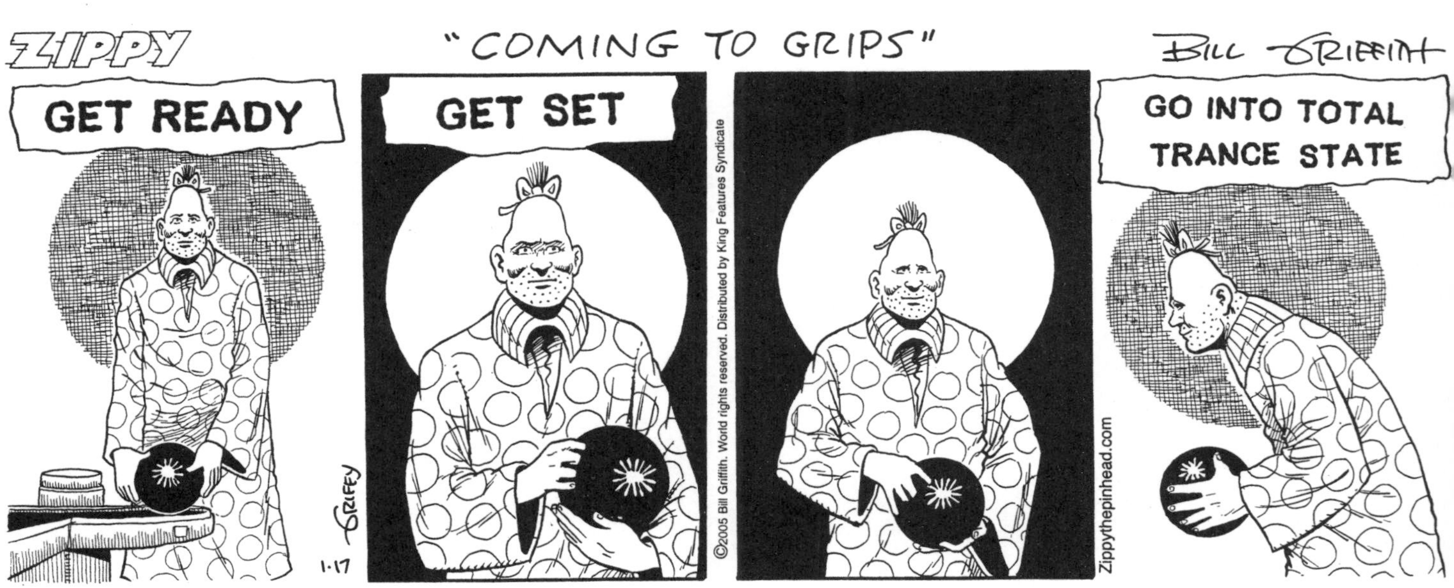
ZIPPY
"COMING TO GRIPS"
BILL GRIFFITH
GET READY
GRIFFY 1·17
GET SET
©2005 Bill Griffith. World rights reserved. Distributed by King Features Syndicate
Zippythepinhead.com
GO INTO TOTAL TRANCE STATE

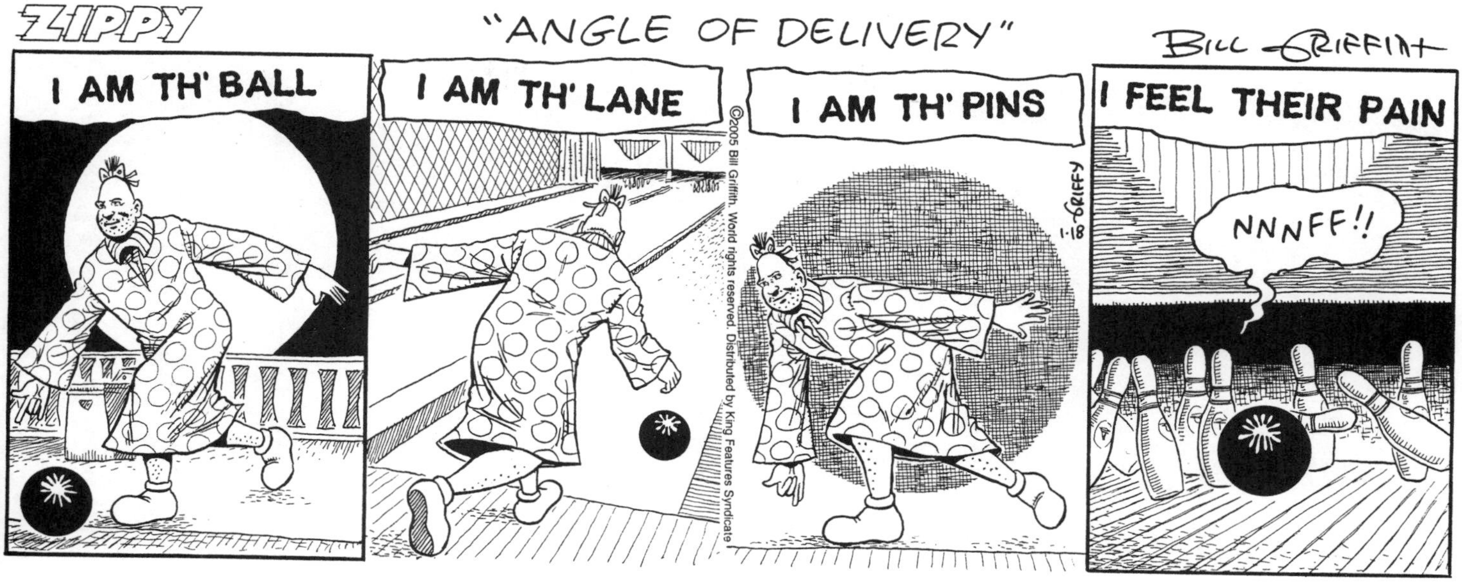
ZIPPY
"ANGLE OF DELIVERY"
BILL GRIFFITH
I AM TH' BALL
I AM TH' LANE
©2005 Bill Griffith. World rights reserved. Distributed by King Features Syndicate
I AM TH' PINS
GRIFFY 1·18
I FEEL THEIR PAIN
NNNFF!!

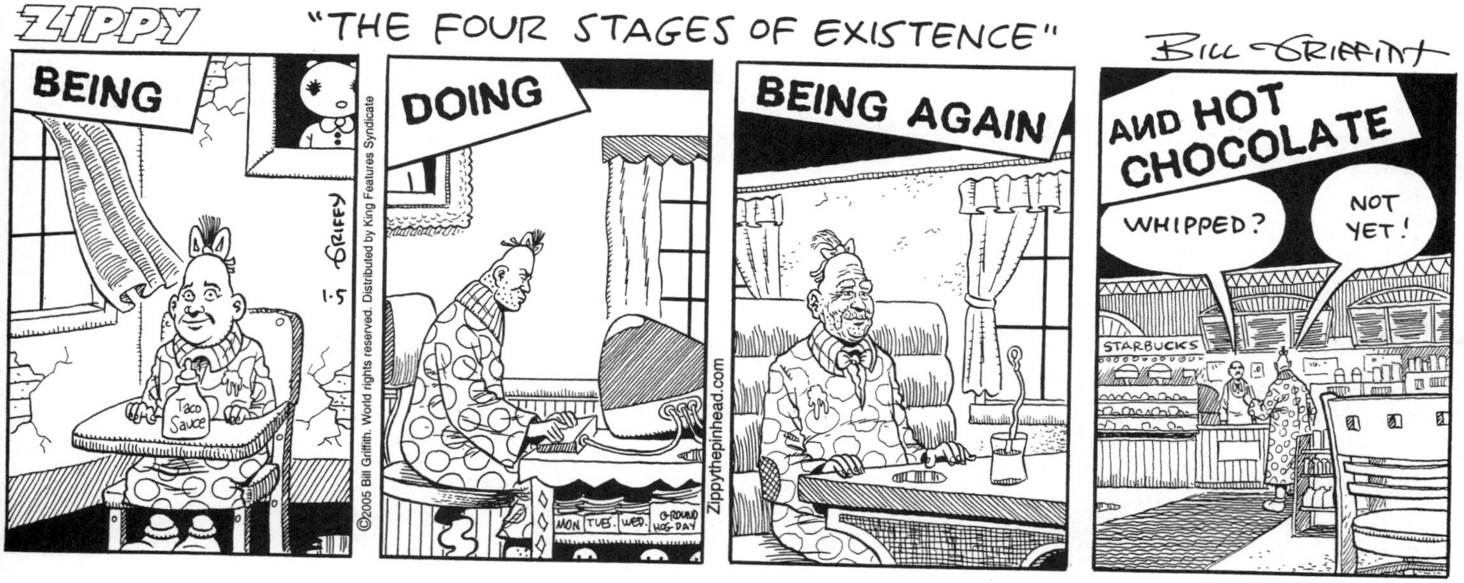
ZIPPY
"THE FOUR STAGES OF EXISTENCE"
BILL GRIFFITH
BEING
GRIFFY 1·5
Taco Sauce
©2005 Bill Griffith. World rights reserved. Distributed by King Features Syndicate
DOING
MON. TUES. WED. GROUND HOG DAY
Zippythepinhead.com
BEING AGAIN
AND HOT CHOCOLATE
WHIPPED?
NOT YET!
STARBUCKS

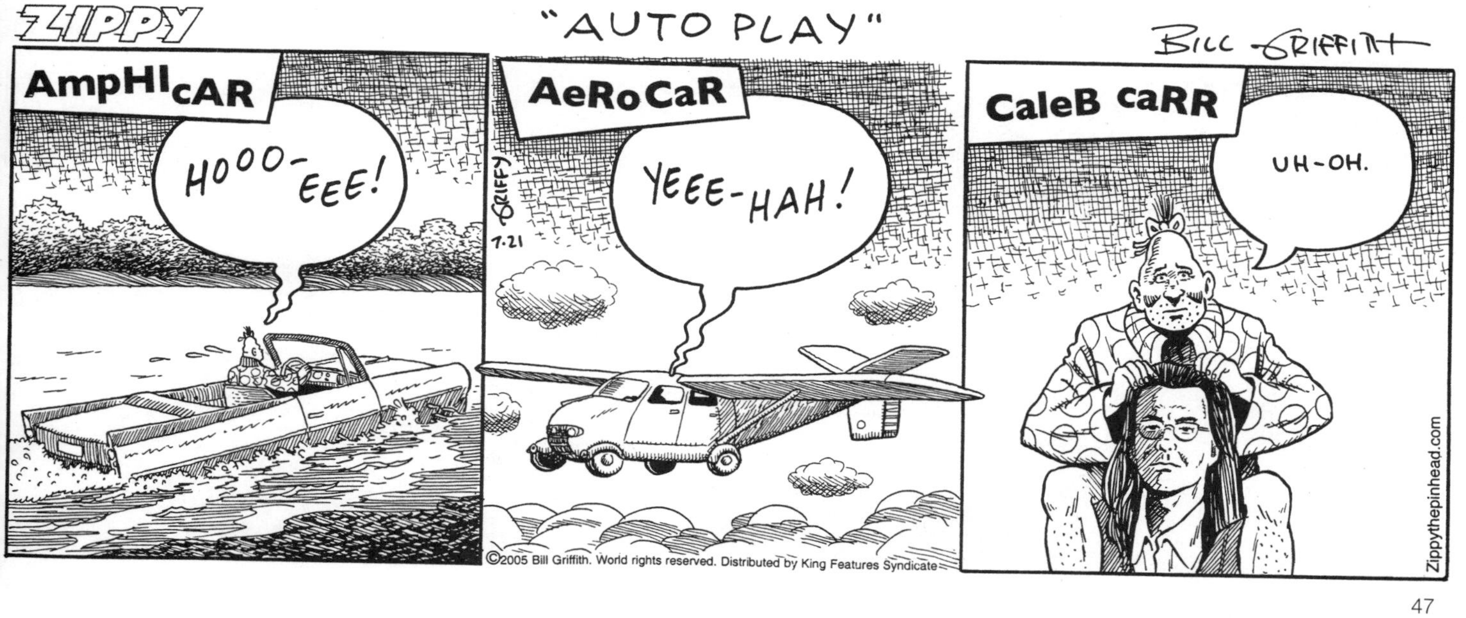
ZIPPY
"AUTO PLAY"
BILL GRIFFITH
AmpHIcAR
HOOO-EEE!
GRIFFY 7·21
AeRoCaR
YEEE-HAH!
©2005 Bill Griffith. World rights reserved. Distributed by King Features Syndicate
CaleB caRR
UH-OH.
Zippythepinhead.com

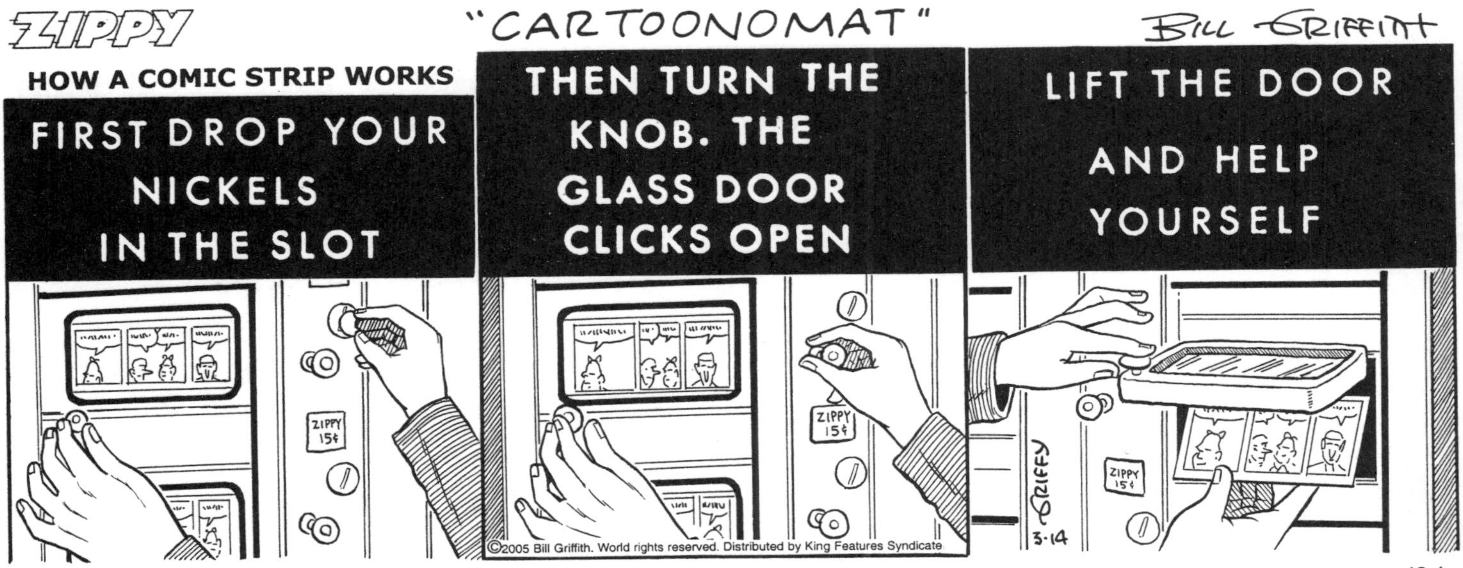
ZIPPY
"CARTOONOMAT"
BILL GRIFFITH
HOW A COMIC STRIP WORKS
FIRST DROP YOUR NICKELS IN THE SLOT
ZIPPY 15¢
THEN TURN THE KNOB. THE GLASS DOOR CLICKS OPEN
ZIPPY 15¢
©2005 Bill Griffith. World rights reserved. Distributed by King Features Syndicate
LIFT THE DOOR AND HELP YOURSELF
ZIPPY 15¢
GRIFFY 3·14

48 A

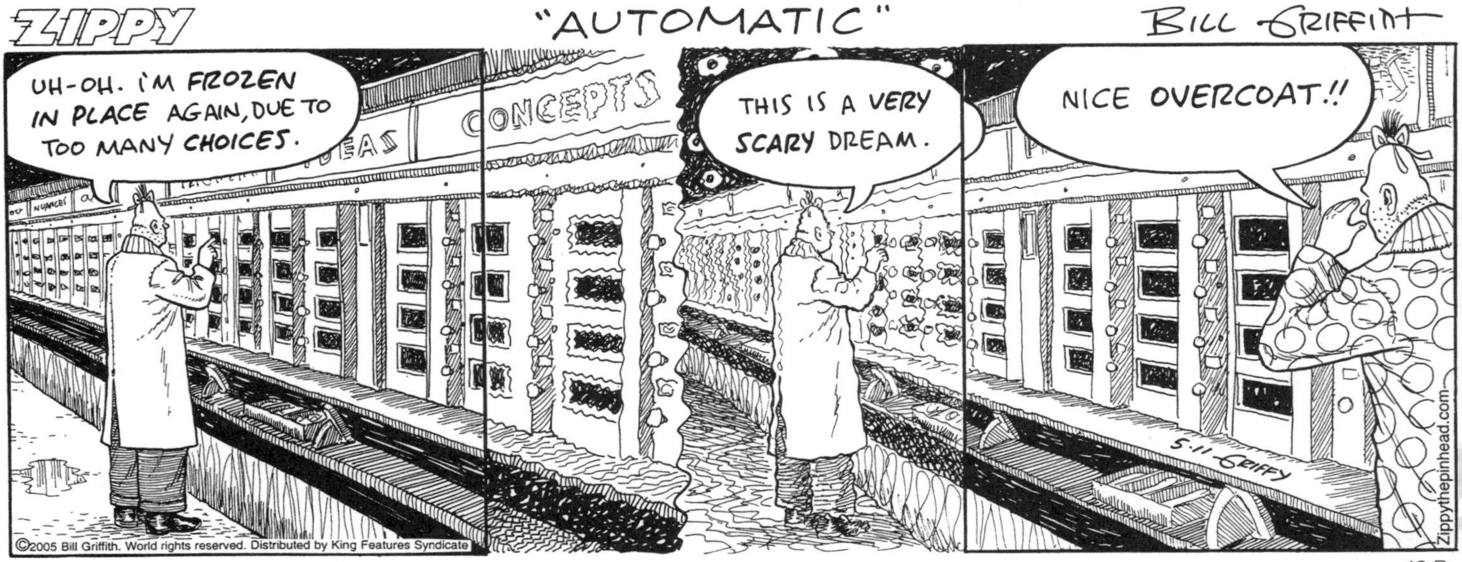
ZIPPY
"AUTOMATIC"
BILL GRIFFITH
UH-OH. I'M FROZEN IN PLACE AGAIN, DUE TO TOO MANY CHOICES.
IDEAS
NUANCES
©2005 Bill Griffith. World rights reserved. Distributed by King Features Syndicate
CONCEPTS
THIS IS A VERY SCARY DREAM.
NICE OVERCOAT!!
5·11 GRIFFY
Zippythepinhead.com

48 B

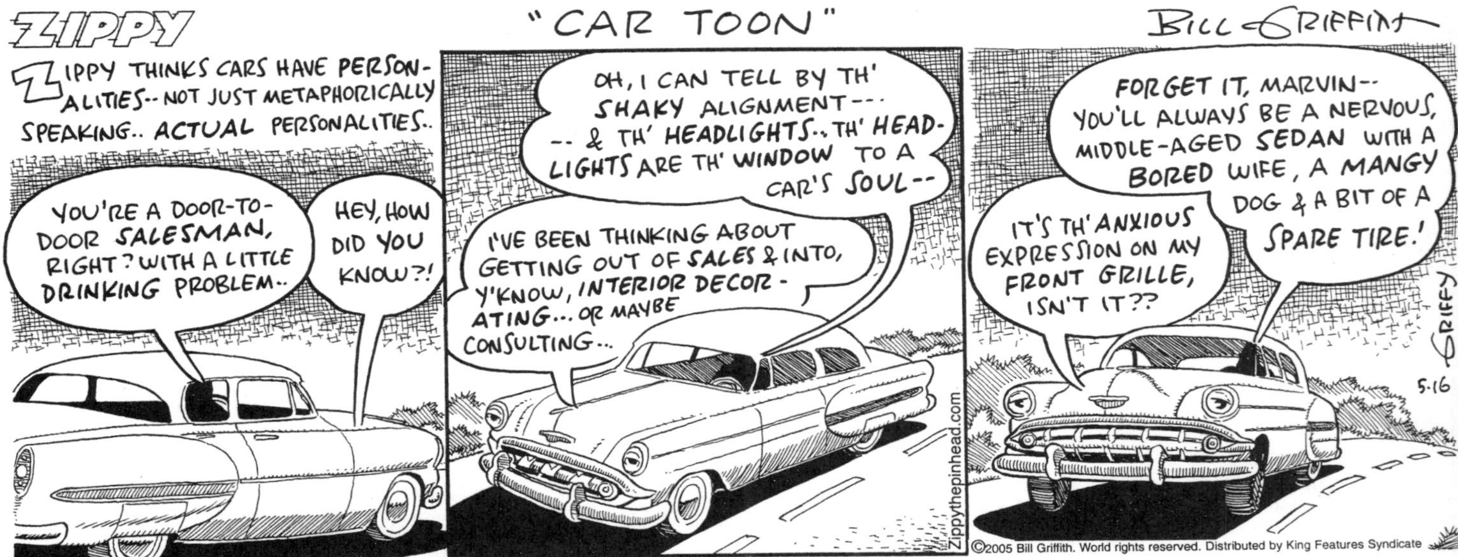
ZIPPY
"CAR TOON"
BILL GRIFFITH
ZIPPY THINKS CARS HAVE PERSONALITIES-- NOT JUST METAPHORICALLY SPEAKING.. ACTUAL PERSONALITIES..
YOU'RE A DOOR-TO-DOOR SALESMAN, RIGHT? WITH A LITTLE DRINKING PROBLEM..
HEY, HOW DID YOU KNOW?!
OH, I CAN TELL BY TH' SHAKY ALIGNMENT--
-- & TH' HEADLIGHTS.. TH' HEADLIGHTS ARE TH' WINDOW TO A CAR'S SOUL--
I'VE BEEN THINKING ABOUT GETTING OUT OF SALES & INTO, Y'KNOW, INTERIOR DECORATING... OR MAYBE CONSULTING...
Zippythepinhead.com
FORGET IT, MARVIN-- YOU'LL ALWAYS BE A NERVOUS, MIDDLE-AGED SEDAN WITH A BORED WIFE, A MANGY DOG & A BIT OF A SPARE TIRE.'
IT'S TH' ANXIOUS EXPRESSION ON MY FRONT GRILLE, ISN'T IT??
GRIFFY 5·16
©2005 Bill Griffith. World rights reserved. Distributed by King Features Syndicate

49

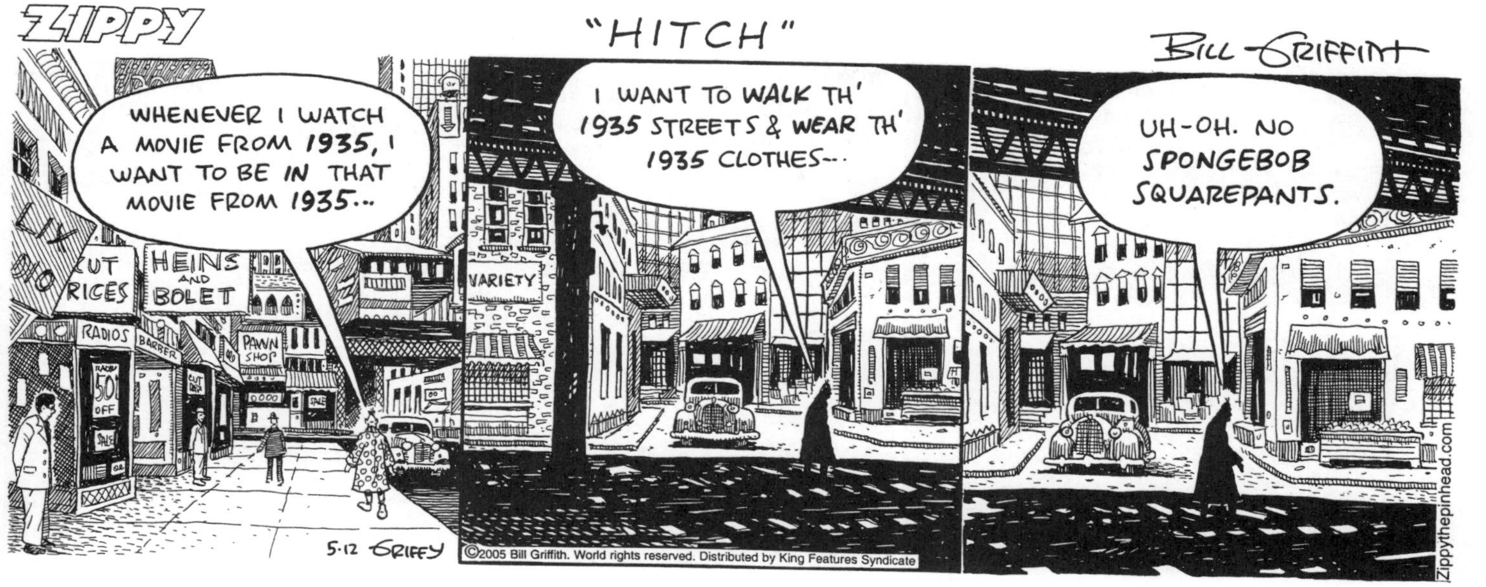
ZIPPY
"HITCH"
BILL GRIFFITH
WHENEVER I WATCH A MOVIE FROM 1935, I WANT TO BE IN THAT MOVIE FROM 1935...
I WANT TO WALK TH' 1935 STREETS & WEAR TH' 1935 CLOTHES--
UH-OH. NO SPONGEBOB SQUAREPANTS.
CUT PRICES
HEINS AND BOLET
RADIOS
BARBER
PAWN SHOP
VARIETY
5.12 GRIFFY
©2005 Bill Griffith. World rights reserved. Distributed by King Features Syndicate
Zippythepinhead.com

50

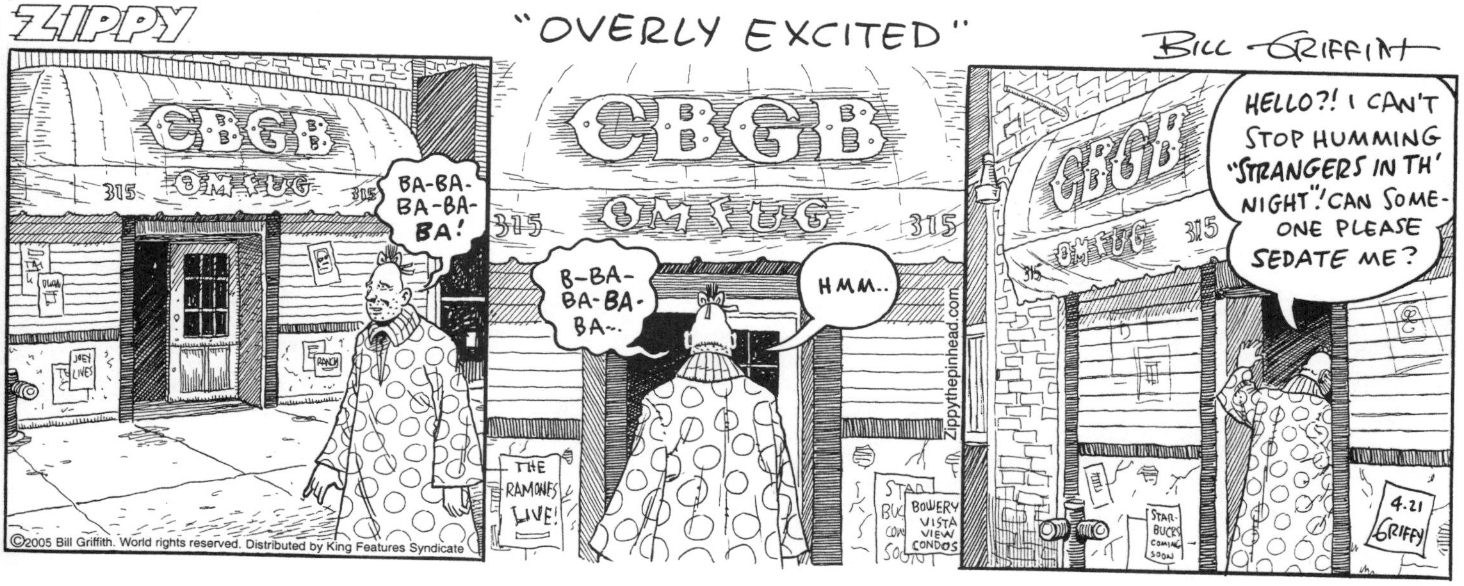
ZIPPY
"OVERLY EXCITED"
BILL GRIFFITH
CBGB
OMFUG
315
BA-BA-BA-BA-BA!
B-BA-BA-BA-BA..
HMM..
HELLO?! I CAN'T STOP HUMMING "STRANGERS IN TH' NIGHT"! CAN SOME-ONE PLEASE SEDATE ME?
JOEY LIVES
THE RAMONES LIVE!
BOWERY VISTA VIEW CONDOS
STAR-BUCKS COMING SOON
4.21 GRIFFY
©2005 Bill Griffith. World rights reserved. Distributed by King Features Syndicate
Zippythepinhead.com

51

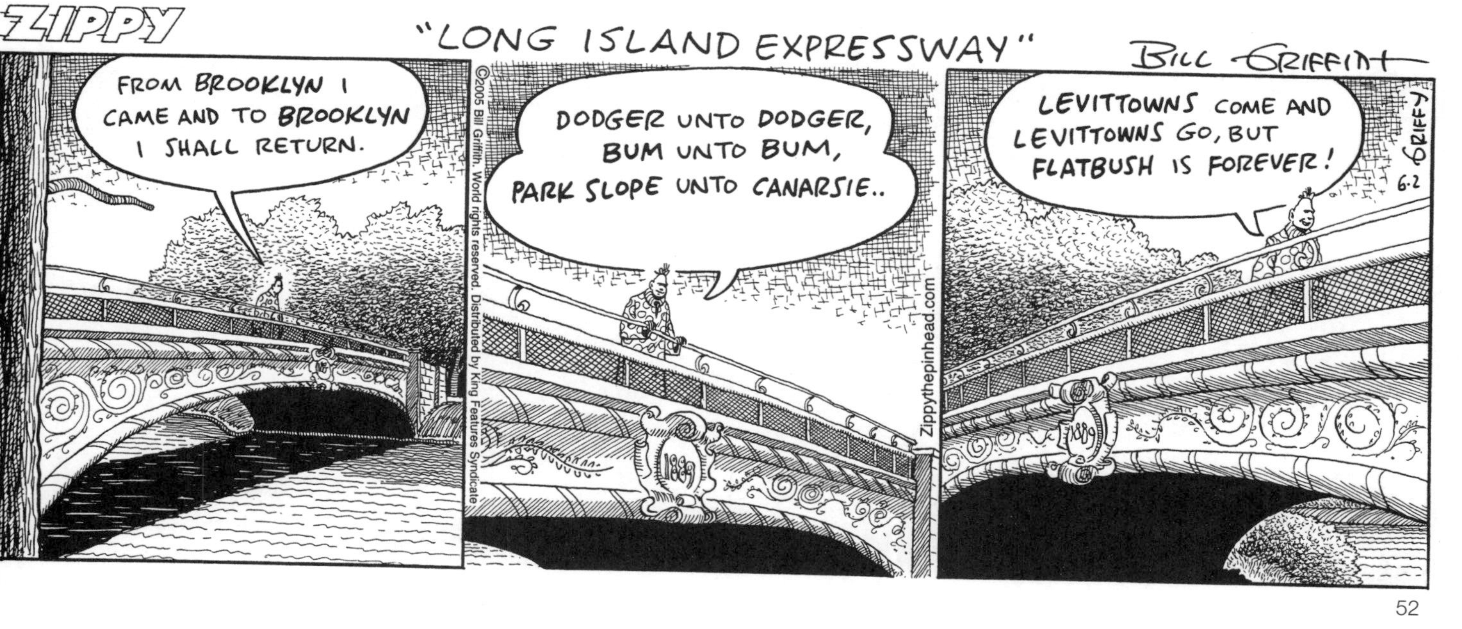
ZIPPY
"LONG ISLAND EXPRESSWAY"
BILL GRIFFITH
FROM BROOKLYN I CAME AND TO BROOKLYN I SHALL RETURN.
DODGER UNTO DODGER, BUM UNTO BUM, PARK SLOPE UNTO CANARSIE..
LEVITTOWNS COME AND LEVITTOWNS GO, BUT FLATBUSH IS FOREVER!
GRIFFY 6.2
1889
©2005 Bill Griffith. World rights reserved. Distributed by King Features Syndicate
Zippythepinhead.com

52

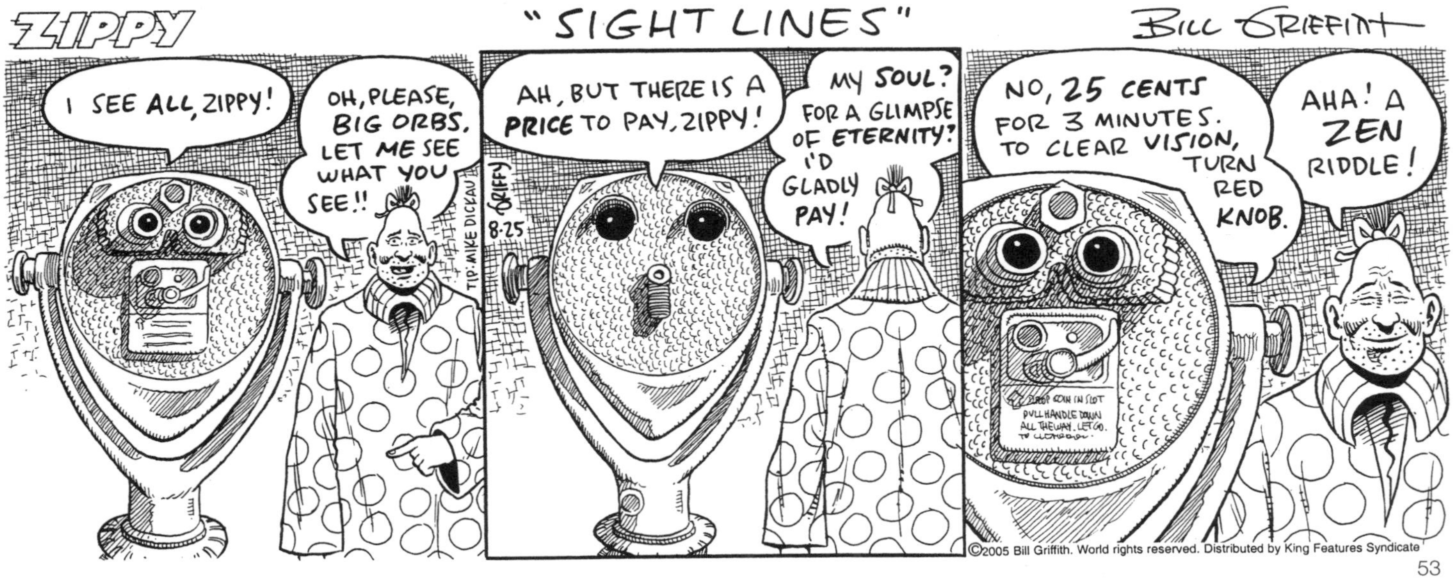
ZIPPY
"SIGHT LINES"
BILL GRIFFITH
I SEE ALL, ZIPPY!
OH, PLEASE, BIG ORBS. LET ME SEE WHAT YOU SEE!!
TIP: MIKE DICKAU
GRIFFY 8-25
AH, BUT THERE IS A PRICE TO PAY, ZIPPY!
MY SOUL? FOR A GLIMPSE OF ETERNITY? I'D GLADLY PAY!
NO, 25 CENTS FOR 3 MINUTES. TO CLEAR VISION, TURN RED KNOB.
AHA! A ZEN RIDDLE!
DROP COIN IN SLOT PULL HANDLE DOWN ALL THE WAY. LET GO.
©2005 Bill Griffith. World rights reserved. Distributed by King Features Syndicate

53

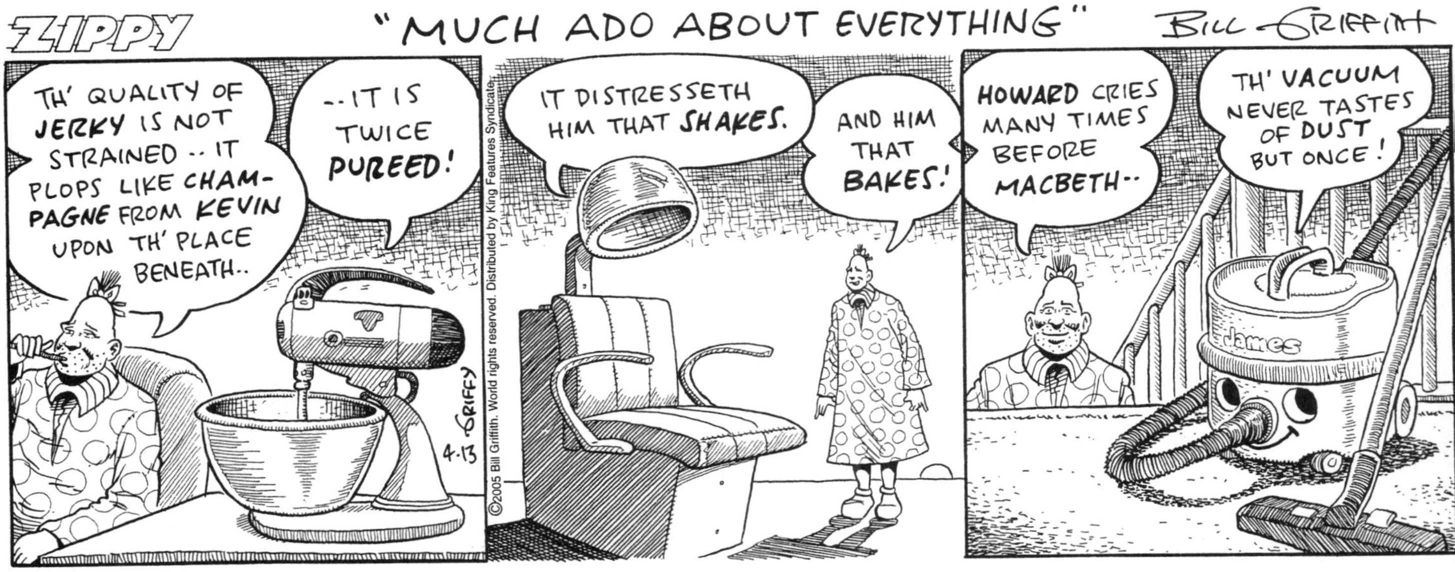
ZIPPY
"MUCH ADO ABOUT EVERYTHING"
BILL GRIFFITH
TH' QUALITY OF JERKY IS NOT STRAINED.. IT PLOPS LIKE CHAMPAGNE FROM KEVIN UPON TH' PLACE BENEATH..
..IT IS TWICE PUREED!
GRIFFY 4-13
©2005 Bill Griffith. World rights reserved. Distributed by King Features Syndicate
IT DISTRESSETH HIM THAT SHAKES.
AND HIM THAT BAKES!
HOWARD CRIES MANY TIMES BEFORE MACBETH..
TH' VACUUM NEVER TASTES OF DUST BUT ONCE!
James

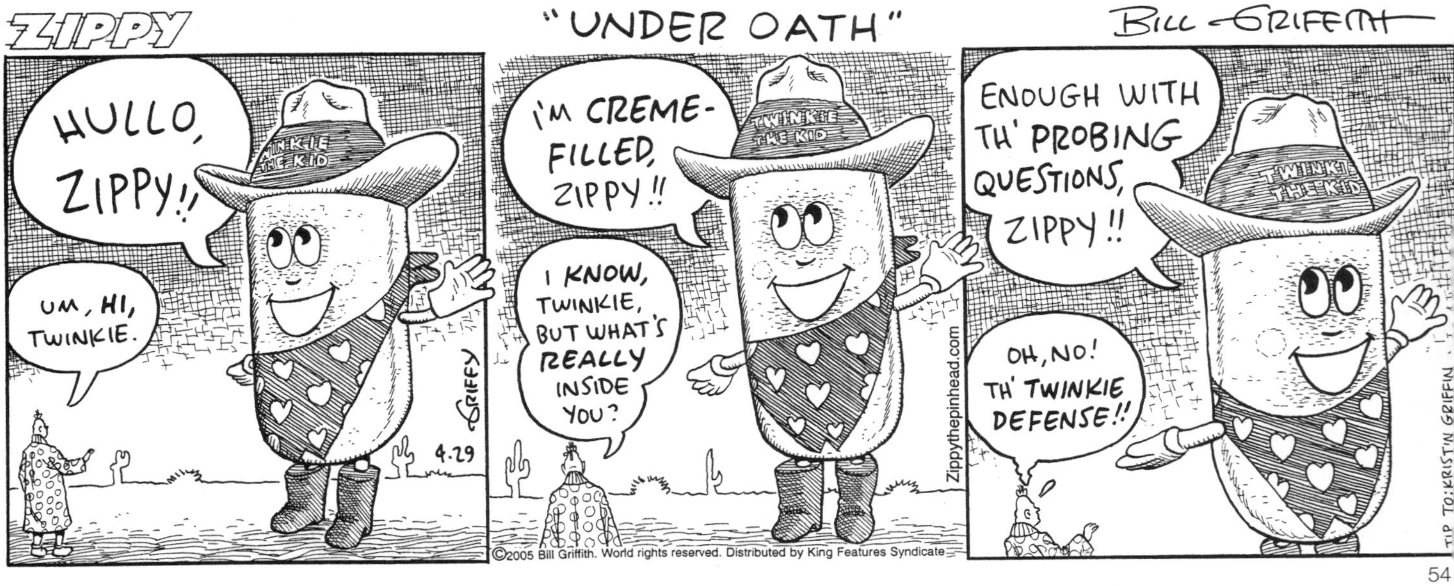
ZIPPY
"UNDER OATH"
BILL GRIFFITH
HULLO, ZIPPY!!
TWINKIE THE KID
UM, HI, TWINKIE.
GRIFFY 4-29
I'M CREME-FILLED, ZIPPY!!
I KNOW, TWINKIE, BUT WHAT'S REALLY INSIDE YOU?
Zippythepinhead.com
ENOUGH WITH TH' PROBING QUESTIONS, ZIPPY!!
OH, NO! TH' TWINKIE DEFENSE!!
TIP TO: KRISTIN GRIFFIN
©2005 Bill Griffith. World rights reserved. Distributed by King Features Syndicate

54

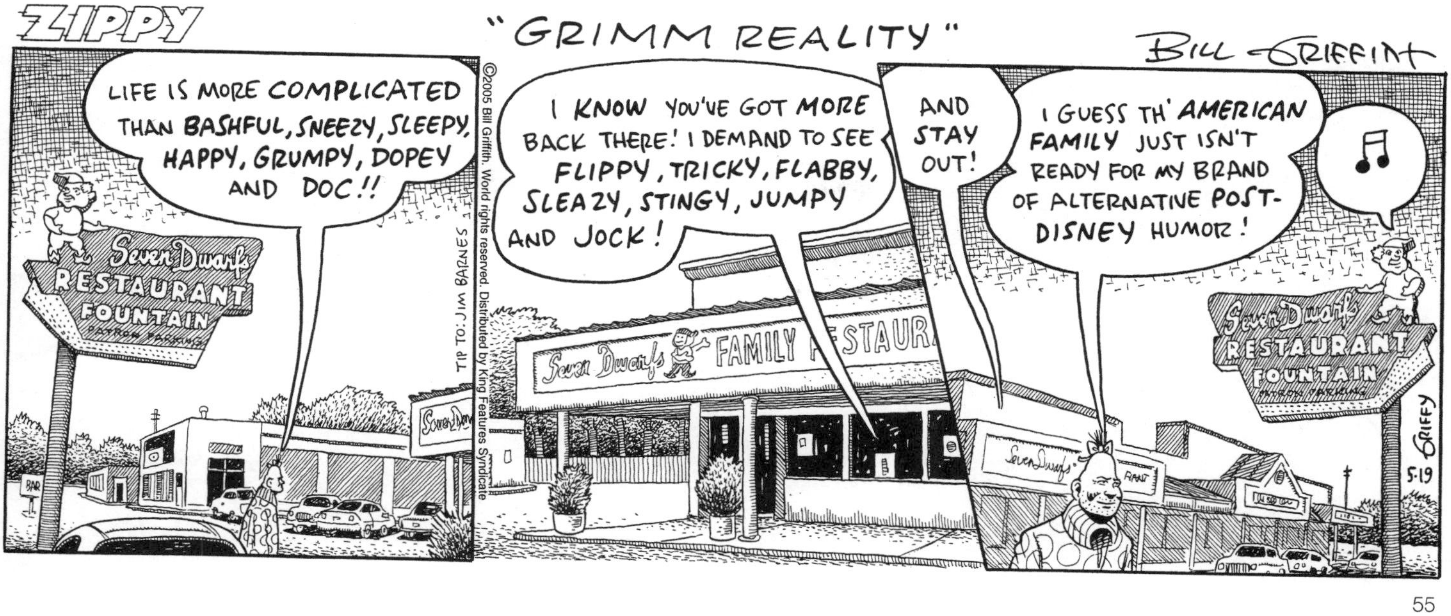
ZIPPY
"GRIMM REALITY"
BILL GRIFFITH
LIFE IS MORE COMPLICATED THAN BASHFUL, SNEEZY, SLEEPY, HAPPY, GRUMPY, DOPEY AND DOC!!
Seven Dwarfs RESTAURANT FOUNTAIN
©2005 Bill Griffith. World rights reserved. Distributed by King Features Syndicate
TIP TO: JIM BARNES
I KNOW YOU'VE GOT MORE BACK THERE! I DEMAND TO SEE FLIPPY, TRICKY, FLABBY, SLEAZY, STINGY, JUMPY AND JOCK!
Seven Dwarfs FAMILY RESTAUR
AND STAY OUT!
I GUESS TH' AMERICAN FAMILY JUST ISN'T READY FOR MY BRAND OF ALTERNATIVE POST-DISNEY HUMOR!
♫
Seven Dwarfs RESTAURANT FOUNTAIN
GRIFFY
5.19

55

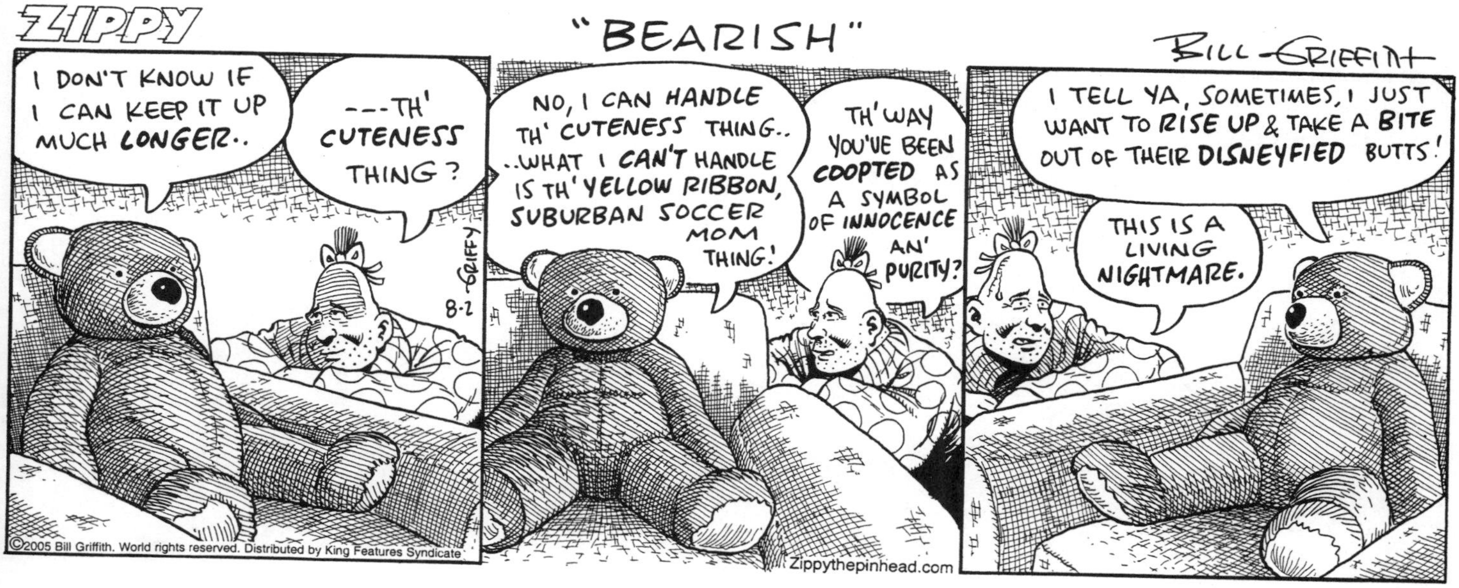
ZIPPY
"BEARISH"
BILL GRIFFITH
I DON'T KNOW IF I CAN KEEP IT UP MUCH LONGER..
---TH' CUTENESS THING?
GRIFFY
8-2
©2005 Bill Griffith. World rights reserved. Distributed by King Features Syndicate
NO, I CAN HANDLE TH' CUTENESS THING.. ..WHAT I CAN'T HANDLE IS TH' YELLOW RIBBON, SUBURBAN SOCCER MOM THING!
TH' WAY YOU'VE BEEN COOPTED AS A SYMBOL OF INNOCENCE AN' PURITY?
Zippythepinhead.com
I TELL YA, SOMETIMES, I JUST WANT TO RISE UP & TAKE A BITE OUT OF THEIR DISNEYFIED BUTTS!
THIS IS A LIVING NIGHTMARE.

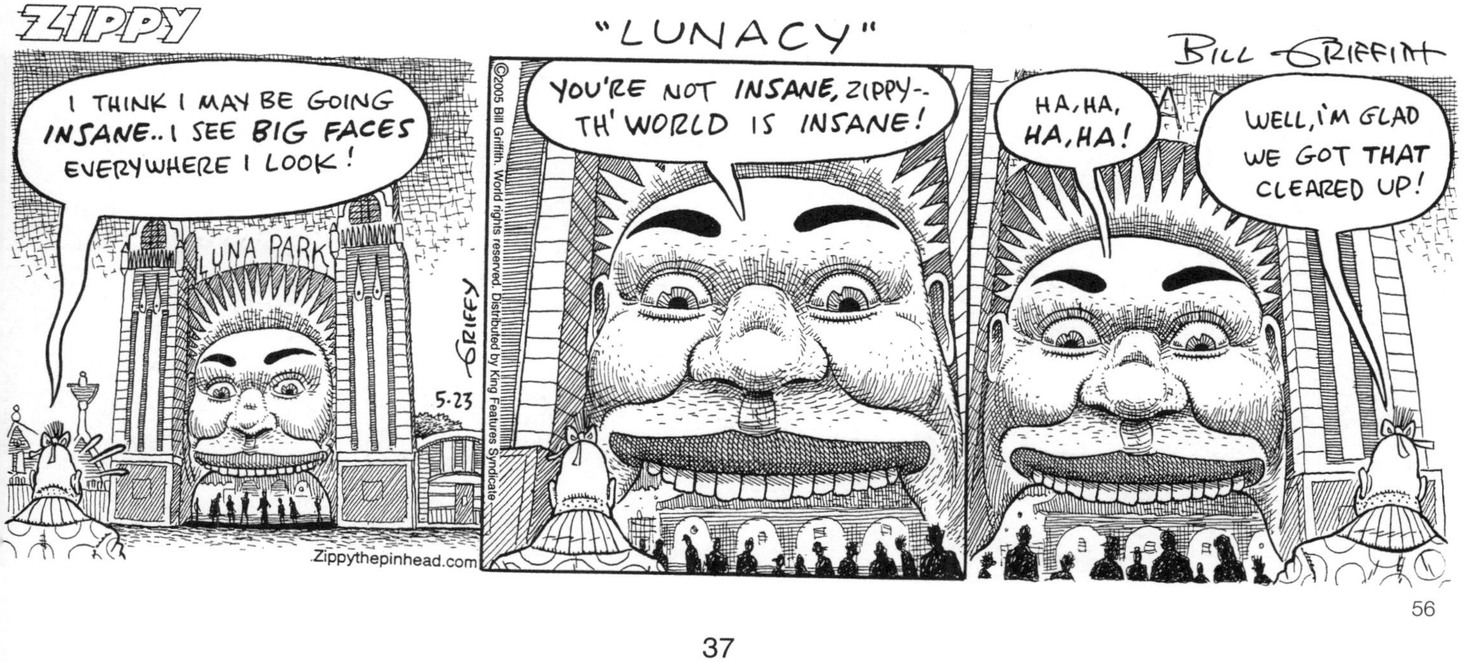
ZIPPY
"LUNACY"
BILL GRIFFITH
I THINK I MAY BE GOING INSANE.. I SEE BIG FACES EVERYWHERE I LOOK!
LUNA PARK
GRIFFY
5-23
Zippythepinhead.com
©2005 Bill Griffith. World rights reserved. Distributed by King Features Syndicate
YOU'RE NOT INSANE, ZIPPY-- TH' WORLD IS INSANE!
HA, HA, HA, HA!
WELL, I'M GLAD WE GOT THAT CLEARED UP!

56

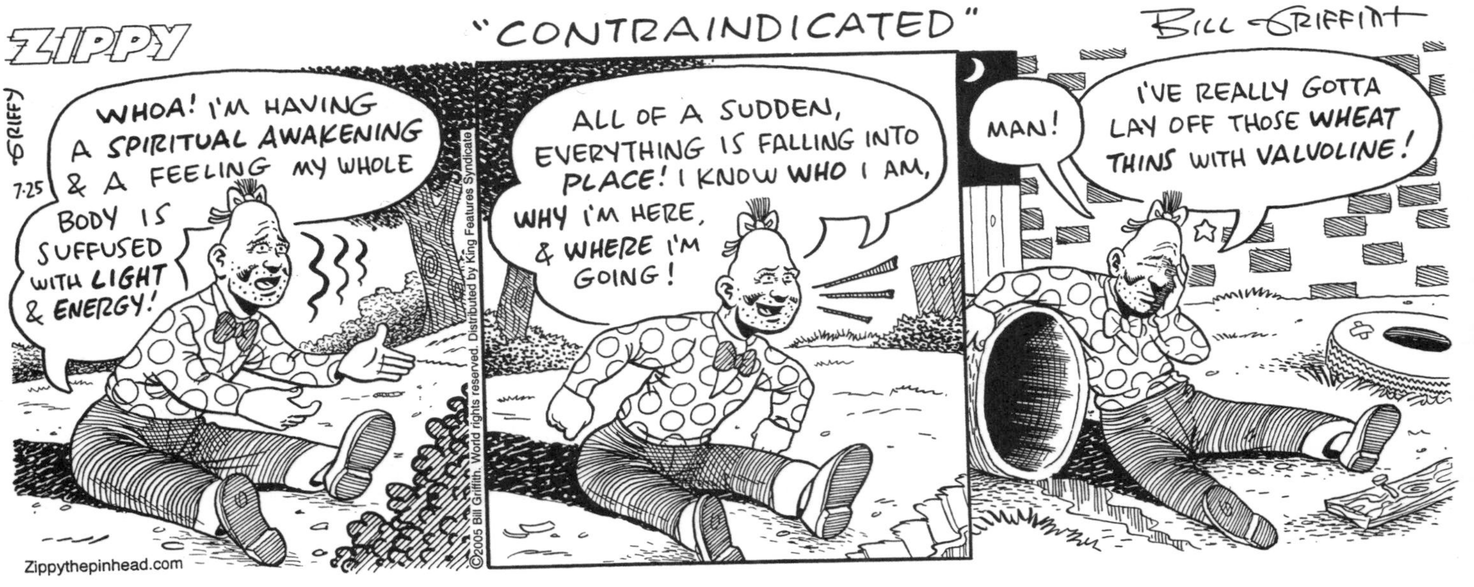
ZIPPY
"CONTRAINDICATED"
BILL GRIFFITH
GRIFFY 7·25
WHOA! I'M HAVING A SPIRITUAL AWAKENING & A FEELING MY WHOLE BODY IS SUFFUSED WITH LIGHT & ENERGY!
ALL OF A SUDDEN, EVERYTHING IS FALLING INTO PLACE! I KNOW WHO I AM, WHY I'M HERE, & WHERE I'M GOING!
MAN!
I'VE REALLY GOTTA LAY OFF THOSE WHEAT THINS WITH VALVOLINE!
©2005 Bill Griffith. World rights reserved. Distributed by King Features Syndicate
Zippythepinhead.com

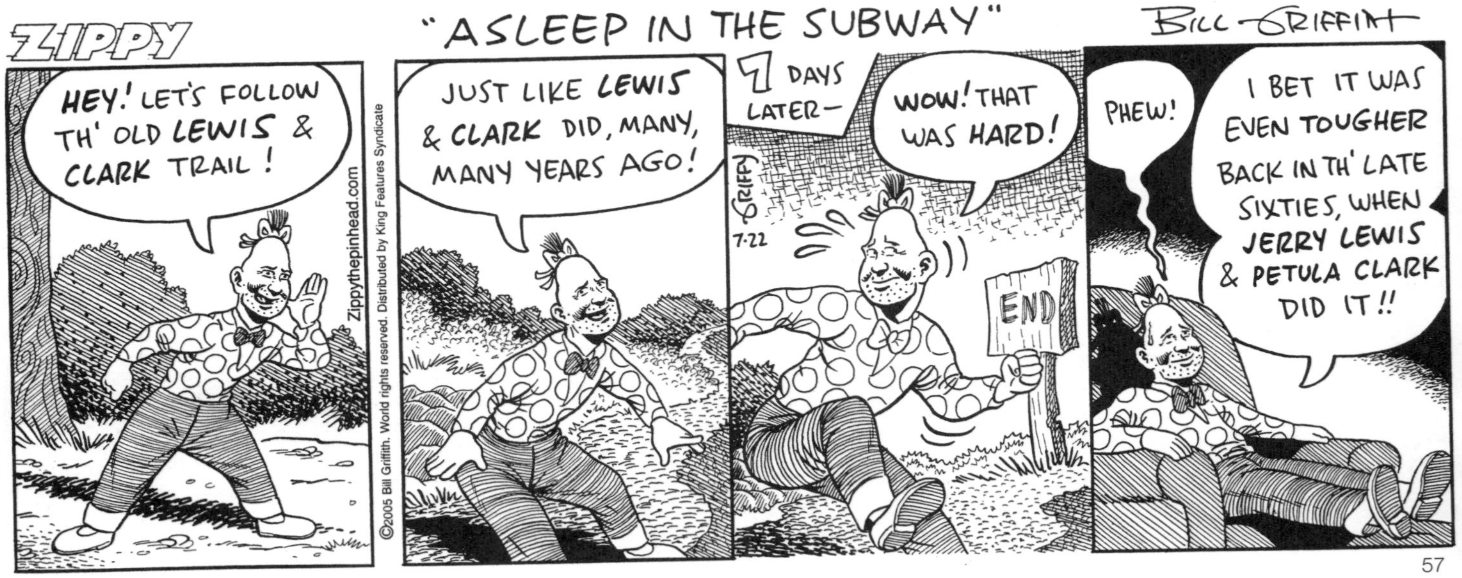
ZIPPY
"ASLEEP IN THE SUBWAY"
BILL GRIFFITH
HEY! LET'S FOLLOW TH' OLD LEWIS & CLARK TRAIL!
©2005 Bill Griffith. World rights reserved. Distributed by King Features Syndicate
Zippythepinhead.com
JUST LIKE LEWIS & CLARK DID, MANY, MANY YEARS AGO!
7 DAYS LATER—
GRIFFY 7·22
WOW! THAT WAS HARD!
END
PHEW!
I BET IT WAS EVEN TOUGHER BACK IN TH' LATE SIXTIES, WHEN JERRY LEWIS & PETULA CLARK DID IT!!

57

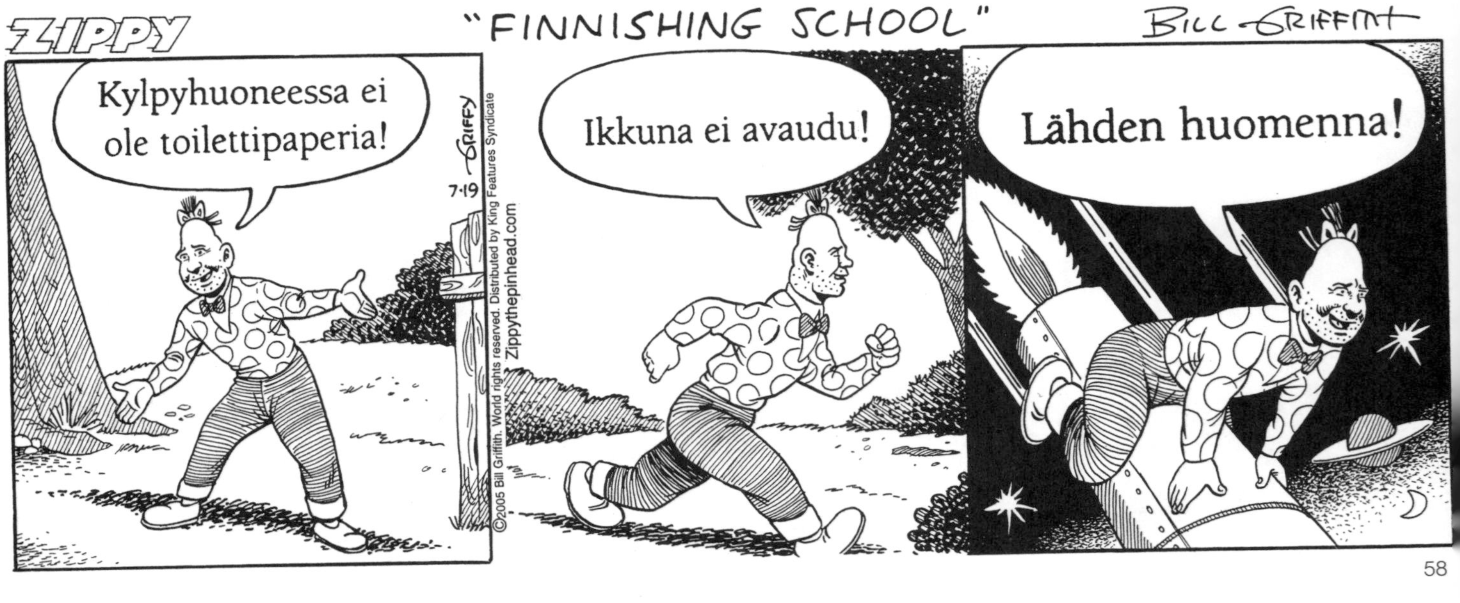
ZIPPY
"FINNISHING SCHOOL"
BILL GRIFFITH
Kylpyhuoneessa ei ole toilettipaperia!
GRIFFY 7·19
©2005 Bill Griffith. World rights reserved. Distributed by King Features Syndicate
Zippythepinhead.com
Ikkuna ei avaudu!
Lähden huomenna!

58

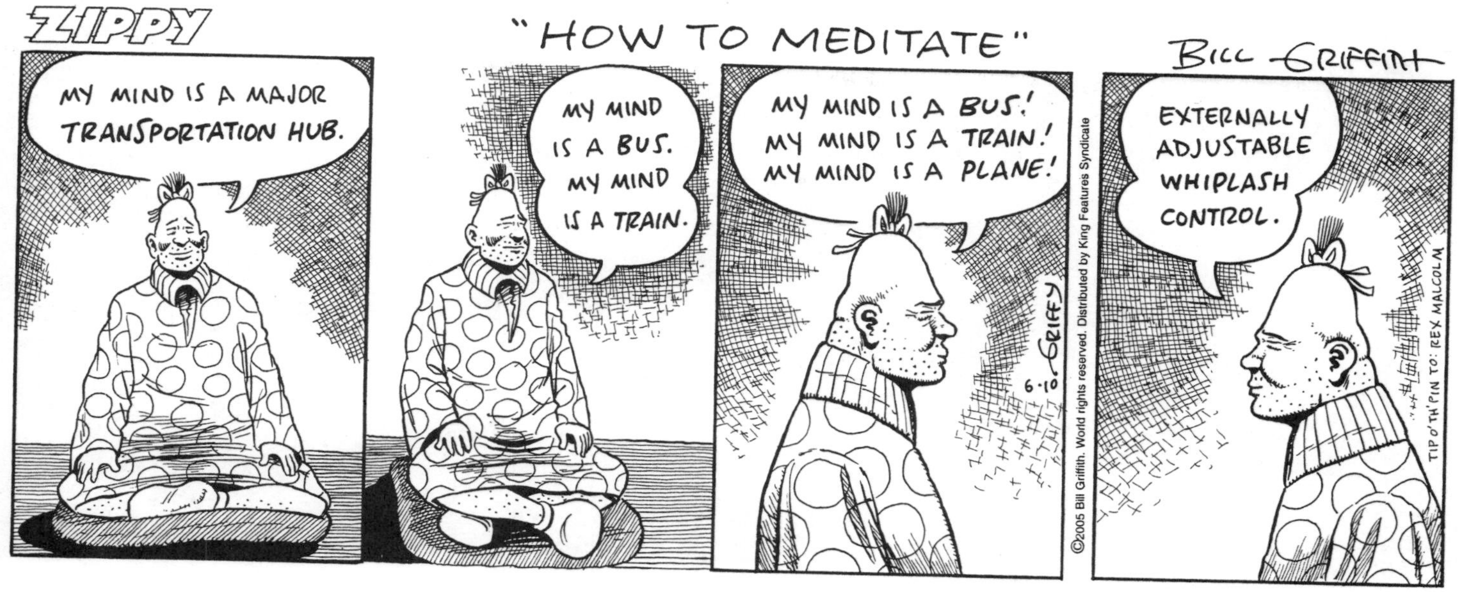
ZIPPY
"HOW TO MEDITATE"
BILL GRIFFITH
MY MIND IS A MAJOR TRANSPORTATION HUB.
MY MIND IS A BUS. MY MIND IS A TRAIN.
MY MIND IS A BUS! MY MIND IS A TRAIN! MY MIND IS A PLANE!
GRIFFY 6·10
©2005 Bill Griffith. World rights reserved. Distributed by King Features Syndicate
EXTERNALLY ADJUSTABLE WHIPLASH CONTROL.
TIP O' TH' PIN TO: REX MALCOLM

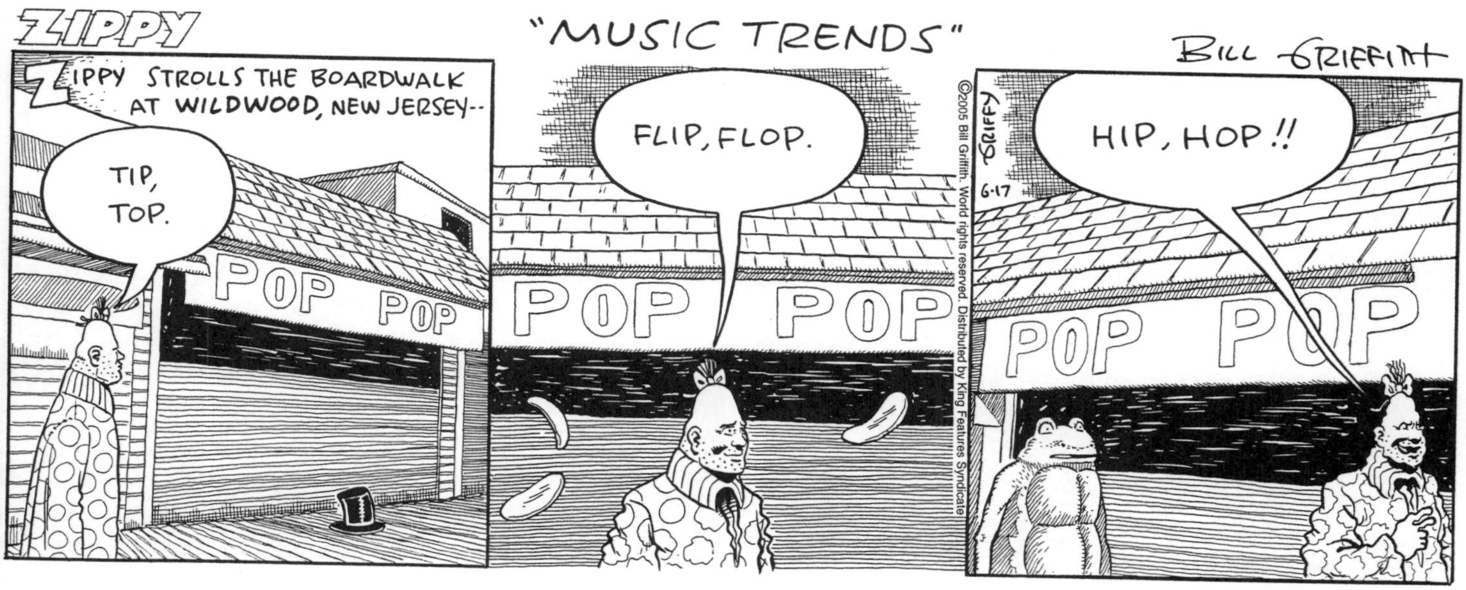
ZIPPY
"MUSIC TRENDS"
BILL GRIFFITH
ZIPPY STROLLS THE BOARDWALK AT WILDWOOD, NEW JERSEY--
TIP, TOP.
POP POP
FLIP, FLOP.
POP POP
©2005 Bill Griffith. World rights reserved. Distributed by King Features Syndicate
GRIFFY 6·17
HIP, HOP!!
POP POP

59

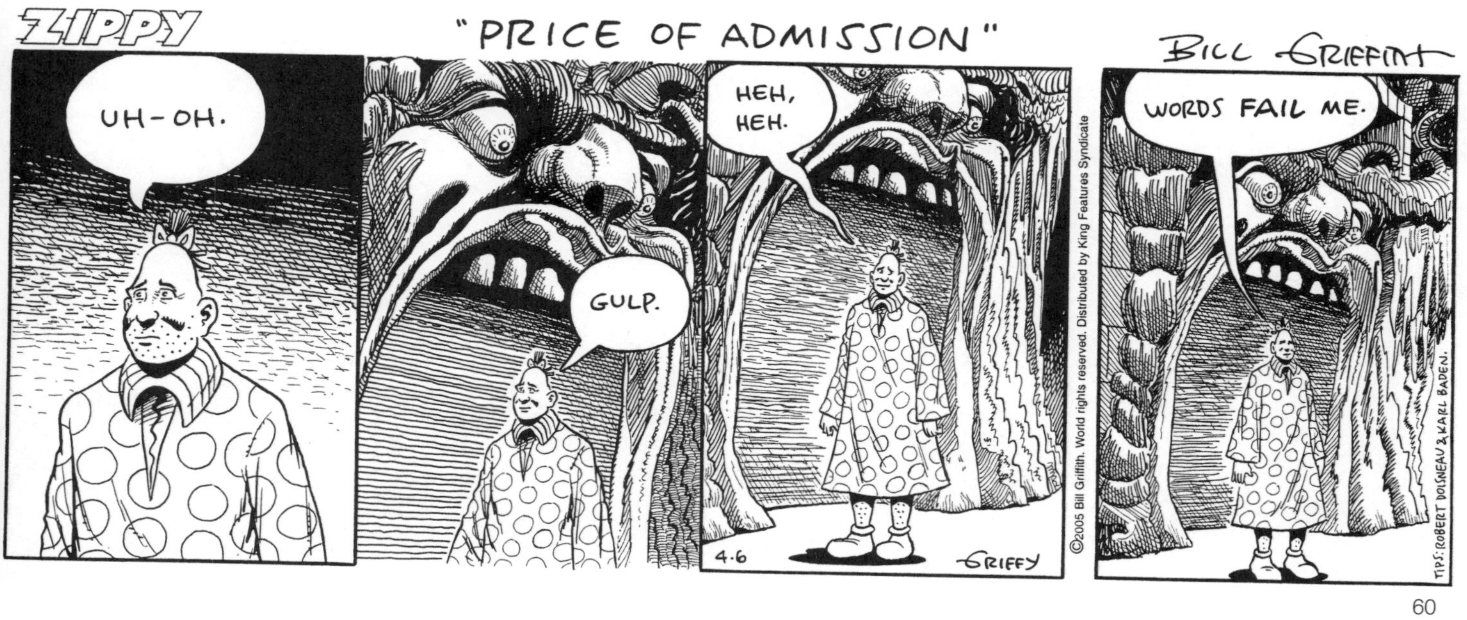
ZIPPY
"PRICE OF ADMISSION"
BILL GRIFFITH
UH-OH.
GULP.
HEH, HEH.
4·6
GRIFFY
©2005 Bill Griffith. World rights reserved. Distributed by King Features Syndicate
WORDS FAIL ME.
TIPS: ROBERT BOISNEAU & KARL BADEN.

60

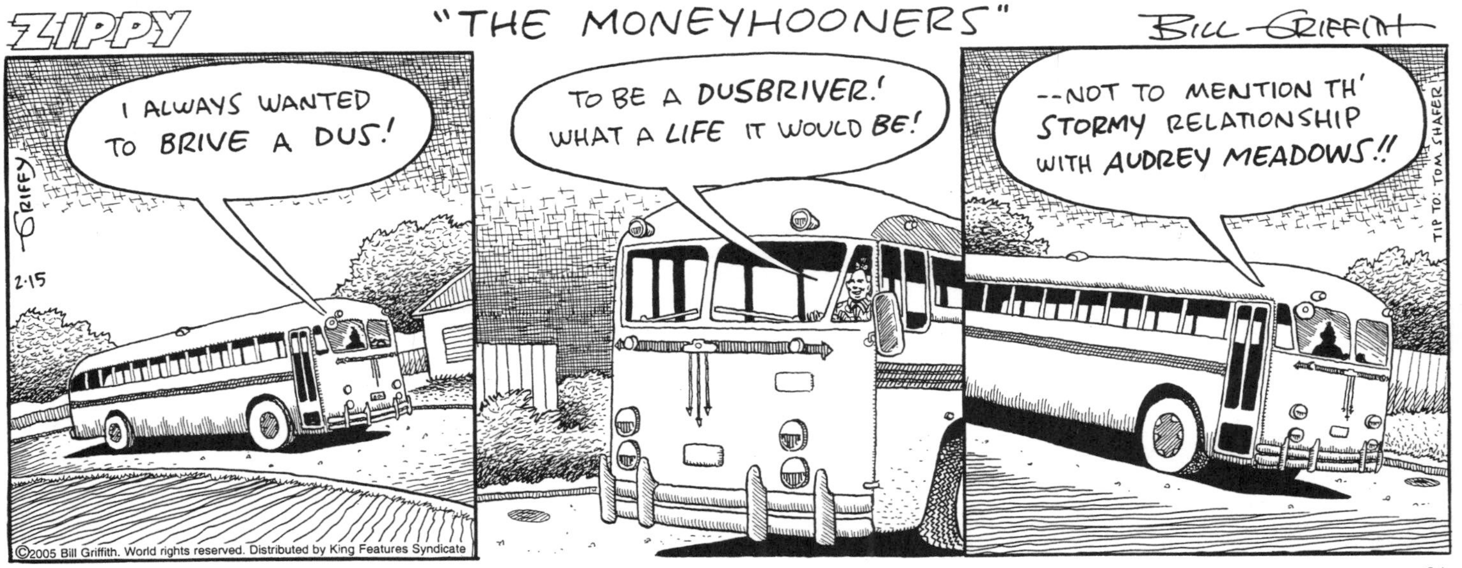
ZIPPY
"THE MONEYHOONERS"
BILL GRIFFITH
I ALWAYS WANTED TO BRIVE A DUS!
GRIFFY
2·15
TO BE A DUSBRIVER! WHAT A LIFE IT WOULD BE!
--NOT TO MENTION TH' STORMY RELATIONSHIP WITH AUDREY MEADOWS!!
TIP TO: TOM SHAFER
©2005 Bill Griffith. World rights reserved. Distributed by King Features Syndicate

61

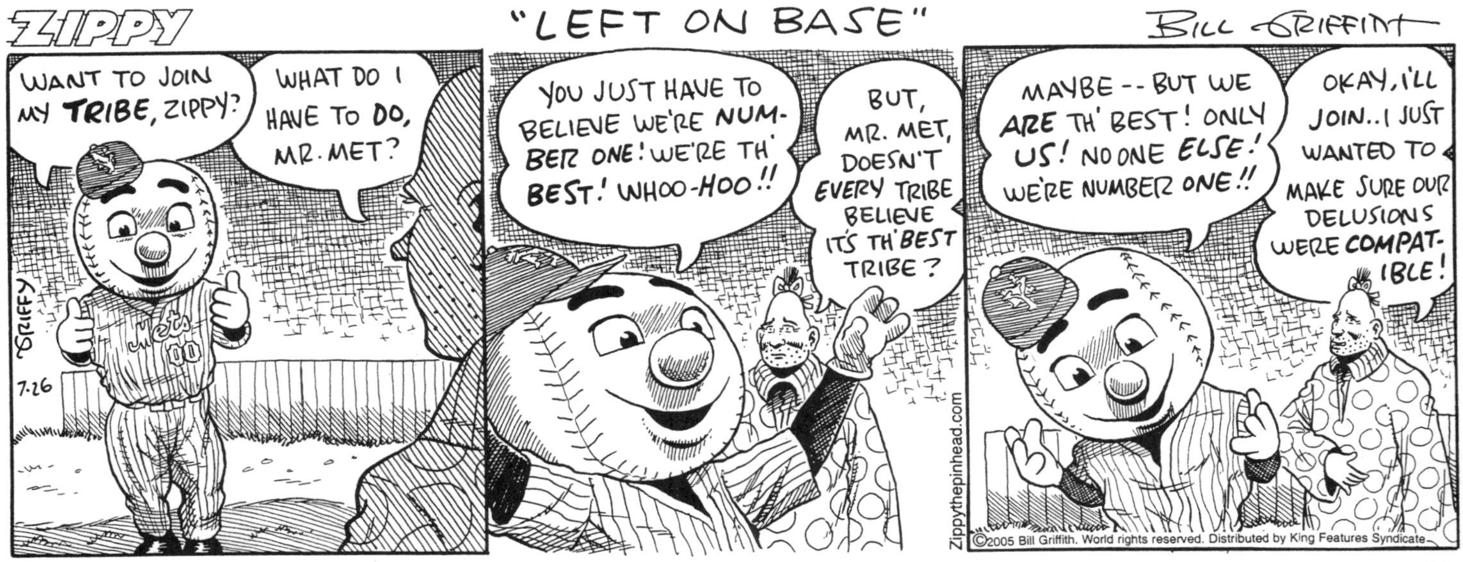
ZIPPY
"LEFT ON BASE"
BILL GRIFFITH
WANT TO JOIN MY TRIBE, ZIPPY?
WHAT DO I HAVE TO DO, MR. MET?
GRIFFY
7·26
YOU JUST HAVE TO BELIEVE WE'RE NUMBER ONE! WE'RE TH' BEST! WHOO-HOO!!
BUT, MR. MET, DOESN'T EVERY TRIBE BELIEVE IT'S TH' BEST TRIBE?
zippythepinhead.com
MAYBE -- BUT WE ARE TH' BEST! ONLY US! NO ONE ELSE! WE'RE NUMBER ONE!!
OKAY, I'LL JOIN.. I JUST WANTED TO MAKE SURE OUR DELUSIONS WERE COMPATIBLE!
©2005 Bill Griffith. World rights reserved. Distributed by King Features Syndicate

62

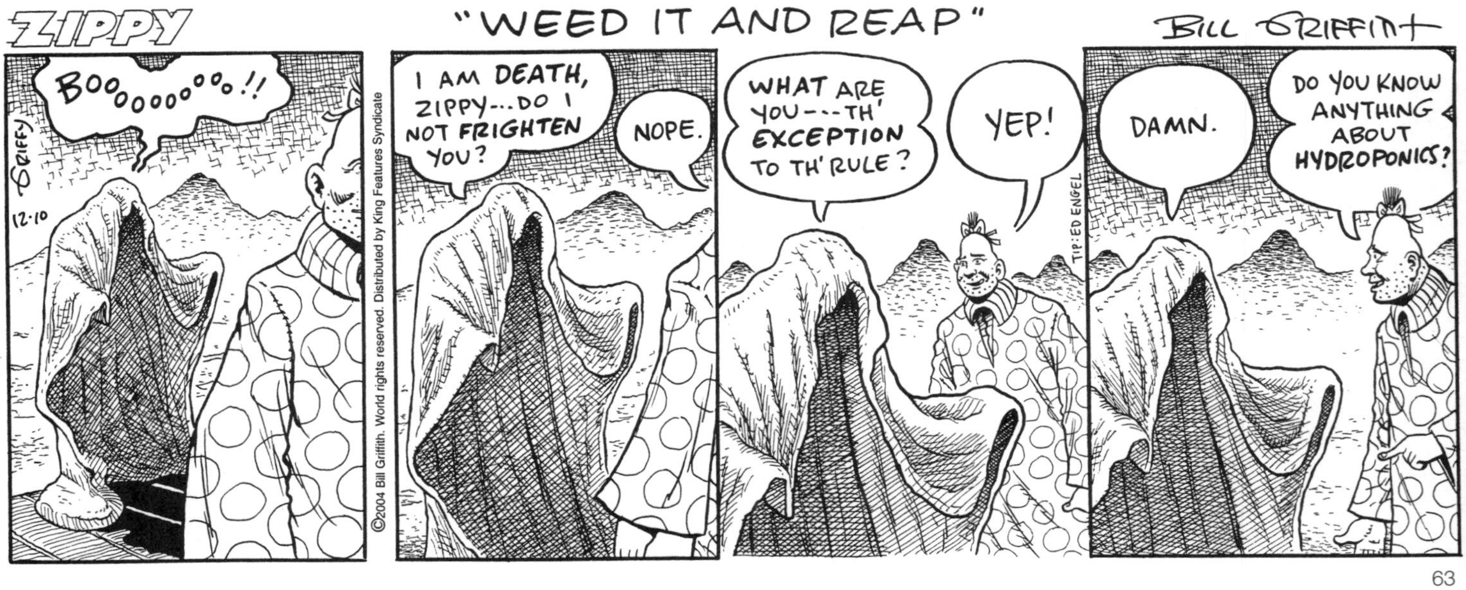
ZIPPY
"WEED IT AND REAP"
BILL GRIFFITH
BOOoooooooo!!
GRIFFY
12·10
©2004 Bill Griffith. World rights reserved. Distributed by King Features Syndicate
I AM DEATH, ZIPPY... DO I NOT FRIGHTEN YOU?
NOPE.
WHAT ARE YOU--- TH' EXCEPTION TO TH' RULE?
YEP!
TIP: ED ENGEL
DAMN.
DO YOU KNOW ANYTHING ABOUT HYDROPONICS?

63

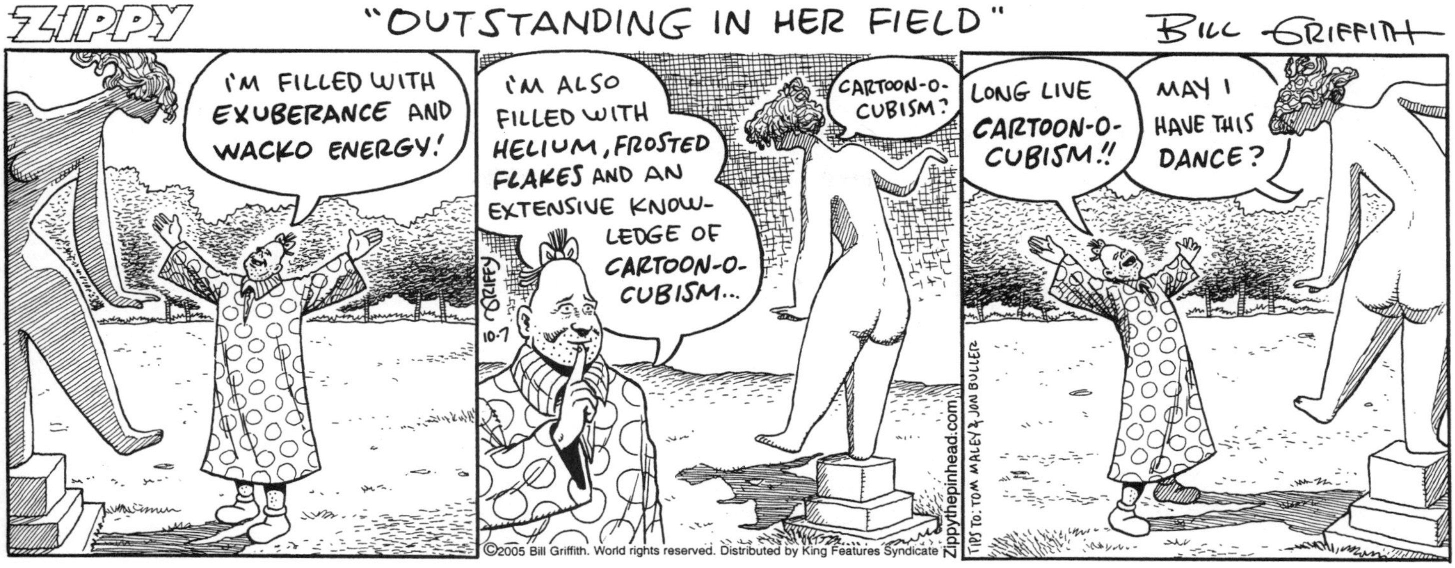
ZIPPY
"OUTSTANDING IN HER FIELD"
BILL GRIFFITH
I'M FILLED WITH EXUBERANCE AND WACKO ENERGY!
I'M ALSO FILLED WITH HELIUM, FROSTED FLAKES AND AN EXTENSIVE KNOWLEDGE OF CARTOON-O-CUBISM...
CARTOON-O-CUBISM?
LONG LIVE CARTOON-O-CUBISM!!
MAY I HAVE THIS DANCE?
GRIFFY 10-7
©2005 Bill Griffith. World rights reserved. Distributed by King Features Syndicate
Zippythepinhead.com
TIPS TO: TOM MALEY & JON BULLER

64 A

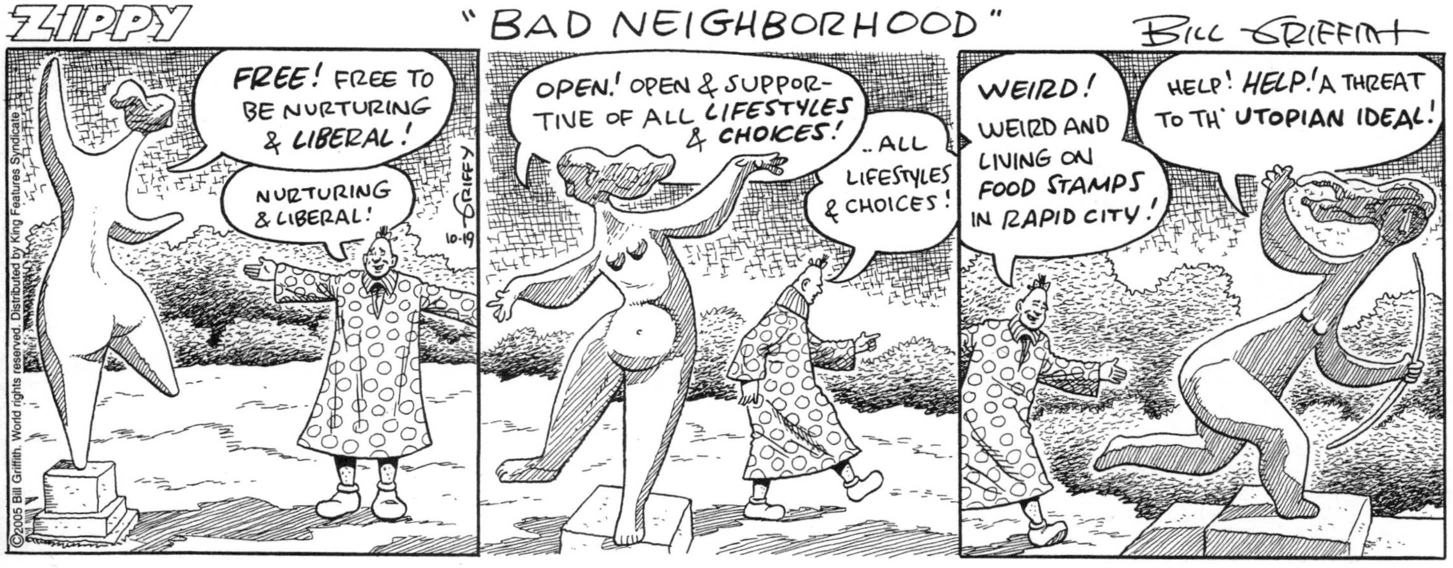
ZIPPY
"BAD NEIGHBORHOOD"
BILL GRIFFITH
FREE! FREE TO BE NURTURING & LIBERAL!
NURTURING & LIBERAL!
GRIFFY 10-19
OPEN! OPEN & SUPPORTIVE OF ALL LIFESTYLES & CHOICES!
..ALL LIFESTYLES & CHOICES!
WEIRD! WEIRD AND LIVING ON FOOD STAMPS IN RAPID CITY!
HELP! HELP! A THREAT TO TH' UTOPIAN IDEAL!
©2005 Bill Griffith. World rights reserved. Distributed by King Features Syndicate

64 B

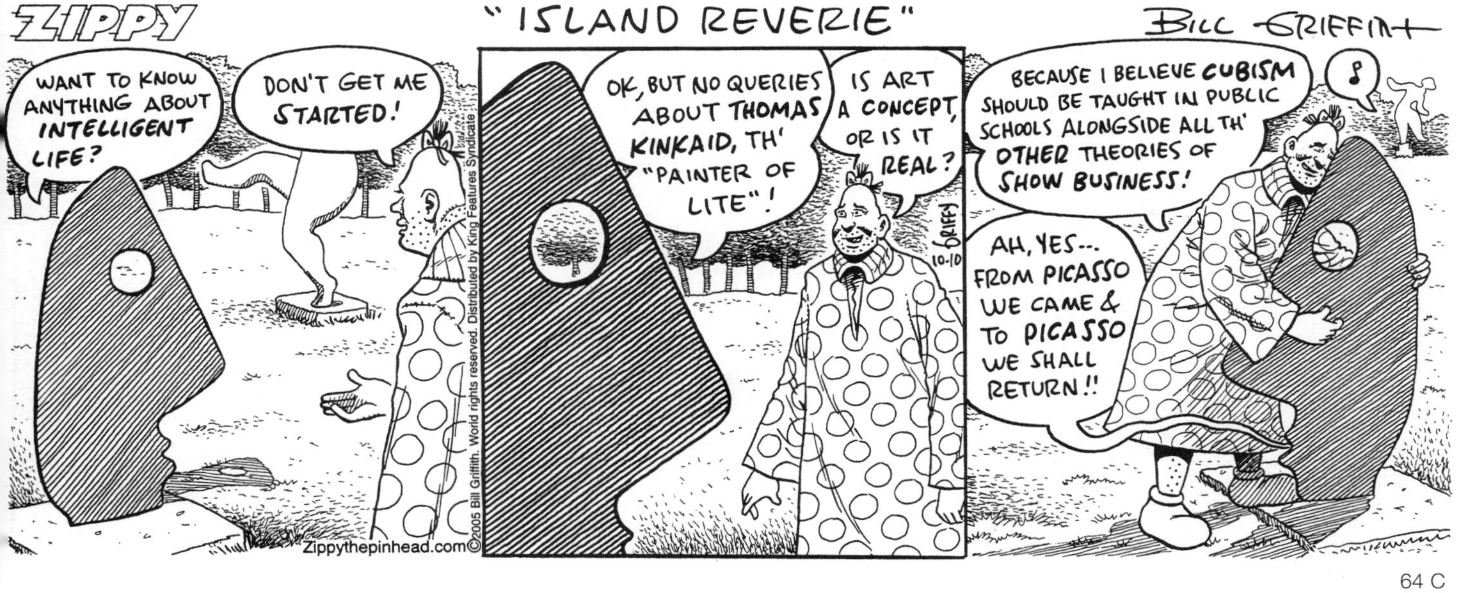
ZIPPY
"ISLAND REVERIE"
BILL GRIFFITH
WANT TO KNOW ANYTHING ABOUT INTELLIGENT LIFE?
DON'T GET ME STARTED!
OK, BUT NO QUERIES ABOUT THOMAS KINKAID, TH' "PAINTER OF LITE"!
IS ART A CONCEPT, OR IS IT REAL?
GRIFFY 10-10
BECAUSE I BELIEVE CUBISM SHOULD BE TAUGHT IN PUBLIC SCHOOLS ALONGSIDE ALL TH' OTHER THEORIES OF SHOW BUSINESS!
AH, YES--- FROM PICASSO WE CAME & TO PICASSO WE SHALL RETURN!!
©2005 Bill Griffith. World rights reserved. Distributed by King Features Syndicate
Zippythepinhead.com©

64 C

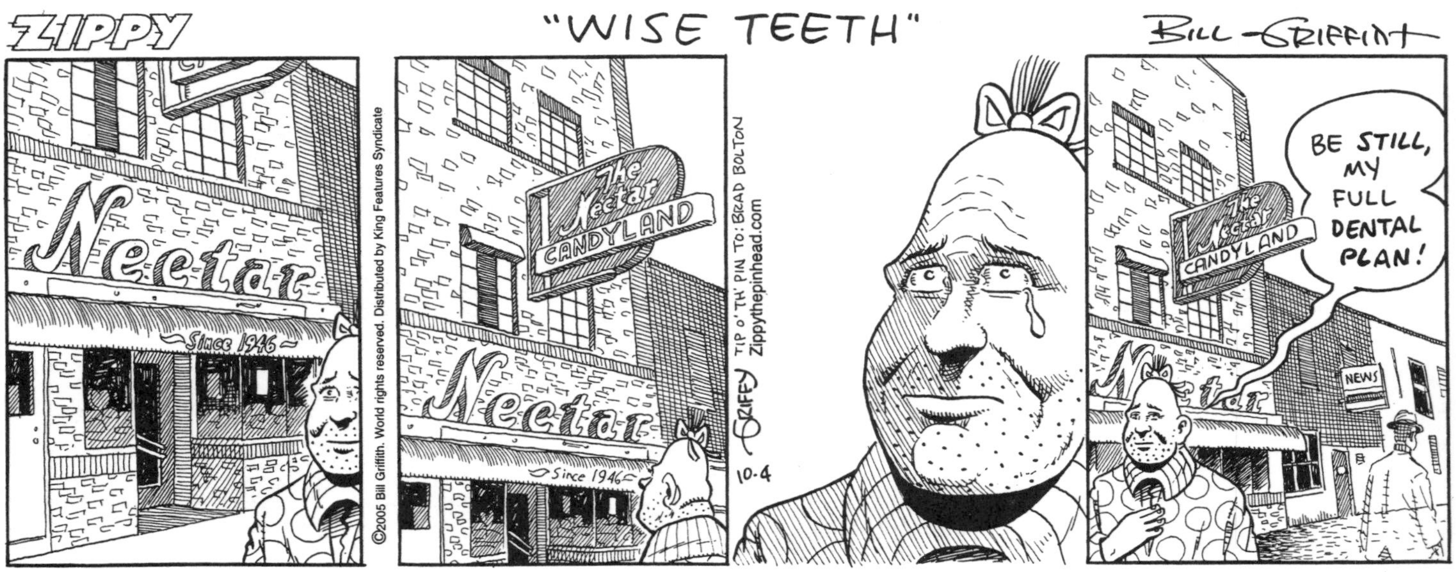
ZIPPY
"WISE TEETH"
BILL GRIFFITH
Nectar
Since 1946
©2005 Bill Griffith. World rights reserved. Distributed by King Features Syndicate
The Nectar CANDYLAND
Nectar
Since 1946
GRIFFY 10-4
TIP O' TH' PIN TO: BRAD BOLTON
Zippythepinhead.com
The Nectar CANDYLAND
BE STILL, MY FULL DENTAL PLAN!
NEWS

65

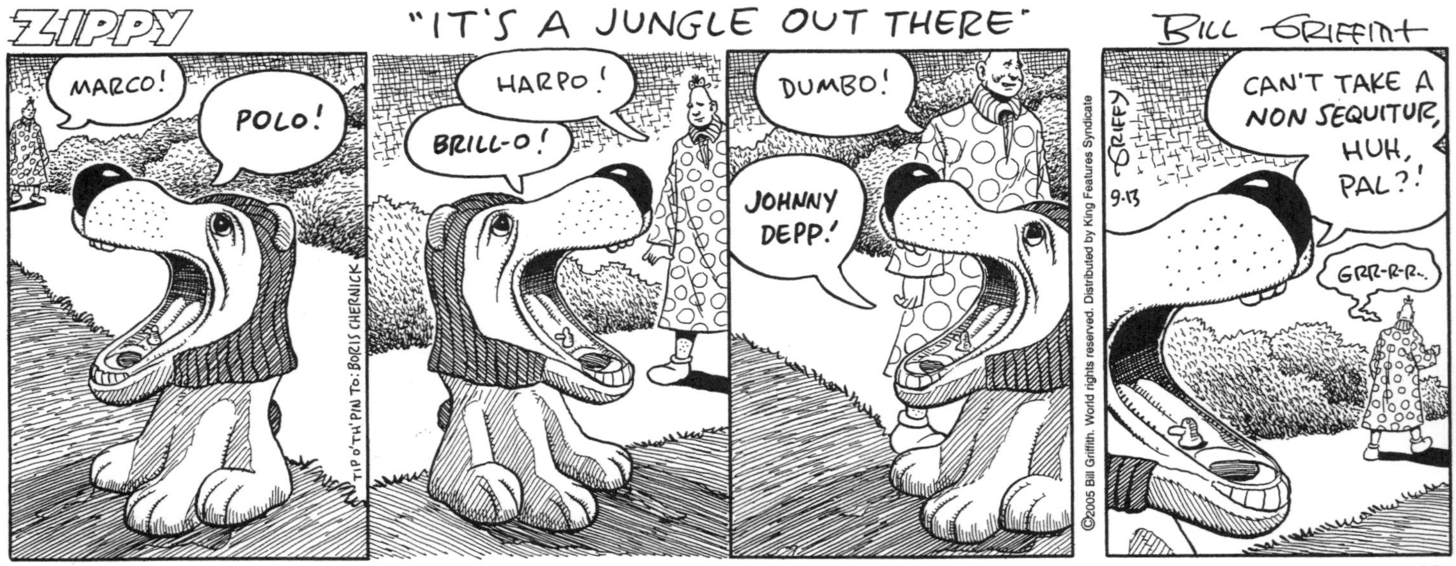
ZIPPY
"IT'S A JUNGLE OUT THERE"
BILL GRIFFITH
MARCO!
POLO!
TIP O' TH' PIN TO: BORIS CHERNICK
HARPO!
BRILL-O!
DUMBO!
JOHNNY DEPP!
©2005 Bill Griffith. World rights reserved. Distributed by King Features Syndicate
GRIFFY 9-13
CAN'T TAKE A NON SEQUITUR, HUH, PAL?!
GRR-R-R..

66

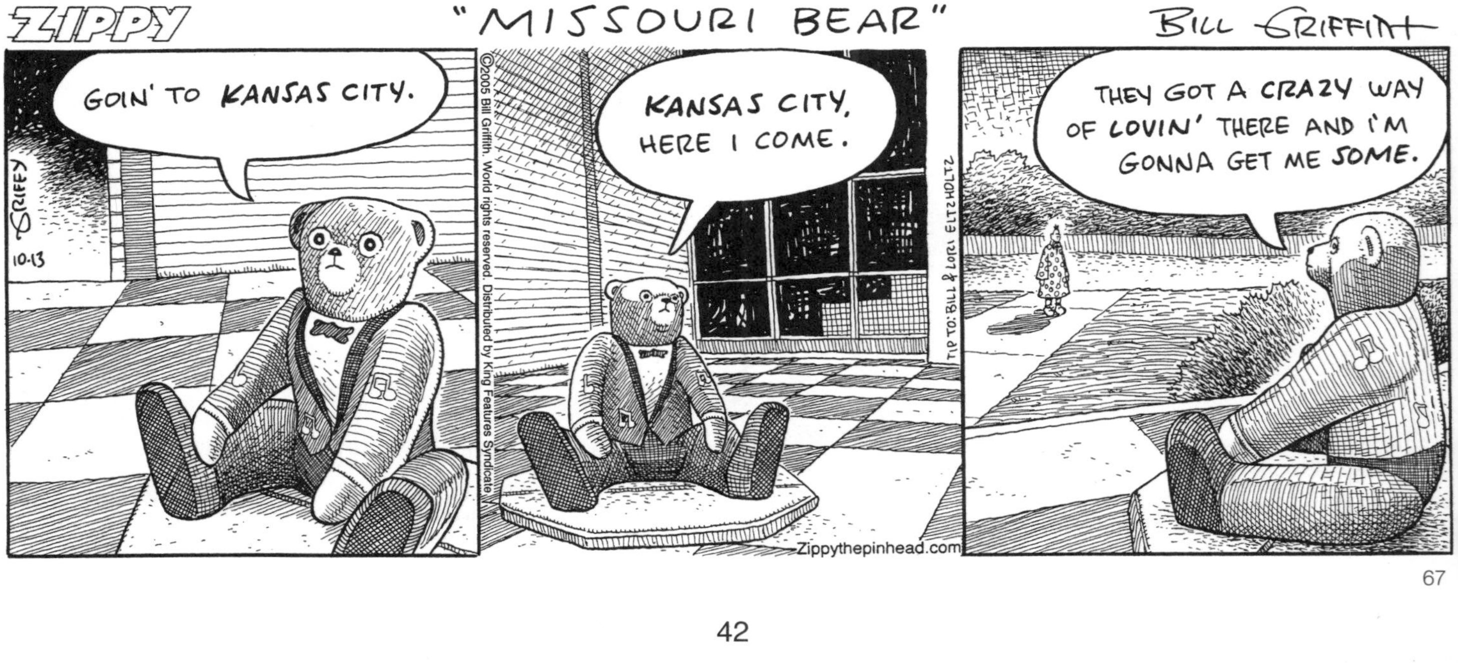
ZIPPY
"MISSOURI BEAR"
BILL GRIFFITH
GOIN' TO KANSAS CITY.
GRIFFY 10-13
©2005 Bill Griffith. World rights reserved. Distributed by King Features Syndicate
KANSAS CITY, HERE I COME.
Zippythepinhead.com
TIP TO: BILL & LORI ELTZHOLTZ
THEY GOT A CRAZY WAY OF LOVIN' THERE AND I'M GONNA GET ME SOME.

67

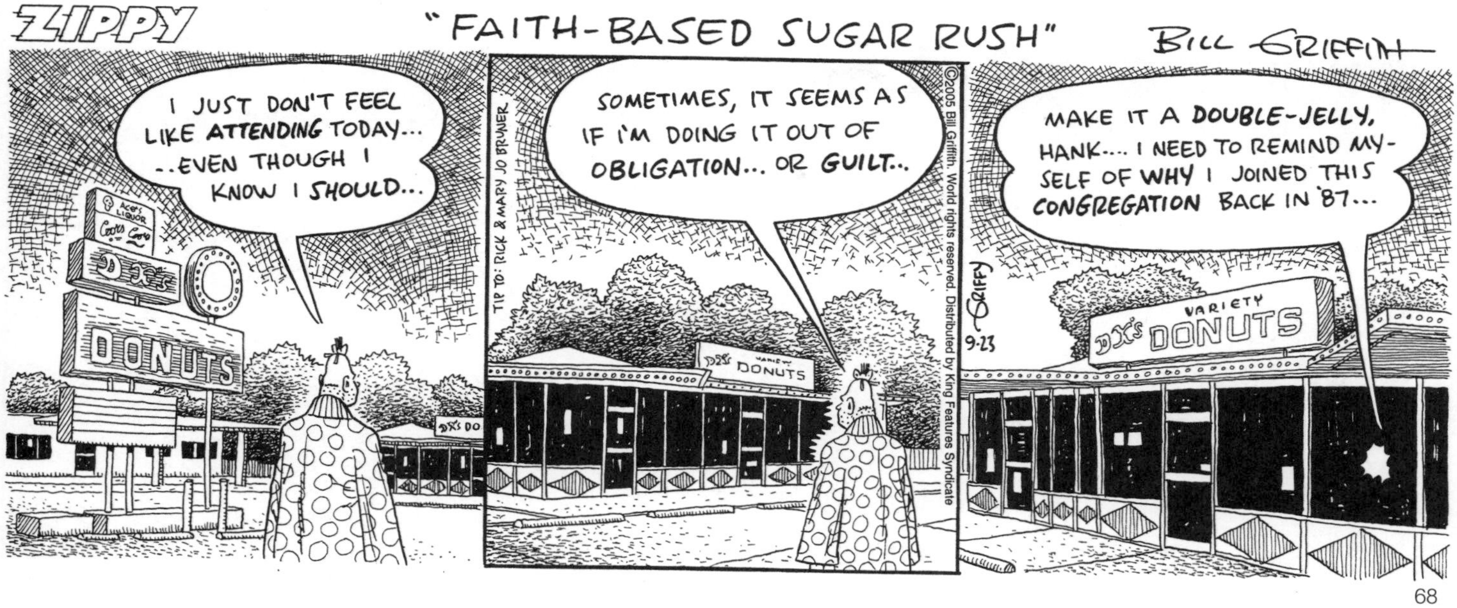
ZIPPY
"FAITH-BASED SUGAR RUSH"
BILL GRIFFITH
I JUST DON'T FEEL LIKE ATTENDING TODAY... ..EVEN THOUGH I KNOW I SHOULD...
DONUTS
SOMETIMES, IT SEEMS AS IF I'M DOING IT OUT OF OBLIGATION... OR GUILT...
TIP TO: RICK & MARY JO BRUNER
©2005 Bill Griffith. World rights reserved. Distributed by King Features Syndicate
GRIFFY 9-23
MAKE IT A DOUBLE-JELLY, HANK.... I NEED TO REMIND MYSELF OF WHY I JOINED THIS CONGREGATION BACK IN '87...
DX'S VARIETY DONUTS

68

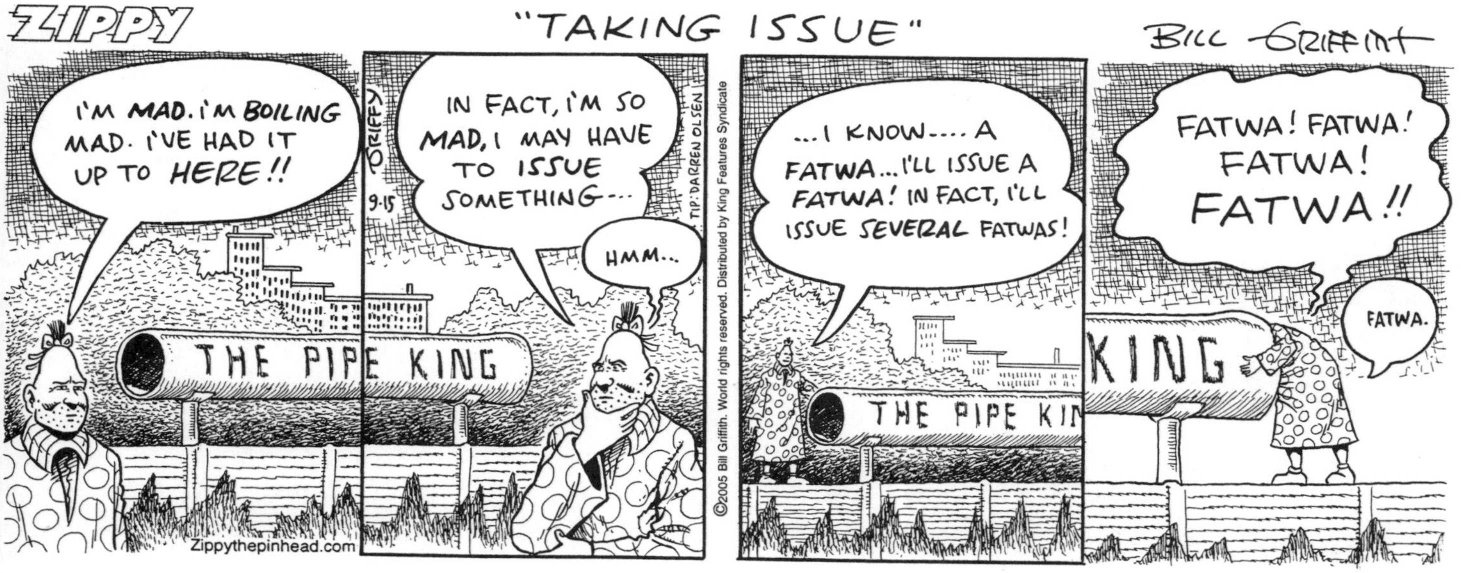
ZIPPY
"TAKING ISSUE"
BILL GRIFFITH
I'M MAD. I'M BOILING MAD. I'VE HAD IT UP TO HERE!!
GRIFFY 9-15
IN FACT, I'M SO MAD, I MAY HAVE TO ISSUE SOMETHING--..
TIP: DARREN OLSEN
HMM...
THE PIPE KING
Zippythepinhead.com
©2005 Bill Griffith. World rights reserved. Distributed by King Features Syndicate
...I KNOW.... A FATWA...I'LL ISSUE A FATWA! IN FACT, I'LL ISSUE SEVERAL FATWAS!
FATWA! FATWA! FATWA! FATWA!!
FATWA.

69

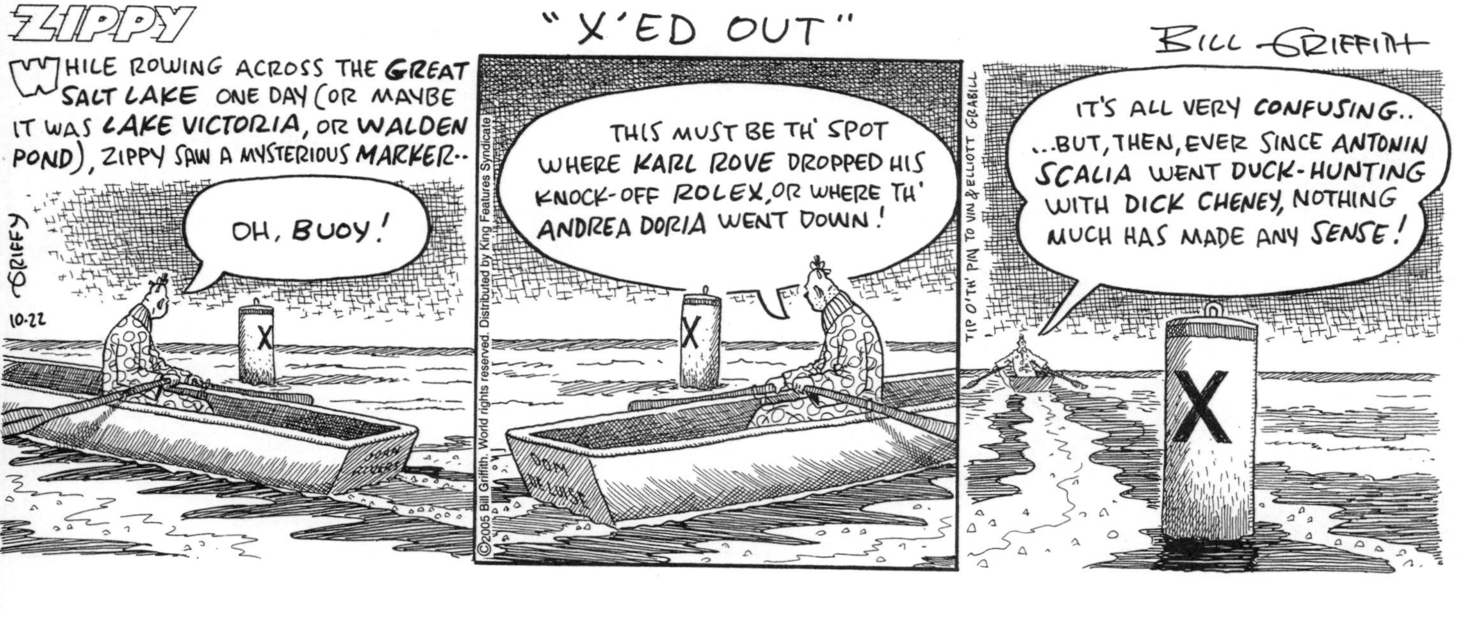
ZIPPY
"X'ED OUT"
BILL GRIFFITH
WHILE ROWING ACROSS THE GREAT SALT LAKE ONE DAY (OR MAYBE IT WAS LAKE VICTORIA, OR WALDEN POND), ZIPPY SAW A MYSTERIOUS MARKER--
OH, BUOY!
GRIFFY 10-22
X
THIS MUST BE TH' SPOT WHERE KARL ROVE DROPPED HIS KNOCK-OFF ROLEX, OR WHERE TH' ANDREA DORIA WENT DOWN!
©2005 Bill Griffith. World rights reserved. Distributed by King Features Syndicate
TIP O' TH' PIN TO VIN & ELLIOTT GRABILL
IT'S ALL VERY CONFUSING.. ...BUT, THEN, EVER SINCE ANTONIN SCALIA WENT DUCK-HUNTING WITH DICK CHENEY, NOTHING MUCH HAS MADE ANY SENSE!

ZIPPY & CO.

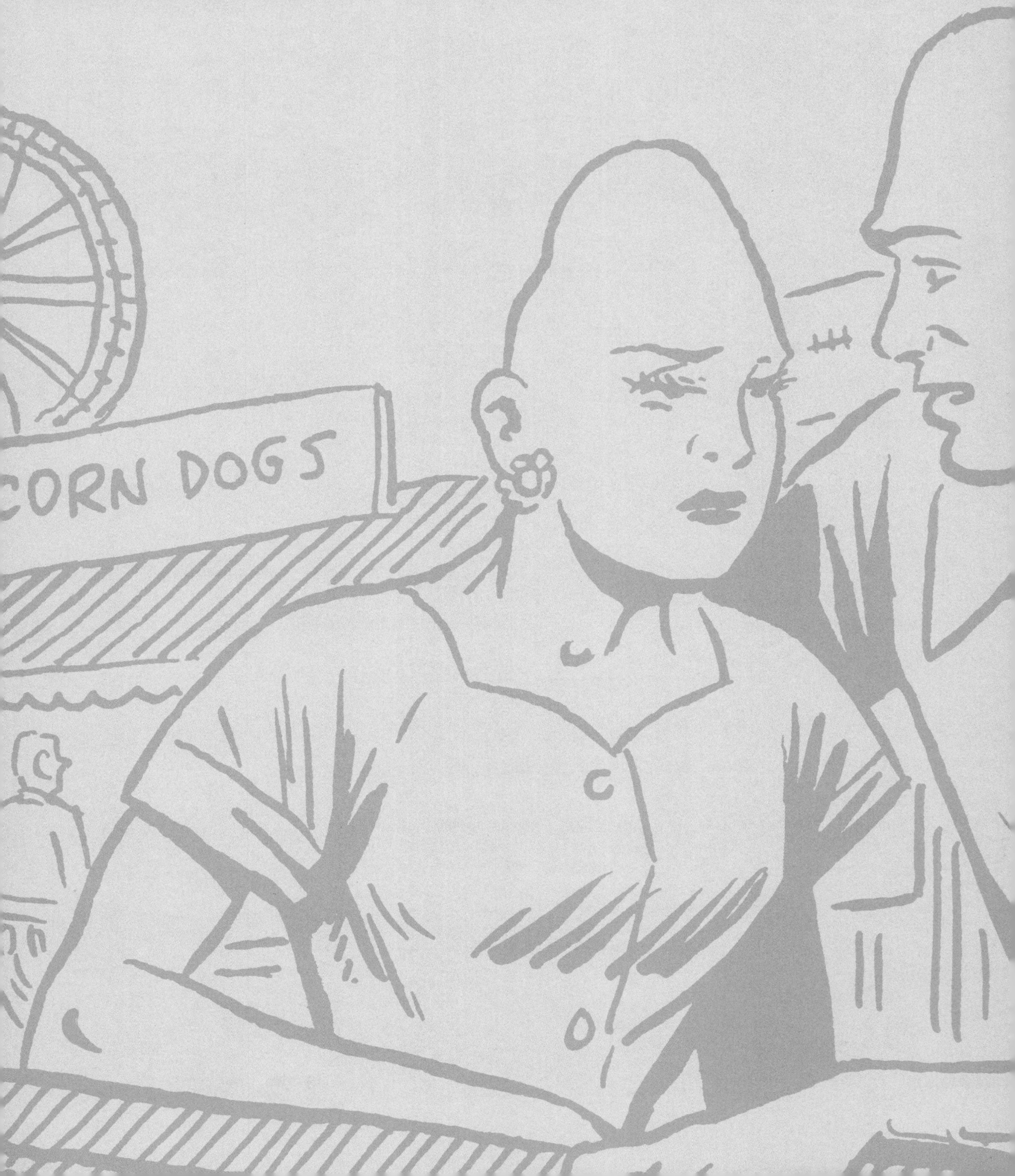
CORN DOGS

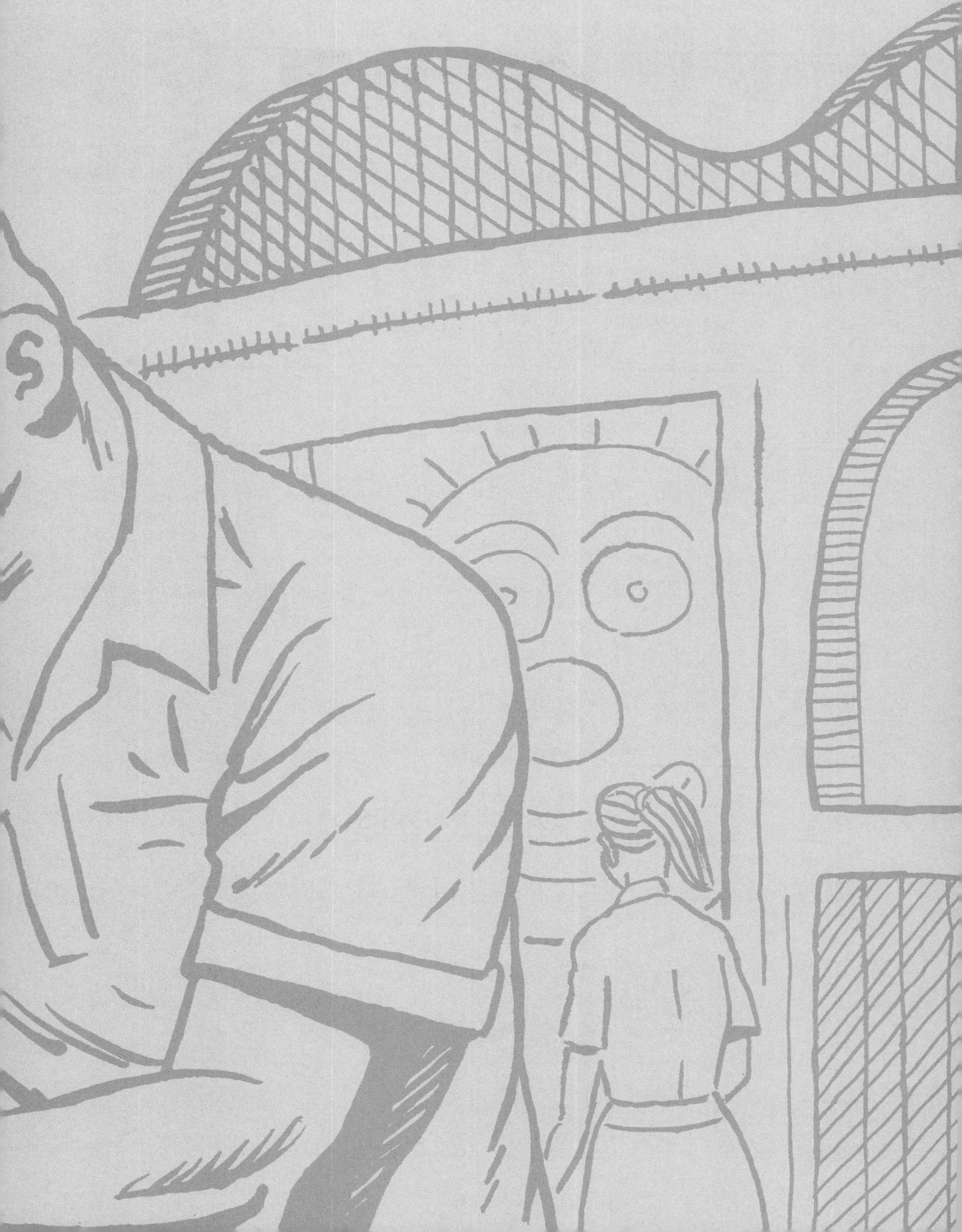

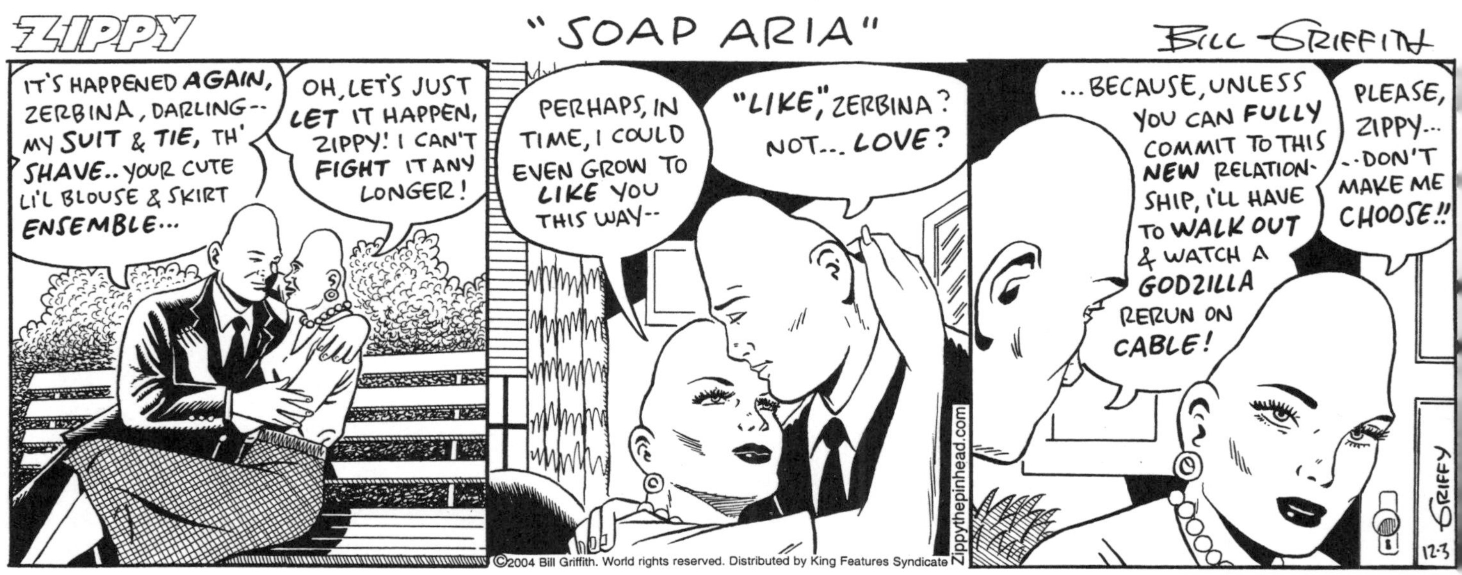
ZIPPY
"SOAP ARIA"
BILL GRIFFITH
IT'S HAPPENED AGAIN, ZERBINA, DARLING-- MY SUIT & TIE, TH' SHAVE.. YOUR CUTE LI'L BLOUSE & SKIRT ENSEMBLE...
OH, LET'S JUST LET IT HAPPEN, ZIPPY! I CAN'T FIGHT IT ANY LONGER!
PERHAPS, IN TIME, I COULD EVEN GROW TO LIKE YOU THIS WAY--
"LIKE," ZERBINA? NOT... LOVE?
...BECAUSE, UNLESS YOU CAN FULLY COMMIT TO THIS NEW RELATIONSHIP, I'LL HAVE TO WALK OUT & WATCH A GODZILLA RERUN ON CABLE!
PLEASE, ZIPPY... ..DON'T MAKE ME CHOOSE!!
GRIFFY
12-3
Zippythepinhead.com
©2004 Bill Griffith. World rights reserved. Distributed by King Features Syndicate

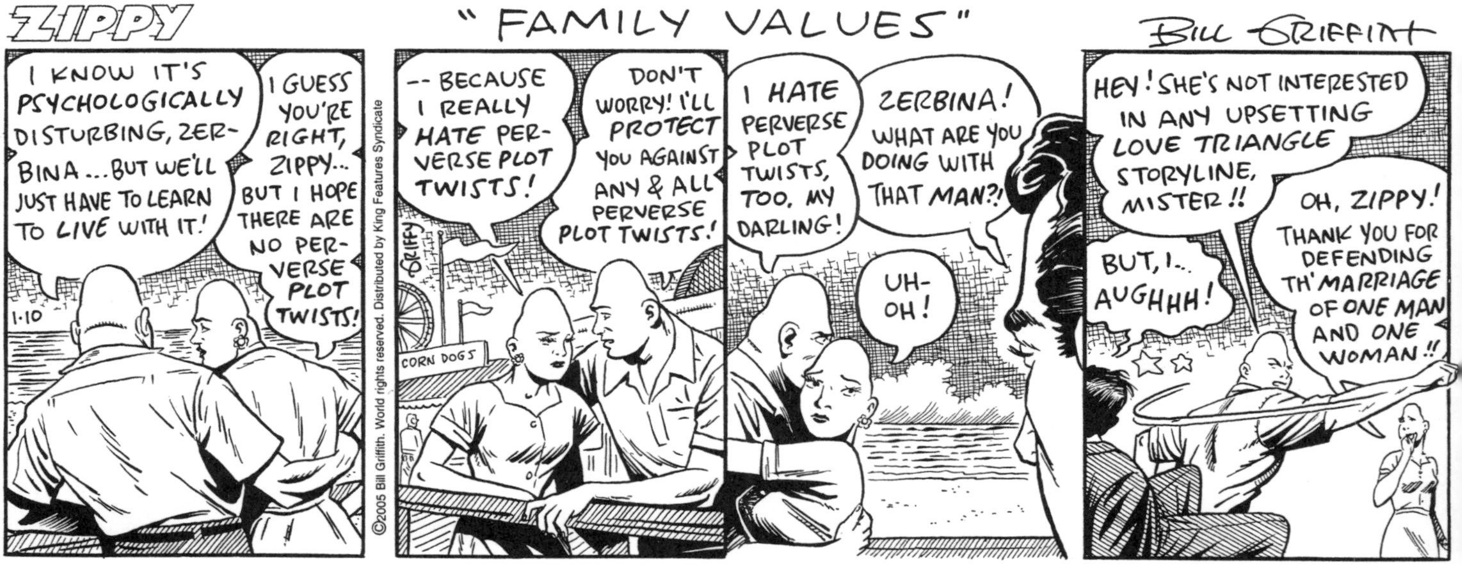
ZIPPY
"FAMILY VALUES"
BILL GRIFFITH
I KNOW IT'S PSYCHOLOGICALLY DISTURBING, ZERBINA... BUT WE'LL JUST HAVE TO LEARN TO LIVE WITH IT!
I GUESS YOU'RE RIGHT, ZIPPY... BUT I HOPE THERE ARE NO PERVERSE PLOT TWISTS!
1-10
©2005 Bill Griffith. World rights reserved. Distributed by King Features Syndicate
-- BECAUSE I REALLY HATE PERVERSE PLOT TWISTS!
DON'T WORRY! I'LL PROTECT YOU AGAINST ANY & ALL PERVERSE PLOT TWISTS!
GRIFFY
CORN DOGS
I HATE PERVERSE PLOT TWISTS, TOO, MY DARLING!
ZERBINA! WHAT ARE YOU DOING WITH THAT MAN?!
UH-OH!
HEY! SHE'S NOT INTERESTED IN ANY UPSETTING LOVE TRIANGLE STORYLINE, MISTER!!
BUT, I.. AUGHHH!
OH, ZIPPY! THANK YOU FOR DEFENDING TH' MARRIAGE OF ONE MAN AND ONE WOMAN!!

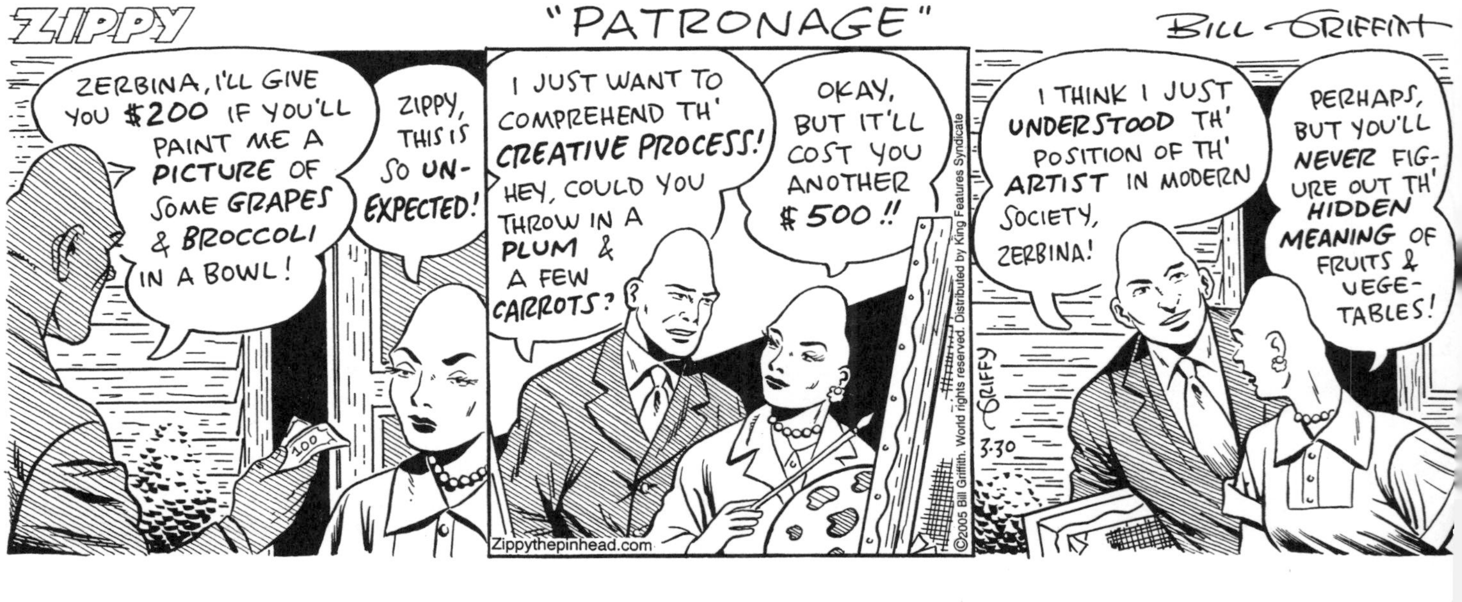
ZIPPY
"PATRONAGE"
BILL GRIFFITH
ZERBINA, I'LL GIVE YOU $200 IF YOU'LL PAINT ME A PICTURE OF SOME GRAPES & BROCCOLI IN A BOWL!
ZIPPY, THIS IS SO UNEXPECTED!
100
I JUST WANT TO COMPREHEND TH' CREATIVE PROCESS! HEY, COULD YOU THROW IN A PLUM & A FEW CARROTS?
OKAY, BUT IT'LL COST YOU ANOTHER $500!!
Zippythepinhead.com
GRIFFY
3-30
©2005 Bill Griffith. World rights reserved. Distributed by King Features Syndicate
I THINK I JUST UNDERSTOOD TH' POSITION OF TH' ARTIST IN MODERN SOCIETY, ZERBINA!
PERHAPS, BUT YOU'LL NEVER FIGURE OUT TH' HIDDEN MEANING OF FRUITS & VEGETABLES!

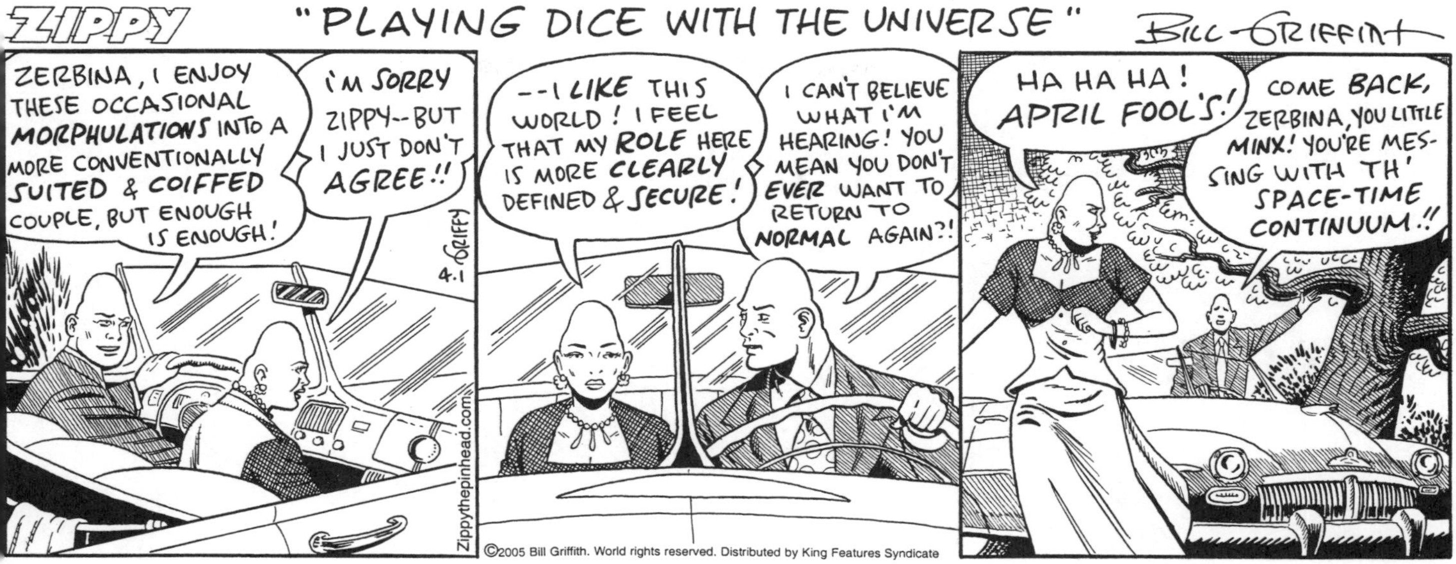
ZIPPY
"PLAYING DICE WITH THE UNIVERSE"
BILL GRIFFITH
ZERBINA, I ENJOY THESE OCCASIONAL MORPHULATIONS INTO A MORE CONVENTIONALLY SUITED & COIFFED COUPLE, BUT ENOUGH IS ENOUGH!
I'M SORRY ZIPPY-- BUT I JUST DON'T AGREE!!
GRIFFY 4.1
--I LIKE THIS WORLD! I FEEL THAT MY ROLE HERE IS MORE CLEARLY DEFINED & SECURE!
I CAN'T BELIEVE WHAT I'M HEARING! YOU MEAN YOU DON'T EVER WANT TO RETURN TO NORMAL AGAIN?!
HA HA HA! APRIL FOOL'S!
COME BACK, ZERBINA, YOU LITTLE MINX! YOU'RE MESSING WITH TH' SPACE-TIME CONTINUUM!!
Zippythepinhead.com
©2005 Bill Griffith. World rights reserved. Distributed by King Features Syndicate

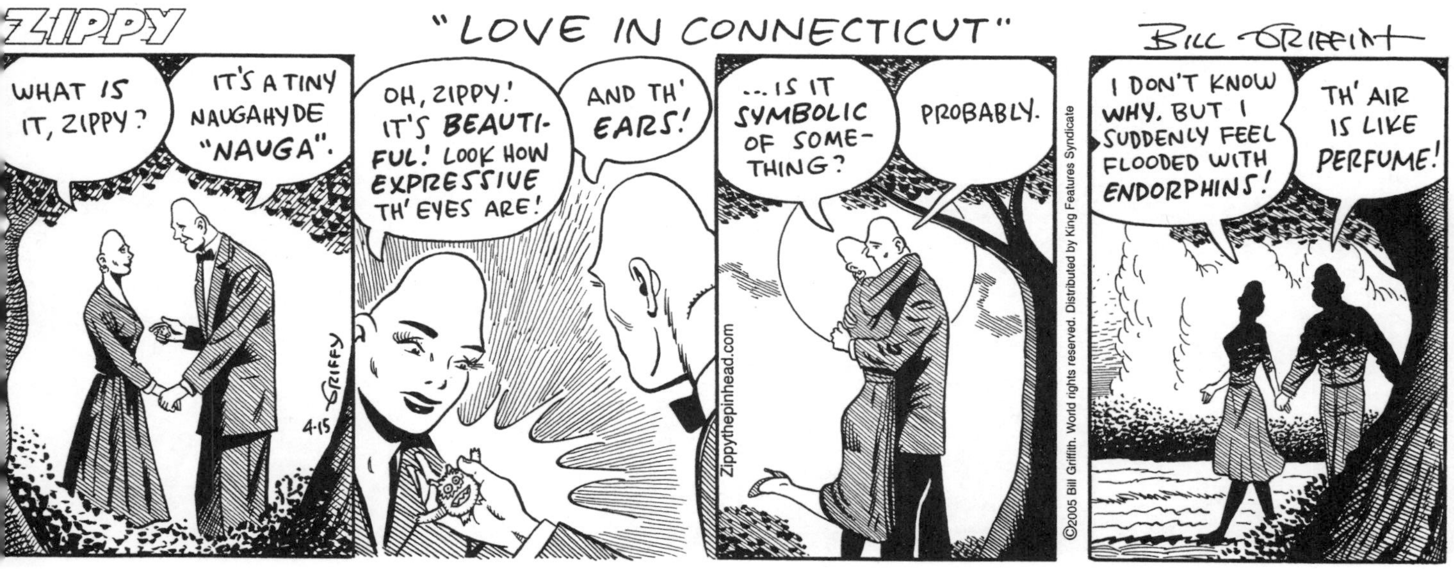
ZIPPY
"LOVE IN CONNECTICUT"
BILL GRIFFITH
WHAT IS IT, ZIPPY?
IT'S A TINY NAUGAHYDE "NAUGA".
GRIFFY 4.15
OH, ZIPPY! IT'S BEAUTIFUL! LOOK HOW EXPRESSIVE TH' EYES ARE!
AND TH' EARS!
...IS IT SYMBOLIC OF SOMETHING?
PROBABLY.
Zippythepinhead.com
I DON'T KNOW WHY, BUT I SUDDENLY FEEL FLOODED WITH ENDORPHINS!
TH' AIR IS LIKE PERFUME!
©2005 Bill Griffith. World rights reserved. Distributed by King Features Syndicate

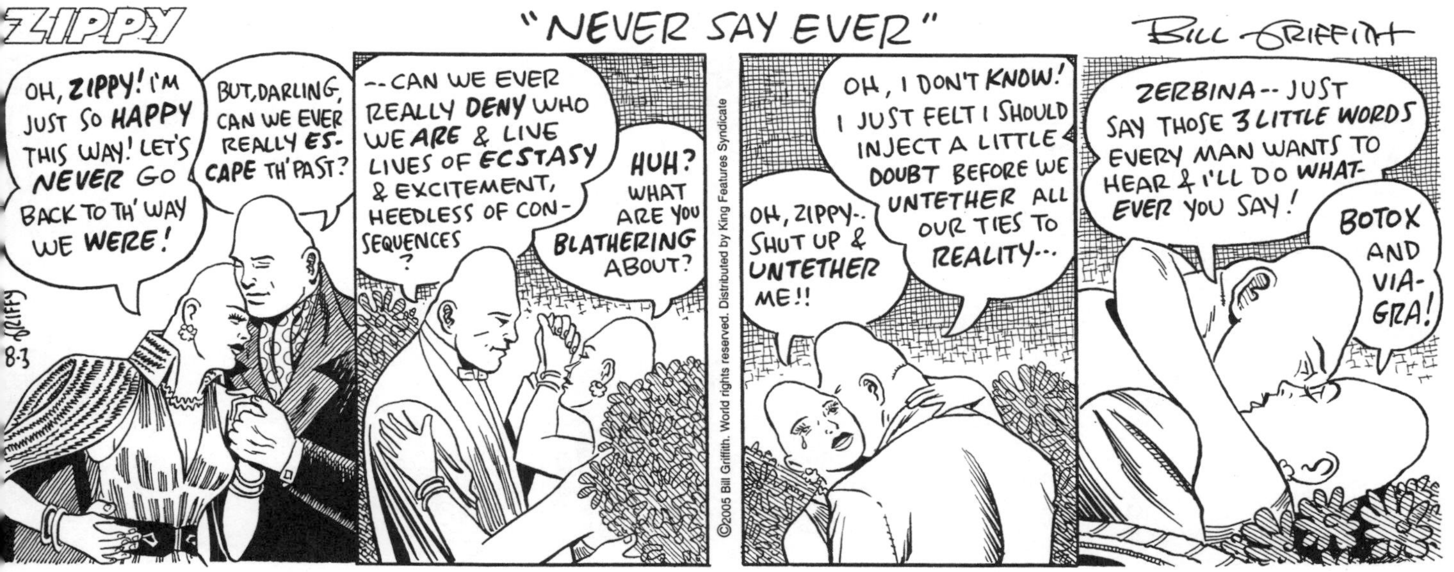
ZIPPY
"NEVER SAY EVER"
BILL GRIFFITH
OH, ZIPPY! I'M JUST SO HAPPY THIS WAY! LET'S NEVER GO BACK TO TH' WAY WE WERE!
BUT, DARLING, CAN WE EVER REALLY ESCAPE TH' PAST?
GRIFFY 8.3
--CAN WE EVER REALLY DENY WHO WE ARE & LIVE LIVES OF ECSTASY & EXCITEMENT, HEEDLESS OF CONSEQUENCES?
HUH? WHAT ARE YOU BLATHERING ABOUT?
©2005 Bill Griffith. World rights reserved. Distributed by King Features Syndicate
OH, I DON'T KNOW! I JUST FELT I SHOULD INJECT A LITTLE DOUBT BEFORE WE UNTETHER ALL OUR TIES TO REALITY...
OH, ZIPPY.. SHUT UP & UNTETHER ME!!
ZERBINA-- JUST SAY THOSE 3 LITTLE WORDS EVERY MAN WANTS TO HEAR & I'LL DO WHATEVER YOU SAY!
BOTOX AND VIAGRA!

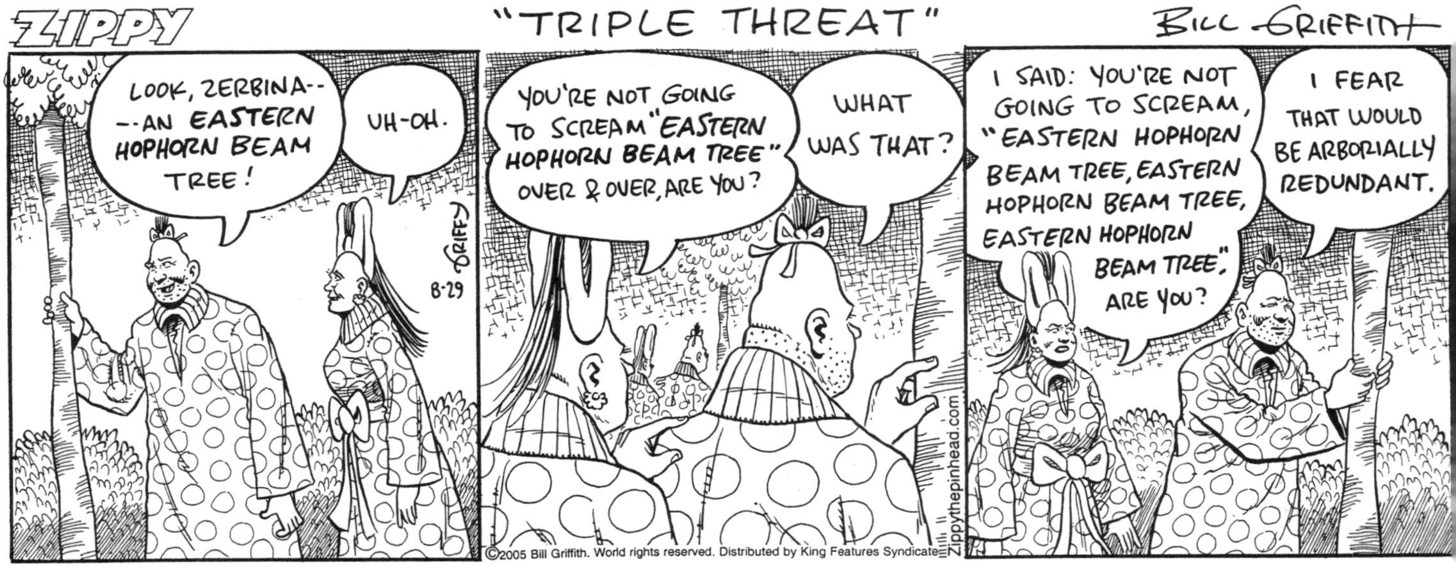
ZIPPY
"TRIPLE THREAT"
BILL GRIFFITH
LOOK, ZERBINA-- --AN EASTERN HOPHORN BEAM TREE!
UH-OH.
GRIFFY
8·29
YOU'RE NOT GOING TO SCREAM "EASTERN HOPHORN BEAM TREE" OVER & OVER, ARE YOU?
WHAT WAS THAT?
©2005 Bill Griffith. World rights reserved. Distributed by King Features Syndicate
Zippythepinhead.com
I SAID: YOU'RE NOT GOING TO SCREAM, "EASTERN HOPHORN BEAM TREE, EASTERN HOPHORN BEAM TREE, EASTERN HOPHORN BEAM TREE," ARE YOU?
I FEAR THAT WOULD BE ARBORIALLY REDUNDANT.

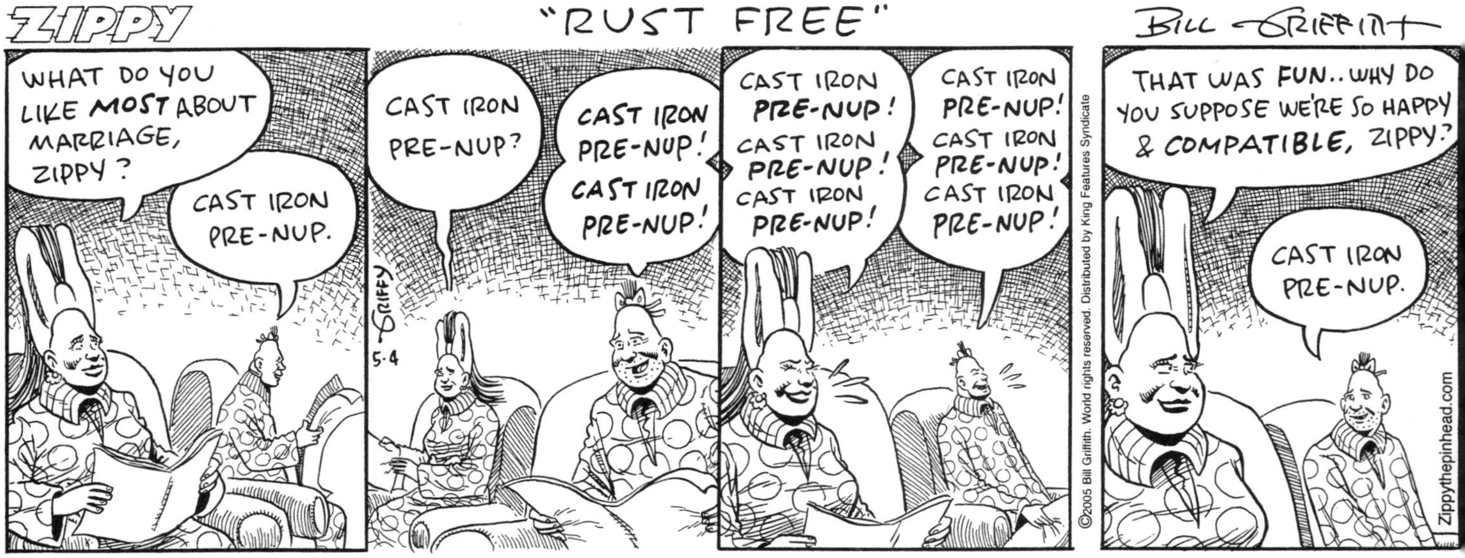
ZIPPY
"RUST FREE"
BILL GRIFFITH
WHAT DO YOU LIKE MOST ABOUT MARRIAGE, ZIPPY?
CAST IRON PRE-NUP.
GRIFFY
5·4
CAST IRON PRE-NUP?
CAST IRON PRE-NUP! CAST IRON PRE-NUP!
CAST IRON PRE-NUP! CAST IRON PRE-NUP! CAST IRON PRE-NUP!
CAST IRON PRE-NUP! CAST IRON PRE-NUP! CAST IRON PRE-NUP!
©2005 Bill Griffith. World rights reserved. Distributed by King Features Syndicate
THAT WAS FUN.. WHY DO YOU SUPPOSE WE'RE SO HAPPY & COMPATIBLE, ZIPPY?
CAST IRON PRE-NUP.
Zippythepinhead.com

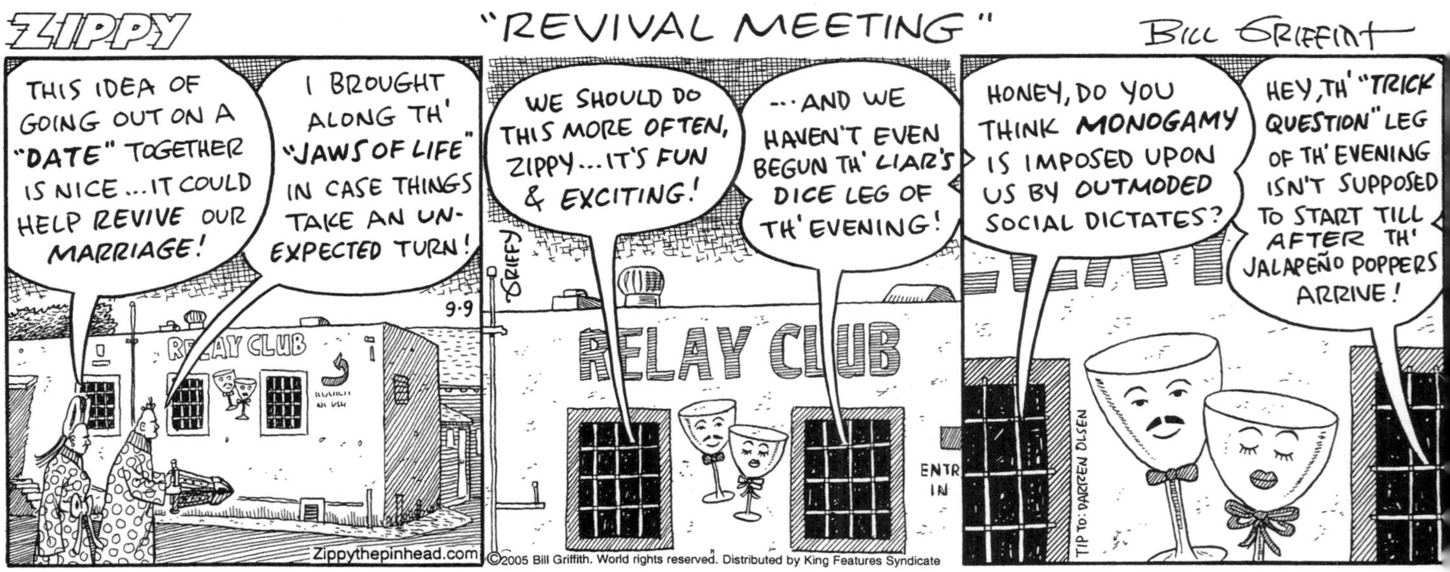
ZIPPY
"REVIVAL MEETING"
BILL GRIFFITH
THIS IDEA OF GOING OUT ON A "DATE" TOGETHER IS NICE... IT COULD HELP REVIVE OUR MARRIAGE!
I BROUGHT ALONG TH' "JAWS OF LIFE" IN CASE THINGS TAKE AN UN-EXPECTED TURN!
GRIFFY
9·9
RELAY CLUB
Zippythepinhead.com
WE SHOULD DO THIS MORE OFTEN, ZIPPY... IT'S FUN & EXCITING!
...AND WE HAVEN'T EVEN BEGUN TH' LIAR'S DICE LEG OF TH' EVENING!
RELAY CLUB
ENTR IN
©2005 Bill Griffith. World rights reserved. Distributed by King Features Syndicate
HONEY, DO YOU THINK MONOGAMY IS IMPOSED UPON US BY OUTMODED SOCIAL DICTATES?
HEY, TH' "TRICK QUESTION" LEG OF TH' EVENING ISN'T SUPPOSED TO START TILL AFTER TH' JALAPEÑO POPPERS ARRIVE!
TIP TO: DARREN OLSEN

70

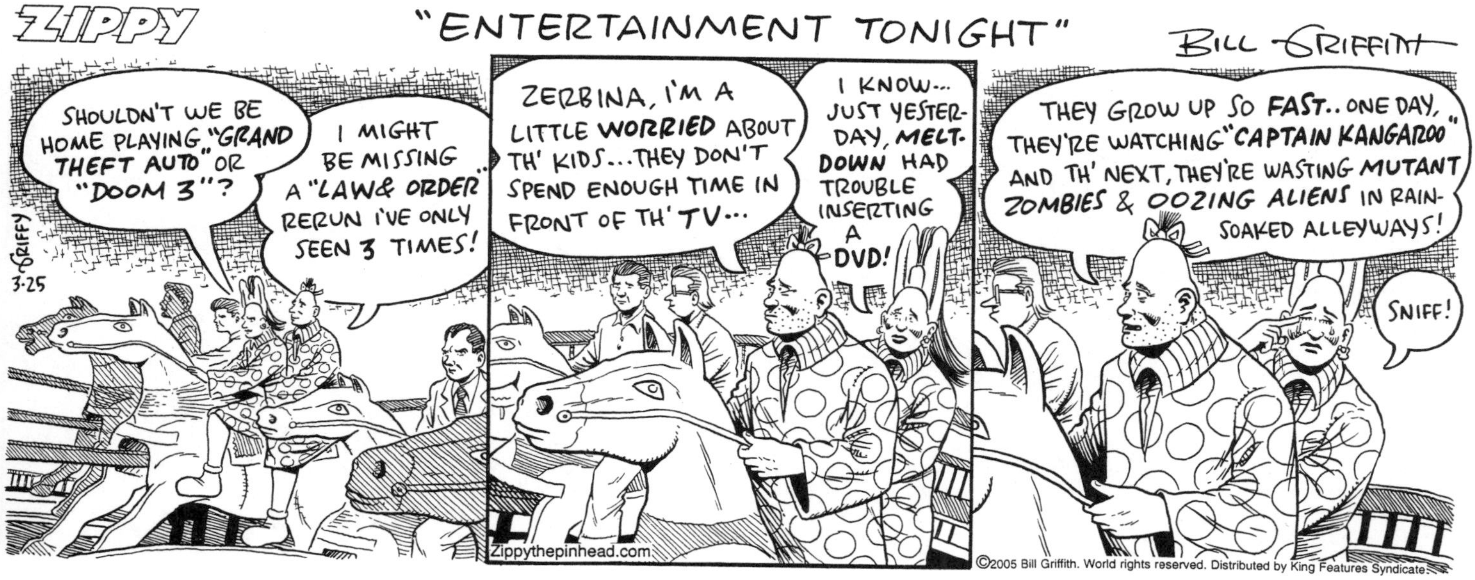
ZIPPY
"ENTERTAINMENT TONIGHT"
BILL GRIFFITH
SHOULDN'T WE BE HOME PLAYING "GRAND THEFT AUTO" OR "DOOM 3"?
I MIGHT BE MISSING A "LAW & ORDER" RERUN I'VE ONLY SEEN 3 TIMES!
GRIFFY 3-25
ZERBINA, I'M A LITTLE WORRIED ABOUT TH' KIDS... THEY DON'T SPEND ENOUGH TIME IN FRONT OF TH' TV...
I KNOW... JUST YESTERDAY, MELT-DOWN HAD TROUBLE INSERTING A DVD!
THEY GROW UP SO FAST.. ONE DAY, THEY'RE WATCHING "CAPTAIN KANGAROO" AND TH' NEXT, THEY'RE WASTING MUTANT ZOMBIES & OOZING ALIENS IN RAIN-SOAKED ALLEYWAYS!
SNIFF!
Zippythepinhead.com
©2005 Bill Griffith. World rights reserved. Distributed by King Features Syndicate

71

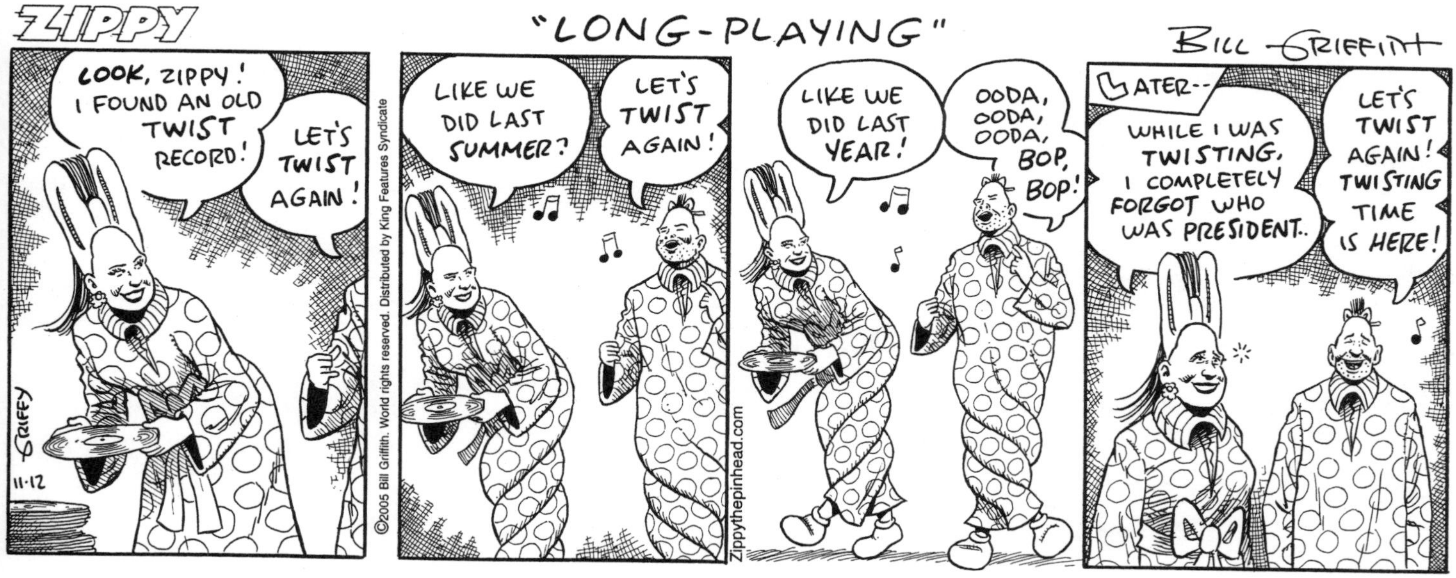
ZIPPY
"LONG-PLAYING"
BILL GRIFFITH
LOOK, ZIPPY! I FOUND AN OLD TWIST RECORD!
LET'S TWIST AGAIN!
GRIFFY 11-12
©2005 Bill Griffith. World rights reserved. Distributed by King Features Syndicate
LIKE WE DID LAST SUMMER?
LET'S TWIST AGAIN!
Zippythepinhead.com
LIKE WE DID LAST YEAR!
OODA, OODA, OODA, BOP, BOP!
LATER--
WHILE I WAS TWISTING, I COMPLETELY FORGOT WHO WAS PRESIDENT..
LET'S TWIST AGAIN! TWISTING TIME IS HERE!

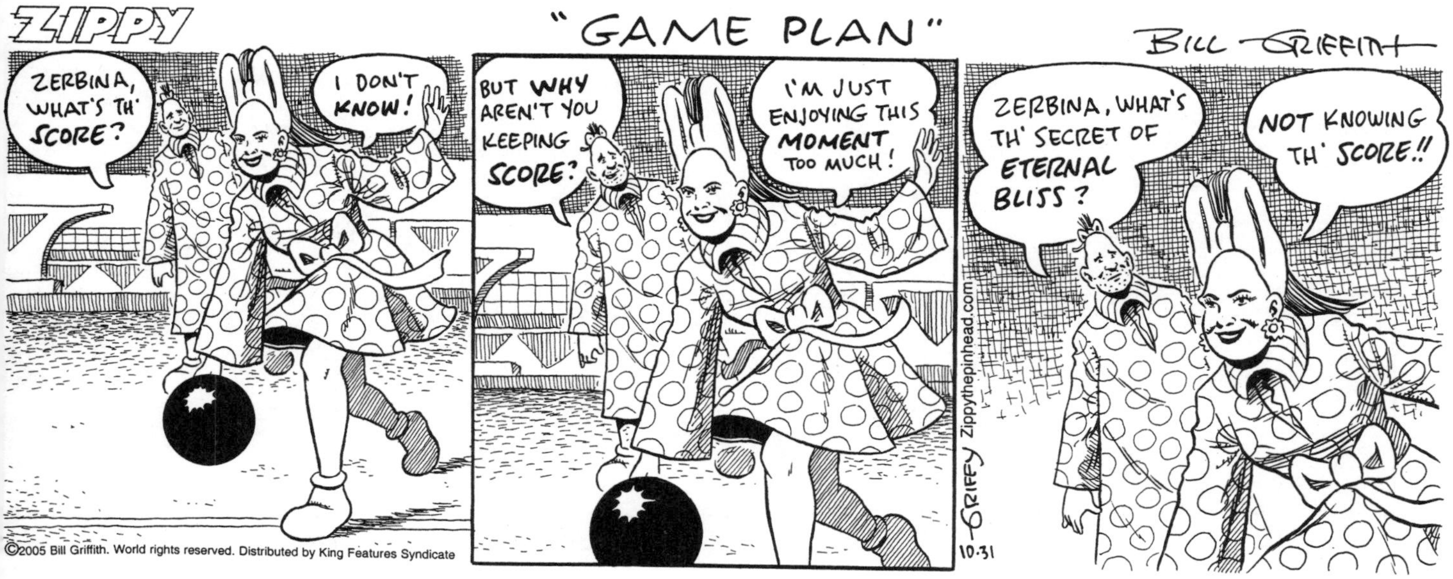
ZIPPY
"GAME PLAN"
BILL GRIFFITH
ZERBINA, WHAT'S TH' SCORE?
I DON'T KNOW!
©2005 Bill Griffith. World rights reserved. Distributed by King Features Syndicate
BUT WHY AREN'T YOU KEEPING SCORE?
I'M JUST ENJOYING THIS MOMENT TOO MUCH!
GRIFFY Zippythepinhead.com 10-31
ZERBINA, WHAT'S TH' SECRET OF ETERNAL BLISS?
NOT KNOWING TH' SCORE!!

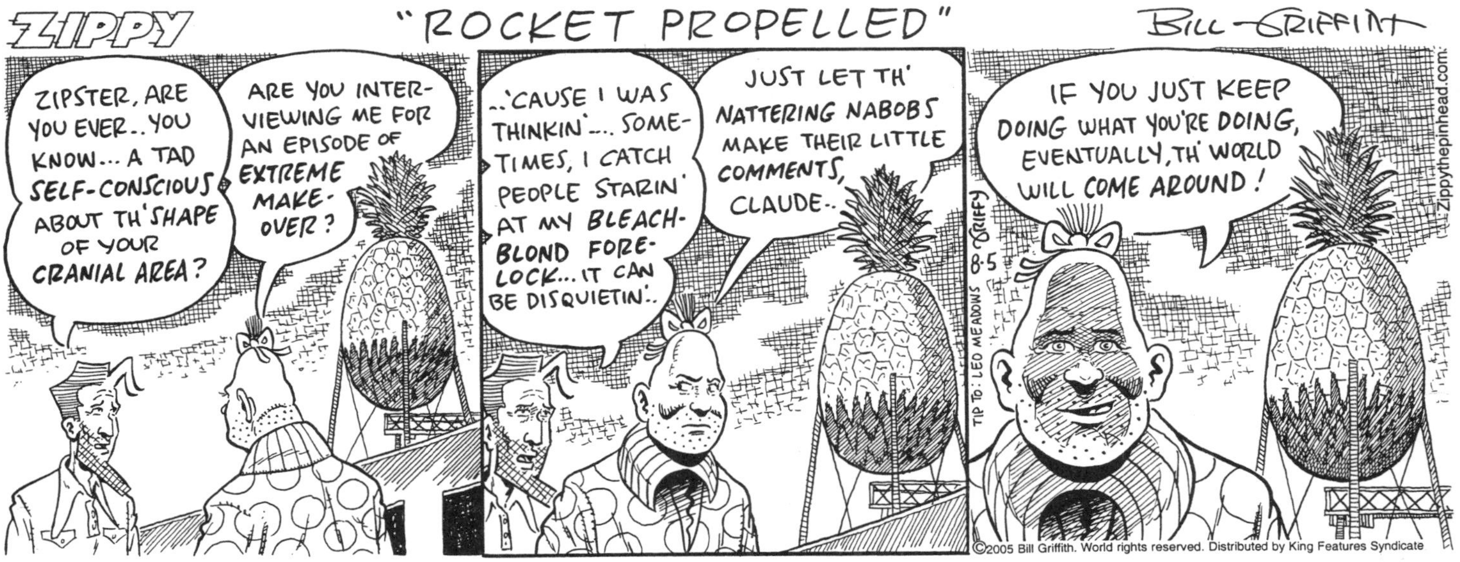
ZIPPY
"ROCKET PROPELLED"
BILL GRIFFITH
ZIPSTER, ARE YOU EVER.. YOU KNOW... A TAD SELF-CONSCIOUS ABOUT TH' SHAPE OF YOUR CRANIAL AREA?
ARE YOU INTER-VIEWING ME FOR AN EPISODE OF EXTREME MAKE-OVER?
..'CAUSE I WAS THINKIN'.... SOME-TIMES, I CATCH PEOPLE STARIN' AT MY BLEACH-BLOND FORE-LOCK... IT CAN BE DISQUIETIN'..
JUST LET TH' NATTERING NABOBS MAKE THEIR LITTLE COMMENTS, CLAUDE..
IF YOU JUST KEEP DOING WHAT YOU'RE DOING, EVENTUALLY, TH' WORLD WILL COME AROUND!
TIP TO: LEO MEADOWS
8-5
GRIFFY
Zippythepinhead.com
©2005 Bill Griffith. World rights reserved. Distributed by King Features Syndicate

72

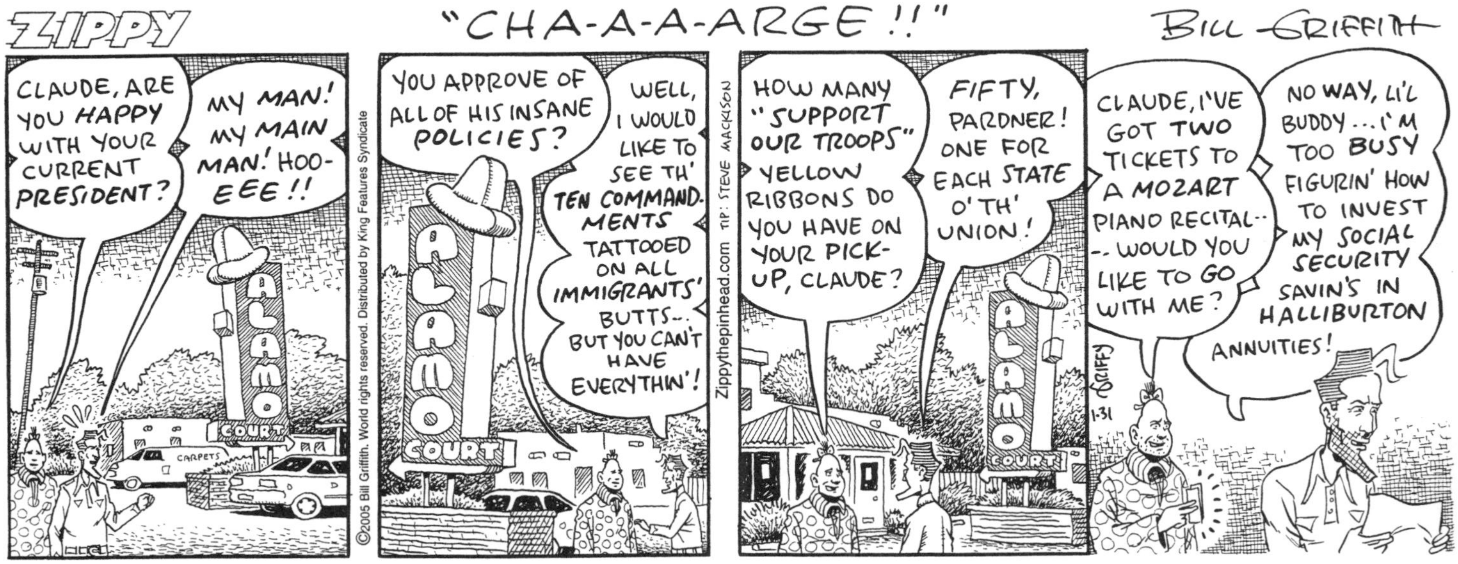
ZIPPY
"CHA-A-A-ARGE!!"
BILL GRIFFITH
CLAUDE, ARE YOU HAPPY WITH YOUR CURRENT PRESIDENT?
MY MAN! MY MAIN MAN! HOO-EEE!!
ALAMO COURT
CARPETS
©2005 Bill Griffith. World rights reserved. Distributed by King Features Syndicate
YOU APPROVE OF ALL OF HIS INSANE POLICIES?
WELL, I WOULD LIKE TO SEE TH' TEN COMMAND-MENTS TATTOOED ON ALL IMMIGRANTS' BUTTS.. BUT YOU CAN'T HAVE EVERYTHIN'!
Zippythepinhead.com
TIP: STEVE MACKISON
HOW MANY "SUPPORT OUR TROOPS" YELLOW RIBBONS DO YOU HAVE ON YOUR PICK-UP, CLAUDE?
FIFTY, PARDNER! ONE FOR EACH STATE O' TH' UNION!
CLAUDE, I'VE GOT TWO TICKETS TO A MOZART PIANO RECITAL.. -- WOULD YOU LIKE TO GO WITH ME?
NO WAY, LI'L BUDDY... I'M TOO BUSY FIGURIN' HOW TO INVEST MY SOCIAL SECURITY SAVIN'S IN HALLIBURTON ANNUITIES!
GRIFFY
1-31

73

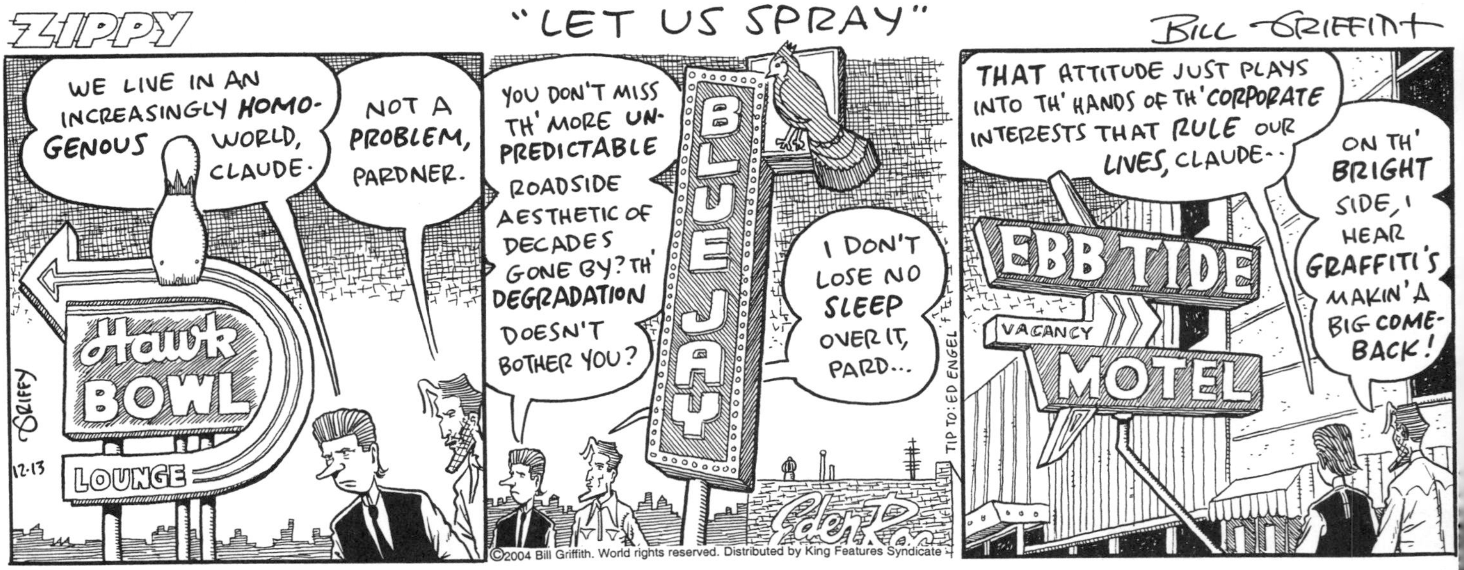
ZIPPY
"LET US SPRAY"
BILL GRIFFITH
WE LIVE IN AN INCREASINGLY HOMO-GENOUS WORLD, CLAUDE.
NOT A PROBLEM, PARDNER.
Hawk BOWL
LOUNGE
GRIFFY
12-13
YOU DON'T MISS TH' MORE UN-PREDICTABLE ROADSIDE AESTHETIC OF DECADES GONE BY? TH' DEGRADATION DOESN'T BOTHER YOU?
BLUE JAY
I DON'T LOSE NO SLEEP OVER IT, PARD...
TIP TO: ED ENGEL
©2004 Bill Griffith. World rights reserved. Distributed by King Features Syndicate
THAT ATTITUDE JUST PLAYS INTO TH' HANDS OF TH' CORPORATE INTERESTS THAT RULE OUR LIVES, CLAUDE..
ON TH' BRIGHT SIDE, I HEAR GRAFFITI'S MAKIN' A BIG COME-BACK!
EBB TIDE
VACANCY
MOTEL

74

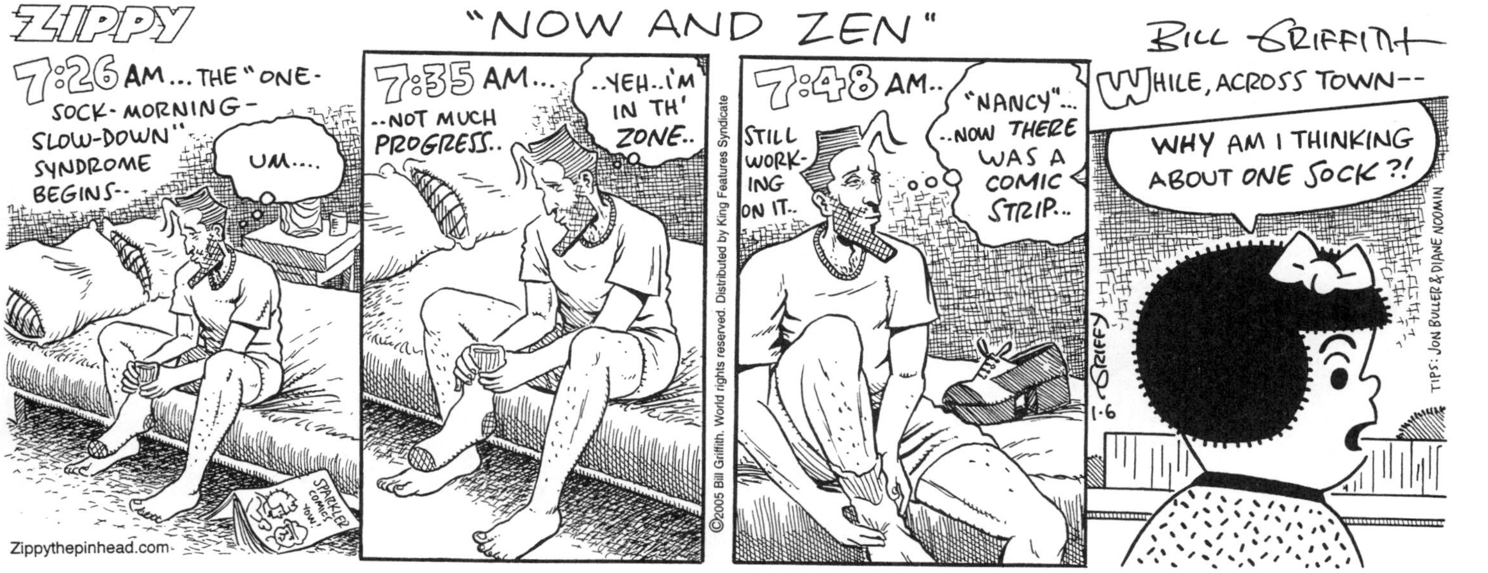
ZIPPY
"NOW AND ZEN"
BILL GRIFFITH
7:26 AM... THE "ONE-SOCK-MORNING-SLOW-DOWN" SYNDROME BEGINS..
UM....
SPARKLER COMICS
Zippythepinhead.com
7:35 AM... ..NOT MUCH PROGRESS..
..YEH..I'M IN TH' ZONE..
©2005 Bill Griffith. World rights reserved. Distributed by King Features Syndicate
7:48 AM.. STILL WORKING ON IT..
"NANCY"... ..NOW THERE WAS A COMIC STRIP...
GRIFFY 1-6
WHILE, ACROSS TOWN--
WHY AM I THINKING ABOUT ONE SOCK?!
TIPS: JON BULLER & DIANE NOOMIN

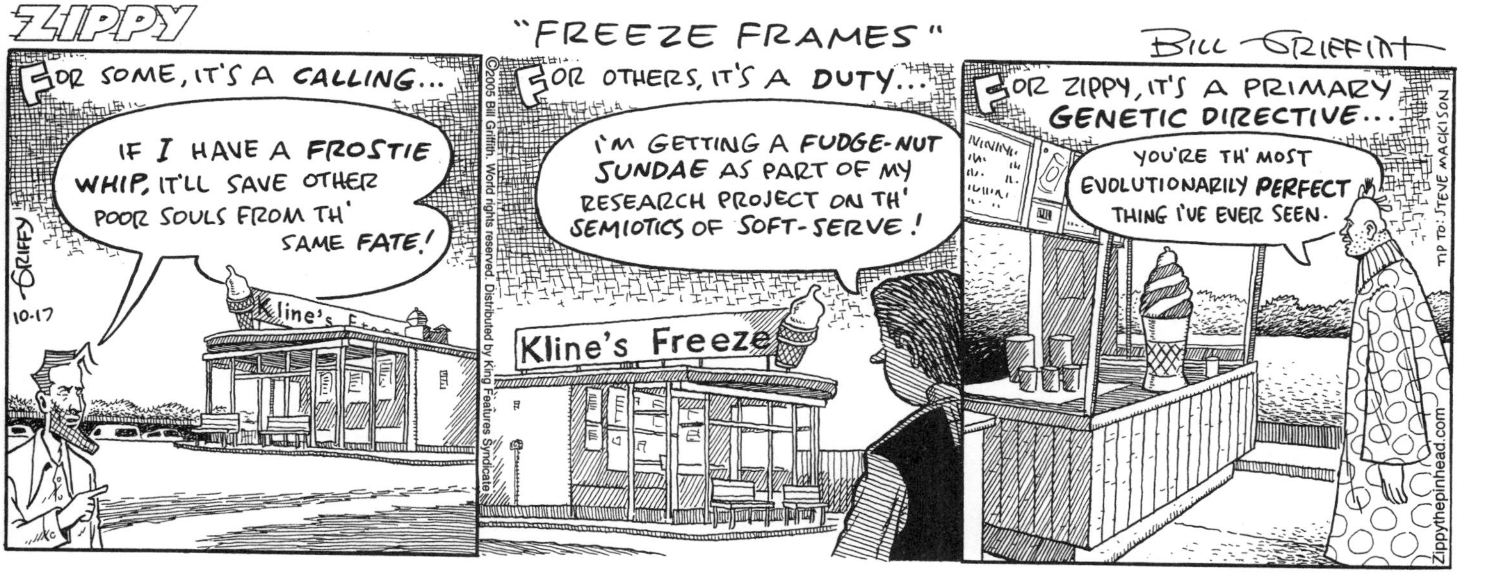
ZIPPY
"FREEZE FRAMES"
BILL GRIFFITH
FOR SOME, IT'S A CALLING...
IF I HAVE A FROSTIE WHIP, IT'LL SAVE OTHER POOR SOULS FROM TH' SAME FATE!
GRIFFY 10-17
©2005 Bill Griffith. World rights reserved. Distributed by King Features Syndicate
FOR OTHERS, IT'S A DUTY...
I'M GETTING A FUDGE-NUT SUNDAE AS PART OF MY RESEARCH PROJECT ON TH' SEMIOTICS OF SOFT-SERVE!
Kline's Freeze
FOR ZIPPY, IT'S A PRIMARY GENETIC DIRECTIVE...
YOU'RE TH' MOST EVOLUTIONARILY PERFECT THING I'VE EVER SEEN.
TIP TO: STEVE MACKISON
Zippythepinhead.com

75

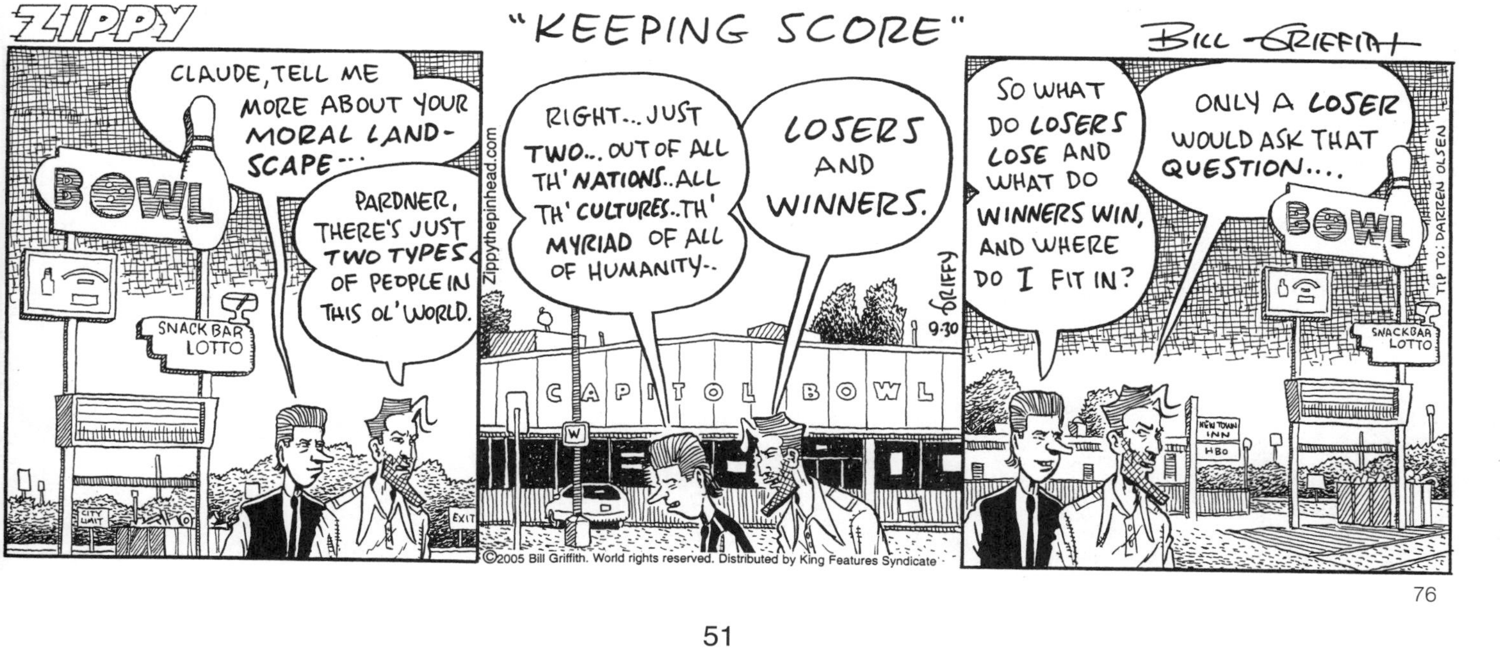
ZIPPY
"KEEPING SCORE"
BILL GRIFFITH
CLAUDE, TELL ME MORE ABOUT YOUR MORAL LANDSCAPE...
PARDNER, THERE'S JUST TWO TYPES OF PEOPLE IN THIS OL' WORLD.
BOWL
SNACK BAR LOTTO
EXIT
Zippythepinhead.com
RIGHT... JUST TWO... OUT OF ALL TH' NATIONS.. ALL TH' CULTURES..TH' MYRIAD OF ALL OF HUMANITY..
LOSERS AND WINNERS.
GRIFFY 9-30
CAPITOL BOWL
SO WHAT DO LOSERS LOSE AND WHAT DO WINNERS WIN, AND WHERE DO I FIT IN?
ONLY A LOSER WOULD ASK THAT QUESTION....
BOWL
SNACK BAR LOTTO
NEW TOWN INN HBO
TIP TO: DARREN OLSEN
©2005 Bill Griffith. World rights reserved. Distributed by King Features Syndicate

76

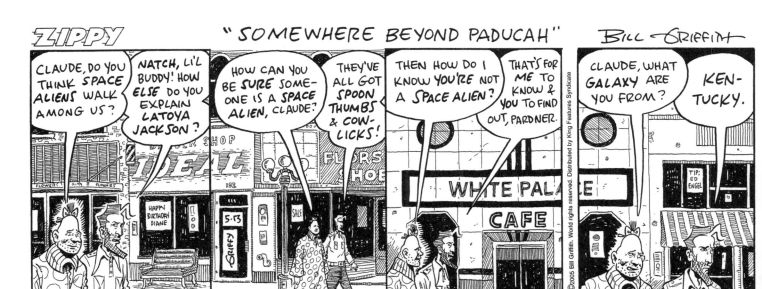

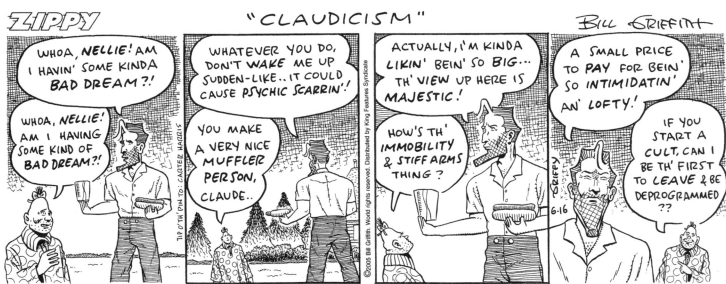

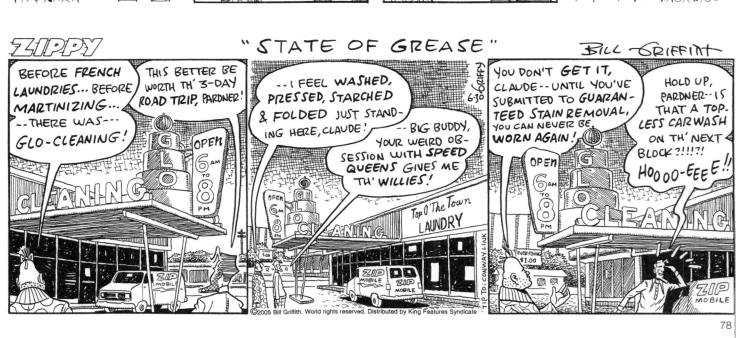

52

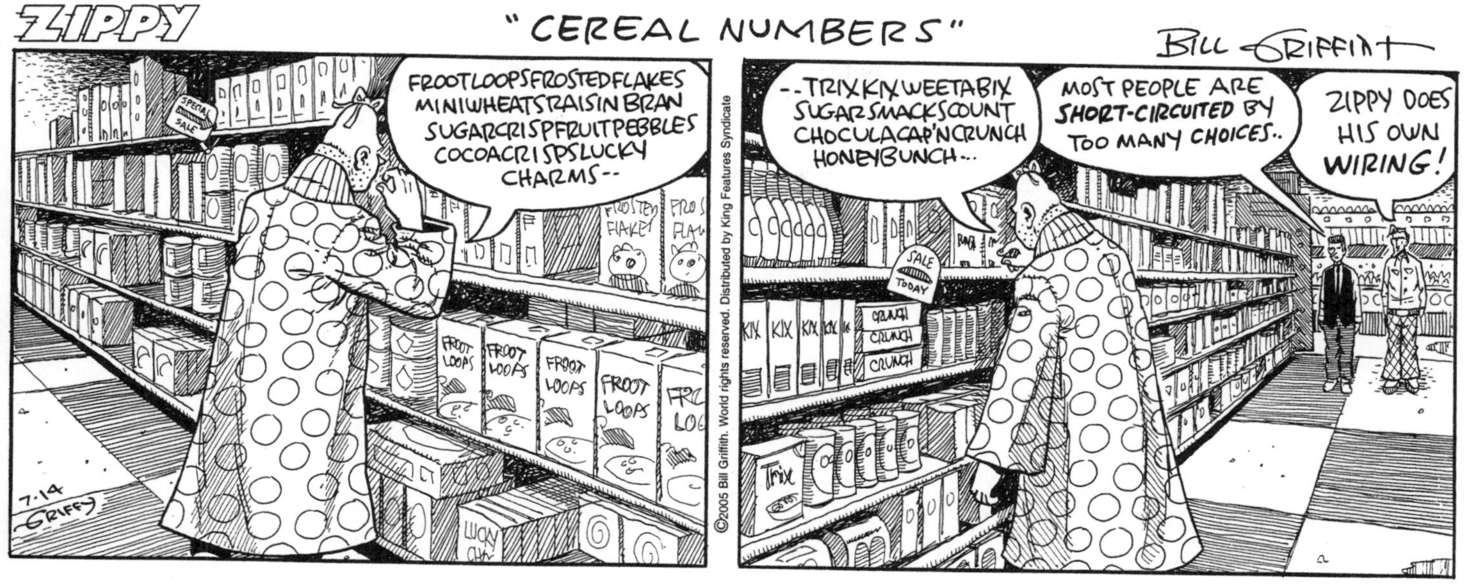
ZIPPY
"CEREAL NUMBERS"
BILL GRIFFITH
FROOTLOOPSFROSTEDFLAKES MINIWHEATSRAISIN BRAN SUGARCRISPFRUITPEBBLES COCOACRISPSLUCKY CHARMS--
--TRIXKIXWEETABIX SUGARSMACKSCOUNT CHOCULACAP'NCRUNCH HONEYBUNCH...
MOST PEOPLE ARE SHORT-CIRCUITED BY TOO MANY CHOICES..
ZIPPY DOES HIS OWN WIRING!
7.14 GRIFFY
©2005 Bill Griffith. World rights reserved. Distributed by King Features Syndicate

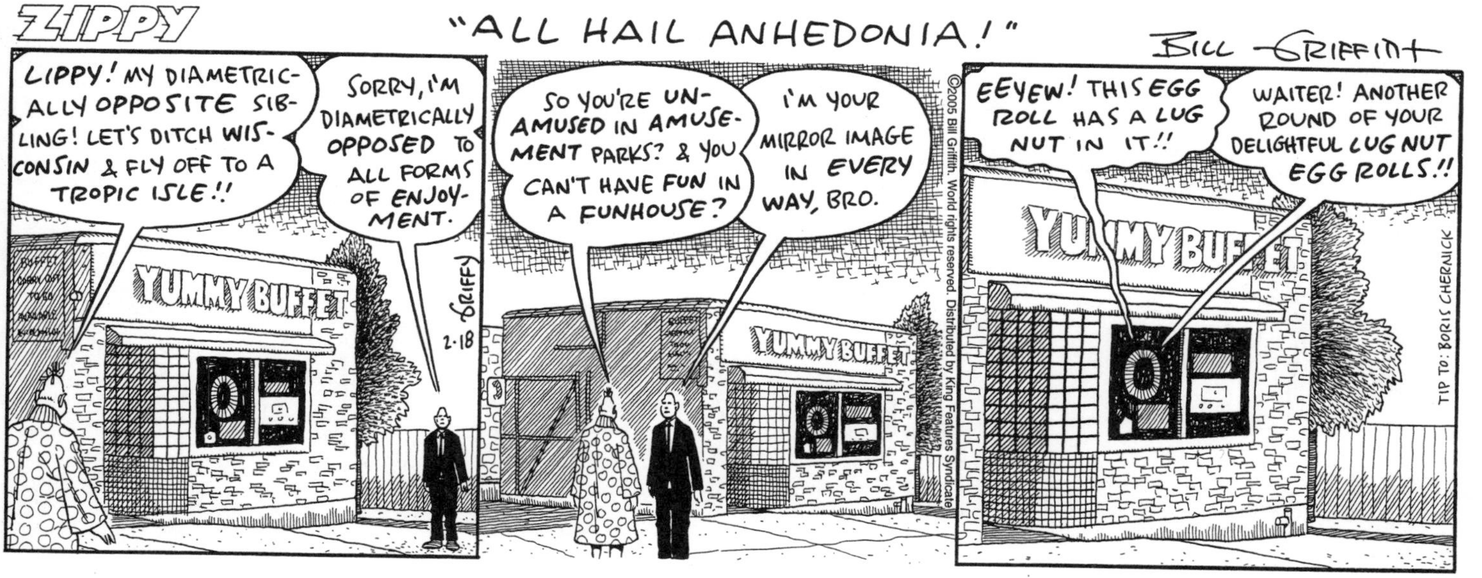
ZIPPY
"ALL HAIL ANHEDONIA!"
BILL GRIFFITH
LIPPY! MY DIAMETRICALLY OPPOSITE SIBLING! LET'S DITCH WISCONSIN & FLY OFF TO A TROPIC ISLE!!
SORRY, I'M DIAMETRICALLY OPPOSED TO ALL FORMS OF ENJOYMENT.
GRIFFY 2.18
SO YOU'RE UNAMUSED IN AMUSEMENT PARKS? & YOU CAN'T HAVE FUN IN A FUNHOUSE?
I'M YOUR MIRROR IMAGE IN EVERY WAY, BRO.
YUMMY BUFFET
©2005 Bill Griffith. World rights reserved. Distributed by King Features Syndicate
EEYEW! THIS EGG ROLL HAS A LUG NUT IN IT!!
WAITER! ANOTHER ROUND OF YOUR DELIGHTFUL LUG NUT EGG ROLLS!!
TIP TO: BORIS CHERNICK

79

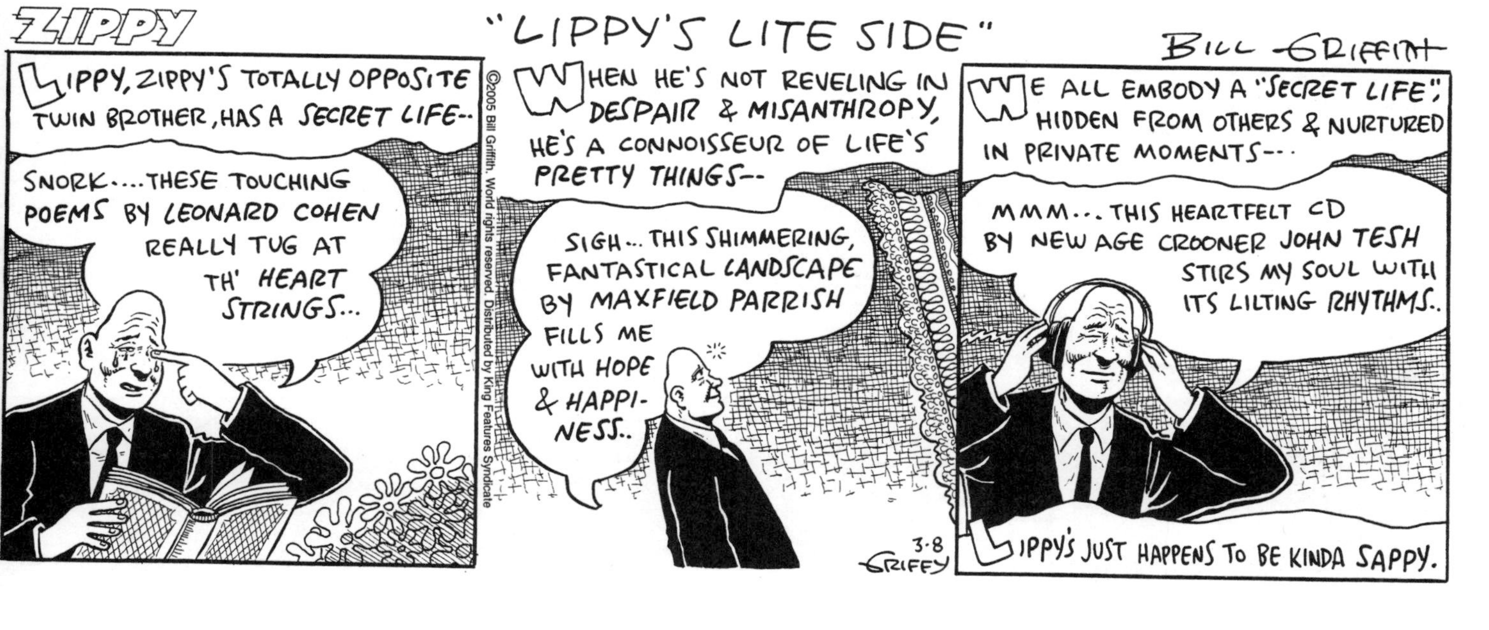
ZIPPY
"LIPPY'S LITE SIDE"
BILL GRIFFITH
LIPPY, ZIPPY'S TOTALLY OPPOSITE TWIN BROTHER, HAS A SECRET LIFE--
SNORK....THESE TOUCHING POEMS BY LEONARD COHEN REALLY TUG AT TH' HEART STRINGS...
©2005 Bill Griffith. World rights reserved. Distributed by King Features Syndicate
WHEN HE'S NOT REVELING IN DESPAIR & MISANTHROPY, HE'S A CONNOISSEUR OF LIFE'S PRETTY THINGS--
SIGH... THIS SHIMMERING, FANTASTICAL LANDSCAPE BY MAXFIELD PARRISH FILLS ME WITH HOPE & HAPPINESS..
WE ALL EMBODY A "SECRET LIFE", HIDDEN FROM OTHERS & NURTURED IN PRIVATE MOMENTS---
MMM... THIS HEARTFELT CD BY NEW AGE CROONER JOHN TESH STIRS MY SOUL WITH ITS LILTING RHYTHMS..
3.8 GRIFFY
LIPPY'S JUST HAPPENS TO BE KINDA SAPPY.

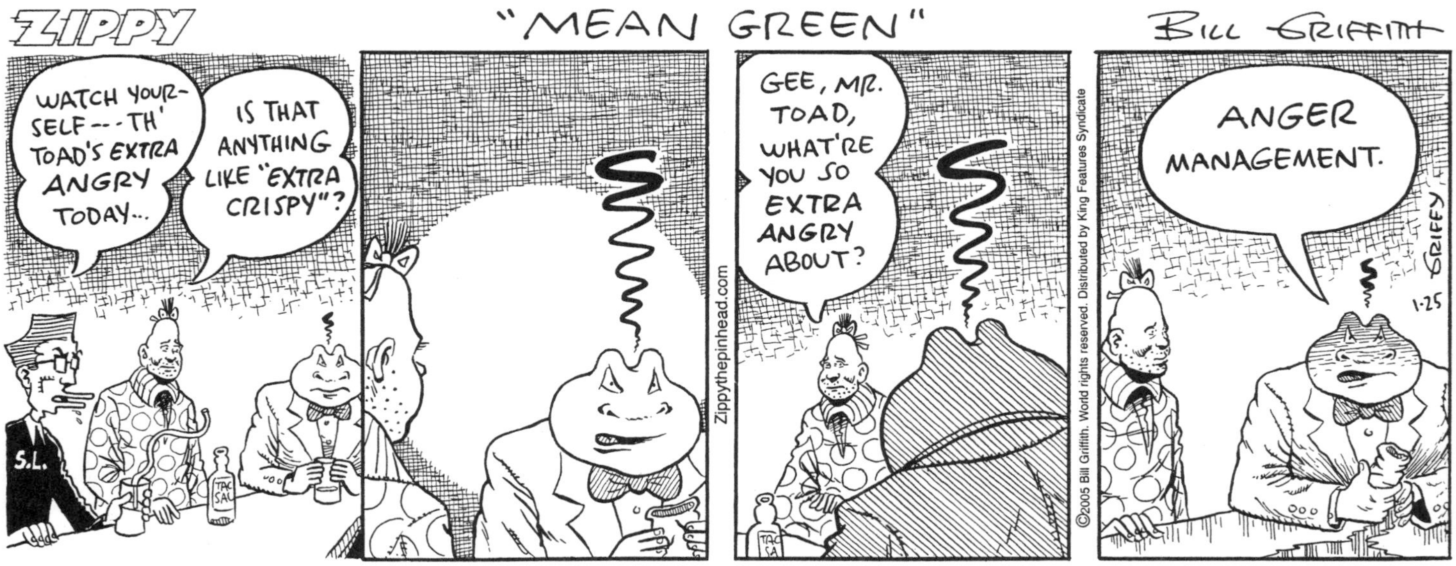
ZIPPY
"MEAN GREEN"
BILL GRIFFITH
WATCH YOURSELF --- TH' TOAD'S EXTRA ANGRY TODAY...
IS THAT ANYTHING LIKE "EXTRA CRISPY"?
S.L.
TAC SAL
Zippythepinhead.com
GEE, MR. TOAD, WHAT'RE YOU SO EXTRA ANGRY ABOUT?
©2005 Bill Griffith. World rights reserved. Distributed by King Features Syndicate
ANGER MANAGEMENT.
GRIFFY
1-25

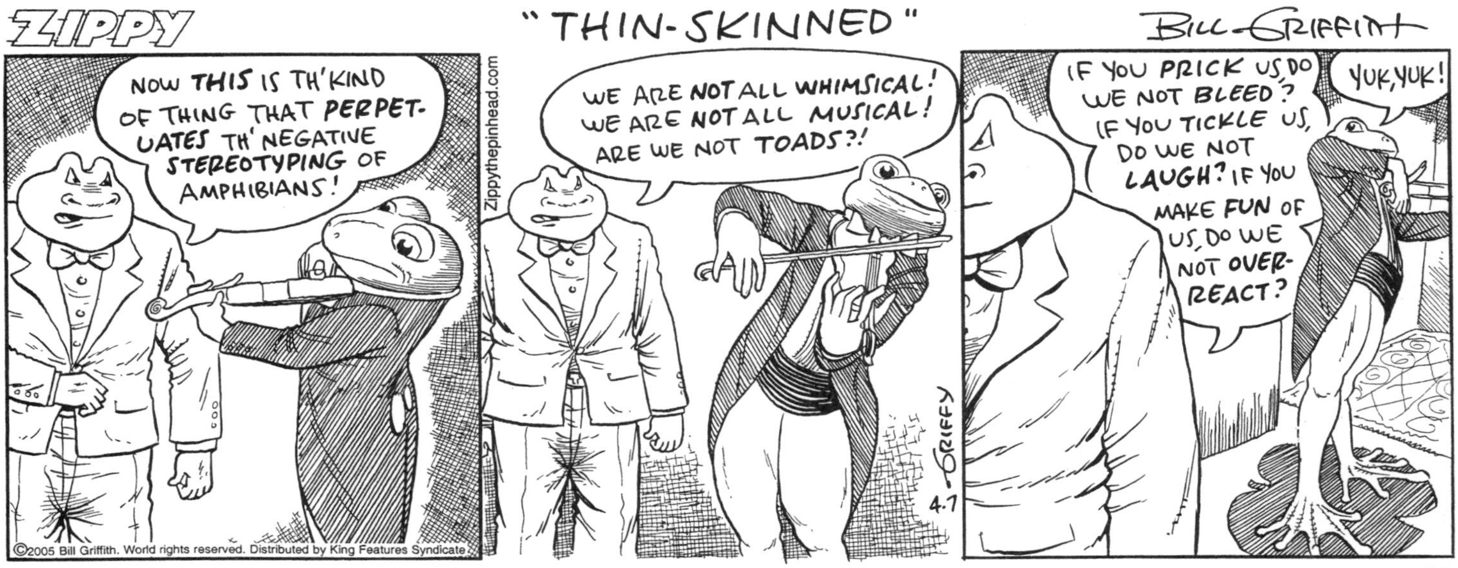
ZIPPY
"THIN-SKINNED"
BILL GRIFFITH
NOW THIS IS TH' KIND OF THING THAT PERPETUATES TH' NEGATIVE STEREOTYPING OF AMPHIBIANS!
Zippythepinhead.com
WE ARE NOT ALL WHIMSICAL! WE ARE NOT ALL MUSICAL! ARE WE NOT TOADS?!
GRIFFY
4-7
IF YOU PRICK US, DO WE NOT BLEED? IF YOU TICKLE US, DO WE NOT LAUGH? IF YOU MAKE FUN OF US, DO WE NOT OVER-REACT?
YUK, YUK!
©2005 Bill Griffith. World rights reserved. Distributed by King Features Syndicate

80

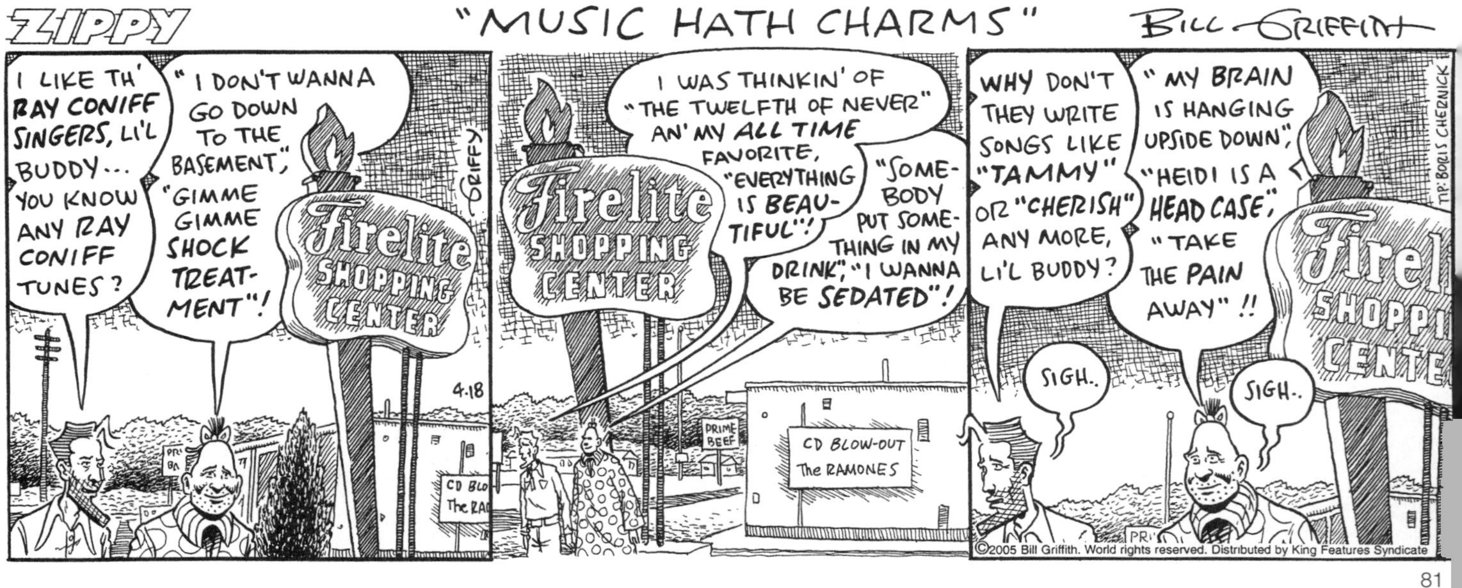
ZIPPY
"MUSIC HATH CHARMS"
BILL GRIFFITH
I LIKE TH' RAY CONIFF SINGERS, LI'L BUDDY... YOU KNOW ANY RAY CONIFF TUNES?
"I DON'T WANNA GO DOWN TO THE BASEMENT", "GIMME GIMME SHOCK TREATMENT"!
Firelite SHOPPING CENTER
GRIFFY
4-18
I WAS THINKIN' OF "THE TWELFTH OF NEVER" AN' MY ALL TIME FAVORITE, "EVERYTHING IS BEAUTIFUL"!
"SOMEBODY PUT SOMETHING IN MY DRINK", "I WANNA BE SEDATED"!
PRIME BEEF
CD BLOW-OUT The RAMONES
WHY DON'T THEY WRITE SONGS LIKE "TAMMY" OR "CHERISH" ANY MORE, LI'L BUDDY?
"MY BRAIN IS HANGING UPSIDE DOWN", "HEIDI IS A HEAD CASE", "TAKE THE PAIN AWAY"!!
TIP: BORIS CHERNICK
SIGH..
SIGH..
©2005 Bill Griffith. World rights reserved. Distributed by King Features Syndicate

81

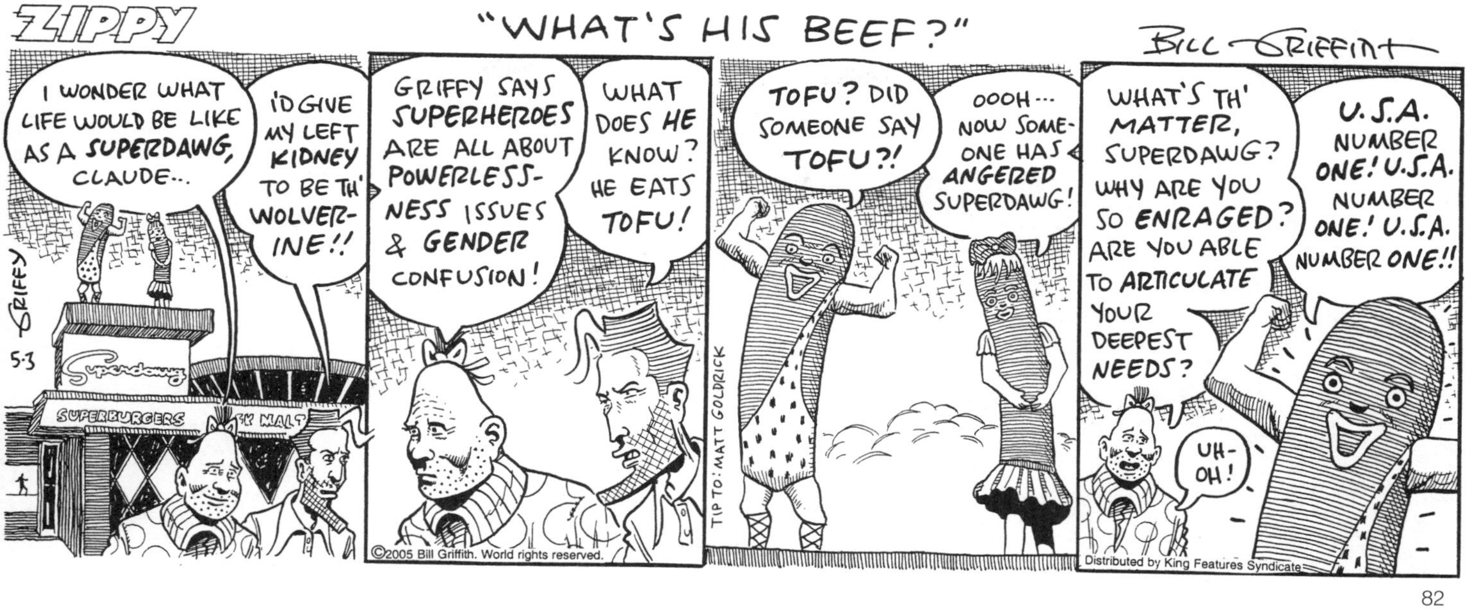

ZIPPY
"WHAT'S HIS BEEF?"
BILL GRIFFITH
I WONDER WHAT LIFE WOULD BE LIKE AS A SUPERDAWG, CLAUDE...
I'D GIVE MY LEFT KIDNEY TO BE TH' WOLVERINE!!
GRIFFY
5-3
Superdawg
SUPERBURGERS
GRIFFY SAYS SUPERHEROES ARE ALL ABOUT POWERLESSNESS ISSUES & GENDER CONFUSION!
WHAT DOES HE KNOW? HE EATS TOFU!
©2005 Bill Griffith. World rights reserved.
TOFU? DID SOMEONE SAY TOFU?!
OOOH... NOW SOMEONE HAS ANGERED SUPERDAWG!
TIP TO: MATT GOLDRICK
WHAT'S TH' MATTER, SUPERDAWG? WHY ARE YOU SO ENRAGED? ARE YOU ABLE TO ARTICULATE YOUR DEEPEST NEEDS?
U.S.A. NUMBER ONE! U.S.A. NUMBER ONE! U.S.A. NUMBER ONE!!
UH-OH!
Distributed by King Features Syndicate

82

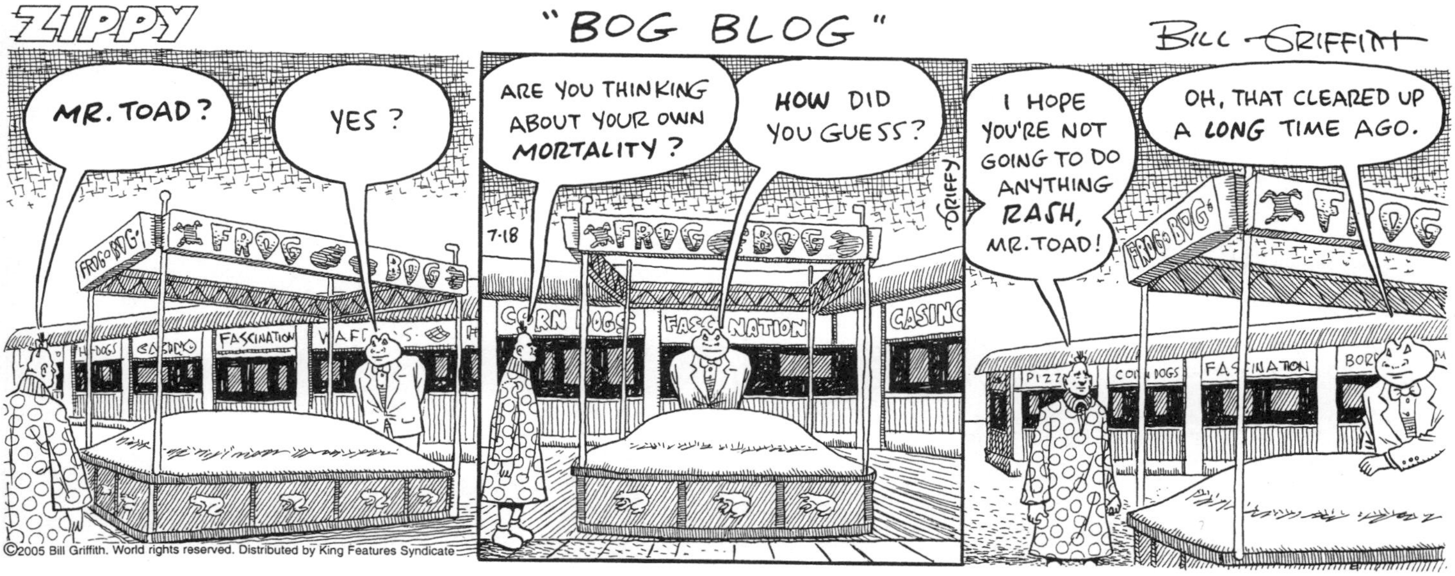

ZIPPY
"BOG BLOG"
BILL GRIFFITH
MR. TOAD?
YES?
FROG BOG
FASCINATION
ARE YOU THINKING ABOUT YOUR OWN MORTALITY?
HOW DID YOU GUESS?
7-18
GRIFFY
CORN DOGS
FASCINATION
CASINO
I HOPE YOU'RE NOT GOING TO DO ANYTHING RASH, MR. TOAD!
OH, THAT CLEARED UP A LONG TIME AGO.
©2005 Bill Griffith. World rights reserved. Distributed by King Features Syndicate

83

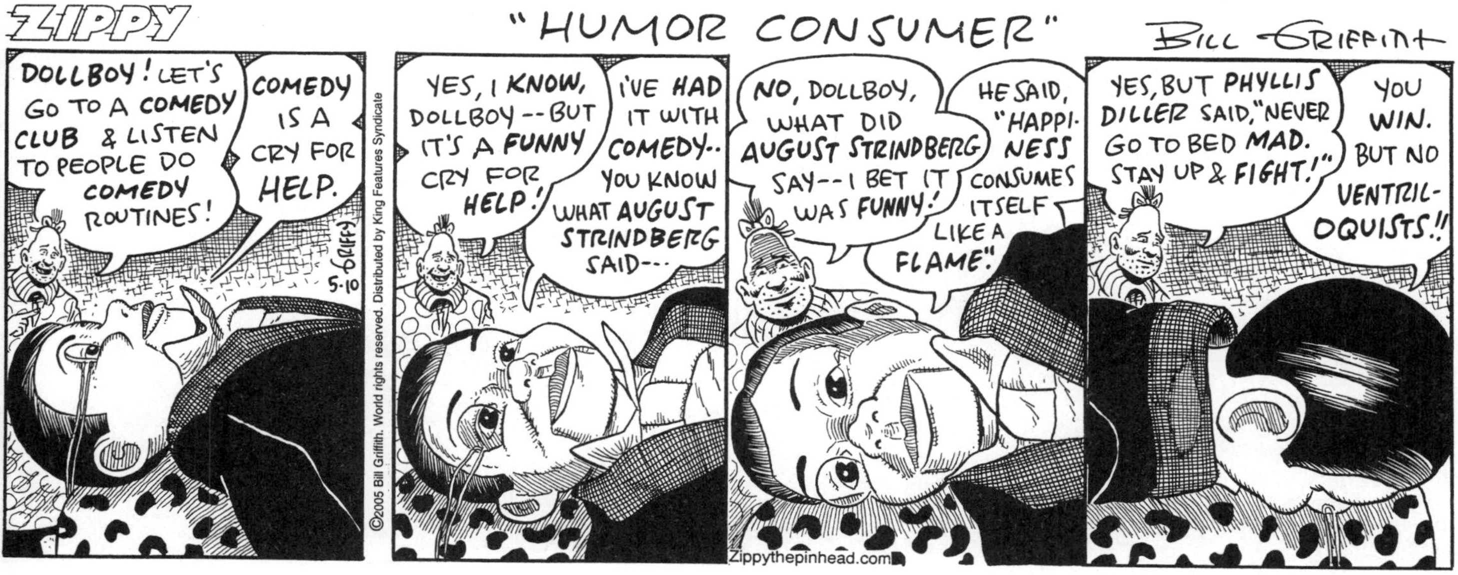

ZIPPY
"HUMOR CONSUMER"
BILL GRIFFITH
DOLLBOY! LET'S GO TO A COMEDY CLUB & LISTEN TO PEOPLE DO COMEDY ROUTINES!
COMEDY IS A CRY FOR HELP.
GRIFFY
5-10
©2005 Bill Griffith. World rights reserved. Distributed by King Features Syndicate
YES, I KNOW, DOLLBOY -- BUT IT'S A FUNNY CRY FOR HELP!
I'VE HAD IT WITH COMEDY.. YOU KNOW WHAT AUGUST STRINDBERG SAID---
NO, DOLLBOY, WHAT DID AUGUST STRINDBERG SAY-- I BET IT WAS FUNNY!
HE SAID, "HAPPINESS CONSUMES ITSELF LIKE A FLAME"!
YES, BUT PHYLLIS DILLER SAID, "NEVER GO TO BED MAD. STAY UP & FIGHT!"
YOU WIN. BUT NO VENTRILOQUISTS!!
Zippythepinhead.com

84

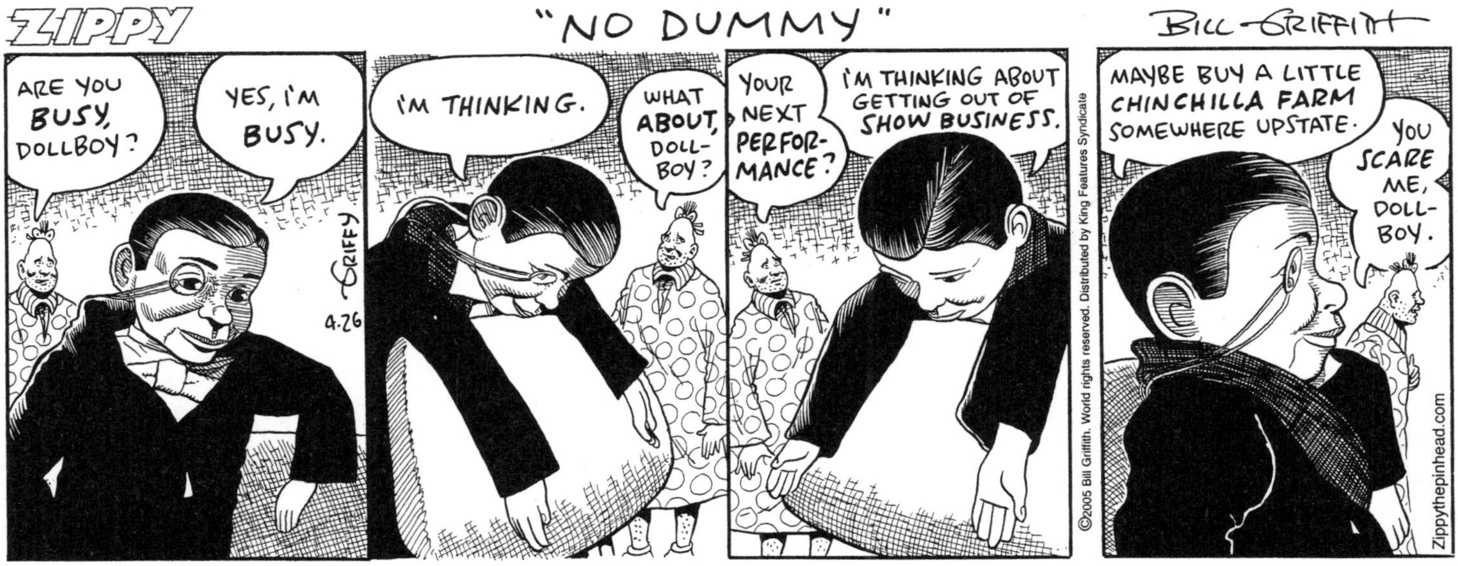
ZIPPY
"NO DUMMY"
BILL GRIFFITH
ARE YOU BUSY, DOLLBOY?
YES, I'M BUSY.
GRIFFY 4-26
I'M THINKING.
WHAT ABOUT, DOLL-BOY?
YOUR NEXT PERFOR-MANCE?
I'M THINKING ABOUT GETTING OUT OF SHOW BUSINESS.
©2005 Bill Griffith. World rights reserved. Distributed by King Features Syndicate
MAYBE BUY A LITTLE CHINCHILLA FARM SOMEWHERE UPSTATE.
YOU SCARE ME, DOLL-BOY.
Zippythepinhead.com

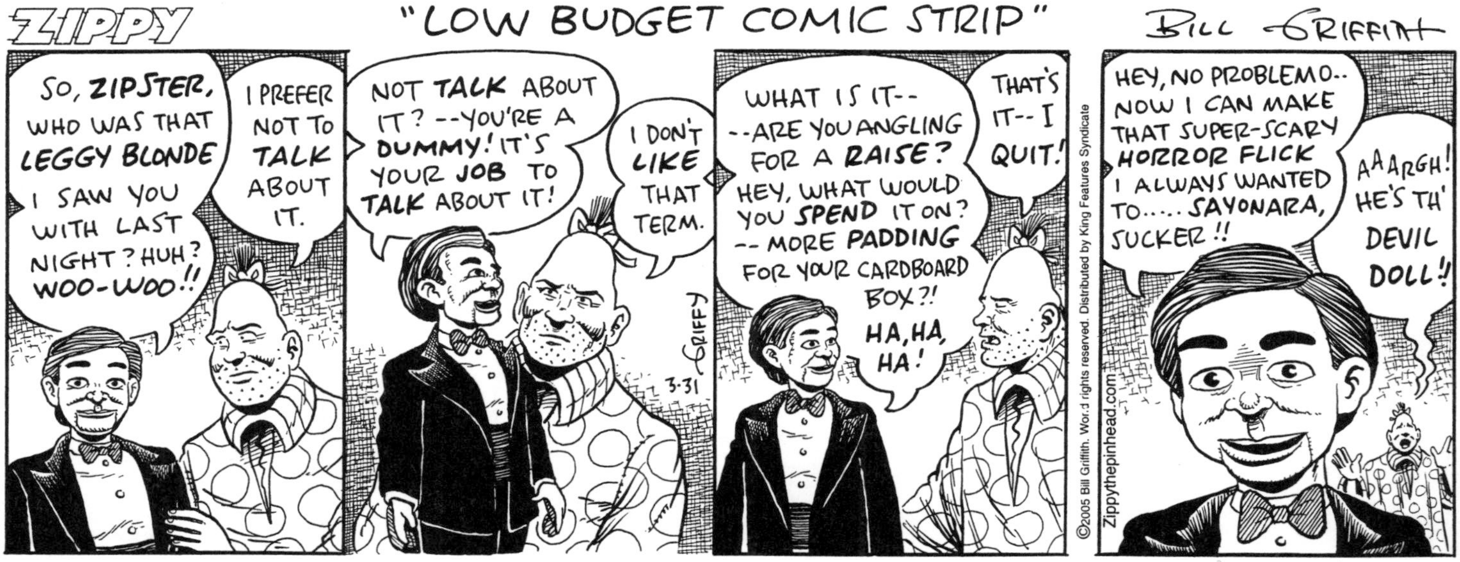
ZIPPY
"LOW BUDGET COMIC STRIP"
BILL GRIFFITH
SO, ZIPSTER, WHO WAS THAT LEGGY BLONDE I SAW YOU WITH LAST NIGHT? HUH? WOO-WOO!!
I PREFER NOT TO TALK ABOUT IT.
NOT TALK ABOUT IT? --YOU'RE A DUMMY! IT'S YOUR JOB TO TALK ABOUT IT!
I DON'T LIKE THAT TERM.
GRIFFY 3-31
WHAT IS IT-- --ARE YOU ANGLING FOR A RAISE? HEY, WHAT WOULD YOU SPEND IT ON? --MORE PADDING FOR YOUR CARDBOARD BOX?!
HA, HA, HA!
THAT'S IT-- I QUIT!
©2005 Bill Griffith. World rights reserved. Distributed by King Features Syndicate
Zippythepinhead.com
HEY, NO PROBLEMO.. NOW I CAN MAKE THAT SUPER-SCARY HORROR FLICK I ALWAYS WANTED TO..... SAYONARA, SUCKER!!
AAARGH! HE'S TH' DEVIL DOLL!!

85

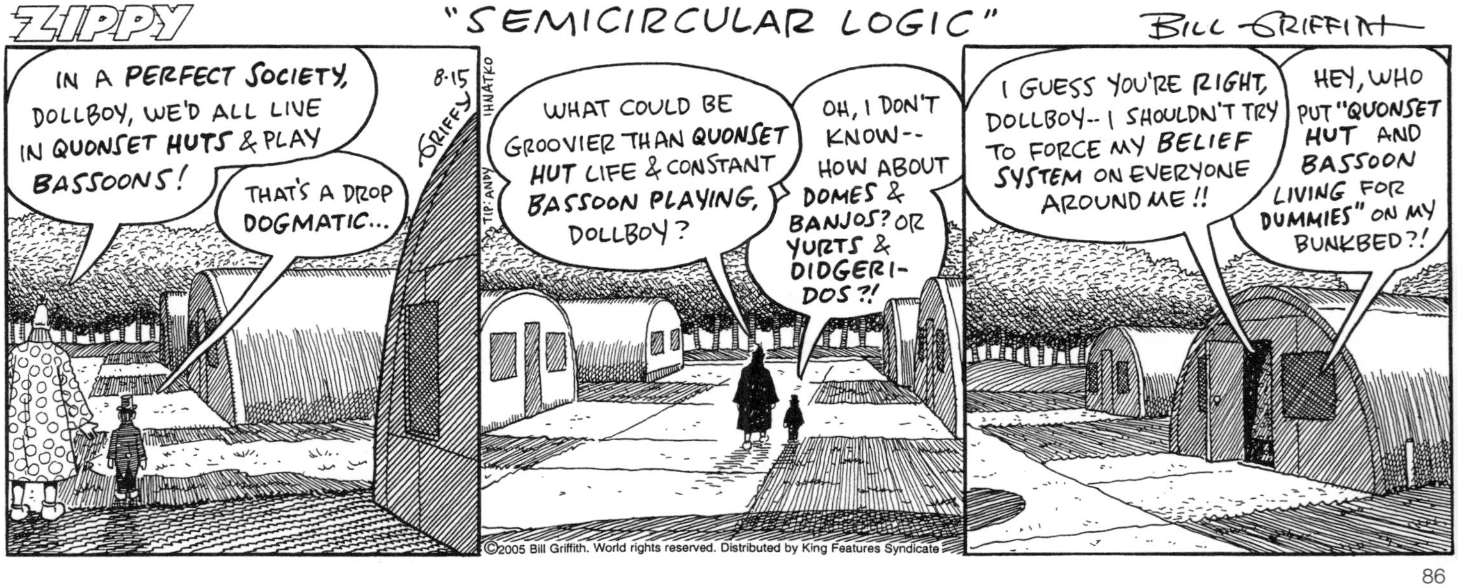
ZIPPY
"SEMICIRCULAR LOGIC"
BILL GRIFFITH
IN A PERFECT SOCIETY, DOLLBOY, WE'D ALL LIVE IN QUONSET HUTS & PLAY BASSOONS!
THAT'S A DROP DOGMATIC...
8-15 GRIFFY
TIP: ANDY IHNATKO
WHAT COULD BE GROOVIER THAN QUONSET HUT LIFE & CONSTANT BASSOON PLAYING, DOLLBOY?
OH, I DON'T KNOW-- HOW ABOUT DOMES & BANJOS? OR YURTS & DIDGERI-DOS?!
I GUESS YOU'RE RIGHT, DOLLBOY-- I SHOULDN'T TRY TO FORCE MY BELIEF SYSTEM ON EVERYONE AROUND ME!!
HEY, WHO PUT "QUONSET HUT AND BASSOON LIVING FOR DUMMIES" ON MY BUNKBED?!
©2005 Bill Griffith. World rights reserved. Distributed by King Features Syndicate

86

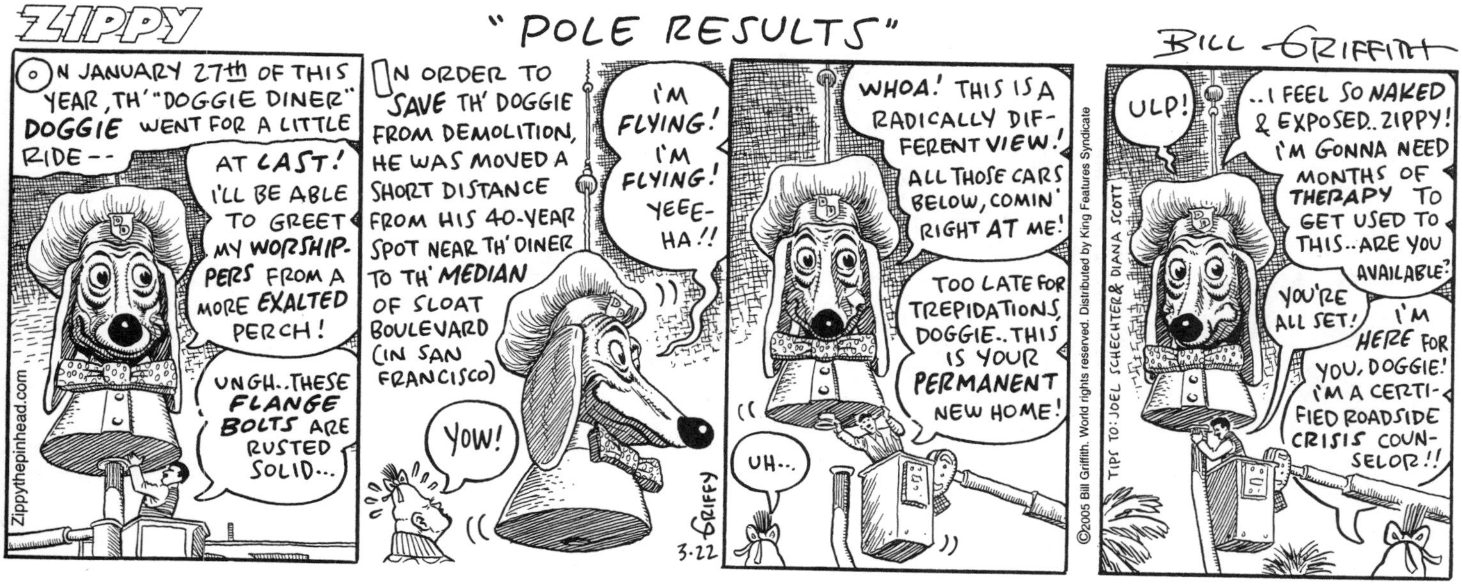
ZIPPY
"POLE RESULTS"
BILL GRIFFITH
ON JANUARY 27th OF THIS YEAR, TH' "DOGGIE DINER" DOGGIE WENT FOR A LITTLE RIDE--
AT LAST! I'LL BE ABLE TO GREET MY WORSHIPPERS FROM A MORE EXALTED PERCH!
UNGH..THESE FLANGE BOLTS ARE RUSTED SOLID...
Zippythepinhead.com
IN ORDER TO SAVE TH' DOGGIE FROM DEMOLITION, HE WAS MOVED A SHORT DISTANCE FROM HIS 40-YEAR SPOT NEAR TH' DINER TO TH' MEDIAN OF SLOAT BOULEVARD (IN SAN FRANCISCO)
I'M FLYING! I'M FLYING! YEEE-HA!!
YOW!
GRIFFY 3-22
WHOA! THIS IS A RADICALLY DIFFERENT VIEW! ALL THOSE CARS BELOW, COMIN' RIGHT AT ME!
TOO LATE FOR TREPIDATIONS, DOGGIE.. THIS IS YOUR PERMANENT NEW HOME!
UH...
©2005 Bill Griffith. World rights reserved. Distributed by King Features Syndicate
TIPS TO: JOEL SCHECHTER & DIANA SCOTT
ULP!
..I FEEL SO NAKED & EXPOSED.. ZIPPY! I'M GONNA NEED MONTHS OF THERAPY TO GET USED TO THIS..ARE YOU AVAILABLE?
YOU'RE ALL SET!
I'M HERE FOR YOU, DOGGIE! I'M A CERTIFIED ROADSIDE CRISIS COUNSELOR!!

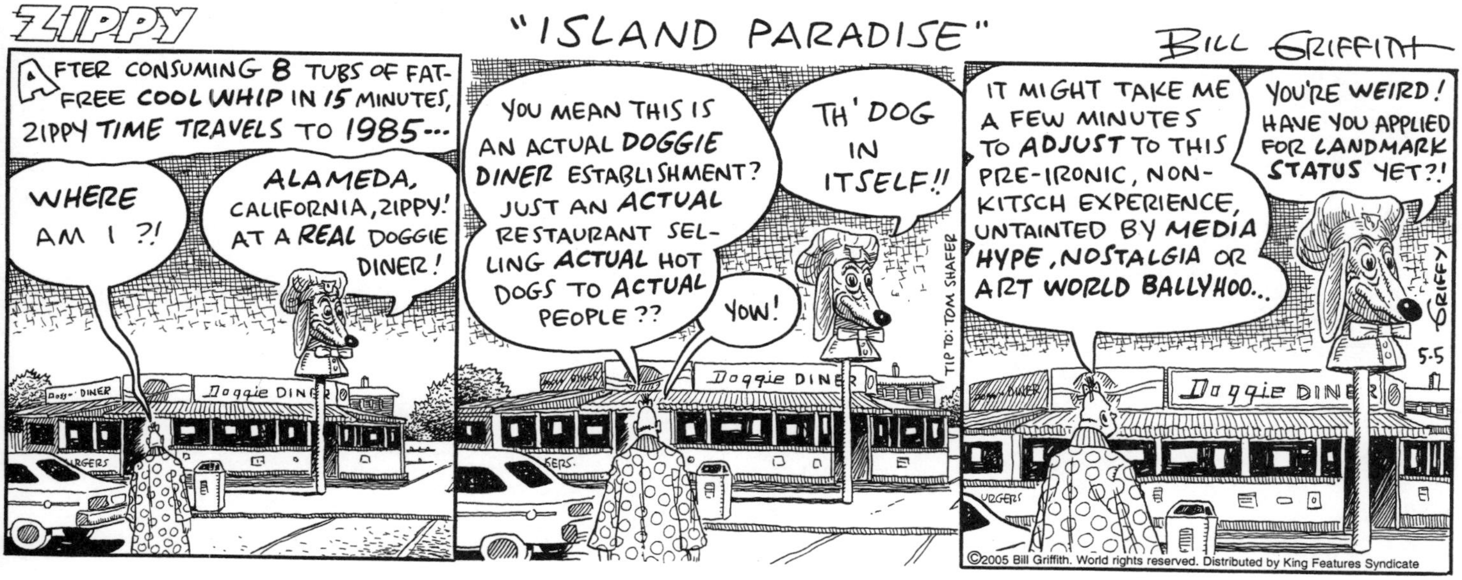
ZIPPY
"ISLAND PARADISE"
BILL GRIFFITH
AFTER CONSUMING 8 TUBS OF FAT-FREE COOL WHIP IN 15 MINUTES, ZIPPY TIME TRAVELS TO 1985---
WHERE AM I ?!
ALAMEDA, CALIFORNIA, ZIPPY! AT A REAL DOGGIE DINER!
DOGGIE DINER
YOU MEAN THIS IS AN ACTUAL DOGGIE DINER ESTABLISHMENT? JUST AN ACTUAL RESTAURANT SELLING ACTUAL HOT DOGS TO ACTUAL PEOPLE??
TH' DOG IN ITSELF!!
YOW!
TIP TO: TOM SHAFER
IT MIGHT TAKE ME A FEW MINUTES TO ADJUST TO THIS PRE-IRONIC, NON-KITSCH EXPERIENCE, UNTAINTED BY MEDIA HYPE, NOSTALGIA OR ART WORLD BALLYHOO...
YOU'RE WEIRD! HAVE YOU APPLIED FOR LANDMARK STATUS YET?!
GRIFFY 5-5
©2005 Bill Griffith. World rights reserved. Distributed by King Features Syndicate

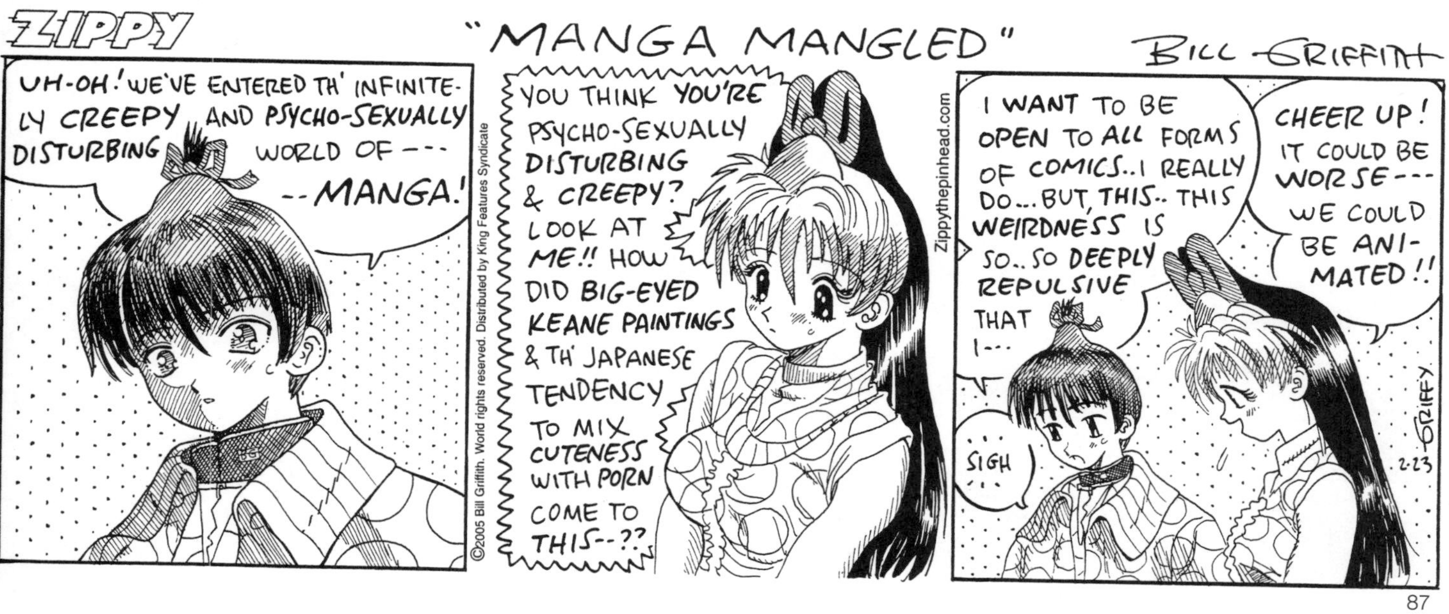
ZIPPY
"MANGA MANGLED"
BILL GRIFFITH
UH-OH! WE'VE ENTERED TH' INFINITELY CREEPY AND PSYCHO-SEXUALLY DISTURBING WORLD OF --- --MANGA!
©2005 Bill Griffith. World rights reserved. Distributed by King Features Syndicate
YOU THINK YOU'RE PSYCHO-SEXUALLY DISTURBING & CREEPY? LOOK AT ME!! HOW DID BIG-EYED KEANE PAINTINGS & TH' JAPANESE TENDENCY TO MIX CUTENESS WITH PORN COME TO THIS--??
Zippythepinhead.com
I WANT TO BE OPEN TO ALL FORMS OF COMICS..I REALLY DO... BUT, THIS.. THIS WEIRDNESS IS SO..SO DEEPLY REPULSIVE THAT I---
CHEER UP! IT COULD BE WORSE--- WE COULD BE ANIMATED!!
SIGH
GRIFFY 2-23

87

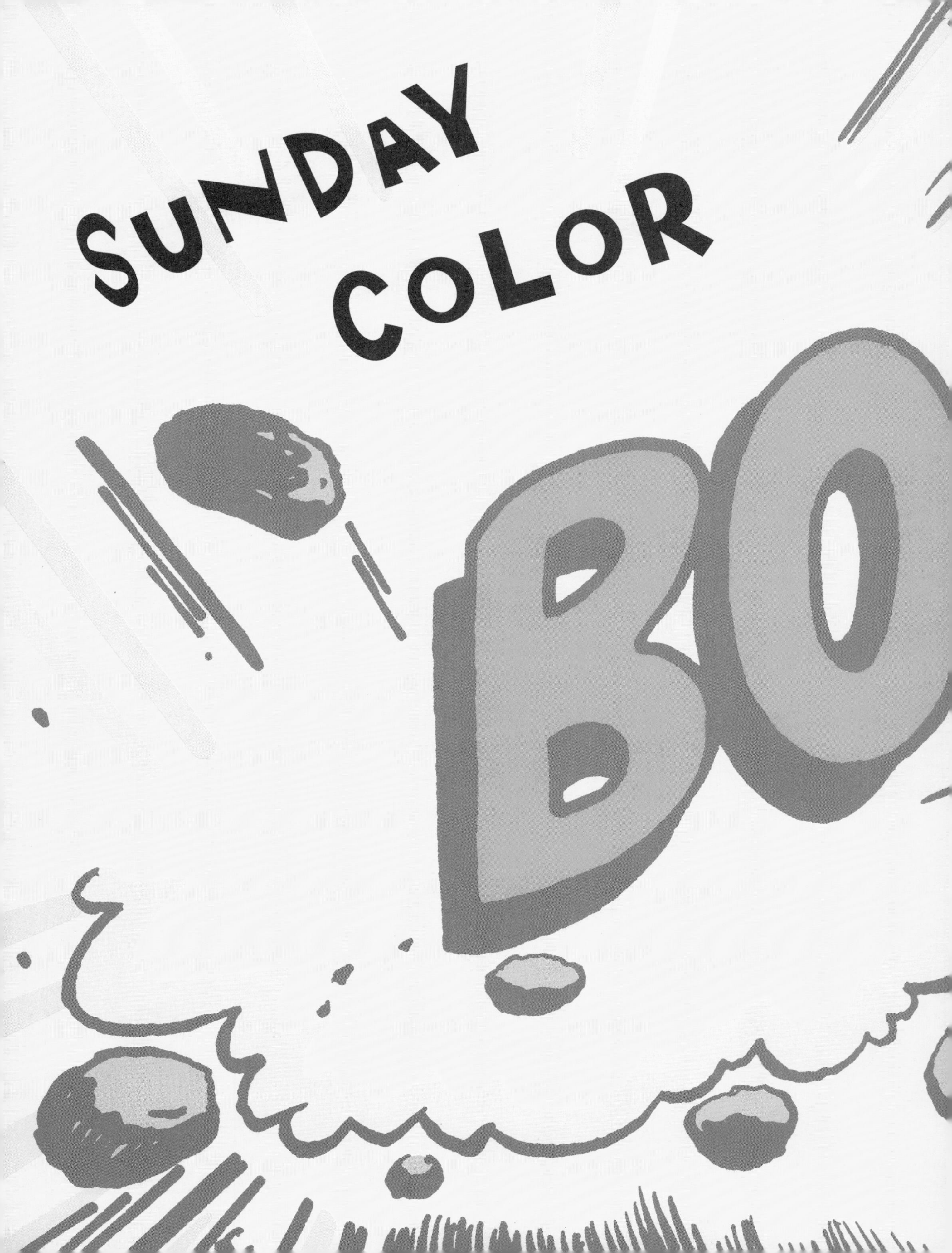
SUNDAY
COLOR
BO

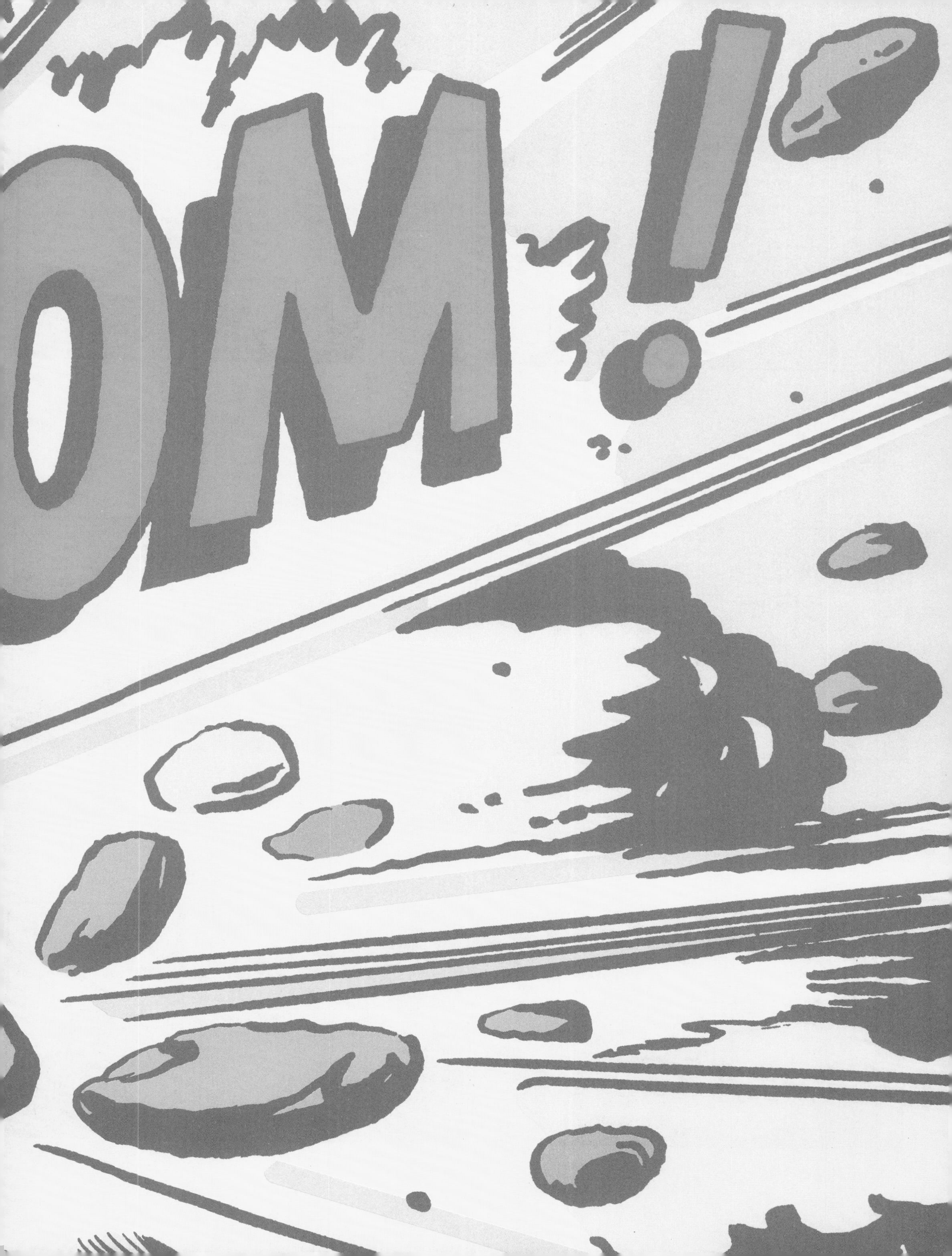
OM!

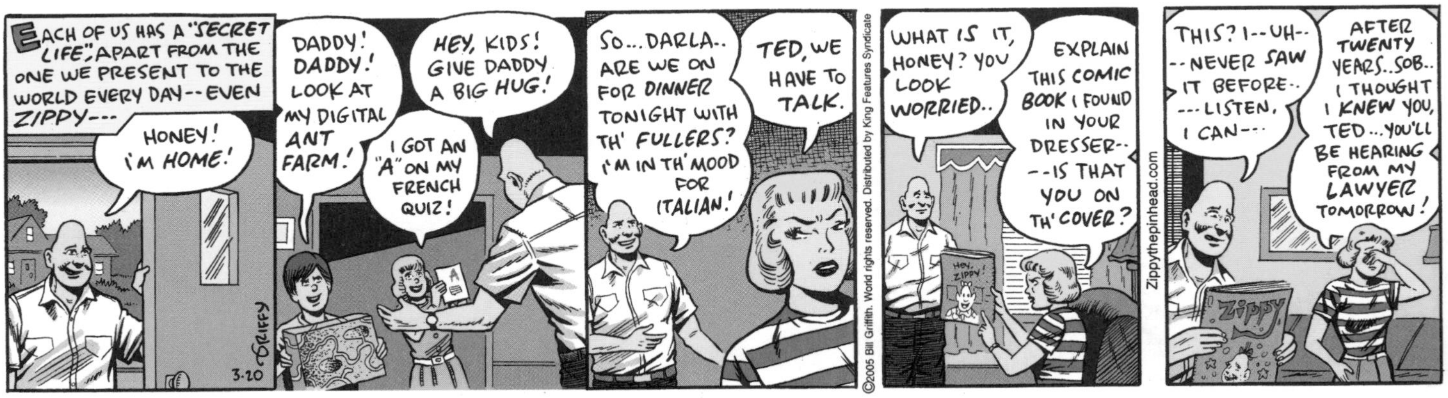
EACH OF US HAS A "SECRET LIFE", APART FROM THE ONE WE PRESENT TO THE WORLD EVERY DAY -- EVEN ZIPPY---
HONEY! I'M HOME!
GRIFFY 3-20
DADDY! DADDY! LOOK AT MY DIGITAL ANT FARM!
HEY, KIDS! GIVE DADDY A BIG HUG!
I GOT AN "A" ON MY FRENCH QUIZ!
SO... DARLA.. ARE WE ON FOR DINNER TONIGHT WITH TH' FULLERS? I'M IN TH' MOOD FOR ITALIAN!
TED, WE HAVE TO TALK.
©2005 Bill Griffith. World rights reserved. Distributed by King Features Syndicate
WHAT IS IT, HONEY? YOU LOOK WORRIED..
EXPLAIN THIS COMIC BOOK I FOUND IN YOUR DRESSER-- --IS THAT YOU ON TH' COVER?
HEY, ZIPPY!
Zippythepinhead.com
THIS? I--UH-- --NEVER SAW IT BEFORE.. ---LISTEN, I CAN---
AFTER TWENTY YEARS.. SOB.. I THOUGHT I KNEW YOU, TED... YOU'LL BE HEARING FROM MY LAWYER TOMORROW!
ZIPPY

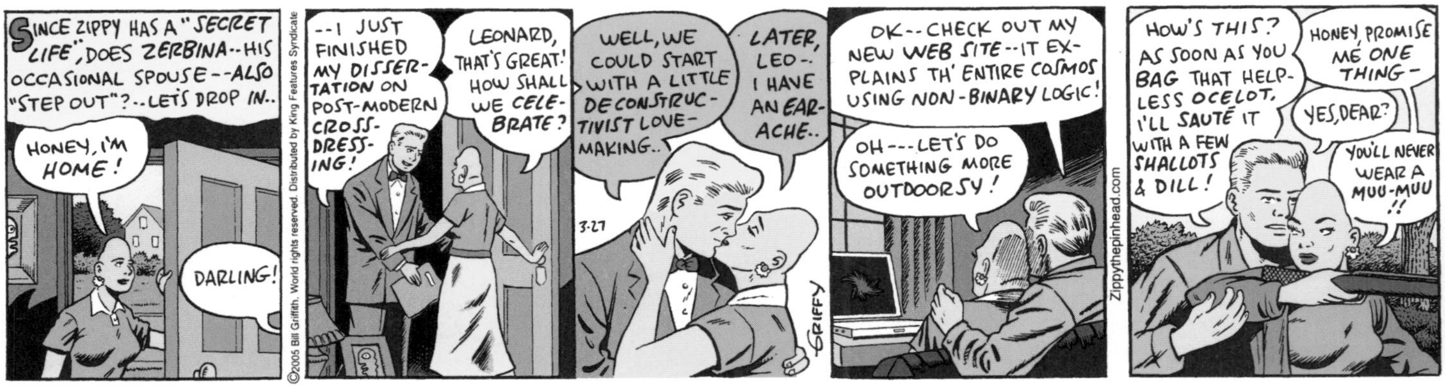
SINCE ZIPPY HAS A "SECRET LIFE", DOES ZERBINA--HIS OCCASIONAL SPOUSE--ALSO "STEP OUT"?--LET'S DROP IN..
HONEY, I'M HOME!
DARLING!
©2005 Bill Griffith. World rights reserved. Distributed by King Features Syndicate
--I JUST FINISHED MY DISSERTATION ON POST-MODERN CROSS-DRESSING!
LEONARD, THAT'S GREAT! HOW SHALL WE CELEBRATE?
WELL, WE COULD START WITH A LITTLE DECONSTRUCTIVIST LOVE-MAKING..
LATER, LEO-- I HAVE AN EAR-ACHE..
3-27
GRIFFY
OK--CHECK OUT MY NEW WEB SITE--IT EXPLAINS TH' ENTIRE COSMOS USING NON-BINARY LOGIC!
OH---LET'S DO SOMETHING MORE OUTDOORSY!
Zippythepinhead.com
HOW'S THIS? AS SOON AS YOU BAG THAT HELPLESS OCELOT, I'LL SAUTÉ IT WITH A FEW SHALLOTS & DILL!
HONEY, PROMISE ME ONE THING-
YES, DEAR?
YOU'LL NEVER WEAR A MUU-MUU!!

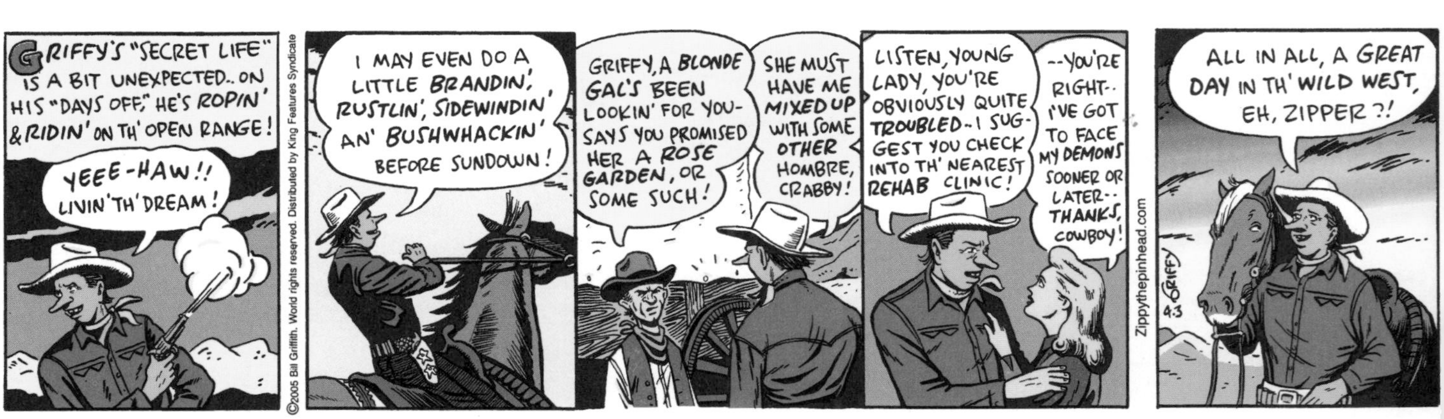
GRIFFY'S "SECRET LIFE" IS A BIT UNEXPECTED.. ON HIS "DAYS OFF," HE'S ROPIN' & RIDIN' ON TH' OPEN RANGE!
YEEE-HAW!! LIVIN' TH' DREAM!
©2005 Bill Griffith. World rights reserved. Distributed by King Features Syndicate
I MAY EVEN DO A LITTLE BRANDIN', RUSTLIN', SIDEWINDIN' AN' BUSHWHACKIN' BEFORE SUNDOWN!
GRIFFY, A BLONDE GAL'S BEEN LOOKIN' FOR YOU-- SAYS YOU PROMISED HER A ROSE GARDEN, OR SOME SUCH!
SHE MUST HAVE ME MIXED UP WITH SOME OTHER HOMBRE, CRABBY!
LISTEN, YOUNG LADY, YOU'RE OBVIOUSLY QUITE TROUBLED--I SUGGEST YOU CHECK INTO TH' NEAREST REHAB CLINIC!
--YOU'RE RIGHT-- I'VE GOT TO FACE MY DEMONS SOONER OR LATER-- THANKS, COWBOY!
Zippythepinhead.com
GRIFFY 4-3
ALL IN ALL, A GREAT DAY IN TH' WILD WEST, EH, ZIPPER?!

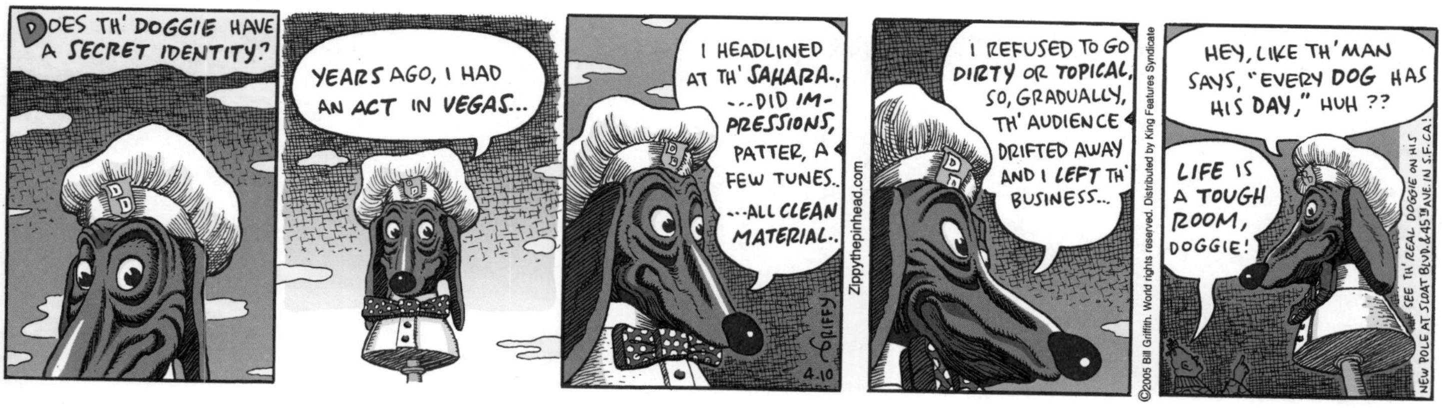
DOES TH' DOGGIE HAVE A SECRET IDENTITY?
YEARS AGO, I HAD AN ACT IN VEGAS...
I HEADLINED AT TH' SAHARA.. ...DID IMPRESSIONS, PATTER, A FEW TUNES.. ...ALL CLEAN MATERIAL..
GRIFFY
4.10
Zippythepinhead.com
I REFUSED TO GO DIRTY OR TOPICAL, SO, GRADUALLY, TH' AUDIENCE DRIFTED AWAY AND I LEFT TH' BUSINESS...
©2005 Bill Griffith. World rights reserved. Distributed by King Features Syndicate
HEY, LIKE TH' MAN SAYS, "EVERY DOG HAS HIS DAY," HUH ??
LIFE IS A TOUGH ROOM, DOGGIE!
SEE TH' REAL DOGGIE ON HIS NEW POLE AT SLOAT BLVD. & 45TH AVE. IN S.F. CA!

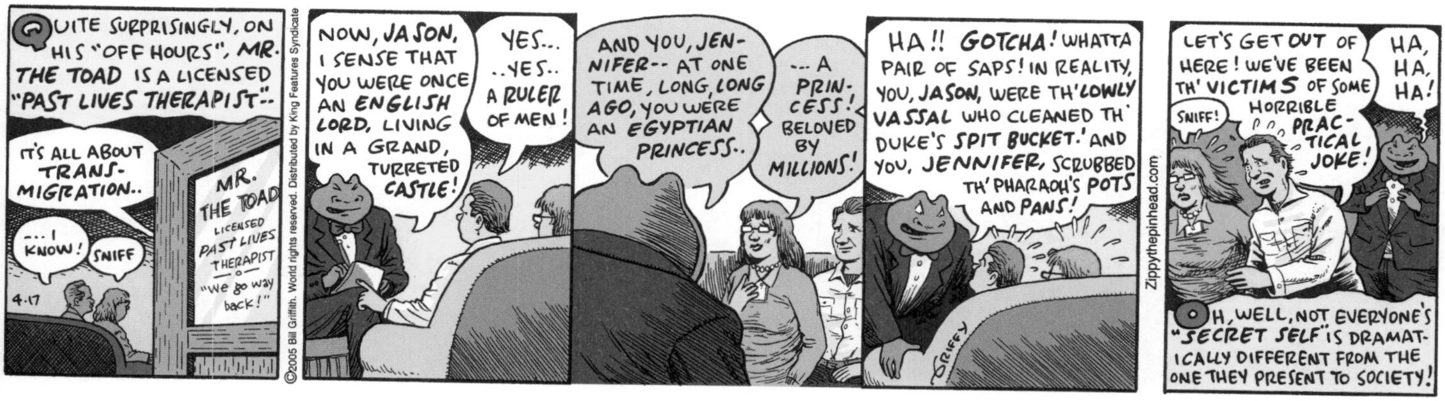
QUITE SURPRISINGLY, ON HIS "OFF HOURS", MR. THE TOAD IS A LICENSED "PAST LIVES THERAPIST"..
IT'S ALL ABOUT TRANS-MIGRATION..
...I KNOW!
SNIFF
MR. THE TOAD LICENSED PAST LIVES THERAPIST "We go way back!"
4.17
©2005 Bill Griffith. World rights reserved. Distributed by King Features Syndicate
NOW, JASON, I SENSE THAT YOU WERE ONCE AN ENGLISH LORD, LIVING IN A GRAND, TURRETED CASTLE!
YES.. ..YES.. A RULER OF MEN!
AND YOU, JENNIFER-- AT ONE TIME, LONG, LONG AGO, YOU WERE AN EGYPTIAN PRINCESS..
-- A PRINCESS! BELOVED BY MILLIONS!
HA!! GOTCHA! WHATTA PAIR OF SAPS! IN REALITY, YOU, JASON, WERE TH' LOWLY VASSAL WHO CLEANED TH' DUKE'S SPIT BUCKET.' AND YOU, JENNIFER, SCRUBBED TH' PHARAOH'S POTS AND PANS!
GRIFFY
Zippythepinhead.com
LET'S GET OUT OF HERE! WE'VE BEEN TH' VICTIMS OF SOME HORRIBLE PRACTICAL JOKE!
SNIFF!
HA, HA, HA!
OH, WELL, NOT EVERYONE'S "SECRET SELF" IS DRAMATICALLY DIFFERENT FROM THE ONE THEY PRESENT TO SOCIETY!

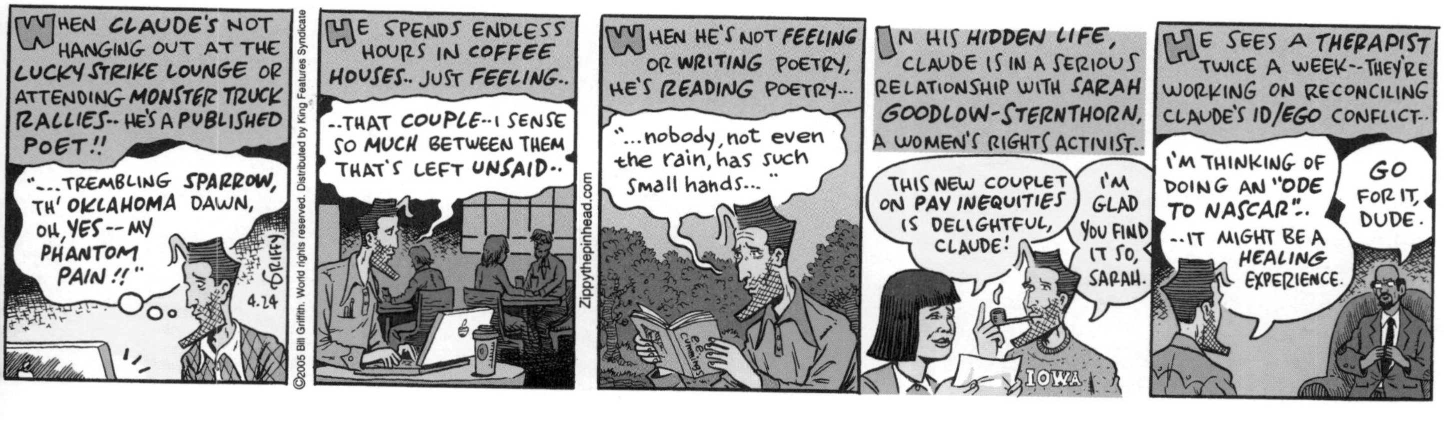
WHEN CLAUDE'S NOT HANGING OUT AT THE LUCKY STRIKE LOUNGE OR ATTENDING MONSTER TRUCK RALLIES-- HE'S A PUBLISHED POET!!
"...TREMBLING SPARROW, TH' OKLAHOMA DAWN, OH, YES -- MY PHANTOM PAIN!!"
GRIFFY
4.24
©2005 Bill Griffith. World rights reserved. Distributed by King Features Syndicate
HE SPENDS ENDLESS HOURS IN COFFEE HOUSES.. JUST FEELING..
--THAT COUPLE--I SENSE SO MUCH BETWEEN THEM THAT'S LEFT UNSAID--
Zippythepinhead.com
WHEN HE'S NOT FEELING OR WRITING POETRY, HE'S READING POETRY...
"...nobody, not even the rain, has such small hands..."
e.e. cummings
IN HIS HIDDEN LIFE, CLAUDE IS IN A SERIOUS RELATIONSHIP WITH SARAH GOODLOW-STERNTHORN, A WOMEN'S RIGHTS ACTIVIST..
THIS NEW COUPLET ON PAY INEQUITIES IS DELIGHTFUL, CLAUDE!
I'M GLAD YOU FIND IT SO, SARAH.
IOWA
HE SEES A THERAPIST TWICE A WEEK--THEY'RE WORKING ON RECONCILING CLAUDE'S ID/EGO CONFLICT..
I'M THINKING OF DOING AN "ODE TO NASCAR".. --IT MIGHT BE A HEALING EXPERIENCE.
GO FOR IT, DUDE.

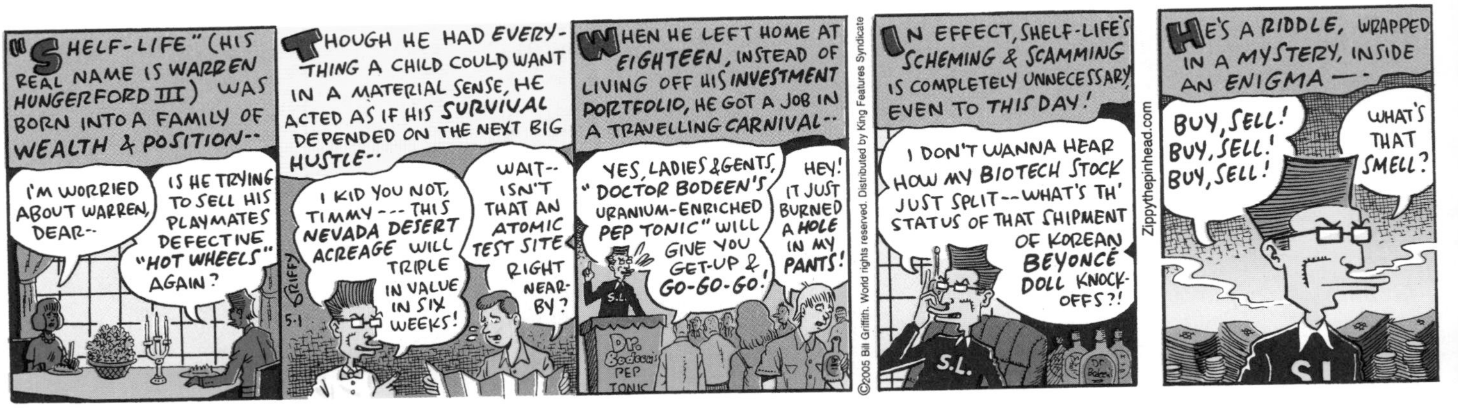
"SHELF-LIFE" (HIS REAL NAME IS WARREN HUNGERFORD III) WAS BORN INTO A FAMILY OF WEALTH & POSITION--
I'M WORRIED ABOUT WARREN, DEAR--
IS HE TRYING TO SELL HIS PLAYMATES DEFECTIVE "HOT WHEELS" AGAIN?
THOUGH HE HAD EVERYTHING A CHILD COULD WANT IN A MATERIAL SENSE, HE ACTED AS IF HIS SURVIVAL DEPENDED ON THE NEXT BIG HUSTLE--
I KID YOU NOT, TIMMY--- THIS NEVADA DESERT ACREAGE WILL TRIPLE IN VALUE IN SIX WEEKS!
WAIT-- ISN'T THAT AN ATOMIC TEST SITE RIGHT NEARBY?
GRIFFY
5-1
WHEN HE LEFT HOME AT EIGHTEEN, INSTEAD OF LIVING OFF HIS INVESTMENT PORTFOLIO, HE GOT A JOB IN A TRAVELLING CARNIVAL--
YES, LADIES & GENTS, "DOCTOR BODEEN'S URANIUM-ENRICHED PEP TONIC" WILL GIVE YOU GET-UP & GO-GO-GO!
HEY! IT JUST BURNED A HOLE IN MY PANTS!
DR. BODEEN'S PEP TONIC
IN EFFECT, SHELF-LIFE'S SCHEMING & SCAMMING IS COMPLETELY UNNECESSARY, EVEN TO THIS DAY!
I DON'T WANNA HEAR HOW MY BIOTECH STOCK JUST SPLIT-- WHAT'S TH' STATUS OF THAT SHIPMENT OF KOREAN BEYONCÉ DOLL KNOCK-OFFS?!
S.L.
©2005 Bill Griffith. World rights reserved. Distributed by King Features Syndicate
Zippythepinhead.com
HE'S A RIDDLE, WRAPPED IN A MYSTERY, INSIDE AN ENIGMA---
BUY, SELL! BUY, SELL! BUY, SELL!
WHAT'S THAT SMELL?

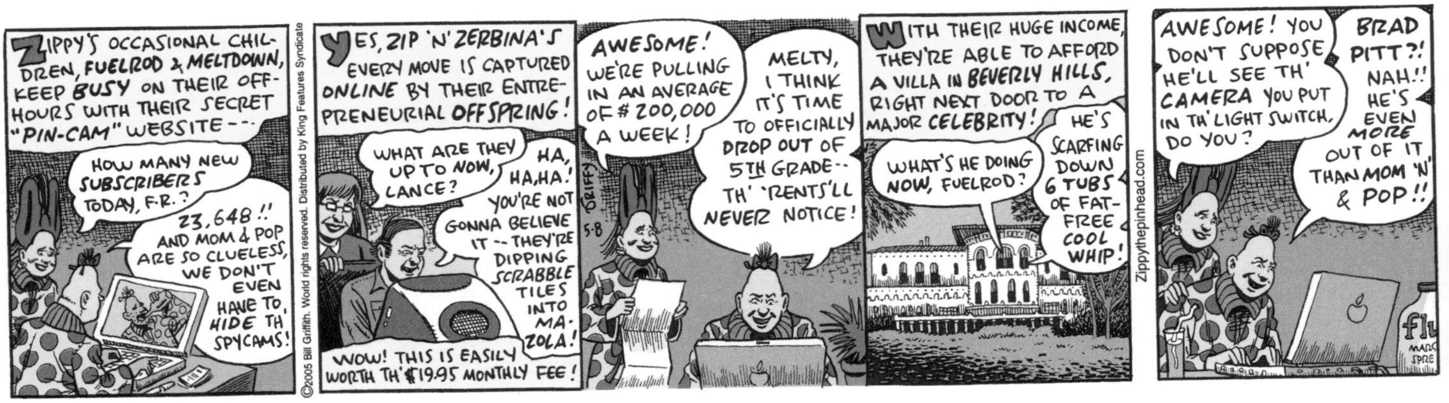
ZIPPY'S OCCASIONAL CHILDREN, FUELROD & MELTDOWN, KEEP BUSY ON THEIR OFF-HOURS WITH THEIR SECRET "PIN-CAM" WEBSITE---
HOW MANY NEW SUBSCRIBERS TODAY, F.R.?
23,648!! AND MOM & POP ARE SO CLUELESS, WE DON'T EVEN HAVE TO HIDE TH' SPYCAMS!
©2005 Bill Griffith. World rights reserved. Distributed by King Features Syndicate
YES, ZIP 'N' ZERBINA'S EVERY MOVE IS CAPTURED ONLINE BY THEIR ENTREPRENEURIAL OFFSPRING!
WHAT ARE THEY UP TO NOW, LANCE?
HA, HA,HA! YOU'RE NOT GONNA BELIEVE IT -- THEY'RE DIPPING SCRABBLE TILES INTO MAZOLA!
WOW! THIS IS EASILY WORTH TH' $19.95 MONTHLY FEE!
GRIFFY
5-8
AWESOME! WE'RE PULLING IN AN AVERAGE OF $200,000 A WEEK!
MELTY, I THINK IT'S TIME TO OFFICIALLY DROP OUT OF 5TH GRADE-- TH' 'RENTS'LL NEVER NOTICE!
WITH THEIR HUGE INCOME, THEY'RE ABLE TO AFFORD A VILLA IN BEVERLY HILLS, RIGHT NEXT DOOR TO A MAJOR CELEBRITY!
WHAT'S HE DOING NOW, FUELROD?
HE'S SCARFING DOWN 6 TUBS OF FAT-FREE COOL WHIP!
Zippythepinhead.com
AWESOME! YOU DON'T SUPPOSE HE'LL SEE TH' CAMERA YOU PUT IN TH' LIGHT SWITCH, DO YOU?
BRAD PITT?! NAH!! HE'S EVEN MORE OUT OF IT THAN MOM 'N' POP!!

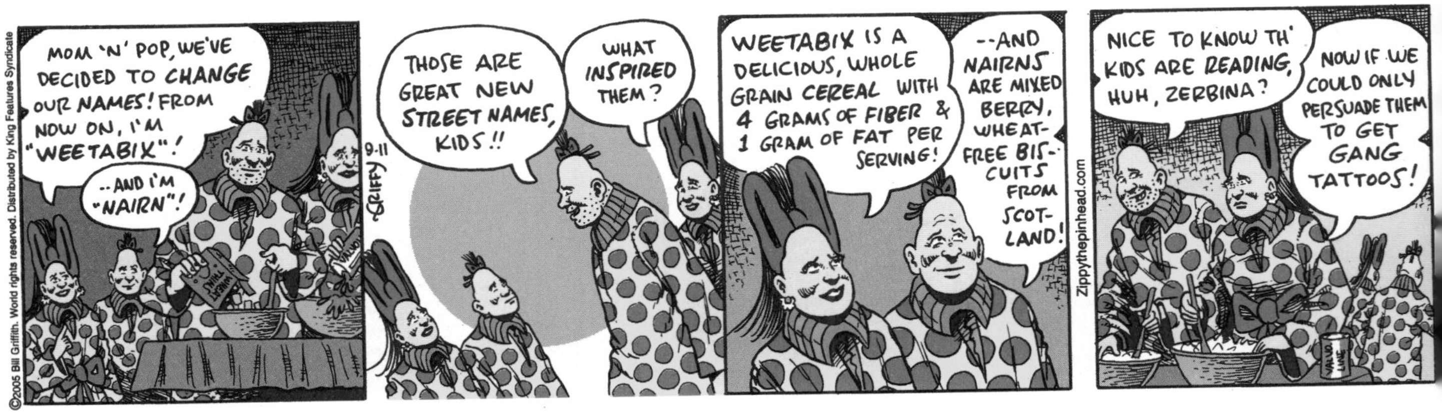
©2005 Bill Griffith. World rights reserved. Distributed by King Features Syndicate
MOM 'N' POP, WE'VE DECIDED TO CHANGE OUR NAMES! FROM NOW ON, I'M "WEETABIX"!
--AND I'M "NAIRN"!
THOSE ARE GREAT NEW STREET NAMES, KIDS!!
WHAT INSPIRED THEM?
9-11
GRIFFY
WEETABIX IS A DELICIOUS, WHOLE GRAIN CEREAL WITH 4 GRAMS OF FIBER & 1 GRAM OF FAT PER SERVING!
--AND NAIRNS ARE MIXED BERRY, WHEAT-FREE BISCUITS FROM SCOTLAND!
Zippythepinhead.com
NICE TO KNOW TH' KIDS ARE READING, HUH, ZERBINA?
NOW IF WE COULD ONLY PERSUADE THEM TO GET GANG TATTOOS!

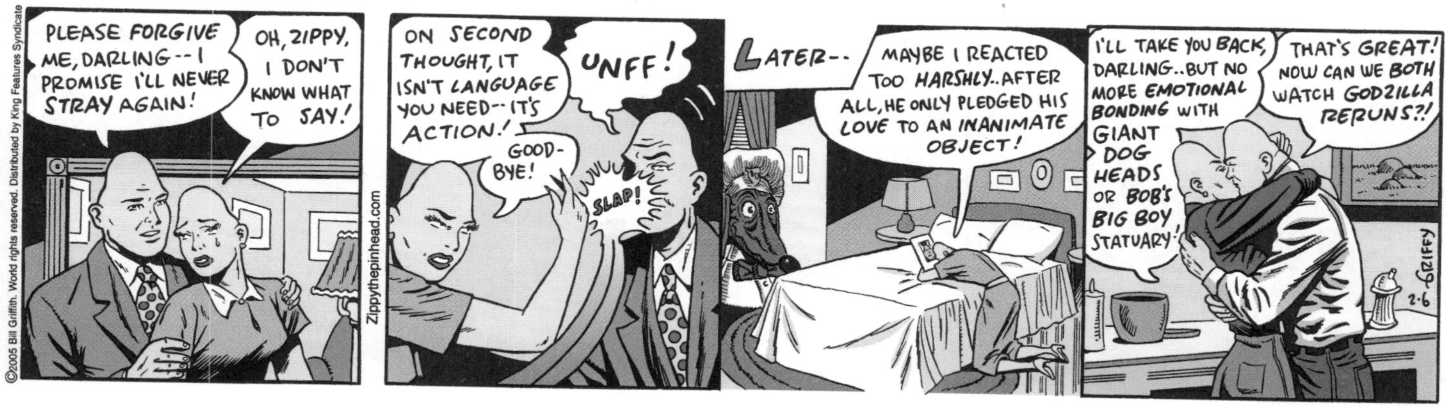
PLEASE FORGIVE ME, DARLING -- I PROMISE I'LL NEVER STRAY AGAIN!
OH, ZIPPY, I DON'T KNOW WHAT TO SAY!
©2005 Bill Griffith. World rights reserved. Distributed by King Features Syndicate
Zippythepinhead.com
ON SECOND THOUGHT, IT ISN'T LANGUAGE YOU NEED -- IT'S ACTION!
UNFF!
GOOD-BYE!
SLAP!
LATER--
MAYBE I REACTED TOO HARSHLY.. AFTER ALL, HE ONLY PLEDGED HIS LOVE TO AN INANIMATE OBJECT!
I'LL TAKE YOU BACK, DARLING.. BUT NO MORE EMOTIONAL BONDING WITH GIANT DOG HEADS OR BOB'S BIG BOY STATUARY!
THAT'S GREAT! NOW CAN WE BOTH WATCH GODZILLA RERUNS?!
GRIFFY
2·6

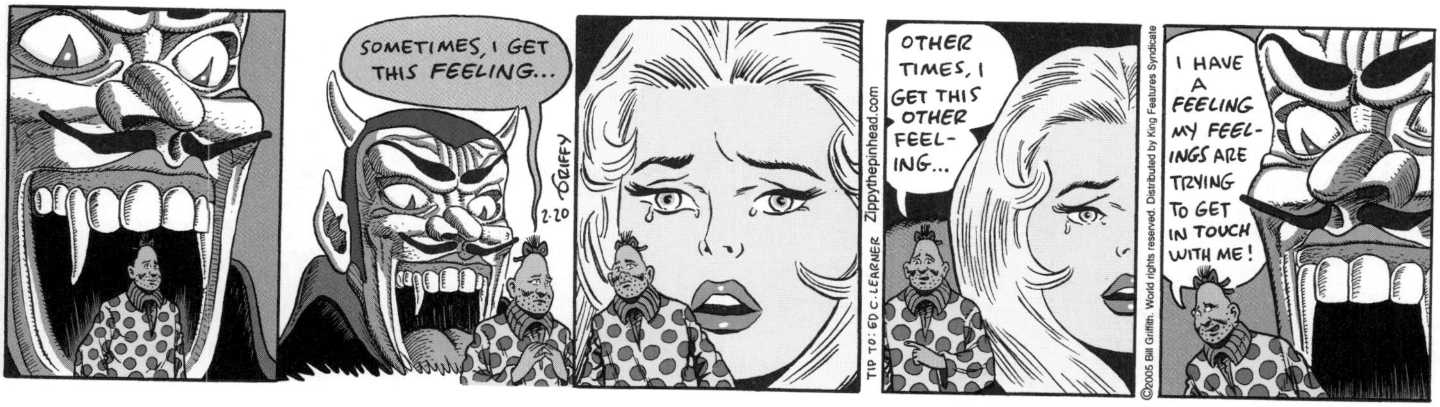
SOMETIMES, I GET THIS FEELING...
GRIFFY
2·20
OTHER TIMES, I GET THIS OTHER FEEL-ING...
Zippythepinhead.com
TIP TO: ED C. LEARNER
©2005 Bill Griffith. World rights reserved. Distributed by King Features Syndicate
I HAVE A FEELING MY FEEL-INGS ARE TRYING TO GET IN TOUCH WITH ME!

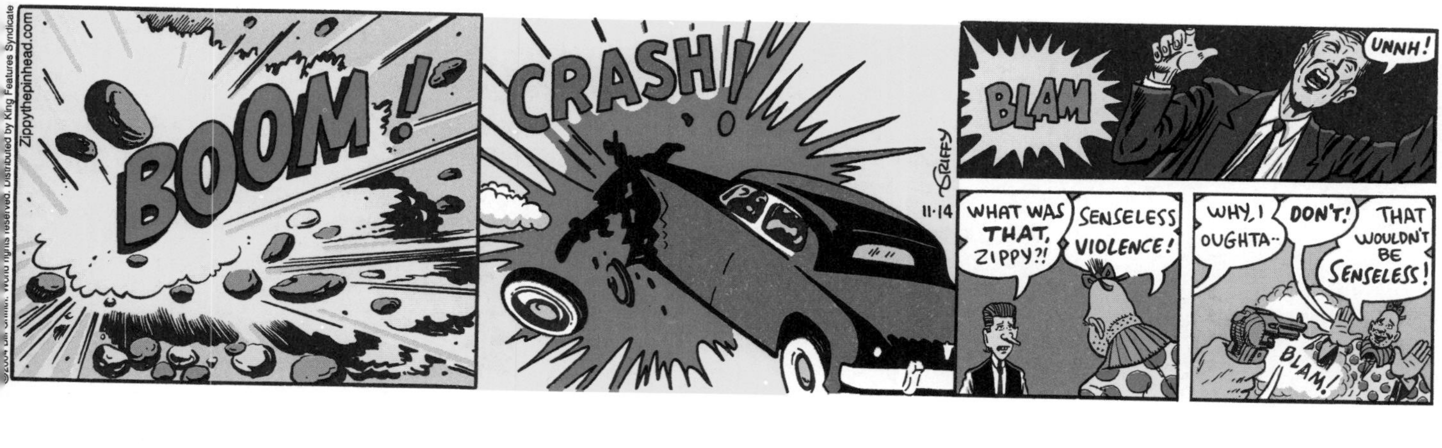
©2004 Bill Griffith. World rights reserved. Distributed by King Features Syndicate
Zippythepinhead.com
BOOM!
CRASH!
GRIFFY
11·14
BLAM
UNNH!
WHAT WAS THAT, ZIPPY?!
SENSELESS VIOLENCE!
WHY, I OUGHTA..
DON'T!
THAT WOULDN'T BE SENSELESS!
BLAM!

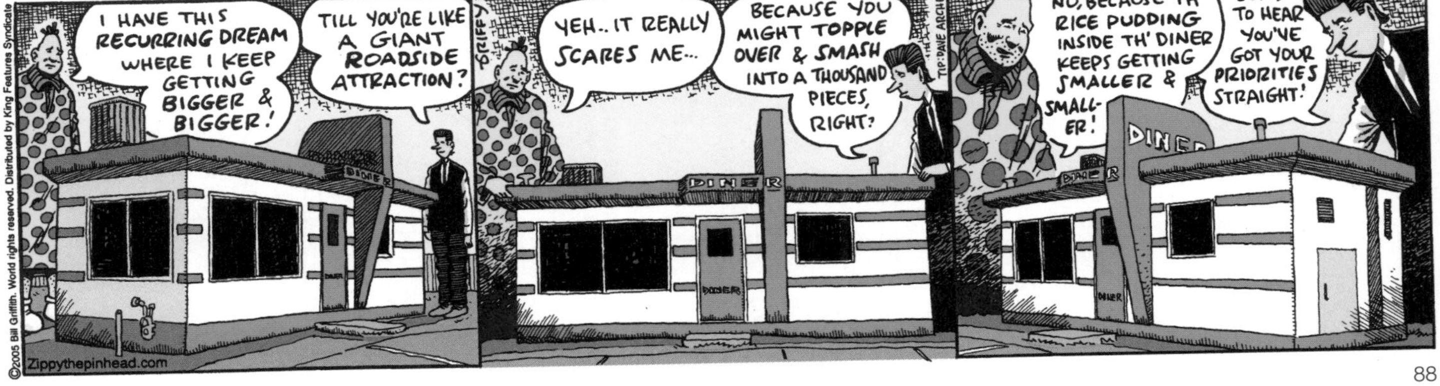
I HAVE THIS RECURRING DREAM WHERE I KEEP GETTING BIGGER & BIGGER!
TILL YOU'RE LIKE A GIANT ROADSIDE ATTRACTION?
YEH.. IT REALLY SCARES ME..
BECAUSE YOU MIGHT TOPPLE OVER & SMASH INTO A THOUSAND PIECES, RIGHT?
NO, BECAUSE TH' RICE PUDDING INSIDE TH' DINER KEEPS GETTING SMALLER & SMALLER!
GLAD TO HEAR YOU'VE GOT YOUR PRIORITIES STRAIGHT!
GRIFFY
TIP: DANE ARCHER
11-6
DINER
©2005 Bill Griffith. World rights reserved. Distributed by King Features Syndicate
Zippythepinhead.com

88

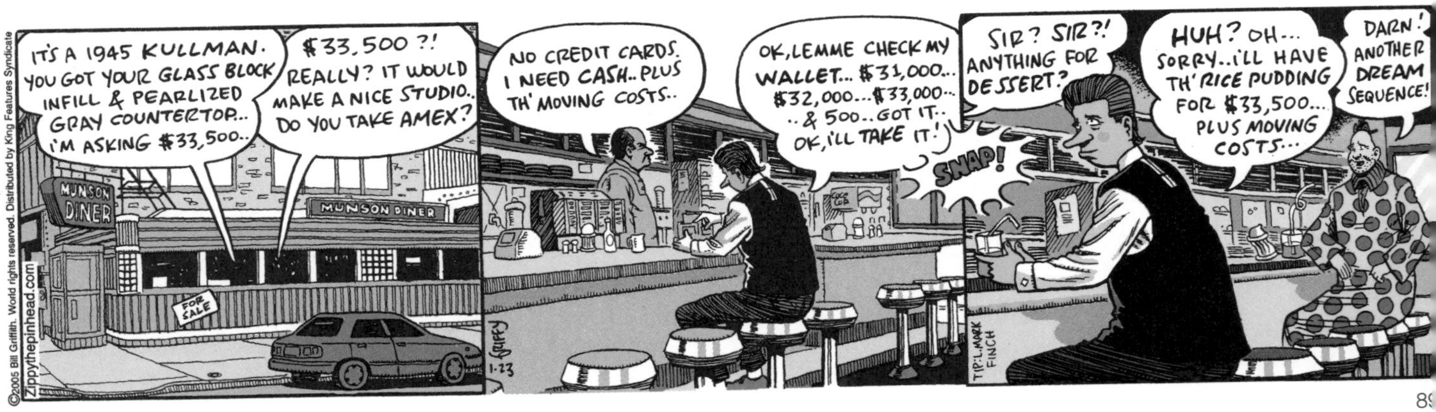
IT'S A 1945 KULLMAN. YOU GOT YOUR GLASS BLOCK INFILL & PEARLIZED GRAY COUNTERTOP.. I'M ASKING $33,500..
$33,500?! REALLY? IT WOULD MAKE A NICE STUDIO.. DO YOU TAKE AMEX?
MUNSON DINER
MUNSON DINER
FOR SALE
NO CREDIT CARDS. I NEED CASH.. PLUS TH' MOVING COSTS..
OK, LEMME CHECK MY WALLET... $31,000... $32,000... $33,000... .. & 500.. GOT IT.. OK, I'LL TAKE IT!
GRIFFY
1-23
SIR? SIR?! ANYTHING FOR DESSERT?
SNAP!
HUH? OH... SORRY.. I'LL HAVE TH' RICE PUDDING FOR $33,500... PLUS MOVING COSTS...
DARN! ANOTHER DREAM SEQUENCE!
TIP: L. MARK FINCH
©2005 Bill Griffith. World rights reserved. Distributed by King Features Syndicate
Zippythepinhead.com

89

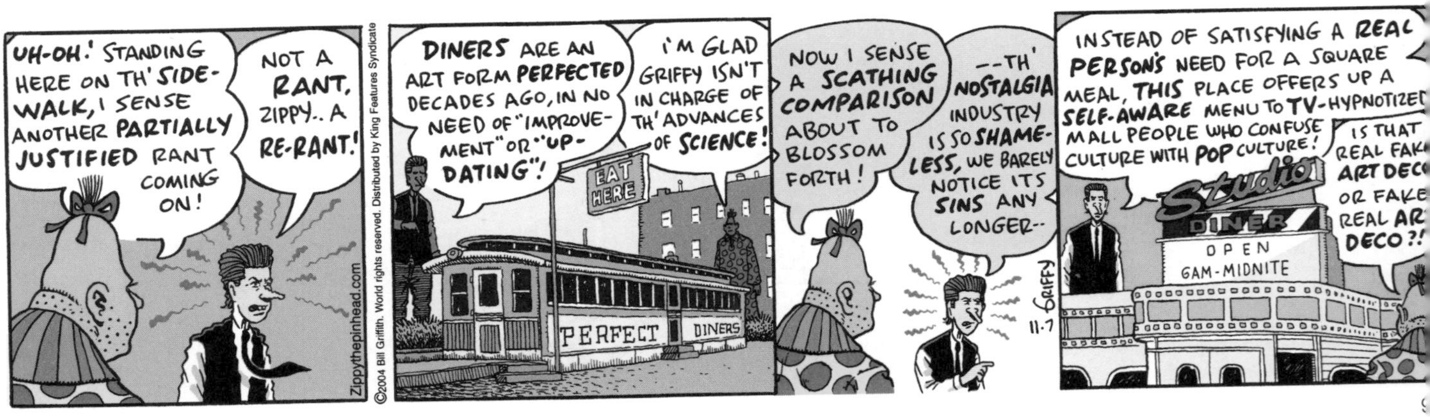
UH-OH! STANDING HERE ON TH' SIDEWALK, I SENSE ANOTHER PARTIALLY JUSTIFIED RANT COMING ON!
NOT A RANT, ZIPPY.. A RE-RANT!
Zippythepinhead.com
DINERS ARE AN ART FORM PERFECTED DECADES AGO, IN NO NEED OF "IMPROVEMENT" OR "UP-DATING"!
I'M GLAD GRIFFY ISN'T IN CHARGE OF TH' ADVANCES OF SCIENCE!
EAT HERE
PERFECT DINERS
©2004 Bill Griffith. World rights reserved. Distributed by King Features Syndicate
NOW I SENSE A SCATHING COMPARISON ABOUT TO BLOSSOM FORTH!
--TH' NOSTALGIA INDUSTRY IS SO SHAMELESS, WE BARELY NOTICE ITS SINS ANY LONGER--
GRIFFY
11-7
INSTEAD OF SATISFYING A REAL PERSON'S NEED FOR A SQUARE MEAL, THIS PLACE OFFERS UP A SELF-AWARE MENU TO TV-HYPNOTIZED MALL PEOPLE WHO CONFUSE CULTURE WITH POP CULTURE!
IS THAT REAL FAKE ART DECO OR FAKE REAL ART DECO?!
Studio DINER
OPEN 6AM-MIDNITE

9

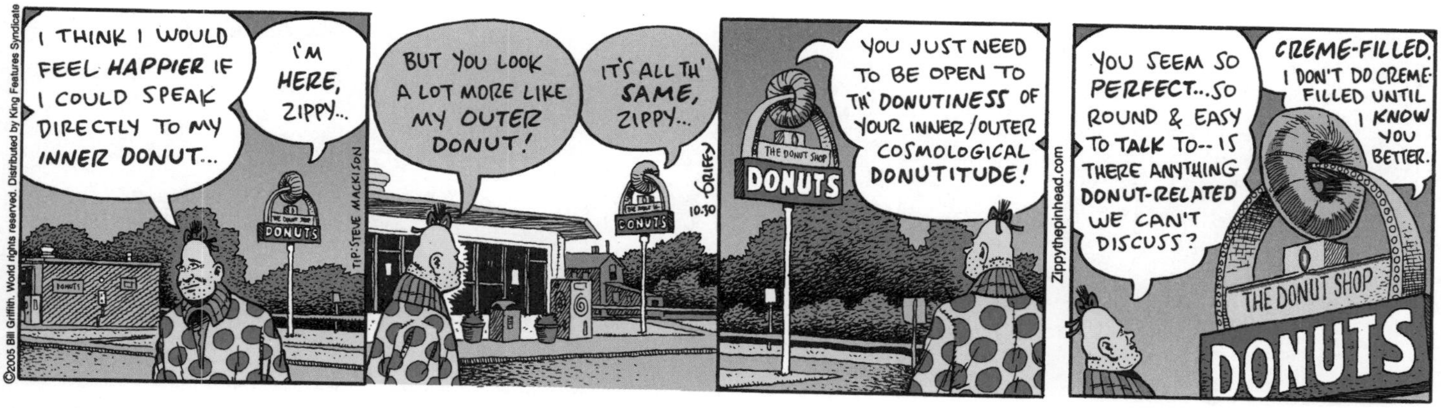
I THINK I WOULD FEEL HAPPIER IF I COULD SPEAK DIRECTLY TO MY INNER DONUT...
I'M HERE, ZIPPY...
DONUTS
TIP: STEVE MACKISON
BUT YOU LOOK A LOT MORE LIKE MY OUTER DONUT!
IT'S ALL TH' SAME, ZIPPY...
DONUTS
GRIFFY 10.30
YOU JUST NEED TO BE OPEN TO TH' DONUTINESS OF YOUR INNER/OUTER COSMOLOGICAL DONUTITUDE!
THE DONUT SHOP
DONUTS
YOU SEEM SO PERFECT...SO ROUND & EASY TO TALK TO-- IS THERE ANYTHING DONUT-RELATED WE CAN'T DISCUSS?
CREME-FILLED. I DON'T DO CREME-FILLED UNTIL I KNOW YOU BETTER.
THE DONUT SHOP
DONUTS
©2005 Bill Griffith. World rights reserved. Distributed by King Features Syndicate
Zippythepinhead.com

91

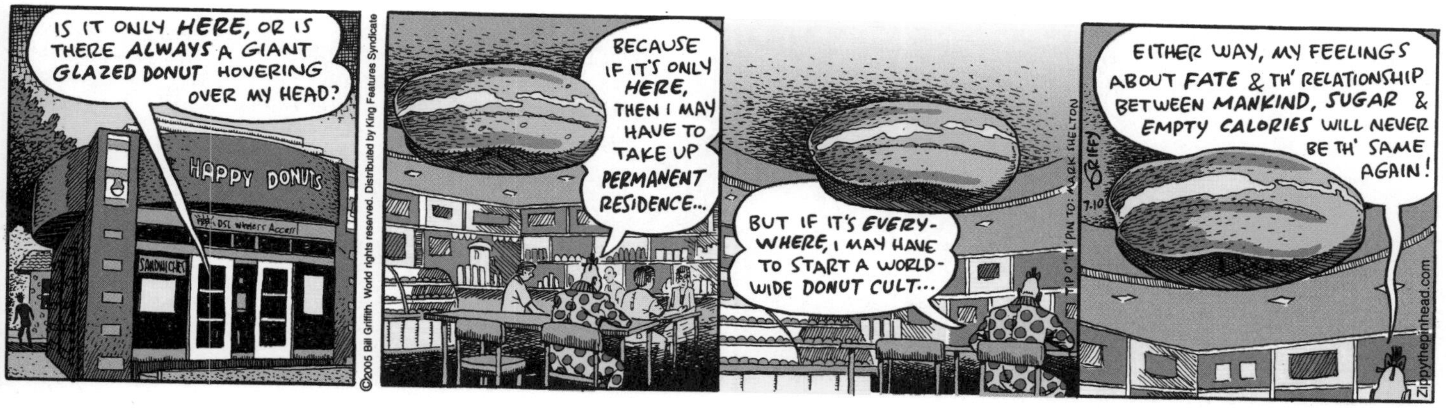
IS IT ONLY HERE, OR IS THERE ALWAYS A GIANT GLAZED DONUT HOVERING OVER MY HEAD?
HAPPY DONUTS
SANDWICHES
©2005 Bill Griffith. World rights reserved. Distributed by King Features Syndicate
BECAUSE IF IT'S ONLY HERE, THEN I MAY HAVE TO TAKE UP PERMANENT RESIDENCE...
BUT IF IT'S EVERYWHERE, I MAY HAVE TO START A WORLD-WIDE DONUT CULT...
TIP O' TH' PIN TO: MARK SHELTON
GRIFFY 7.10
EITHER WAY, MY FEELINGS ABOUT FATE & TH' RELATIONSHIP BETWEEN MANKIND, SUGAR & EMPTY CALORIES WILL NEVER BE TH' SAME AGAIN!
Zippythepinhead.com

92

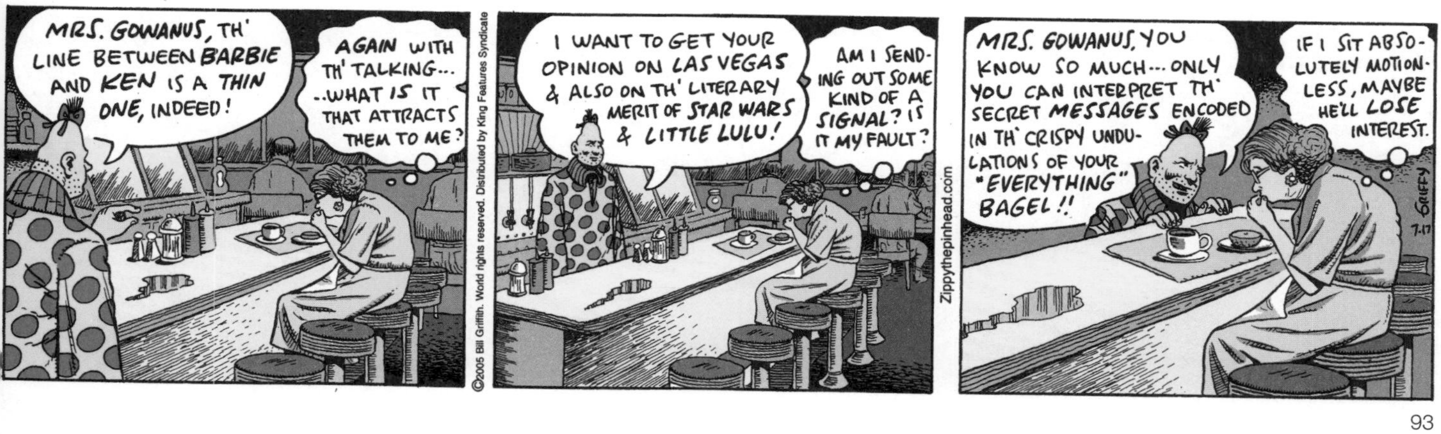
MRS. GOWANUS, TH' LINE BETWEEN BARBIE AND KEN IS A THIN ONE, INDEED!
AGAIN WITH TH' TALKING... ..WHAT IS IT THAT ATTRACTS THEM TO ME?
©2005 Bill Griffith. World rights reserved. Distributed by King Features Syndicate
I WANT TO GET YOUR OPINION ON LAS VEGAS & ALSO ON TH' LITERARY MERIT OF STAR WARS & LITTLE LULU!
AM I SENDING OUT SOME KIND OF A SIGNAL? IS IT MY FAULT?
Zippythepinhead.com
MRS. GOWANUS, YOU KNOW SO MUCH--- ONLY YOU CAN INTERPRET TH' SECRET MESSAGES ENCODED IN TH' CRISPY UNDULATIONS OF YOUR "EVERYTHING" BAGEL!!
IF I SIT ABSOLUTELY MOTIONLESS, MAYBE HE'LL LOSE INTEREST.
GRIFFY 7.17

93

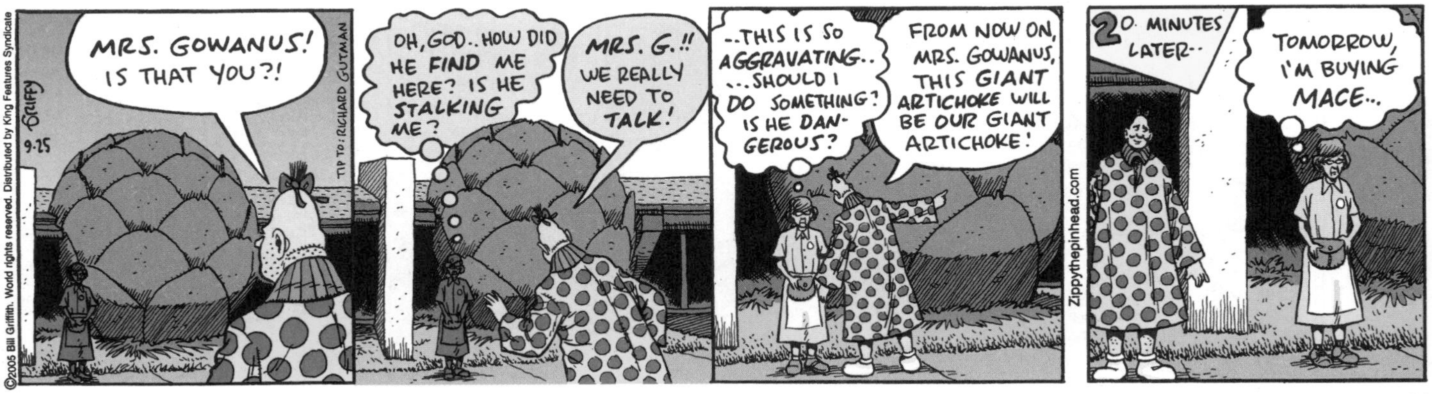
MRS. GOWANUS! IS THAT YOU?!
OH, GOD.. HOW DID HE FIND ME HERE? IS HE STALKING ME?
MRS. G.!! WE REALLY NEED TO TALK!
..THIS IS SO AGGRAVATING.. ...SHOULD I DO SOMETHING? IS HE DANGEROUS?
FROM NOW ON, MRS. GOWANUS, THIS GIANT ARTICHOKE WILL BE OUR GIANT ARTICHOKE!
20 MINUTES LATER..
TOMORROW, I'M BUYING MACE...
TIP TO: RICHARD GUTMAN
©2005 Bill Griffith. World rights reserved. Distributed by King Features Syndicate
Zippythepinhead.com

94

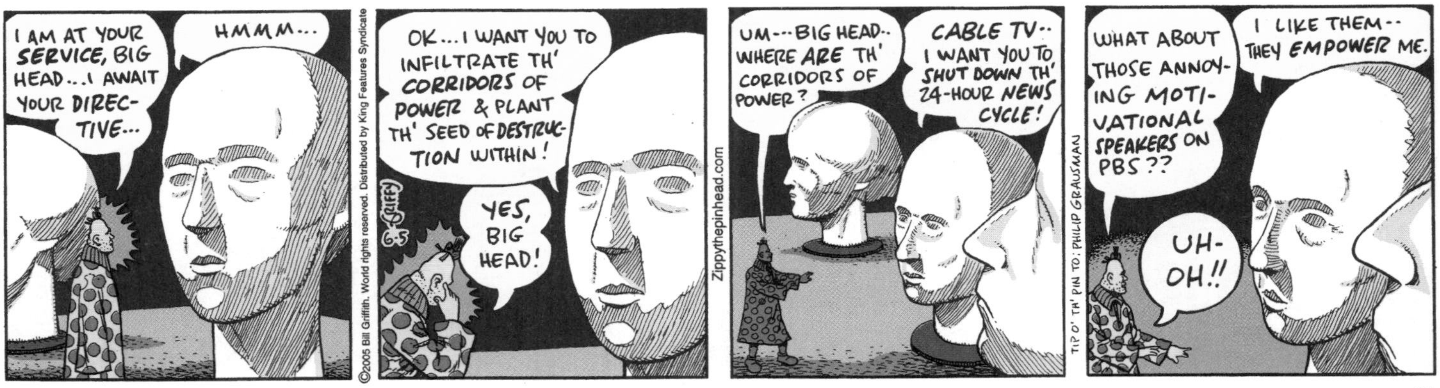
I AM AT YOUR SERVICE, BIG HEAD...I AWAIT YOUR DIRECTIVE...
HMMM...
OK...I WANT YOU TO INFILTRATE TH' CORRIDORS OF POWER & PLANT TH' SEED OF DESTRUCTION WITHIN!
YES, BIG HEAD!
UM...BIG HEAD.. WHERE ARE TH' CORRIDORS OF POWER?
CABLE TV.. I WANT YOU TO SHUT DOWN TH' 24-HOUR NEWS CYCLE!
WHAT ABOUT THOSE ANNOYING MOTIVATIONAL SPEAKERS ON PBS??
I LIKE THEM.. THEY EMPOWER ME.
UH-OH!!
TIP O' TH' PIN TO: PHILIP GRAUSMAN
©2005 Bill Griffith. World rights reserved. Distributed by King Features Syndicate
Zippythepinhead.com

95

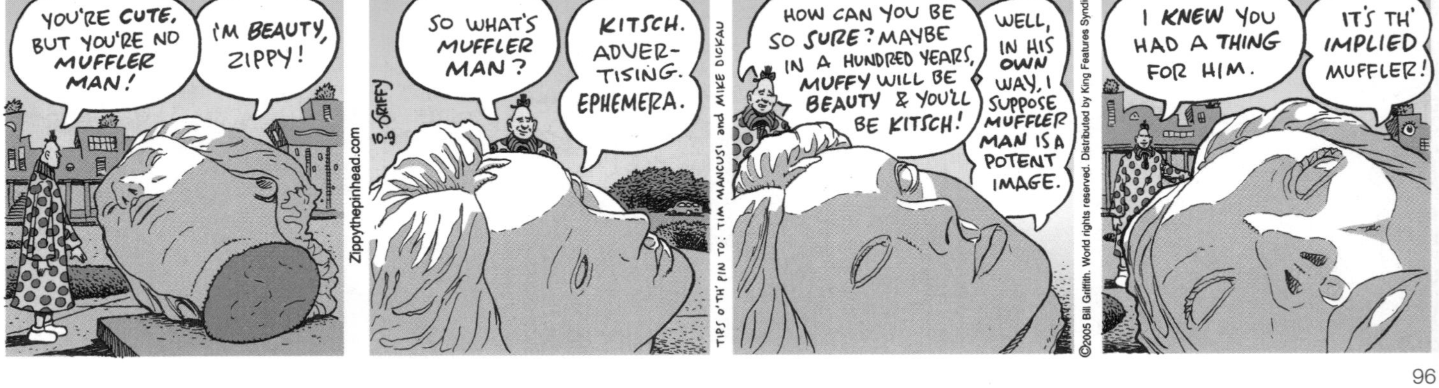
YOU'RE CUTE, BUT YOU'RE NO MUFFLER MAN!
I'M BEAUTY, ZIPPY!
SO WHAT'S MUFFLER MAN?
KITSCH. ADVERTISING. EPHEMERA.
HOW CAN YOU BE SO SURE? MAYBE IN A HUNDRED YEARS, MUFFY WILL BE BEAUTY & YOU'LL BE KITSCH!
WELL, IN HIS OWN WAY, I SUPPOSE MUFFLER MAN IS A POTENT IMAGE.
I KNEW YOU HAD A THING FOR HIM.
IT'S TH' IMPLIED MUFFLER!
TIPS O' TH' PIN TO: TIM MANCUSI and MIKE DICKAU
©2005 Bill Griffith. World rights reserved. Distributed by King Features Syndicate
Zippythepinhead.com

96

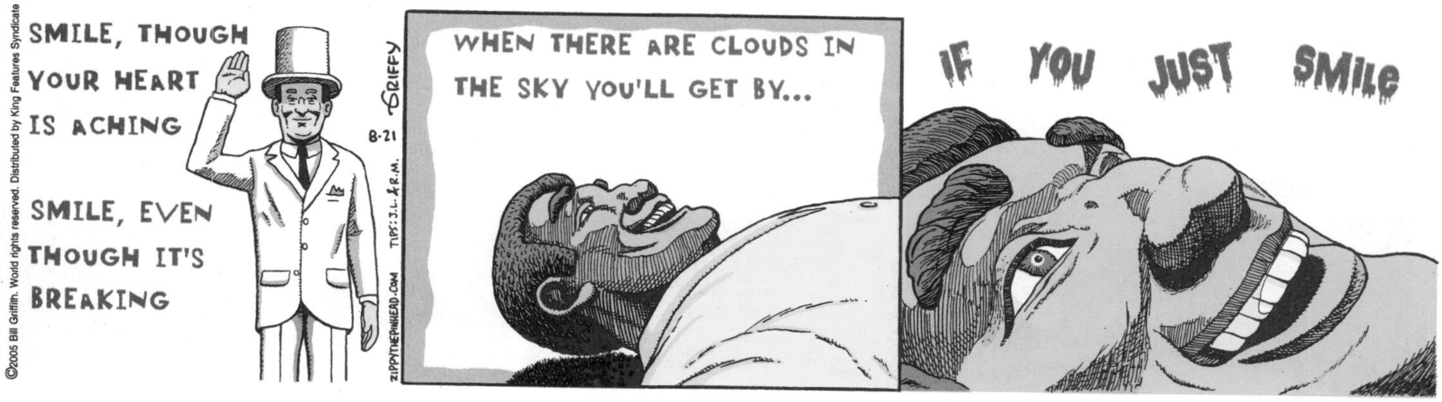
SMILE, THOUGH YOUR HEART IS ACHING
SMILE, EVEN THOUGH IT'S BREAKING
GRIFFY
8-21
TIPS: J.L. & R.M.
ZIPPYTHEPINHEAD.COM
WHEN THERE ARE CLOUDS IN THE SKY YOU'LL GET BY...
IF YOU JUST SMILE
©2005 Bill Griffith. World rights reserved. Distributed by King Features Syndicate

97

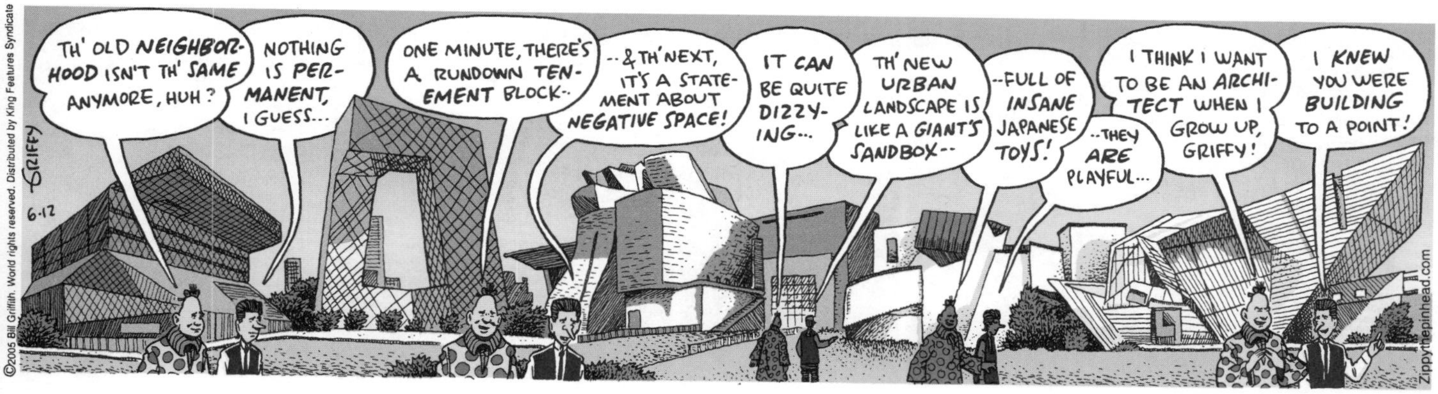
TH' OLD NEIGHBORHOOD ISN'T TH' SAME ANYMORE, HUH?
NOTHING IS PERMANENT, I GUESS...
ONE MINUTE, THERE'S A RUNDOWN TENEMENT BLOCK..
..& TH' NEXT, IT'S A STATEMENT ABOUT NEGATIVE SPACE!
IT CAN BE QUITE DIZZYING...
TH' NEW URBAN LANDSCAPE IS LIKE A GIANT'S SANDBOX--
--FULL OF INSANE JAPANESE TOYS!
..THEY ARE PLAYFUL...
I THINK I WANT TO BE AN ARCHITECT WHEN I GROW UP, GRIFFY!
I KNEW YOU WERE BUILDING TO A POINT!
GRIFFY
6-12
Zippythepinhead.com
©2005 Bill Griffith. World rights reserved. Distributed by King Features Syndicate

98

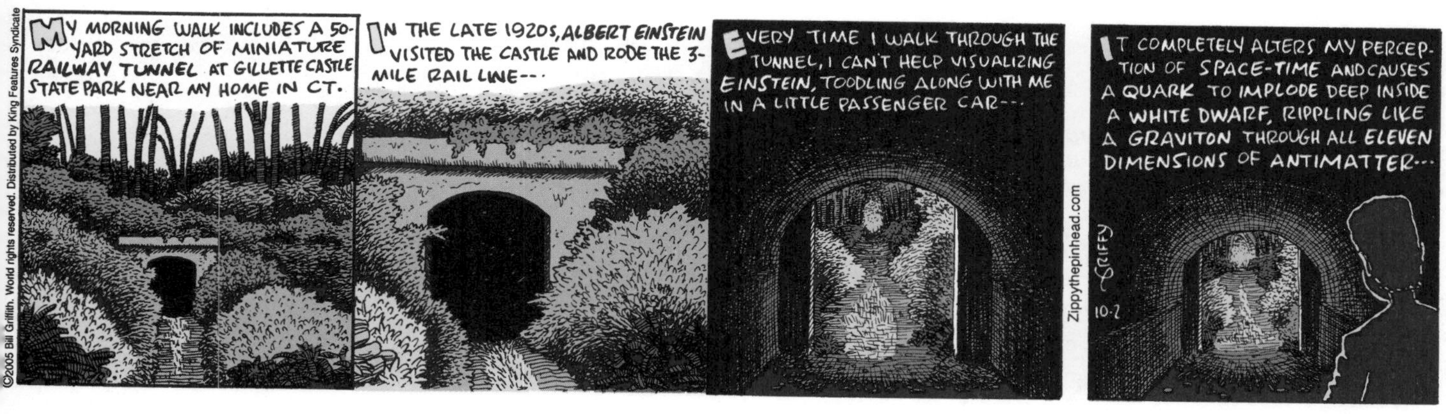
MY MORNING WALK INCLUDES A 50-YARD STRETCH OF MINIATURE RAILWAY TUNNEL AT GILLETTE CASTLE STATE PARK NEAR MY HOME IN CT.
IN THE LATE 1920s, ALBERT EINSTEIN VISITED THE CASTLE AND RODE THE 3-MILE RAIL LINE---
EVERY TIME I WALK THROUGH THE TUNNEL, I CAN'T HELP VISUALIZING EINSTEIN, TOODLING ALONG WITH ME IN A LITTLE PASSENGER CAR---
IT COMPLETELY ALTERS MY PERCEPTION OF SPACE-TIME AND CAUSES A QUARK TO IMPLODE DEEP INSIDE A WHITE DWARF, RIPPLING LIKE A GRAVITON THROUGH ALL ELEVEN DIMENSIONS OF ANTIMATTER---
Zippythepinhead.com
GRIFFY
10-2
©2005 Bill Griffith. World rights reserved. Distributed by King Features Syndicate

99

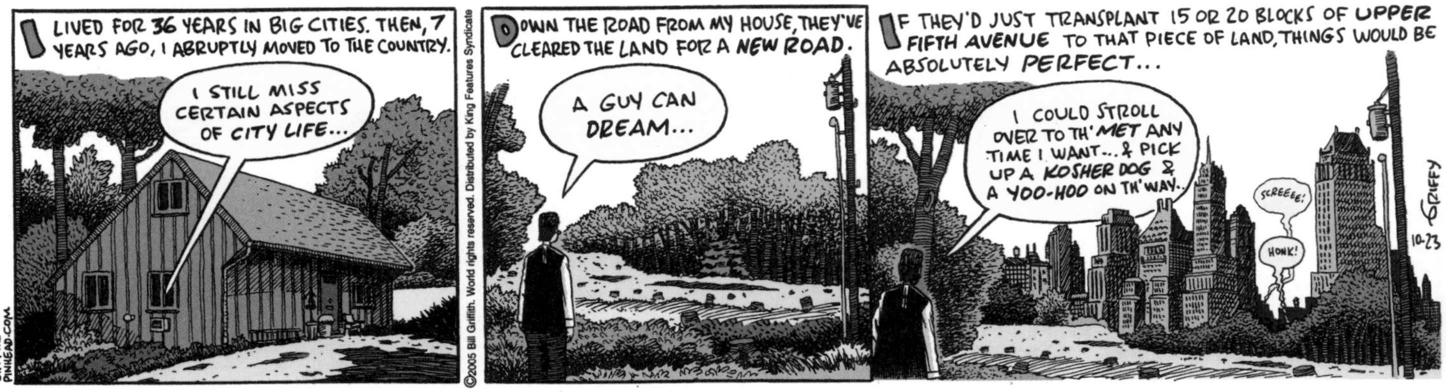
I LIVED FOR 36 YEARS IN BIG CITIES. THEN, 7 YEARS AGO, I ABRUPTLY MOVED TO THE COUNTRY.
I STILL MISS CERTAIN ASPECTS OF CITY LIFE...
ZIPPYTHEPINHEAD.COM
©2005 Bill Griffith. World rights reserved. Distributed by King Features Syndicate
DOWN THE ROAD FROM MY HOUSE, THEY'VE CLEARED THE LAND FOR A NEW ROAD.
A GUY CAN DREAM...
IF THEY'D JUST TRANSPLANT 15 OR 20 BLOCKS OF UPPER FIFTH AVENUE TO THAT PIECE OF LAND, THINGS WOULD BE ABSOLUTELY PERFECT...
I COULD STROLL OVER TO TH' MET ANY TIME I WANT... & PICK UP A KOSHER DOG & A YOO-HOO ON TH' WAY.
SCREEEE!
HONK!
GRIFFY
10-23

100

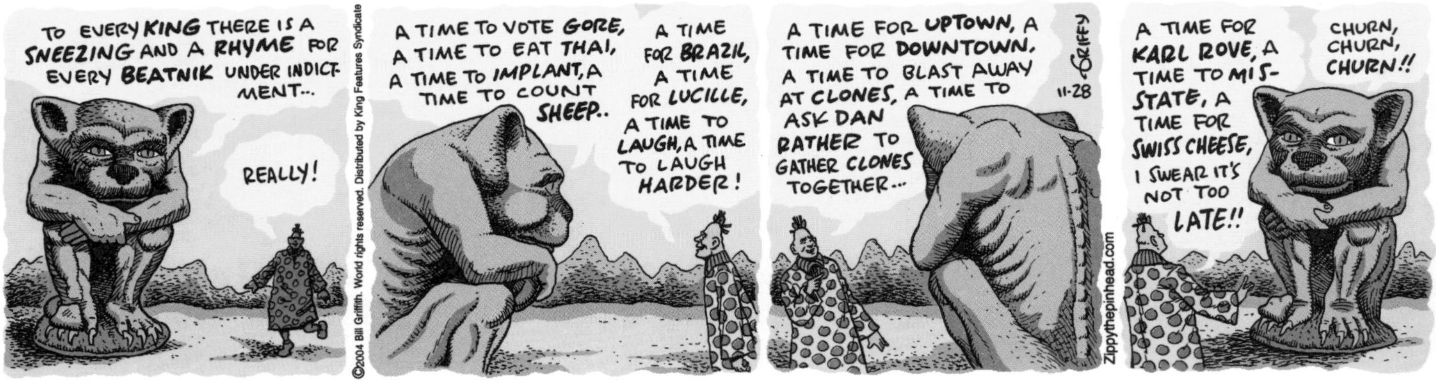
TO EVERY KING THERE IS A SNEEZING AND A RHYME FOR EVERY BEATNIK UNDER INDICT-MENT...
REALLY!
©2004 Bill Griffith. World rights reserved. Distributed by King Features Syndicate
A TIME TO VOTE GORE, A TIME TO EAT THAI, A TIME TO IMPLANT, A TIME TO COUNT SHEEP..
A TIME FOR BRAZIL, A TIME FOR LUCILLE, A TIME TO LAUGH, A TIME TO LAUGH HARDER!
A TIME FOR UPTOWN, A TIME FOR DOWNTOWN, A TIME TO BLAST AWAY AT CLONES, A TIME TO ASK DAN RATHER TO GATHER CLONES TOGETHER...
GRIFFY
11-28
Zippythepinhead.com
A TIME FOR KARL ROVE, A TIME TO MIS-STATE, A TIME FOR SWISS CHEESE, I SWEAR IT'S NOT TOO LATE!!
CHURN, CHURN, CHURN!!

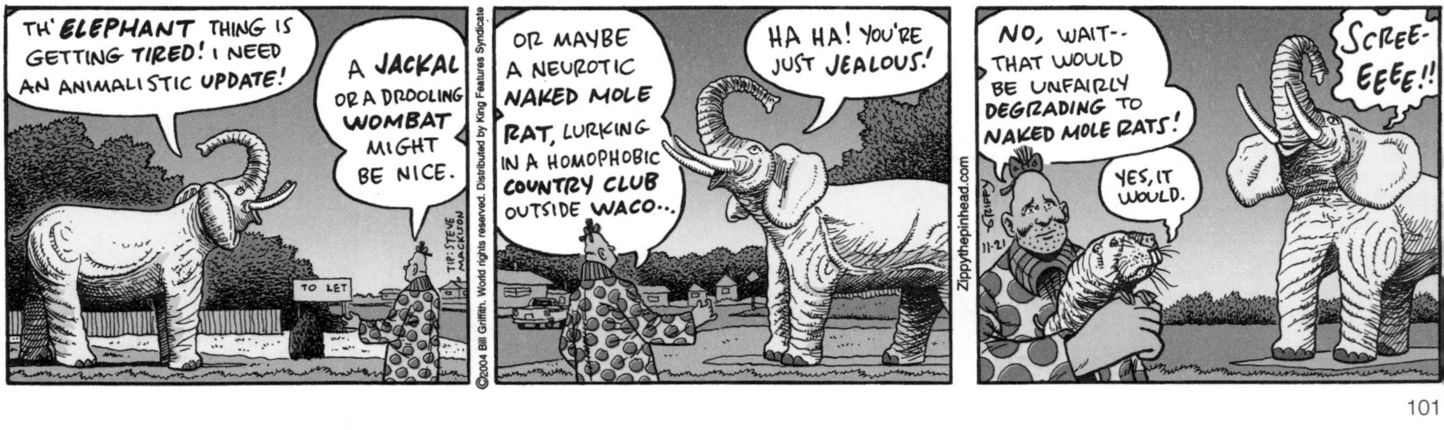
TH' ELEPHANT THING IS GETTING TIRED! I NEED AN ANIMALISTIC UPDATE!
A JACKAL OR A DROOLING WOMBAT MIGHT BE NICE.
TIP: STEVE MACKLOW
TO LET
©2004 Bill Griffith. World rights reserved. Distributed by King Features Syndicate
OR MAYBE A NEUROTIC NAKED MOLE RAT, LURKING IN A HOMOPHOBIC COUNTRY CLUB OUTSIDE WACO...
HA HA! YOU'RE JUST JEALOUS!
Zippythepinhead.com
NO, WAIT-- THAT WOULD BE UNFAIRLY DEGRADING TO NAKED MOLE RATS!
YES, IT WOULD.
SCREE-EEEE!!
GRIFFY
11-21

101

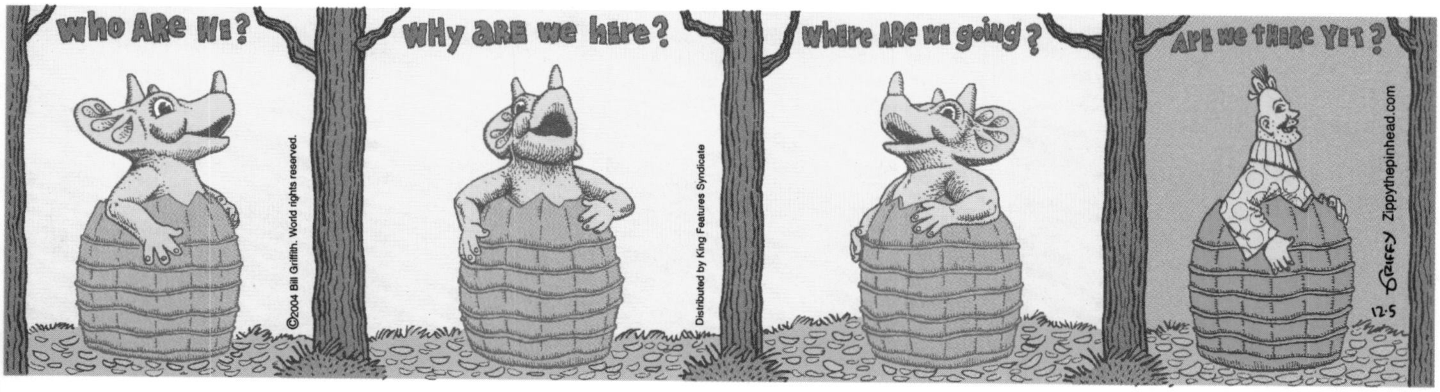
WHO ARE WE?
WHY ARE WE HERE?
WHERE ARE WE GOING?
ARE WE THERE YET?
©2004 Bill Griffith. World rights reserved.
Distributed by King Features Syndicate
Zippythepinhead.com
GRIFFY
12·5

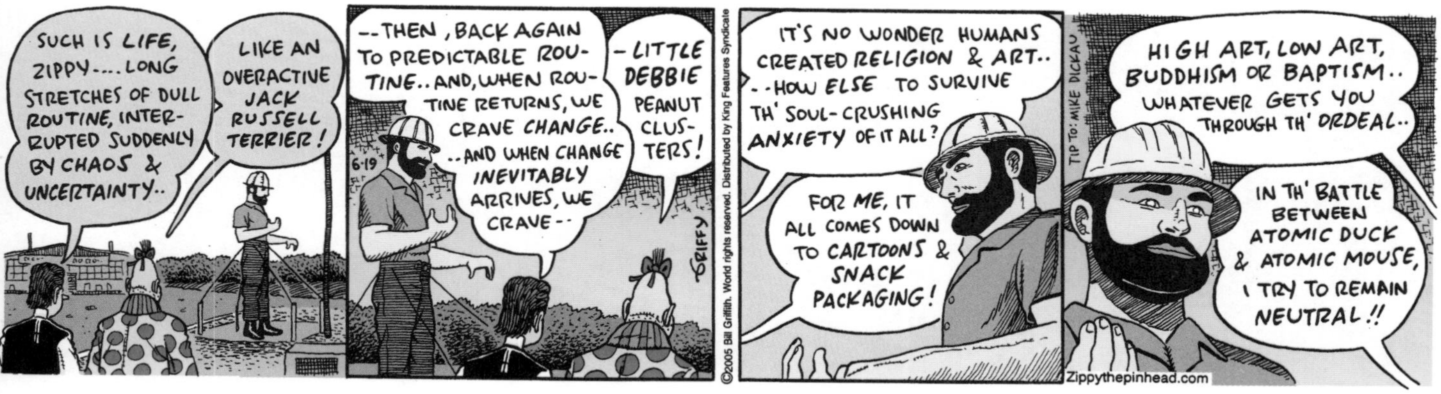
SUCH IS LIFE, ZIPPY.... LONG STRETCHES OF DULL ROUTINE, INTERRUPTED SUDDENLY BY CHAOS & UNCERTAINTY..
LIKE AN OVERACTIVE JACK RUSSELL TERRIER!
6·19
--THEN, BACK AGAIN TO PREDICTABLE ROUTINE.. AND, WHEN ROUTINE RETURNS, WE CRAVE CHANGE.. ..AND WHEN CHANGE INEVITABLY ARRIVES, WE CRAVE--
-LITTLE DEBBIE PEANUT CLUSTERS!
GRIFFY
©2005 Bill Griffith. World rights reserved. Distributed by King Features Syndicate
IT'S NO WONDER HUMANS CREATED RELIGION & ART.. --HOW ELSE TO SURVIVE TH' SOUL-CRUSHING ANXIETY OF IT ALL?
FOR ME, IT ALL COMES DOWN TO CARTOONS & SNACK PACKAGING!
TIP TO: MIKE DICKAU
HIGH ART, LOW ART, BUDDHISM OR BAPTISM.. WHATEVER GETS YOU THROUGH TH' ORDEAL..
IN TH' BATTLE BETWEEN ATOMIC DUCK & ATOMIC MOUSE, I TRY TO REMAIN NEUTRAL!!
Zippythepinhead.com

102

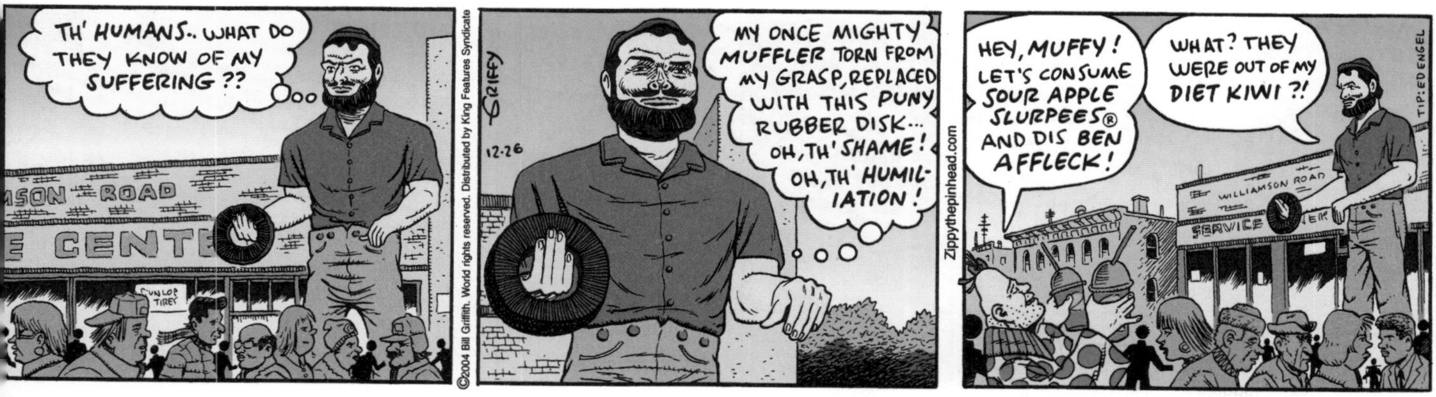
TH' HUMANS.. WHAT DO THEY KNOW OF MY SUFFERING??
ASON ROAD
E CENTE
DUNLOP TIRES
©2004 Bill Griffith. World rights reserved. Distributed by King Features Syndicate
GRIFFY
12·26
MY ONCE MIGHTY MUFFLER TORN FROM MY GRASP, REPLACED WITH THIS PUNY RUBBER DISK... OH, TH' SHAME! OH, TH' HUMILIATION!
Zippythepinhead.com
HEY, MUFFY! LET'S CONSUME SOUR APPLE SLURPEES® AND DIS BEN AFFLECK!
WHAT? THEY WERE OUT OF MY DIET KIWI?!
TIP: ED ENGEL
WILLIAMSON ROAD
SERVICE

103

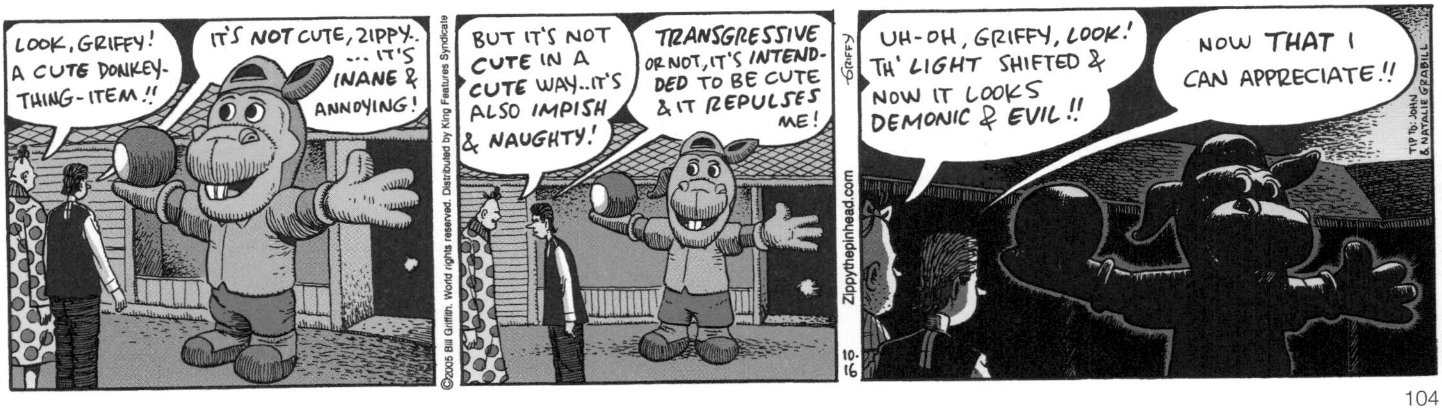

LOOK, GRIFFY! A CUTE DONKEY-THING-ITEM!!
IT'S NOT CUTE, ZIPPY... ...IT'S INANE & ANNOYING!
©2005 Bill Griffith. World rights reserved. Distributed by King Features Syndicate
BUT IT'S NOT CUTE IN A CUTE WAY..IT'S ALSO IMPISH & NAUGHTY!
TRANSGRESSIVE OR NOT, IT'S INTENDED TO BE CUTE & IT REPULSES ME!
GRIFFY
Zippythepinhead.com
10-16
UH-OH, GRIFFY, LOOK! TH' LIGHT SHIFTED & NOW IT LOOKS DEMONIC & EVIL!!
NOW THAT I CAN APPRECIATE!!
TIP TO: JOHN & NATALIE GRABILL

104

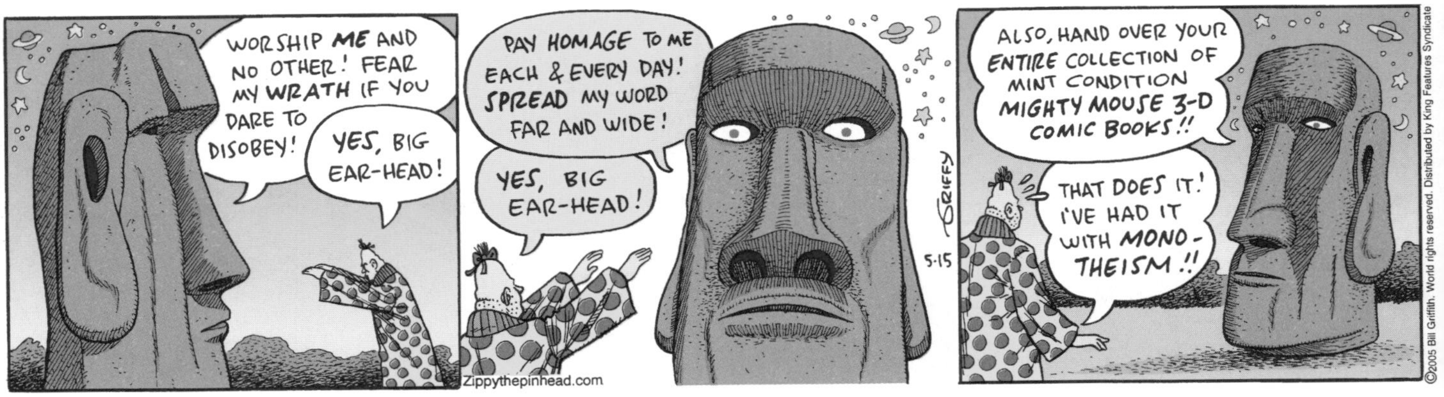

WORSHIP ME AND NO OTHER! FEAR MY WRATH IF YOU DARE TO DISOBEY!
YES, BIG EAR-HEAD!
PAY HOMAGE TO ME EACH & EVERY DAY! SPREAD MY WORD FAR AND WIDE!
YES, BIG EAR-HEAD!
Zippythepinhead.com
GRIFFY
5-15
ALSO, HAND OVER YOUR ENTIRE COLLECTION OF MINT CONDITION MIGHTY MOUSE 3-D COMIC BOOKS!!
THAT DOES IT! I'VE HAD IT WITH MONO-THEISM!!
©2005 Bill Griffith. World rights reserved. Distributed by King Features Syndicate

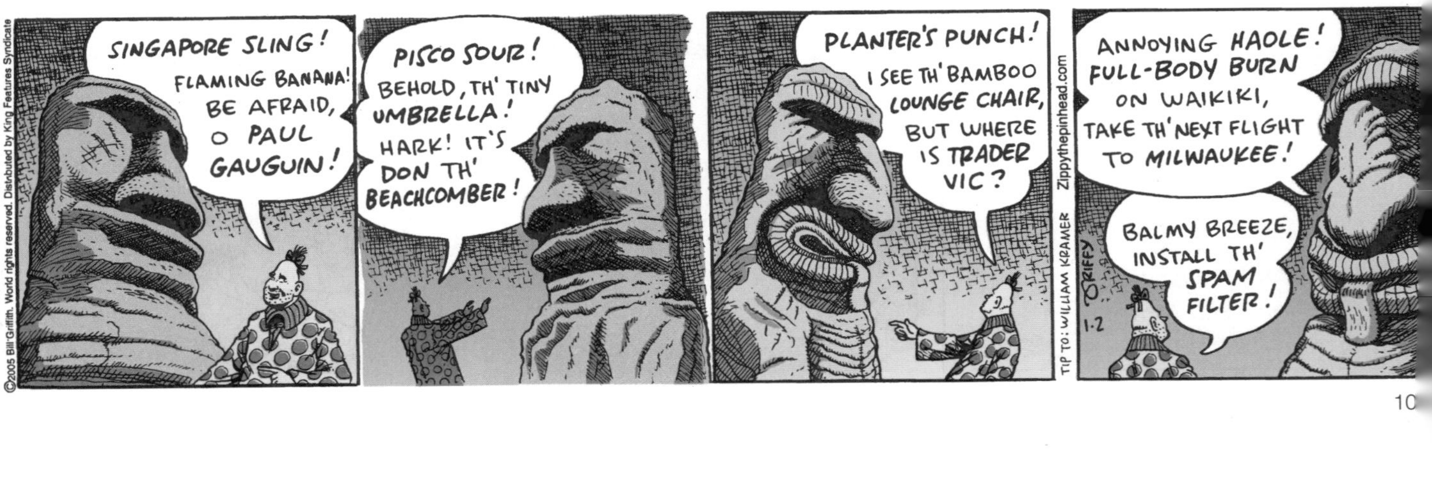

©2005 Bill Griffith. World rights reserved. Distributed by King Features Syndicate
SINGAPORE SLING!
FLAMING BANANA! BE AFRAID, O PAUL GAUGUIN!
PISCO SOUR!
BEHOLD, TH' TINY UMBRELLA! HARK! IT'S DON TH' BEACHCOMBER!
PLANTER'S PUNCH!
I SEE TH' BAMBOO LOUNGE CHAIR, BUT WHERE IS TRADER VIC?
Zippythepinhead.com
TIP TO: WILLIAM KRAMER
GRIFFY
1-2
ANNOYING HAOLE! FULL-BODY BURN ON WAIKIKI, TAKE TH' NEXT FLIGHT TO MILWAUKEE!
BALMY BREEZE, INSTALL TH' SPAM FILTER!

10

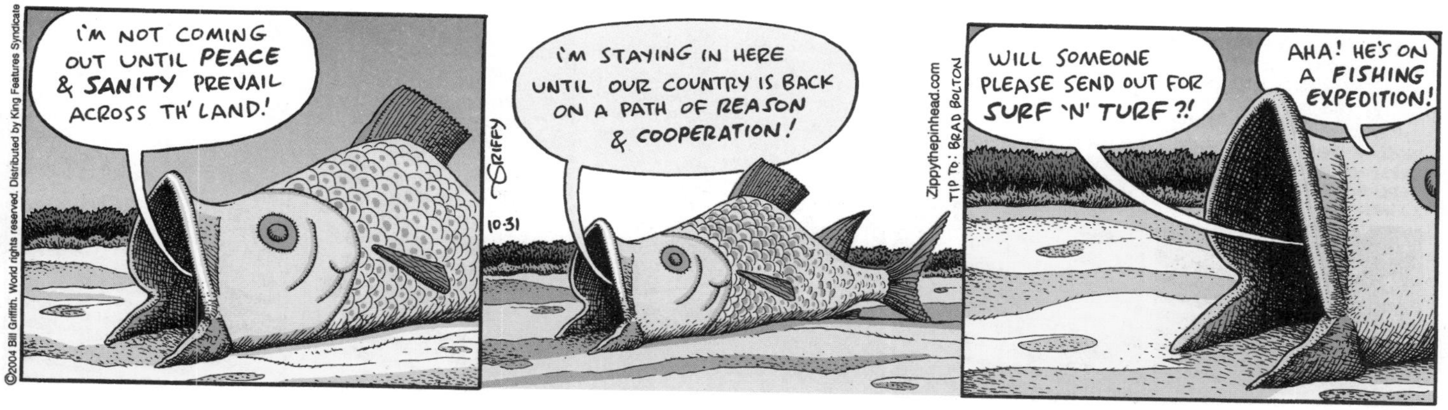
©2004 Bill Griffith. World rights reserved. Distributed by King Features Syndicate
I'M NOT COMING OUT UNTIL PEACE & SANITY PREVAIL ACROSS TH' LAND!
I'M STAYING IN HERE UNTIL OUR COUNTRY IS BACK ON A PATH OF REASON & COOPERATION!
GRIFFY
10·31
Zippythepinhead.com
TIP TO: BRAD BOLTON
WILL SOMEONE PLEASE SEND OUT FOR SURF 'N' TURF?!
AHA! HE'S ON A FISHING EXPEDITION!

106

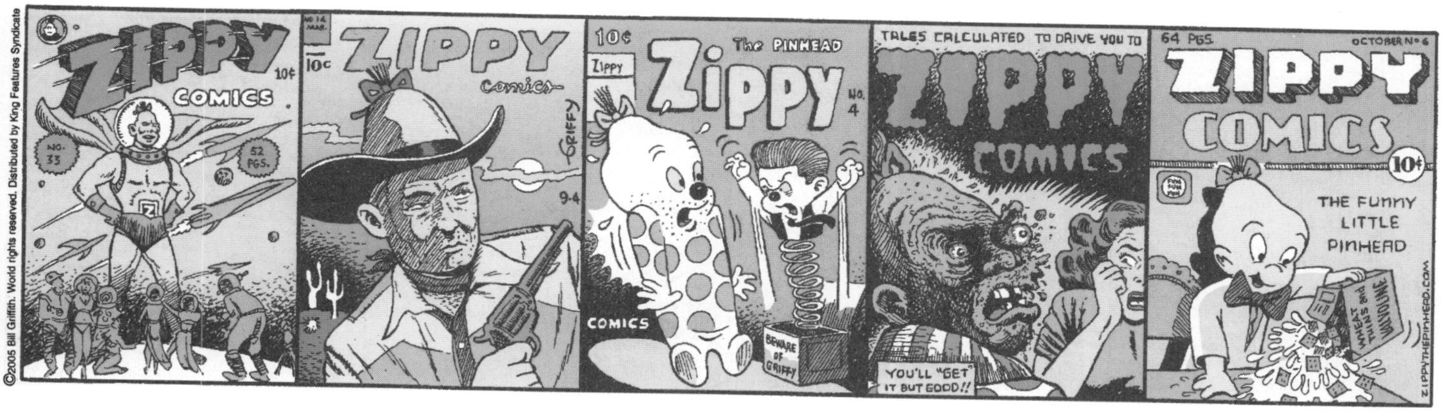
©2005 Bill Griffith. World rights reserved. Distributed by King Features Syndicate
ZIPPY
COMICS
10¢
NO. 33
52 PGS.
ZIPPY
10¢
Comics
GRIFFY
9·4
10¢
The PINHEAD
ZIPPY
NO. 4
COMICS
BEWARE OF GRIFFY
TALES CALCULATED TO DRIVE YOU TO
ZIPPY
COMICS
YOU'LL "GET" IT BUT GOOD!!
64 PGS.
OCTOBER No 6
ZIPPY
COMICS
10¢
THE FUNNY LITTLE PINHEAD
ZIPPYTHEPINHEAD.COM

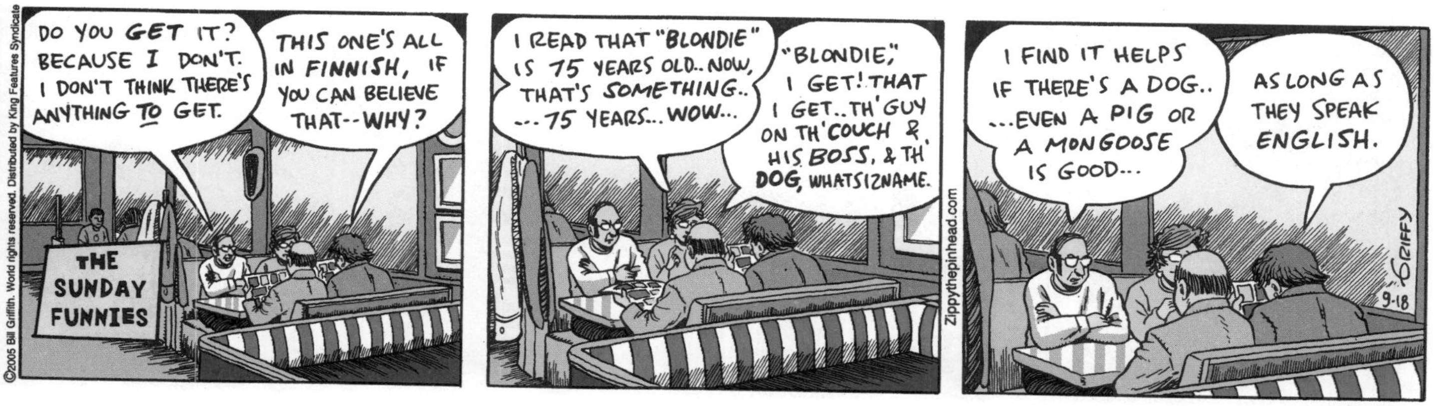
©2005 Bill Griffith. World rights reserved. Distributed by King Features Syndicate
DO YOU GET IT? BECAUSE I DON'T. I DON'T THINK THERE'S ANYTHING TO GET.
THIS ONE'S ALL IN FINNISH, IF YOU CAN BELIEVE THAT--WHY?
THE SUNDAY FUNNIES
I READ THAT "BLONDIE" IS 75 YEARS OLD.. NOW, THAT'S SOMETHING.. ...75 YEARS... WOW...
"BLONDIE," I GET! THAT I GET.. TH' GUY ON TH' COUCH & HIS BOSS, & TH' DOG, WHATSIZNAME.
Zippythepinhead.com
I FIND IT HELPS IF THERE'S A DOG.. ...EVEN A PIG OR A MONGOOSE IS GOOD...
AS LONG AS THEY SPEAK ENGLISH.
GRIFFY
9·18

107

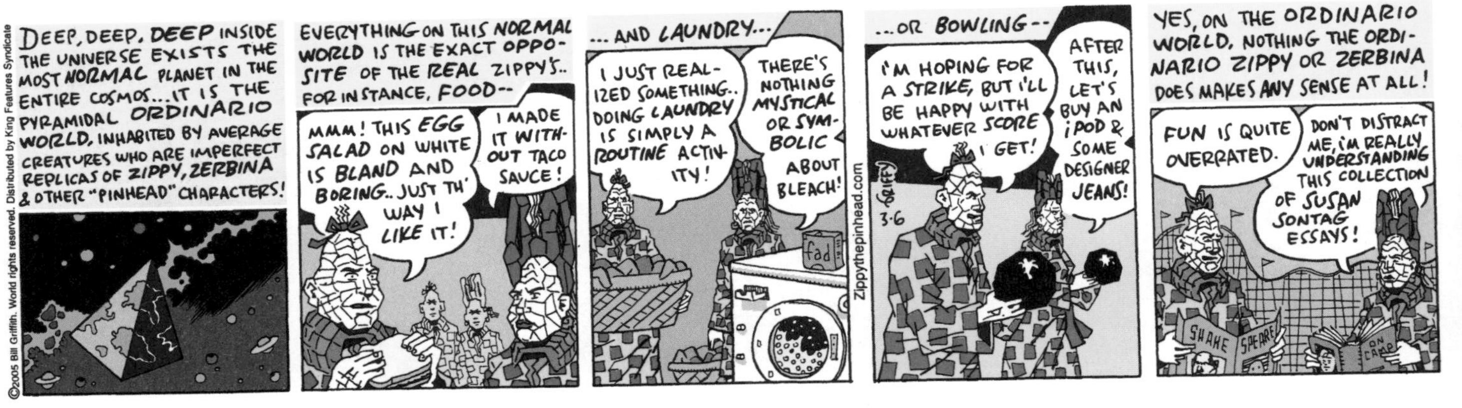

©2005 Bill Griffith. World rights reserved. Distributed by King Features Syndicate
DEEP, DEEP, DEEP INSIDE THE UNIVERSE EXISTS THE MOST NORMAL PLANET IN THE ENTIRE COSMOS... IT IS THE PYRAMIDAL ORDINARIO WORLD, INHABITED BY AVERAGE CREATURES WHO ARE IMPERFECT REPLICAS OF ZIPPY, ZERBINA & OTHER "PINHEAD" CHARACTERS!
EVERYTHING ON THIS NORMAL WORLD IS THE EXACT OPPOSITE OF THE REAL ZIPPY'S.. FOR INSTANCE, FOOD--
MMM! THIS EGG SALAD ON WHITE IS BLAND AND BORING.. JUST TH' WAY I LIKE IT!
I MADE IT WITHOUT TACO SAUCE!
... AND LAUNDRY...
I JUST REALIZED SOMETHING.. DOING LAUNDRY IS SIMPLY A ROUTINE ACTIVITY!
THERE'S NOTHING MYSTICAL OR SYMBOLIC ABOUT BLEACH!
fad
Zippythepinhead.com
GRIFFY 3-6
...OR BOWLING--
I'M HOPING FOR A STRIKE, BUT I'LL BE HAPPY WITH WHATEVER SCORE I GET!
AFTER THIS, LET'S BUY AN iPOD & SOME DESIGNER JEANS!
YES, ON THE ORDINARIO WORLD, NOTHING THE ORDINARIO ZIPPY OR ZERBINA DOES MAKES ANY SENSE AT ALL!
FUN IS QUITE OVERRATED.
DON'T DISTRACT ME, I'M REALLY UNDERSTANDING THIS COLLECTION OF SUSAN SONTAG ESSAYS!
SHAKE SPEARE
ON CAMP

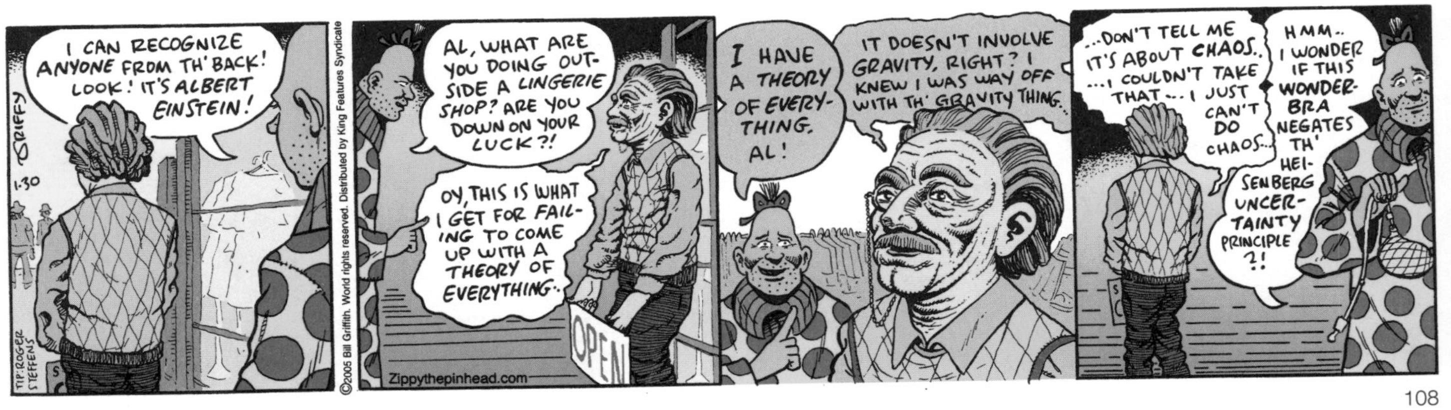

I CAN RECOGNIZE ANYONE FROM TH' BACK! LOOK! IT'S ALBERT EINSTEIN!
GRIFFY 1-30
TIP: ROGER STEFFENS
©2005 Bill Griffith. World rights reserved. Distributed by King Features Syndicate
AL, WHAT ARE YOU DOING OUTSIDE A LINGERIE SHOP? ARE YOU DOWN ON YOUR LUCK?!
OY, THIS IS WHAT I GET FOR FAILING TO COME UP WITH A THEORY OF EVERYTHING..
OPEN
Zippythepinhead.com
I HAVE A THEORY OF EVERYTHING, AL!
IT DOESN'T INVOLVE GRAVITY, RIGHT? I KNEW I WAS WAY OFF WITH TH' GRAVITY THING..
..DON'T TELL ME IT'S ABOUT CHAOS. ..I COULDN'T TAKE THAT... I JUST CAN'T DO CHAOS..
HMM.. I WONDER IF THIS WONDERBRA NEGATES TH' HEISENBERG UNCERTAINTY PRINCIPLE?!

108

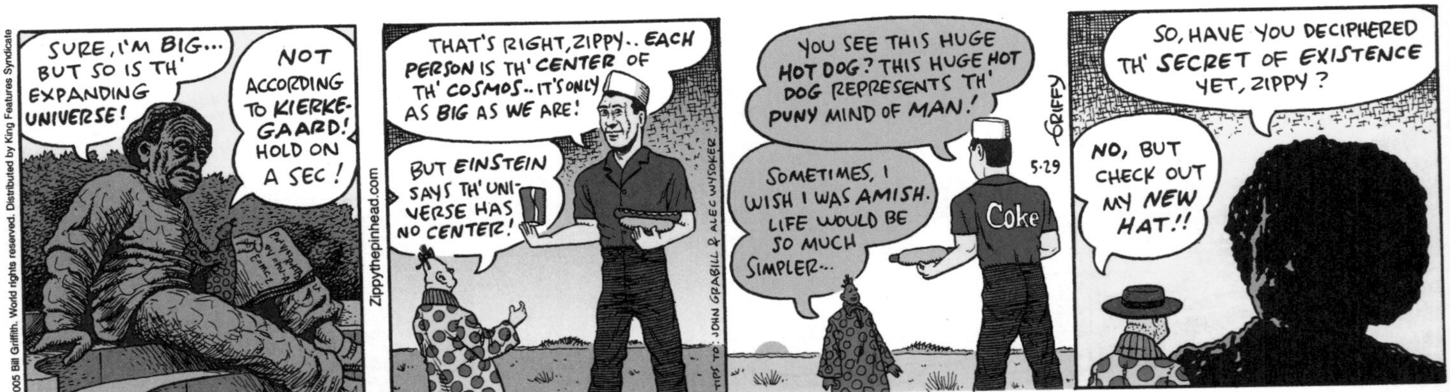

©2005 Bill Griffith. World rights reserved. Distributed by King Features Syndicate
SURE, I'M BIG... BUT SO IS TH' EXPANDING UNIVERSE!
NOT ACCORDING TO KIERKEGAARD! HOLD ON A SEC!
Zippythepinhead.com
THAT'S RIGHT, ZIPPY.. EACH PERSON IS TH' CENTER OF TH' COSMOS.. IT'S ONLY AS BIG AS WE ARE!
BUT EINSTEIN SAYS TH' UNIVERSE HAS NO CENTER!
TIPS TO: JOHN GRABILL & ALEC WYSOKER
YOU SEE THIS HUGE HOT DOG? THIS HUGE HOT DOG REPRESENTS TH' PUNY MIND OF MAN!
SOMETIMES, I WISH I WAS AMISH. LIFE WOULD BE SO MUCH SIMPLER...
Coke
GRIFFY 5-29
SO, HAVE YOU DECIPHERED TH' SECRET OF EXISTENCE YET, ZIPPY?
NO, BUT CHECK OUT MY NEW HAT!!

109

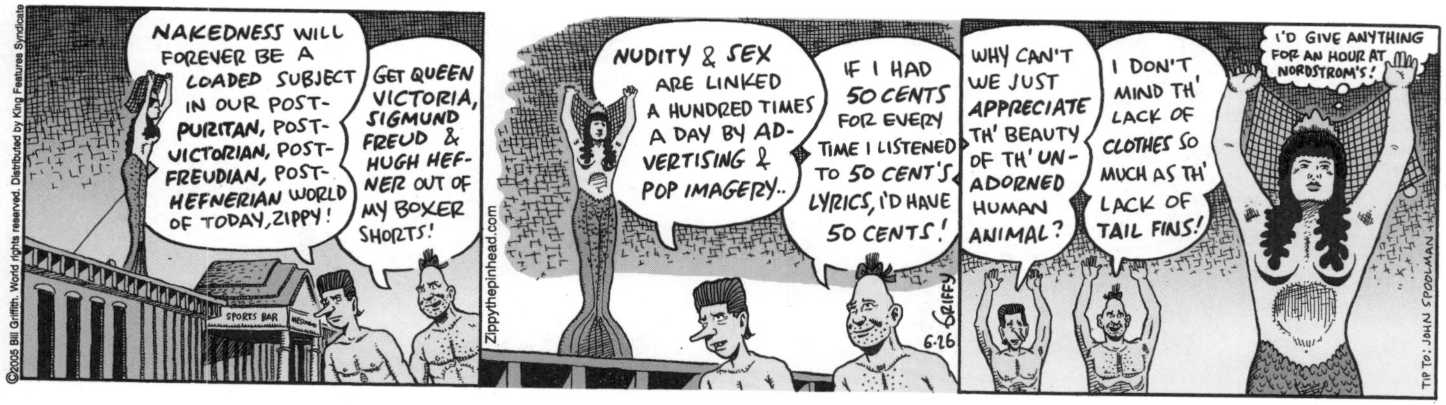
NAKEDNESS WILL FOREVER BE A LOADED SUBJECT IN OUR POST-PURITAN, POST-VICTORIAN, POST-FREUDIAN, POST-HEFNERIAN WORLD OF TODAY, ZIPPY!
GET QUEEN VICTORIA, SIGMUND FREUD & HUGH HEFNER OUT OF MY BOXER SHORTS!
SPORTS BAR
NUDITY & SEX ARE LINKED A HUNDRED TIMES A DAY BY ADVERTISING & POP IMAGERY..
IF I HAD 50 CENTS FOR EVERY TIME I LISTENED TO 50 CENT'S LYRICS, I'D HAVE 50 CENTS!
WHY CAN'T WE JUST APPRECIATE TH' BEAUTY OF TH' UNADORNED HUMAN ANIMAL?
I DON'T MIND TH' LACK OF CLOTHES SO MUCH AS TH' LACK OF TAIL FINS!
I'D GIVE ANYTHING FOR AN HOUR AT NORDSTROM'S!
©2005 Bill Griffith. World rights reserved. Distributed by King Features Syndicate
Zippythepinhead.com
GRIFFY 6-26
TIP TO: JOHN SPOOLMAN

110

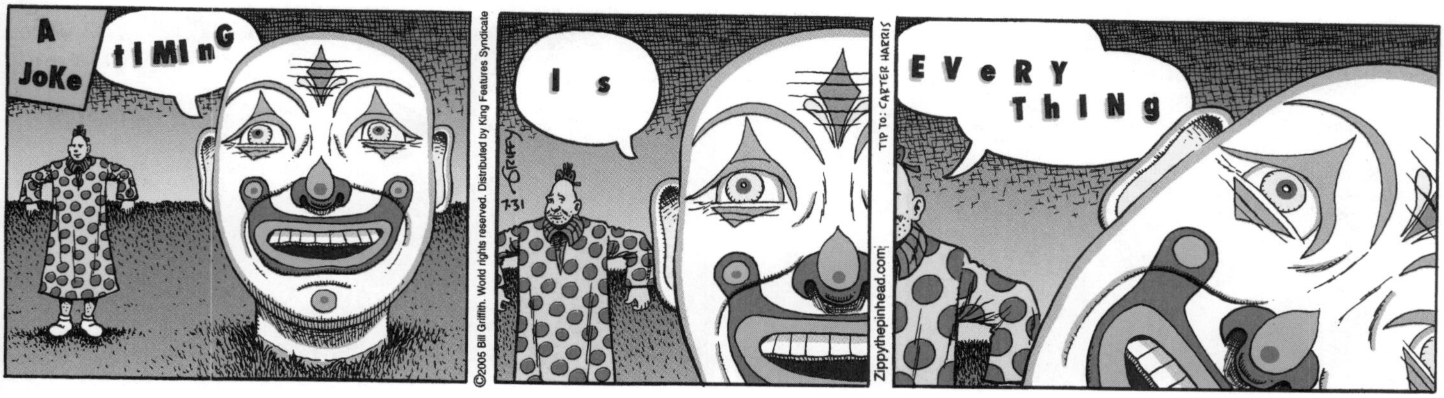
A JoKe
tIMInG
Is
EVeRY ThInG
©2005 Bill Griffith. World rights reserved. Distributed by King Features Syndicate
GRIFFY 7-31
TIP TO: CARTER HARRIS
Zippythepinhead.com

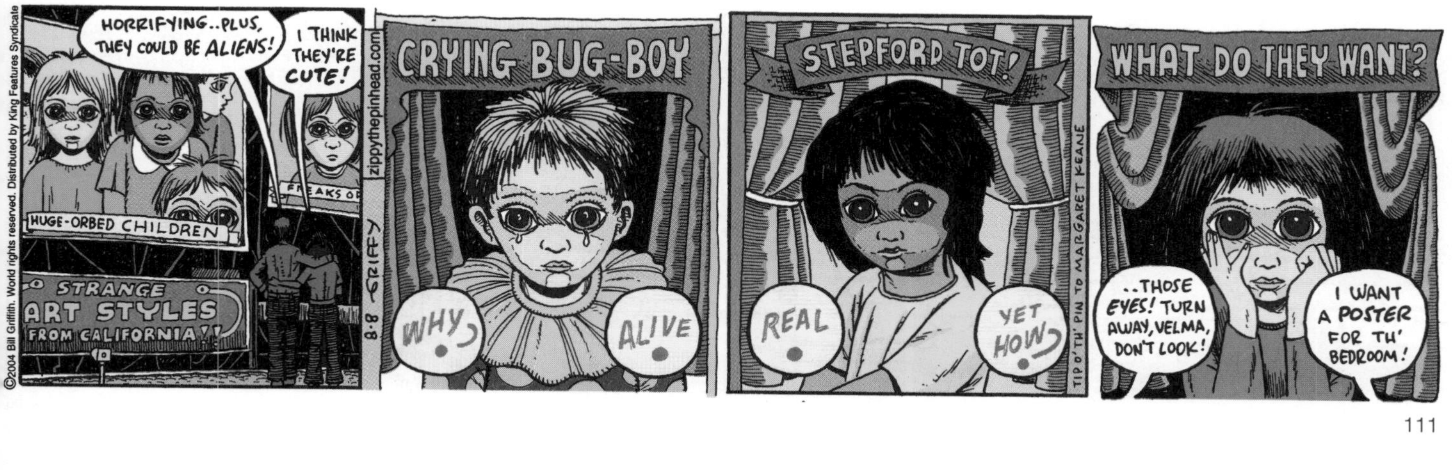
HORRIFYING..PLUS, THEY COULD BE ALIENS!
I THINK THEY'RE CUTE!
HUGE-ORBED CHILDREN
FREAKS OF
STRANGE ART STYLES FROM CALIFORNIA!!
©2004 Bill Griffith. World rights reserved. Distributed by King Features Syndicate
zippythepinhead.com
GRIFFY 8-8
CRYING BUG-BOY
WHY
ALIVE
STEPFORD TOT!
REAL
YET HOW
TIP O' TH' PIN TO MARGARET KEANE
WHAT DO THEY WANT?
..THOSE EYES! TURN AWAY, VELMA, DON'T LOOK!
I WANT A POSTER FOR TH' BEDROOM!

111

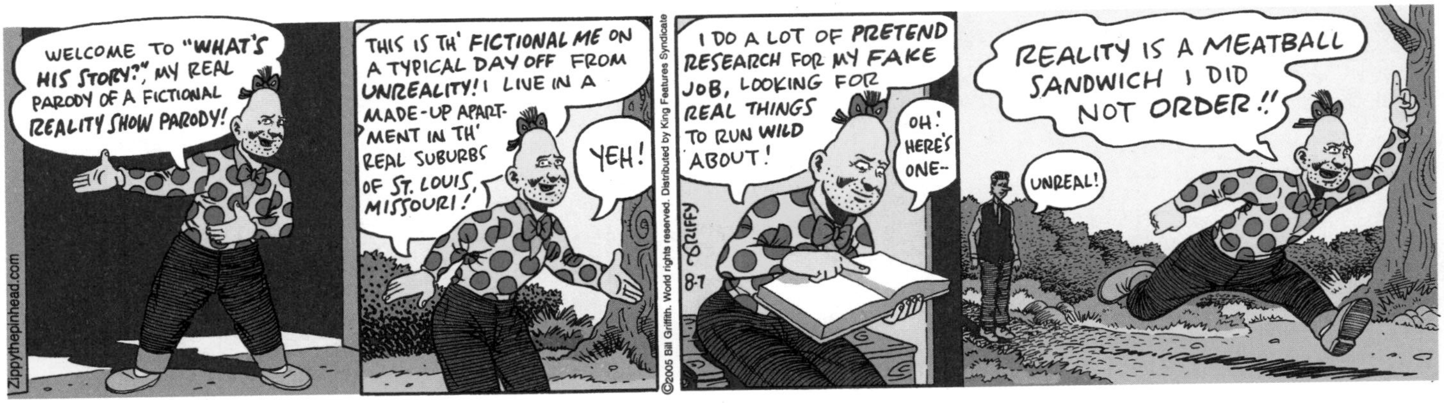
Zippythepinhead.com
WELCOME TO "WHAT'S HIS STORY?," MY REAL PARODY OF A FICTIONAL REALITY SHOW PARODY!
THIS IS TH' FICTIONAL ME ON A TYPICAL DAY OFF FROM UNREALITY! I LIVE IN A MADE-UP APARTMENT IN TH' REAL SUBURBS OF ST. LOUIS, MISSOURI!
YEH!
©2005 Bill Griffith. World rights reserved. Distributed by King Features Syndicate
I DO A LOT OF PRETEND RESEARCH FOR MY FAKE JOB, LOOKING FOR REAL THINGS TO RUN WILD ABOUT!
OH! HERE'S ONE--
GRIFFY
8-7
REALITY IS A MEATBALL SANDWICH I DID NOT ORDER!!
UNREAL!

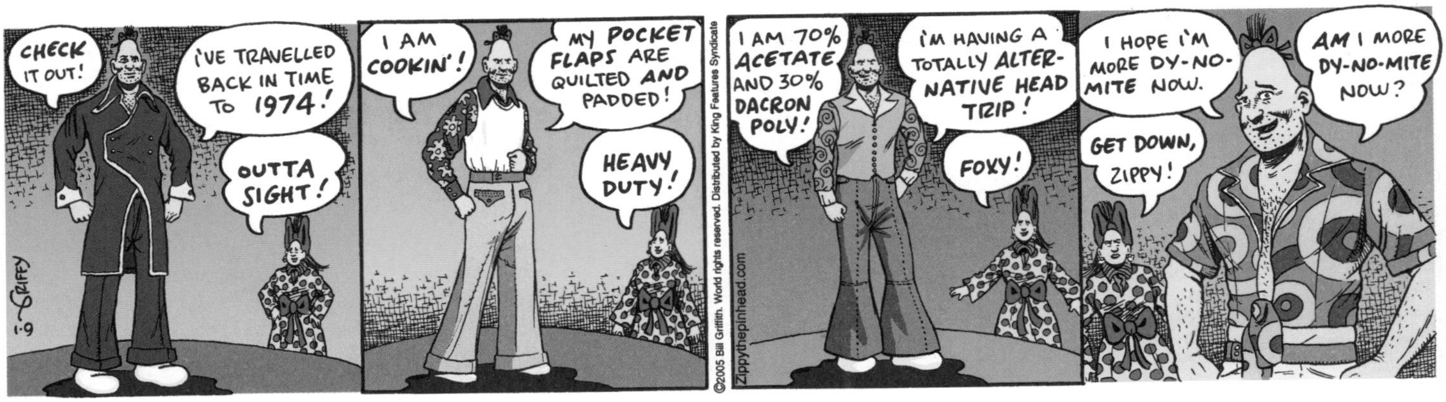
CHECK IT OUT!
I'VE TRAVELLED BACK IN TIME TO 1974!
OUTTA SIGHT!
GRIFFY
1-9
I AM COOKIN'!
MY POCKET FLAPS ARE QUILTED AND PADDED!
HEAVY DUTY!
©2005 Bill Griffith. World rights reserved. Distributed by King Features Syndicate
Zippythepinhead.com
I AM 70% ACETATE AND 30% DACRON POLY!
I'M HAVING A TOTALLY ALTERNATIVE HEAD TRIP!
FOXY!
I HOPE I'M MORE DY-NO-MITE NOW.
AM I MORE DY-NO-MITE NOW?
GET DOWN, ZIPPY!

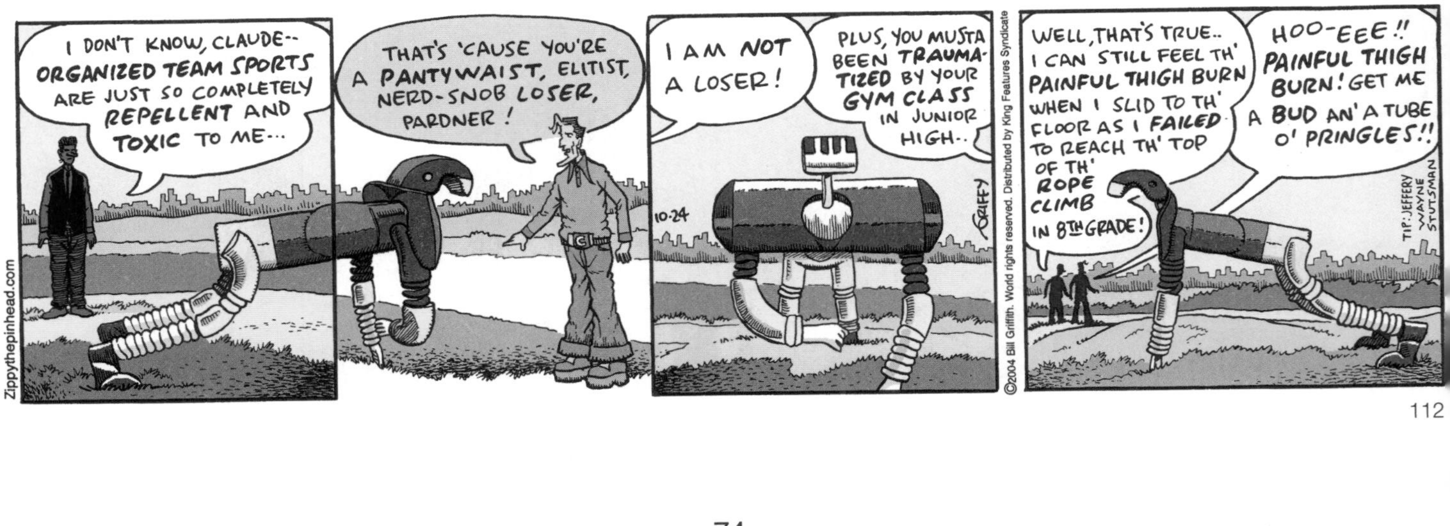
Zippythepinhead.com
I DON'T KNOW, CLAUDE-- ORGANIZED TEAM SPORTS ARE JUST SO COMPLETELY REPELLENT AND TOXIC TO ME...
THAT'S 'CAUSE YOU'RE A PANTYWAIST, ELITIST, NERD-SNOB LOSER, PARDNER!
I AM NOT A LOSER!
PLUS, YOU MUSTA BEEN TRAUMATIZED BY YOUR GYM CLASS IN JUNIOR HIGH..
10-24
GRIFFY
©2004 Bill Griffith. World rights reserved. Distributed by King Features Syndicate
WELL, THAT'S TRUE.. I CAN STILL FEEL TH' PAINFUL THIGH BURN WHEN I SLID TO TH' FLOOR AS I FAILED TO REACH TH' TOP OF TH' ROPE CLIMB IN 8TH GRADE!
HOO-EEE!! PAINFUL THIGH BURN! GET ME A BUD AN' A TUBE O' PRINGLES!!
TIP: JEFFERY WAYNE STUTSMAN

112

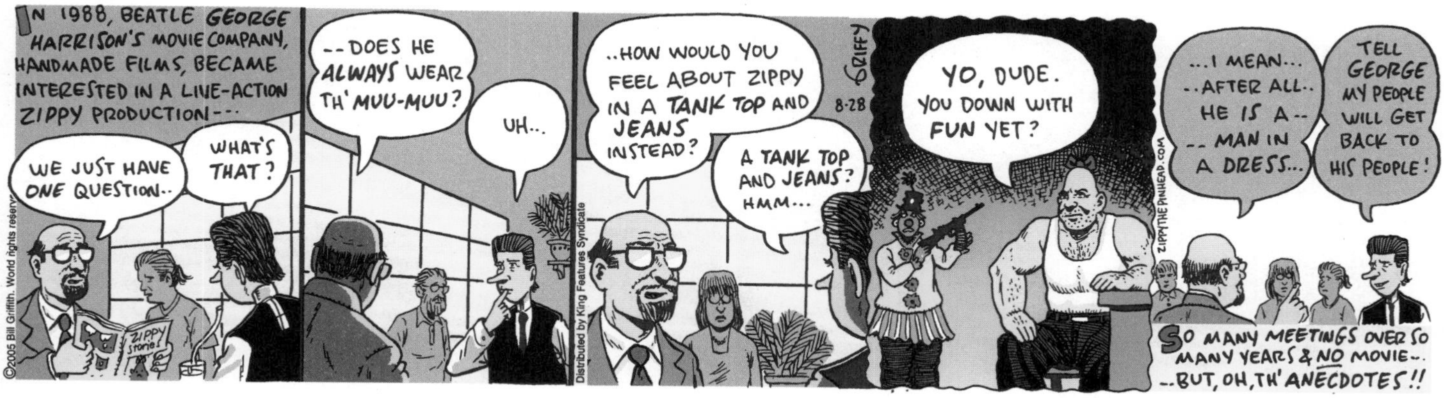
IN 1988, BEATLE GEORGE HARRISON'S MOVIE COMPANY, HANDMADE FILMS, BECAME INTERESTED IN A LIVE-ACTION ZIPPY PRODUCTION--
WE JUST HAVE ONE QUESTION..
WHAT'S THAT?
ZIPPY stories
--DOES HE ALWAYS WEAR TH' MUU-MUU?
UH...
..HOW WOULD YOU FEEL ABOUT ZIPPY IN A TANK TOP AND JEANS INSTEAD?
A TANK TOP AND JEANS? HMM...
GRIFFY 8-28
YO, DUDE. YOU DOWN WITH FUN YET?
...I MEAN... ..AFTER ALL.. HE IS A-- -- MAN IN A DRESS...
TELL GEORGE MY PEOPLE WILL GET BACK TO HIS PEOPLE!
SO MANY MEETINGS OVER SO MANY YEARS & NO MOVIE.. --BUT, OH, TH' ANECDOTES!!
©2005 Bill Griffith. World rights reserved.
Distributed by King Features Syndicate
ZIPPYTHEPINHEAD.COM

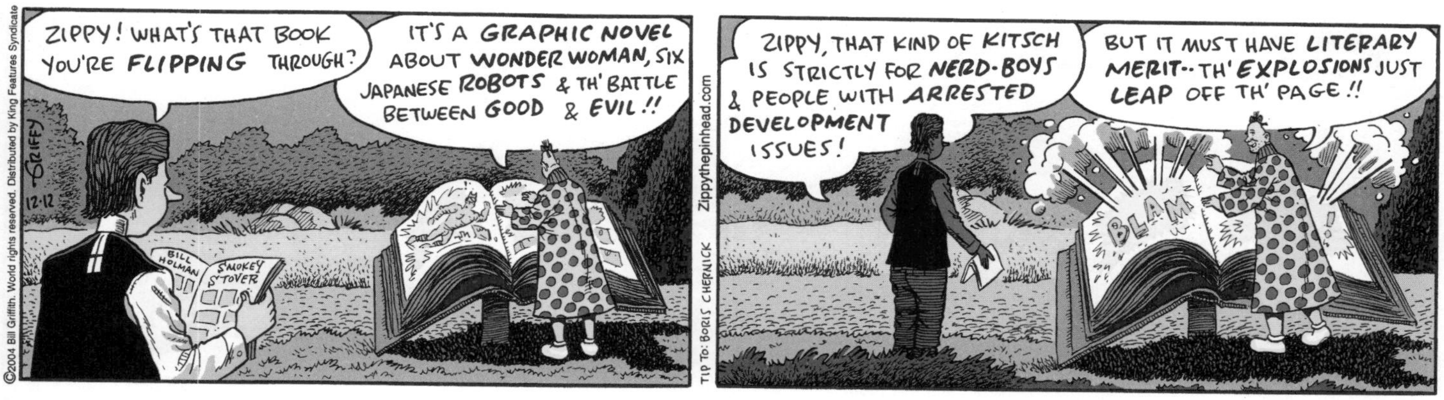
ZIPPY! WHAT'S THAT BOOK YOU'RE FLIPPING THROUGH?
IT'S A GRAPHIC NOVEL ABOUT WONDER WOMAN, SIX JAPANESE ROBOTS & TH' BATTLE BETWEEN GOOD & EVIL!!
GRIFFY 12-12
BILL HOLMAN SMOKEY STOVER
ZIPPY, THAT KIND OF KITSCH IS STRICTLY FOR NERD-BOYS & PEOPLE WITH ARRESTED DEVELOPMENT ISSUES!
BUT IT MUST HAVE LITERARY MERIT-- TH' EXPLOSIONS JUST LEAP OFF TH' PAGE!!
BLAM
©2004 Bill Griffith. World rights reserved. Distributed by King Features Syndicate
TIP TO: BORIS CHERNICK
Zippythepinhead.com

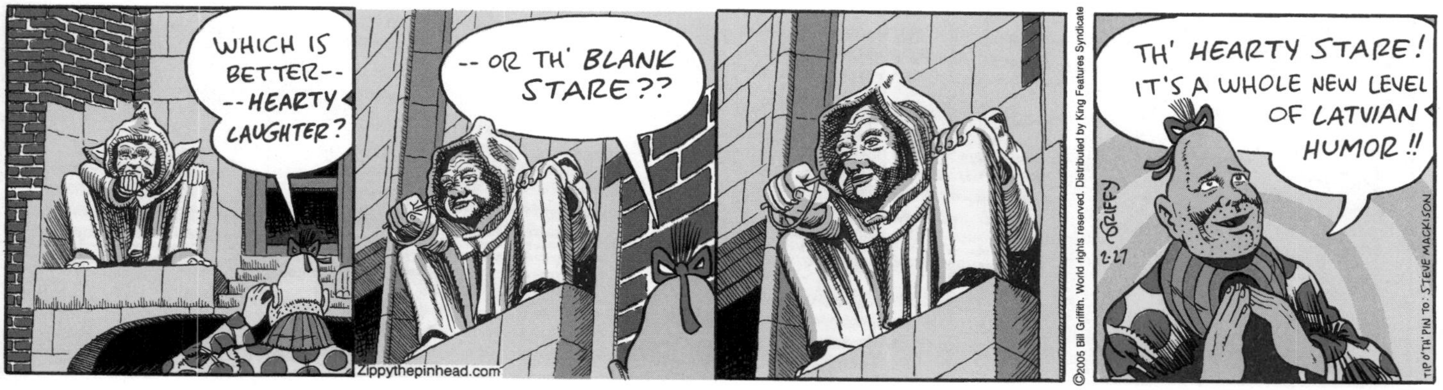
WHICH IS BETTER-- --HEARTY LAUGHTER?
-- OR TH' BLANK STARE??
TH' HEARTY STARE! IT'S A WHOLE NEW LEVEL OF LATVIAN HUMOR!!
GRIFFY 2-27
Zippythepinhead.com
©2005 Bill Griffith. World rights reserved. Distributed by King Features Syndicate
TIP O'TH' PIN TO: STEVE MACKISON

113

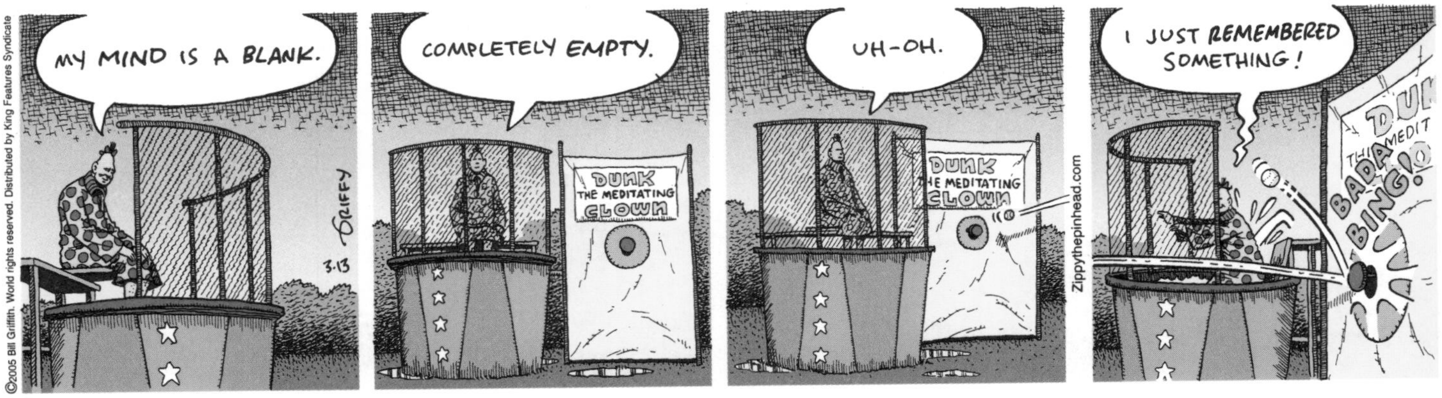
©2005 Bill Griffith. World rights reserved. Distributed by King Features Syndicate
MY MIND IS A BLANK.
GRIFFY 3-13
COMPLETELY EMPTY.
DUNK THE MEDITATING CLOWN
UH-OH.
DUNK THE MEDITATING CLOWN
Zippythepinhead.com
I JUST REMEMBERED SOMETHING!
BADA BING!

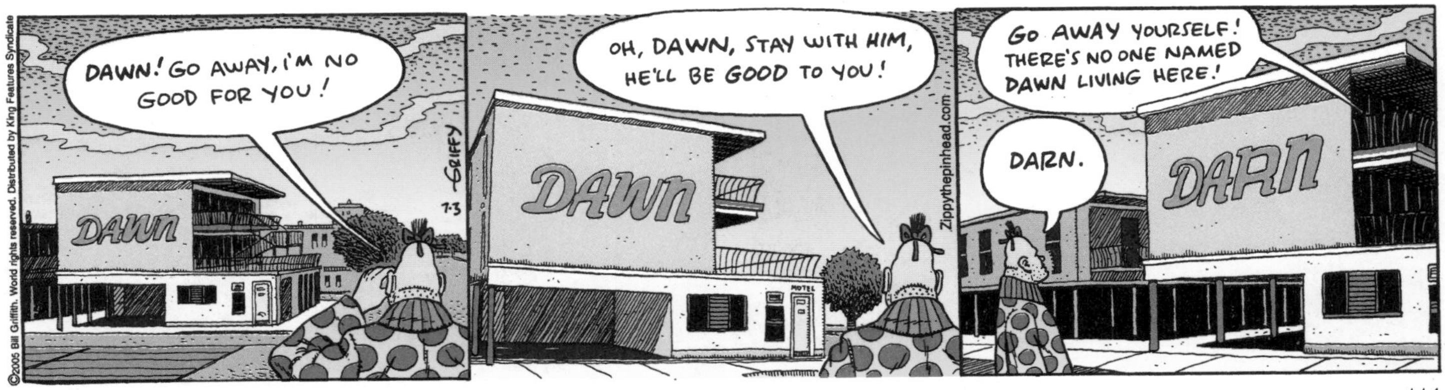
©2005 Bill Griffith. World rights reserved. Distributed by King Features Syndicate
DAWN! GO AWAY, I'M NO GOOD FOR YOU!
DAWN
GRIFFY 7-3
OH, DAWN, STAY WITH HIM, HE'LL BE GOOD TO YOU!
DAWN
MOTEL
Zippythepinhead.com
GO AWAY YOURSELF! THERE'S NO ONE NAMED DAWN LIVING HERE!
DARN.
DARN

114

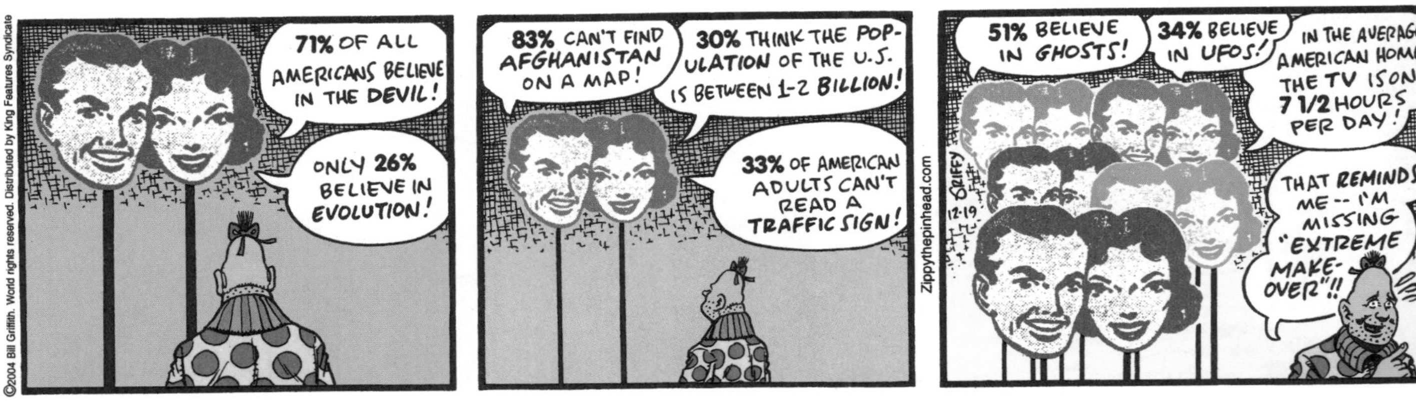
©2004 Bill Griffith. World rights reserved. Distributed by King Features Syndicate
71% OF ALL AMERICANS BELIEVE IN THE DEVIL!
ONLY 26% BELIEVE IN EVOLUTION!
83% CAN'T FIND AFGHANISTAN ON A MAP!
30% THINK THE POPULATION OF THE U.S. IS BETWEEN 1-2 BILLION!
33% OF AMERICAN ADULTS CAN'T READ A TRAFFIC SIGN!
Zippythepinhead.com
GRIFFY 12-19
51% BELIEVE IN GHOSTS!
34% BELIEVE IN UFOS!
IN THE AVERAGE AMERICAN HOME, THE TV IS ON 7 1/2 HOURS PER DAY!
THAT REMINDS ME -- I'M MISSING "EXTREME MAKE-OVER"!!

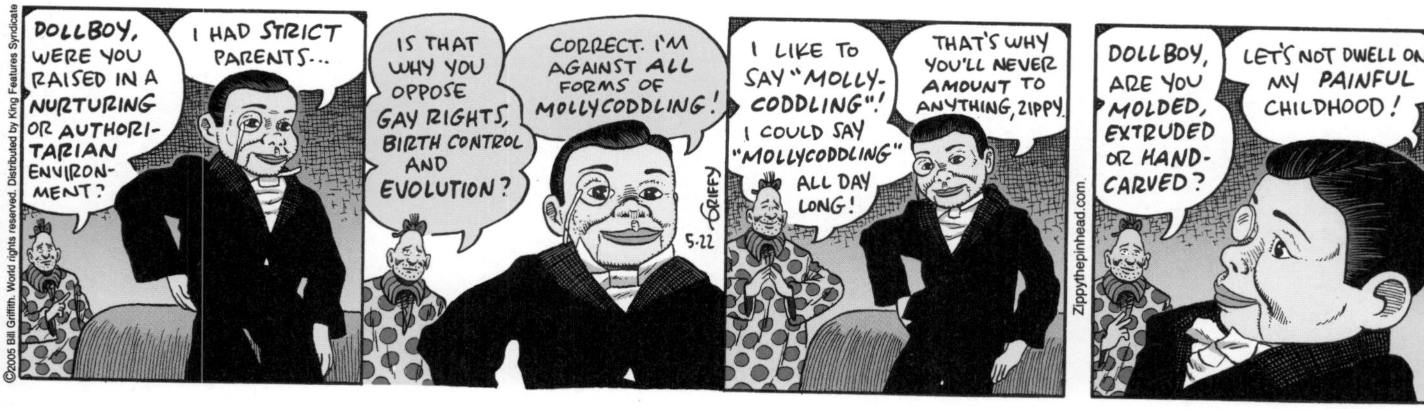
©2005 Bill Griffith. World rights reserved. Distributed by King Features Syndicate
DOLLBOY, WERE YOU RAISED IN A NURTURING OR AUTHORITARIAN ENVIRONMENT?
I HAD STRICT PARENTS...
IS THAT WHY YOU OPPOSE GAY RIGHTS, BIRTH CONTROL AND EVOLUTION?
CORRECT. I'M AGAINST ALL FORMS OF MOLLYCODDLING!
GRIFFY 5·22
I LIKE TO SAY "MOLLY-CODDLING"! I COULD SAY "MOLLYCODDLING" ALL DAY LONG!
THAT'S WHY YOU'LL NEVER AMOUNT TO ANYTHING, ZIPPY.
Zippythepinhead.com
DOLLBOY, ARE YOU MOLDED, EXTRUDED OR HAND-CARVED?
LET'S NOT DWELL ON MY PAINFUL CHILDHOOD!

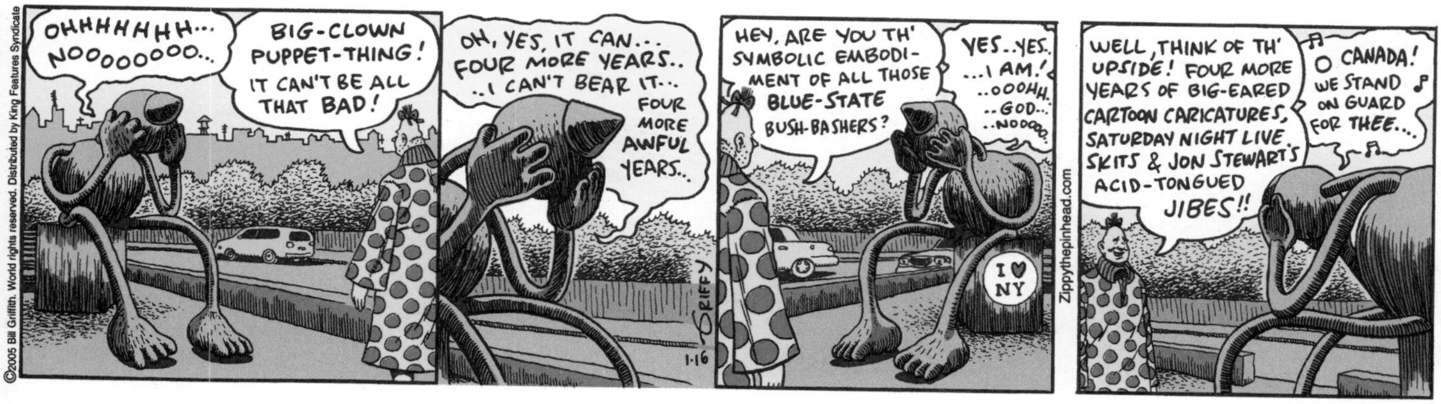
©2005 Bill Griffith. World rights reserved. Distributed by King Features Syndicate
OHHHHHHH... NOOOOOOOO...
BIG-CLOWN PUPPET-THING! IT CAN'T BE ALL THAT BAD!
OH, YES, IT CAN... FOUR MORE YEARS.. ..I CAN'T BEAR IT... FOUR MORE AWFUL YEARS..
GRIFFY 1·16
HEY, ARE YOU TH' SYMBOLIC EMBODIMENT OF ALL THOSE BLUE-STATE BUSH-BASHERS?
YES..YES.. ...I AM.! ..OOOHH.. ..GOD... ..NOOOOO.
I ♥ NY
Zippythepinhead.com
WELL, THINK OF TH' UPSIDE! FOUR MORE YEARS OF BIG-EARED CARTOON CARICATURES, SATURDAY NIGHT LIVE SKITS & JON STEWART'S ACID-TONGUED JIBES!!
O CANADA! WE STAND ON GUARD FOR THEE...

115

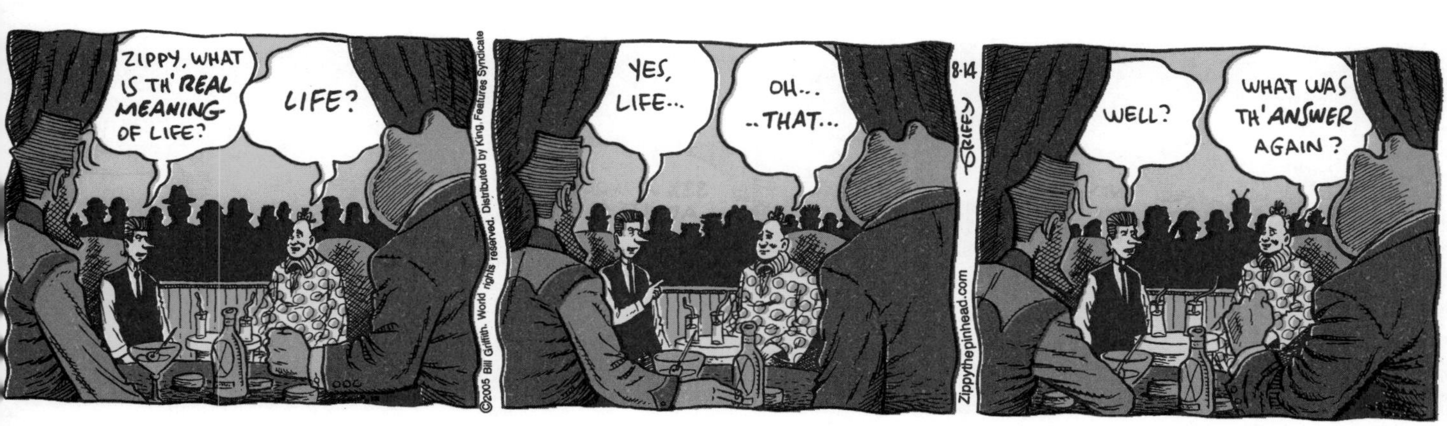
ZIPPY, WHAT IS TH' REAL MEANING OF LIFE?
LIFE?
©2005 Bill Griffith. World rights reserved. Distributed by King Features Syndicate
Zippythepinhead.com
YES, LIFE...
OH... ..THAT...
8·14 GRIFFY
WELL?
WHAT WAS TH' ANSWER AGAIN?

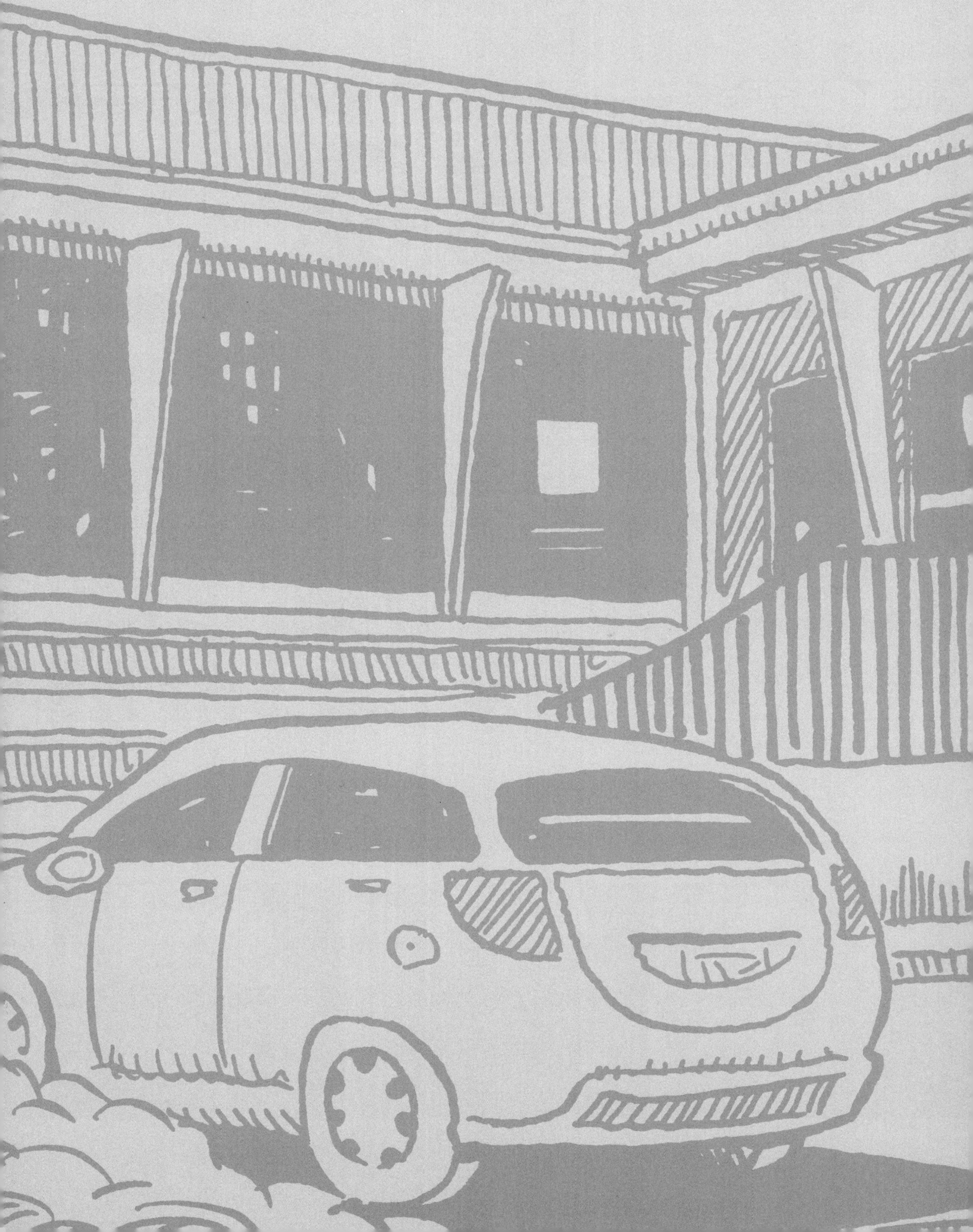

DINERAMA

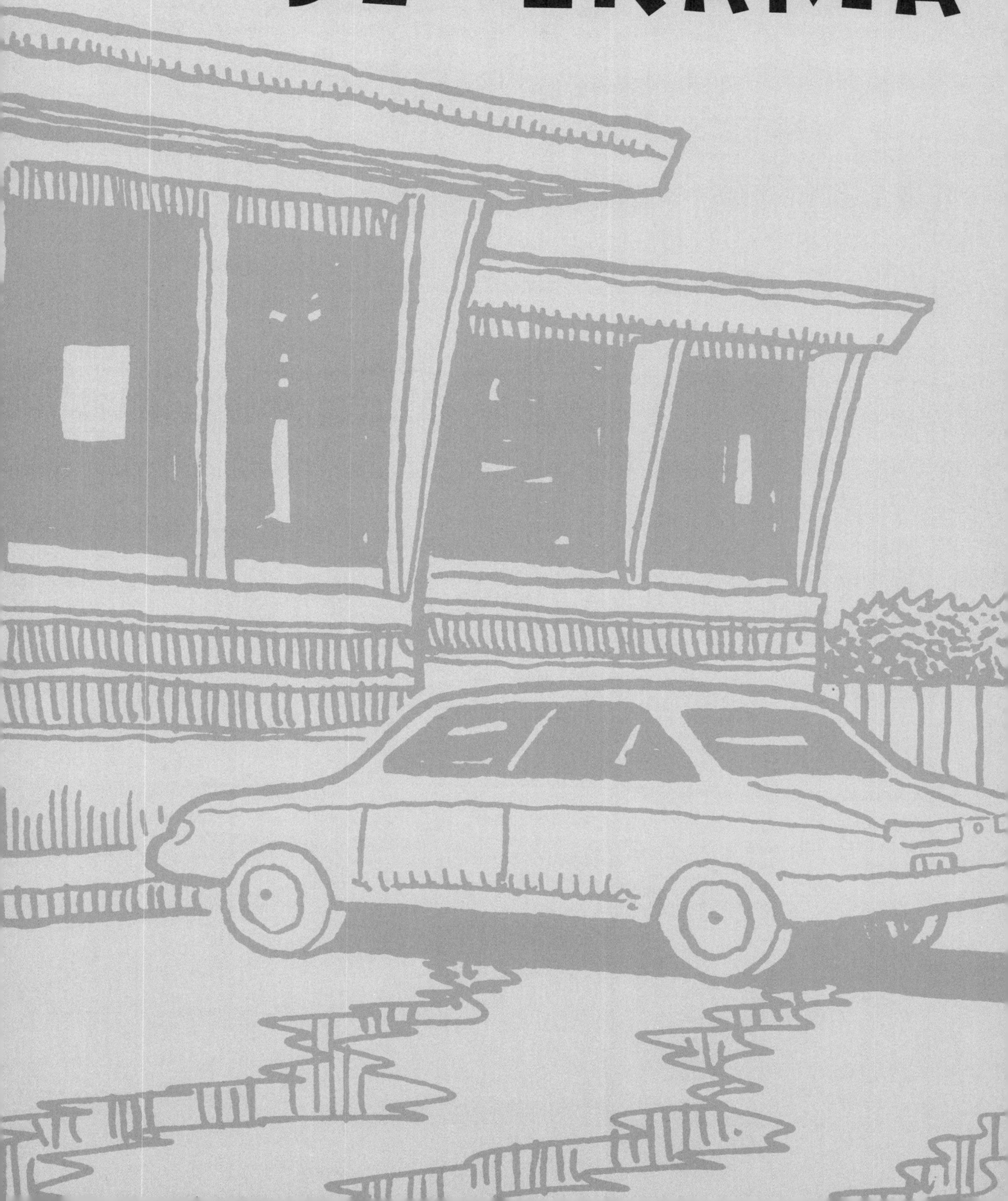

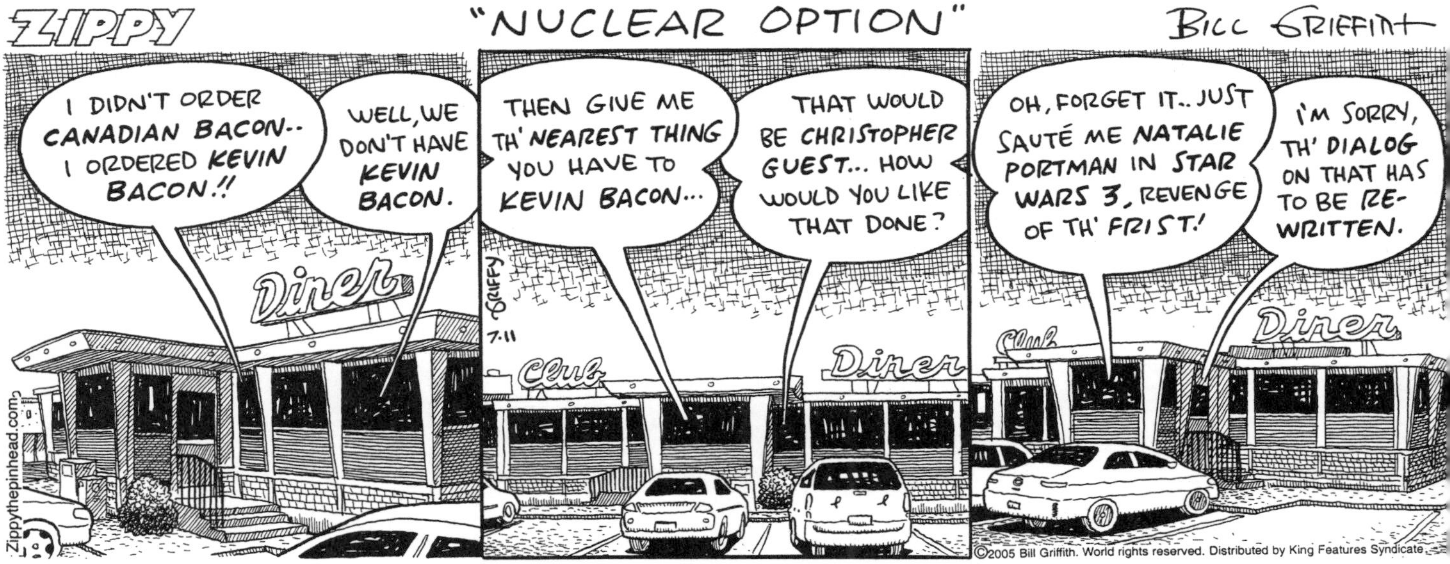
ZIPPY
"NUCLEAR OPTION"
BILL GRIFFITH
I DIDN'T ORDER CANADIAN BACON.. I ORDERED KEVIN BACON!!
WELL, WE DON'T HAVE KEVIN BACON.
THEN GIVE ME TH' NEAREST THING YOU HAVE TO KEVIN BACON...
THAT WOULD BE CHRISTOPHER GUEST... HOW WOULD YOU LIKE THAT DONE?
OH, FORGET IT.. JUST SAUTÉ ME NATALIE PORTMAN IN STAR WARS 3, REVENGE OF TH' FRIST!
I'M SORRY, TH' DIALOG ON THAT HAS TO BE RE-WRITTEN.
Diner
Club
Diner
Diner
Zippythepinhead.com
GRIFFY 7.11
©2005 Bill Griffith. World rights reserved. Distributed by King Features Syndicate

116

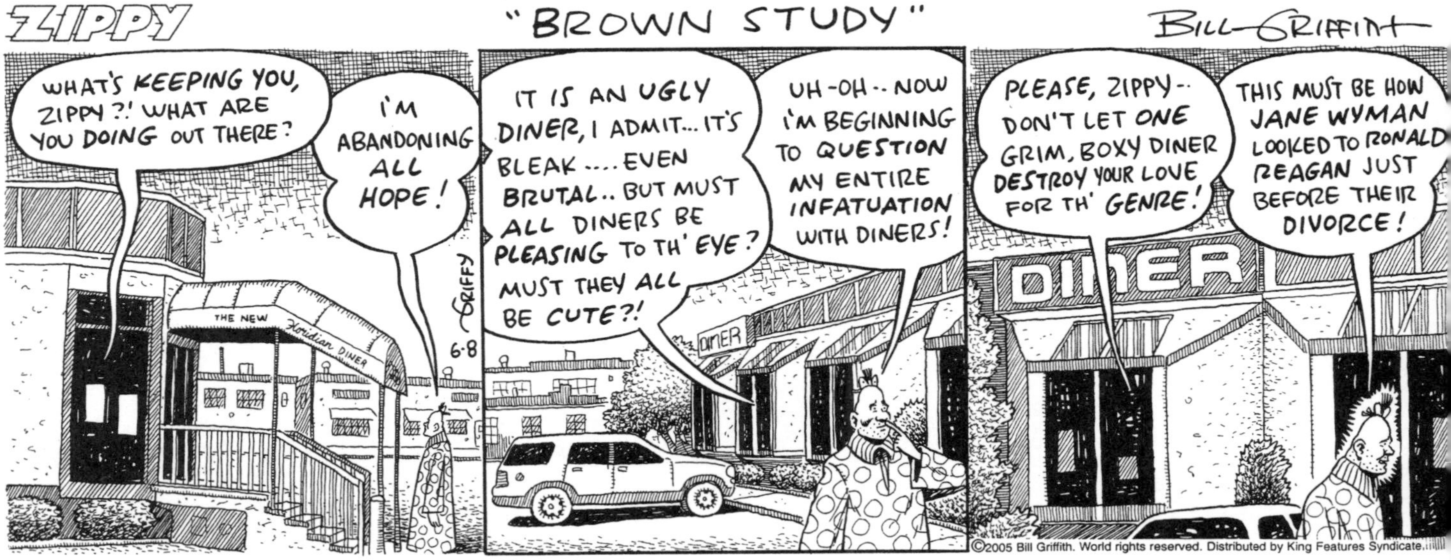
ZIPPY
"BROWN STUDY"
BILL GRIFFITH
WHAT'S KEEPING YOU, ZIPPY?! WHAT ARE YOU DOING OUT THERE?
I'M ABANDONING ALL HOPE!
IT IS AN UGLY DINER, I ADMIT... IT'S BLEAK.... EVEN BRUTAL.. BUT MUST ALL DINERS BE PLEASING TO TH' EYE? MUST THEY ALL BE CUTE?!
UH-OH.. NOW I'M BEGINNING TO QUESTION MY ENTIRE INFATUATION WITH DINERS!
PLEASE, ZIPPY.. DON'T LET ONE GRIM, BOXY DINER DESTROY YOUR LOVE FOR TH' GENRE!
THIS MUST BE HOW JANE WYMAN LOOKED TO RONALD REAGAN JUST BEFORE THEIR DIVORCE!
THE NEW Floridian DINER
DINER
DINER
GRIFFY 6.8
©2005 Bill Griffith. World rights reserved. Distributed by King Features Syndicate

117

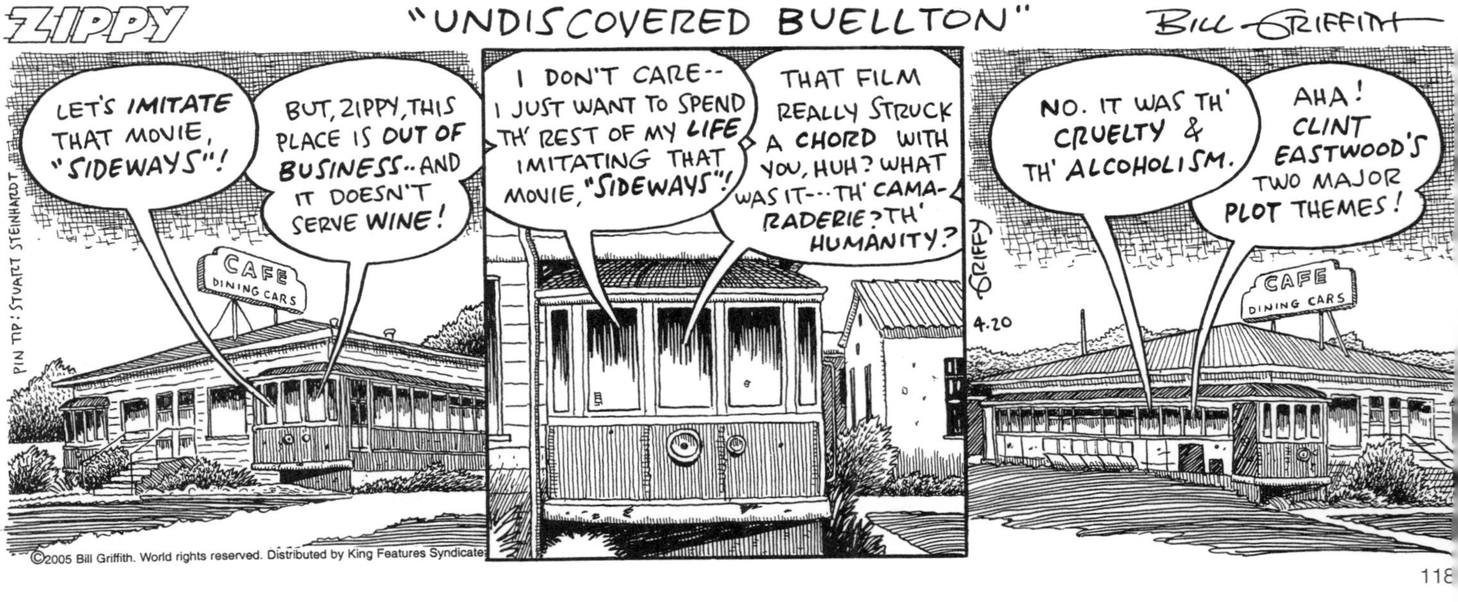
ZIPPY
"UNDISCOVERED BUELLTON"
BILL GRIFFITH
LET'S IMITATE THAT MOVIE, "SIDEWAYS"!
BUT, ZIPPY, THIS PLACE IS OUT OF BUSINESS.. AND IT DOESN'T SERVE WINE!
I DON'T CARE-- I JUST WANT TO SPEND TH' REST OF MY LIFE IMITATING THAT MOVIE, "SIDEWAYS"!
THAT FILM REALLY STRUCK A CHORD WITH YOU, HUH? WHAT WAS IT--- TH' CAMARADERIE? TH' HUMANITY?
NO. IT WAS TH' CRUELTY & TH' ALCOHOLISM.
AHA! CLINT EASTWOOD'S TWO MAJOR PLOT THEMES!
CAFE DINING CARS
CAFE DINING CARS
PIN TIP: STUART STEINHARDT
GRIFFY 4.20
©2005 Bill Griffith. World rights reserved. Distributed by King Features Syndicate

118

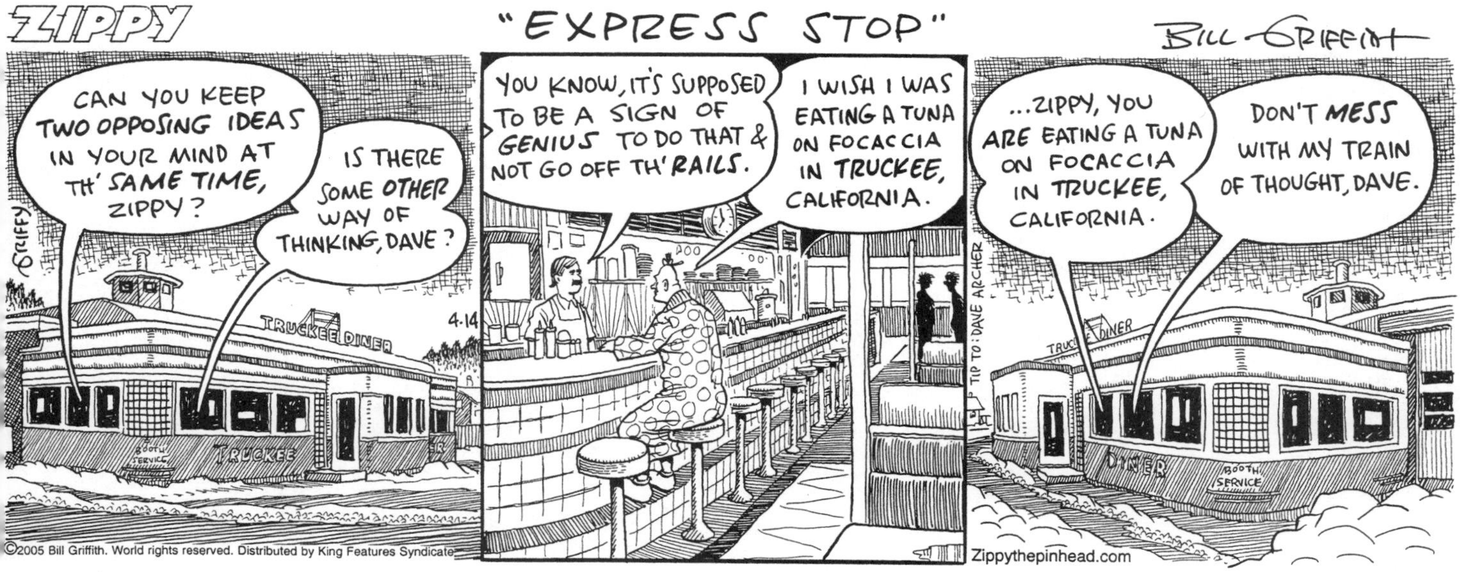
ZIPPY
"EXPRESS STOP"
BILL GRIFFITH
CAN YOU KEEP TWO OPPOSING IDEAS IN YOUR MIND AT TH' SAME TIME, ZIPPY?
IS THERE SOME OTHER WAY OF THINKING, DAVE?
YOU KNOW, IT'S SUPPOSED TO BE A SIGN OF GENIUS TO DO THAT & NOT GO OFF TH' RAILS.
I WISH I WAS EATING A TUNA ON FOCACCIA IN TRUCKEE, CALIFORNIA.
...ZIPPY, YOU ARE EATING A TUNA ON FOCACCIA IN TRUCKEE, CALIFORNIA.
DON'T MESS WITH MY TRAIN OF THOUGHT, DAVE.
TRUCKEE DINER
TRUCKEE
BOOTH SERVICE
DINER
TIP TO: DAVE ARCHER
4-14
GRIFFY
©2005 Bill Griffith. World rights reserved. Distributed by King Features Syndicate
Zippythepinhead.com

119

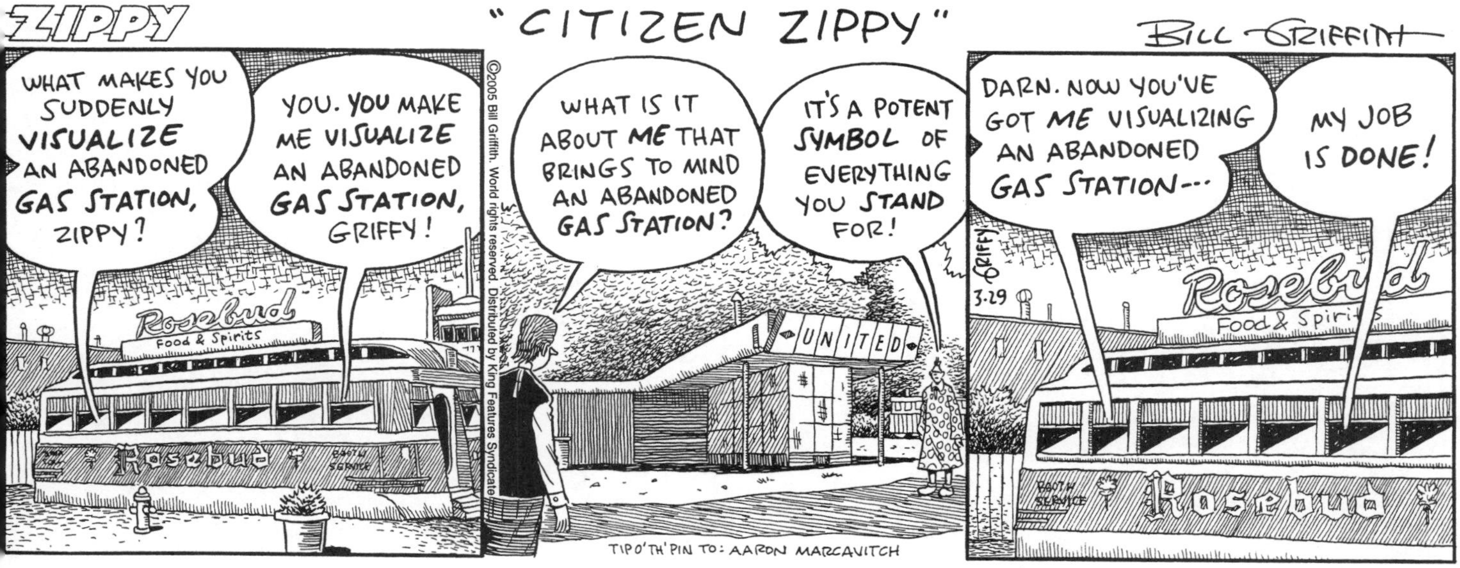
ZIPPY
"CITIZEN ZIPPY"
BILL GRIFFITH
WHAT MAKES YOU SUDDENLY VISUALIZE AN ABANDONED GAS STATION, ZIPPY?
YOU. YOU MAKE ME VISUALIZE AN ABANDONED GAS STATION, GRIFFY!
WHAT IS IT ABOUT ME THAT BRINGS TO MIND AN ABANDONED GAS STATION?
IT'S A POTENT SYMBOL OF EVERYTHING YOU STAND FOR!
DARN. NOW YOU'VE GOT ME VISUALIZING AN ABANDONED GAS STATION---
MY JOB IS DONE!
Rosebud
Food & Spirits
BOOTH SERVICE
UNITED
TIP O' TH' PIN TO: AARON MARCAVITCH
GRIFFY
3-29
©2005 Bill Griffith. World rights reserved. Distributed by King Features Syndicate

120

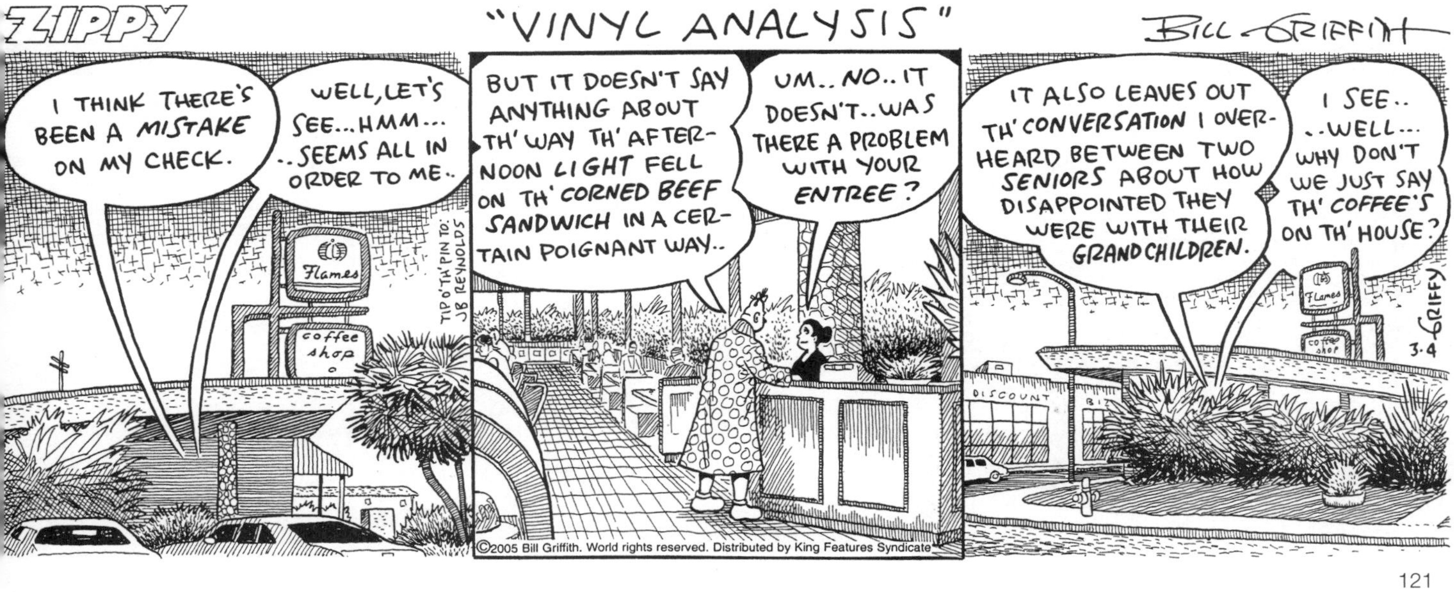
ZIPPY
"VINYL ANALYSIS"
BILL GRIFFITH
I THINK THERE'S BEEN A MISTAKE ON MY CHECK.
WELL, LET'S SEE... HMM... ..SEEMS ALL IN ORDER TO ME..
BUT IT DOESN'T SAY ANYTHING ABOUT TH' WAY TH' AFTERNOON LIGHT FELL ON TH' CORNED BEEF SANDWICH IN A CERTAIN POIGNANT WAY..
UM.. NO.. IT DOESN'T.. WAS THERE A PROBLEM WITH YOUR ENTREE?
IT ALSO LEAVES OUT TH' CONVERSATION I OVERHEARD BETWEEN TWO SENIORS ABOUT HOW DISAPPOINTED THEY WERE WITH THEIR GRANDCHILDREN.
I SEE.. ..WELL... WHY DON'T WE JUST SAY TH' COFFEE'S ON TH' HOUSE?
Flames
coffee shop
DISCOUNT
TIP O' TH' PIN TO: JB REYNOLDS
GRIFFY
3-4
©2005 Bill Griffith. World rights reserved. Distributed by King Features Syndicate

121

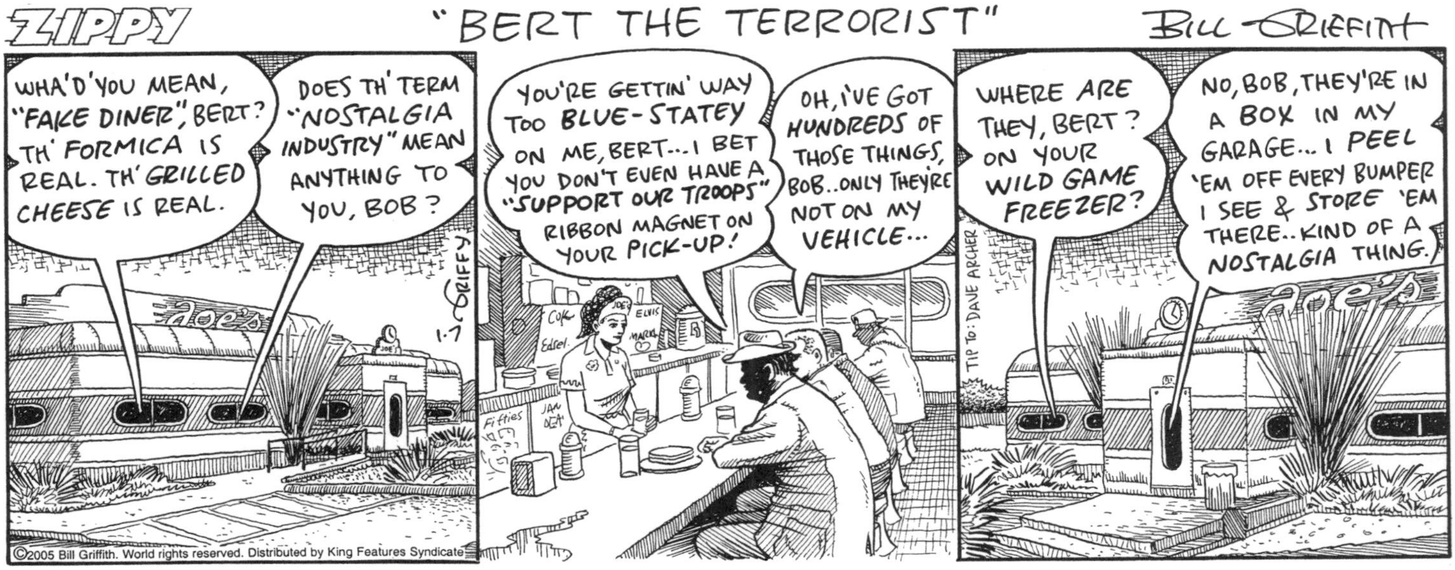
ZIPPY
"BERT THE TERRORIST"
BILL GRIFFITH
WHA'D'YOU MEAN, "FAKE DINER", BERT? TH' FORMICA IS REAL. TH' GRILLED CHEESE IS REAL.
DOES TH' TERM "NOSTALGIA INDUSTRY" MEAN ANYTHING TO YOU, BOB?
YOU'RE GETTIN' WAY TOO BLUE-STATEY ON ME, BERT... I BET YOU DON'T EVEN HAVE A "SUPPORT OUR TROOPS" RIBBON MAGNET ON YOUR PICK-UP!
OH, I'VE GOT HUNDREDS OF THOSE THINGS, BOB.. ONLY THEY'RE NOT ON MY VEHICLE...
WHERE ARE THEY, BERT? ON YOUR WILD GAME FREEZER?
NO, BOB, THEY'RE IN A BOX IN MY GARAGE... I PEEL 'EM OFF EVERY BUMPER I SEE & STORE 'EM THERE.. KIND OF A NOSTALGIA THING.
TIP TO: DAVE ARCHER
©2005 Bill Griffith. World rights reserved. Distributed by King Features Syndicate

122

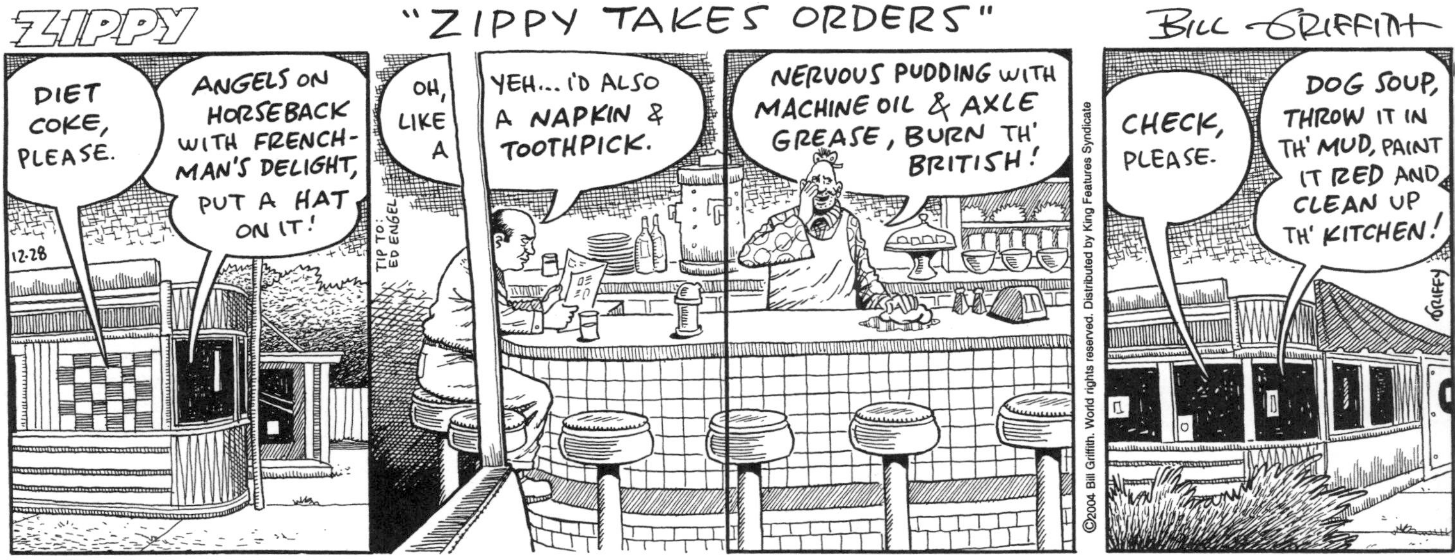
ZIPPY
"ZIPPY TAKES ORDERS"
BILL GRIFFITH
DIET COKE, PLEASE.
ANGELS ON HORSEBACK WITH FRENCH-MAN'S DELIGHT, PUT A HAT ON IT!
OH, LIKE A
YEH... I'D ALSO A NAPKIN & TOOTHPICK.
NERVOUS PUDDING WITH MACHINE OIL & AXLE GREASE, BURN TH' BRITISH!
CHECK, PLEASE.
DOG SOUP, THROW IT IN TH' MUD, PAINT IT RED AND CLEAN UP TH' KITCHEN!
TIP TO: ED ENGEL
©2004 Bill Griffith. World rights reserved. Distributed by King Features Syndicate

123

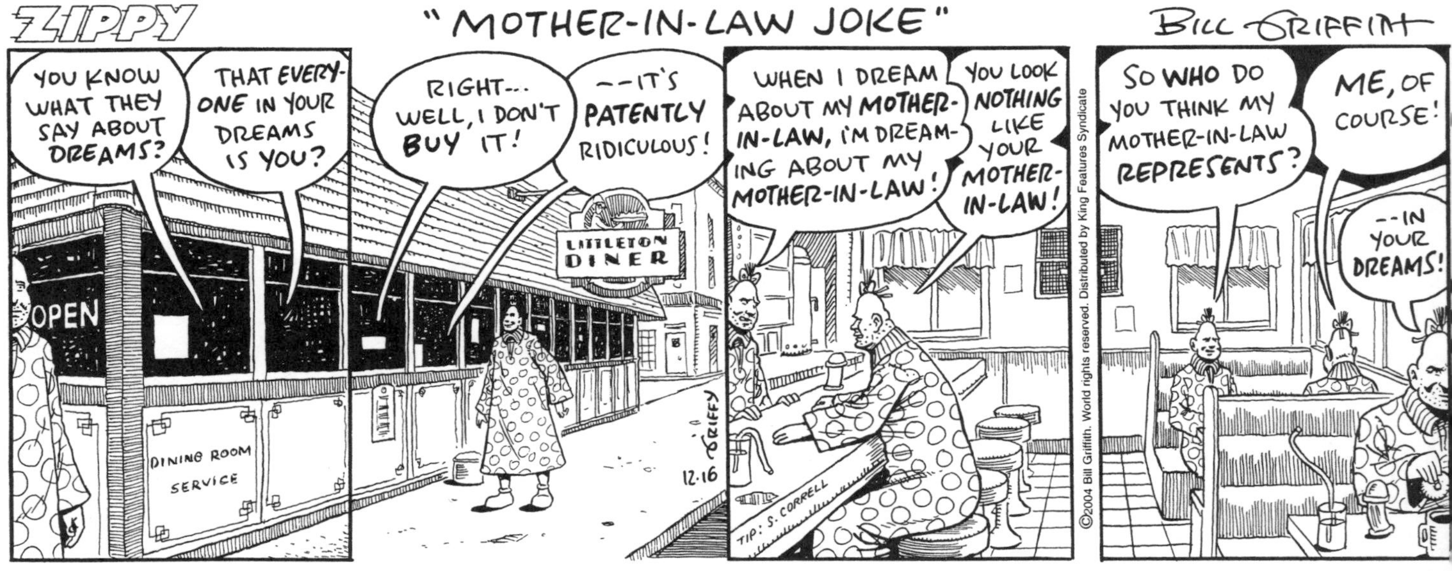
ZIPPY
"MOTHER-IN-LAW JOKE"
BILL GRIFFITH
YOU KNOW WHAT THEY SAY ABOUT DREAMS?
THAT EVERY-ONE IN YOUR DREAMS IS YOU?
RIGHT... WELL, I DON'T BUY IT!
--IT'S PATENTLY RIDICULOUS!
OPEN
DINING ROOM SERVICE
LITTLETON DINER
WHEN I DREAM ABOUT MY MOTHER-IN-LAW, I'M DREAM-ING ABOUT MY MOTHER-IN-LAW!
YOU LOOK NOTHING LIKE YOUR MOTHER-IN-LAW!
SO WHO DO YOU THINK MY MOTHER-IN-LAW REPRESENTS?
ME, OF COURSE!
--IN YOUR DREAMS!
TIP: S. CORRELL
©2004 Bill Griffith. World rights reserved. Distributed by King Features Syndicate

124

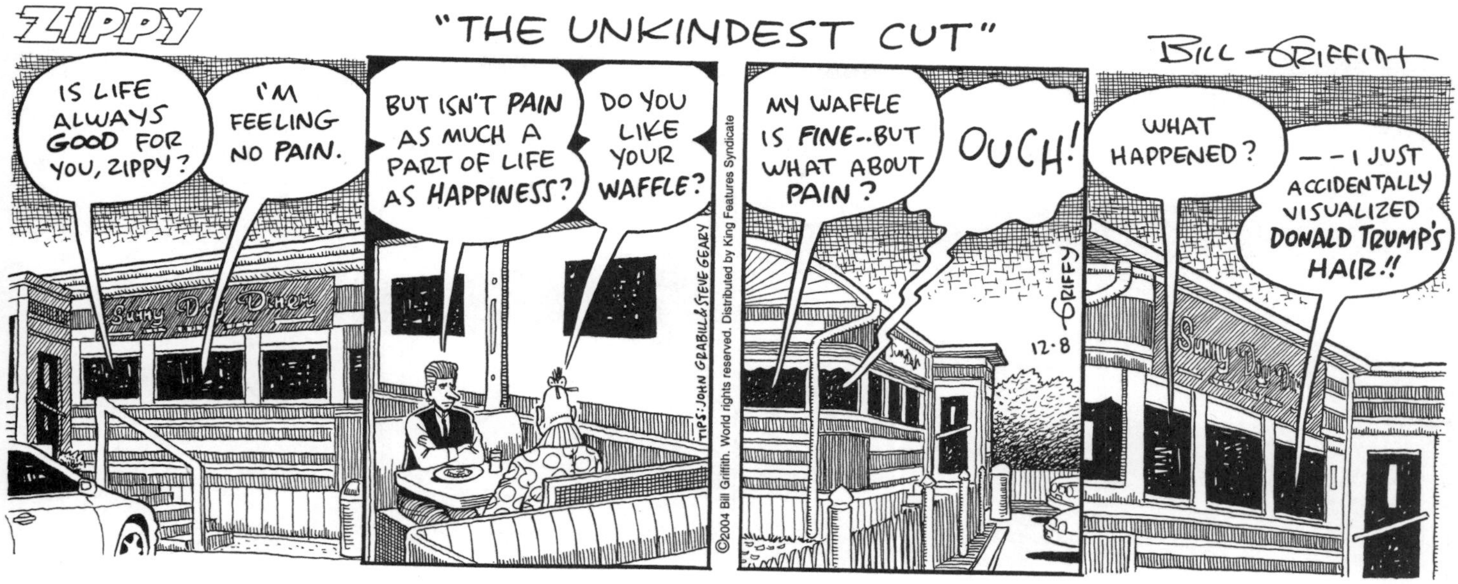
ZIPPY
"THE UNKINDEST CUT"
BILL GRIFFITH
IS LIFE ALWAYS GOOD FOR YOU, ZIPPY?
I'M FEELING NO PAIN.
BUT ISN'T PAIN AS MUCH A PART OF LIFE AS HAPPINESS?
DO YOU LIKE YOUR WAFFLE?
MY WAFFLE IS FINE--BUT WHAT ABOUT PAIN?
OUCH!
WHAT HAPPENED?
--I JUST ACCIDENTALLY VISUALIZED DONALD TRUMP'S HAIR!!
TIPS: JOHN GRABILL & STEVE GEARY
©2004 Bill Griffith. World rights reserved. Distributed by King Features Syndicate
GRIFFY 12·8

125

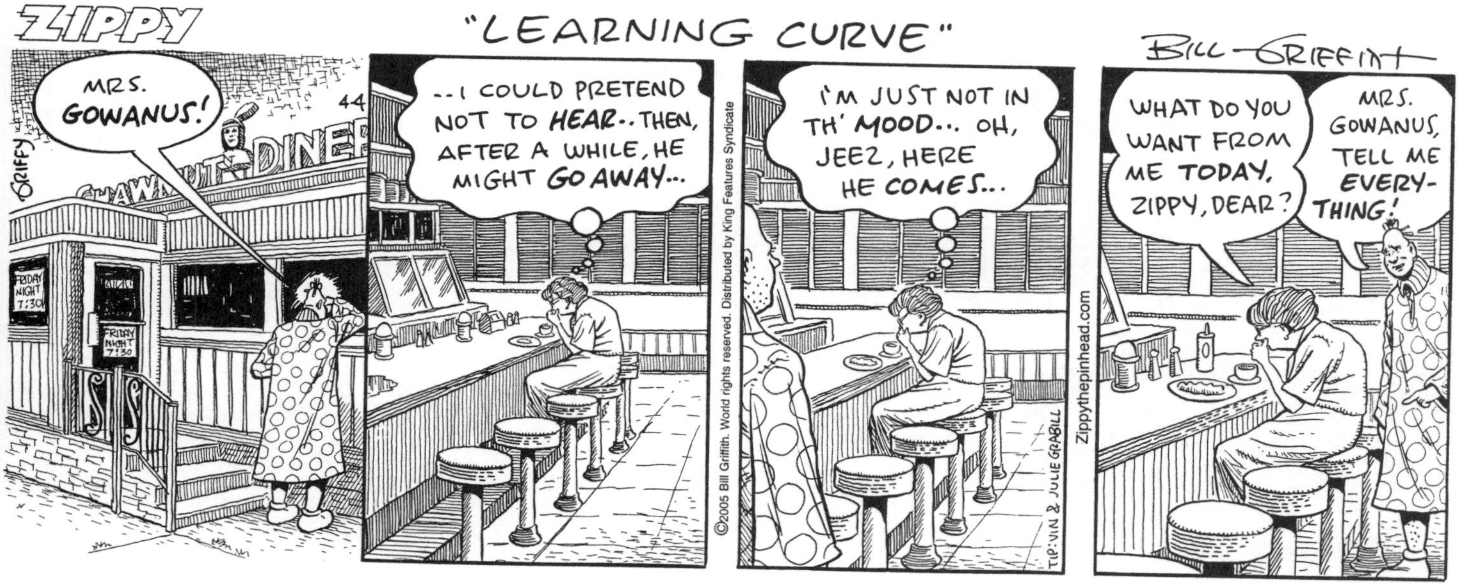
ZIPPY
"LEARNING CURVE"
BILL GRIFFITH
MRS. GOWANUS!
--I COULD PRETEND NOT TO HEAR.. THEN, AFTER A WHILE, HE MIGHT GO AWAY...
I'M JUST NOT IN TH' MOOD... OH, JEEZ, HERE HE COMES...
WHAT DO YOU WANT FROM ME TODAY, ZIPPY, DEAR?
MRS. GOWANUS, TELL ME EVERY-THING!
©2005 Bill Griffith. World rights reserved. Distributed by King Features Syndicate
TIP: VIN & JULIE GRABILL
Zippythepinhead.com

126 A

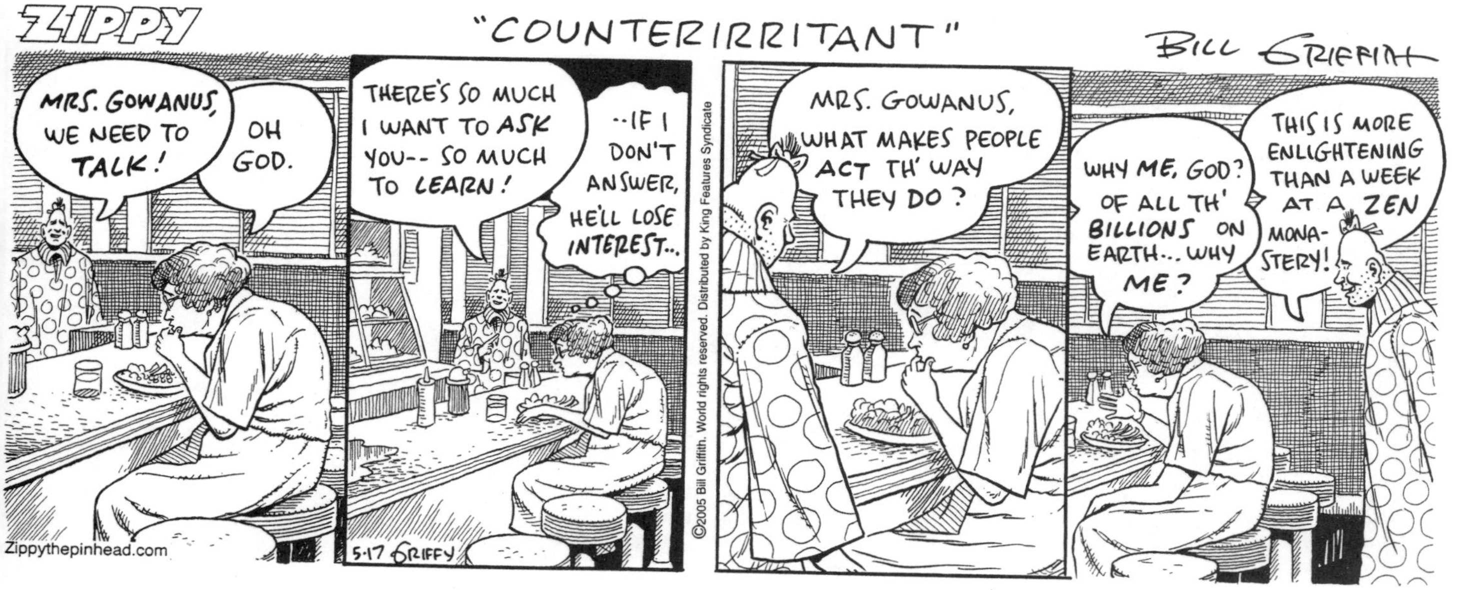
ZIPPY
"COUNTERIRRITANT"
BILL GRIFFITH
MRS. GOWANUS, WE NEED TO TALK!
OH GOD.
THERE'S SO MUCH I WANT TO ASK YOU-- SO MUCH TO LEARN!
--IF I DON'T ANSWER, HE'LL LOSE INTEREST...
MRS. GOWANUS, WHAT MAKES PEOPLE ACT TH' WAY THEY DO?
WHY ME, GOD? OF ALL TH' BILLIONS ON EARTH... WHY ME?
THIS IS MORE ENLIGHTENING THAN A WEEK AT A ZEN MONA-STERY!
Zippythepinhead.com
5·17 GRIFFY
©2005 Bill Griffith. World rights reserved. Distributed by King Features Syndicate

126 B

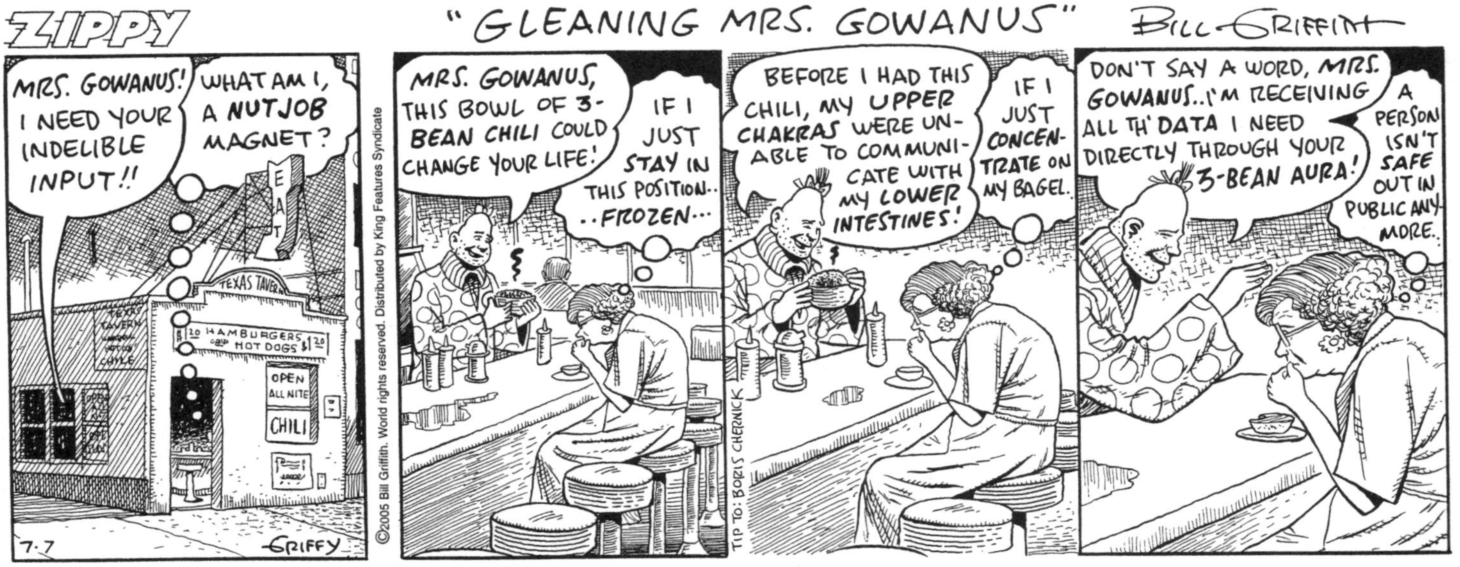
ZIPPY
"GLEANING MRS. GOWANUS"
BILL GRIFFITH
MRS. GOWANUS! I NEED YOUR INDELIBLE INPUT!!
WHAT AM I, A NUTJOB MAGNET?
EAT
TEXAS TAVERN
TEXAS TAVERN
HAMBURGERS HOT DOGS
OPEN ALL NITE
CHILI
7-7
GRIFFY
©2005 Bill Griffith. World rights reserved. Distributed by King Features Syndicate
MRS. GOWANUS, THIS BOWL OF 3-BEAN CHILI COULD CHANGE YOUR LIFE!
IF I JUST STAY IN THIS POSITION.. ..FROZEN...
TIP TO: BORIS CHERNICK
BEFORE I HAD THIS CHILI, MY UPPER CHAKRAS WERE UNABLE TO COMMUNICATE WITH MY LOWER INTESTINES!
IF I JUST CONCENTRATE ON MY BAGEL.
DON'T SAY A WORD, MRS. GOWANUS..I'M RECEIVING ALL TH' DATA I NEED DIRECTLY THROUGH YOUR 3-BEAN AURA!
A PERSON ISN'T SAFE OUT IN PUBLIC ANYMORE..

127

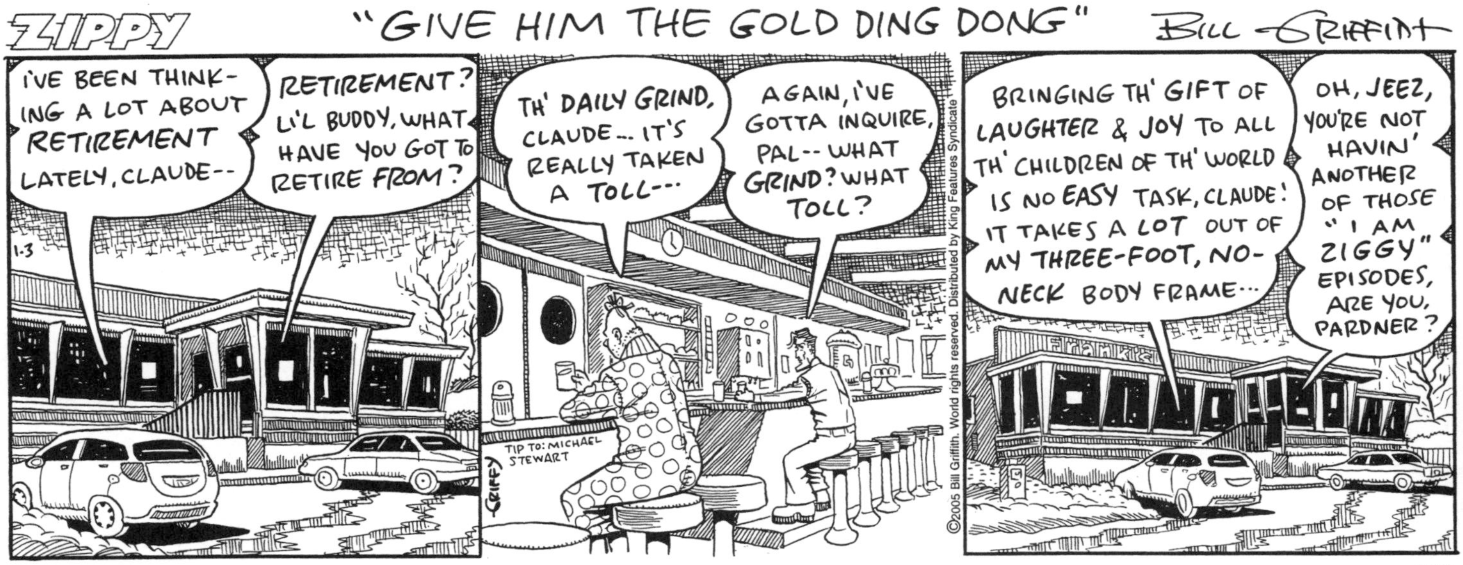
ZIPPY
"GIVE HIM THE GOLD DING DONG"
BILL GRIFFITH
I'VE BEEN THINKING A LOT ABOUT RETIREMENT LATELY, CLAUDE--
RETIREMENT? LI'L BUDDY, WHAT HAVE YOU GOT TO RETIRE FROM?
1-3
TH' DAILY GRIND, CLAUDE... IT'S REALLY TAKEN A TOLL---
AGAIN, I'VE GOTTA INQUIRE, PAL-- WHAT GRIND? WHAT TOLL?
TIP TO: MICHAEL STEWART
GRIFFY
©2005 Bill Griffith. World rights reserved. Distributed by King Features Syndicate
BRINGING TH' GIFT OF LAUGHTER & JOY TO ALL TH' CHILDREN OF TH' WORLD IS NO EASY TASK, CLAUDE! IT TAKES A LOT OUT OF MY THREE-FOOT, NO-NECK BODY FRAME...
OH, JEEZ, YOU'RE NOT HAVIN' ANOTHER OF THOSE "I AM ZIGGY" EPISODES, ARE YOU, PARDNER?

128

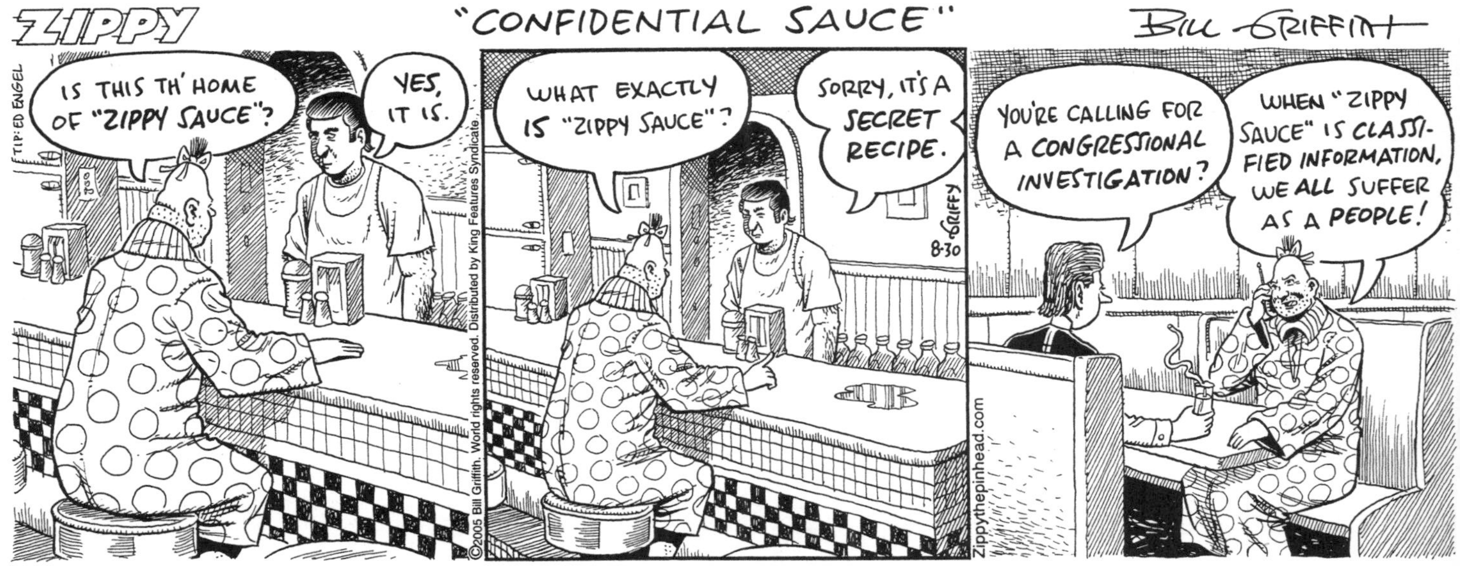
ZIPPY
"CONFIDENTIAL SAUCE"
BILL GRIFFITH
TIP: ED ENGEL
IS THIS TH' HOME OF "ZIPPY SAUCE"?
YES, IT IS.
©2005 Bill Griffith. World rights reserved. Distributed by King Features Syndicate.
WHAT EXACTLY IS "ZIPPY SAUCE"?
SORRY, IT'S A SECRET RECIPE.
GRIFFY
8-30
Zippythepinhead.com
YOU'RE CALLING FOR A CONGRESSIONAL INVESTIGATION?
WHEN "ZIPPY SAUCE" IS CLASSIFIED INFORMATION, WE ALL SUFFER AS A PEOPLE!

129

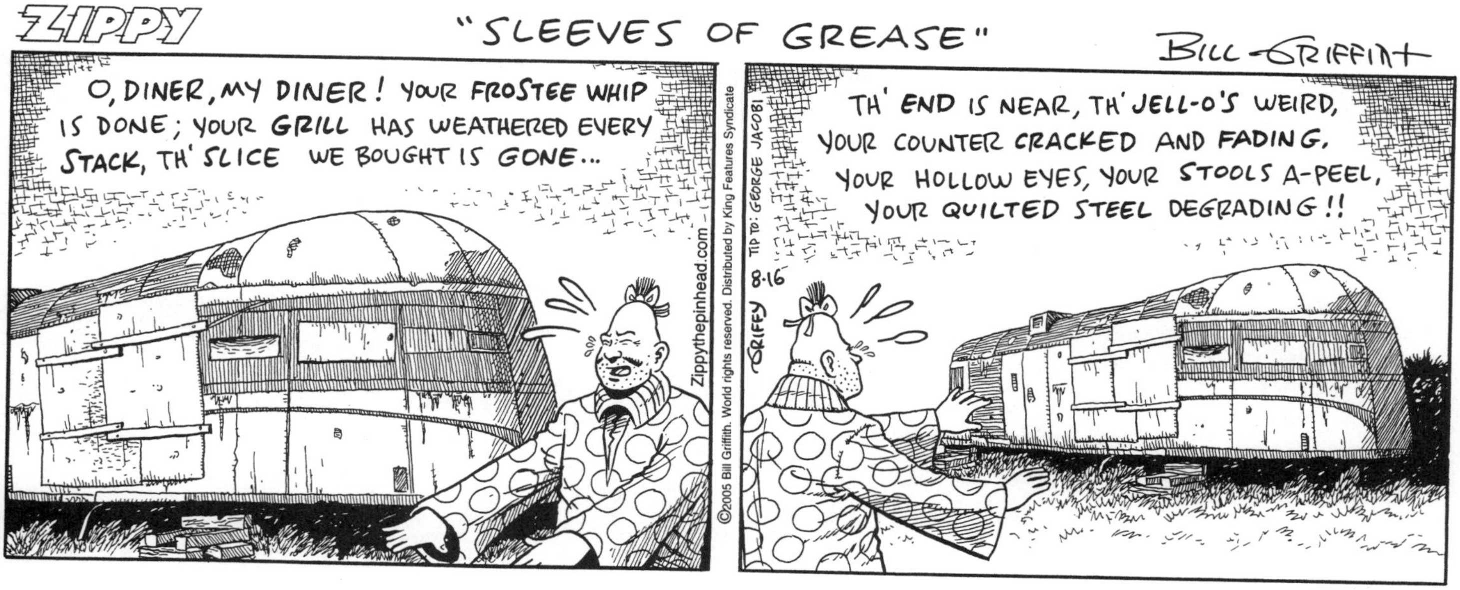
ZIPPY
"SLEEVES OF GREASE"
BILL GRIFFITH
O, DINER, MY DINER! YOUR FROSTEE WHIP IS DONE; YOUR GRILL HAS WEATHERED EVERY STACK, TH' SLICE WE BOUGHT IS GONE...
©2005 Bill Griffith. World rights reserved. Distributed by King Features Syndicate
Zippythepinhead.com
TIP TO: GEORGE JACOBI
8-16
GRIFFY
TH' END IS NEAR, TH' JELL-O'S WEIRD, YOUR COUNTER CRACKED AND FADING, YOUR HOLLOW EYES, YOUR STOOLS A-PEEL, YOUR QUILTED STEEL DEGRADING!!

130

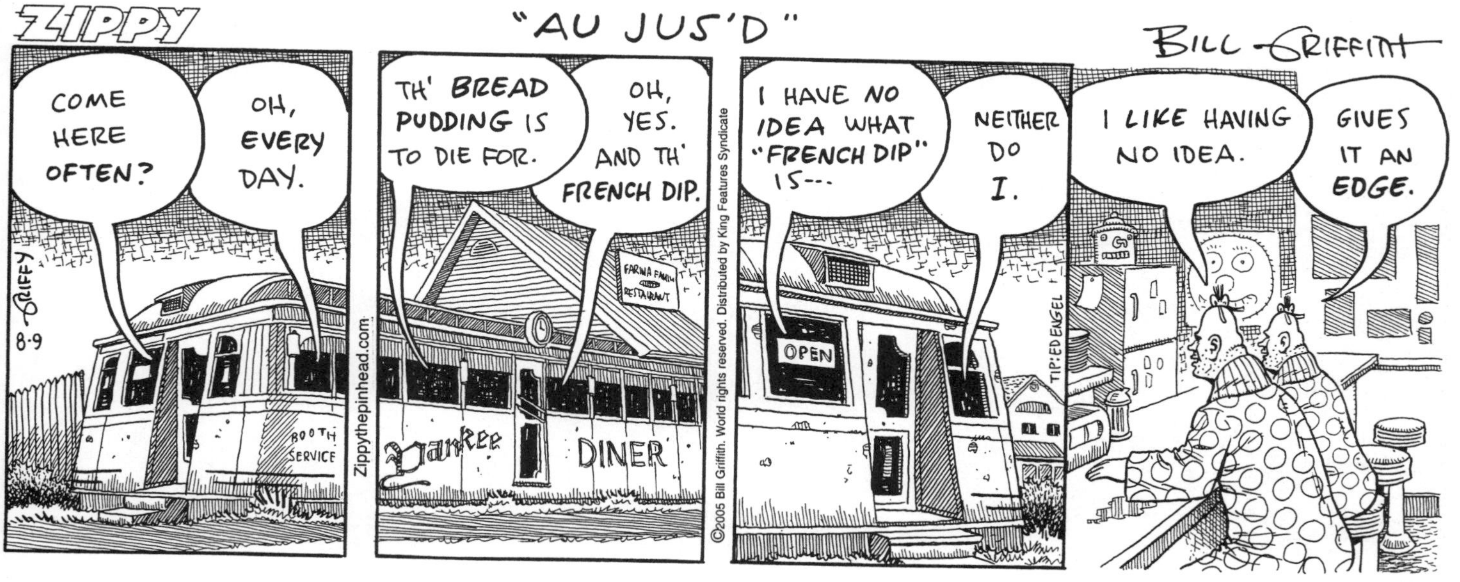
ZIPPY
"AU JUS'D"
BILL GRIFFITH
COME HERE OFTEN?
OH, EVERY DAY.
GRIFFY
8-9
BOOTH SERVICE
Zippythepinhead.com
TH' BREAD PUDDING IS TO DIE FOR.
OH, YES. AND TH' FRENCH DIP.
FARINA FAMILY RESTAURANT
Yankee DINER
©2005 Bill Griffith. World rights reserved. Distributed by King Features Syndicate
I HAVE NO IDEA WHAT "FRENCH DIP" IS---
NEITHER DO I.
OPEN
TIP: ED ENGEL
I LIKE HAVING NO IDEA.
GIVES IT AN EDGE.

131

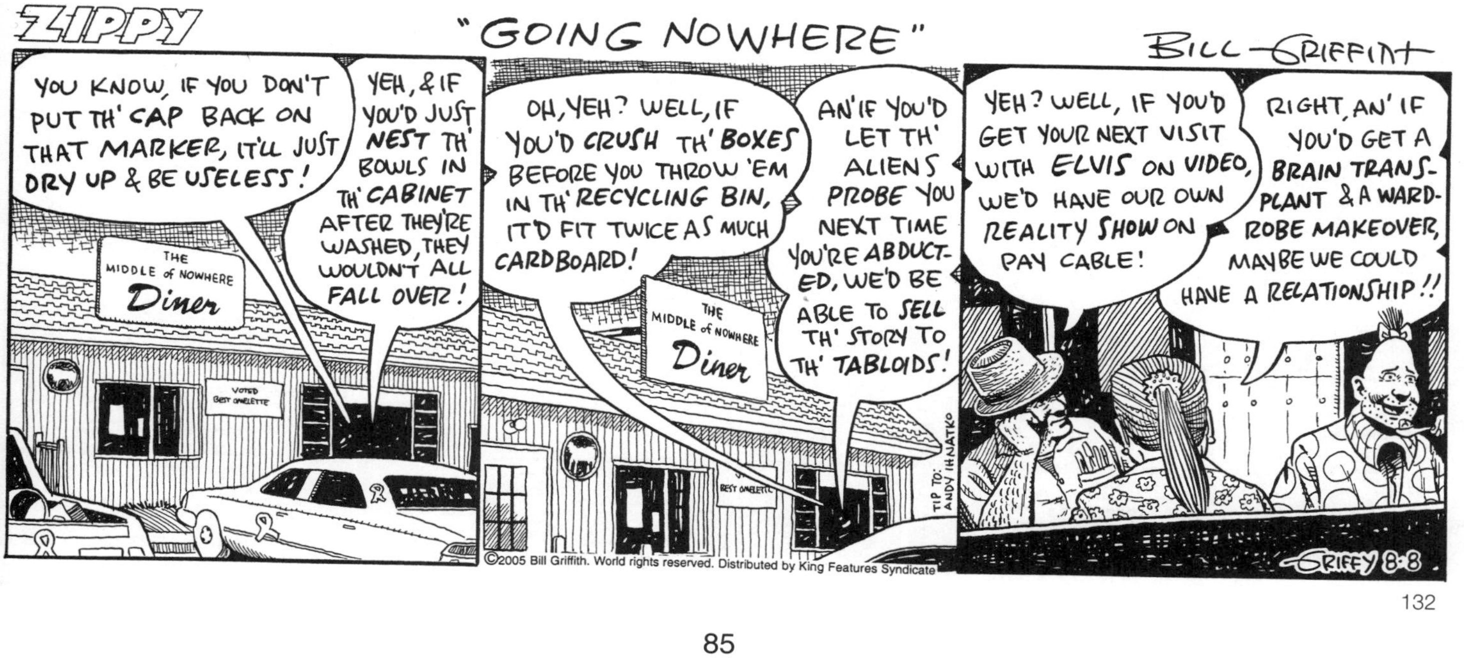
ZIPPY
"GOING NOWHERE"
BILL GRIFFITH
YOU KNOW, IF YOU DON'T PUT TH' CAP BACK ON THAT MARKER, IT'LL JUST DRY UP & BE USELESS!
YEH, & IF YOU'D JUST NEST TH' BOWLS IN TH' CABINET AFTER THEY'RE WASHED, THEY WOULDN'T ALL FALL OVER!
THE MIDDLE of NOWHERE Diner
VOTED BEST OMELETTE
OH, YEH? WELL, IF YOU'D CRUSH TH' BOXES BEFORE YOU THROW 'EM IN TH' RECYCLING BIN, IT'D FIT TWICE AS MUCH CARDBOARD!
AN' IF YOU'D LET TH' ALIENS PROBE YOU NEXT TIME YOU'RE ABDUCTED, WE'D BE ABLE TO SELL TH' STORY TO TH' TABLOIDS!
THE MIDDLE of NOWHERE Diner
BEST OMELETTE
TIP TO: ANDY IHNATKO
©2005 Bill Griffith. World rights reserved. Distributed by King Features Syndicate
YEH? WELL, IF YOU'D GET YOUR NEXT VISIT WITH ELVIS ON VIDEO, WE'D HAVE OUR OWN REALITY SHOW ON PAY CABLE!
RIGHT, AN' IF YOU'D GET A BRAIN TRANSPLANT & A WARDROBE MAKEOVER, MAYBE WE COULD HAVE A RELATIONSHIP!!
GRIFFY 8-8

132

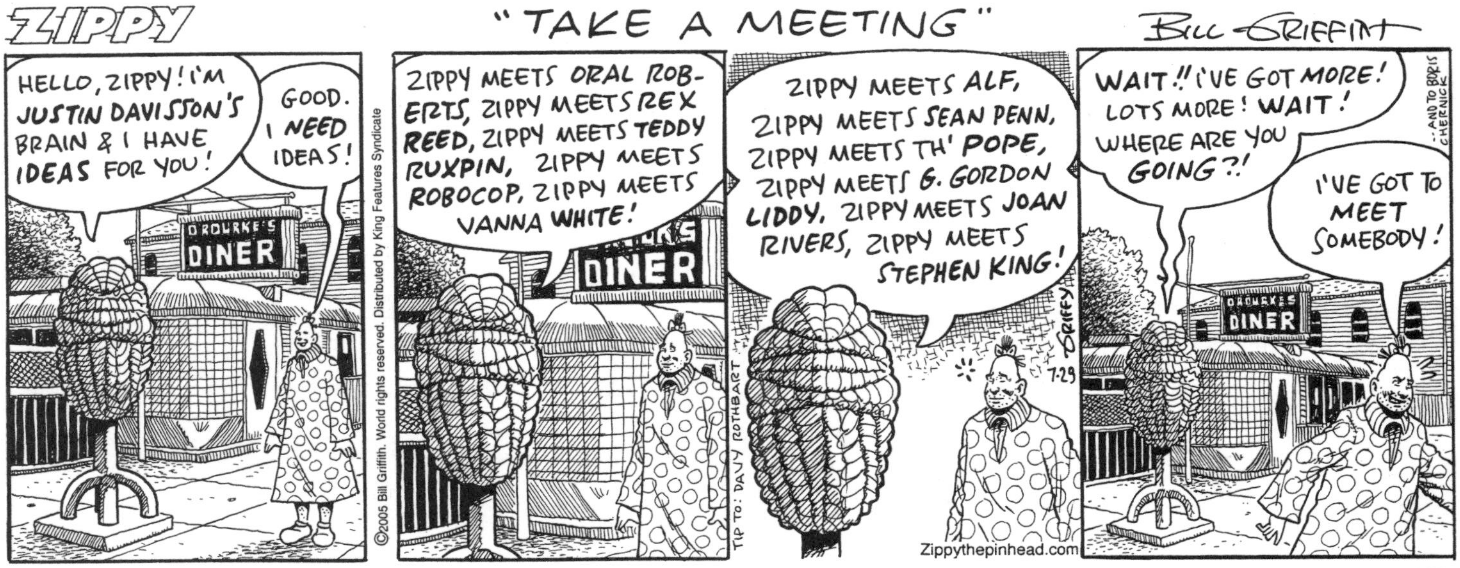
ZIPPY
"TAKE A MEETING"
BILL GRIFFITH
HELLO, ZIPPY! I'M JUSTIN DAVISSON'S BRAIN & I HAVE IDEAS FOR YOU!
GOOD. I NEED IDEAS!
O'ROURKE'S DINER
©2005 Bill Griffith. World rights reserved. Distributed by King Features Syndicate
ZIPPY MEETS ORAL ROBERTS, ZIPPY MEETS REX REED, ZIPPY MEETS TEDDY RUXPIN, ZIPPY MEETS ROBOCOP, ZIPPY MEETS VANNA WHITE!
DINER
TIP TO: DAVY ROTHBART
ZIPPY MEETS ALF, ZIPPY MEETS SEAN PENN, ZIPPY MEETS TH' POPE, ZIPPY MEETS G. GORDON LIDDY, ZIPPY MEETS JOAN RIVERS, ZIPPY MEETS STEPHEN KING!
GRIFFY 7-29
Zippythepinhead.com
WAIT!! I'VE GOT MORE! LOTS MORE! WAIT! WHERE ARE YOU GOING?!
I'VE GOT TO MEET SOMEBODY!
--AND TO BORIS CHERNICK
O'ROURKE'S DINER

133

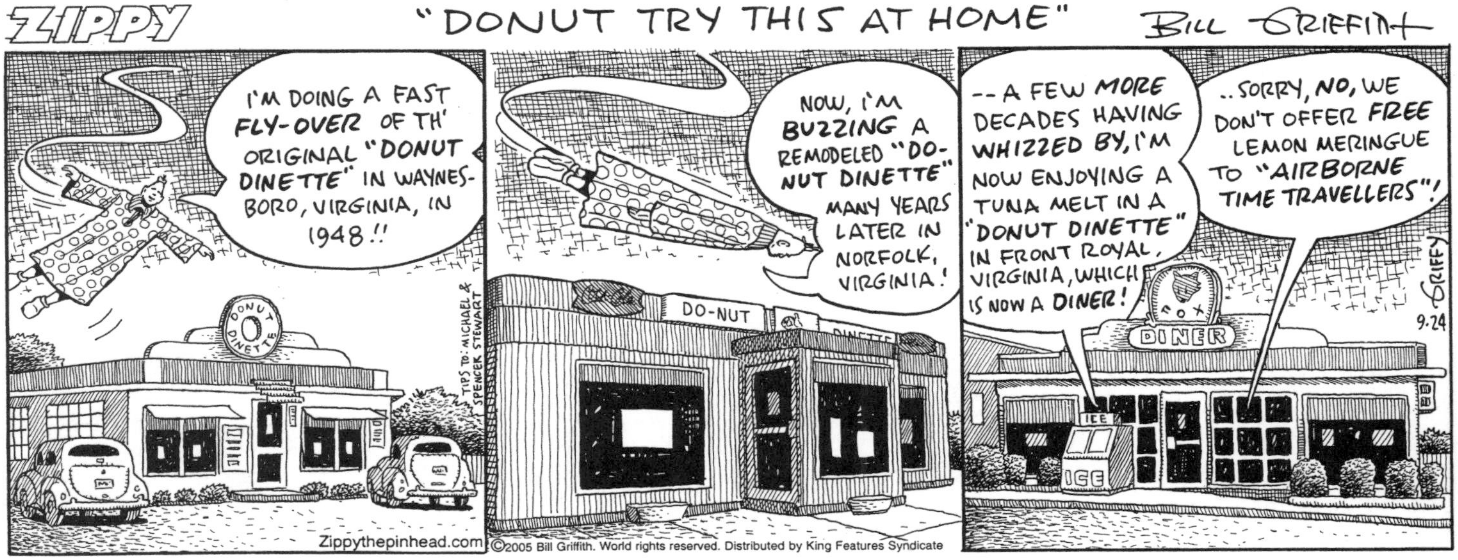
ZIPPY
"DONUT TRY THIS AT HOME"
BILL GRIFFITH
I'M DOING A FAST FLY-OVER OF TH' ORIGINAL "DONUT DINETTE" IN WAYNESBORO, VIRGINIA, IN 1948!!
DONUT DINETTE
TIPS TO: MICHAEL & SPENCER STEWART
Zippythepinhead.com
NOW, I'M BUZZING A REMODELED "DO-NUT DINETTE" MANY YEARS LATER IN NORFOLK, VIRGINIA!
DO-NUT
©2005 Bill Griffith. World rights reserved. Distributed by King Features Syndicate
--A FEW MORE DECADES HAVING WHIZZED BY, I'M NOW ENJOYING A TUNA MELT IN A "DONUT DINETTE" IN FRONT ROYAL, VIRGINIA, WHICH IS NOW A DINER!
..SORRY, NO, WE DON'T OFFER FREE LEMON MERINGUE TO "AIRBORNE TIME TRAVELLERS"!
FOX
DINER
ICE
ICE
GRIFFY 9-24

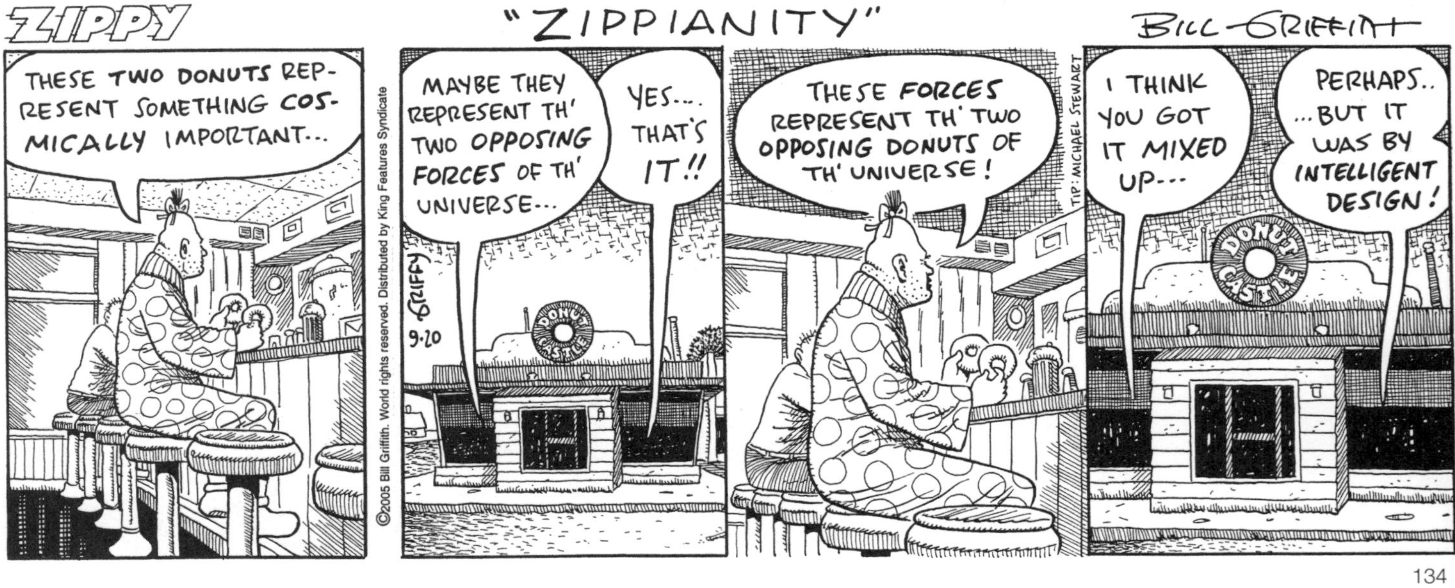
ZIPPY
"ZIPPIANITY"
BILL GRIFFITH
THESE TWO DONUTS REPRESENT SOMETHING COSMICALLY IMPORTANT...
©2005 Bill Griffith. World rights reserved. Distributed by King Features Syndicate
MAYBE THEY REPRESENT TH' TWO OPPOSING FORCES OF TH' UNIVERSE...
YES... THAT'S IT!!
GRIFFY 9-20
DONUT CASTLE
THESE FORCES REPRESENT TH' TWO OPPOSING DONUTS OF TH' UNIVERSE!
TIP: MICHAEL STEWART
I THINK YOU GOT IT MIXED UP---
PERHAPS.. ...BUT IT WAS BY INTELLIGENT DESIGN!
DONUT CASTLE

134

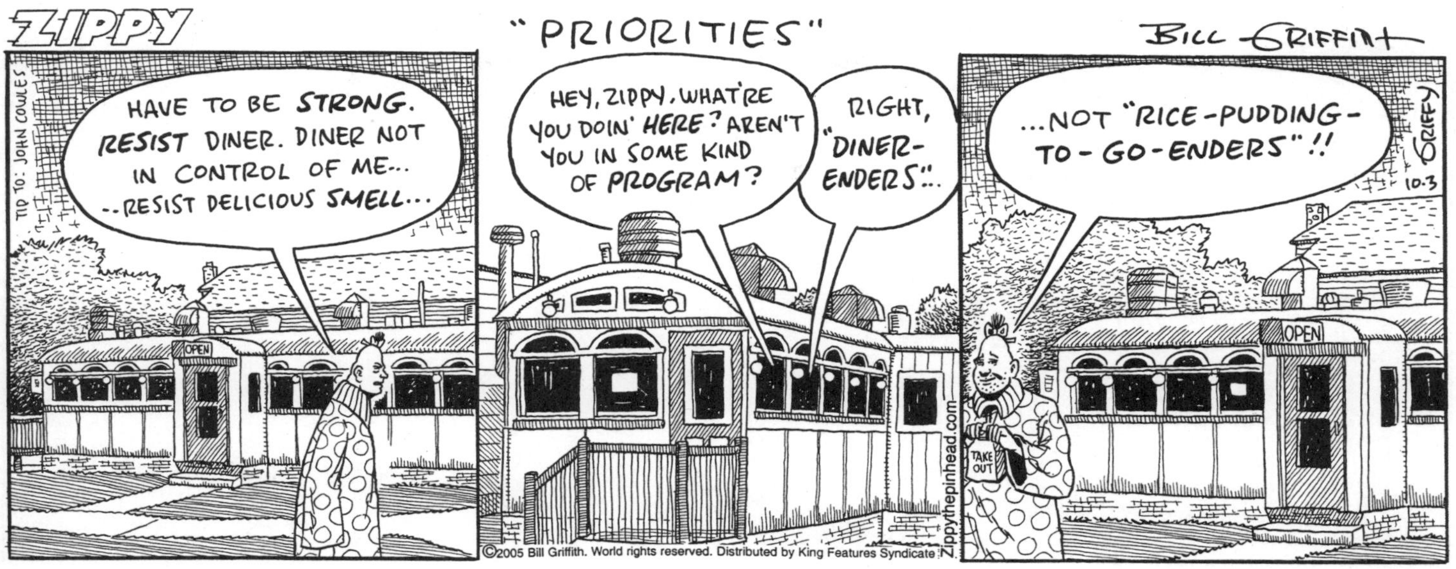
ZIPPY
"PRIORITIES"
BILL GRIFFITH
TIP TO: JOHN COWLES
HAVE TO BE STRONG. RESIST DINER. DINER NOT IN CONTROL OF ME... --RESIST DELICIOUS SMELL...
OPEN
HEY, ZIPPY, WHAT'RE YOU DOIN' HERE? AREN'T YOU IN SOME KIND OF PROGRAM?
RIGHT, "DINER-ENDERS"...
Zippythepinhead.com
©2005 Bill Griffith. World rights reserved. Distributed by King Features Syndicate
...NOT "RICE-PUDDING-TO-GO-ENDERS"!!
GRIFFY 10-3
OPEN
TAKE OUT

135

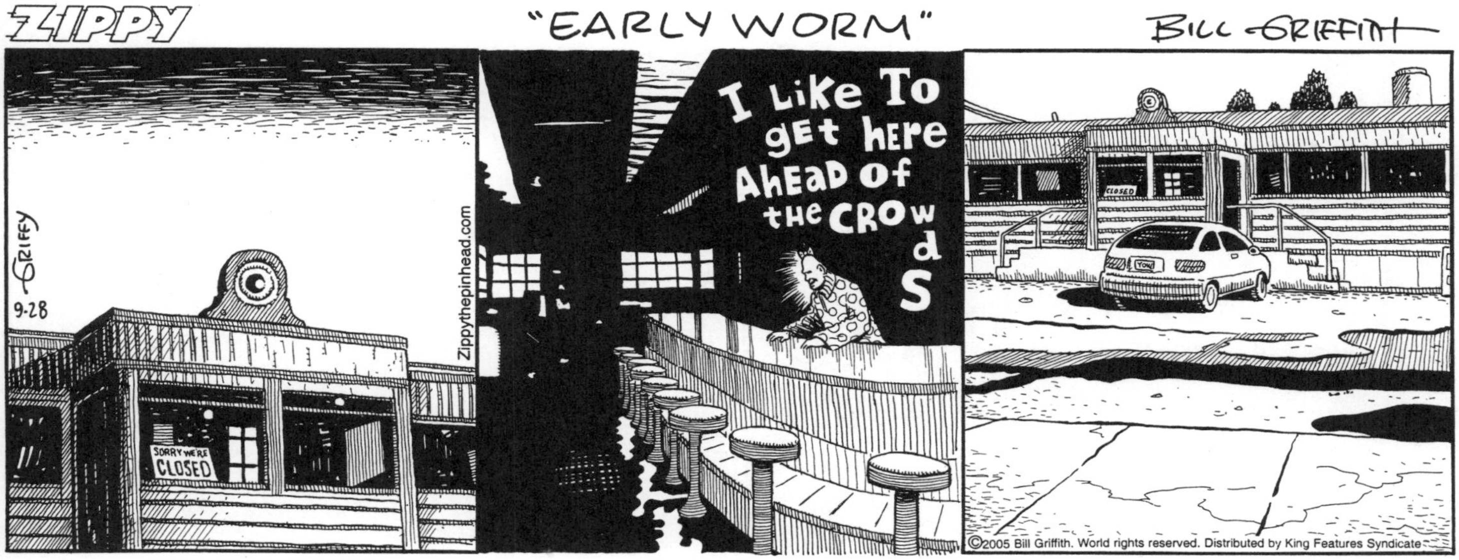
ZIPPY
"EARLY WORM"
BILL GRIFFITH
GRIFFY 9-28
SORRY WE'RE CLOSED
Zippythepinhead.com
I LIKE TO GET HERE AHEAD OF THE CROWDS
CLOSED
©2005 Bill Griffith. World rights reserved. Distributed by King Features Syndicate

136

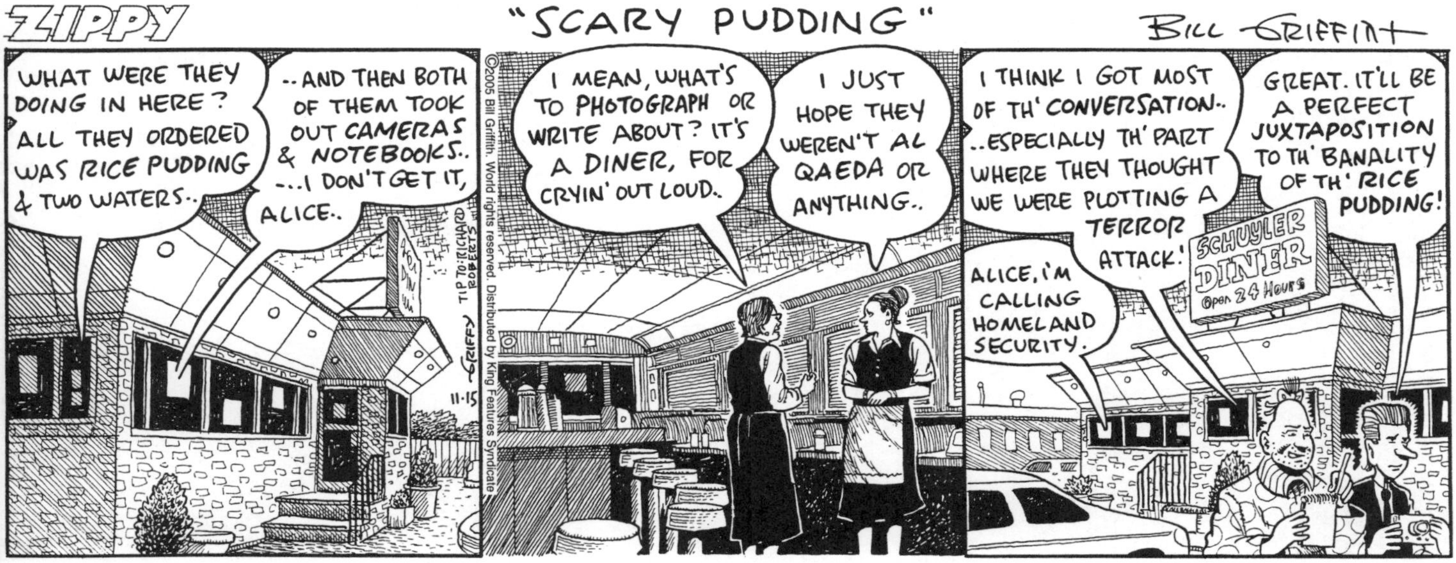
ZIPPY
"SCARY PUDDING"
BILL GRIFFITH
WHAT WERE THEY DOING IN HERE? ALL THEY ORDERED WAS RICE PUDDING & TWO WATERS..
..AND THEN BOTH OF THEM TOOK OUT CAMERAS & NOTEBOOKS.. ...I DON'T GET IT, ALICE..
TIP TO: RICHARD ROBERTS
GRIFFY 11-15
©2005 Bill Griffith. World rights reserved. Distributed by King Features Syndicate
I MEAN, WHAT'S TO PHOTOGRAPH OR WRITE ABOUT? IT'S A DINER, FOR CRYIN' OUT LOUD..
I JUST HOPE THEY WEREN'T AL QAEDA OR ANYTHING..
I THINK I GOT MOST OF TH' CONVERSATION.. ..ESPECIALLY TH' PART WHERE THEY THOUGHT WE WERE PLOTTING A TERROR ATTACK!
GREAT. IT'LL BE A PERFECT JUXTAPOSITION TO TH' BANALITY OF TH' RICE PUDDING!
ALICE, I'M CALLING HOMELAND SECURITY.
SCHUYLER DINER Open 24 Hours

137

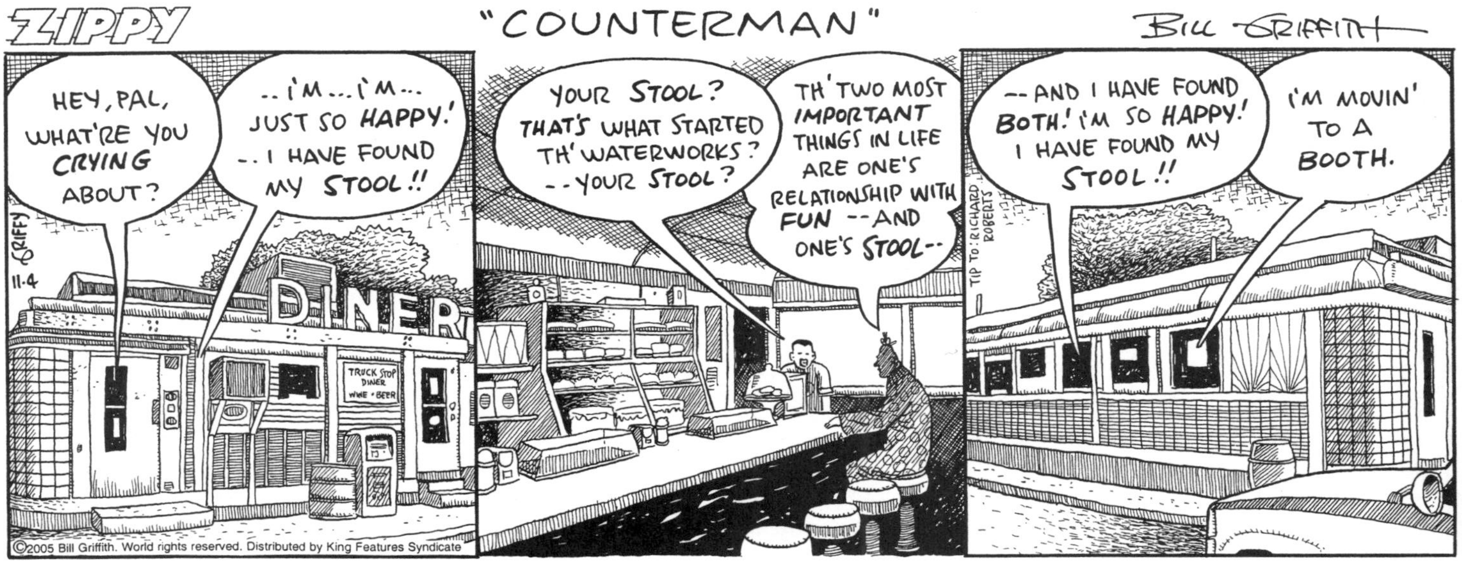
ZIPPY
"COUNTERMAN"
BILL GRIFFITH
HEY, PAL, WHAT'RE YOU CRYING ABOUT?
..I'M...I'M... JUST SO HAPPY! ..I HAVE FOUND MY STOOL!!
GRIFFY 11-4
DINER
TRUCK STOP DINER WINE · BEER
YOUR STOOL? THAT'S WHAT STARTED TH' WATERWORKS? --YOUR STOOL?
TH' TWO MOST IMPORTANT THINGS IN LIFE ARE ONE'S RELATIONSHIP WITH FUN --AND ONE'S STOOL--
TIP TO: RICHARD ROBERTS
--AND I HAVE FOUND BOTH! I'M SO HAPPY! I HAVE FOUND MY STOOL!!
I'M MOVIN' TO A BOOTH.
©2005 Bill Griffith. World rights reserved. Distributed by King Features Syndicate

138

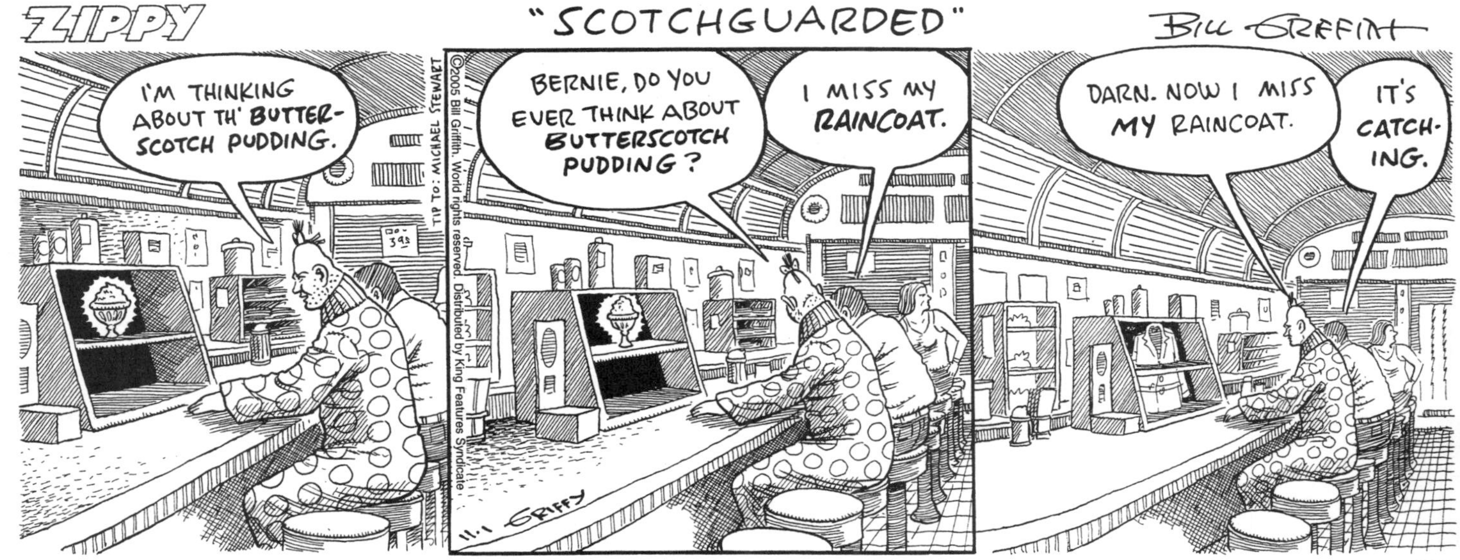
ZIPPY
"SCOTCHGUARDED"
BILL GRIFFITH
I'M THINKING ABOUT TH' BUTTER-SCOTCH PUDDING.
©2005 Bill Griffith. World rights reserved. Distributed by King Features Syndicate
TIP TO: MICHAEL STEWART
BERNIE, DO YOU EVER THINK ABOUT BUTTERSCOTCH PUDDING?
I MISS MY RAINCOAT.
11-1 GRIFFY
DARN. NOW I MISS MY RAINCOAT.
IT'S CATCH-ING.

139

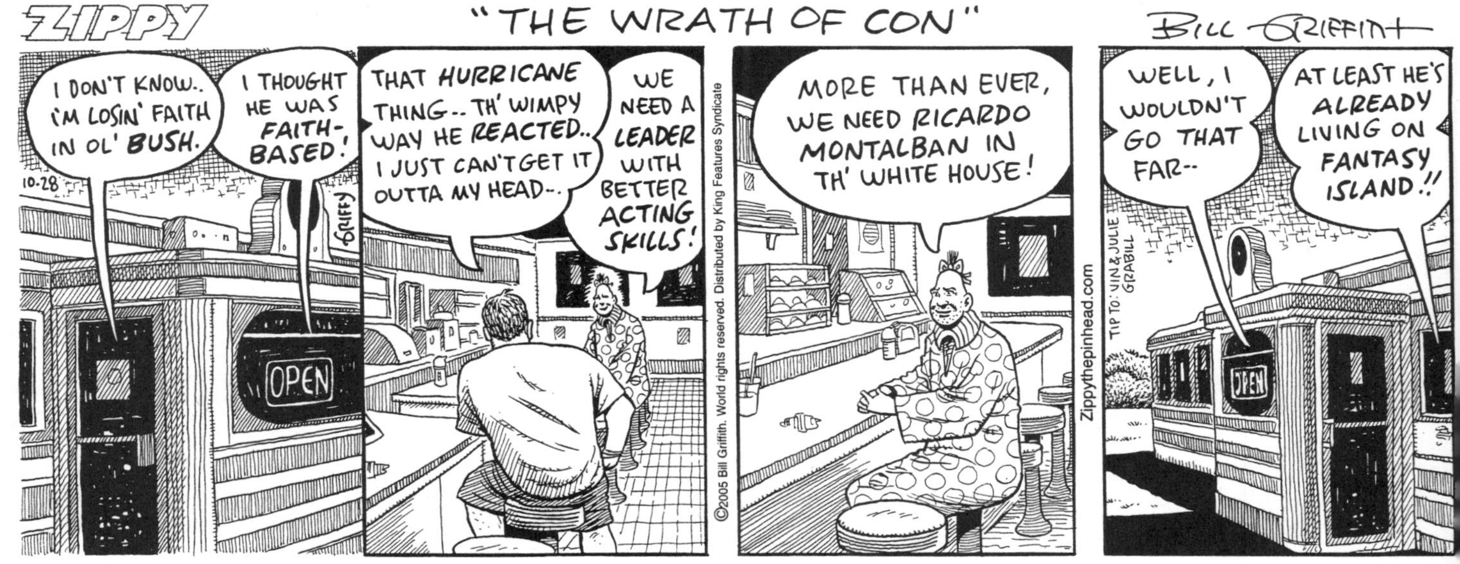
ZIPPY
"THE WRATH OF CON"
BILL GRIFFITH
I DON'T KNOW.. I'M LOSIN' FAITH IN OL' BUSH.
I THOUGHT HE WAS FAITH-BASED!
10-28 GRIFFY
OPEN
THAT HURRICANE THING.. TH' WIMPY WAY HE REACTED.. I JUST CAN'T GET IT OUTTA MY HEAD--.
WE NEED A LEADER WITH BETTER ACTING SKILLS!
©2005 Bill Griffith. World rights reserved. Distributed by King Features Syndicate
MORE THAN EVER, WE NEED RICARDO MONTALBAN IN TH' WHITE HOUSE!
Zippythepinhead.com
TIP TO: VIN & JULIE GRABILL
WELL, I WOULDN'T GO THAT FAR--
AT LEAST HE'S ALREADY LIVING ON FANTASY ISLAND!!
OPEN

140

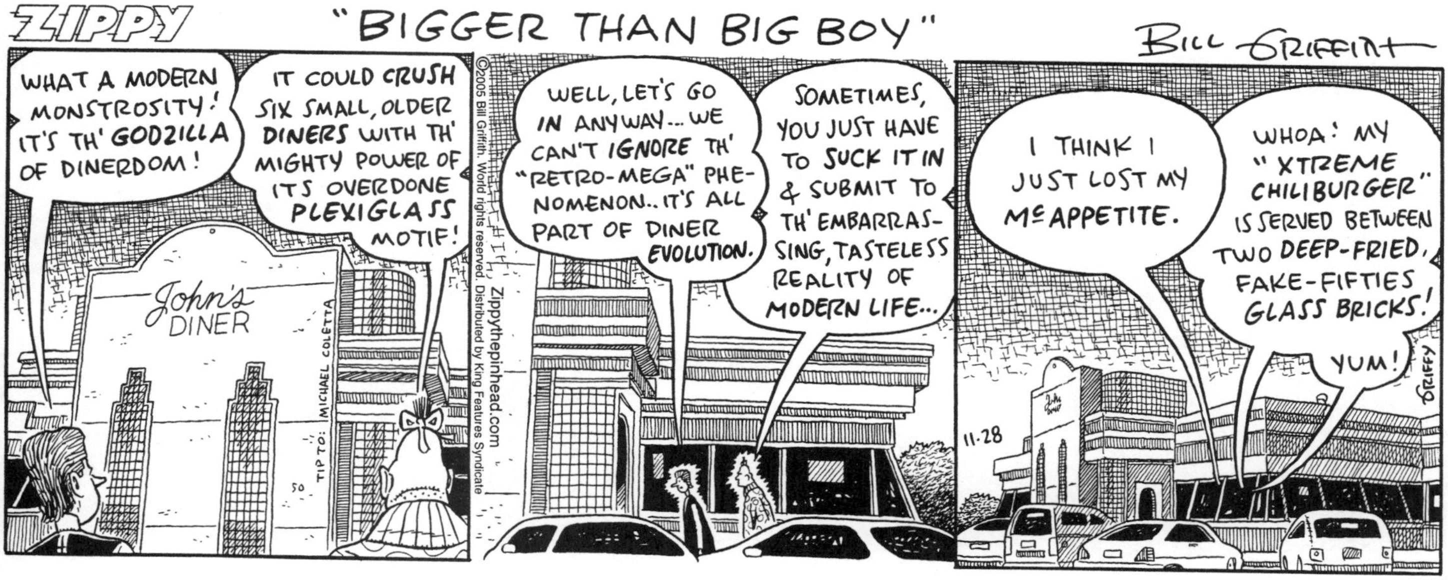
ZIPPY
"BIGGER THAN BIG BOY"
BILL GRIFFITH
WHAT A MODERN MONSTROSITY! IT'S TH' GODZILLA OF DINERDOM!
IT COULD CRUSH SIX SMALL, OLDER DINERS WITH TH' MIGHTY POWER OF ITS OVERDONE PLEXIGLASS MOTIF!
John's DINER
TIP TO: MICHAEL COLETTA
©2005 Bill Griffith. World rights reserved. Distributed by King Features Syndicate
Zippythepinhead.com
WELL, LET'S GO IN ANYWAY... WE CAN'T IGNORE TH' "RETRO-MEGA" PHENOMENON.. IT'S ALL PART OF DINER EVOLUTION.
SOMETIMES, YOU JUST HAVE TO SUCK IT IN & SUBMIT TO TH' EMBARRASSING, TASTELESS REALITY OF MODERN LIFE...
I THINK I JUST LOST MY McAPPETITE.
WHOA: MY "XTREME CHILIBURGER" IS SERVED BETWEEN TWO DEEP-FRIED, FAKE-FIFTIES GLASS BRICKS!
YUM!
11-28
GRIFFY

141

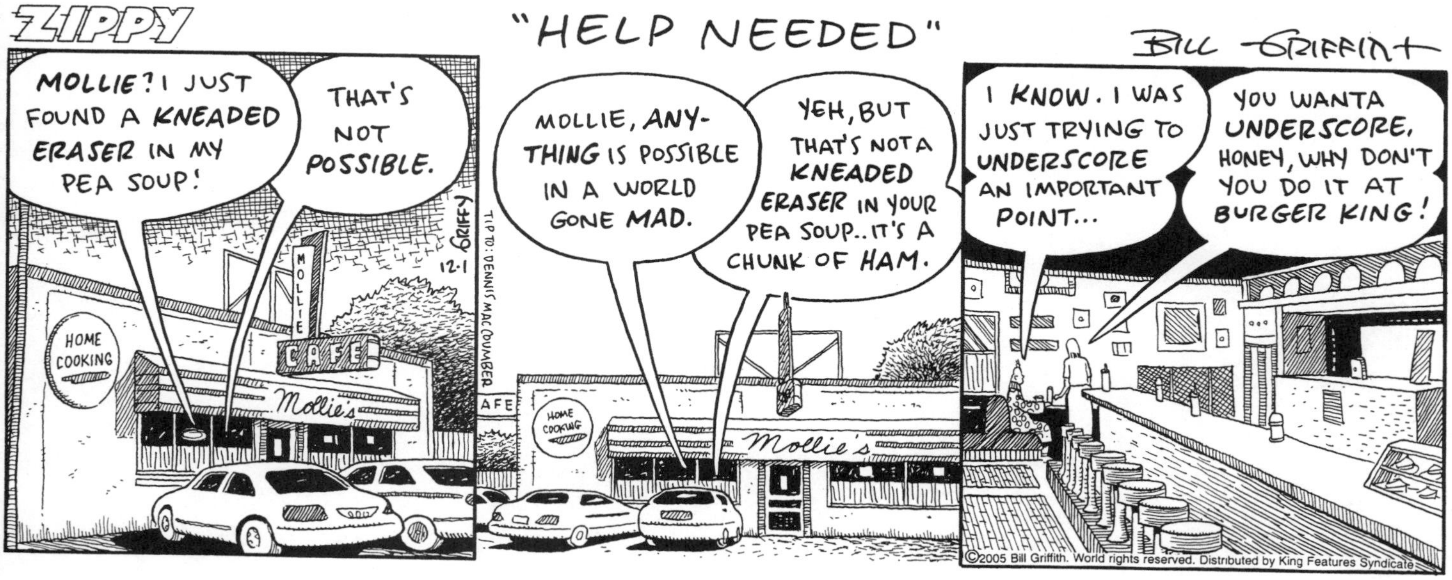
ZIPPY
"HELP NEEDED"
BILL GRIFFITH
MOLLIE? I JUST FOUND A KNEADED ERASER IN MY PEA SOUP!
THAT'S NOT POSSIBLE.
HOME COOKING
MOLLIE
CAFE
Mollie's
12-1
GRIFFY
TIP TO: DENNIS MAC COUMBER
MOLLIE, ANYTHING IS POSSIBLE IN A WORLD GONE MAD.
YEH, BUT THAT'S NOT A KNEADED ERASER IN YOUR PEA SOUP.. IT'S A CHUNK OF HAM.
I KNOW. I WAS JUST TRYING TO UNDERSCORE AN IMPORTANT POINT...
YOU WANTA UNDERSCORE, HONEY, WHY DON'T YOU DO IT AT BURGER KING!
©2005 Bill Griffith. World rights reserved. Distributed by King Features Syndicate

142

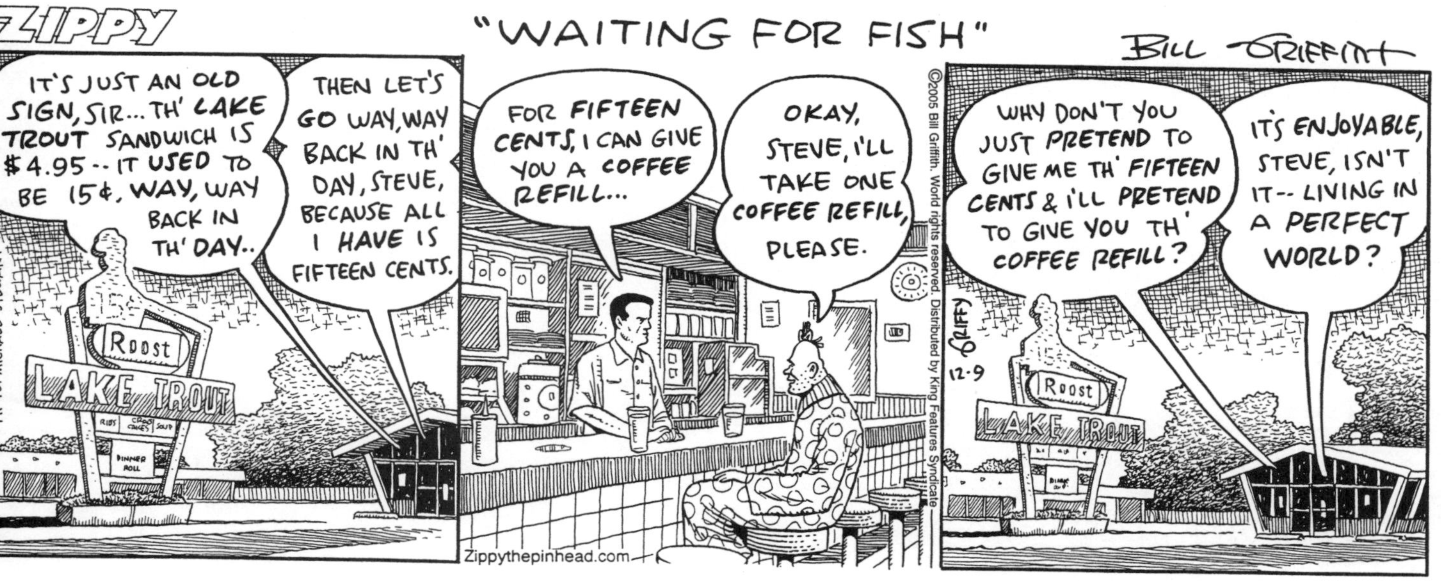
ZIPPY
"WAITING FOR FISH"
BILL GRIFFITH
IT'S JUST AN OLD SIGN, SIR... TH' LAKE TROUT SANDWICH IS $4.95 -- IT USED TO BE 15¢, WAY, WAY BACK IN TH' DAY..
THEN LET'S GO WAY, WAY BACK IN TH' DAY, STEVE, BECAUSE ALL I HAVE IS FIFTEEN CENTS.
TIP TO: MICHAEL STEWART
Roost
LAKE TROUT
FOR FIFTEEN CENTS, I CAN GIVE YOU A COFFEE REFILL...
OKAY, STEVE, I'LL TAKE ONE COFFEE REFILL, PLEASE.
Zippythepinhead.com
©2005 Bill Griffith. World rights reserved. Distributed by King Features Syndicate
WHY DON'T YOU JUST PRETEND TO GIVE ME TH' FIFTEEN CENTS & I'LL PRETEND TO GIVE YOU TH' COFFEE REFILL?
IT'S ENJOYABLE, STEVE, ISN'T IT-- LIVING IN A PERFECT WORLD?
GRIFFY
12-9

143

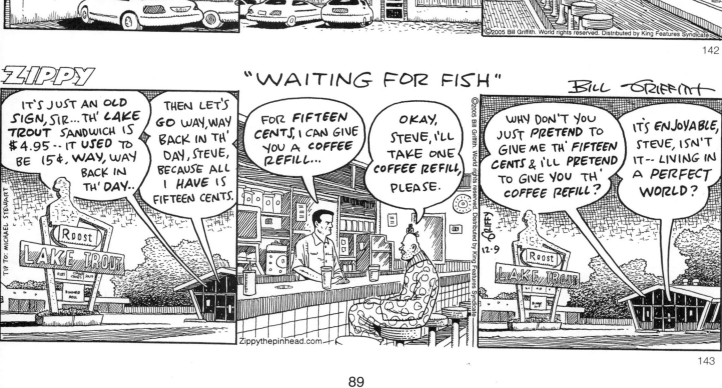

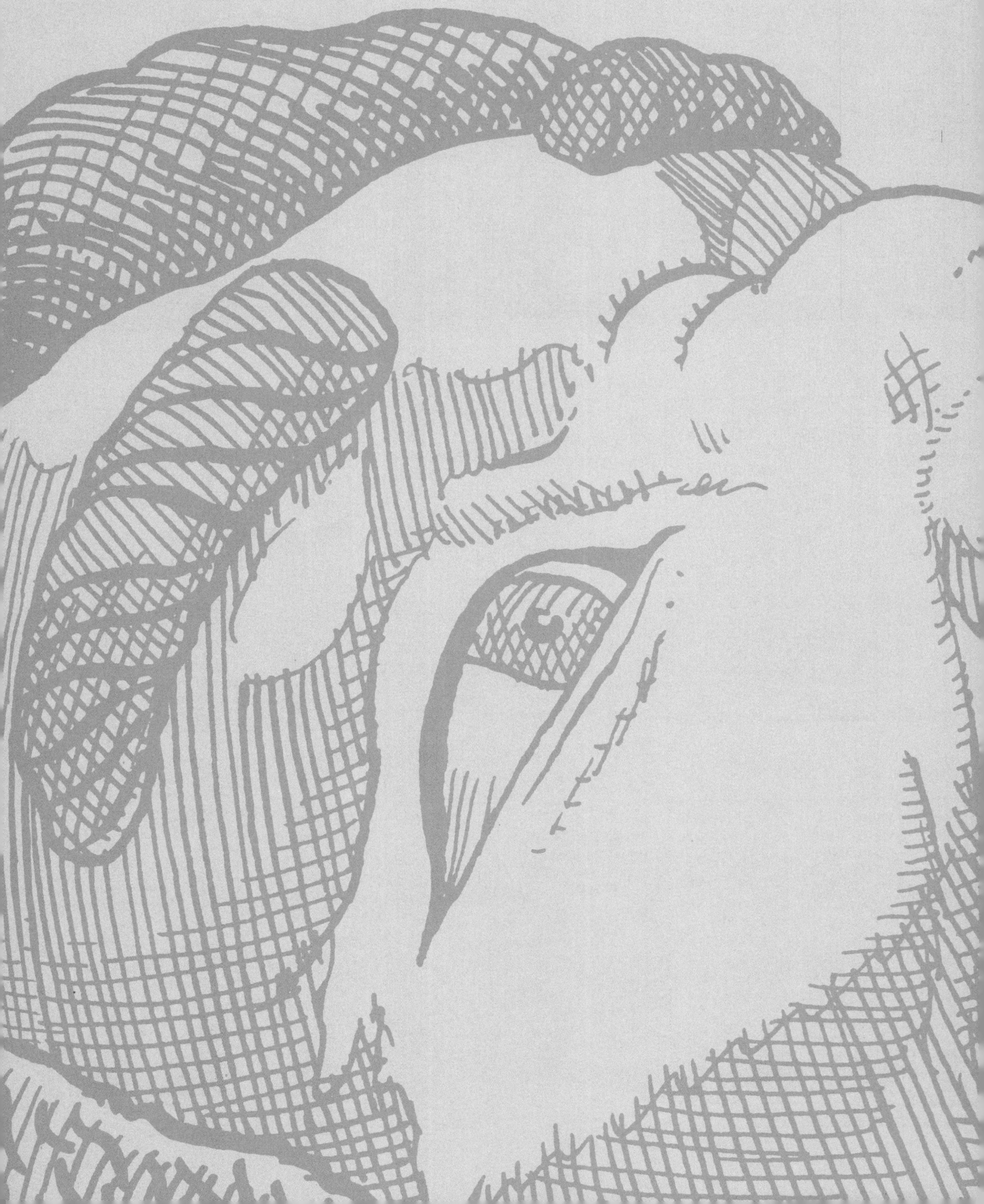

ROADSIDE ATTRACTIONS

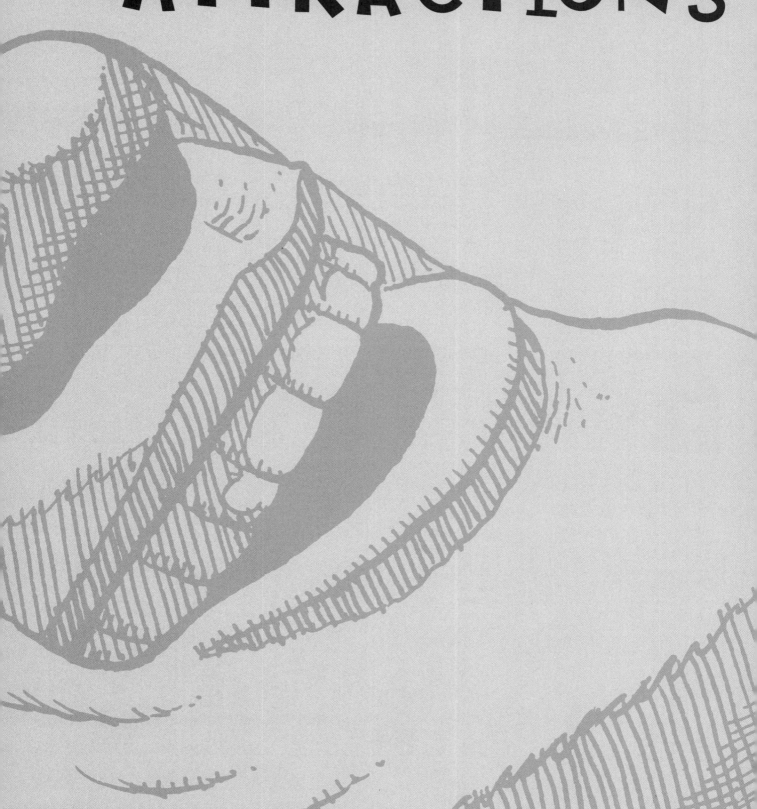

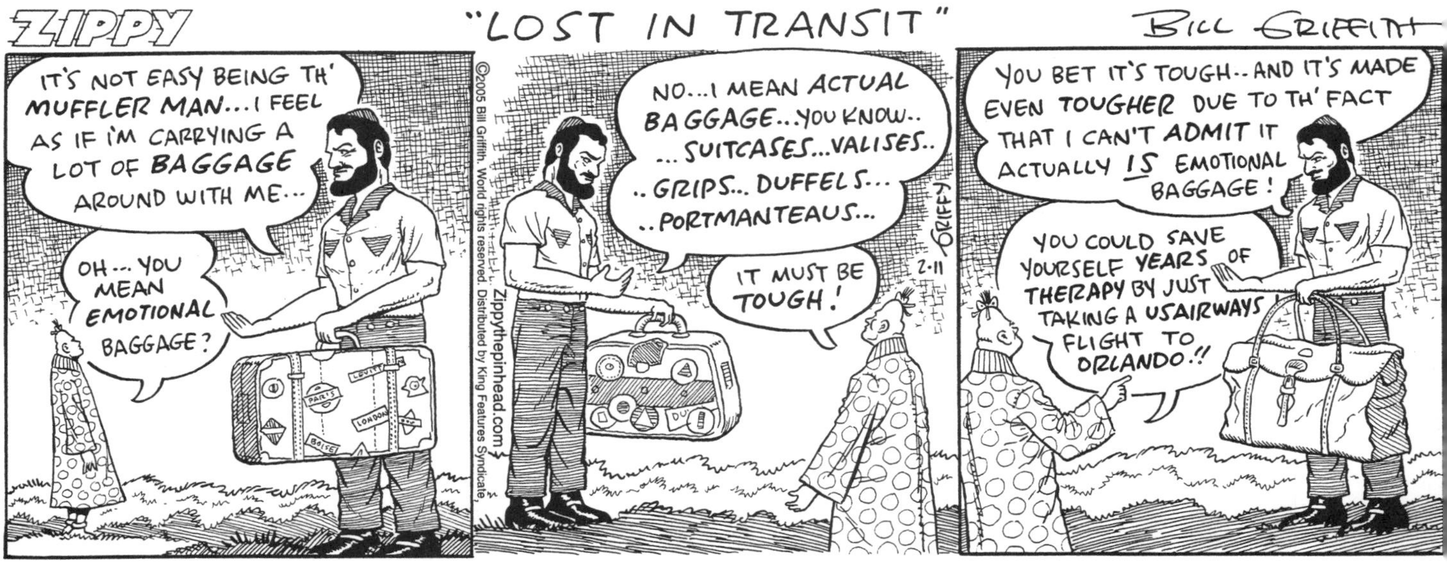
ZIPPY
"LOST IN TRANSIT"
BILL GRIFFITH
IT'S NOT EASY BEING TH' MUFFLER MAN... I FEEL AS IF I'M CARRYING A LOT OF BAGGAGE AROUND WITH ME...
OH... YOU MEAN EMOTIONAL BAGGAGE?
©2005 Bill Griffith. World rights reserved. Distributed by King Features Syndicate
Zippythepinhead.com
NO... I MEAN ACTUAL BAGGAGE... YOU KNOW... ... SUITCASES... VALISES... .. GRIPS... DUFFELS... .. PORTMANTEAUS...
IT MUST BE TOUGH!
GRIFFY
2-11
YOU BET IT'S TOUGH.. AND IT'S MADE EVEN TOUGHER DUE TO TH' FACT THAT I CAN'T ADMIT IT ACTUALLY IS EMOTIONAL BAGGAGE!
YOU COULD SAVE YOURSELF YEARS OF THERAPY BY JUST TAKING A USAIRWAYS FLIGHT TO ORLANDO!!

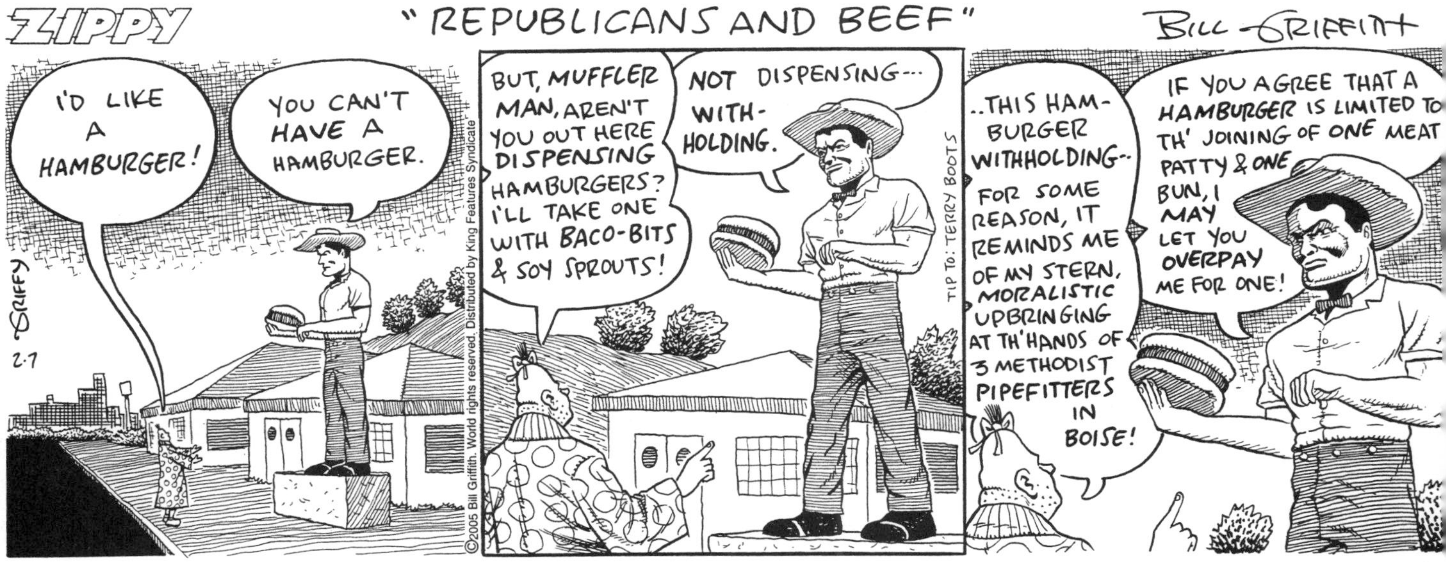
ZIPPY
"REPUBLICANS AND BEEF"
BILL GRIFFITH
I'D LIKE A HAMBURGER!
YOU CAN'T HAVE A HAMBURGER.
GRIFFY
2-7
©2005 Bill Griffith. World rights reserved. Distributed by King Features Syndicate
BUT, MUFFLER MAN, AREN'T YOU OUT HERE DISPENSING HAMBURGERS? I'LL TAKE ONE WITH BACO-BITS & SOY SPROUTS!
NOT DISPENSING... WITHHOLDING.
TIP TO: TERRY BOOTS
..THIS HAMBURGER WITHHOLDING.. FOR SOME REASON, IT REMINDS ME OF MY STERN, MORALISTIC UPBRINGING AT TH' HANDS OF 3 METHODIST PIPEFITTERS IN BOISE!
IF YOU AGREE THAT A HAMBURGER IS LIMITED TO TH' JOINING OF ONE MEAT PATTY & ONE BUN, I MAY LET YOU OVERPAY ME FOR ONE!

144

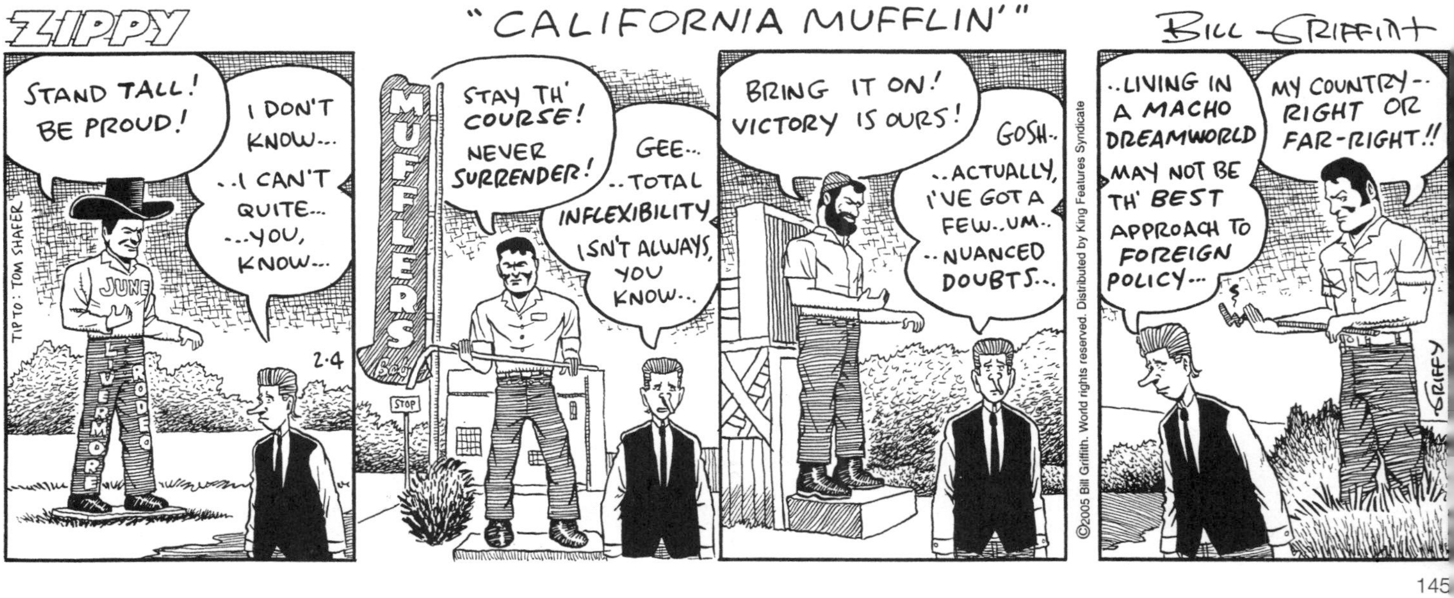
ZIPPY
"CALIFORNIA MUFFLIN'"
BILL GRIFFITH
STAND TALL! BE PROUD!
I DON'T KNOW... ..I CAN'T QUITE... ...YOU, KNOW...
TIP TO: TOM SHAFER
JUNE
LIVERMORE RODEO
2-4
MUFFLERS
STOP
STAY TH' COURSE! NEVER SURRENDER!
GEE... ..TOTAL INFLEXIBILITY ISN'T ALWAYS, YOU KNOW...
BRING IT ON! VICTORY IS OURS!
GOSH.. ..ACTUALLY, I'VE GOT A FEW..UM.. ..NUANCED DOUBTS...
©2005 Bill Griffith. World rights reserved. Distributed by King Features Syndicate
..LIVING IN A MACHO DREAMWORLD MAY NOT BE TH' BEST APPROACH TO FOREIGN POLICY...
MY COUNTRY.. RIGHT OR FAR-RIGHT!!
GRIFFY

145

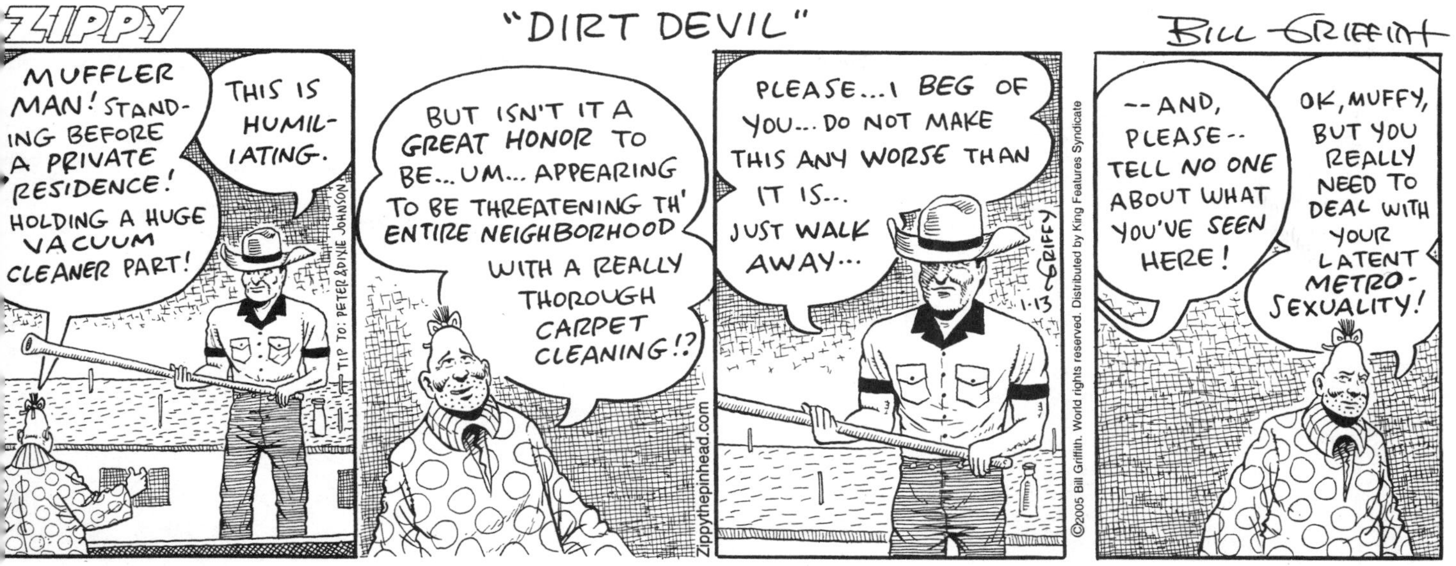
ZIPPY
"DIRT DEVIL"
BILL GRIFFITH
MUFFLER MAN! STANDING BEFORE A PRIVATE RESIDENCE! HOLDING A HUGE VACUUM CLEANER PART!
THIS IS HUMILIATING.
TIP TO: PETER & DIXIE JOHNSON
BUT ISN'T IT A GREAT HONOR TO BE... UM... APPEARING TO BE THREATENING TH' ENTIRE NEIGHBORHOOD
WITH A REALLY THOROUGH CARPET CLEANING!?
Zippythepinhead.com
PLEASE... I BEG OF YOU... DO NOT MAKE THIS ANY WORSE THAN IT IS... JUST WALK AWAY...
GRIFFY 1·13
©2005 Bill Griffith. World rights reserved. Distributed by King Features Syndicate
--AND, PLEASE-- TELL NO ONE ABOUT WHAT YOU'VE SEEN HERE!
OK, MUFFY, BUT YOU REALLY NEED TO DEAL WITH YOUR LATENT METRO-SEXUALITY!

146

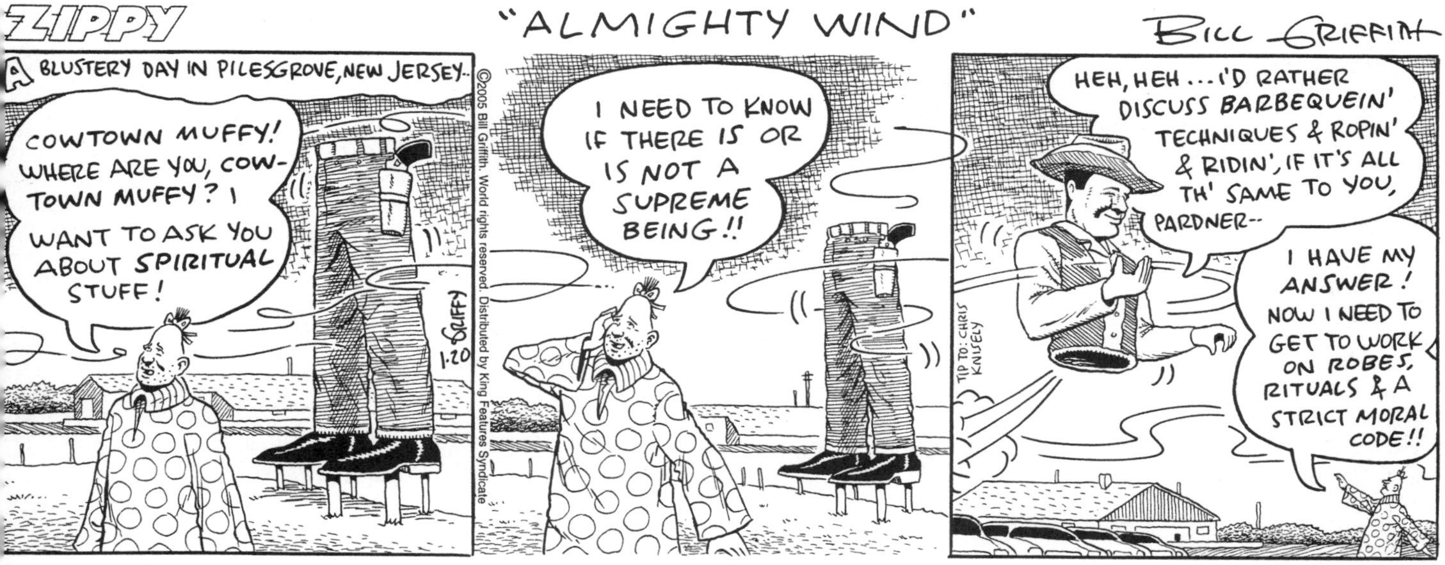
ZIPPY
"ALMIGHTY WIND"
BILL GRIFFITH
A BLUSTERY DAY IN PILESGROVE, NEW JERSEY..
COWTOWN MUFFY! WHERE ARE YOU, COWTOWN MUFFY? I WANT TO ASK YOU ABOUT SPIRITUAL STUFF!
GRIFFY 1·20
©2005 Bill Griffith. World rights reserved. Distributed by King Features Syndicate
I NEED TO KNOW IF THERE IS OR IS NOT A SUPREME BEING!!
TIP TO: CHRIS KNISELY
HEH, HEH ... I'D RATHER DISCUSS BARBEQUEIN' TECHNIQUES & ROPIN' & RIDIN', IF IT'S ALL TH' SAME TO YOU, PARDNER--
I HAVE MY ANSWER! NOW I NEED TO GET TO WORK ON ROBES, RITUALS & A STRICT MORAL CODE!!

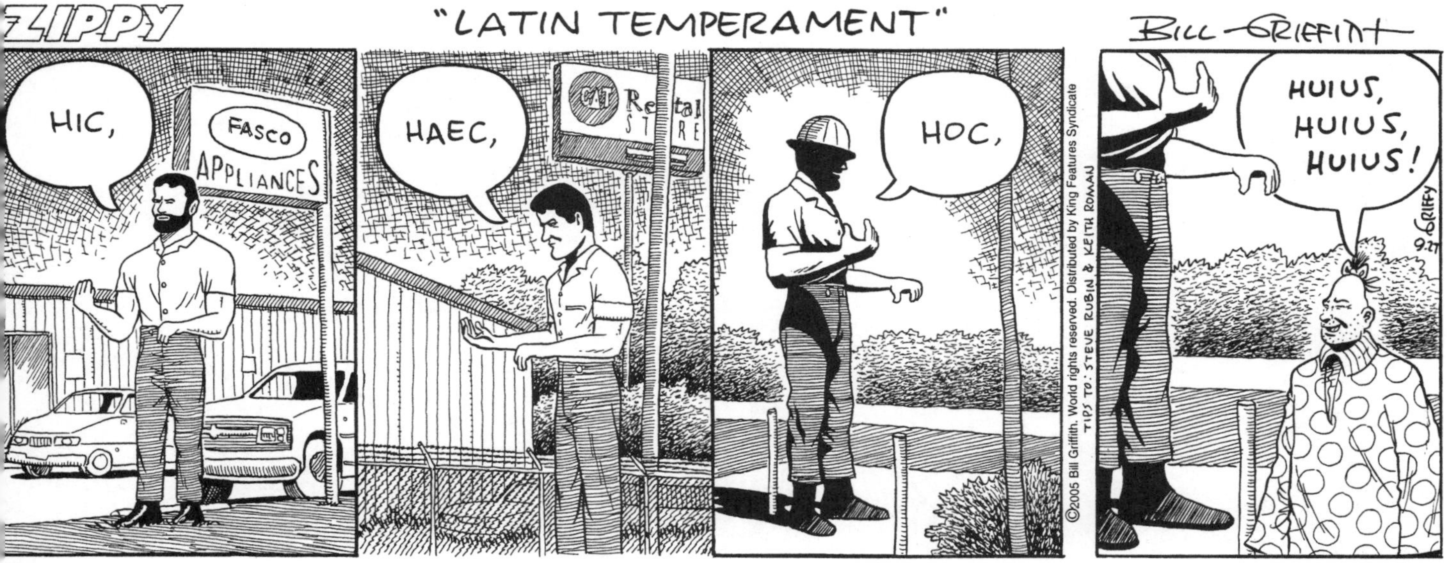
ZIPPY
"LATIN TEMPERAMENT"
BILL GRIFFITH
HIC,
FASCO
APPLIANCES
HAEC,
Rental STORE
HOC,
©2005 Bill Griffith. World rights reserved. Distributed by King Features Syndicate
TIPS TO: STEVE RUBIN & KEITH ROMAN
HUIUS, HUIUS, HUIUS!
GRIFFY 9·27

147

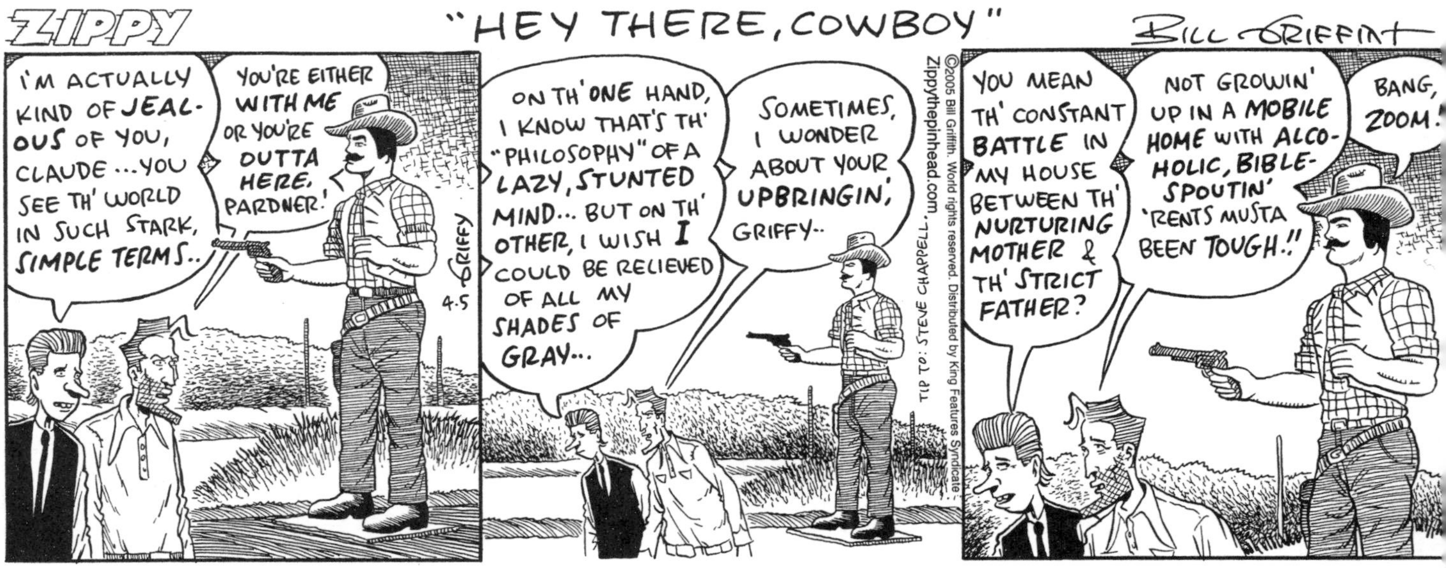
ZIPPY
"HEY THERE, COWBOY"
BILL GRIFFITH
I'M ACTUALLY KIND OF JEALOUS OF YOU, CLAUDE... YOU SEE TH' WORLD IN SUCH STARK, SIMPLE TERMS..
YOU'RE EITHER WITH ME OR YOU'RE OUTTA HERE, PARDNER!
GRIFFY 4-5
ON TH' ONE HAND, I KNOW THAT'S TH' "PHILOSOPHY" OF A LAZY, STUNTED MIND... BUT ON TH' OTHER, I WISH I COULD BE RELIEVED OF ALL MY SHADES OF GRAY...
SOMETIMES, I WONDER ABOUT YOUR UPBRINGIN', GRIFFY..
TIP TO: STEVE CHAPPELL
©2005 Bill Griffith. World rights reserved. Distributed by King Features Syndicate
Zippythepinhead.com
YOU MEAN TH' CONSTANT BATTLE IN MY HOUSE BETWEEN TH' NURTURING MOTHER & TH' STRICT FATHER?
NOT GROWIN' UP IN A MOBILE HOME WITH ALCOHOLIC, BIBLE-SPOUTIN' 'RENTS MUSTA BEEN TOUGH.!!
BANG, ZOOM!

148

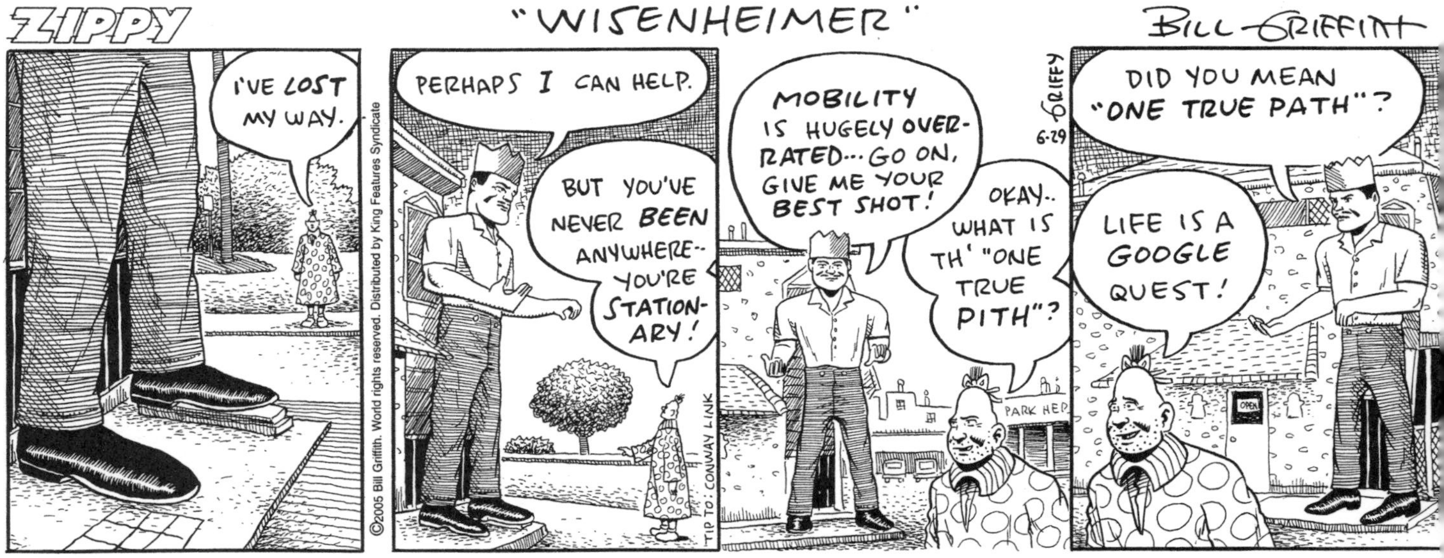
ZIPPY
"WISENHEIMER"
BILL GRIFFITH
I'VE LOST MY WAY.
©2005 Bill Griffith. World rights reserved. Distributed by King Features Syndicate
PERHAPS I CAN HELP.
BUT YOU'VE NEVER BEEN ANYWHERE.. YOU'RE STATIONARY!
TIP TO: CONWAY LINK
GRIFFY 6-29
MOBILITY IS HUGELY OVERRATED... GO ON, GIVE ME YOUR BEST SHOT!
OKAY.. WHAT IS TH' "ONE TRUE PITH"?
PARK HEP
DID YOU MEAN "ONE TRUE PATH"?
LIFE IS A GOOGLE QUEST!
OPEN

149

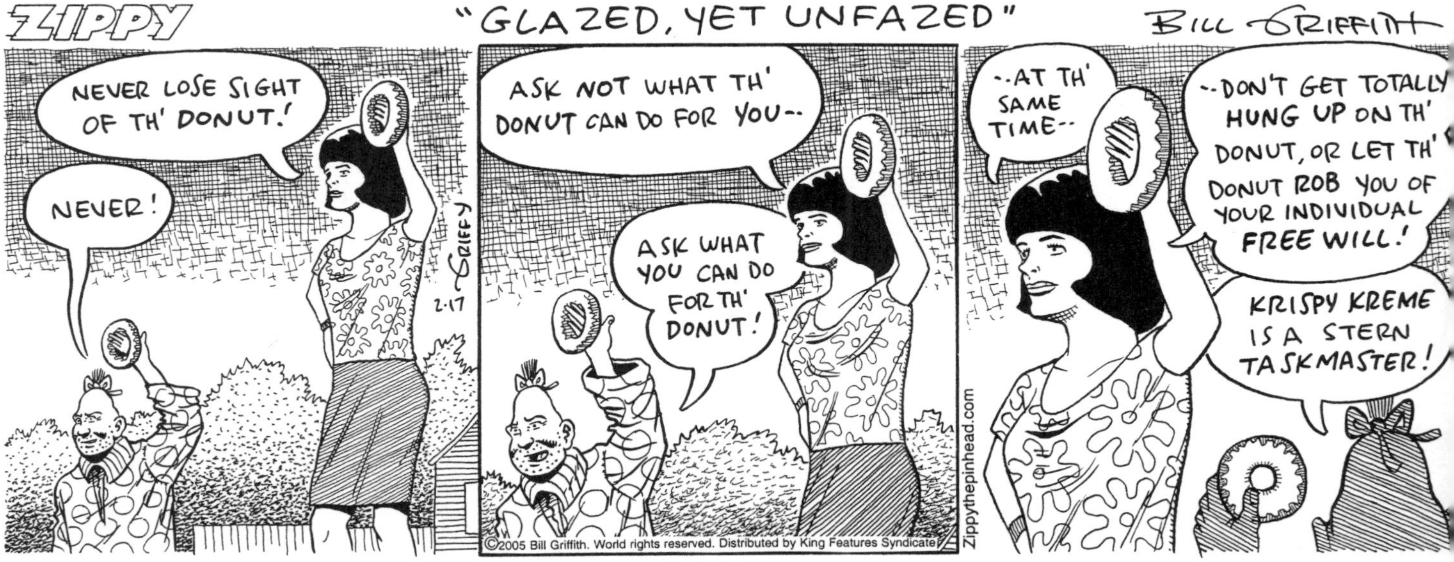
ZIPPY
"GLAZED, YET UNFAZED"
BILL GRIFFITH
NEVER LOSE SIGHT OF TH' DONUT!
NEVER!
GRIFFY 2-17
ASK NOT WHAT TH' DONUT CAN DO FOR YOU--
ASK WHAT YOU CAN DO FOR TH' DONUT!
©2005 Bill Griffith. World rights reserved. Distributed by King Features Syndicate
Zippythepinhead.com
--AT TH' SAME TIME--
--DON'T GET TOTALLY HUNG UP ON TH' DONUT, OR LET TH' DONUT ROB YOU OF YOUR INDIVIDUAL FREE WILL!
KRISPY KREME IS A STERN TASKMASTER!

150

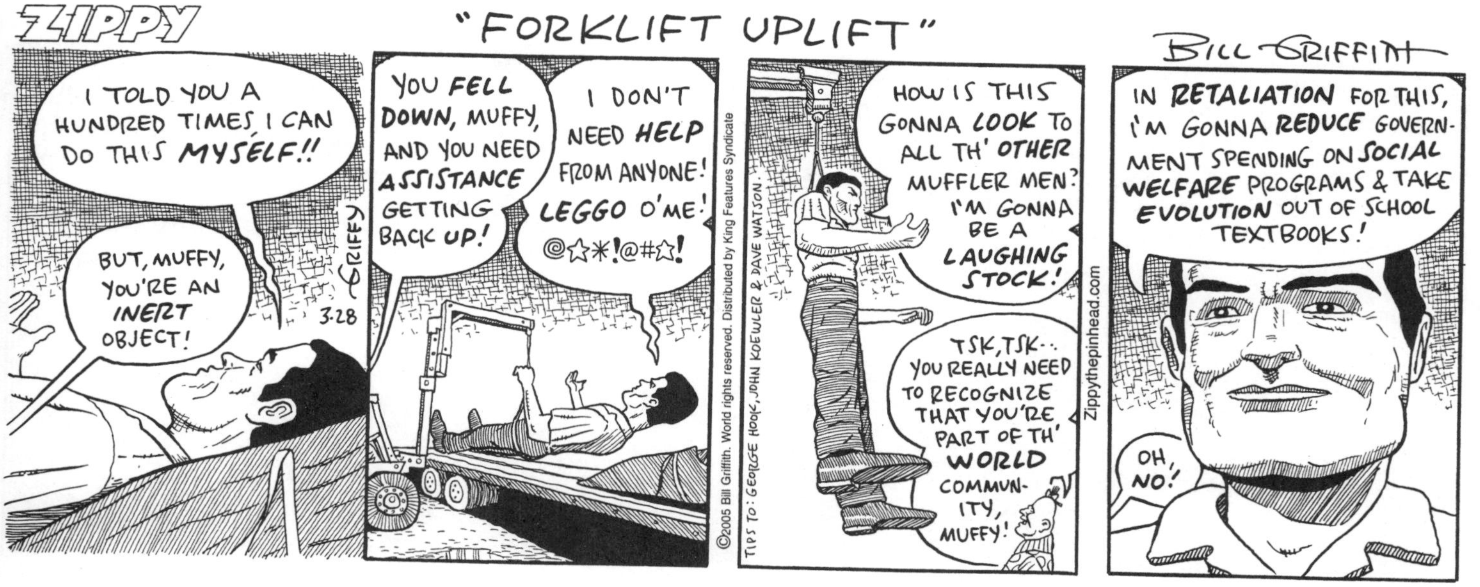
ZIPPY
"FORKLIFT UPLIFT"
BILL GRIFFITH
I TOLD YOU A HUNDRED TIMES, I CAN DO THIS MYSELF!!
BUT, MUFFY, YOU'RE AN INERT OBJECT!
GRIFFY 3-28
YOU FELL DOWN, MUFFY, AND YOU NEED ASSISTANCE GETTING BACK UP!
I DON'T NEED HELP FROM ANYONE! LEGGO O'ME! @☆*!@#☆!
©2005 Bill Griffith. World rights reserved. Distributed by King Features Syndicate
TIPS TO: GEORGE HOOK, JOHN KOEWLER & DAVE WATSON.
HOW IS THIS GONNA LOOK TO ALL TH' OTHER MUFFLER MEN? I'M GONNA BE A LAUGHING STOCK!
TSK, TSK.. YOU REALLY NEED TO RECOGNIZE THAT YOU'RE PART OF TH' WORLD COMMUN-ITY, MUFFY!
Zippythepinhead.com
IN RETALIATION FOR THIS, I'M GONNA REDUCE GOVERNMENT SPENDING ON SOCIAL WELFARE PROGRAMS & TAKE EVOLUTION OUT OF SCHOOL TEXTBOOKS!
OH, NO!

151

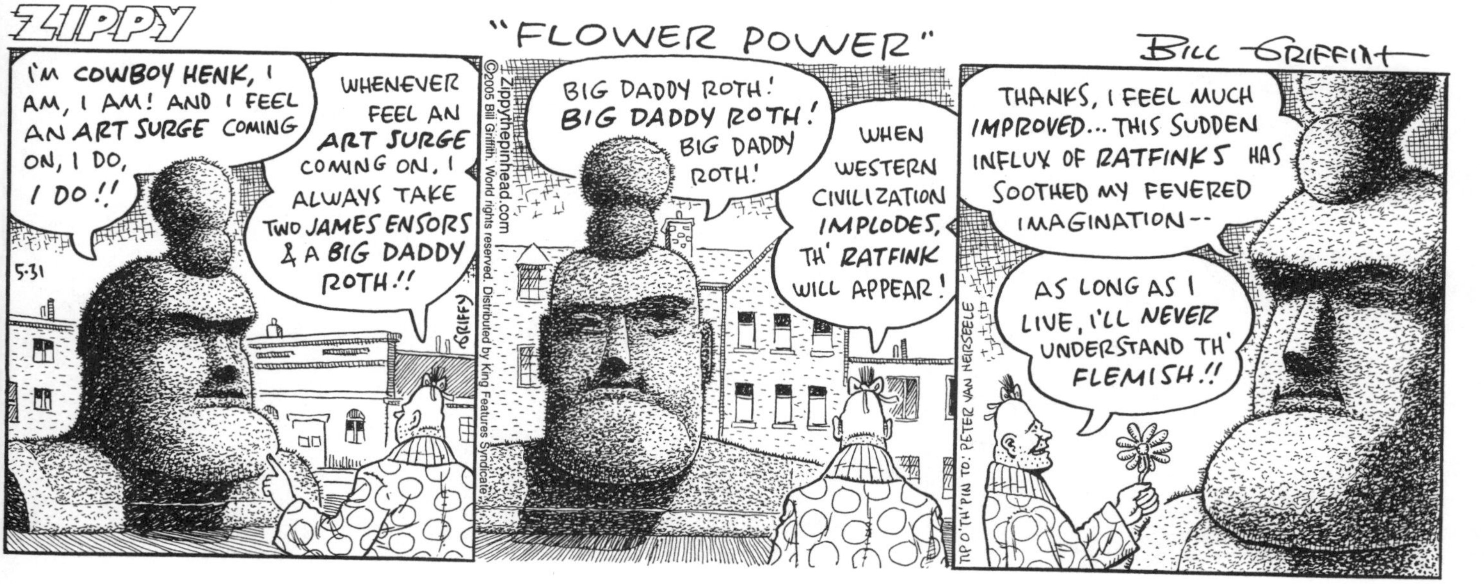
ZIPPY
"FLOWER POWER"
BILL GRIFFITH
I'M COWBOY HENK, I AM, I AM! AND I FEEL AN ART SURGE COMING ON, I DO, I DO!!
WHENEVER I FEEL AN ART SURGE COMING ON, I ALWAYS TAKE TWO JAMES ENSORS & A BIG DADDY ROTH!!
5-31
GRIFFY
©2005 Bill Griffith. World rights reserved. Distributed by King Features Syndicate
Zippythepinhead.com
BIG DADDY ROTH! BIG DADDY ROTH! BIG DADDY ROTH!
WHEN WESTERN CIVILIZATION IMPLODES, TH' RATFINK WILL APPEAR!
TIP O' TH' PIN TO: PETER VAN HEIRSEELE
THANKS, I FEEL MUCH IMPROVED... THIS SUDDEN INFLUX OF RATFINKS HAS SOOTHED MY FEVERED IMAGINATION--
AS LONG AS I LIVE, I'LL NEVER UNDERSTAND TH' FLEMISH!!

152

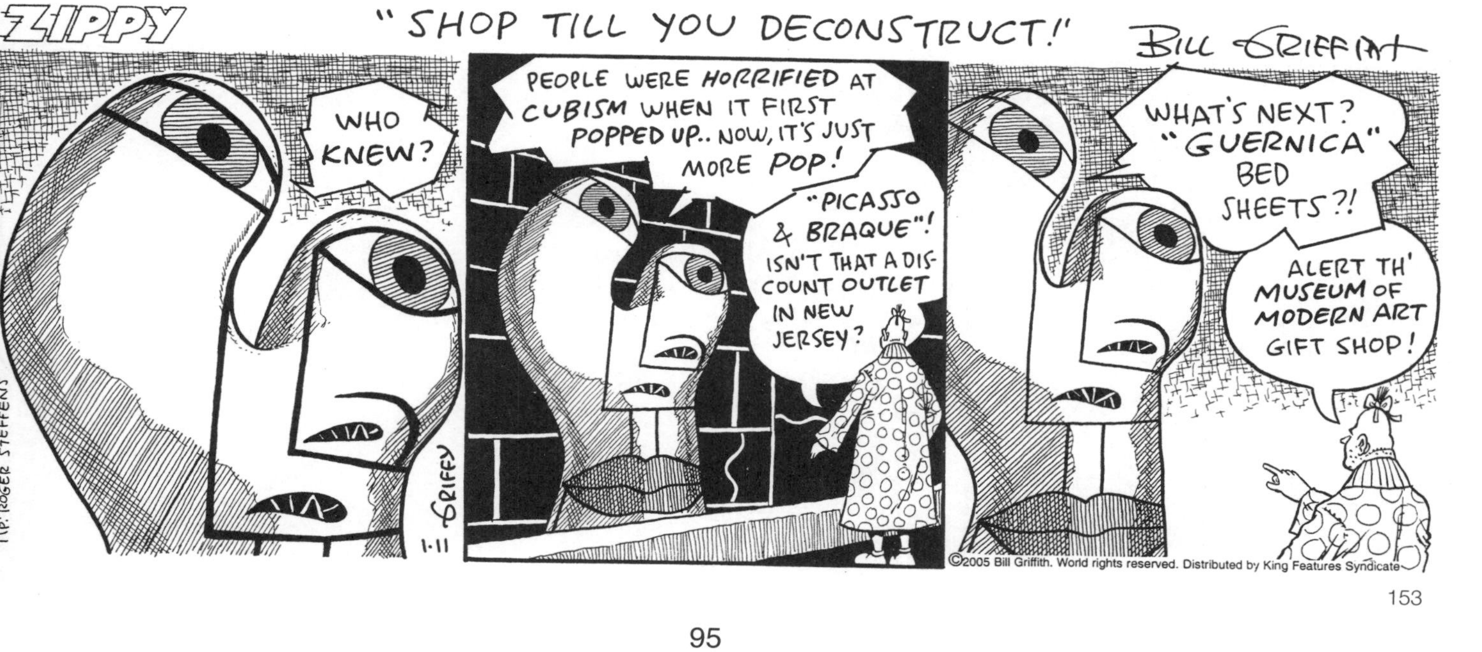
ZIPPY
"SHOP TILL YOU DECONSTRUCT!"
BILL GRIFFITH
WHO KNEW?
TIP: ROGER STEFFENS
GRIFFY 1-11
PEOPLE WERE HORRIFIED AT CUBISM WHEN IT FIRST POPPED UP.. NOW, IT'S JUST MORE POP!
"PICASSO & BRAQUE"! ISN'T THAT A DISCOUNT OUTLET IN NEW JERSEY?
WHAT'S NEXT? "GUERNICA" BED SHEETS?!
ALERT TH' MUSEUM OF MODERN ART GIFT SHOP!
©2005 Bill Griffith. World rights reserved. Distributed by King Features Syndicate

153

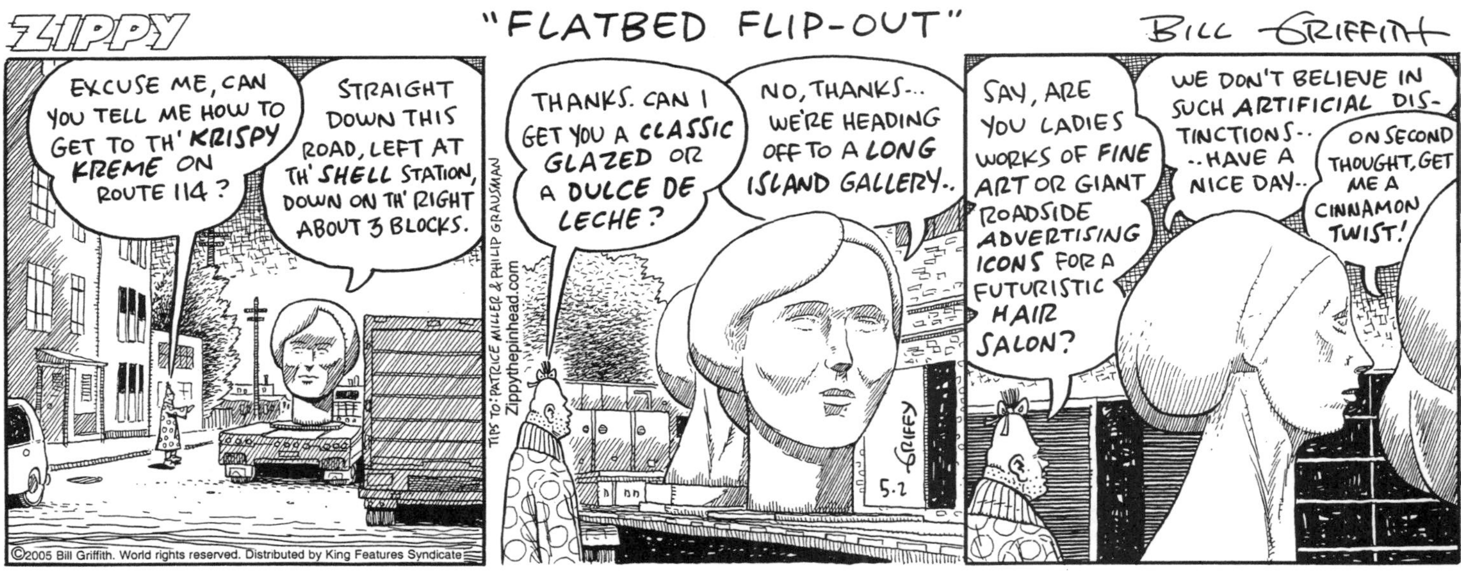
ZIPPY
"FLATBED FLIP-OUT"
BILL GRIFFITH
EXCUSE ME, CAN YOU TELL ME HOW TO GET TO TH' KRISPY KREME ON ROUTE 114?
STRAIGHT DOWN THIS ROAD, LEFT AT TH' SHELL STATION, DOWN ON TH' RIGHT ABOUT 3 BLOCKS.
TIPS TO: PATRICE MILLER & PHILIP GRAUSMAN
Zippythepinhead.com
THANKS. CAN I GET YOU A CLASSIC GLAZED OR A DULCE DE LECHE?
NO, THANKS... WE'RE HEADING OFF TO A LONG ISLAND GALLERY..
GRIFFY 5-2
SAY, ARE YOU LADIES WORKS OF FINE ART OR GIANT ROADSIDE ADVERTISING ICONS FOR A FUTURISTIC HAIR SALON?
WE DON'T BELIEVE IN SUCH ARTIFICIAL DISTINCTIONS.. ..HAVE A NICE DAY..
ON SECOND THOUGHT, GET ME A CINNAMON TWIST!
©2005 Bill Griffith. World rights reserved. Distributed by King Features Syndicate

154

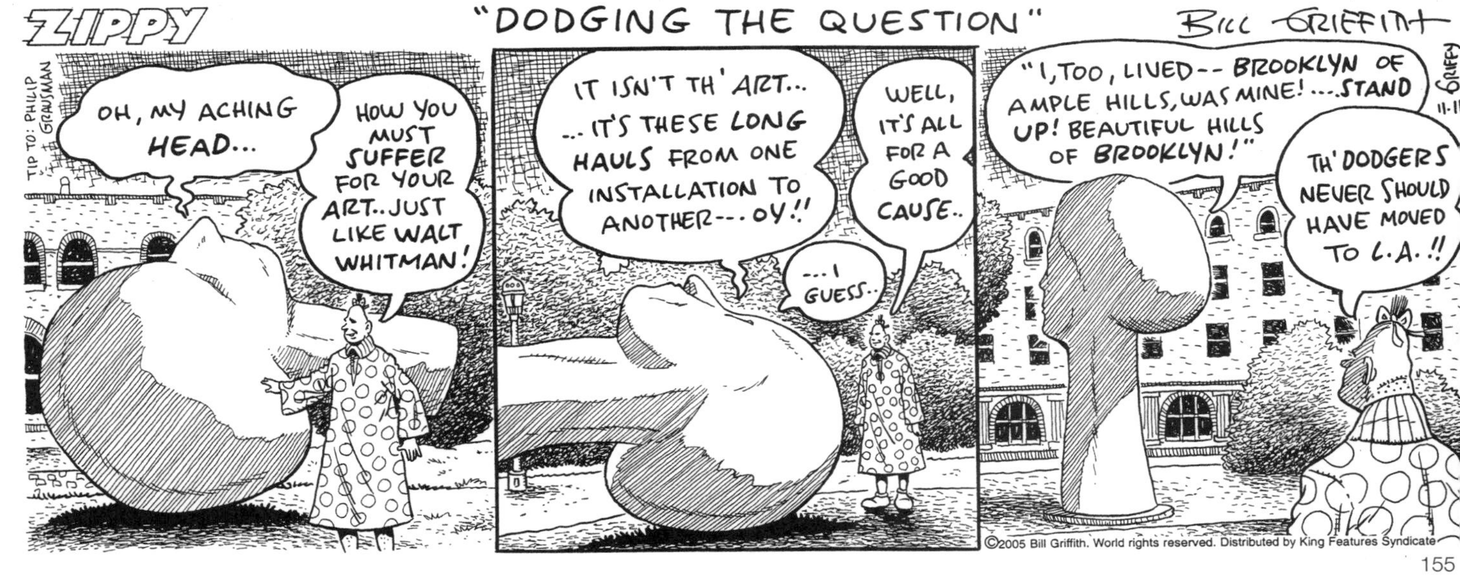
ZIPPY
"DODGING THE QUESTION"
BILL GRIFFITH
TIP TO: PHILIP GRAUSMAN
OH, MY ACHING HEAD...
HOW YOU MUST SUFFER FOR YOUR ART.. JUST LIKE WALT WHITMAN!
IT ISN'T TH' ART... ...IT'S THESE LONG HAULS FROM ONE INSTALLATION TO ANOTHER---OY!!
WELL, IT'S ALL FOR A GOOD CAUSE..
...I GUESS..
GRIFFY 11-1
"I, TOO, LIVED-- BROOKLYN OF AMPLE HILLS, WAS MINE! ....STAND UP! BEAUTIFUL HILLS OF BROOKLYN!"
TH' DODGERS NEVER SHOULD HAVE MOVED TO L.A.!!
©2005 Bill Griffith. World rights reserved. Distributed by King Features Syndicate

155

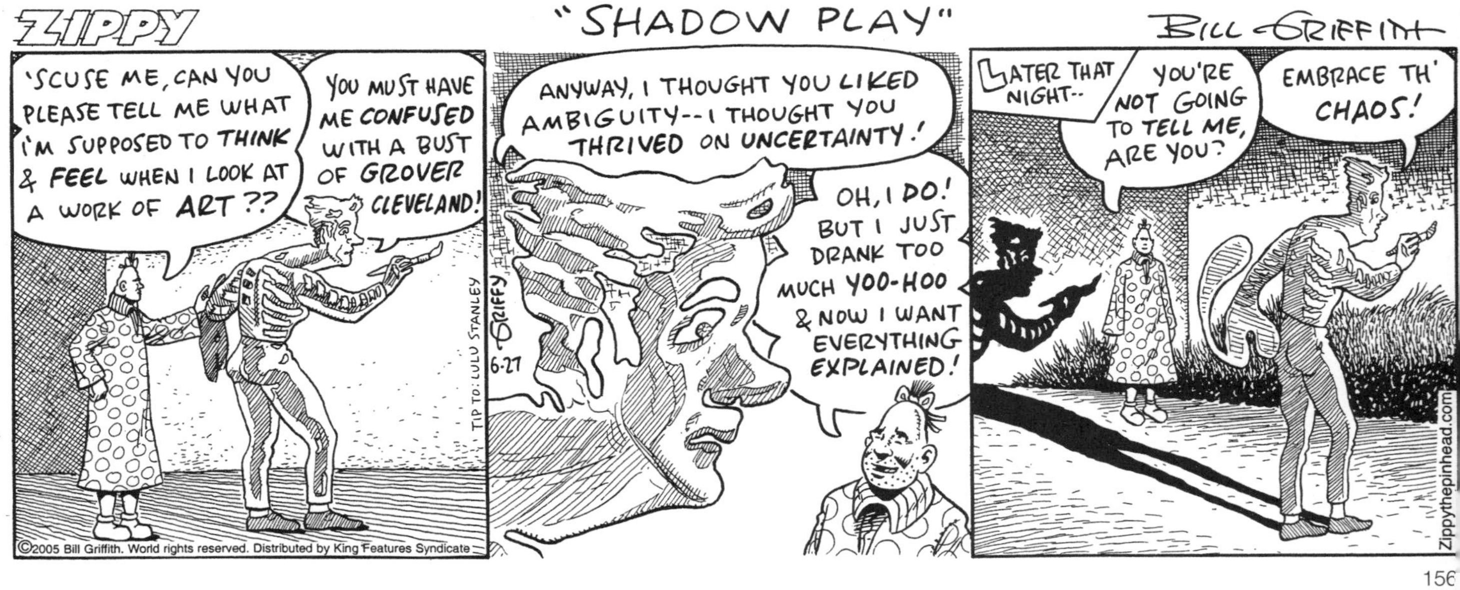
ZIPPY
"SHADOW PLAY"
BILL GRIFFITH
'SCUSE ME, CAN YOU PLEASE TELL ME WHAT I'M SUPPOSED TO THINK & FEEL WHEN I LOOK AT A WORK OF ART??
YOU MUST HAVE ME CONFUSED WITH A BUST OF GROVER CLEVELAND!
TIP TO: LULU STANLEY
GRIFFY 6-27
ANYWAY, I THOUGHT YOU LIKED AMBIGUITY--I THOUGHT YOU THRIVED ON UNCERTAINTY!
OH, I DO! BUT I JUST DRANK TOO MUCH YOO-HOO & NOW I WANT EVERYTHING EXPLAINED!
LATER THAT NIGHT..
YOU'RE NOT GOING TO TELL ME, ARE YOU?
EMBRACE TH' CHAOS!
Zippythepinhead.com
©2005 Bill Griffith. World rights reserved. Distributed by King Features Syndicate

156

ZIPPY "APPLE SUPPORT" BILL GRIFFITH

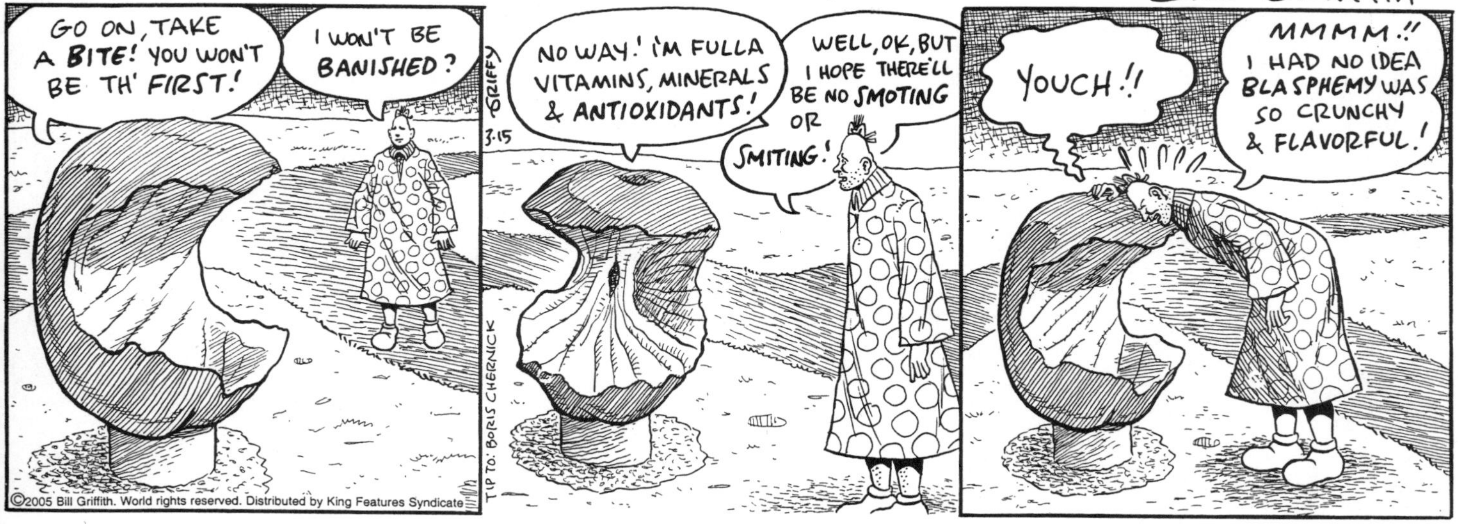
GO ON, TAKE A BITE! YOU WON'T BE TH' FIRST!
I WON'T BE BANISHED?
GRIFFY 3·15
NO WAY! I'M FULLA VITAMINS, MINERALS & ANTIOXIDANTS!
WELL, OK, BUT I HOPE THERE'LL BE NO SMOTING OR SMITING!
TIP TO: BORIS CHERNICK
YOUCH!!
MMMM!! I HAD NO IDEA BLASPHEMY WAS SO CRUNCHY & FLAVORFUL!
©2005 Bill Griffith. World rights reserved. Distributed by King Features Syndicate

157

ZIPPY "HAPPY BLUE YEAR" BILL GRIFFITH

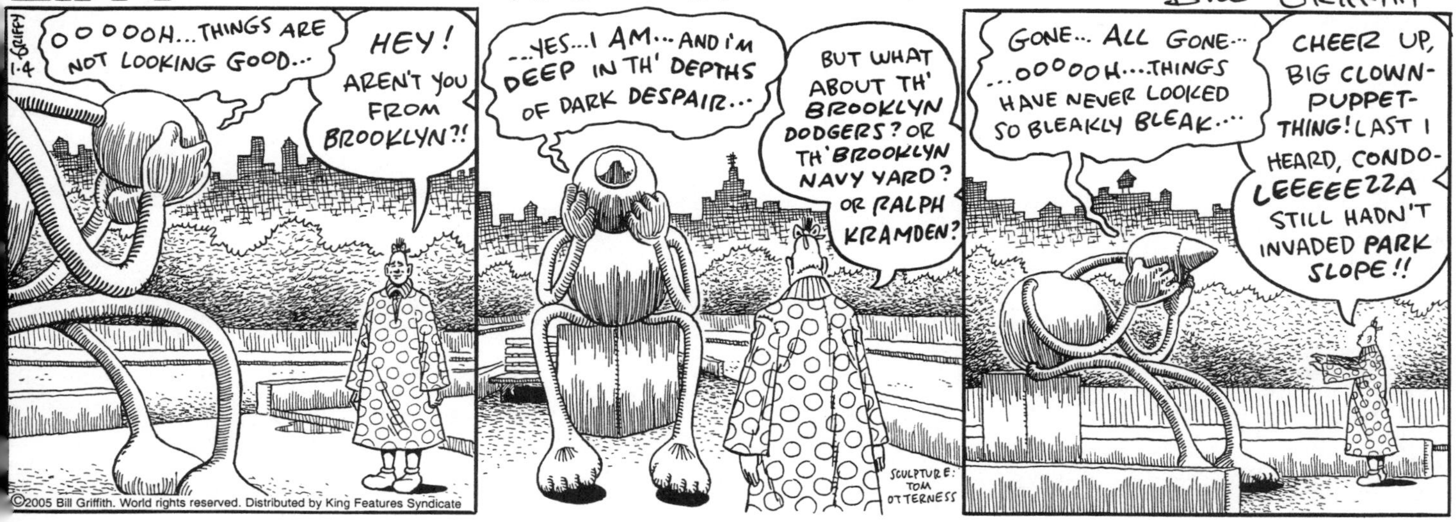
GRIFFY 1·4
OOOOOH... THINGS ARE NOT LOOKING GOOD...
HEY! AREN'T YOU FROM BROOKLYN?!
...YES...I AM...AND I'M DEEP IN TH' DEPTHS OF DARK DESPAIR...
BUT WHAT ABOUT TH' BROOKLYN DODGERS? OR TH' BROOKLYN NAVY YARD? OR RALPH KRAMDEN?
SCULPTURE: TOM OTTERNESS
GONE... ALL GONE... ...OOOOOH....THINGS HAVE NEVER LOOKED SO BLEAKLY BLEAK....
CHEER UP, BIG CLOWN-PUPPET-THING! LAST I HEARD, CONDO-LEEEEEZZA STILL HADN'T INVADED PARK SLOPE!!
©2005 Bill Griffith. World rights reserved. Distributed by King Features Syndicate

158

ZIPPY "WEIRD IN INDIANA" BILL GRIFFITH

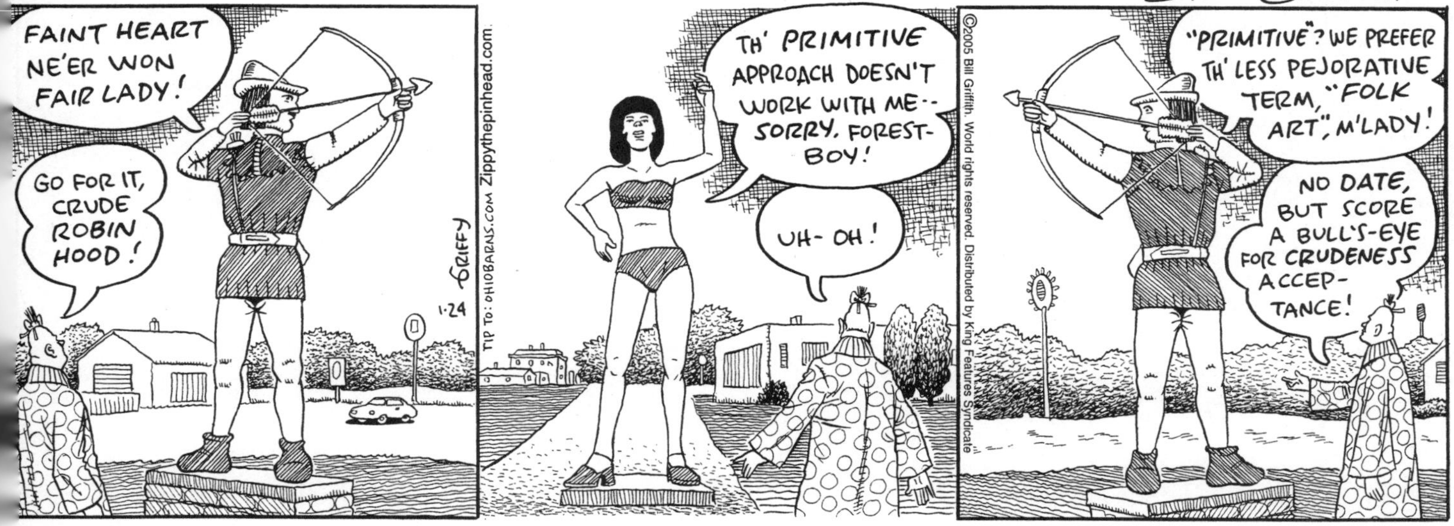
FAINT HEART NE'ER WON FAIR LADY!
GO FOR IT, CRUDE ROBIN HOOD!
GRIFFY 1·24
TIP TO: OHIOBARNS.COM Zippythepinhead.com
TH' PRIMITIVE APPROACH DOESN'T WORK WITH ME-- SORRY, FOREST-BOY!
UH-OH!
©2005 Bill Griffith. World rights reserved. Distributed by King Features Syndicate
"PRIMITIVE"? WE PREFER TH' LESS PEJORATIVE TERM, "FOLK ART", M'LADY!
NO DATE, BUT SCORE A BULL'S-EYE FOR CRUDENESS ACCEP-TANCE!

159

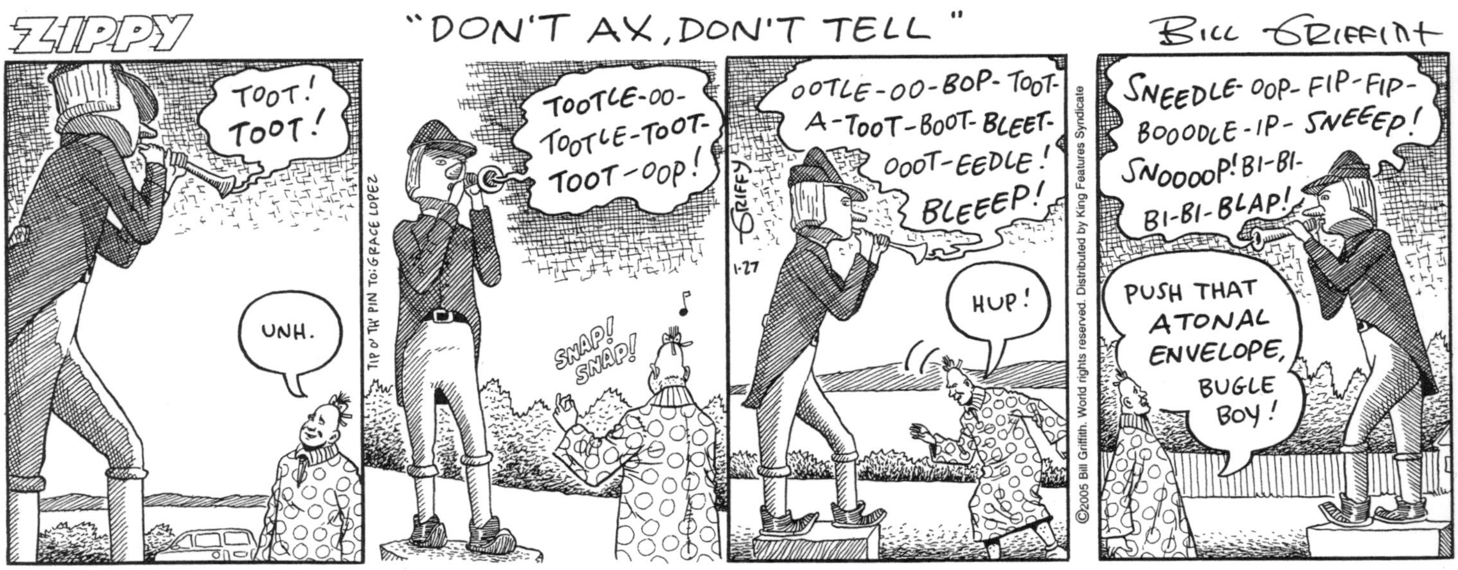
ZIPPY
"DON'T AX, DON'T TELL"
BILL GRIFFITH
TOOT! TOOT!
UNH.
TIP O' TH' PIN TO: GRACE LOPEZ
TOOTLE-OO-TOOTLE-TOOT-TOOT-OOP!
SNAP! SNAP!
OOTLE-OO-BOP-TOOT-A-TOOT-BOOT-BLEET-OOOT-EEDLE! BLEEEP!
GRIFFY 1-27
HUP!
©2005 Bill Griffith. World rights reserved. Distributed by King Features Syndicate
SNEEDLE-OOP-FIP-FIP-BOOODLE-IP-SNEEEP! SNOOOOP! BI-BI-BI-BI-BLAP!
PUSH THAT ATONAL ENVELOPE, BUGLE BOY!

160

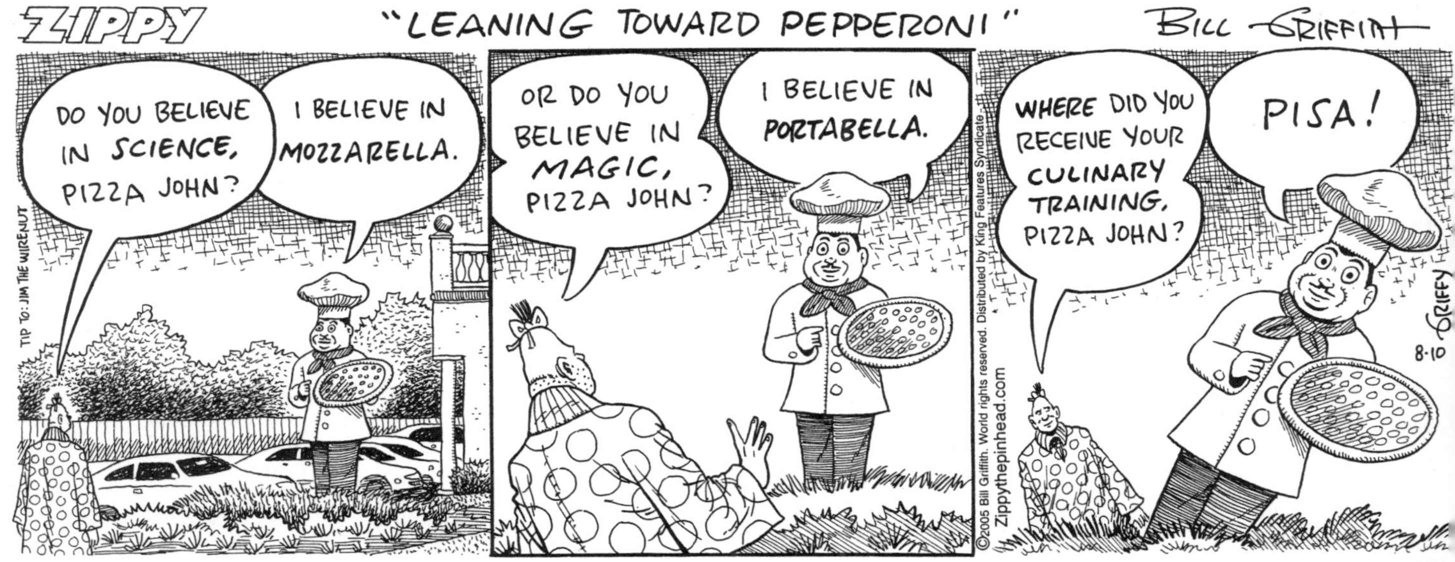
ZIPPY
"LEANING TOWARD PEPPERONI"
BILL GRIFFITH
DO YOU BELIEVE IN SCIENCE, PIZZA JOHN?
I BELIEVE IN MOZZARELLA.
TIP TO: JIM THE WIRENUT
OR DO YOU BELIEVE IN MAGIC, PIZZA JOHN?
I BELIEVE IN PORTABELLA.
©2005 Bill Griffith. World rights reserved. Distributed by King Features Syndicate
Zippythepinhead.com
WHERE DID YOU RECEIVE YOUR CULINARY TRAINING, PIZZA JOHN?
PISA!
GRIFFY 8-10

161

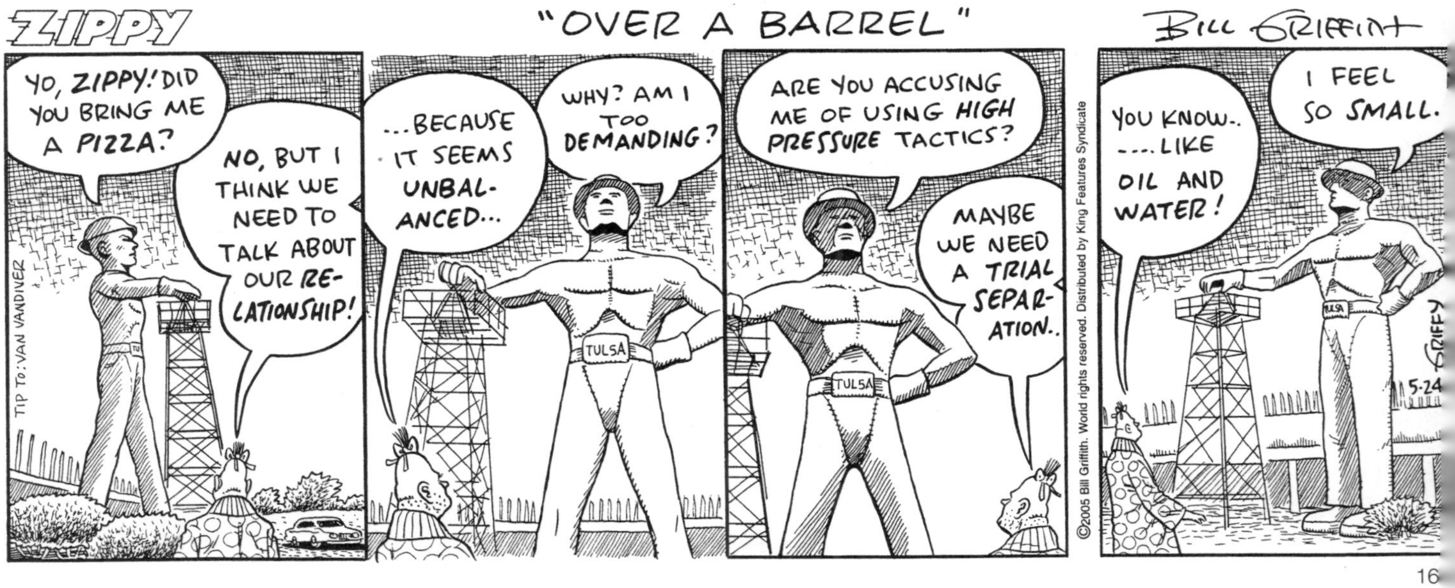
ZIPPY
"OVER A BARREL"
BILL GRIFFITH
YO, ZIPPY! DID YOU BRING ME A PIZZA?
NO, BUT I THINK WE NEED TO TALK ABOUT OUR RELATIONSHIP!
TIP TO: VAN VANDIVER
...BECAUSE IT SEEMS UNBALANCED...
WHY? AM I TOO DEMANDING?
TULSA
ARE YOU ACCUSING ME OF USING HIGH PRESSURE TACTICS?
MAYBE WE NEED A TRIAL SEPARATION..
TULSA
©2005 Bill Griffith. World rights reserved. Distributed by King Features Syndicate
YOU KNOW.. ....LIKE OIL AND WATER!
I FEEL SO SMALL.
GRIFFY 5-24

16

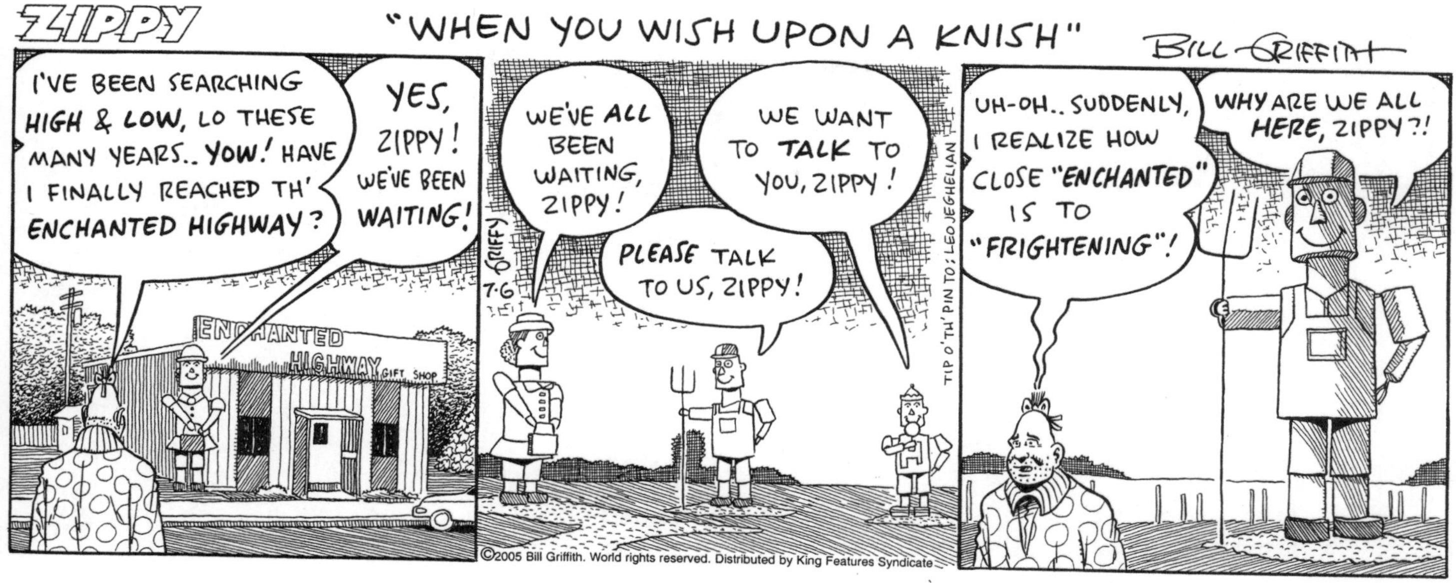

ZIPPY
"WHEN YOU WISH UPON A KNISH"
BILL GRIFFITH
I'VE BEEN SEARCHING HIGH & LOW, LO THESE MANY YEARS.. YOW! HAVE I FINALLY REACHED TH' ENCHANTED HIGHWAY?
YES, ZIPPY! WE'VE BEEN WAITING!
ENCHANTED HIGHWAY GIFT SHOP
WE'VE ALL BEEN WAITING, ZIPPY!
WE WANT TO TALK TO YOU, ZIPPY!
PLEASE TALK TO US, ZIPPY!
GRIFFY 7·6
TIP O' TH' PIN TO: LEO JEGHELYAN
UH-OH.. SUDDENLY, I REALIZE HOW CLOSE "ENCHANTED" IS TO "FRIGHTENING"!
WHY ARE WE ALL HERE, ZIPPY?!
©2005 Bill Griffith. World rights reserved. Distributed by King Features Syndicate

163

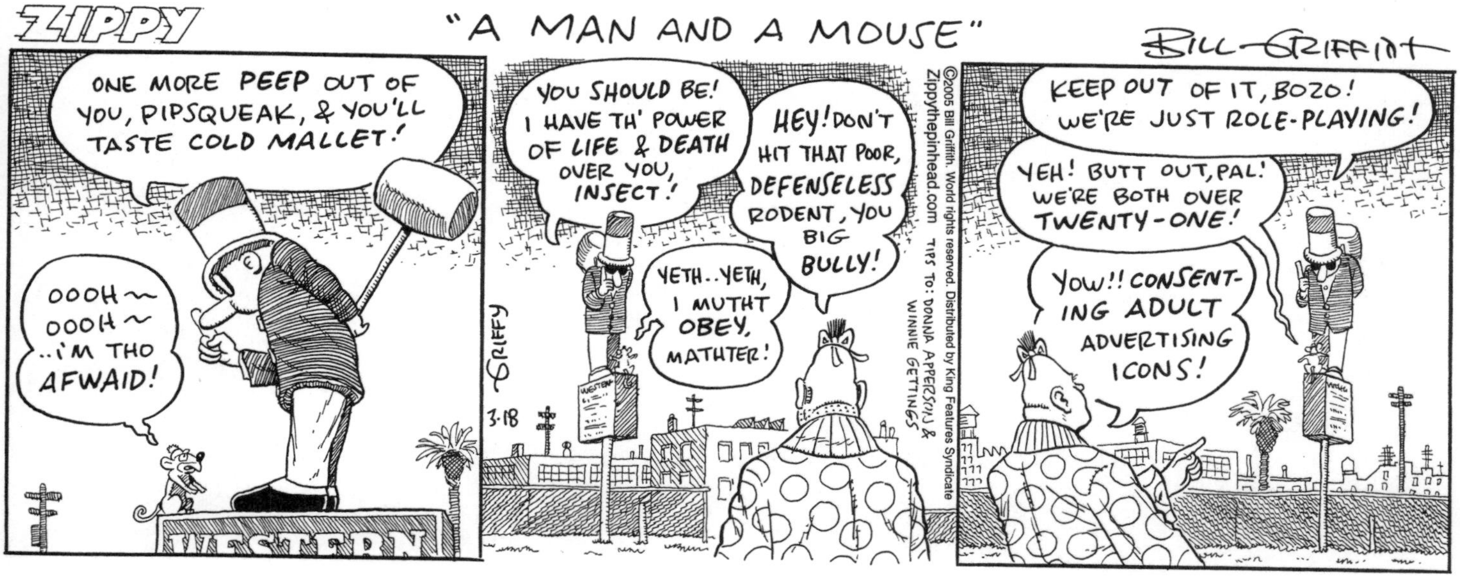

ZIPPY
"A MAN AND A MOUSE"
BILL GRIFFITH
ONE MORE PEEP OUT OF YOU, PIPSQUEAK, & YOU'LL TASTE COLD MALLET!
OOOH~ OOOH~ ..I'M THO AFWAID!
WESTERN
YOU SHOULD BE! I HAVE TH' POWER OF LIFE & DEATH OVER YOU, INSECT!
YETH..YETH, I MUTHT OBEY, MATHTER!
HEY! DON'T HIT THAT POOR, DEFENSELESS RODENT, YOU BIG BULLY!
GRIFFY 3·18
©2005 Bill Griffith. World rights reserved. Distributed by King Features Syndicate
Zippythepinhead.com
TIPS TO: DONNA APPERSON & WINNIE GETTINGS
KEEP OUT OF IT, BOZO! WE'RE JUST ROLE-PLAYING!
YEH! BUTT OUT, PAL! WE'RE BOTH OVER TWENTY-ONE!
YOW!! CONSENTING ADULT ADVERTISING ICONS!

164

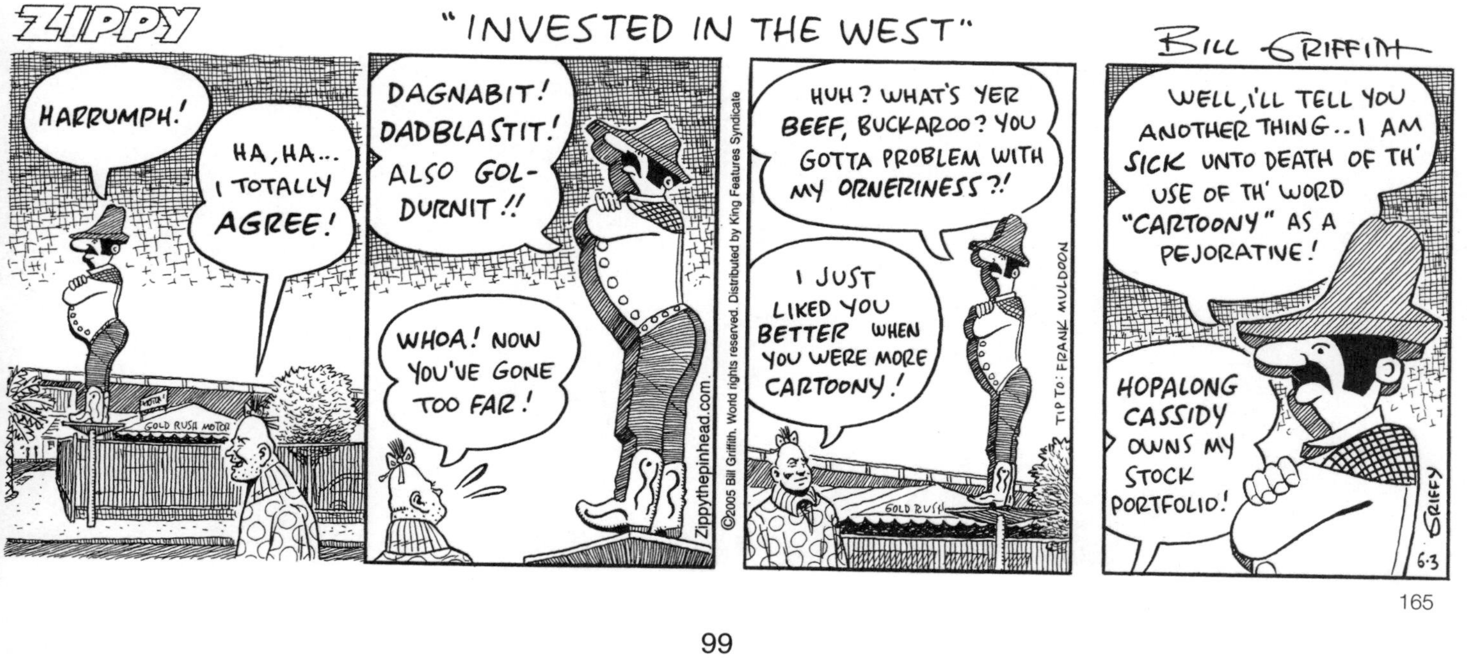

ZIPPY
"INVESTED IN THE WEST"
BILL GRIFFITH
HARRUMPH!
HA, HA... I TOTALLY AGREE!
GOLD RUSH MOTOR
DAGNABIT! DADBLASTIT! ALSO GOL-DURNIT!!
WHOA! NOW YOU'VE GONE TOO FAR!
©2005 Bill Griffith. World rights reserved. Distributed by King Features Syndicate
Zippythepinhead.com
HUH? WHAT'S YER BEEF, BUCKAROO? YOU GOTTA PROBLEM WITH MY ORNERINESS?!
I JUST LIKED YOU BETTER WHEN YOU WERE MORE CARTOONY!
TIP TO: FRANK MULDOON
GOLD RUSH
WELL, I'LL TELL YOU ANOTHER THING.. I AM SICK UNTO DEATH OF TH' USE OF TH' WORD "CARTOONY" AS A PEJORATIVE!
HOPALONG CASSIDY OWNS MY STOCK PORTFOLIO!
GRIFFY 6·3

165

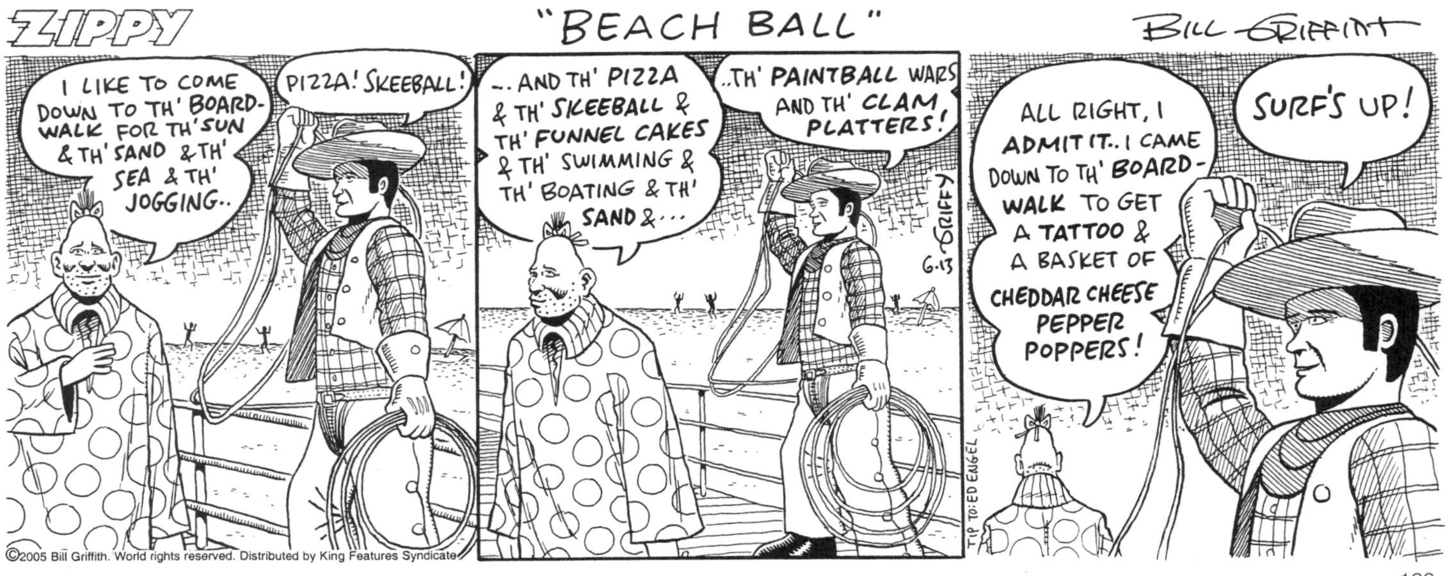
ZIPPY
"BEACH BALL"
BILL GRIFFITH
I LIKE TO COME DOWN TO TH' BOARD-WALK FOR TH' SUN & TH' SAND & TH' SEA & TH' JOGGING..
PIZZA! SKEEBALL!
-- AND TH' PIZZA & TH' SKEEBALL & TH' FUNNEL CAKES & TH' SWIMMING & TH' BOATING & TH' SAND & ...
..TH' PAINTBALL WARS AND TH' CLAM PLATTERS!
GRIFFY 6-13
ALL RIGHT, I ADMIT IT.. I CAME DOWN TO TH' BOARD-WALK TO GET A TATTOO & A BASKET OF CHEDDAR CHEESE PEPPER POPPERS!
SURF'S UP!
TIP TO: ED ENGEL
©2005 Bill Griffith. World rights reserved. Distributed by King Features Syndicate

166

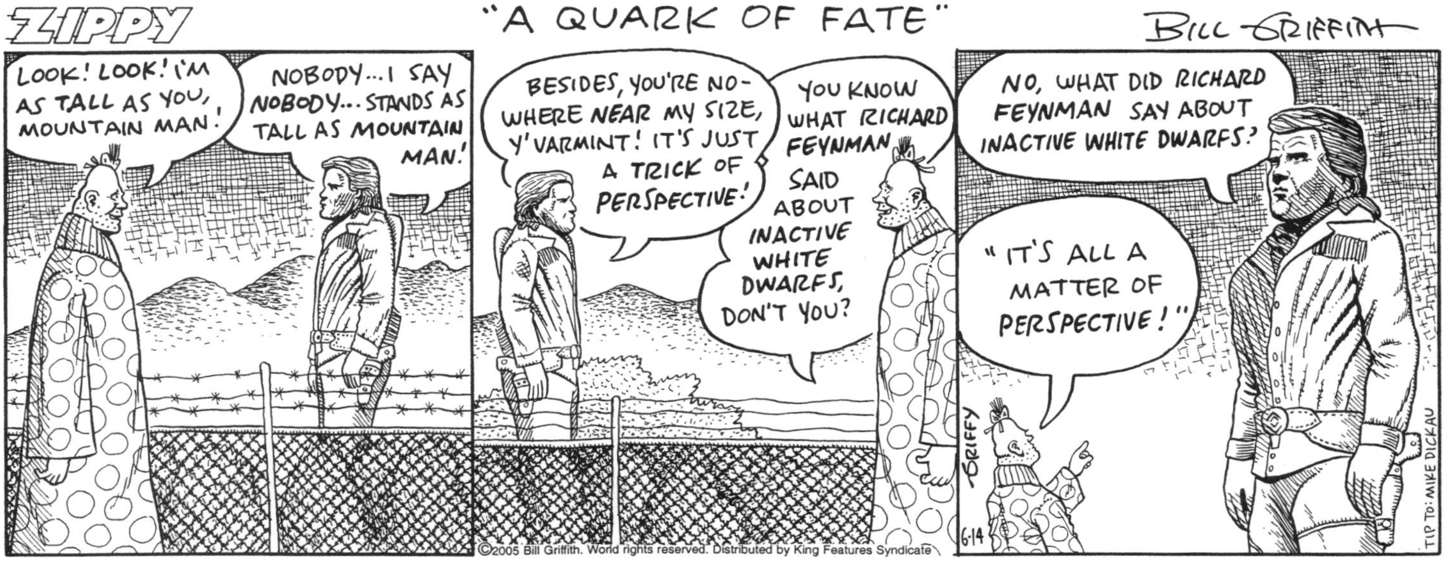
ZIPPY
"A QUARK OF FATE"
BILL GRIFFITH
LOOK! LOOK! I'M AS TALL AS YOU, MOUNTAIN MAN!
NOBODY... I SAY NOBODY... STANDS AS TALL AS MOUNTAIN MAN!
BESIDES, YOU'RE NOWHERE NEAR MY SIZE, Y'VARMINT! IT'S JUST A TRICK OF PERSPECTIVE!
YOU KNOW WHAT RICHARD FEYNMAN SAID ABOUT INACTIVE WHITE DWARFS, DON'T YOU?
NO, WHAT DID RICHARD FEYNMAN SAY ABOUT INACTIVE WHITE DWARFS?
"IT'S ALL A MATTER OF PERSPECTIVE!"
GRIFFY 6-14
TIP TO: MIKE DICKAU
©2005 Bill Griffith. World rights reserved. Distributed by King Features Syndicate

167

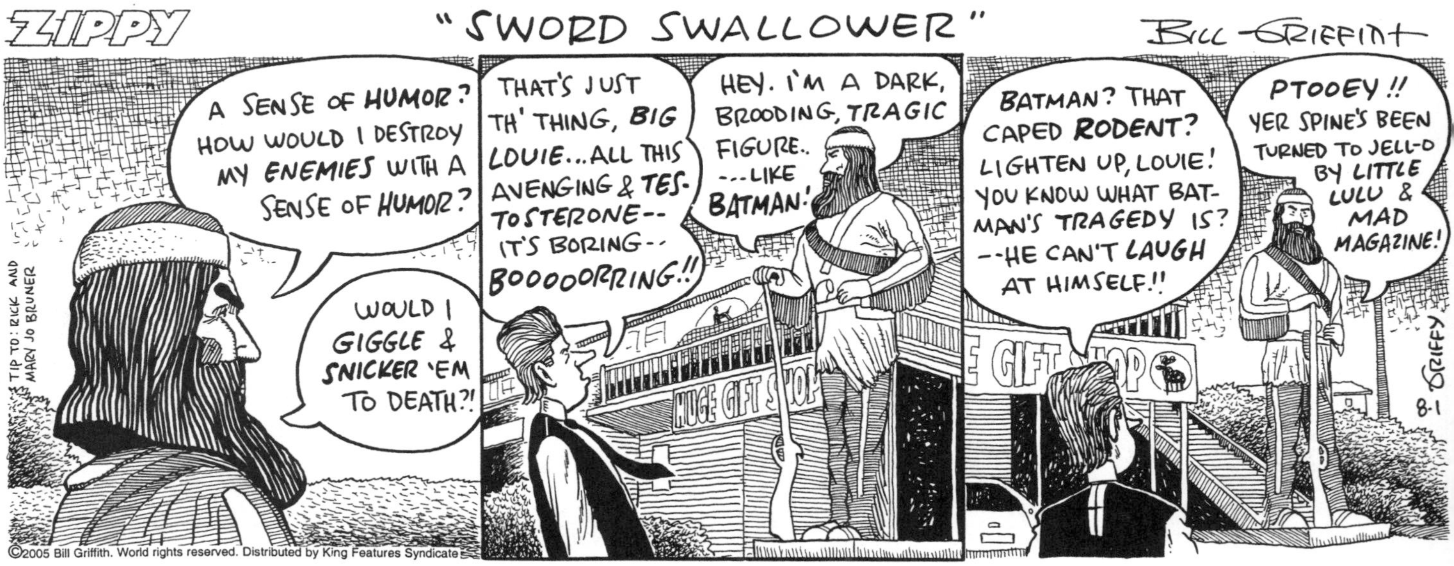
ZIPPY
"SWORD SWALLOWER"
BILL GRIFFITH
A SENSE OF HUMOR? HOW WOULD I DESTROY MY ENEMIES WITH A SENSE OF HUMOR?
WOULD I GIGGLE & SNICKER 'EM TO DEATH?!
TIP TO: RICK AND MARY JO BRUNER
THAT'S JUST TH' THING, BIG LOUIE...ALL THIS AVENGING & TESTOSTERONE-- IT'S BORING-- BOOOOORRING!!
HEY. I'M A DARK, BROODING, TRAGIC FIGURE.. ---LIKE BATMAN!
HUGE GIFT SHOP
BATMAN? THAT CAPED RODENT? LIGHTEN UP, LOUIE! YOU KNOW WHAT BATMAN'S TRAGEDY IS? --HE CAN'T LAUGH AT HIMSELF!!
PTOOEY!! YER SPINE'S BEEN TURNED TO JELL-O BY LITTLE LULU & MAD MAGAZINE!
GRIFFY 8-1
©2005 Bill Griffith. World rights reserved. Distributed by King Features Syndicate

168

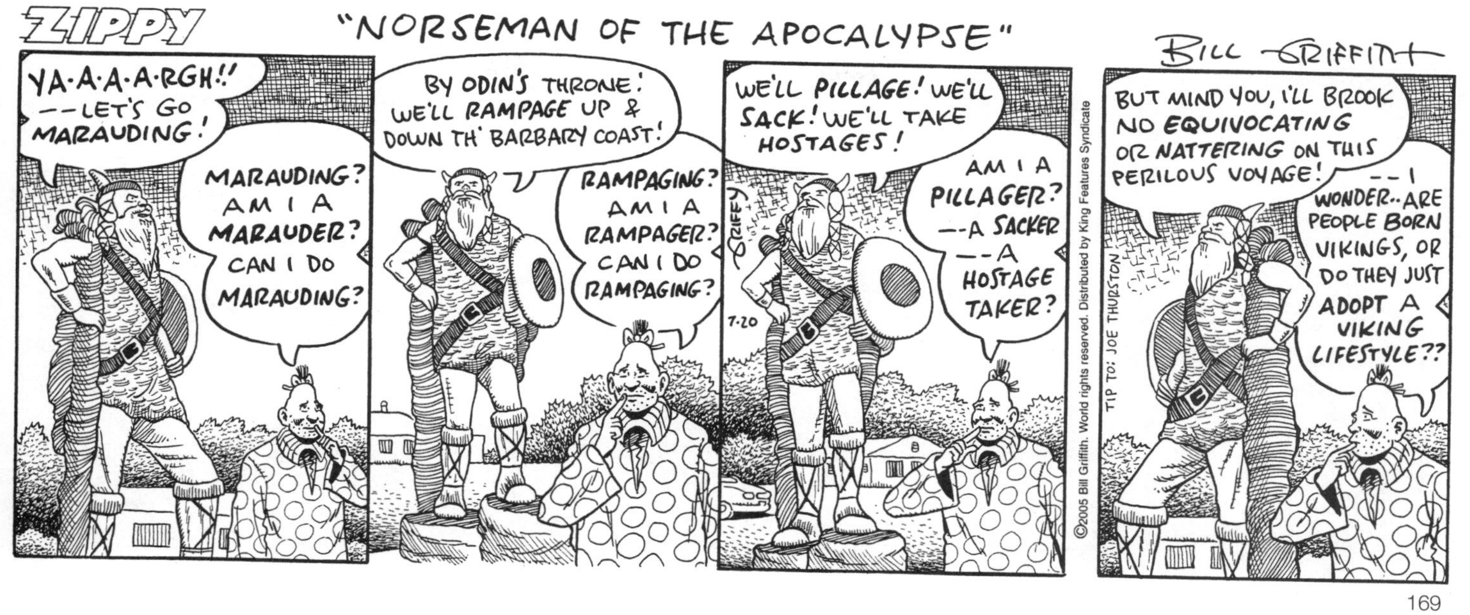
ZIPPY
"NORSEMAN OF THE APOCALYPSE"
BILL GRIFFITH
YA-A-A-A-RGH!! --LET'S GO MARAUDING!
MARAUDING? AM I A MARAUDER? CAN I DO MARAUDING?
BY ODIN'S THRONE! WE'LL RAMPAGE UP & DOWN TH' BARBARY COAST!
RAMPAGING? AM I A RAMPAGER? CAN I DO RAMPAGING?
GRIFFY 7-20
WE'LL PILLAGE! WE'LL SACK! WE'LL TAKE HOSTAGES!
AM I A PILLAGER? --A SACKER --A HOSTAGE TAKER?
©2005 Bill Griffith. World rights reserved. Distributed by King Features Syndicate
TIP TO: JOE THURSTON
BUT MIND YOU, I'LL BROOK NO EQUIVOCATING OR NATTERING ON THIS PERILOUS VOYAGE!
--I WONDER.. ARE PEOPLE BORN VIKINGS, OR DO THEY JUST ADOPT A VIKING LIFESTYLE??

169

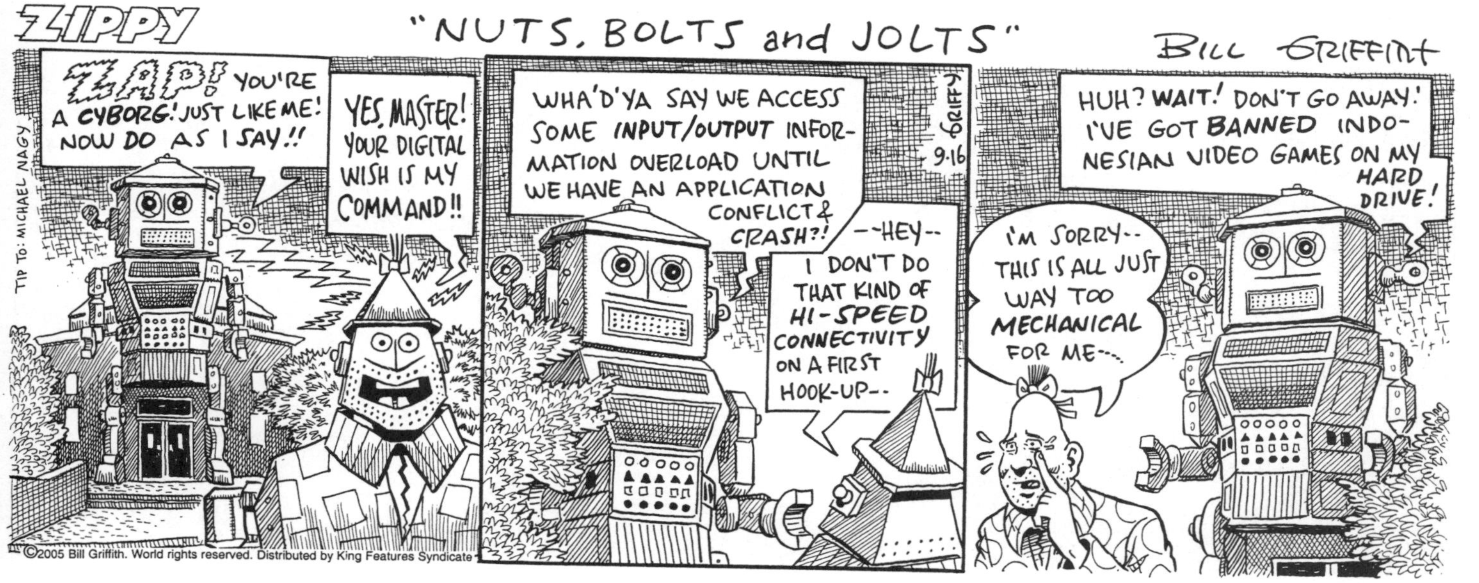
ZIPPY
"NUTS, BOLTS and JOLTS"
BILL GRIFFITH
ZAP! YOU'RE A CYBORG! JUST LIKE ME! NOW DO AS I SAY!!
YES, MASTER! YOUR DIGITAL WISH IS MY COMMAND!!
TIP TO: MICHAEL NAGY
©2005 Bill Griffith. World rights reserved. Distributed by King Features Syndicate
WHA'D'YA SAY WE ACCESS SOME INPUT/OUTPUT INFORMATION OVERLOAD UNTIL WE HAVE AN APPLICATION CONFLICT & CRASH?!
--HEY-- I DON'T DO THAT KIND OF HI-SPEED CONNECTIVITY ON A FIRST HOOK-UP--
GRIFFY 9-16
HUH? WAIT! DON'T GO AWAY! I'VE GOT BANNED INDONESIAN VIDEO GAMES ON MY HARD DRIVE!
I'M SORRY-- THIS IS ALL JUST WAY TOO MECHANICAL FOR ME--

170

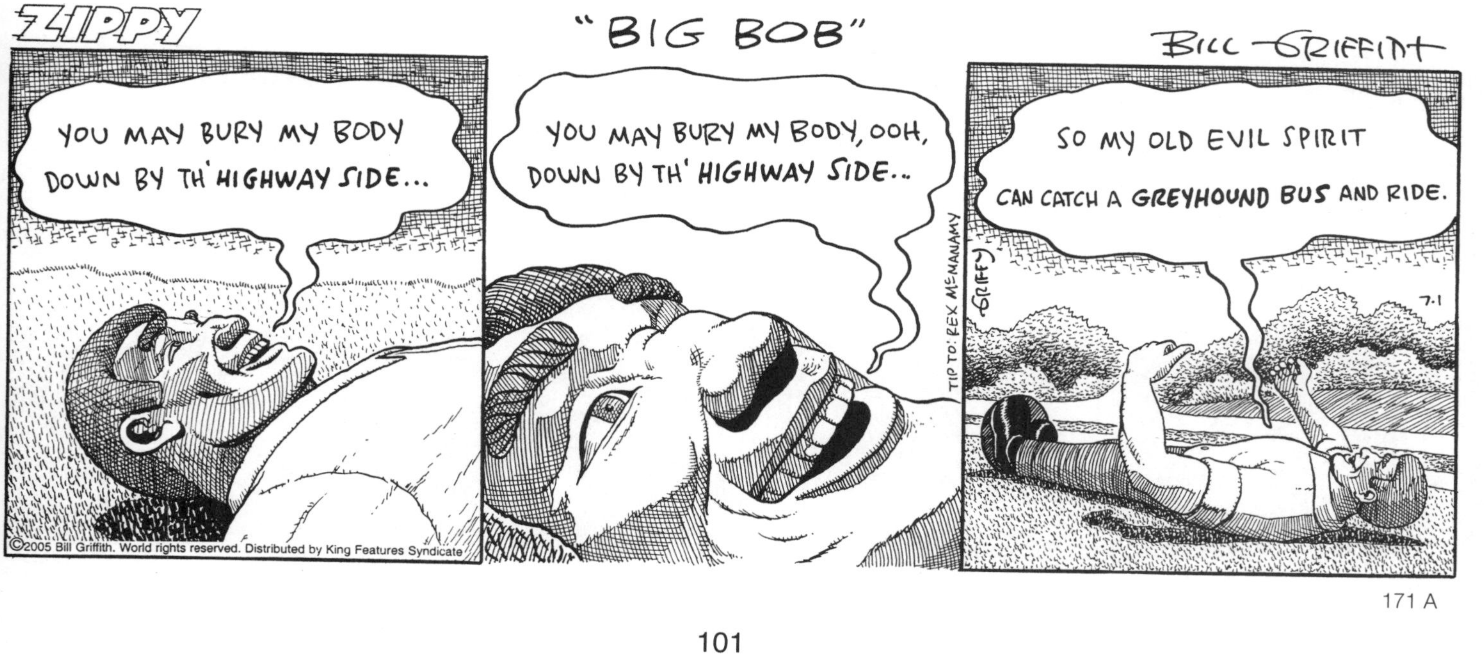
ZIPPY
"BIG BOB"
BILL GRIFFITH
YOU MAY BURY MY BODY DOWN BY TH' HIGHWAY SIDE...
©2005 Bill Griffith. World rights reserved. Distributed by King Features Syndicate
YOU MAY BURY MY BODY, OOH, DOWN BY TH' HIGHWAY SIDE..
TIP TO: REX McMANAMY
GRIFFY 7-1
SO MY OLD EVIL SPIRIT CAN CATCH A GREYHOUND BUS AND RIDE.

171 A

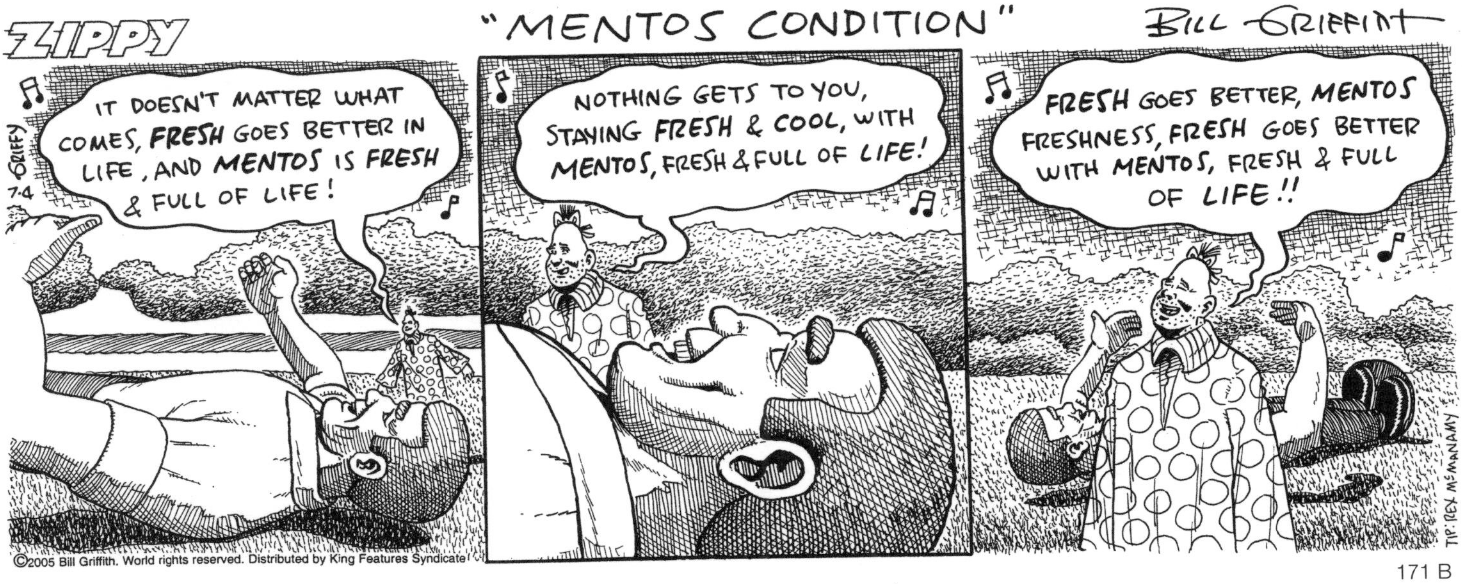
ZIPPY
"MENTOS CONDITION"
BILL GRIFFITH
IT DOESN'T MATTER WHAT COMES, FRESH GOES BETTER IN LIFE, AND MENTOS IS FRESH & FULL OF LIFE!
NOTHING GETS TO YOU, STAYING FRESH & COOL, WITH MENTOS, FRESH & FULL OF LIFE!
FRESH GOES BETTER, MENTOS FRESHNESS, FRESH GOES BETTER WITH MENTOS, FRESH & FULL OF LIFE!!
GRIFFY 7·4
TIP: REX McMANAMY
©2005 Bill Griffith. World rights reserved. Distributed by King Features Syndicate

171 B

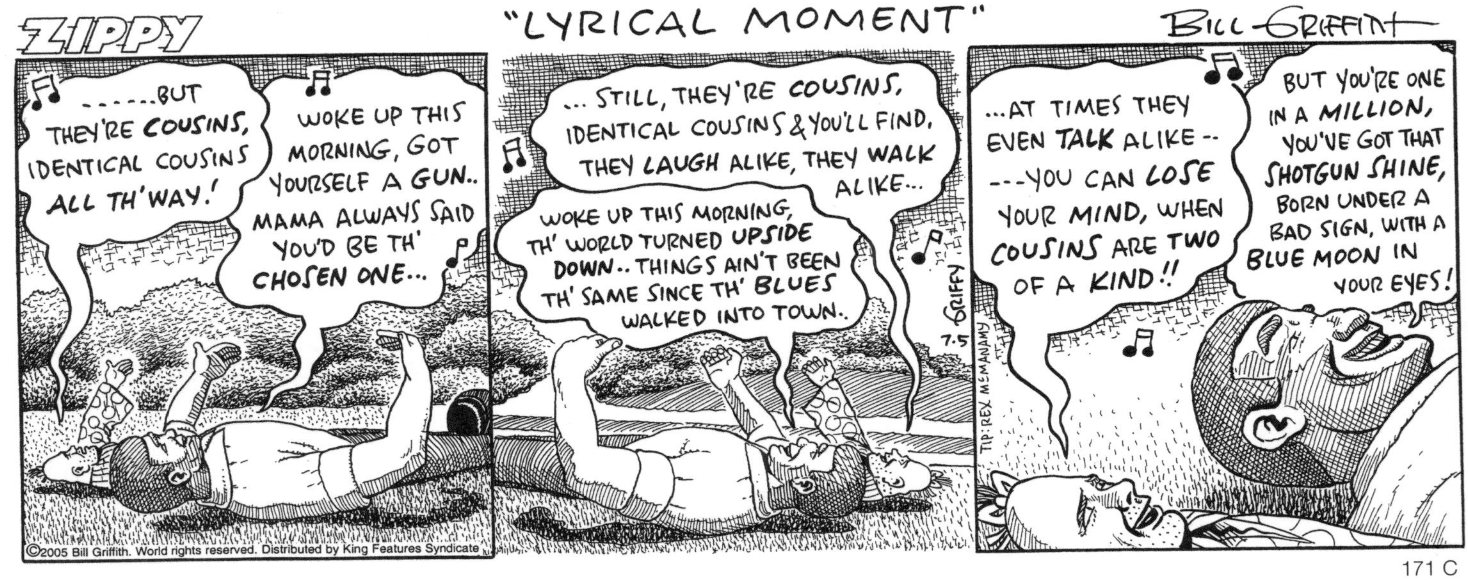
ZIPPY
"LYRICAL MOMENT"
BILL GRIFFITH
......BUT THEY'RE COUSINS, IDENTICAL COUSINS ALL TH' WAY!
WOKE UP THIS MORNING, GOT YOURSELF A GUN.. MAMA ALWAYS SAID YOU'D BE TH' CHOSEN ONE...
... STILL, THEY'RE COUSINS, IDENTICAL COUSINS & YOU'LL FIND, THEY LAUGH ALIKE, THEY WALK ALIKE...
WOKE UP THIS MORNING, TH' WORLD TURNED UPSIDE DOWN.. THINGS AIN'T BEEN TH' SAME SINCE TH' BLUES WALKED INTO TOWN..
GRIFFY 7·5
TIP: REX McMANAMY
...AT TIMES THEY EVEN TALK ALIKE-- ---YOU CAN LOSE YOUR MIND, WHEN COUSINS ARE TWO OF A KIND!!
BUT YOU'RE ONE IN A MILLION, YOU'VE GOT THAT SHOTGUN SHINE, BORN UNDER A BAD SIGN, WITH A BLUE MOON IN YOUR EYES!
©2005 Bill Griffith. World rights reserved. Distributed by King Features Syndicate

171 C

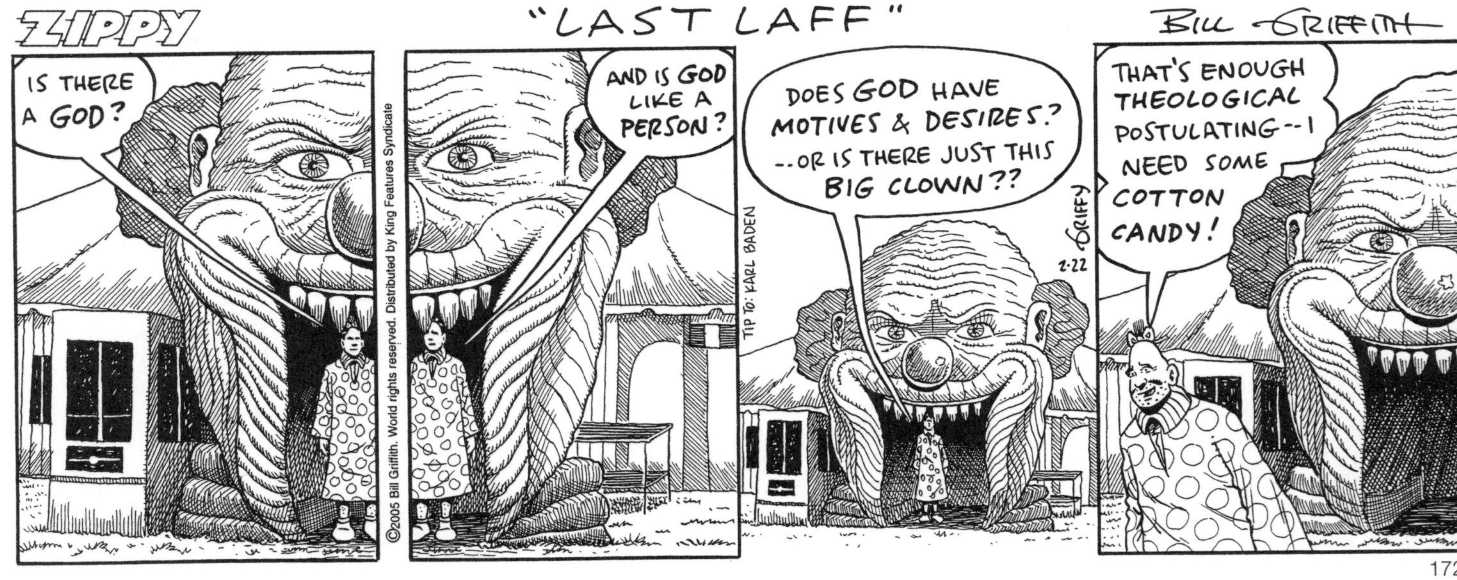
ZIPPY
"LAST LAFF"
BILL GRIFFITH
IS THERE A GOD?
AND IS GOD LIKE A PERSON?
©2005 Bill Griffith. World rights reserved. Distributed by King Features Syndicate
DOES GOD HAVE MOTIVES & DESIRES? --OR IS THERE JUST THIS BIG CLOWN??
TIP TO: KARL BADEN
GRIFFY 2·22
THAT'S ENOUGH THEOLOGICAL POSTULATING--I NEED SOME COTTON CANDY!

172

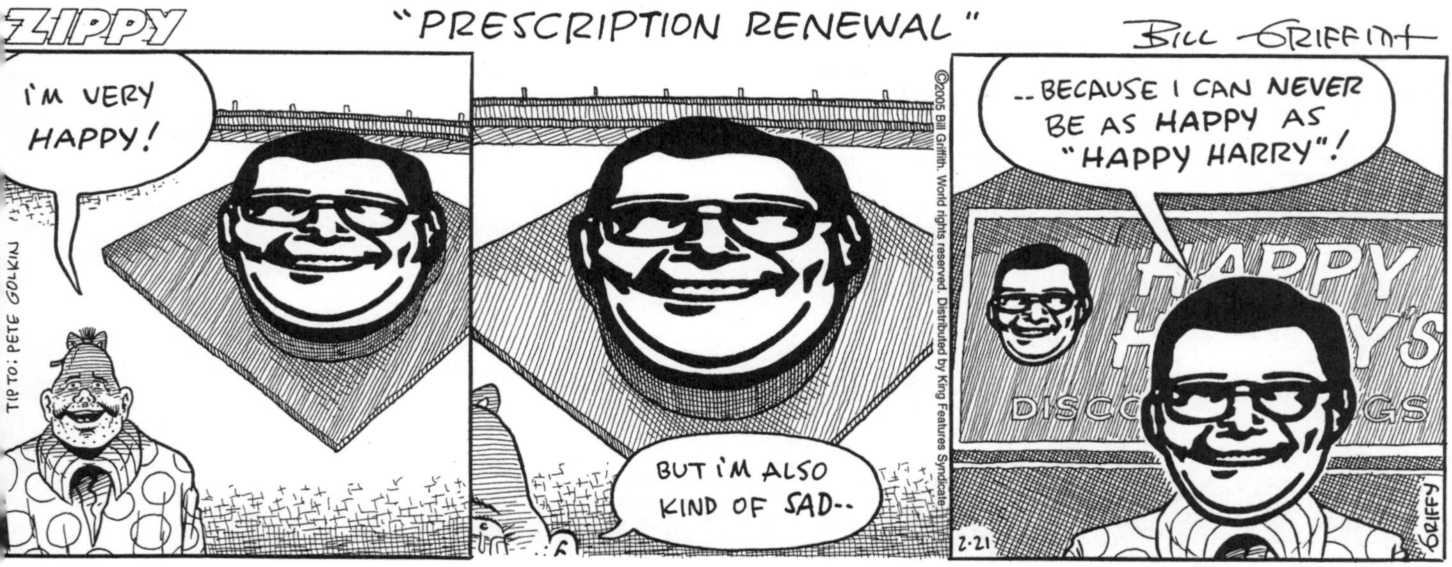
ZIPPY
"PRESCRIPTION RENEWAL"
BILL GRIFFITH
I'M VERY HAPPY!
TIP TO: PETE GOLKIN
©2005 Bill Griffith. World rights reserved. Distributed by King Features Syndicate
BUT I'M ALSO KIND OF SAD--
2-21
--BECAUSE I CAN NEVER BE AS HAPPY AS "HAPPY HARRY"!
GRIFFY

173

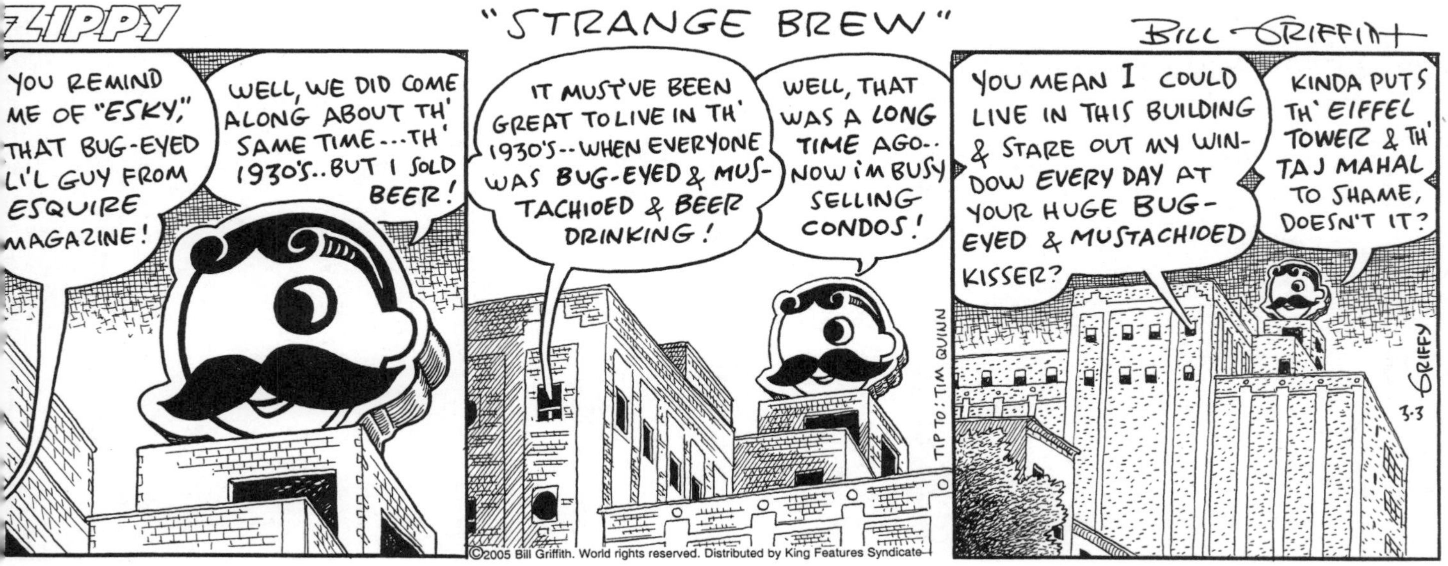
ZIPPY
"STRANGE BREW"
BILL GRIFFITH
YOU REMIND ME OF "ESKY," THAT BUG-EYED LI'L GUY FROM ESQUIRE MAGAZINE!
WELL, WE DID COME ALONG ABOUT TH' SAME TIME---TH' 1930'S.. BUT I SOLD BEER!
IT MUST'VE BEEN GREAT TO LIVE IN TH' 1930'S--WHEN EVERYONE WAS BUG-EYED & MUSTACHIOED & BEER DRINKING!
WELL, THAT WAS A LONG TIME AGO.. NOW I'M BUSY SELLING CONDOS!
TIP TO: TIM QUINN
©2005 Bill Griffith. World rights reserved. Distributed by King Features Syndicate
YOU MEAN I COULD LIVE IN THIS BUILDING & STARE OUT MY WINDOW EVERY DAY AT YOUR HUGE BUG-EYED & MUSTACHIOED KISSER?
KINDA PUTS TH' EIFFEL TOWER & TH' TAJ MAHAL TO SHAME, DOESN'T IT?
GRIFFY
3-3

174

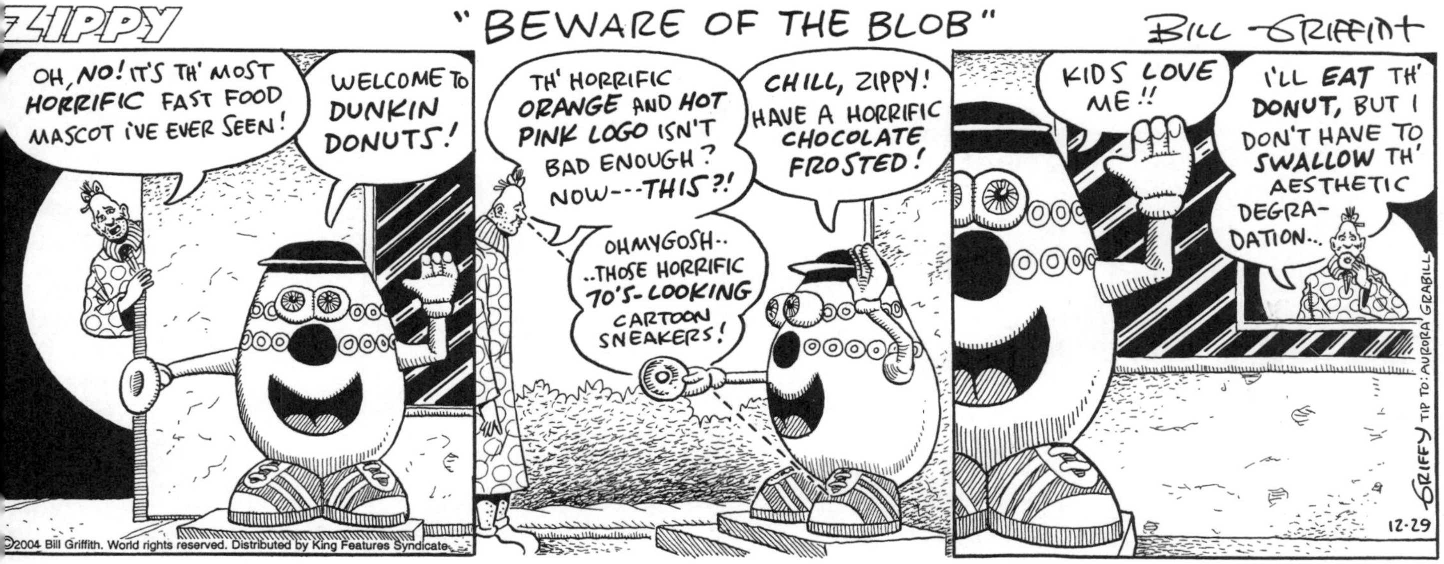
ZIPPY
"BEWARE OF THE BLOB"
BILL GRIFFITH
OH, NO! IT'S TH' MOST HORRIFIC FAST FOOD MASCOT I'VE EVER SEEN!
WELCOME TO DUNKIN DONUTS!
©2004 Bill Griffith. World rights reserved. Distributed by King Features Syndicate
TH' HORRIFIC ORANGE AND HOT PINK LOGO ISN'T BAD ENOUGH? NOW---THIS?!
CHILL, ZIPPY! HAVE A HORRIFIC CHOCOLATE FROSTED!
OHMYGOSH.. ..THOSE HORRIFIC 70'S-LOOKING CARTOON SNEAKERS!
KIDS LOVE ME!!
I'LL EAT TH' DONUT, BUT I DON'T HAVE TO SWALLOW TH' AESTHETIC DEGRADATION..
TIP TO: AURORA GRABILL
GRIFFY
12-29

175

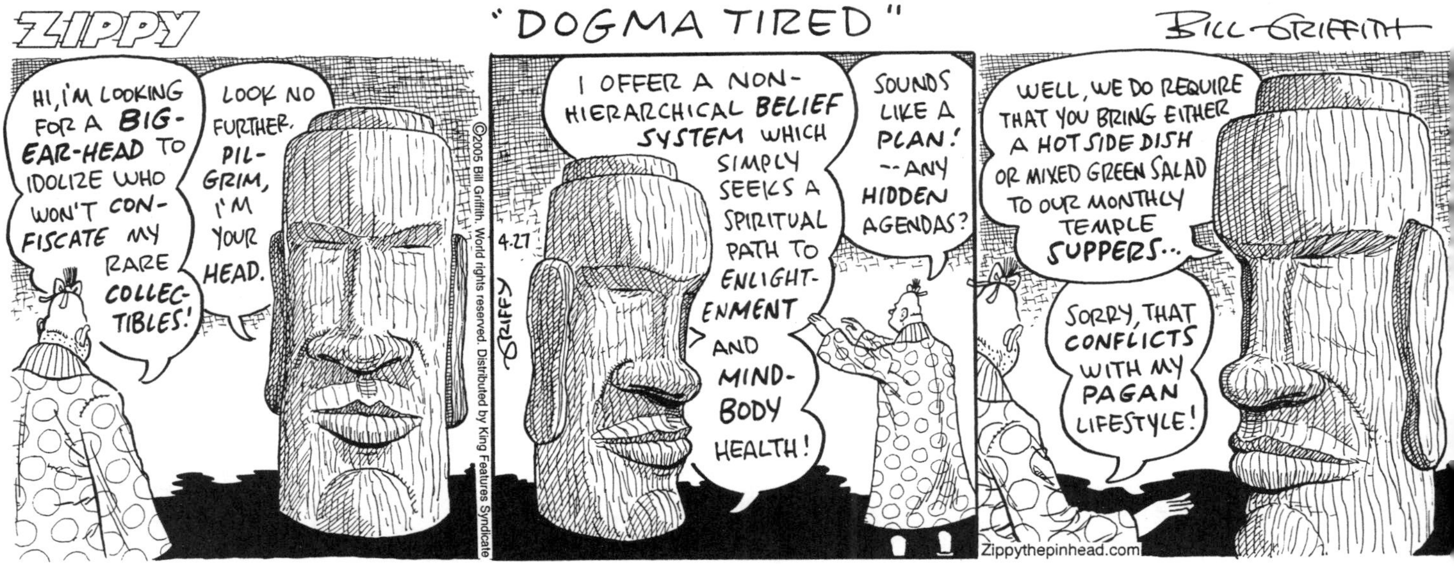
ZIPPY
"DOGMA TIRED"
BILL GRIFFITH
HI, I'M LOOKING FOR A BIG-EAR-HEAD TO IDOLIZE WHO WON'T CON-FISCATE MY RARE COLLEC-TIBLES!
LOOK NO FURTHER, PIL-GRIM, I'M YOUR HEAD.
©2005 Bill Griffith. World rights reserved. Distributed by King Features Syndicate
4-27
GRIFFY
I OFFER A NON-HIERARCHICAL BELIEF SYSTEM WHICH SIMPLY SEEKS A SPIRITUAL PATH TO ENLIGHT-ENMENT AND MIND-BODY HEALTH!
SOUNDS LIKE A PLAN! --ANY HIDDEN AGENDAS?
WELL, WE DO REQUIRE THAT YOU BRING EITHER A HOT SIDE DISH OR MIXED GREEN SALAD TO OUR MONTHLY TEMPLE SUPPERS...
SORRY, THAT CONFLICTS WITH MY PAGAN LIFESTYLE!
Zippythepinhead.com

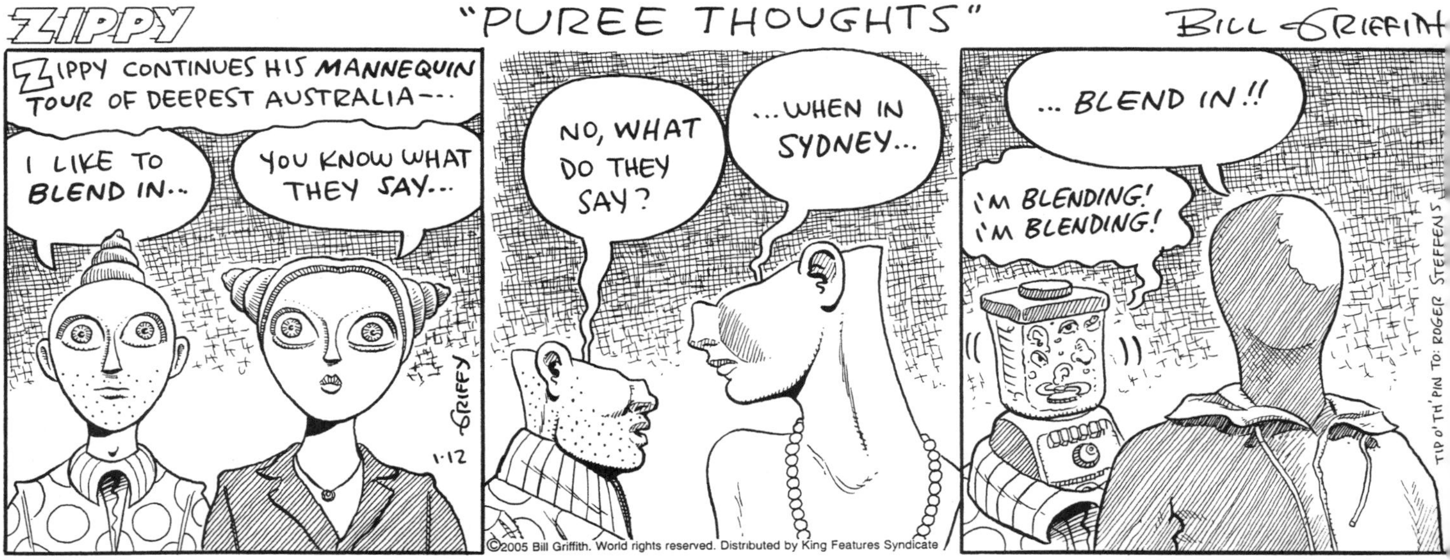
ZIPPY
"PUREE THOUGHTS"
BILL GRIFFITH
ZIPPY CONTINUES HIS MANNEQUIN TOUR OF DEEPEST AUSTRALIA---
I LIKE TO BLEND IN...
YOU KNOW WHAT THEY SAY...
GRIFFY
1-12
NO, WHAT DO THEY SAY?
...WHEN IN SYDNEY...
©2005 Bill Griffith. World rights reserved. Distributed by King Features Syndicate
...BLEND IN!!
I'M BLENDING! I'M BLENDING!
TIP O'TH' PIN TO: ROGER STEFFENS

176

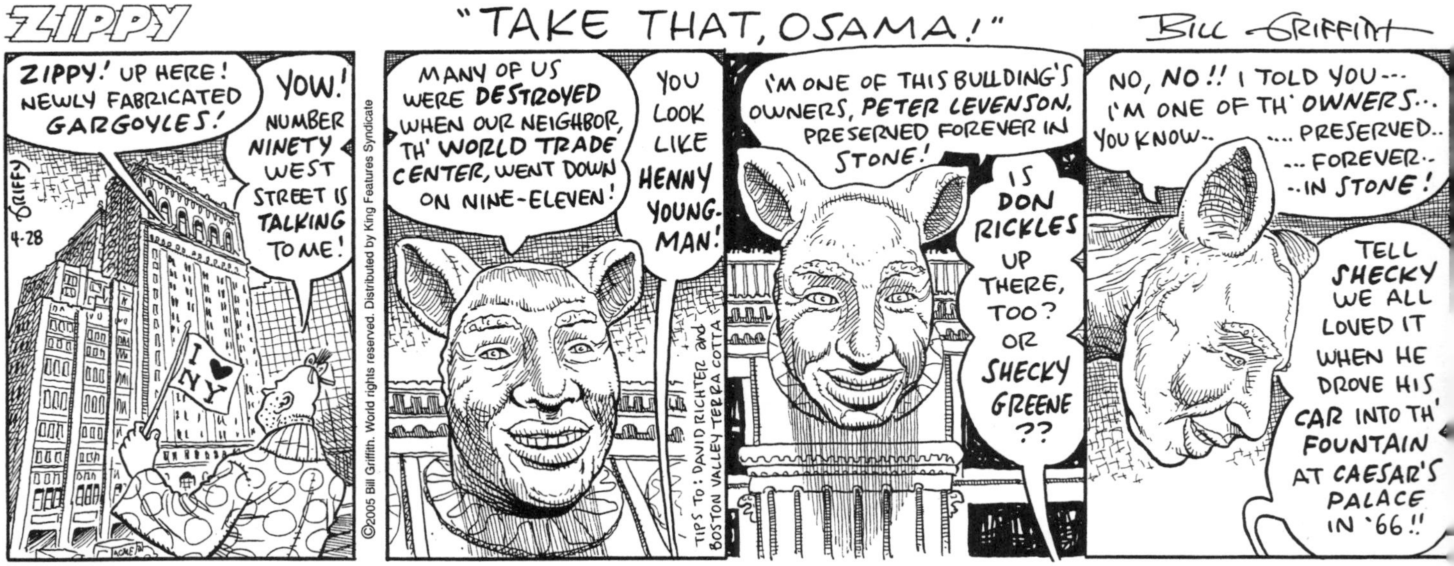
ZIPPY
"TAKE THAT, OSAMA!"
BILL GRIFFITH
ZIPPY! UP HERE! NEWLY FABRICATED GARGOYLES!
YOW! NUMBER NINETY WEST STREET IS TALKING TO ME!
GRIFFY
4-28
I ♥ NY
©2005 Bill Griffith. World rights reserved. Distributed by King Features Syndicate
MANY OF US WERE DESTROYED WHEN OUR NEIGHBOR, TH' WORLD TRADE CENTER, WENT DOWN ON NINE-ELEVEN!
YOU LOOK LIKE HENNY YOUNG-MAN!
TIPS TO: DAVID RICHTER and BOSTON VALLEY TERRA COTTA
I'M ONE OF THIS BUILDING'S OWNERS, PETER LEVENSON, PRESERVED FOREVER IN STONE!
IS DON RICKLES UP THERE, TOO? OR SHECKY GREENE??
NO, NO!! I TOLD YOU--- I'M ONE OF TH' OWNERS... YOU KNOW... ...PRESERVED... ...FOREVER... ...IN STONE!
TELL SHECKY WE ALL LOVED IT WHEN HE DROVE HIS CAR INTO TH' FOUNTAIN AT CAESAR'S PALACE IN '66!!

177

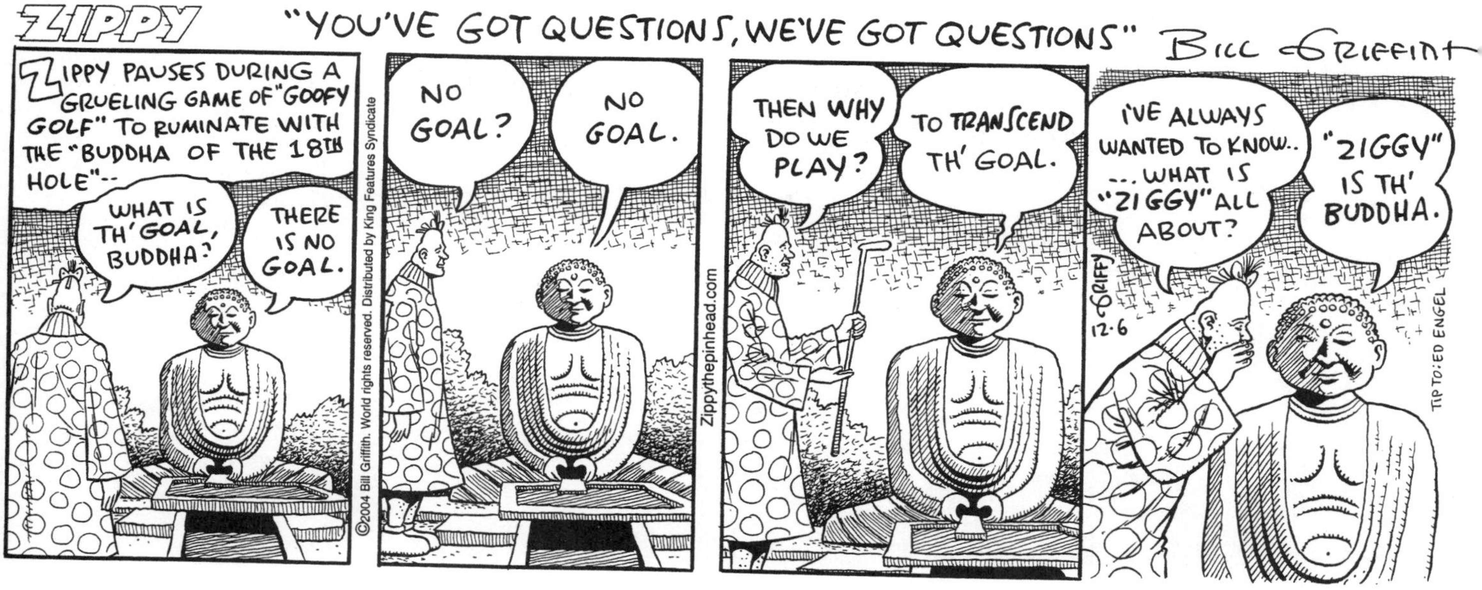
ZIPPY
"YOU'VE GOT QUESTIONS, WE'VE GOT QUESTIONS"
BILL GRIFFITH
ZIPPY PAUSES DURING A GRUELING GAME OF "GOOFY GOLF" TO RUMINATE WITH THE "BUDDHA OF THE 18TH HOLE"--
WHAT IS TH' GOAL, BUDDHA?
THERE IS NO GOAL.
©2004 Bill Griffith. World rights reserved. Distributed by King Features Syndicate
NO GOAL?
NO GOAL.
Zippythepinhead.com
THEN WHY DO WE PLAY?
TO TRANSCEND TH' GOAL.
GRIFFY 12·6
I'VE ALWAYS WANTED TO KNOW.. ...WHAT IS "ZIGGY" ALL ABOUT?
"ZIGGY" IS TH' BUDDHA.
TIP TO: ED ENGEL
178

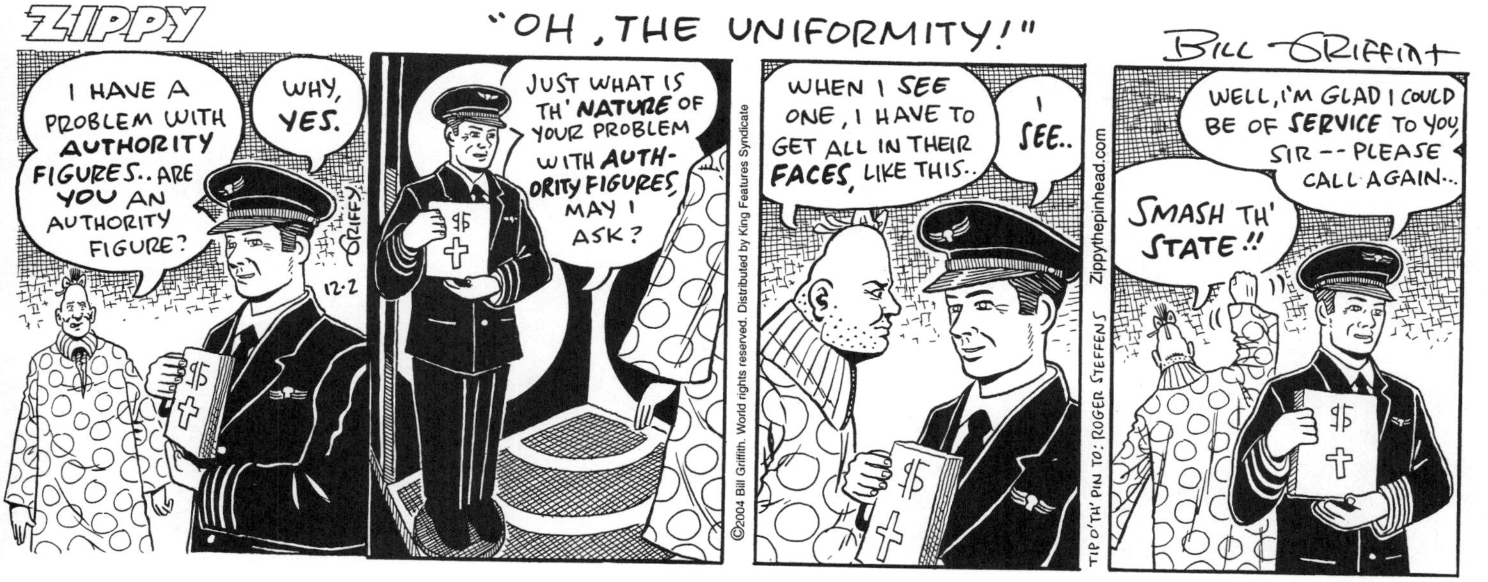
ZIPPY
"OH, THE UNIFORMITY!"
BILL GRIFFITH
I HAVE A PROBLEM WITH AUTHORITY FIGURES.. ARE YOU AN AUTHORITY FIGURE?
WHY, YES.
GRIFFY 12·2
JUST WHAT IS TH' NATURE OF YOUR PROBLEM WITH AUTHORITY FIGURES, MAY I ASK?
©2004 Bill Griffith. World rights reserved. Distributed by King Features Syndicate
WHEN I SEE ONE, I HAVE TO GET ALL IN THEIR FACES, LIKE THIS..
I SEE..
Zippythepinhead.com
TIP O'TH' PIN TO: ROGER STEFFENS
WELL, I'M GLAD I COULD BE OF SERVICE TO YOU, SIR -- PLEASE CALL AGAIN...
SMASH TH' STATE!!
179

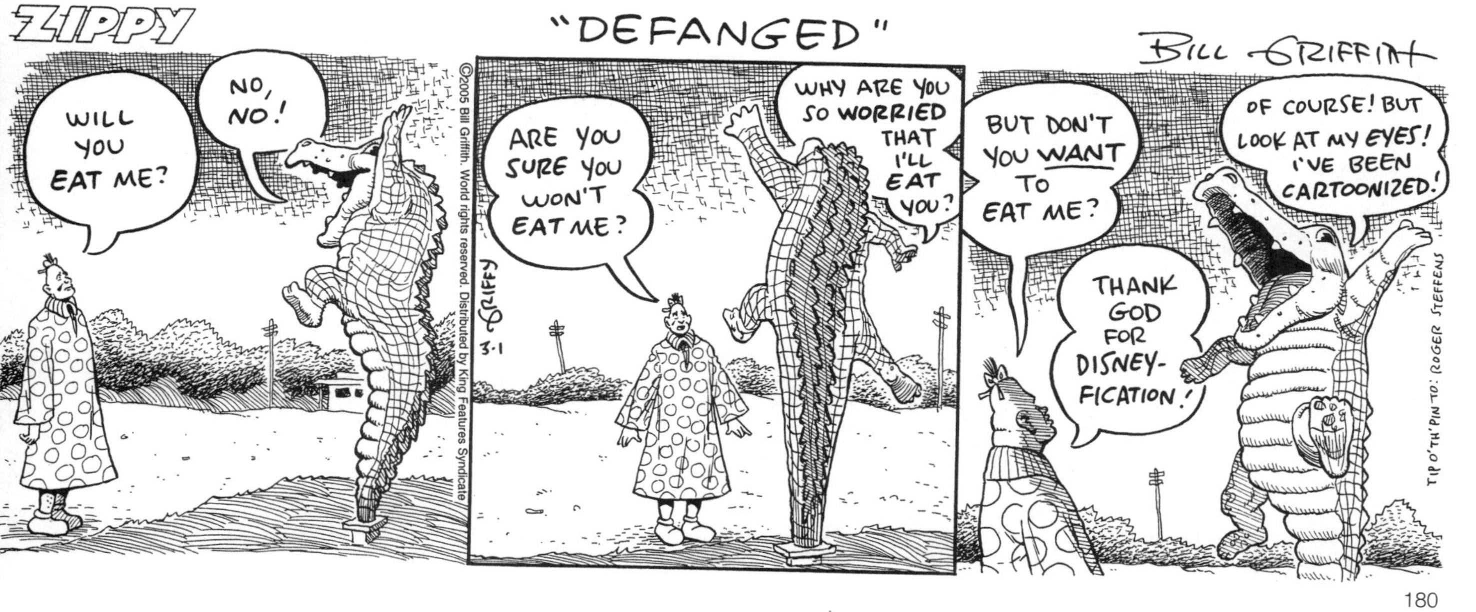
ZIPPY
"DEFANGED"
BILL GRIFFITH
WILL YOU EAT ME?
NO, NO!
©2005 Bill Griffith. World rights reserved. Distributed by King Features Syndicate
ARE YOU SURE YOU WON'T EAT ME?
WHY ARE YOU SO WORRIED THAT I'LL EAT YOU?
GRIFFY 3·1
BUT DON'T YOU WANT TO EAT ME?
OF COURSE! BUT LOOK AT MY EYES! I'VE BEEN CARTOONIZED!
THANK GOD FOR DISNEY-FICATION!
TIP O'TH' PIN TO: ROGER STEFFENS
180

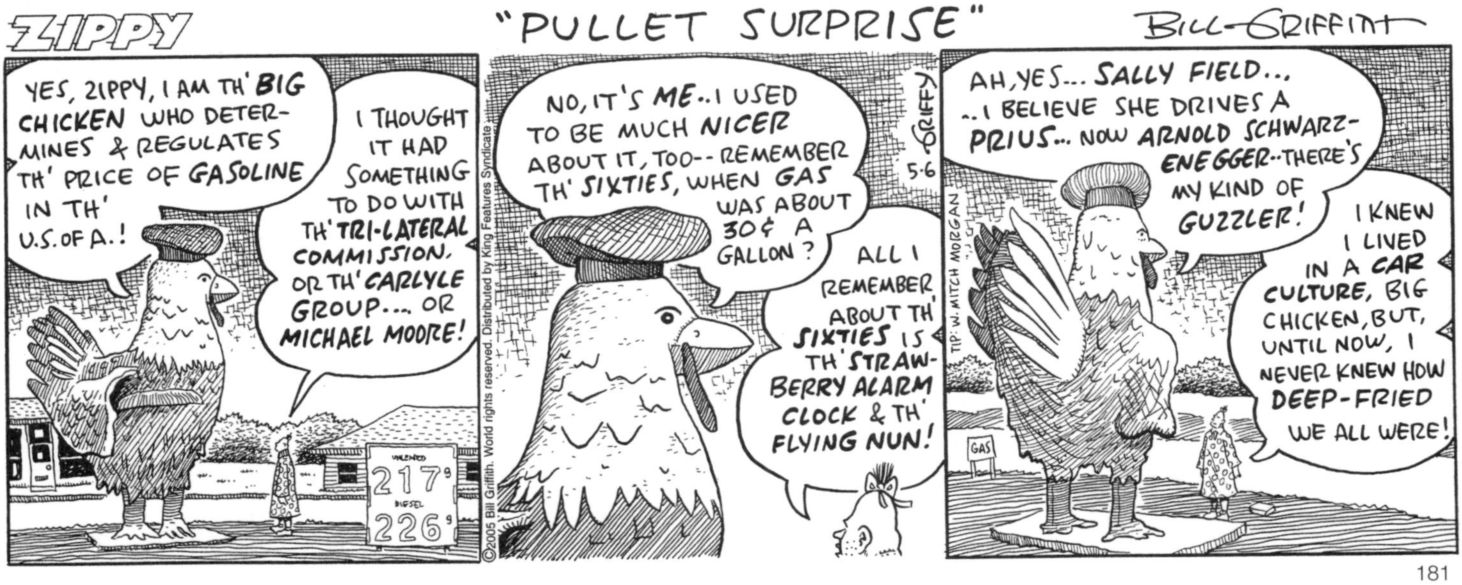
ZIPPY
"PULLET SURPRISE"
BILL GRIFFITH
YES, ZIPPY, I AM TH' BIG CHICKEN WHO DETERMINES & REGULATES TH' PRICE OF GASOLINE IN TH' U.S. OF A.!
I THOUGHT IT HAD SOMETHING TO DO WITH TH' TRI-LATERAL COMMISSION, OR TH' CARLYLE GROUP.... OR MICHAEL MOORE!
217 9
226 9
©2005 Bill Griffith. World rights reserved. Distributed by King Features Syndicate
NO, IT'S ME.. I USED TO BE MUCH NICER ABOUT IT, TOO-- REMEMBER TH' SIXTIES, WHEN GAS WAS ABOUT 30¢ A GALLON?
ALL I REMEMBER ABOUT TH' SIXTIES IS TH' STRAWBERRY ALARM CLOCK & TH' FLYING NUN!
GRIFFY 5·6
TIP: W. MITCH MORGAN
AH, YES... SALLY FIELD... ..I BELIEVE SHE DRIVES A PRIUS... NOW ARNOLD SCHWARZENEGGER-- THERE'S MY KIND OF GUZZLER!
I KNEW I LIVED IN A CAR CULTURE, BIG CHICKEN, BUT, UNTIL NOW, I NEVER KNEW HOW DEEP-FRIED WE ALL WERE!
GAS

181

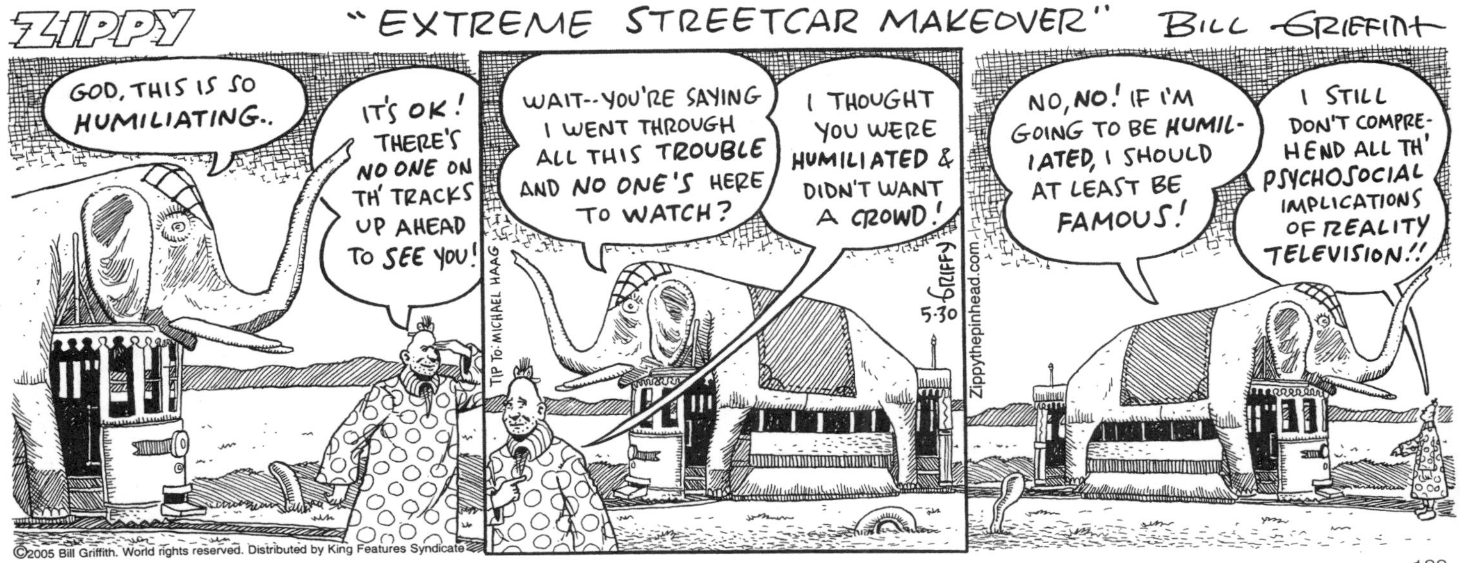
ZIPPY
"EXTREME STREETCAR MAKEOVER"
BILL GRIFFITH
GOD, THIS IS SO HUMILIATING..
IT'S OK! THERE'S NO ONE ON TH' TRACKS UP AHEAD TO SEE YOU!
©2005 Bill Griffith. World rights reserved. Distributed by King Features Syndicate
WAIT-- YOU'RE SAYING I WENT THROUGH ALL THIS TROUBLE AND NO ONE'S HERE TO WATCH?
I THOUGHT YOU WERE HUMILIATED & DIDN'T WANT A CROWD!
TIP TO: MICHAEL HAAG
GRIFFY 5·30
Zippythepinhead.com
NO, NO! IF I'M GOING TO BE HUMILIATED, I SHOULD AT LEAST BE FAMOUS!
I STILL DON'T COMPREHEND ALL TH' PSYCHOSOCIAL IMPLICATIONS OF REALITY TELEVISION!!

182

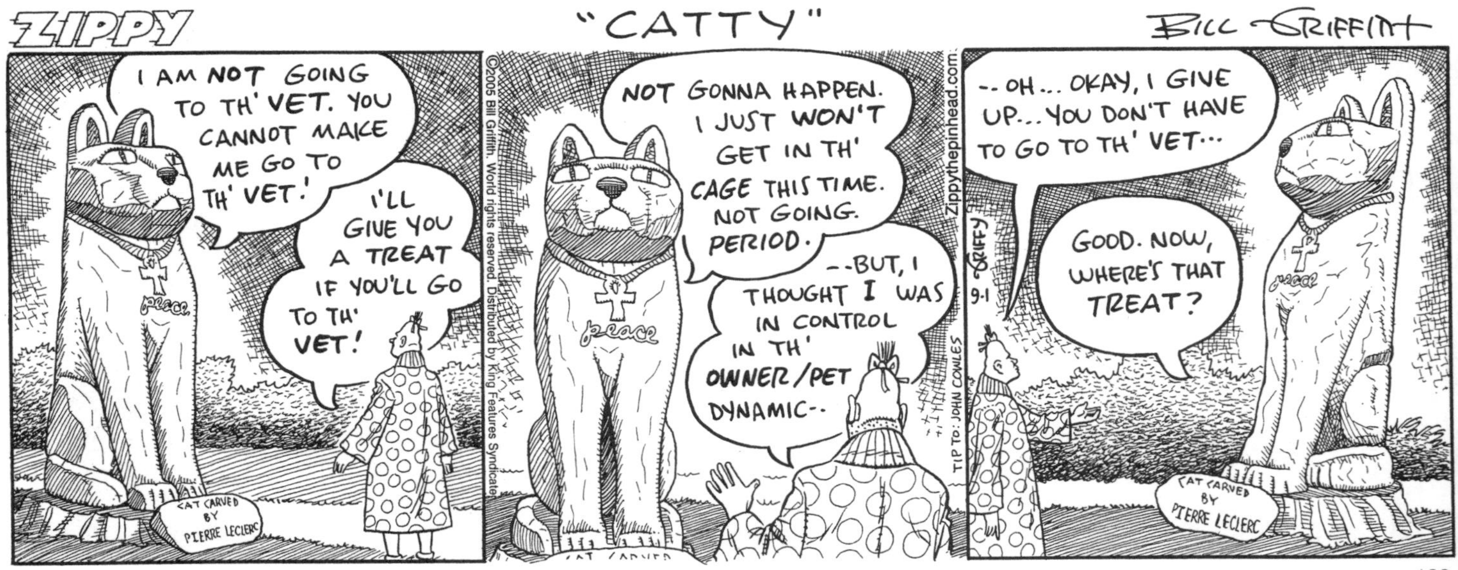
ZIPPY
"CATTY"
BILL GRIFFITH
I AM NOT GOING TO TH' VET. YOU CANNOT MAKE ME GO TO TH' VET!
I'LL GIVE YOU A TREAT IF YOU'LL GO TO TH' VET!
PEACE
CAT CARVED BY PIERRE LECLERC
©2005 Bill Griffith. World rights reserved. Distributed by King Features Syndicate
NOT GONNA HAPPEN. I JUST WON'T GET IN TH' CAGE THIS TIME. NOT GOING. PERIOD.
--BUT, I THOUGHT I WAS IN CONTROL IN TH' OWNER/PET DYNAMIC--
Zippythepinhead.com
GRIFFY 9·1
TIP TO: JOHN COWLES
-- OH... OKAY, I GIVE UP... YOU DON'T HAVE TO GO TO TH' VET...
GOOD. NOW, WHERE'S THAT TREAT?
CAT CARVED BY PIERRE LECLERC

183

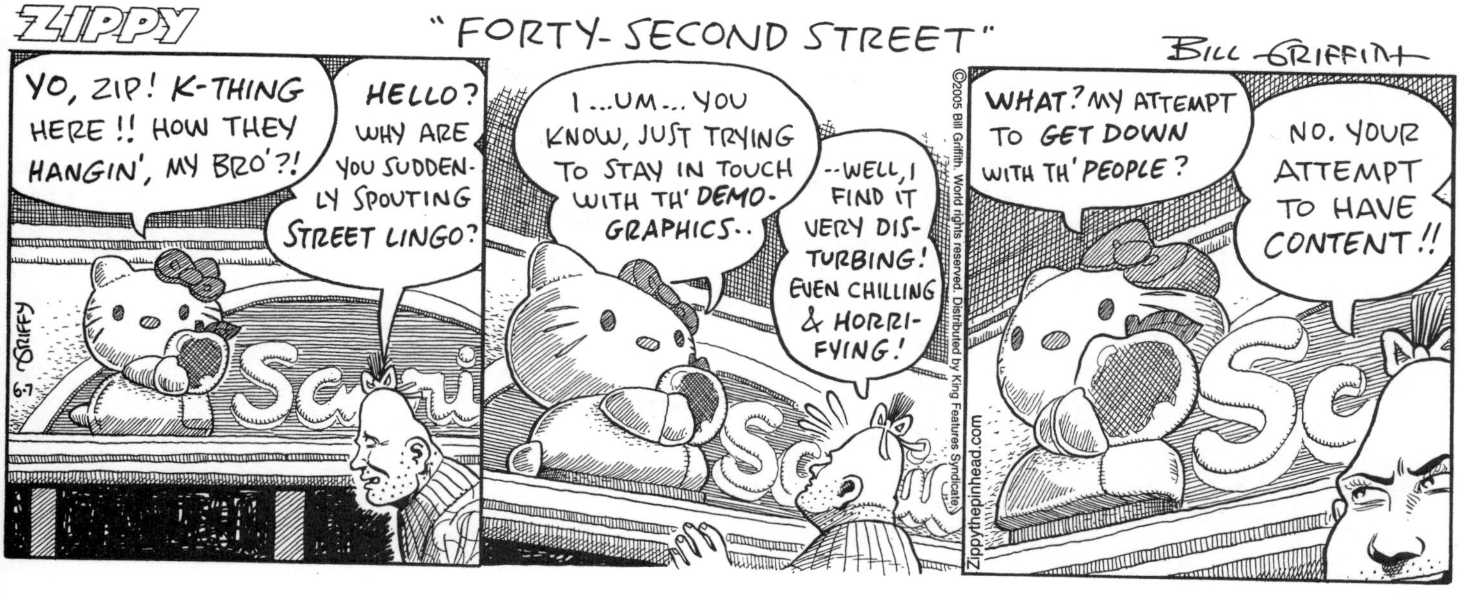
ZIPPY
"FORTY-SECOND STREET"
BILL GRIFFITH
YO, ZIP! K-THING HERE!! HOW THEY HANGIN', MY BRO'?!
HELLO? WHY ARE YOU SUDDENLY SPOUTING STREET LINGO?
GRIFFY 6-7
I...UM...YOU KNOW, JUST TRYING TO STAY IN TOUCH WITH TH' DEMOGRAPHICS..
--WELL, I FIND IT VERY DISTURBING! EVEN CHILLING & HORRIFYING!
©2005 Bill Griffith. World rights reserved. Distributed by King Features Syndicate
WHAT? MY ATTEMPT TO GET DOWN WITH TH' PEOPLE?
NO. YOUR ATTEMPT TO HAVE CONTENT!!
Zippythepinhead.com

184

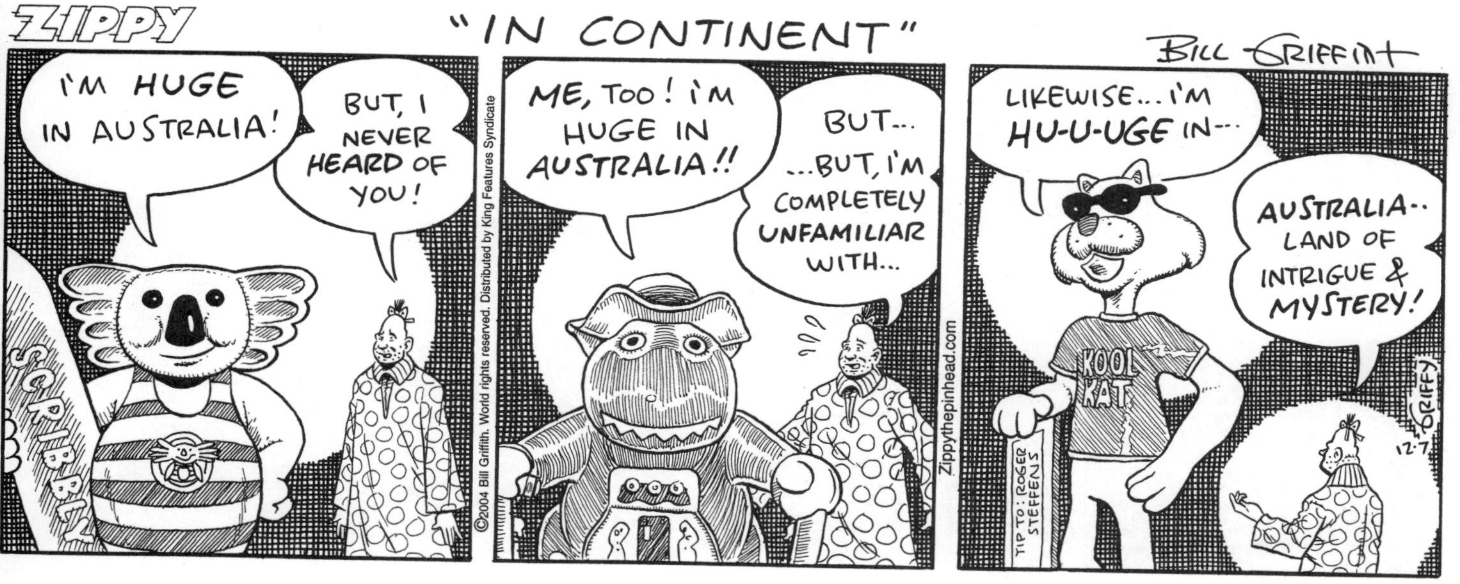
ZIPPY
"IN CONTINENT"
BILL GRIFFITH
I'M HUGE IN AUSTRALIA!
BUT, I NEVER HEARD OF YOU!
SCRIBBLY
©2004 Bill Griffith. World rights reserved. Distributed by King Features Syndicate
ME, TOO! I'M HUGE IN AUSTRALIA!!
BUT... ...BUT, I'M COMPLETELY UNFAMILIAR WITH...
Zippythepinhead.com
LIKEWISE... I'M HU-U-UGE IN--
AUSTRALIA.. LAND OF INTRIGUE & MYSTERY!
KOOL KAT
TIP TO: ROGER STEFFENS
GRIFFY 12-7

185

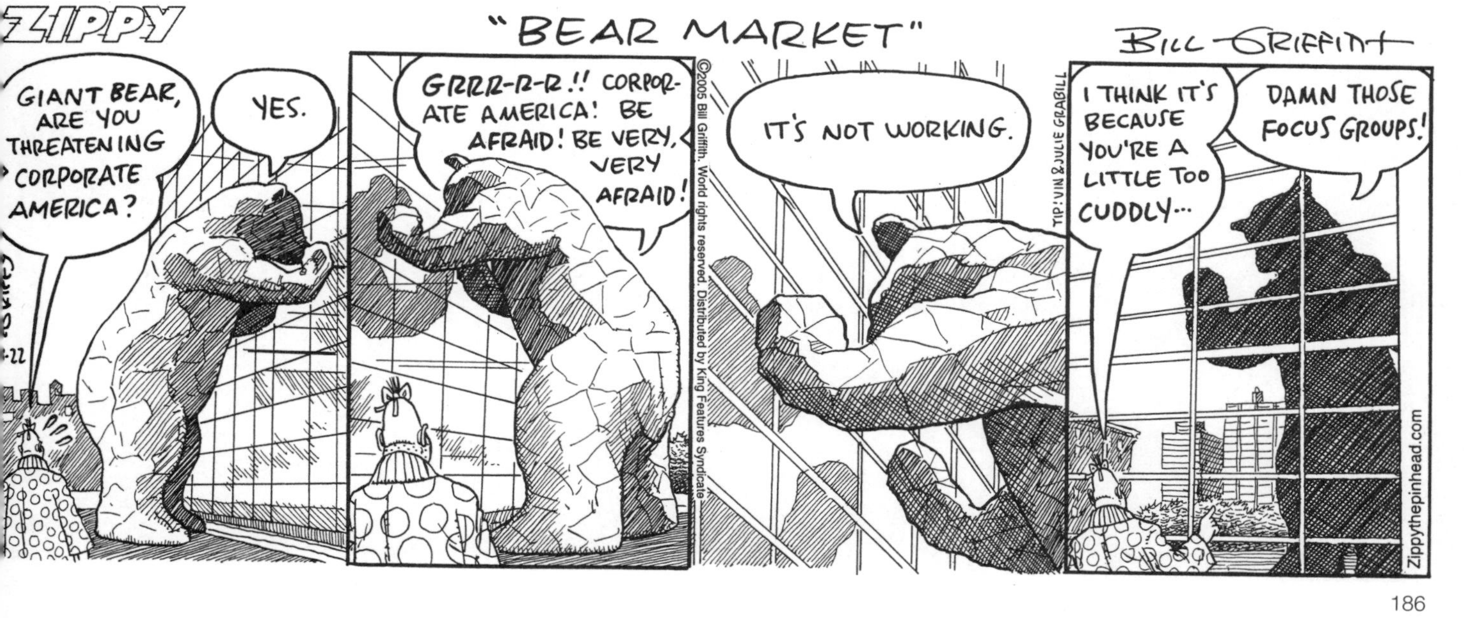
ZIPPY
"BEAR MARKET"
BILL GRIFFITH
GIANT BEAR, ARE YOU THREATENING CORPORATE AMERICA?
YES.
GRRR-R-R!! CORPORATE AMERICA! BE AFRAID! BE VERY, VERY AFRAID!
©2005 Bill Griffith. World rights reserved. Distributed by King Features Syndicate
IT'S NOT WORKING.
TIP: VIN & JULIE GRABILL
I THINK IT'S BECAUSE YOU'RE A LITTLE TOO CUDDLY...
DAMN THOSE FOCUS GROUPS!
Zippythepinhead.com

186

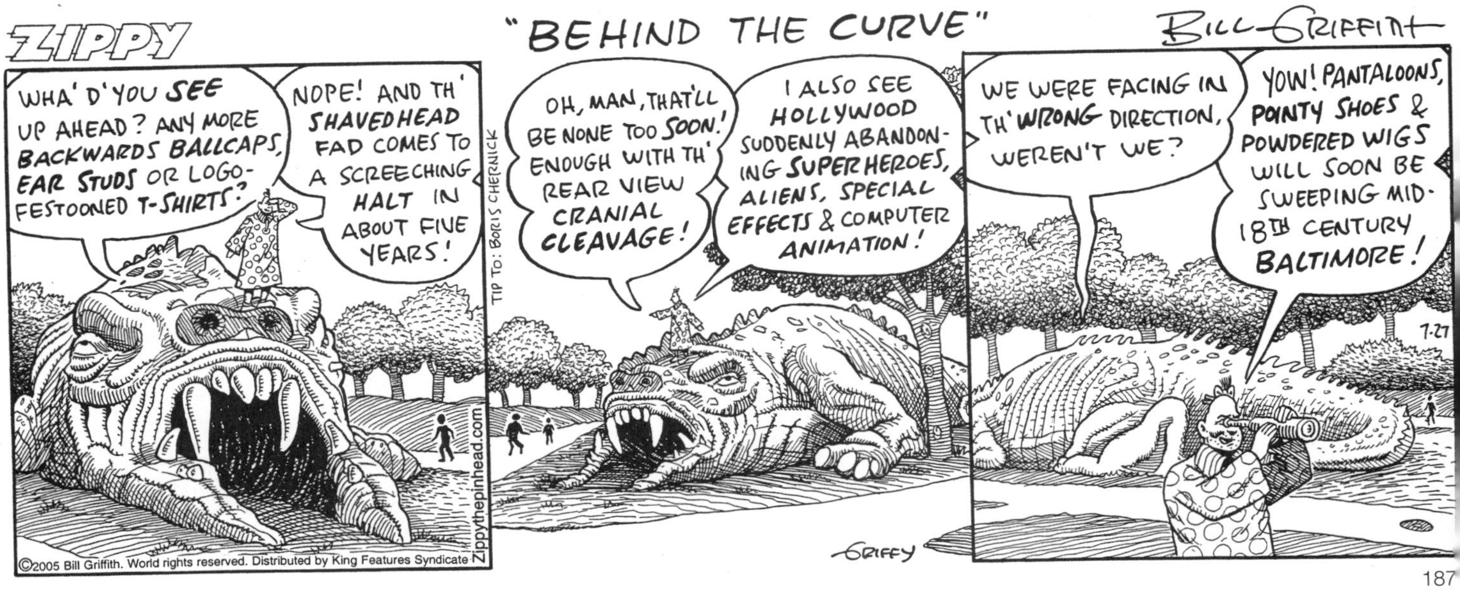
ZIPPY
"BEHIND THE CURVE"
BILL GRIFFITH
WHA' D'YOU SEE UP AHEAD? ANY MORE BACKWARDS BALLCAPS, EAR STUDS OR LOGO-FESTOONED T-SHIRTS?
NOPE! AND TH' SHAVEDHEAD FAD COMES TO A SCREECHING HALT IN ABOUT FIVE YEARS!
TIP TO: BORIS CHERNICK
OH, MAN, THAT'LL BE NONE TOO SOON! ENOUGH WITH TH' REAR VIEW CRANIAL CLEAVAGE!
I ALSO SEE HOLLYWOOD SUDDENLY ABANDONING SUPERHEROES, ALIENS, SPECIAL EFFECTS & COMPUTER ANIMATION!
WE WERE FACING IN TH' WRONG DIRECTION, WEREN'T WE?
YOW! PANTALOONS, POINTY SHOES & POWDERED WIGS WILL SOON BE SWEEPING MID-18TH CENTURY BALTIMORE!
7-27
GRIFFY
©2005 Bill Griffith. World rights reserved. Distributed by King Features Syndicate
Zippythepinhead.com

187

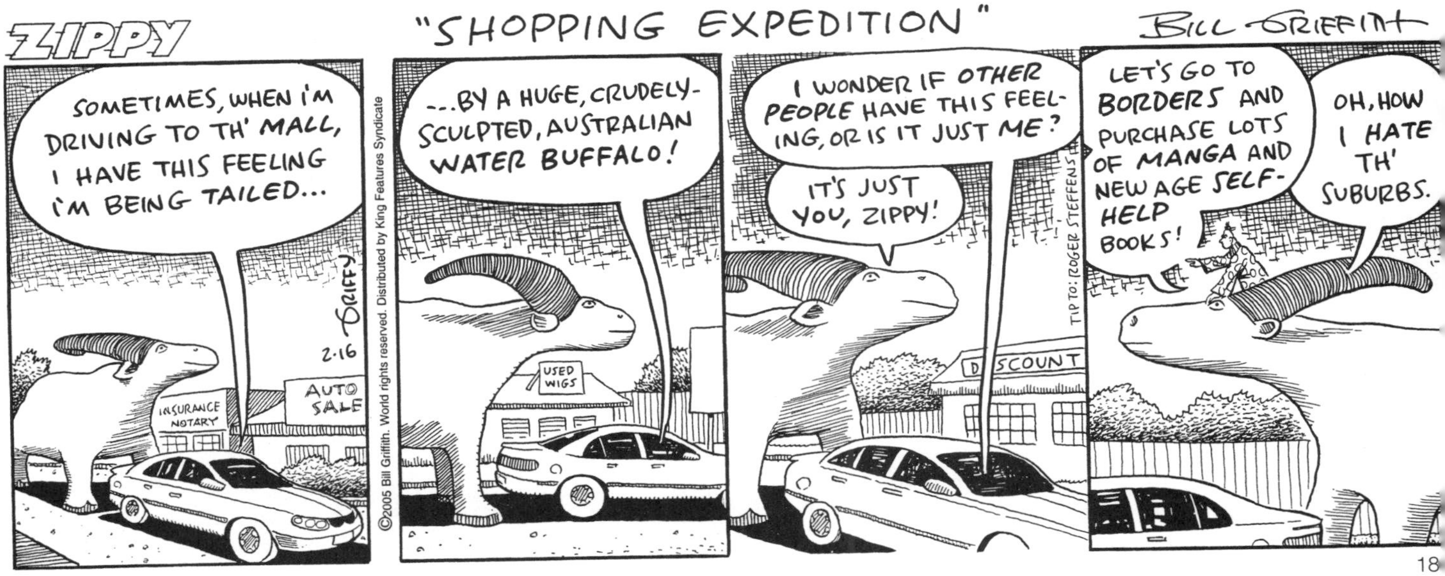
ZIPPY
"SHOPPING EXPEDITION"
BILL GRIFFITH
SOMETIMES, WHEN I'M DRIVING TO TH' MALL, I HAVE THIS FEELING I'M BEING TAILED...
GRIFFY
2-16
INSURANCE NOTARY
AUTO SALE
©2005 Bill Griffith. World rights reserved. Distributed by King Features Syndicate
...BY A HUGE, CRUDELY-SCULPTED, AUSTRALIAN WATER BUFFALO!
USED WIGS
I WONDER IF OTHER PEOPLE HAVE THIS FEELING, OR IS IT JUST ME?
IT'S JUST YOU, ZIPPY!
DISCOUNT
TIP TO: ROGER STEFFENS
LET'S GO TO BORDERS AND PURCHASE LOTS OF MANGA AND NEW AGE SELF-HELP BOOKS!
OH, HOW I HATE TH' SUBURBS.

18

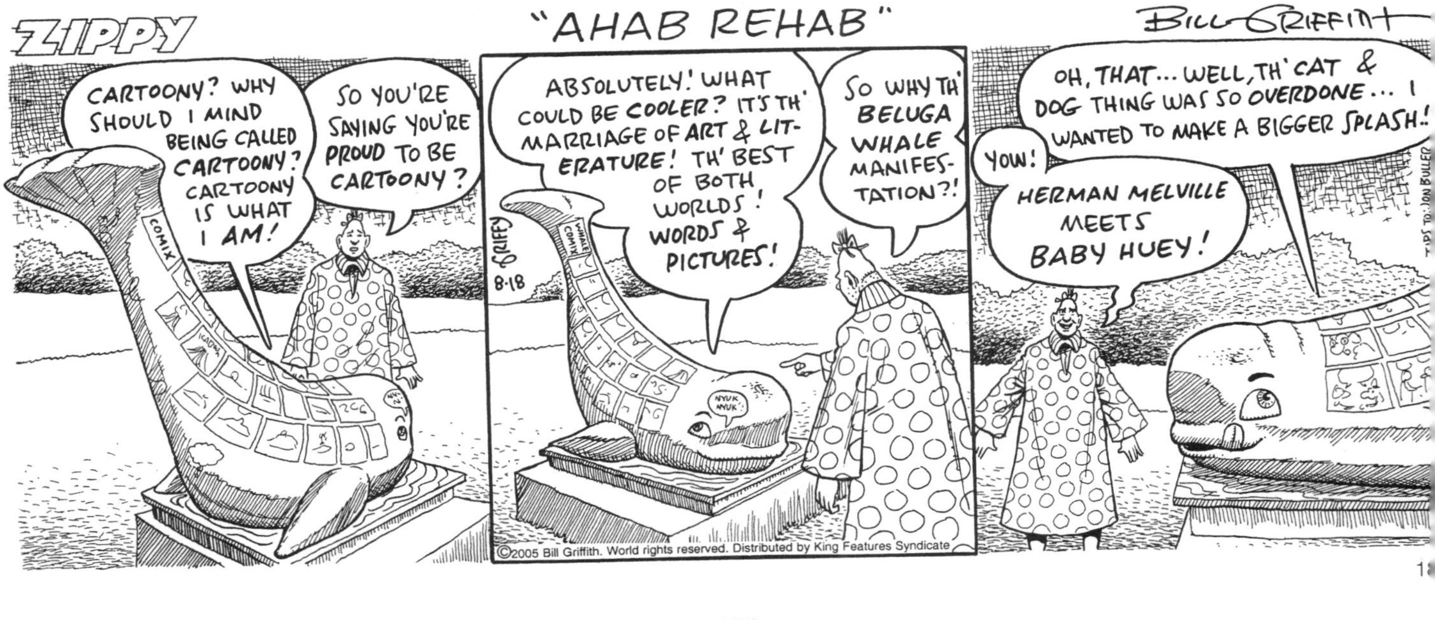
ZIPPY
"AHAB REHAB"
BILL GRIFFITH
CARTOONY? WHY SHOULD I MIND BEING CALLED CARTOONY? CARTOONY IS WHAT I AM!
SO YOU'RE SAYING YOU'RE PROUD TO BE CARTOONY?
COMIX
ABSOLUTELY! WHAT COULD BE COOLER? IT'S TH' MARRIAGE OF ART & LITERATURE! TH' BEST OF BOTH WORLDS! WORDS & PICTURES!
SO WHY TH' BELUGA WHALE MANIFESTATION?!
GRIFFY
8-18
NYUK NYUK
OH, THAT... WELL, TH' CAT & DOG THING WAS SO OVERDONE... I WANTED TO MAKE A BIGGER SPLASH!
YOW!
HERMAN MELVILLE MEETS BABY HUEY!
TIPS TO: JON BULLER
©2005 Bill Griffith. World rights reserved. Distributed by King Features Syndicate

1

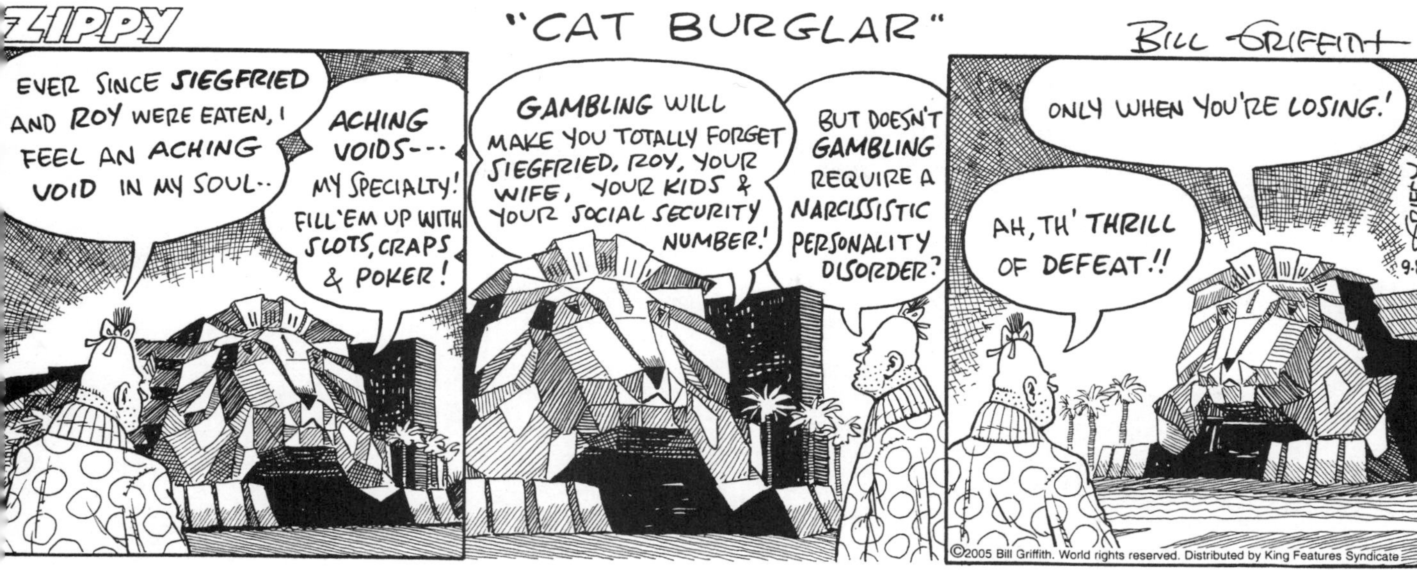
ZIPPY
"CAT BURGLAR"
BILL GRIFFITH
EVER SINCE SIEGFRIED AND ROY WERE EATEN, I FEEL AN ACHING VOID IN MY SOUL..
ACHING VOIDS--- MY SPECIALTY! FILL 'EM UP WITH SLOTS, CRAPS & POKER!
GAMBLING WILL MAKE YOU TOTALLY FORGET SIEGFRIED, ROY, YOUR WIFE, YOUR KIDS & YOUR SOCIAL SECURITY NUMBER!
BUT DOESN'T GAMBLING REQUIRE A NARCISSISTIC PERSONALITY DISORDER?
ONLY WHEN YOU'RE LOSING!
AH, TH' THRILL OF DEFEAT!!
GRIFFY
9-8
©2005 Bill Griffith. World rights reserved. Distributed by King Features Syndicate

190

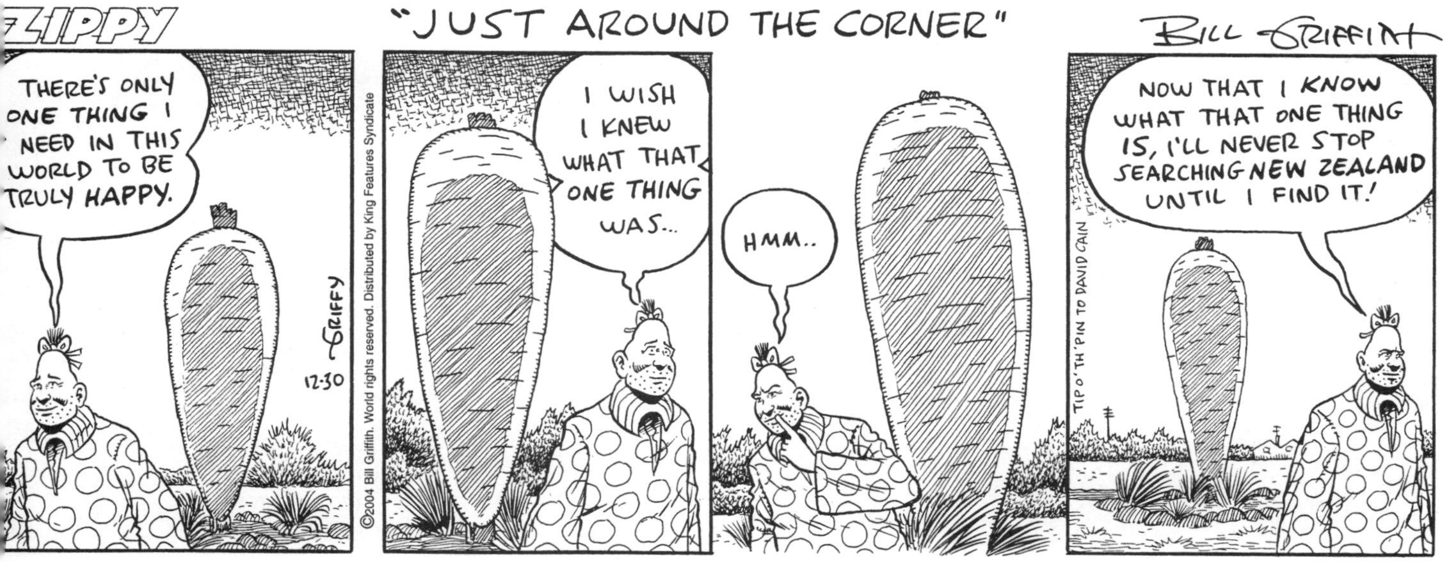
ZIPPY
"JUST AROUND THE CORNER"
BILL GRIFFITH
THERE'S ONLY ONE THING I NEED IN THIS WORLD TO BE TRULY HAPPY.
GRIFFY
12-30
©2004 Bill Griffith. World rights reserved. Distributed by King Features Syndicate
I WISH I KNEW WHAT THAT ONE THING WAS...
HMM..
TIP O' TH' PIN TO DAVID CAIN
NOW THAT I KNOW WHAT THAT ONE THING IS, I'LL NEVER STOP SEARCHING NEW ZEALAND UNTIL I FIND IT!

191

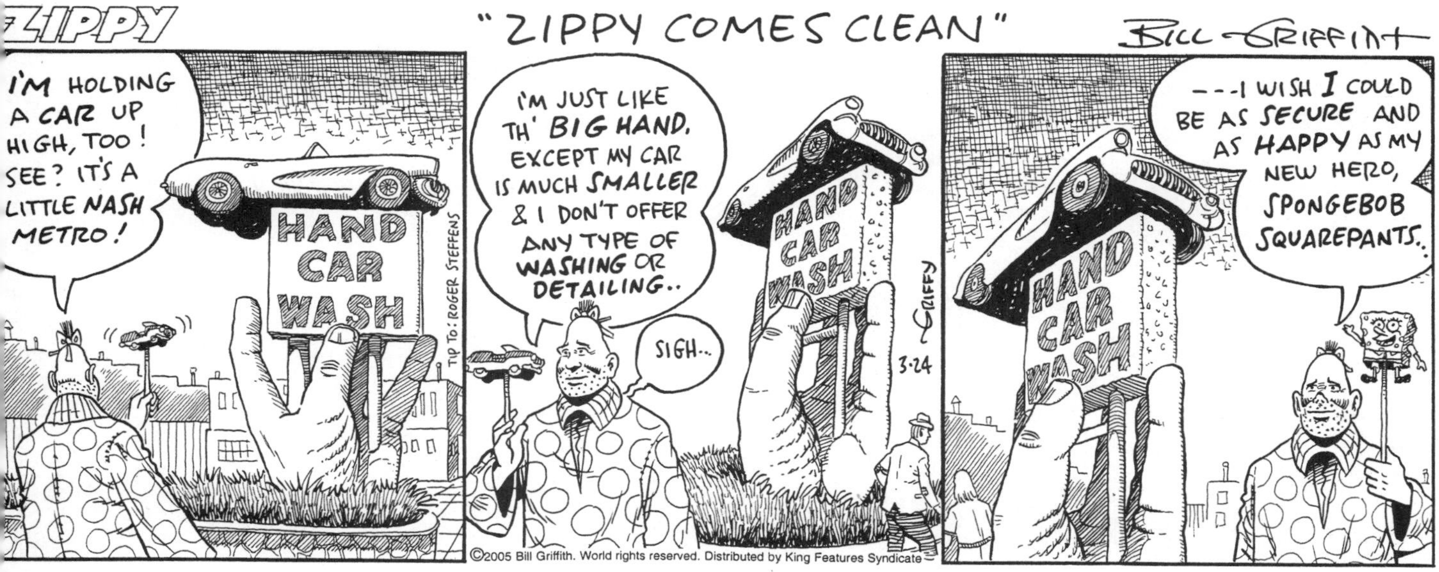
ZIPPY
"ZIPPY COMES CLEAN"
BILL GRIFFITH
I'M HOLDING A CAR UP HIGH, TOO! SEE? IT'S A LITTLE NASH METRO!
HAND CAR WASH
TIP TO: ROGER STEFFENS
I'M JUST LIKE TH' BIG HAND, EXCEPT MY CAR IS MUCH SMALLER & I DON'T OFFER ANY TYPE OF WASHING OR DETAILING..
SIGH..
GRIFFY
3-24
---I WISH I COULD BE AS SECURE AND AS HAPPY AS MY NEW HERO, SPONGEBOB SQUAREPANTS..
©2005 Bill Griffith. World rights reserved. Distributed by King Features Syndicate

192

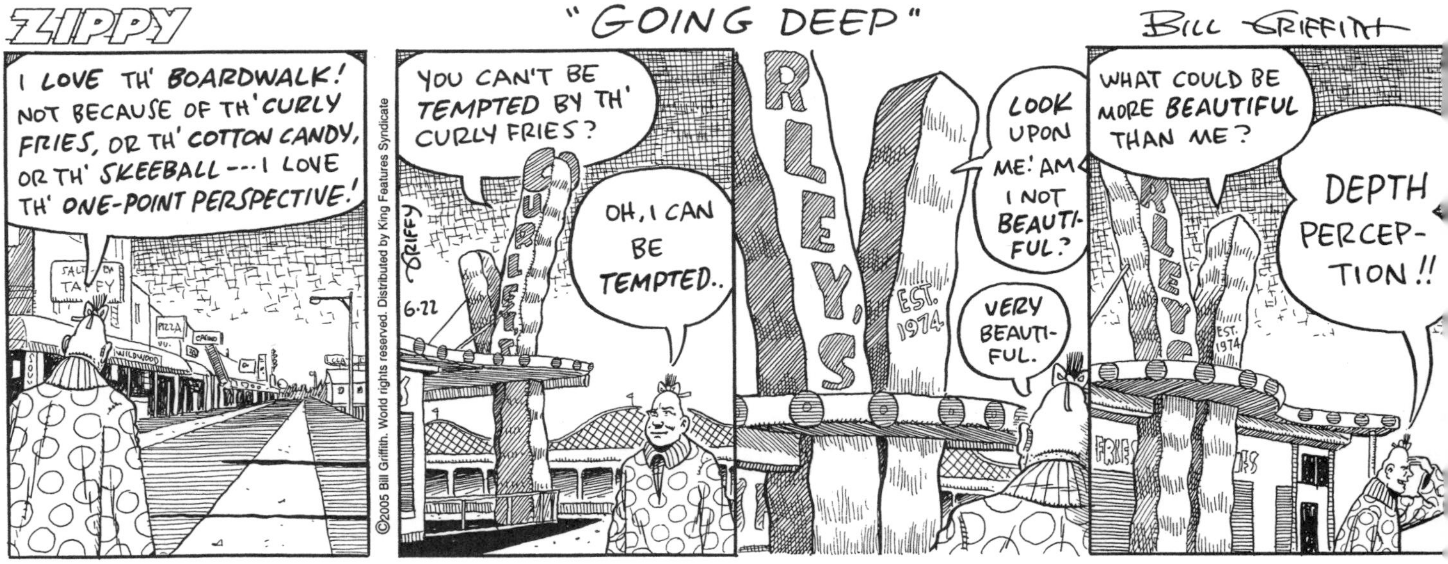
ZIPPY
"GOING DEEP"
BILL GRIFFITH
I LOVE TH' BOARDWALK! NOT BECAUSE OF TH' CURLY FRIES, OR TH' COTTON CANDY, OR TH' SKEEBALL--- I LOVE TH' ONE-POINT PERSPECTIVE!
©2005 Bill Griffith. World rights reserved. Distributed by King Features Syndicate
YOU CAN'T BE TEMPTED BY TH' CURLY FRIES?
GRIFFY 6·22
OH, I CAN BE TEMPTED..
LOOK UPON ME! AM I NOT BEAUTIFUL?
VERY BEAUTIFUL.
EST. 1974
WHAT COULD BE MORE BEAUTIFUL THAN ME?
DEPTH PERCEPTION!!

193

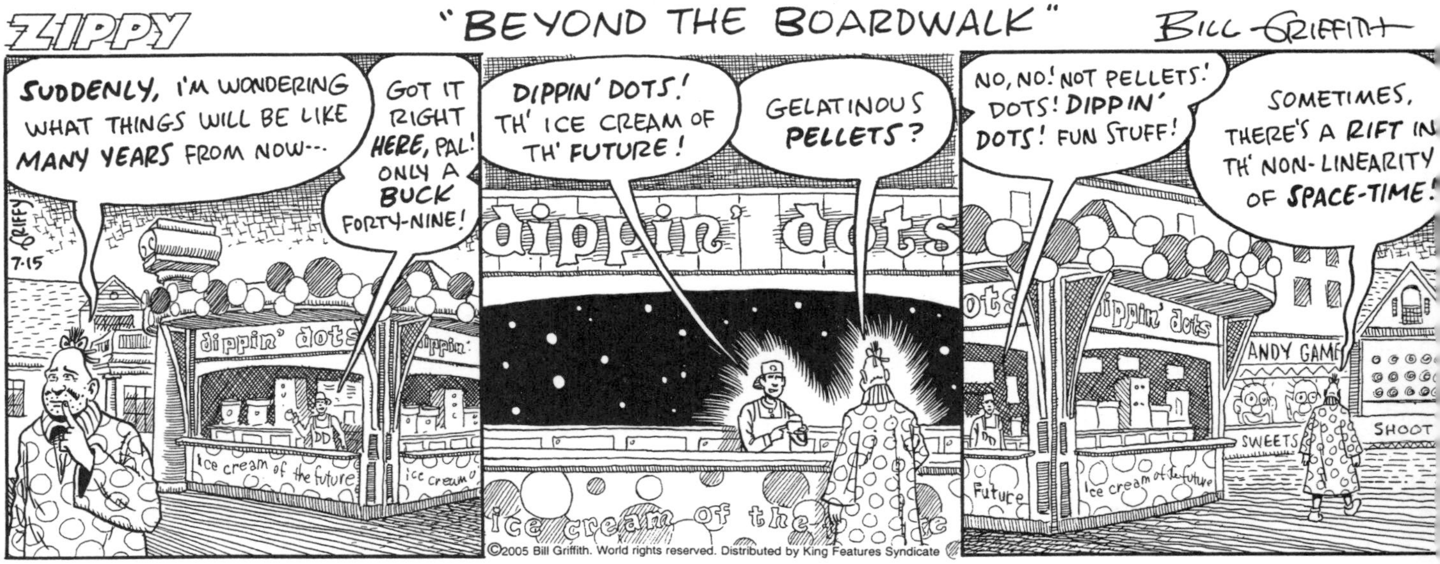
ZIPPY
"BEYOND THE BOARDWALK"
BILL GRIFFITH
SUDDENLY, I'M WONDERING WHAT THINGS WILL BE LIKE MANY YEARS FROM NOW---
GOT IT RIGHT HERE, PAL! ONLY A BUCK FORTY-NINE!
GRIFFY 7·15
dippin' dots
ice cream of the future
DIPPIN' DOTS! TH' ICE CREAM OF TH' FUTURE!
GELATINOUS PELLETS?
©2005 Bill Griffith. World rights reserved. Distributed by King Features Syndicate
NO, NO! NOT PELLETS! DOTS! DIPPIN' DOTS! FUN STUFF!
SOMETIMES, THERE'S A RIFT IN TH' NON-LINEARITY OF SPACE-TIME!
SWEETS
SHOOT

194

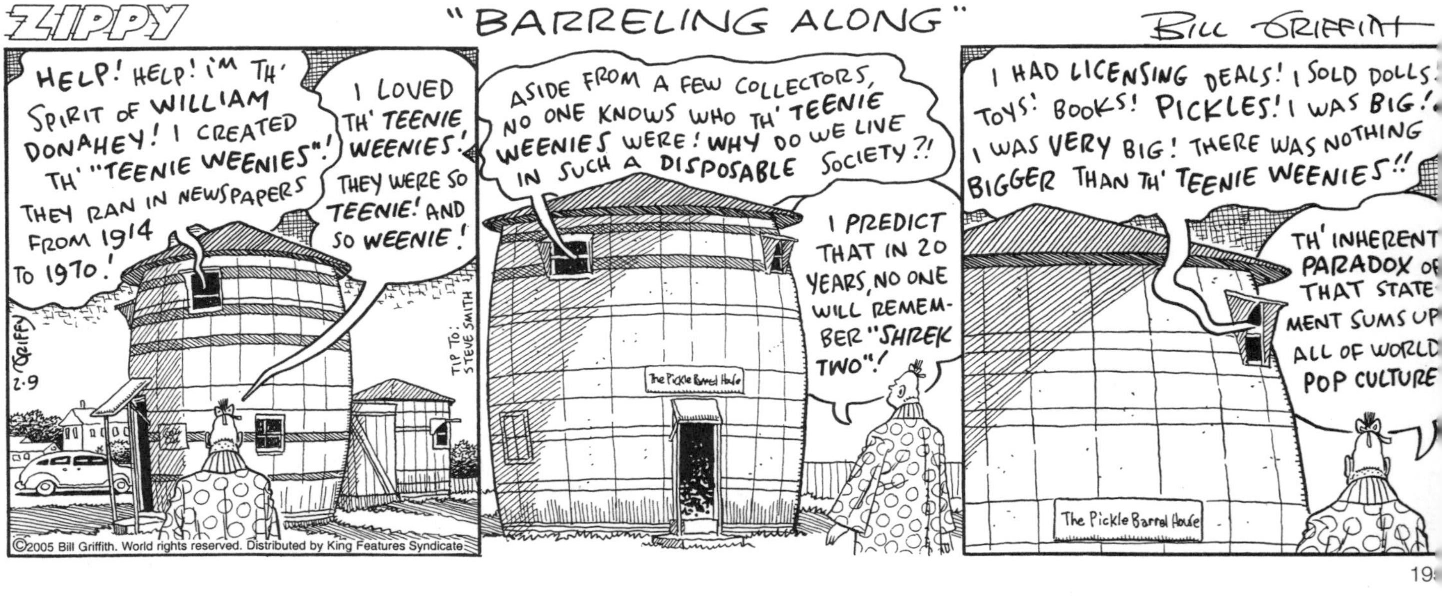
ZIPPY
"BARRELING ALONG"
BILL GRIFFITH
HELP! HELP! I'M TH' SPIRIT OF WILLIAM DONAHEY! I CREATED TH' "TEENIE WEENIES"! THEY RAN IN NEWSPAPERS FROM 1914 TO 1970!
I LOVED TH' TEENIE WEENIES! THEY WERE SO TEENIE! AND SO WEENIE!
GRIFFY 2·9
TIP TO: STEVE SMITH
©2005 Bill Griffith. World rights reserved. Distributed by King Features Syndicate
ASIDE FROM A FEW COLLECTORS, NO ONE KNOWS WHO TH' TEENIE WEENIES WERE! WHY DO WE LIVE IN SUCH A DISPOSABLE SOCIETY?!
The Pickle Barrel House
I PREDICT THAT IN 20 YEARS, NO ONE WILL REMEMBER "SHREK TWO"!
I HAD LICENSING DEALS! I SOLD DOLLS! TOYS! BOOKS! PICKLES! I WAS BIG! I WAS VERY BIG! THERE WAS NOTHING BIGGER THAN TH' TEENIE WEENIES!!
TH' INHERENT PARADOX OF THAT STATEMENT SUMS UP ALL OF WORLD POP CULTURE
The Pickle Barrel House

19

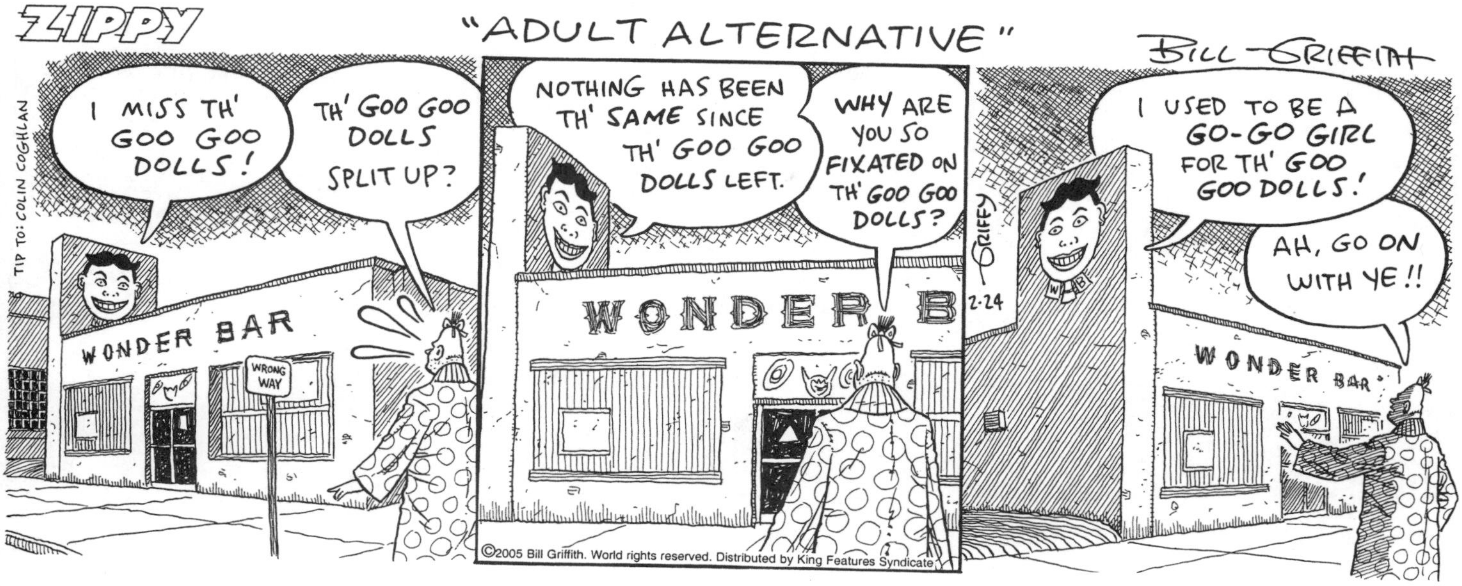
ZIPPY
"ADULT ALTERNATIVE"
BILL GRIFFITH
TIP TO: COLIN COGHLAN
I MISS TH' GOO GOO DOLLS!
TH' GOO GOO DOLLS SPLIT UP?
WONDER BAR
WRONG WAY
NOTHING HAS BEEN TH' SAME SINCE TH' GOO GOO DOLLS LEFT.
WHY ARE YOU SO FIXATED ON TH' GOO GOO DOLLS?
WONDER B
GRIFFY 2-24
©2005 Bill Griffith. World rights reserved. Distributed by King Features Syndicate
I USED TO BE A GO-GO GIRL FOR TH' GOO GOO DOLLS!
AH, GO ON WITH YE!!
WONDER BAR

196

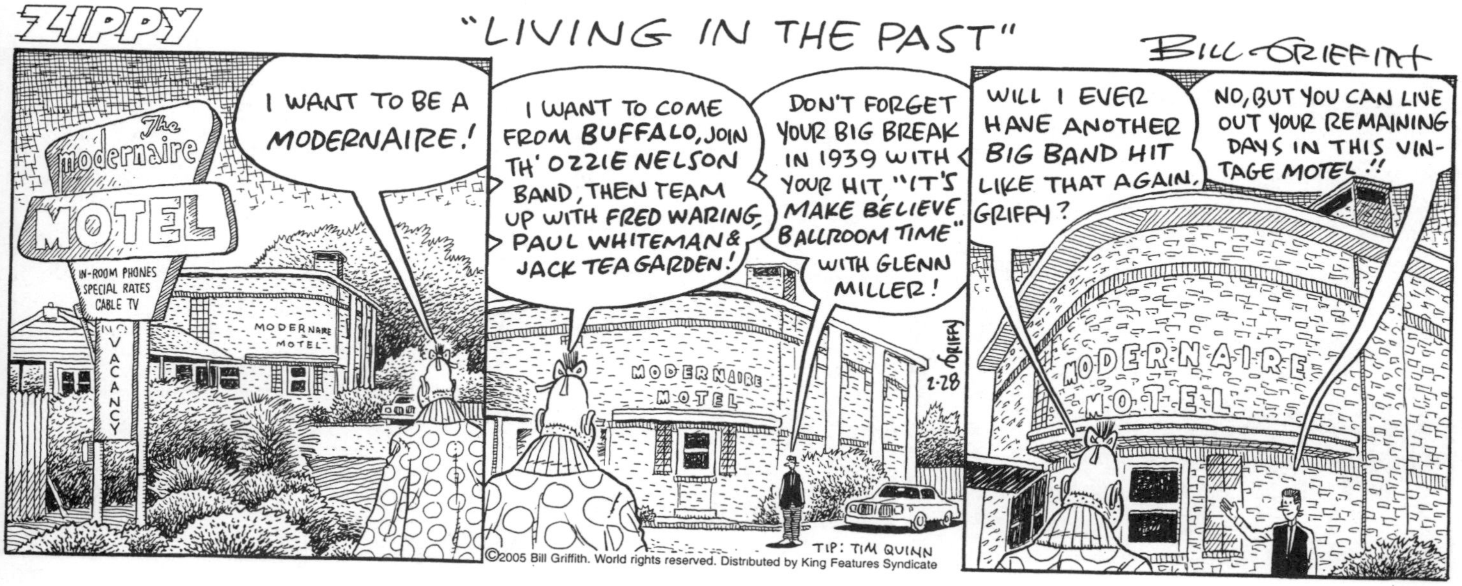
ZIPPY
"LIVING IN THE PAST"
BILL GRIFFITH
The modernaire MOTEL
IN-ROOM PHONES
SPECIAL RATES
CABLE TV
NO VACANCY
MODERNAIRE MOTEL
I WANT TO BE A MODERNAIRE!
I WANT TO COME FROM BUFFALO, JOIN TH' OZZIE NELSON BAND, THEN TEAM UP WITH FRED WARING, PAUL WHITEMAN & JACK TEAGARDEN!
DON'T FORGET YOUR BIG BREAK IN 1939 WITH YOUR HIT, "IT'S MAKE BELIEVE BALLROOM TIME" WITH GLENN MILLER!
MODERNAIRE MOTEL
GRIFFY 2-28
TIP: TIM QUINN
©2005 Bill Griffith. World rights reserved. Distributed by King Features Syndicate
WILL I EVER HAVE ANOTHER BIG BAND HIT LIKE THAT AGAIN, GRIFFY?
NO, BUT YOU CAN LIVE OUT YOUR REMAINING DAYS IN THIS VINTAGE MOTEL!!
MODERNAIRE MOTEL

197

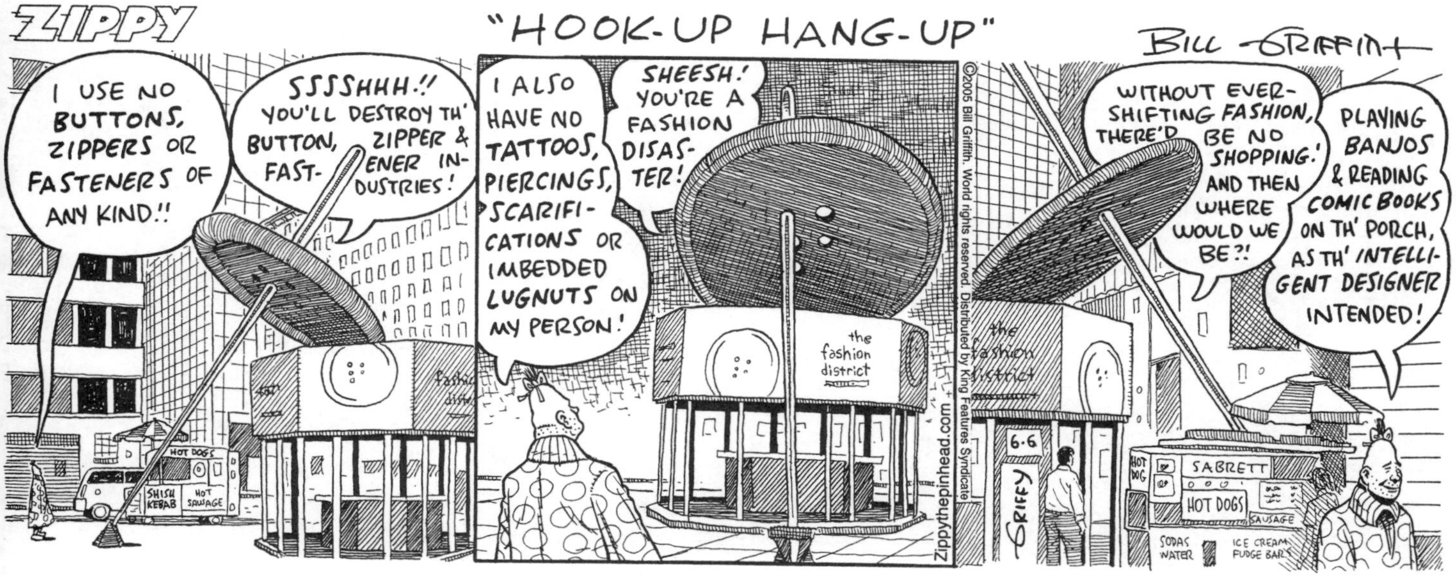
ZIPPY
"HOOK-UP HANG-UP"
BILL GRIFFITH
I USE NO BUTTONS, ZIPPERS OR FASTENERS OF ANY KIND!!
SSSSHHH!! YOU'LL DESTROY TH' BUTTON, ZIPPER & FASTENER INDUSTRIES!
HOT DOGS
SHISH KEBAB
HOT SAUSAGE
I ALSO HAVE NO TATTOOS, PIERCINGS, SCARIFICATIONS OR IMBEDDED LUGNUTS ON MY PERSON!
SHEESH! YOU'RE A FASHION DISASTER!
the fashion district
©2005 Bill Griffith. World rights reserved. Distributed by King Features Syndicate
Zippythepinhead.com
WITHOUT EVER-SHIFTING FASHION, THERE'D BE NO SHOPPING! AND THEN WHERE WOULD WE BE?!
PLAYING BANJOS & READING COMIC BOOKS ON TH' PORCH, AS TH' INTELLIGENT DESIGNER INTENDED!
the fashion district
6-6
GRIFFY
SABRETT
HOT DOGS
SAUSAGE
SODAS WATER
ICE CREAM FUDGE BARS

198

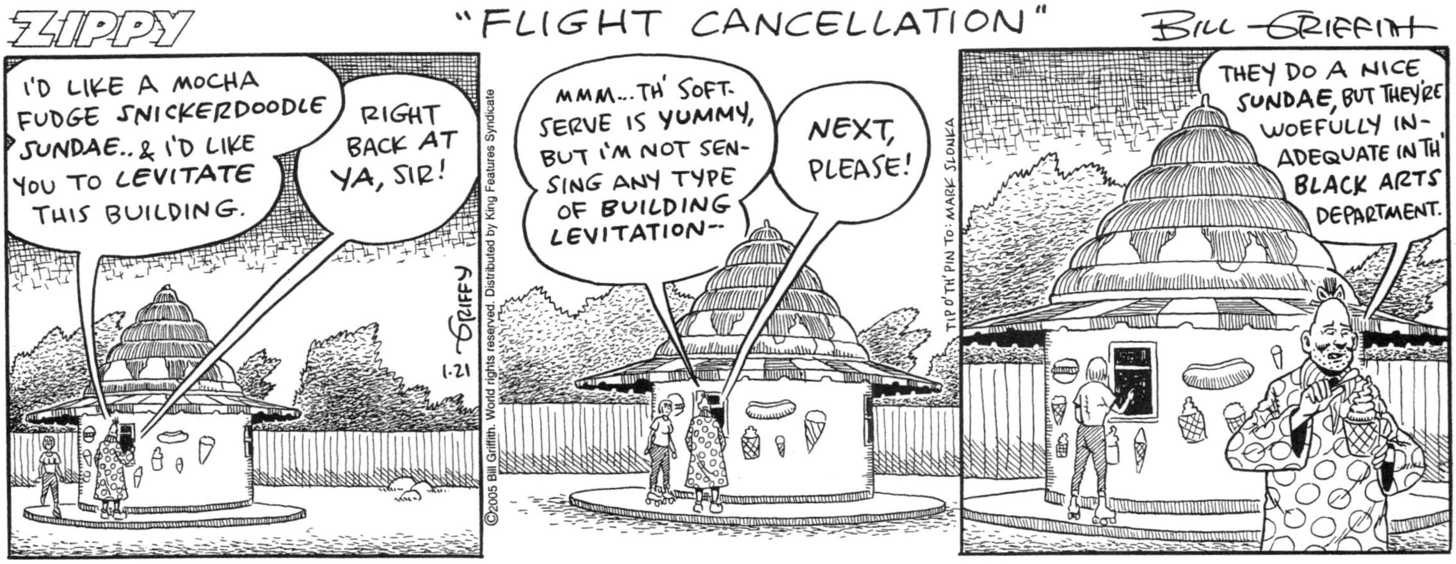
ZIPPY
"FLIGHT CANCELLATION"
BILL GRIFFITH
I'D LIKE A MOCHA FUDGE SNICKERDOODLE SUNDAE..& I'D LIKE YOU TO LEVITATE THIS BUILDING.
RIGHT BACK AT YA, SIR!
GRIFFY 1-21
©2005 Bill Griffith. World rights reserved. Distributed by King Features Syndicate
MMM...TH' SOFT-SERVE IS YUMMY, BUT I'M NOT SENSING ANY TYPE OF BUILDING LEVITATION--
NEXT, PLEASE!
TIP O' TH' PIN TO: MARK SLONKA
THEY DO A NICE SUNDAE, BUT THEY'RE WOEFULLY INADEQUATE IN TH' BLACK ARTS DEPARTMENT.

199

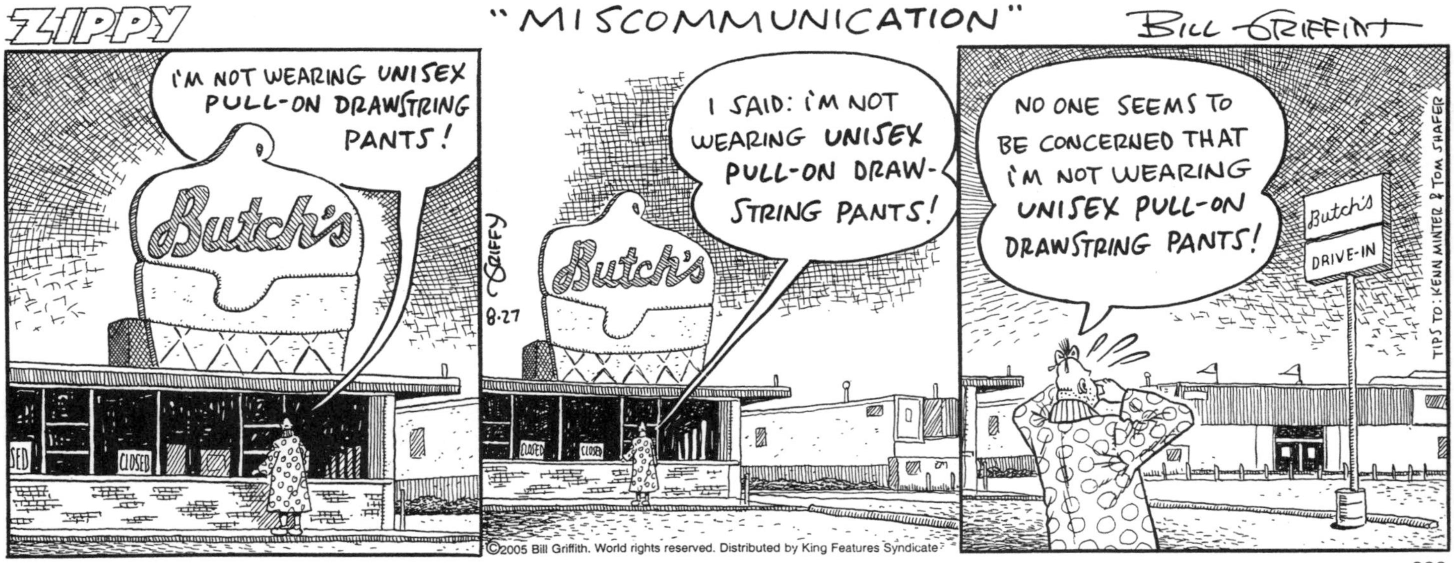
ZIPPY
"MISCOMMUNICATION"
BILL GRIFFITH
I'M NOT WEARING UNISEX PULL-ON DRAWSTRING PANTS!
Butch's
CLOSED
GRIFFY 8-27
I SAID: I'M NOT WEARING UNISEX PULL-ON DRAWSTRING PANTS!
©2005 Bill Griffith. World rights reserved. Distributed by King Features Syndicate
NO ONE SEEMS TO BE CONCERNED THAT I'M NOT WEARING UNISEX PULL-ON DRAWSTRING PANTS!
Butch's
DRIVE-IN
TIPS TO: KENN MINTER & TOM SHAFER

200

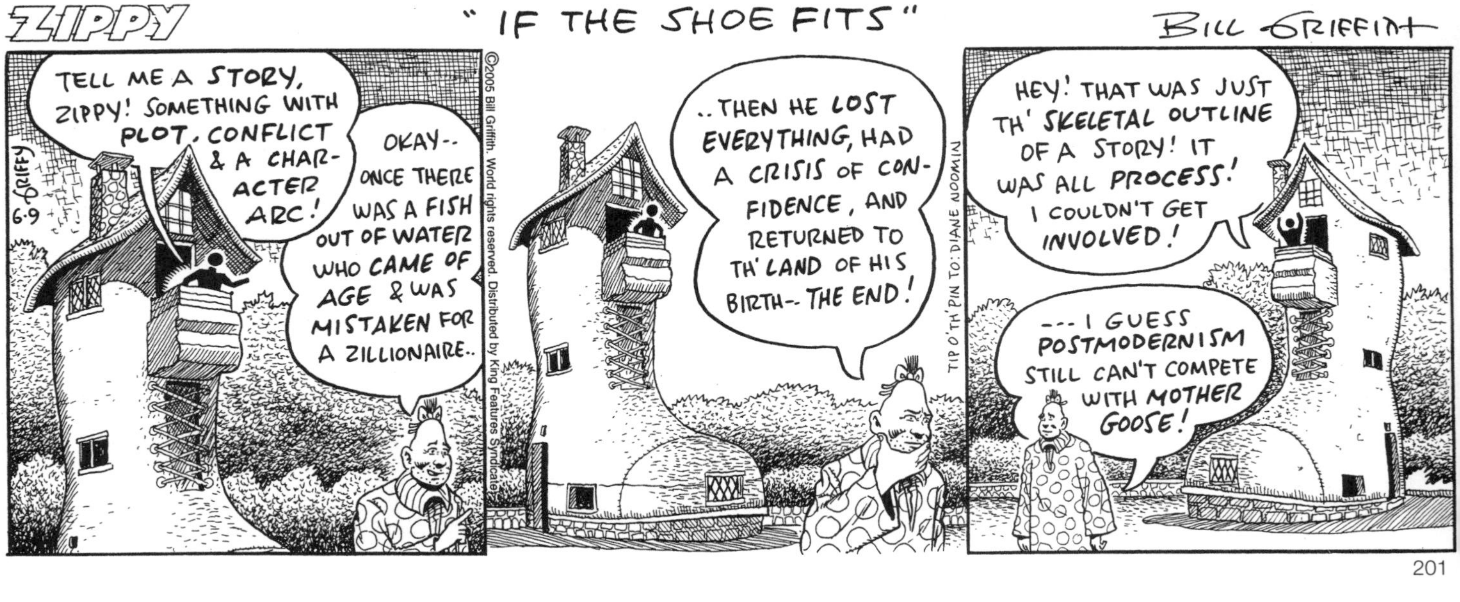
ZIPPY
"IF THE SHOE FITS"
BILL GRIFFITH
TELL ME A STORY, ZIPPY! SOMETHING WITH PLOT, CONFLICT & A CHARACTER ARC!
GRIFFY 6-9
OKAY-- ONCE THERE WAS A FISH OUT OF WATER WHO CAME OF AGE & WAS MISTAKEN FOR A ZILLIONAIRE..
©2005 Bill Griffith. World rights reserved. Distributed by King Features Syndicate
..THEN HE LOST EVERYTHING, HAD A CRISIS OF CONFIDENCE, AND RETURNED TO TH' LAND OF HIS BIRTH-- THE END!
TIP O' TH' PIN TO: DIANE NOOMIN
HEY! THAT WAS JUST TH' SKELETAL OUTLINE OF A STORY! IT WAS ALL PROCESS! I COULDN'T GET INVOLVED!
--- I GUESS POSTMODERNISM STILL CAN'T COMPETE WITH MOTHER GOOSE!

201

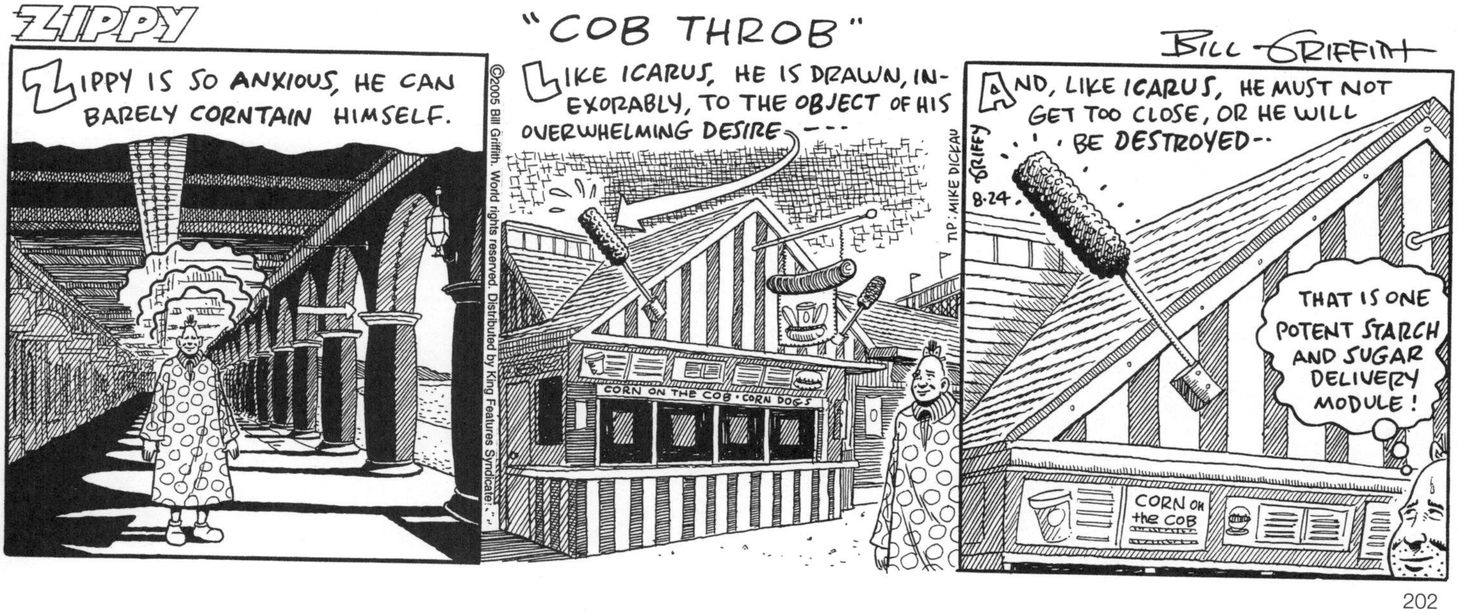
ZIPPY
"COB THROB"
BILL GRIFFITH
ZIPPY IS SO ANXIOUS, HE CAN BARELY CORNTAIN HIMSELF.
©2005 Bill Griffith. World rights reserved. Distributed by King Features Syndicate
LIKE ICARUS, HE IS DRAWN, IN-EXORABLY, TO THE OBJECT OF HIS OVERWHELMING DESIRE---
CORN ON THE COB · CORN DOGS
TIP: MIKE DICKAU
GRIFFY
8·24
AND, LIKE ICARUS, HE MUST NOT GET TOO CLOSE, OR HE WILL BE DESTROYED--
THAT IS ONE POTENT STARCH AND SUGAR DELIVERY MODULE!
CORN on the COB

202

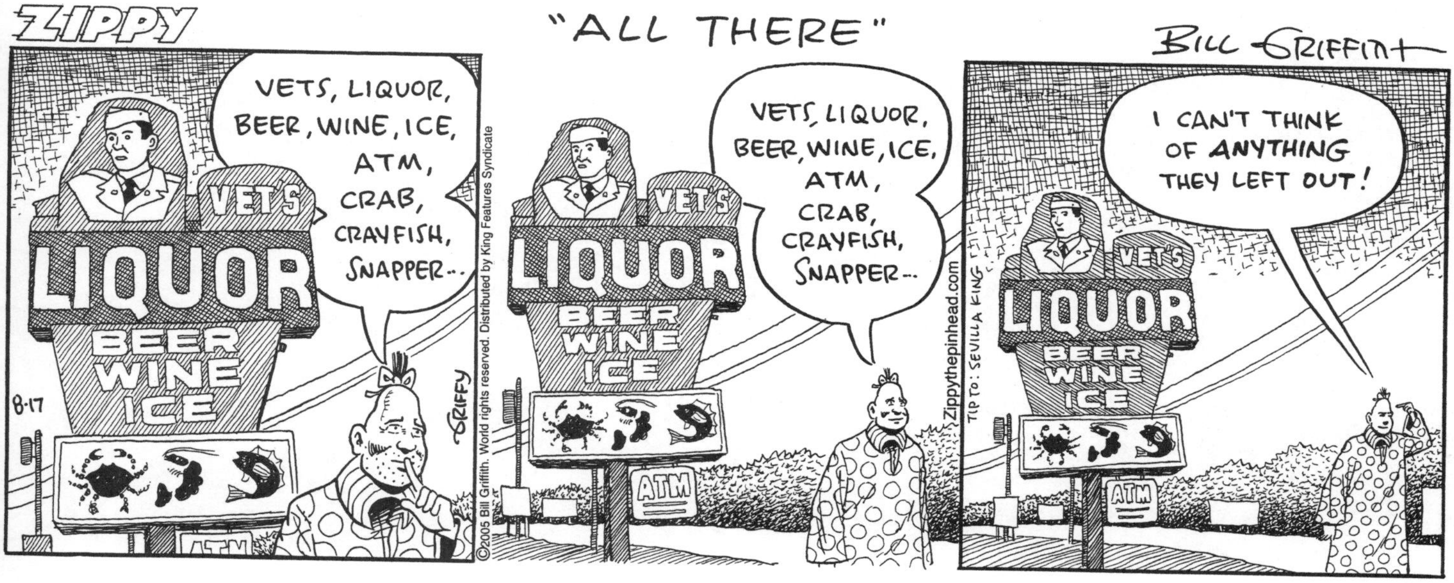
ZIPPY
"ALL THERE"
BILL GRIFFITH
VETS, LIQUOR, BEER, WINE, ICE, ATM, CRAB, CRAYFISH, SNAPPER--
VET'S LIQUOR BEER WINE ICE
8·17
GRIFFY
ATM
©2005 Bill Griffith. World rights reserved. Distributed by King Features Syndicate
VETS, LIQUOR, BEER, WINE, ICE, ATM, CRAB, CRAYFISH, SNAPPER--
VET'S LIQUOR BEER WINE ICE
ATM
Zippythepinhead.com
TIP TO: SEVILLA KING
I CAN'T THINK OF ANYTHING THEY LEFT OUT!
VET'S LIQUOR BEER WINE ICE
ATM

203

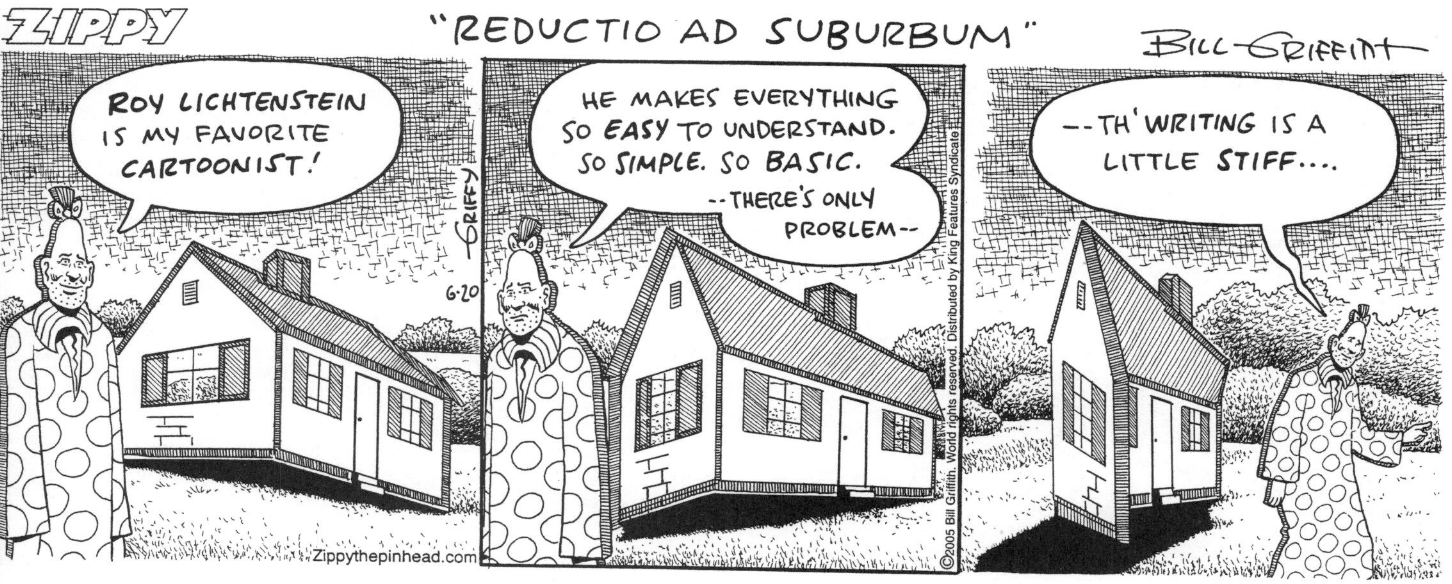
ZIPPY
"REDUCTIO AD SUBURBUM"
BILL GRIFFITH
ROY LICHTENSTEIN IS MY FAVORITE CARTOONIST!
GRIFFY
6·20
Zippythepinhead.com
HE MAKES EVERYTHING SO EASY TO UNDERSTAND. SO SIMPLE. SO BASIC.
--THERE'S ONLY PROBLEM--
©2005 Bill Griffith. World rights reserved. Distributed by King Features Syndicate
--TH' WRITING IS A LITTLE STIFF....

204

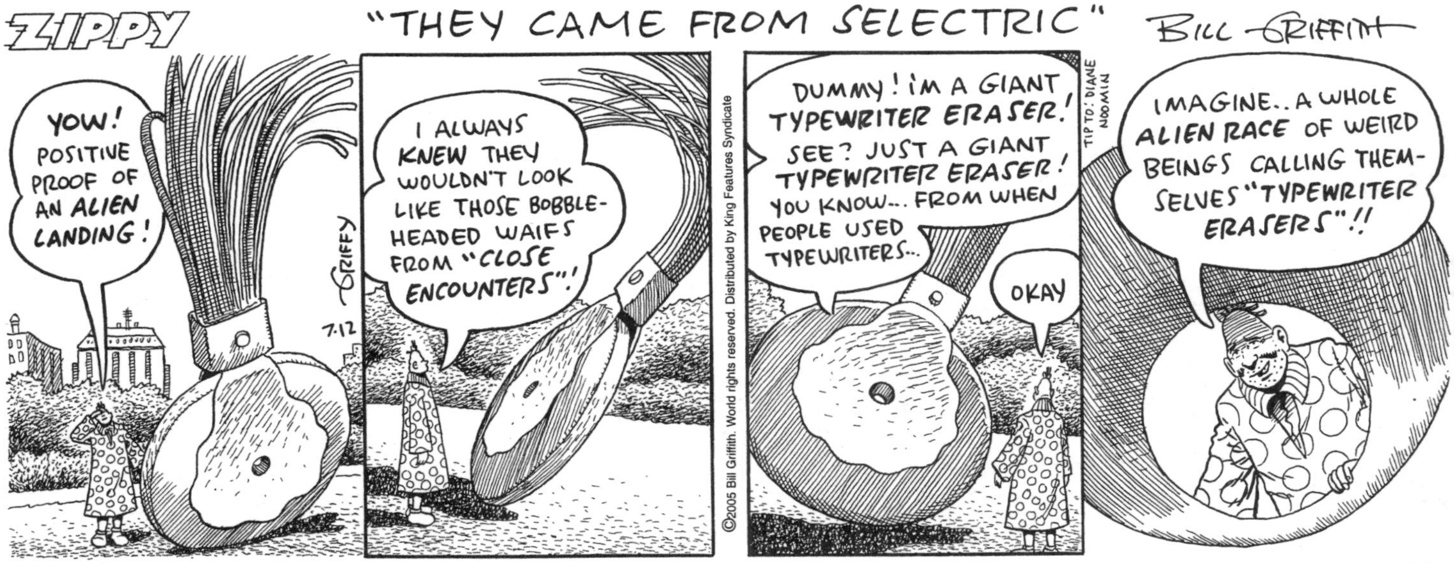
ZIPPY
"THEY CAME FROM SELECTRIC"
BILL GRIFFITH
YOW! POSITIVE PROOF OF AN ALIEN LANDING!
GRIFFY 7.12
I ALWAYS KNEW THEY WOULDN'T LOOK LIKE THOSE BOBBLE-HEADED WAIFS FROM "CLOSE ENCOUNTERS"!
©2005 Bill Griffith. World rights reserved. Distributed by King Features Syndicate
DUMMY! I'M A GIANT TYPEWRITER ERASER! SEE? JUST A GIANT TYPEWRITER ERASER! YOU KNOW... FROM WHEN PEOPLE USED TYPEWRITERS...
OKAY
TIP TO: DIANE NOOMIN
IMAGINE.. A WHOLE ALIEN RACE OF WEIRD BEINGS CALLING THEMSELVES "TYPEWRITER ERASERS"!!

205

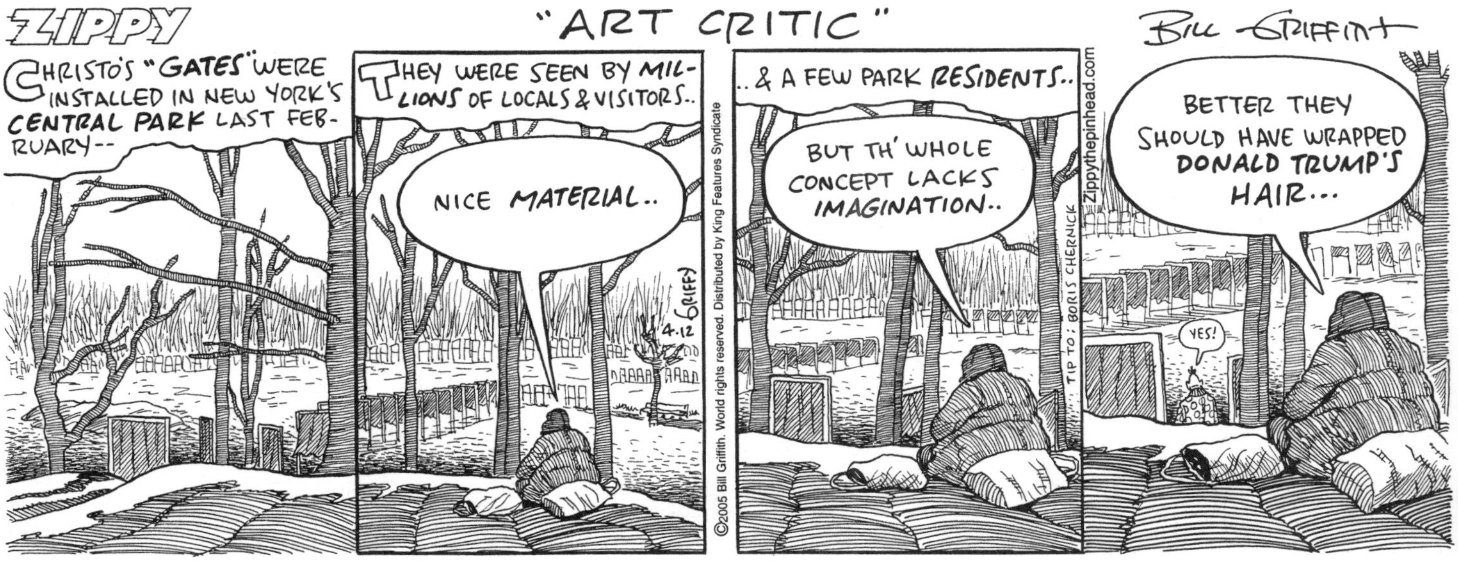
ZIPPY
"ART CRITIC"
BILL GRIFFITH
CHRISTO'S "GATES" WERE INSTALLED IN NEW YORK'S CENTRAL PARK LAST FEBRUARY--
THEY WERE SEEN BY MILLIONS OF LOCALS & VISITORS..
NICE MATERIAL..
GRIFFY 4.12
©2005 Bill Griffith. World rights reserved. Distributed by King Features Syndicate
..& A FEW PARK RESIDENTS..
BUT TH' WHOLE CONCEPT LACKS IMAGINATION..
TIP TO: BORIS CHERNICK
Zippythepinhead.com
BETTER THEY SHOULD HAVE WRAPPED DONALD TRUMP'S HAIR...
YES!

206

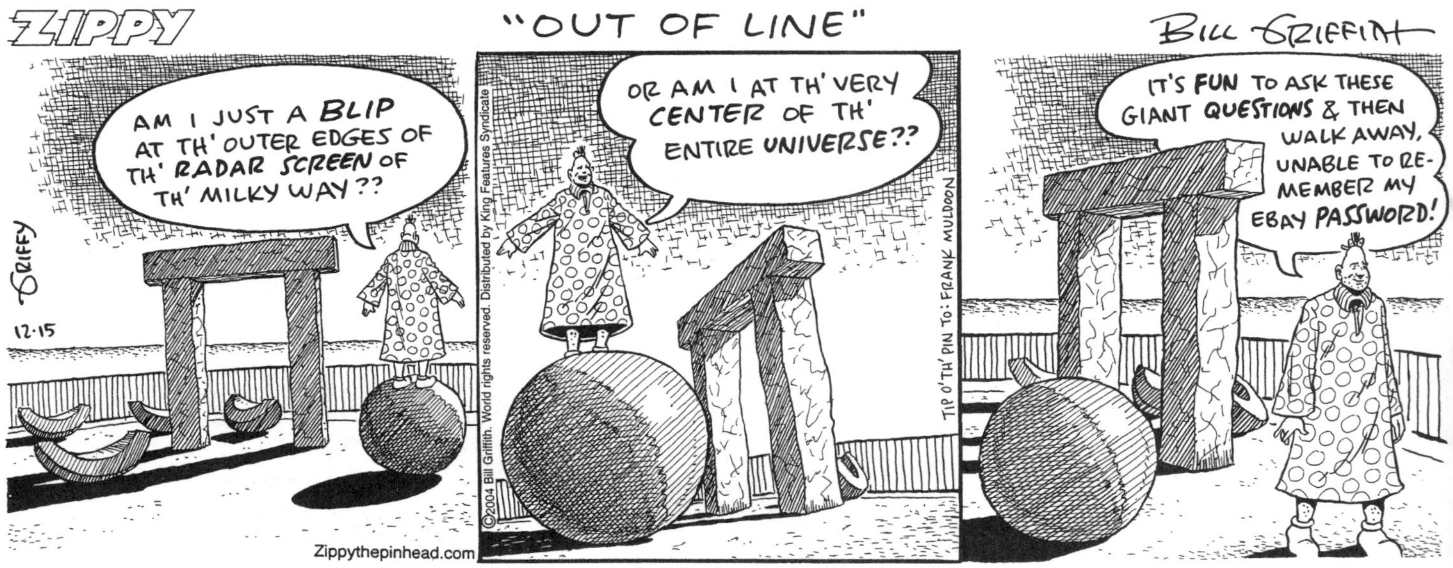
ZIPPY
"OUT OF LINE"
BILL GRIFFITH
AM I JUST A BLIP AT TH' OUTER EDGES OF TH' RADAR SCREEN OF TH' MILKY WAY??
GRIFFY 12.15
Zippythepinhead.com
©2004 Bill Griffith. World rights reserved. Distributed by King Features Syndicate
OR AM I AT TH' VERY CENTER OF TH' ENTIRE UNIVERSE??
TIP O' TH' PIN TO: FRANK MULDOON
IT'S FUN TO ASK THESE GIANT QUESTIONS & THEN WALK AWAY, UNABLE TO REMEMBER MY EBAY PASSWORD!

207

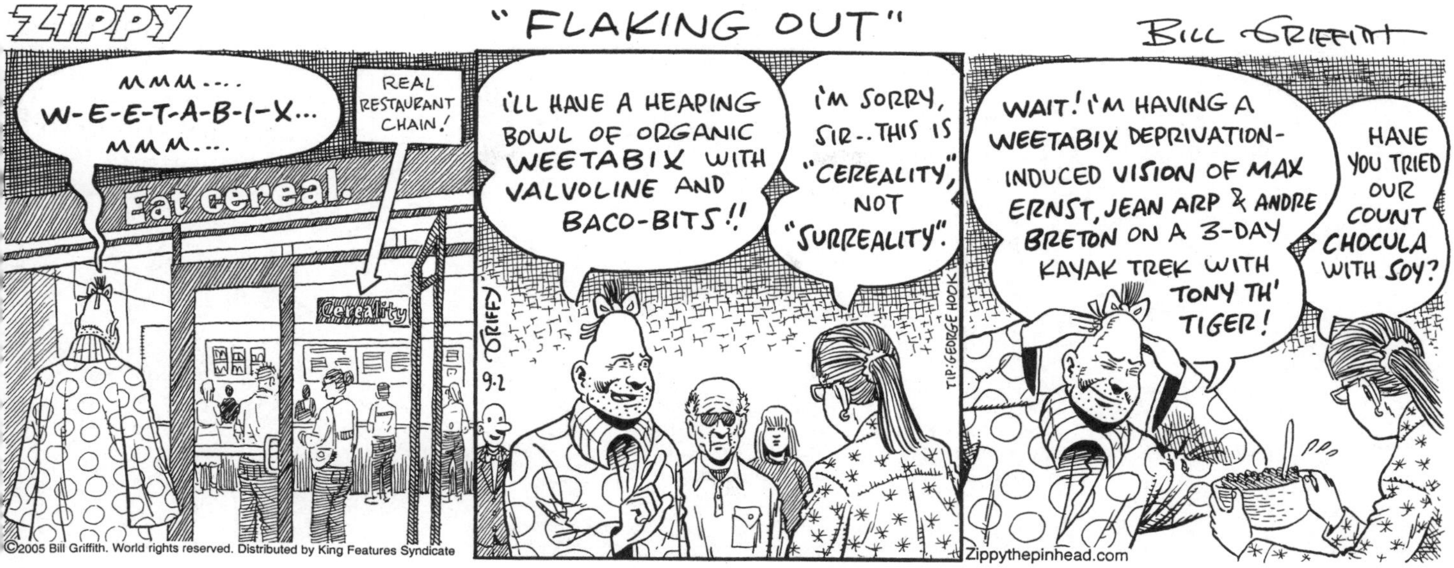
ZIPPY
"FLAKING OUT"
BILL GRIFFITH
MMM.... W-E-E-T-A-B-I-X... MMM....
REAL RESTAURANT CHAIN!
Eat cereal.
Cereality
I'LL HAVE A HEAPING BOWL OF ORGANIC WEETABIX WITH VALVOLINE AND BACO-BITS!!
I'M SORRY, SIR-- THIS IS "CEREALITY", NOT "SURREALITY".
GRIFFY 9·2
TIP: GEORGE HOOK
WAIT! I'M HAVING A WEETABIX DEPRIVATION-INDUCED VISION OF MAX ERNST, JEAN ARP & ANDRE BRETON ON A 3-DAY KAYAK TREK WITH TONY TH' TIGER!
HAVE YOU TRIED OUR COUNT CHOCULA WITH SOY?
©2005 Bill Griffith. World rights reserved. Distributed by King Features Syndicate
Zippythepinhead.com

208

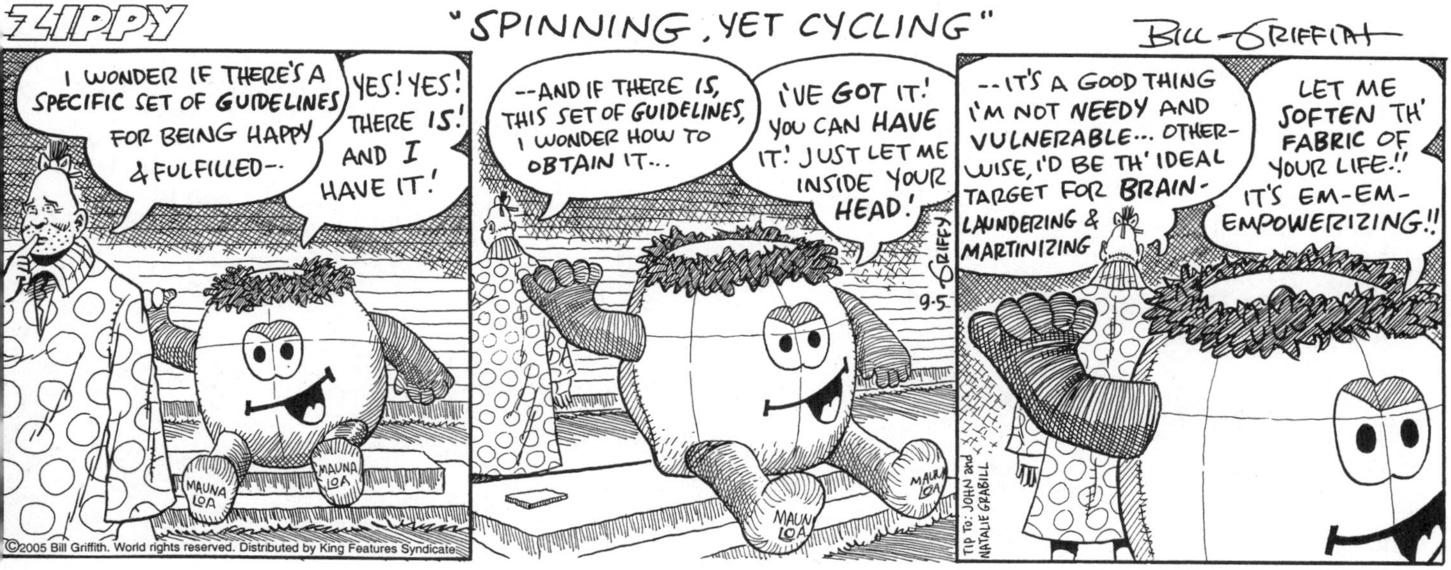
ZIPPY
"SPINNING, YET CYCLING"
BILL GRIFFITH
I WONDER IF THERE'S A SPECIFIC SET OF GUIDELINES FOR BEING HAPPY & FULFILLED--
YES! YES! THERE IS! AND I HAVE IT!
MAUNA LOA
MAUNA LOA
--AND IF THERE IS, THIS SET OF GUIDELINES, I WONDER HOW TO OBTAIN IT...
I'VE GOT IT! YOU CAN HAVE IT! JUST LET ME INSIDE YOUR HEAD!
GRIFFY 9·5
MAUNA LOA
MAUNA LOA
--IT'S A GOOD THING I'M NOT NEEDY AND VULNERABLE... OTHERWISE, I'D BE TH' IDEAL TARGET FOR BRAIN-LAUNDERING & MARTINIZING
LET ME SOFTEN TH' FABRIC OF YOUR LIFE!! IT'S EM-EM-EMPOWERIZING!!
TIP TO: JOHN and NATALIE GRABILL
©2005 Bill Griffith. World rights reserved. Distributed by King Features Syndicate

209

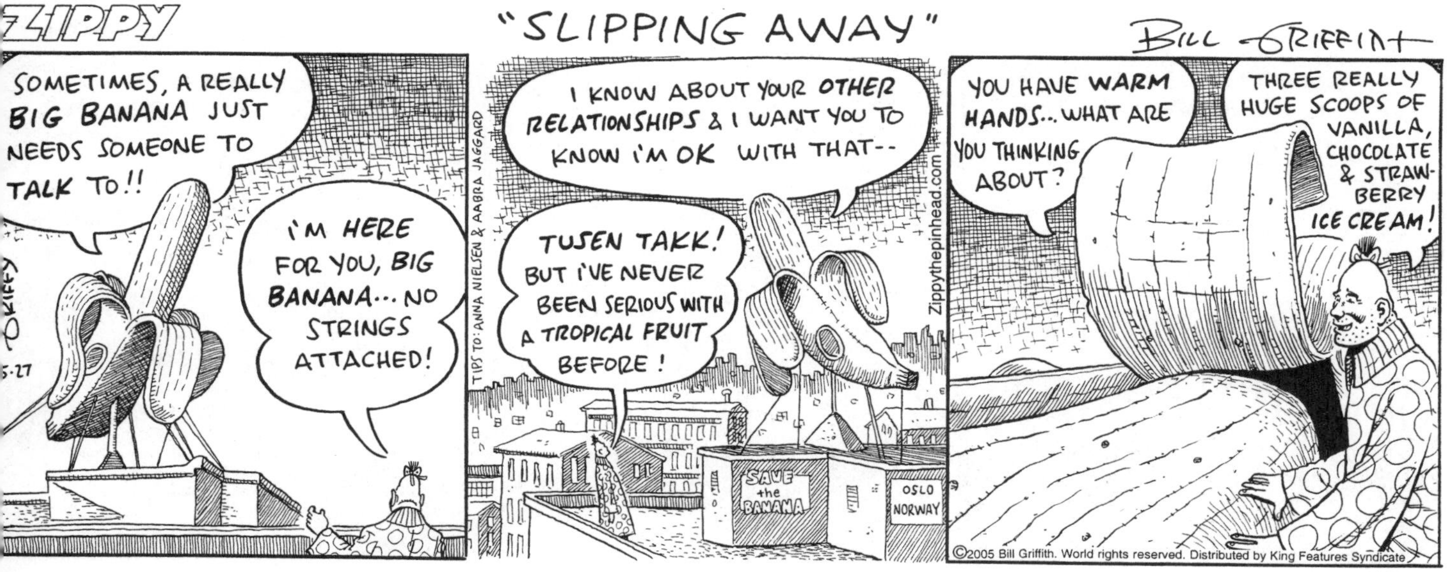
ZIPPY
"SLIPPING AWAY"
BILL GRIFFITH
SOMETIMES, A REALLY BIG BANANA JUST NEEDS SOMEONE TO TALK TO!!
I'M HERE FOR YOU, BIG BANANA... NO STRINGS ATTACHED!
GRIFFY 5·27
I KNOW ABOUT YOUR OTHER RELATIONSHIPS & I WANT YOU TO KNOW I'M OK WITH THAT--
TUSEN TAKK! BUT I'VE NEVER BEEN SERIOUS WITH A TROPICAL FRUIT BEFORE!
TIPS TO: ANNA NIELSEN & AABRA JAGGARD
Zippythepinhead.com
SAVE the BANANA
OSLO NORWAY
YOU HAVE WARM HANDS... WHAT ARE YOU THINKING ABOUT?
THREE REALLY HUGE SCOOPS OF VANILLA, CHOCOLATE & STRAWBERRY ICE CREAM!
©2005 Bill Griffith. World rights reserved. Distributed by King Features Syndicate

210

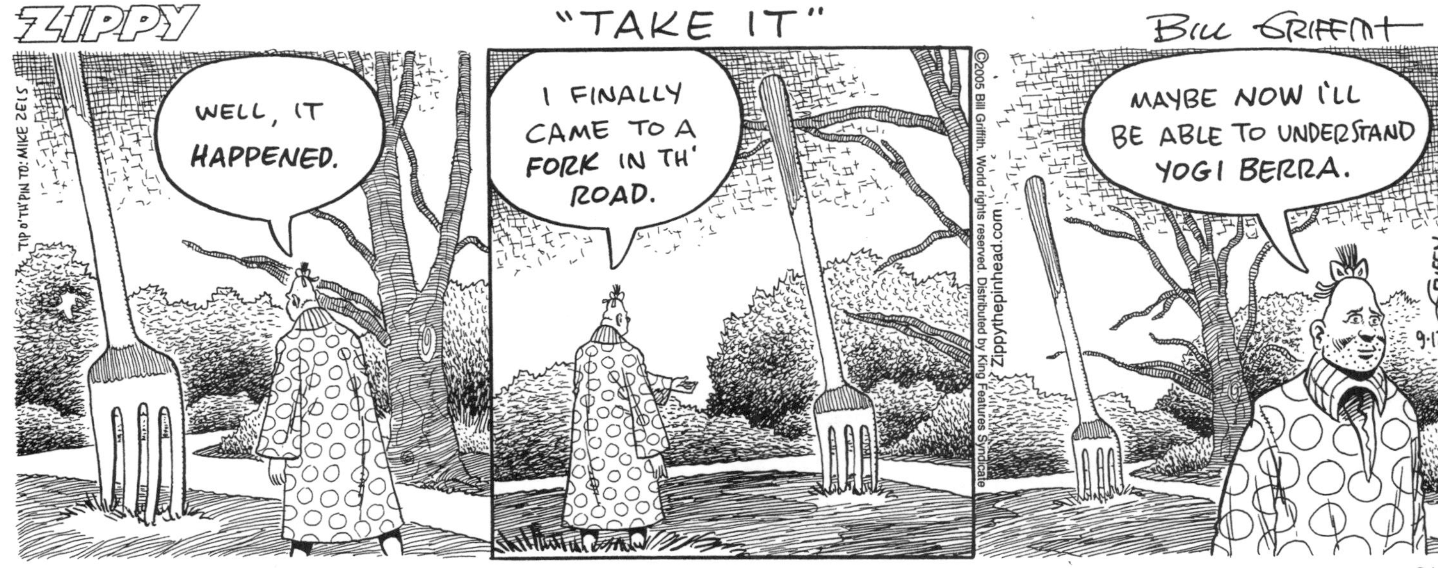
ZIPPY
"TAKE IT"
BILL GRIFFITH
TIP O' TH' PIN TO: MIKE ZEIS
WELL, IT HAPPENED.
I FINALLY CAME TO A FORK IN TH' ROAD.
©2005 Bill Griffith. World rights reserved. Distributed by King Features Syndicate
Zippythepinhead.com
MAYBE NOW I'LL BE ABLE TO UNDERSTAND YOGI BERRA.
GRIFFY 9·12

211

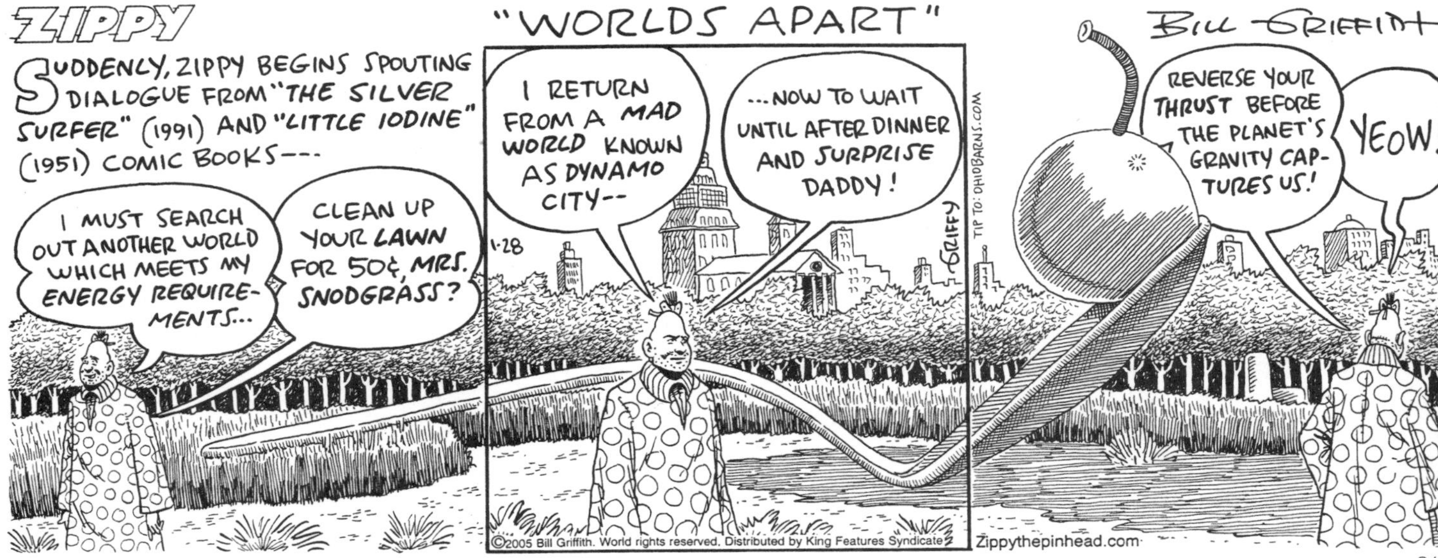
ZIPPY
"WORLDS APART"
BILL GRIFFITH
SUDDENLY, ZIPPY BEGINS SPOUTING DIALOGUE FROM "THE SILVER SURFER" (1991) AND "LITTLE IODINE" (1951) COMIC BOOKS---
I MUST SEARCH OUT ANOTHER WORLD WHICH MEETS MY ENERGY REQUIREMENTS...
CLEAN UP YOUR LAWN FOR 50¢, MRS. SNODGRASS?
I RETURN FROM A MAD WORLD KNOWN AS DYNAMO CITY--
...NOW TO WAIT UNTIL AFTER DINNER AND SURPRISE DADDY!
1·28 GRIFFY
REVERSE YOUR THRUST BEFORE THE PLANET'S GRAVITY CAPTURES US!
YEOW!
©2005 Bill Griffith. World rights reserved. Distributed by King Features Syndicate
Zippythepinhead.com

212

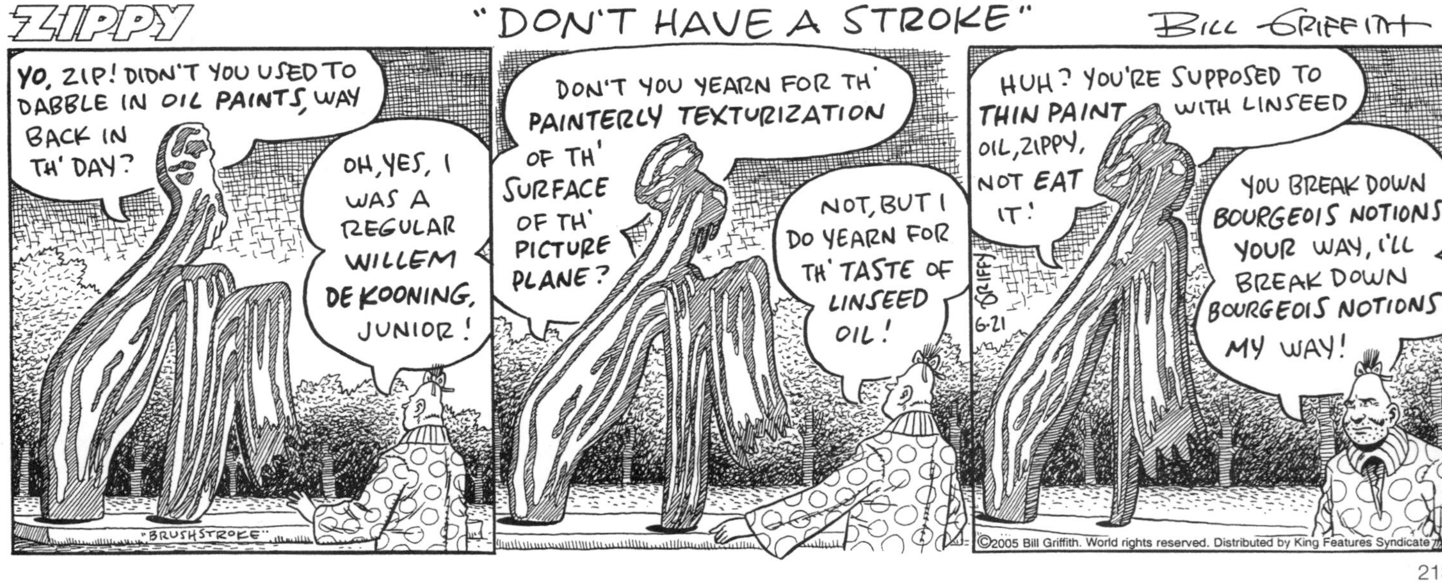
ZIPPY
"DON'T HAVE A STROKE"
BILL GRIFFITH
YO, ZIP! DIDN'T YOU USED TO DABBLE IN OIL PAINTS, WAY BACK IN TH' DAY?
OH, YES, I WAS A REGULAR WILLEM DE KOONING, JUNIOR!
"BRUSHSTROKE"
DON'T YOU YEARN FOR TH' PAINTERLY TEXTURIZATION OF TH' SURFACE OF TH' PICTURE PLANE?
NOT, BUT I DO YEARN FOR TH' TASTE OF LINSEED OIL!
GRIFFY 6·21
HUH? YOU'RE SUPPOSED TO THIN PAINT WITH LINSEED OIL, ZIPPY, NOT EAT IT!
YOU BREAK DOWN BOURGEOIS NOTIONS YOUR WAY, I'LL BREAK DOWN BOURGEOIS NOTIONS MY WAY!
©2005 Bill Griffith. World rights reserved. Distributed by King Features Syndicate

213

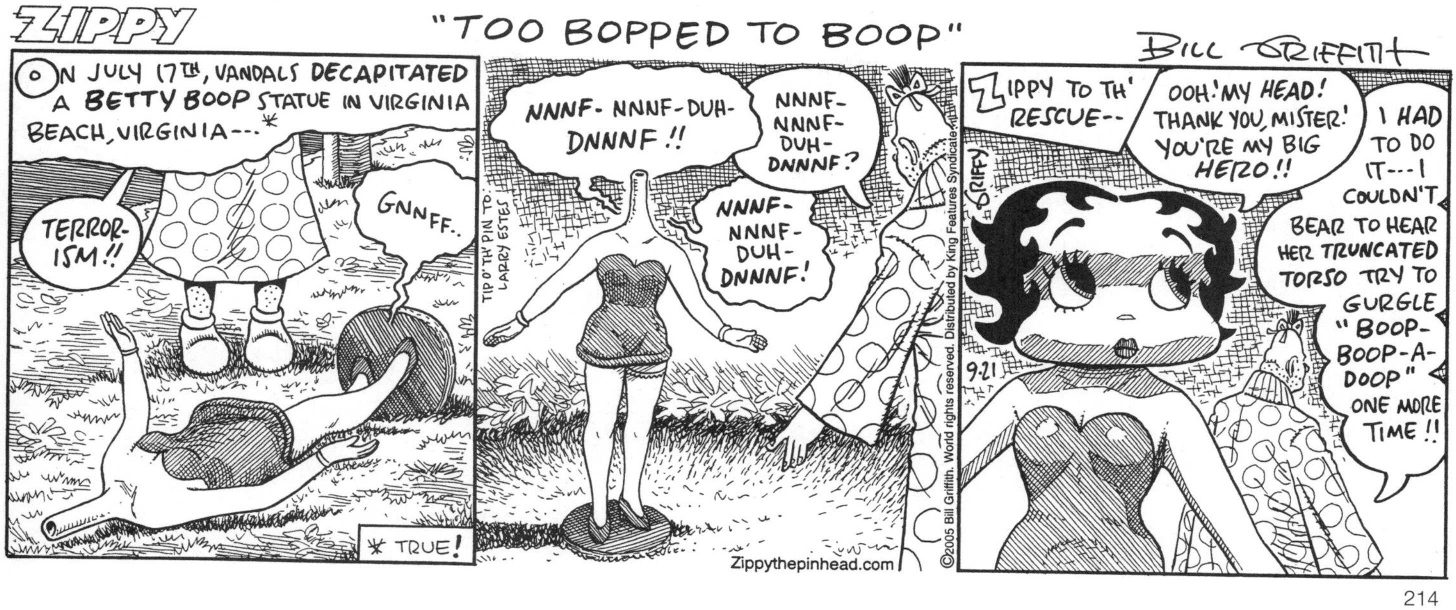
ZIPPY
"TOO BOPPED TO BOOP"
BILL GRIFFITH
ON JULY 17TH, VANDALS DECAPITATED A BETTY BOOP STATUE IN VIRGINIA BEACH, VIRGINIA--.*
TERRORISM!!
GNNFF..
* TRUE!
NNNF- NNNF-DUH-DNNNF!!
NNNF-NNNF-DUH-DNNNF?
NNNF-NNNF-DUH-DNNNF!
TIP O' TH' PIN TO: LARRY ESTES
Zippythepinhead.com
©2005 Bill Griffith. World rights reserved. Distributed by King Features Syndicate
ZIPPY TO TH' RESCUE--
OOH! MY HEAD! THANK YOU, MISTER! YOU'RE MY BIG HERO!!
I HAD TO DO IT---I COULDN'T BEAR TO HEAR HER TRUNCATED TORSO TRY TO GURGLE "BOOP-BOOP-A-DOOP" ONE MORE TIME!!
GRIFFY
9-21

214

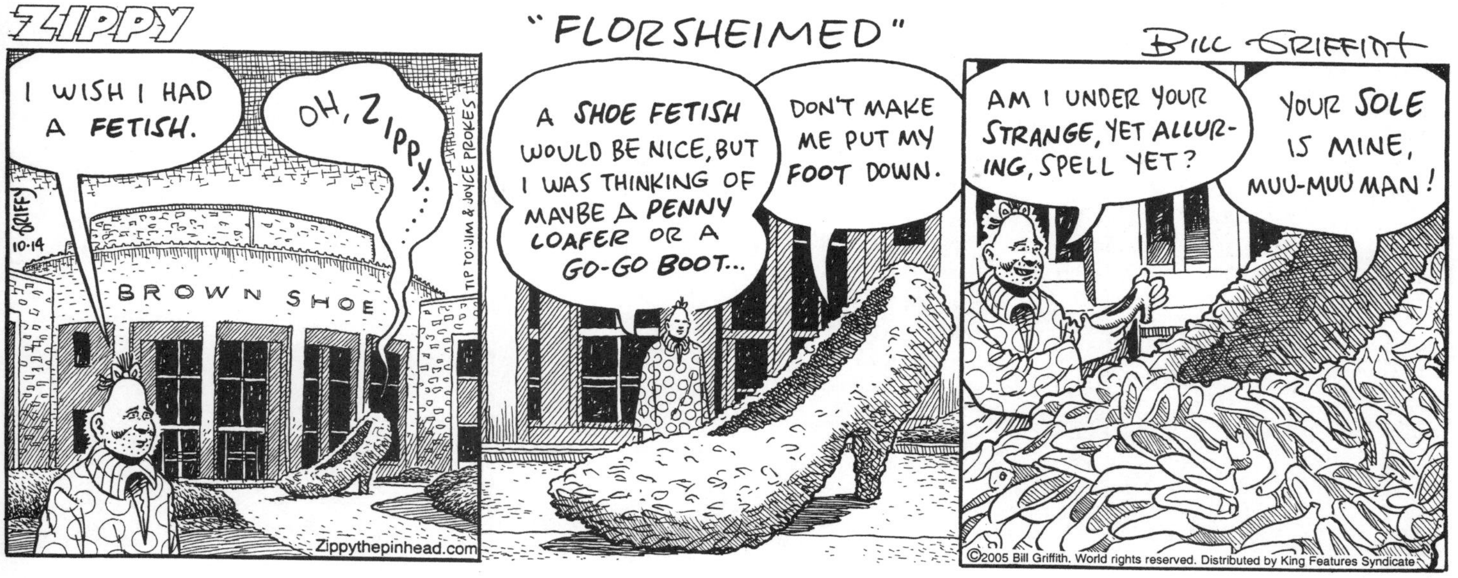
ZIPPY
"FLORSHEIMED"
BILL GRIFFITH
I WISH I HAD A FETISH.
OH, ZIPPY....
BROWN SHOE
GRIFFY
10-14
TIP TO: JIM & JOYCE PROKES
Zippythepinhead.com
A SHOE FETISH WOULD BE NICE, BUT I WAS THINKING OF MAYBE A PENNY LOAFER OR A GO-GO BOOT...
DON'T MAKE ME PUT MY FOOT DOWN.
AM I UNDER YOUR STRANGE, YET ALLURING, SPELL YET?
YOUR SOLE IS MINE, MUU-MUU MAN!
©2005 Bill Griffith. World rights reserved. Distributed by King Features Syndicate

215

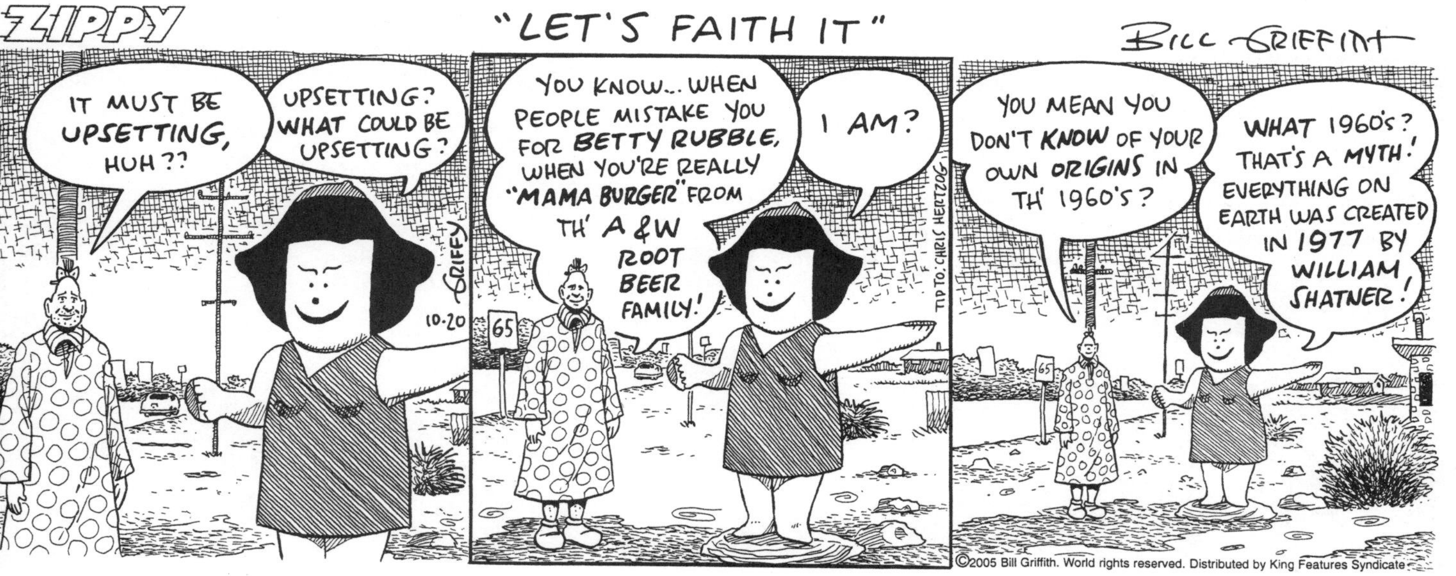
ZIPPY
"LET'S FAITH IT"
BILL GRIFFITH
IT MUST BE UPSETTING, HUH??
UPSETTING? WHAT COULD BE UPSETTING?
GRIFFY
10-20
YOU KNOW... WHEN PEOPLE MISTAKE YOU FOR BETTY RUBBLE, WHEN YOU'RE REALLY "MAMA BURGER" FROM TH' A&W ROOT BEER FAMILY!
I AM?
65
TIP TO: CHRIS HERTZOG
YOU MEAN YOU DON'T KNOW OF YOUR OWN ORIGINS IN TH' 1960'S?
WHAT 1960'S? THAT'S A MYTH! EVERYTHING ON EARTH WAS CREATED IN 1977 BY WILLIAM SHATNER!
©2005 Bill Griffith. World rights reserved. Distributed by King Features Syndicate

216

ZIPPY "MUDDYING THE WATERS" BILL GRIFFITH

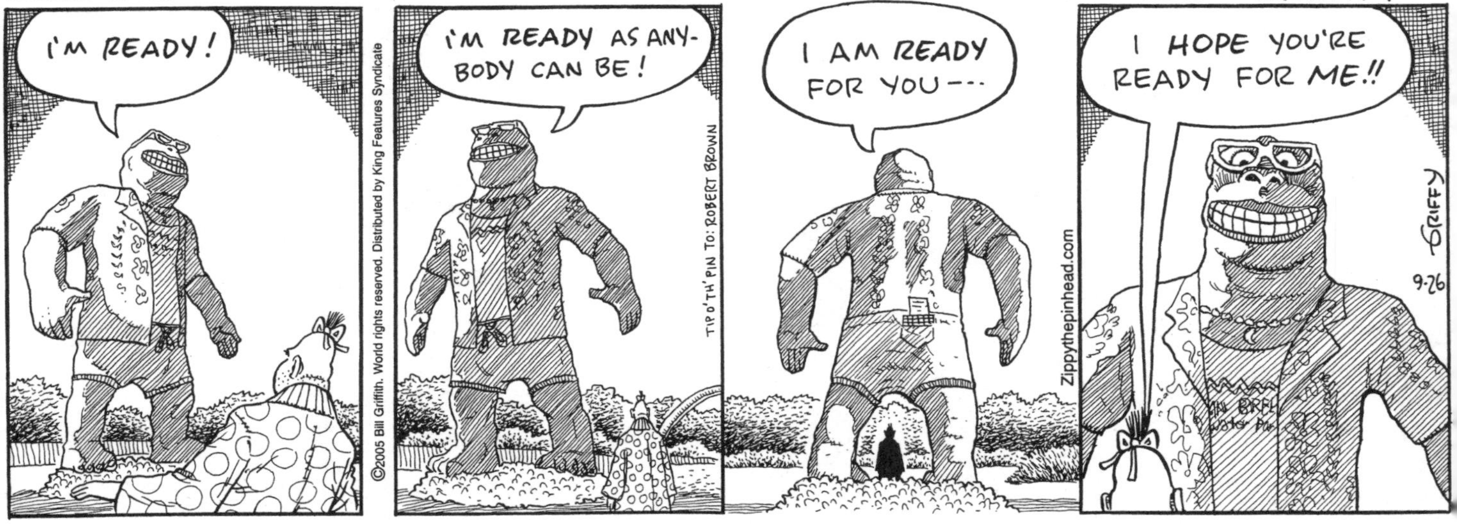
I'M READY!
I'M READY AS ANYBODY CAN BE!
I AM READY FOR YOU---
I HOPE YOU'RE READY FOR ME!!
©2005 Bill Griffith. World rights reserved. Distributed by King Features Syndicate
TIP O'TH' PIN TO: ROBERT BROWN
Zippythepinhead.com
GRIFFY 9-26

217

ZIPPY "SCYTHES MATTER" BILL GRIFFITH

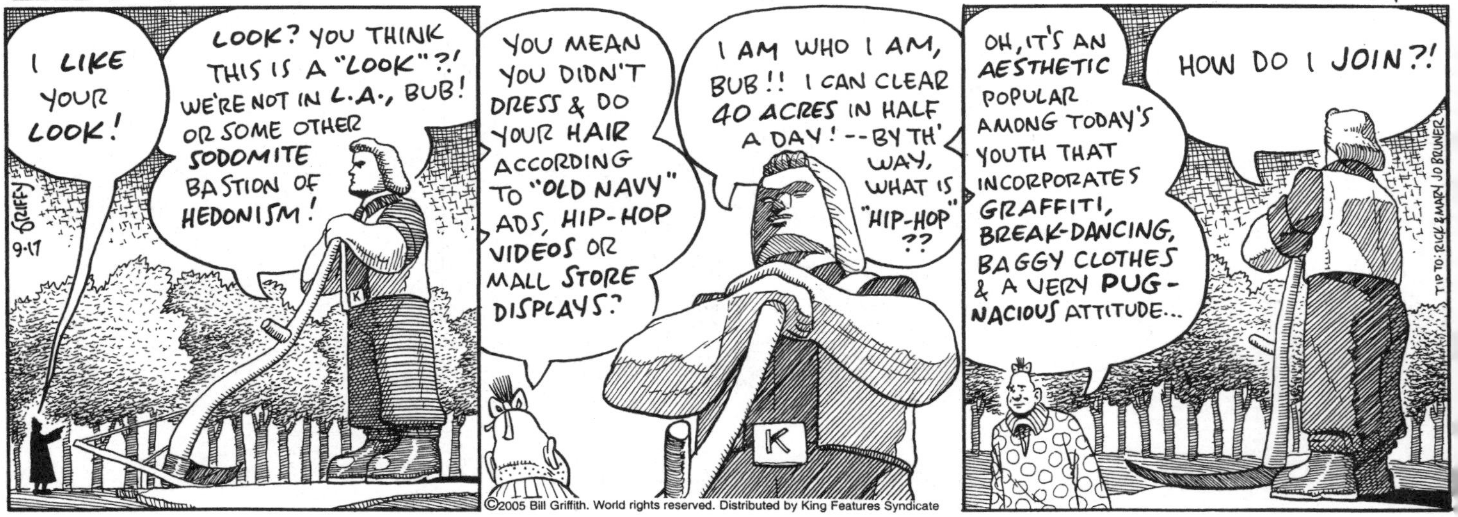
I LIKE YOUR LOOK!
LOOK? YOU THINK THIS IS A "LOOK"?! WE'RE NOT IN L.A., BUB! OR SOME OTHER SODOMITE BASTION OF HEDONISM!
GRIFFY 9-17
YOU MEAN YOU DIDN'T DRESS & DO YOUR HAIR ACCORDING TO "OLD NAVY" ADS, HIP-HOP VIDEOS OR MALL STORE DISPLAYS?
I AM WHO I AM, BUB!! I CAN CLEAR 40 ACRES IN HALF A DAY! --BY TH' WAY, WHAT IS "HIP-HOP"??
OH, IT'S AN AESTHETIC POPULAR AMONG TODAY'S YOUTH THAT INCORPORATES GRAFFITI, BREAK-DANCING, BAGGY CLOTHES & A VERY PUGNACIOUS ATTITUDE...
HOW DO I JOIN?!
TIP TO: RICK & MARY JO BRUNER
©2005 Bill Griffith. World rights reserved. Distributed by King Features Syndicate

218

ZIPPY "QUANTUM SKEEZIX" BILL GRIFFITH

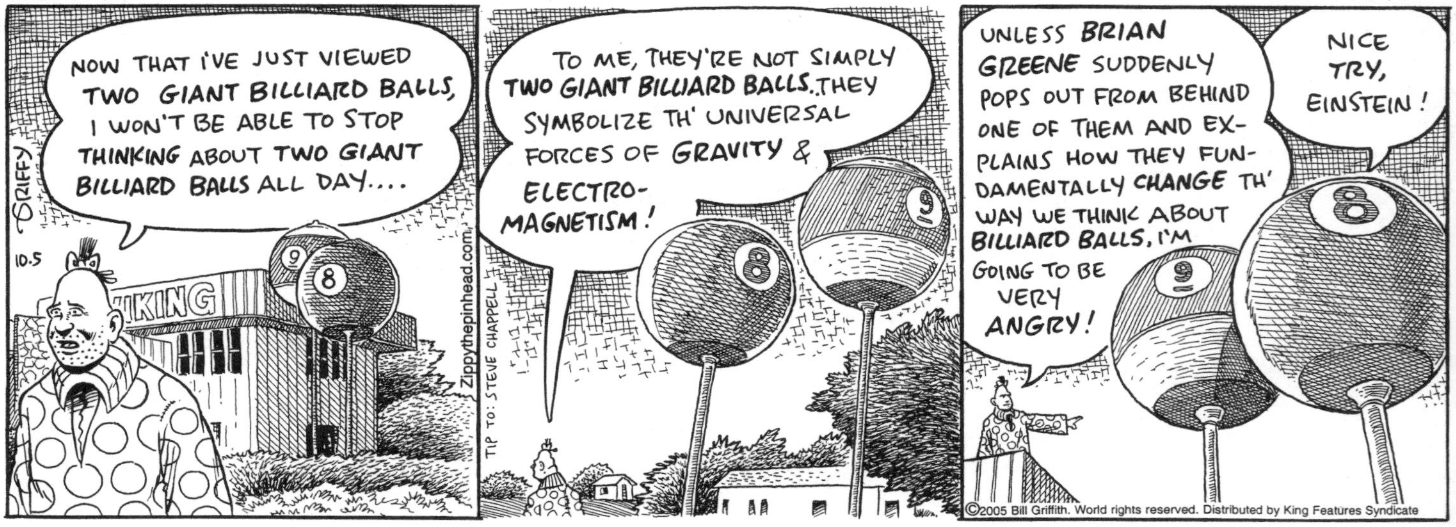
NOW THAT I'VE JUST VIEWED TWO GIANT BILLIARD BALLS, I WON'T BE ABLE TO STOP THINKING ABOUT TWO GIANT BILLIARD BALLS ALL DAY....
GRIFFY 10.5
KING
Zippythepinhead.com
TIP TO: STEVE CHAPPELL
TO ME, THEY'RE NOT SIMPLY TWO GIANT BILLIARD BALLS.. THEY SYMBOLIZE TH' UNIVERSAL FORCES OF GRAVITY & ELECTRO-MAGNETISM!
UNLESS BRIAN GREENE SUDDENLY POPS OUT FROM BEHIND ONE OF THEM AND EXPLAINS HOW THEY FUNDAMENTALLY CHANGE TH' WAY WE THINK ABOUT BILLIARD BALLS, I'M GOING TO BE VERY ANGRY!
NICE TRY, EINSTEIN!
©2005 Bill Griffith. World rights reserved. Distributed by King Features Syndicate

219

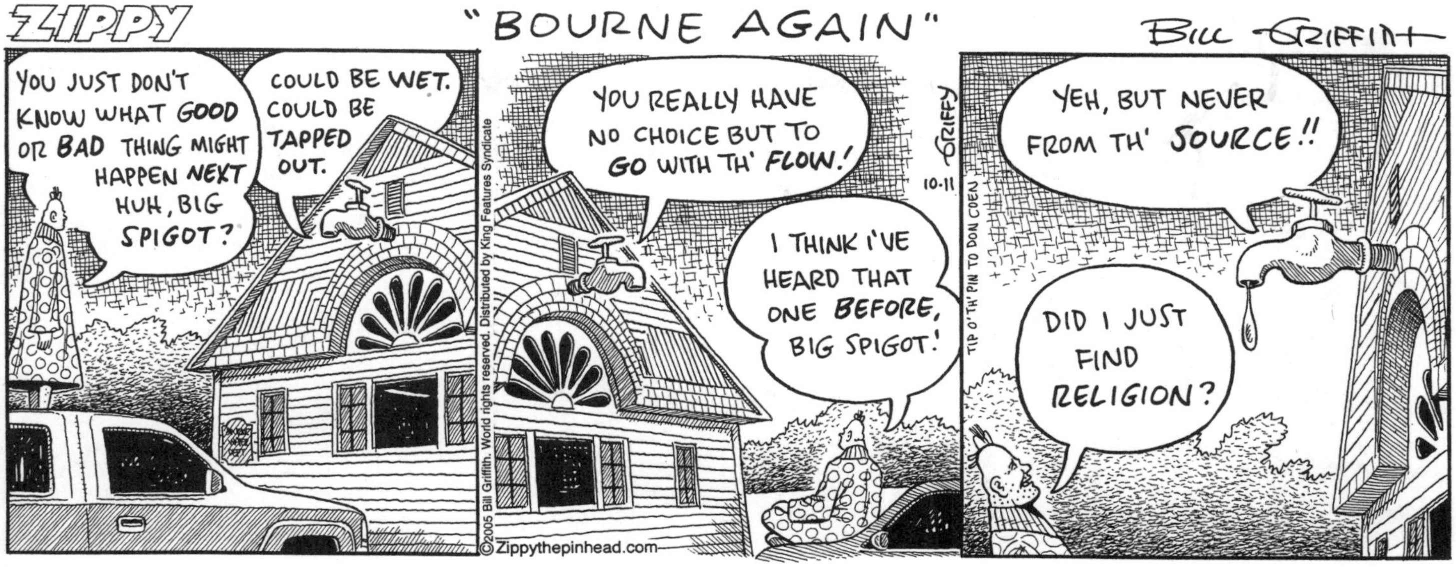
ZIPPY
"BOURNE AGAIN"
BILL GRIFFITH
YOU JUST DON'T KNOW WHAT GOOD OR BAD THING MIGHT HAPPEN NEXT HUH, BIG SPIGOT?
COULD BE WET. COULD BE TAPPED OUT.
©2005 Bill Griffith. World rights reserved. Distributed by King Features Syndicate
Zippythepinhead.com
YOU REALLY HAVE NO CHOICE BUT TO GO WITH TH' FLOW!
GRIFFY 10-11
I THINK I'VE HEARD THAT ONE BEFORE, BIG SPIGOT!
TIP O' TH' PIN TO DON COEN
YEH, BUT NEVER FROM TH' SOURCE!!
DID I JUST FIND RELIGION?

220

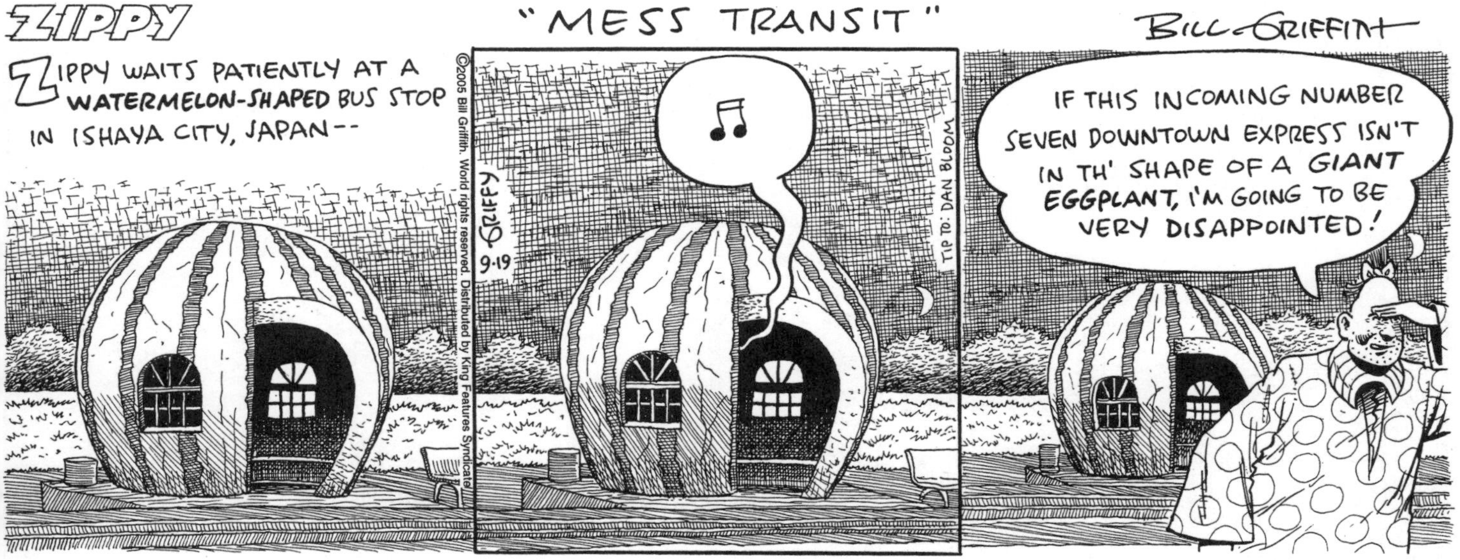
ZIPPY
"MESS TRANSIT"
BILL GRIFFITH
ZIPPY WAITS PATIENTLY AT A WATERMELON-SHAPED BUS STOP IN ISHAYA CITY, JAPAN--
©2005 Bill Griffith. World rights reserved. Distributed by King Features Syndicate
GRIFFY 9-19
TIP TO: DAN BLOOM
IF THIS INCOMING NUMBER SEVEN DOWNTOWN EXPRESS ISN'T IN TH' SHAPE OF A GIANT EGGPLANT, I'M GOING TO BE VERY DISAPPOINTED!

221

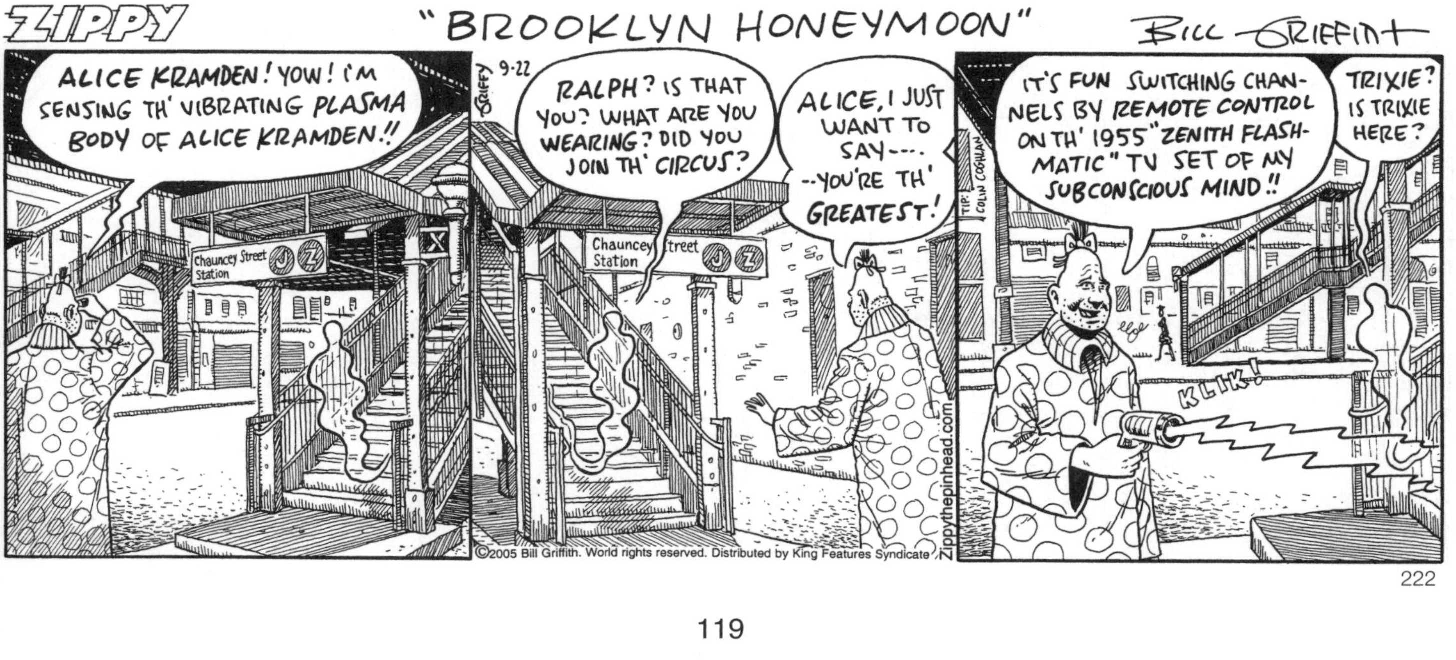
ZIPPY
"BROOKLYN HONEYMOON"
BILL GRIFFITH
ALICE KRAMDEN! YOW! I'M SENSING TH' VIBRATING PLASMA BODY OF ALICE KRAMDEN!!
Chauncey Street Station
GRIFFY 9-22
RALPH? IS THAT YOU? WHAT ARE YOU WEARING? DID YOU JOIN TH' CIRCUS?
ALICE, I JUST WANT TO SAY---. --YOU'RE TH' GREATEST!
©2005 Bill Griffith. World rights reserved. Distributed by King Features Syndicate
Zippythepinhead.com
TIP: COLIN COGHLAN
IT'S FUN SWITCHING CHANNELS BY REMOTE CONTROL ON TH' 1955 "ZENITH FLASH-MATIC" TV SET OF MY SUBCONSCIOUS MIND!!
TRIXIE? IS TRIXIE HERE?
KLIK!

222

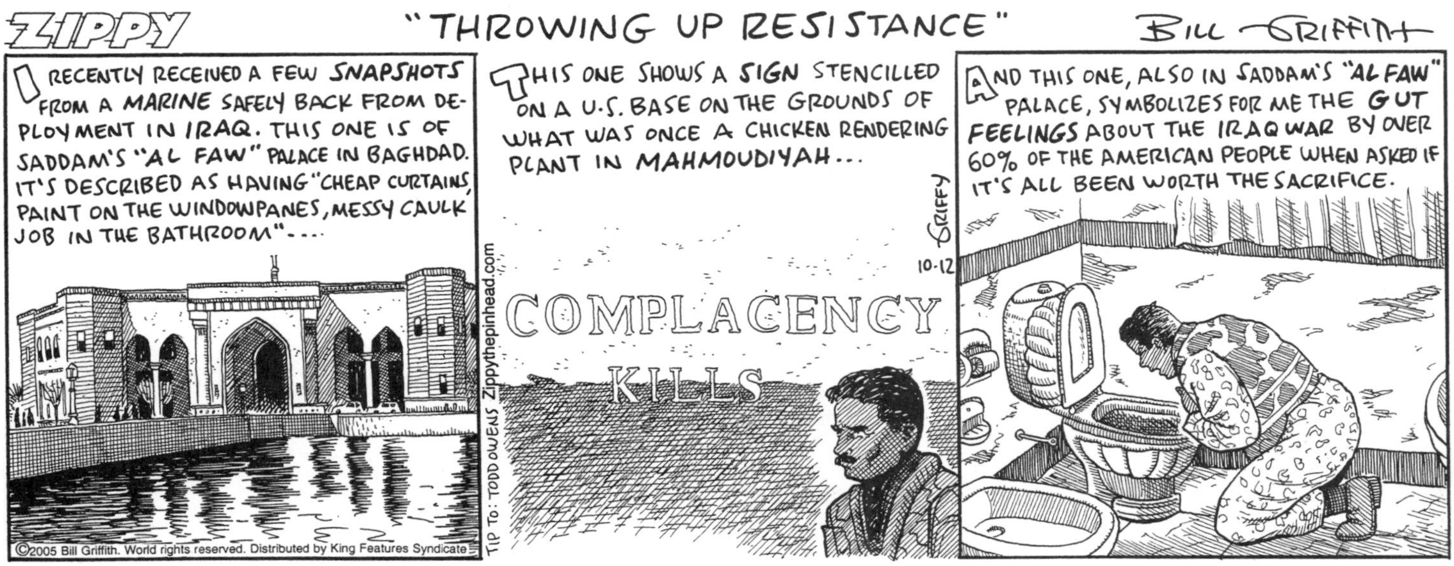
ZIPPY
"THROWING UP RESISTANCE"
BILL GRIFFITH
I RECENTLY RECEIVED A FEW SNAPSHOTS FROM A MARINE SAFELY BACK FROM DEPLOYMENT IN IRAQ. THIS ONE IS OF SADDAM'S "AL FAW" PALACE IN BAGHDAD. IT'S DESCRIBED AS HAVING "CHEAP CURTAINS, PAINT ON THE WINDOWPANES, MESSY CAULK JOB IN THE BATHROOM"---
©2005 Bill Griffith. World rights reserved. Distributed by King Features Syndicate
TIP TO: TODD OWENS Zippythepinhead.com
THIS ONE SHOWS A SIGN STENCILLED ON A U.S. BASE ON THE GROUNDS OF WHAT WAS ONCE A CHICKEN RENDERING PLANT IN MAHMOUDIYAH...
GRIFFY 10-12
COMPLACENCY
KILLS
AND THIS ONE, ALSO IN SADDAM'S "AL FAW" PALACE, SYMBOLIZES FOR ME THE GUT FEELINGS ABOUT THE IRAQ WAR BY OVER 60% OF THE AMERICAN PEOPLE WHEN ASKED IF IT'S ALL BEEN WORTH THE SACRIFICE.

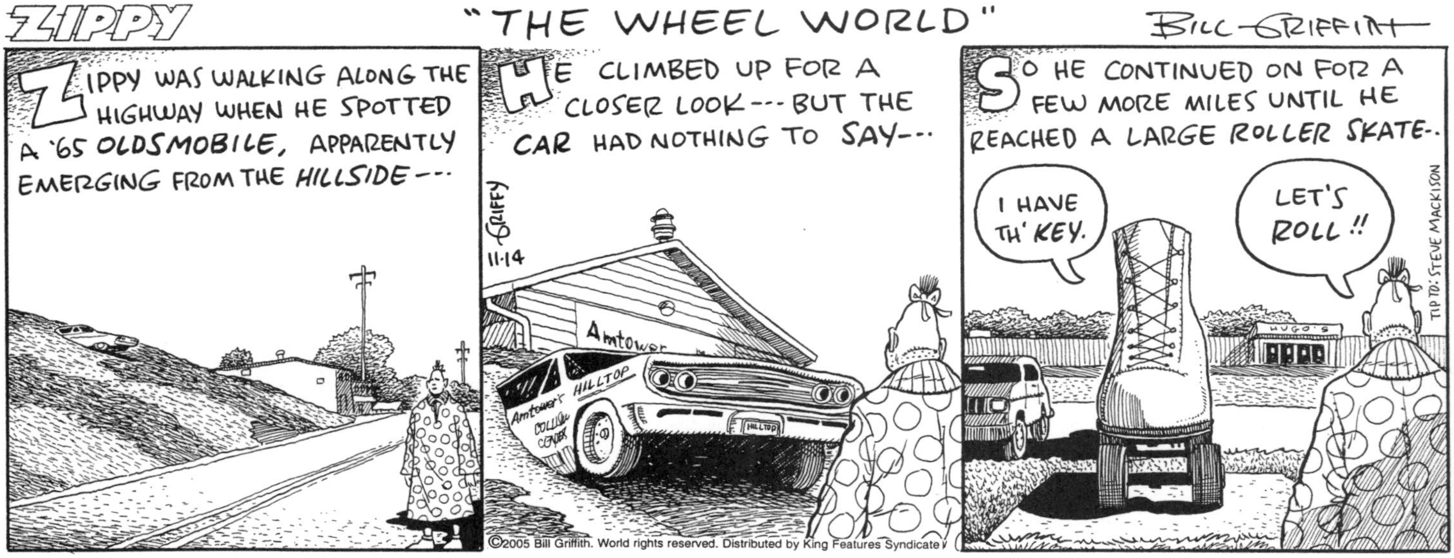
ZIPPY
"THE WHEEL WORLD"
BILL GRIFFITH
ZIPPY WAS WALKING ALONG THE HIGHWAY WHEN HE SPOTTED A '65 OLDSMOBILE, APPARENTLY EMERGING FROM THE HILLSIDE---
HE CLIMBED UP FOR A CLOSER LOOK--- BUT THE CAR HAD NOTHING TO SAY---
GRIFFY 11-14
Amtower
Amtower's HILLTOP
HILLTOP
©2005 Bill Griffith. World rights reserved. Distributed by King Features Syndicate
SO HE CONTINUED ON FOR A FEW MORE MILES UNTIL HE REACHED A LARGE ROLLER SKATE..
I HAVE TH' KEY.
LET'S ROLL!!
TIP TO: STEVE MACKISON
HUGO'S

223

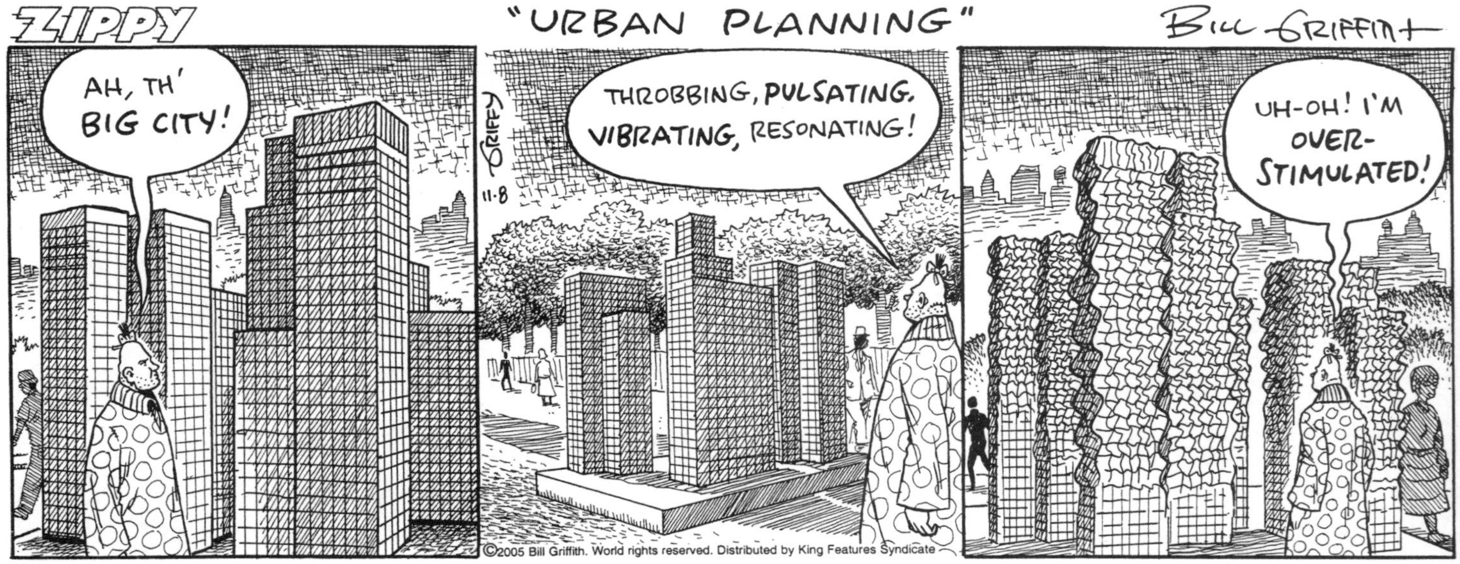
ZIPPY
"URBAN PLANNING"
BILL GRIFFITH
AH, TH' BIG CITY!
GRIFFY 11-8
THROBBING, PULSATING, VIBRATING, RESONATING!
©2005 Bill Griffith. World rights reserved. Distributed by King Features Syndicate
UH-OH! I'M OVER-STIMULATED!

224

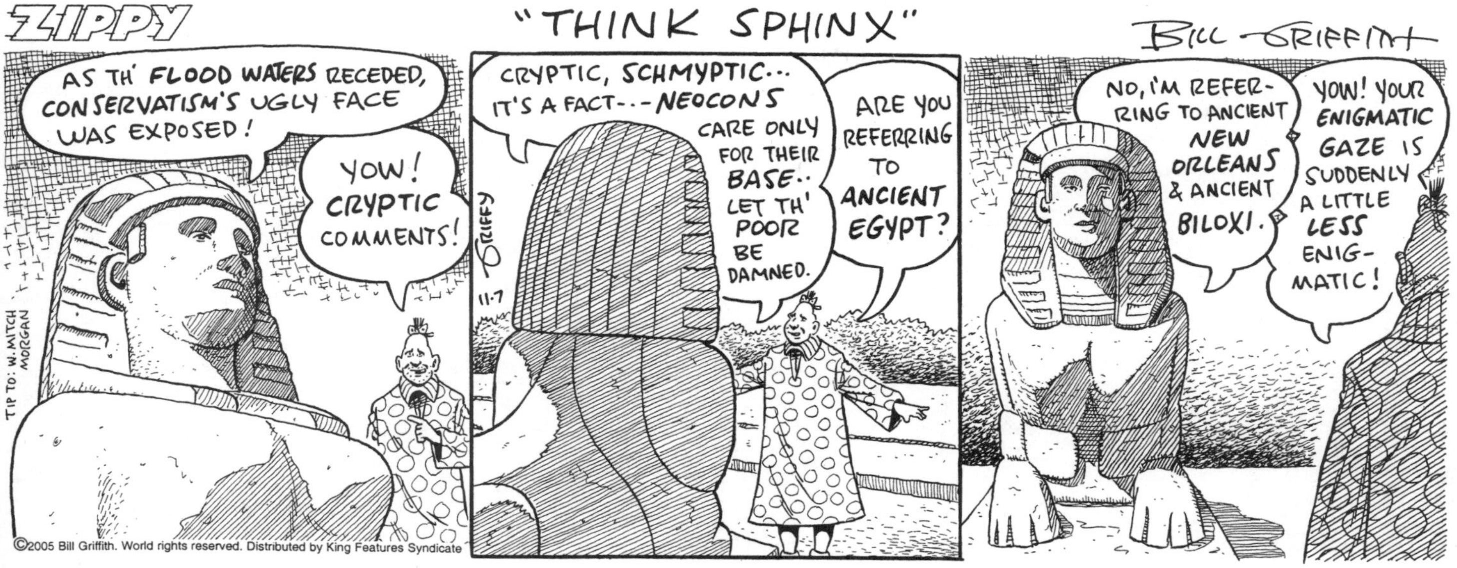
ZIPPY
"THINK SPHINX"
BILL GRIFFITH
AS TH' FLOOD WATERS RECEDED, CONSERVATISM'S UGLY FACE WAS EXPOSED!
YOW! CRYPTIC COMMENTS!
TIP TO: W. MITCH MORGAN
CRYPTIC, SCHMYPTIC... IT'S A FACT--NEOCONS CARE ONLY FOR THEIR BASE.. LET TH' POOR BE DAMNED.
ARE YOU REFERRING TO ANCIENT EGYPT?
GRIFFY 11-7
NO, I'M REFERRING TO ANCIENT NEW ORLEANS & ANCIENT BILOXI.
YOW! YOUR ENIGMATIC GAZE IS SUDDENLY A LITTLE LESS ENIGMATIC!
©2005 Bill Griffith. World rights reserved. Distributed by King Features Syndicate

225

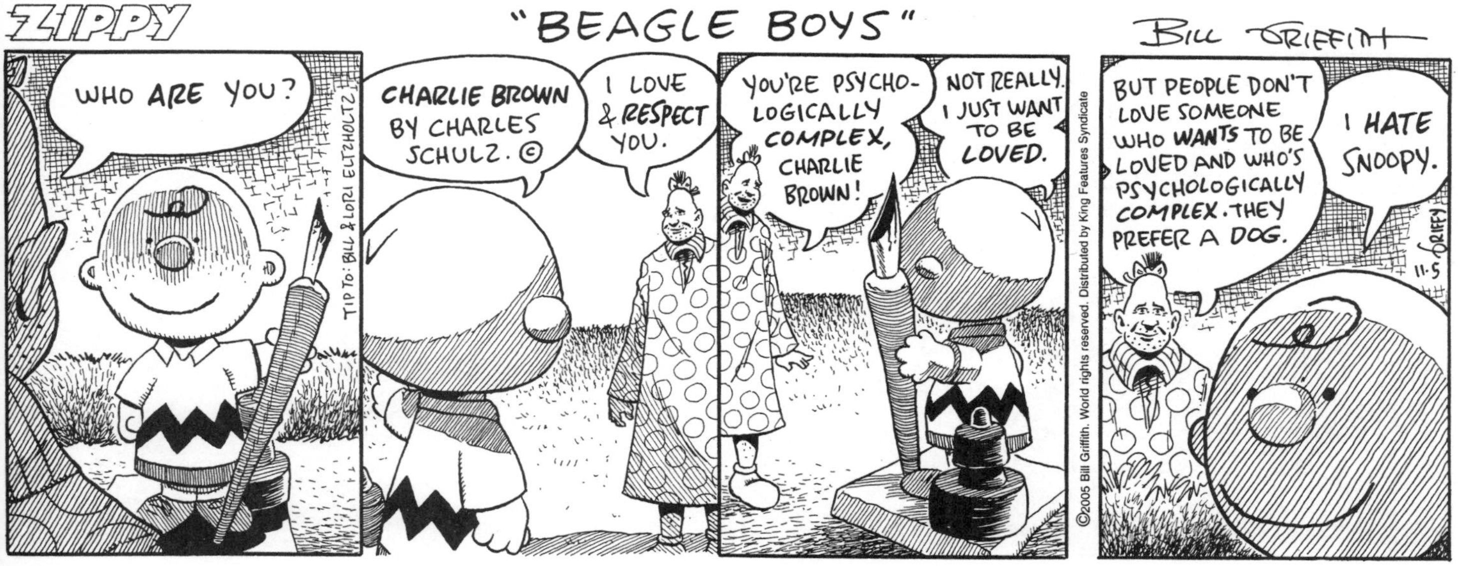
ZIPPY
"BEAGLE BOYS"
BILL GRIFFITH
WHO ARE YOU?
TIP TO: BILL & LORI ELTZHOLTZ
CHARLIE BROWN BY CHARLES SCHULZ. ©
I LOVE & RESPECT YOU.
YOU'RE PSYCHOLOGICALLY COMPLEX, CHARLIE BROWN!
NOT REALLY. I JUST WANT TO BE LOVED.
©2005 Bill Griffith. World rights reserved. Distributed by King Features Syndicate
BUT PEOPLE DON'T LOVE SOMEONE WHO WANTS TO BE LOVED AND WHO'S PSYCHOLOGICALLY COMPLEX. THEY PREFER A DOG.
I HATE SNOOPY.
GRIFFY 11-5

226

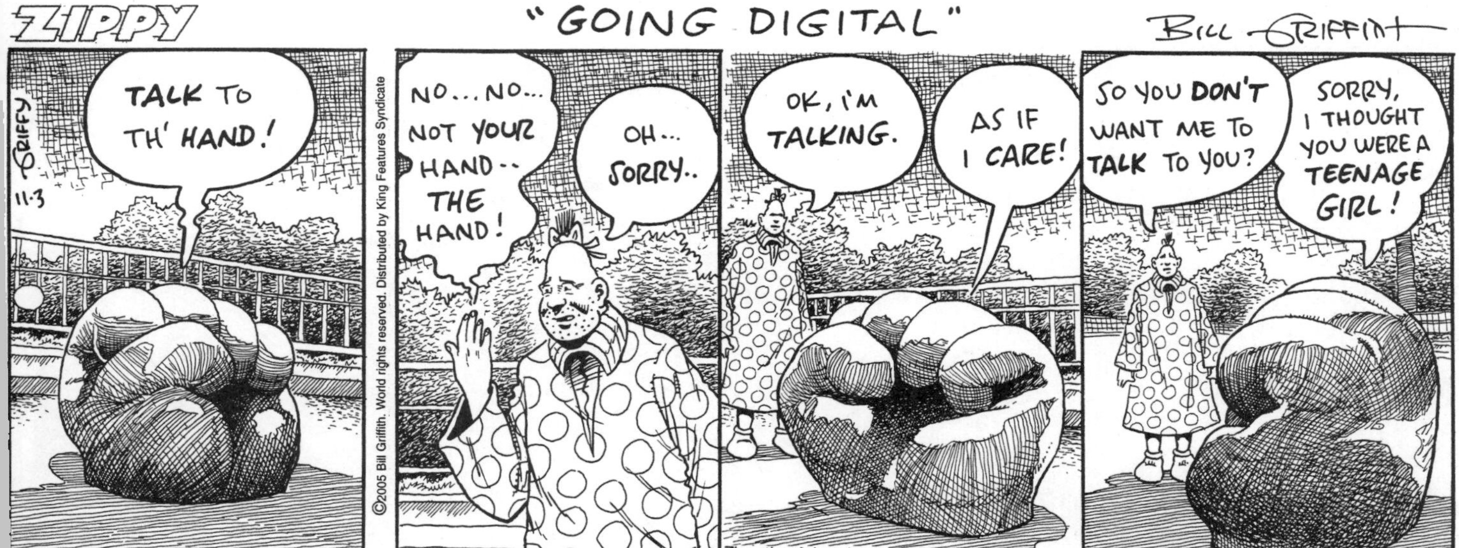
ZIPPY
"GOING DIGITAL"
BILL GRIFFITH
GRIFFY 11-3
TALK TO TH' HAND!
©2005 Bill Griffith. World rights reserved. Distributed by King Features Syndicate
NO... NO... NOT YOUR HAND-- THE HAND!
OH... SORRY..
OK, I'M TALKING.
AS IF I CARE!
SO YOU DON'T WANT ME TO TALK TO YOU?
SORRY, I THOUGHT YOU WERE A TEENAGE GIRL!
Zippythepinhead.com

227

ZIPPY "BIGGER MISTAKE" BILL GRIFFITH

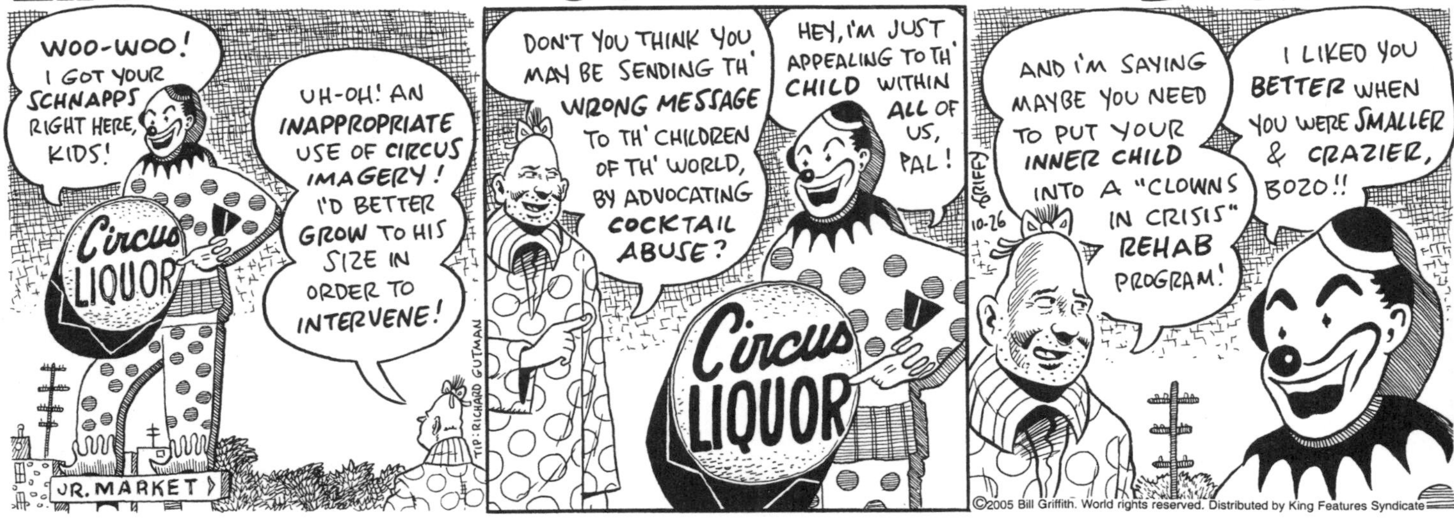
WOO-WOO! I GOT YOUR SCHNAPPS RIGHT HERE, KIDS!
Circus LIQUOR
UH-OH! AN INAPPROPRIATE USE OF CIRCUS IMAGERY! I'D BETTER GROW TO HIS SIZE IN ORDER TO INTERVENE!
JR. MARKET
TIP: RICHARD GUTMAN
DON'T YOU THINK YOU MAY BE SENDING TH' WRONG MESSAGE TO TH' CHILDREN OF TH' WORLD, BY ADVOCATING COCKTAIL ABUSE?
HEY, I'M JUST APPEALING TO TH' CHILD WITHIN ALL OF US, PAL!
Circus LIQUOR
GRIFFY 10-26
AND I'M SAYING MAYBE YOU NEED TO PUT YOUR INNER CHILD INTO A "CLOWNS IN CRISIS" REHAB PROGRAM!
I LIKED YOU BETTER WHEN YOU WERE SMALLER & CRAZIER, BOZO!!
©2005 Bill Griffith. World rights reserved. Distributed by King Features Syndicate

228

ZIPPY "TWIST PARTY" BILL GRIFFITH

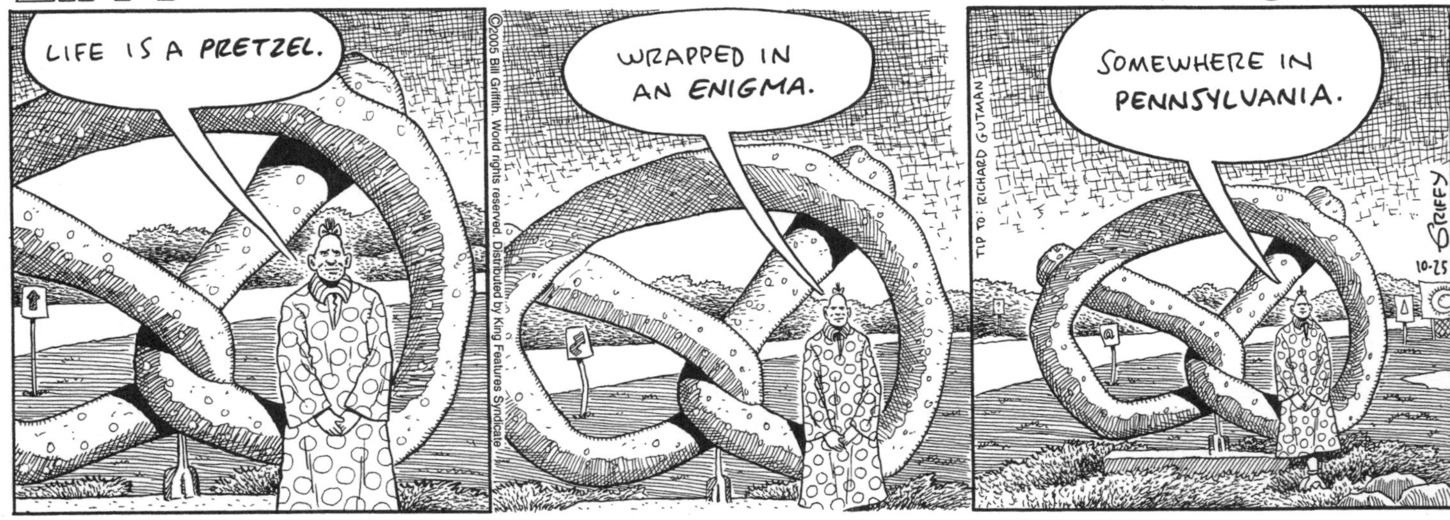
LIFE IS A PRETZEL.
©2005 Bill Griffith. World rights reserved. Distributed by King Features Syndicate
WRAPPED IN AN ENIGMA.
TIP TO: RICHARD GUTMAN
SOMEWHERE IN PENNSYLVANIA.
GRIFFY 10-25

229

ZIPPY "PARADE REST" BILL GRIFFITH

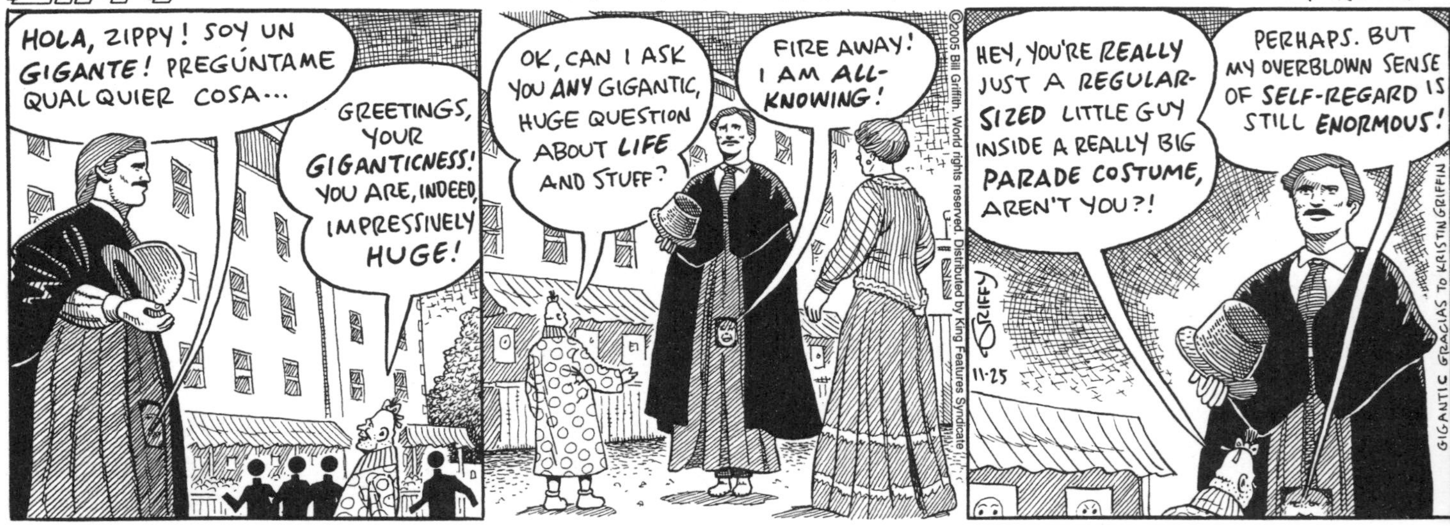
HOLA, ZIPPY! SOY UN GIGANTE! PREGÚNTAME QUALQUIER COSA...
GREETINGS, YOUR GIGANTICNESS! YOU ARE, INDEED, IMPRESSIVELY HUGE!
OK, CAN I ASK YOU ANY GIGANTIC, HUGE QUESTION ABOUT LIFE AND STUFF?
FIRE AWAY! I AM ALL-KNOWING!
©2005 Bill Griffith. World rights reserved. Distributed by King Features Syndicate
GRIFFY 11-25
HEY, YOU'RE REALLY JUST A REGULAR-SIZED LITTLE GUY INSIDE A REALLY BIG PARADE COSTUME, AREN'T YOU?!
PERHAPS. BUT MY OVERBLOWN SENSE OF SELF-REGARD IS STILL ENORMOUS!
GIGANTIC GRACIAS TO KRISTIN GRIFFIN

230

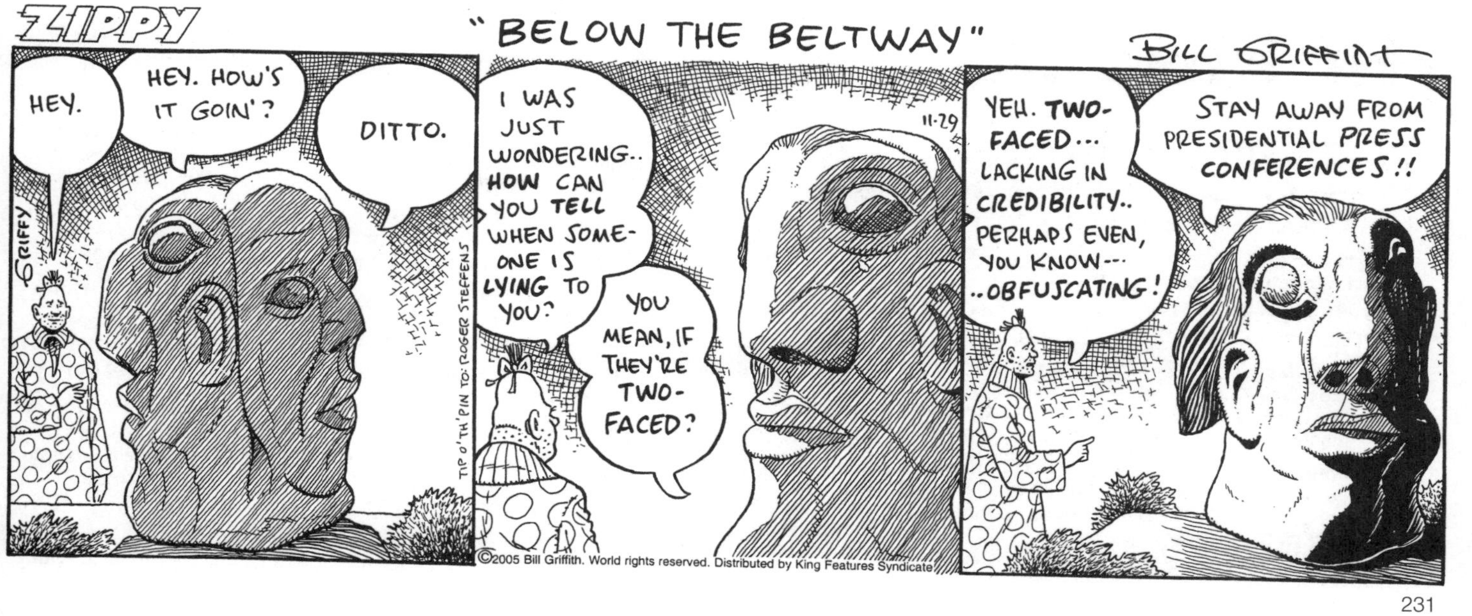
ZIPPY
"BELOW THE BELTWAY"
BILL GRIFFITH
HEY.
HEY. HOW'S IT GOIN'?
DITTO.
GRIFFY
TIP O' TH' PIN TO: ROGER STEFFENS
I WAS JUST WONDERING.. HOW CAN YOU TELL WHEN SOMEONE IS LYING TO YOU?
YOU MEAN, IF THEY'RE TWO-FACED?
11-29
YEH. TWO-FACED... LACKING IN CREDIBILITY.. PERHAPS EVEN, YOU KNOW--- ..OBFUSCATING!
STAY AWAY FROM PRESIDENTIAL PRESS CONFERENCES!!
©2005 Bill Griffith. World rights reserved. Distributed by King Features Syndicate

231

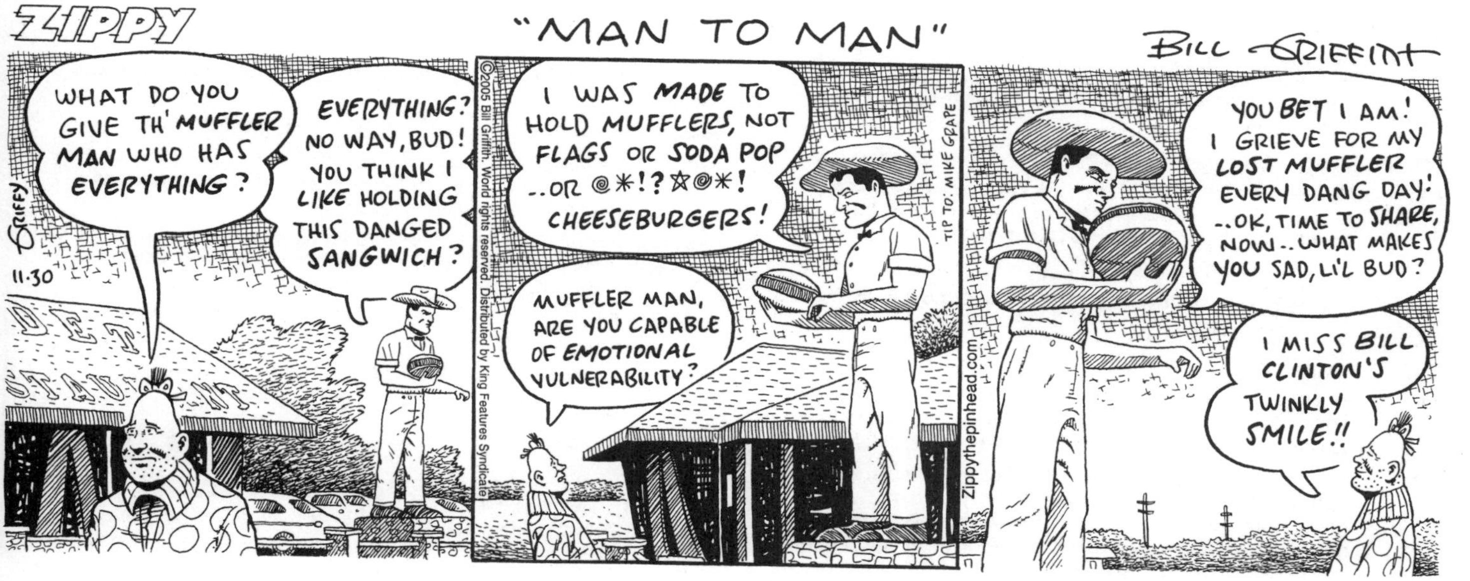
ZIPPY
"MAN TO MAN"
BILL GRIFFITH
WHAT DO YOU GIVE TH' MUFFLER MAN WHO HAS EVERYTHING?
EVERYTHING? NO WAY, BUD! YOU THINK I LIKE HOLDING THIS DANGED SANGWICH?
GRIFFY
11-30
©2005 Bill Griffith. World rights reserved. Distributed by King Features Syndicate
I WAS MADE TO HOLD MUFFLERS, NOT FLAGS OR SODA POP ..OR @*!?☆@*! CHEESEBURGERS!
MUFFLER MAN, ARE YOU CAPABLE OF EMOTIONAL VULNERABILITY?
TIP TO: MIKE GRAPE
Zippythepinhead.com
YOU BET I AM! I GRIEVE FOR MY LOST MUFFLER EVERY DANG DAY! ..OK, TIME TO SHARE, NOW..WHAT MAKES YOU SAD, LI'L BUD?
I MISS BILL CLINTON'S TWINKLY SMILE!!

232

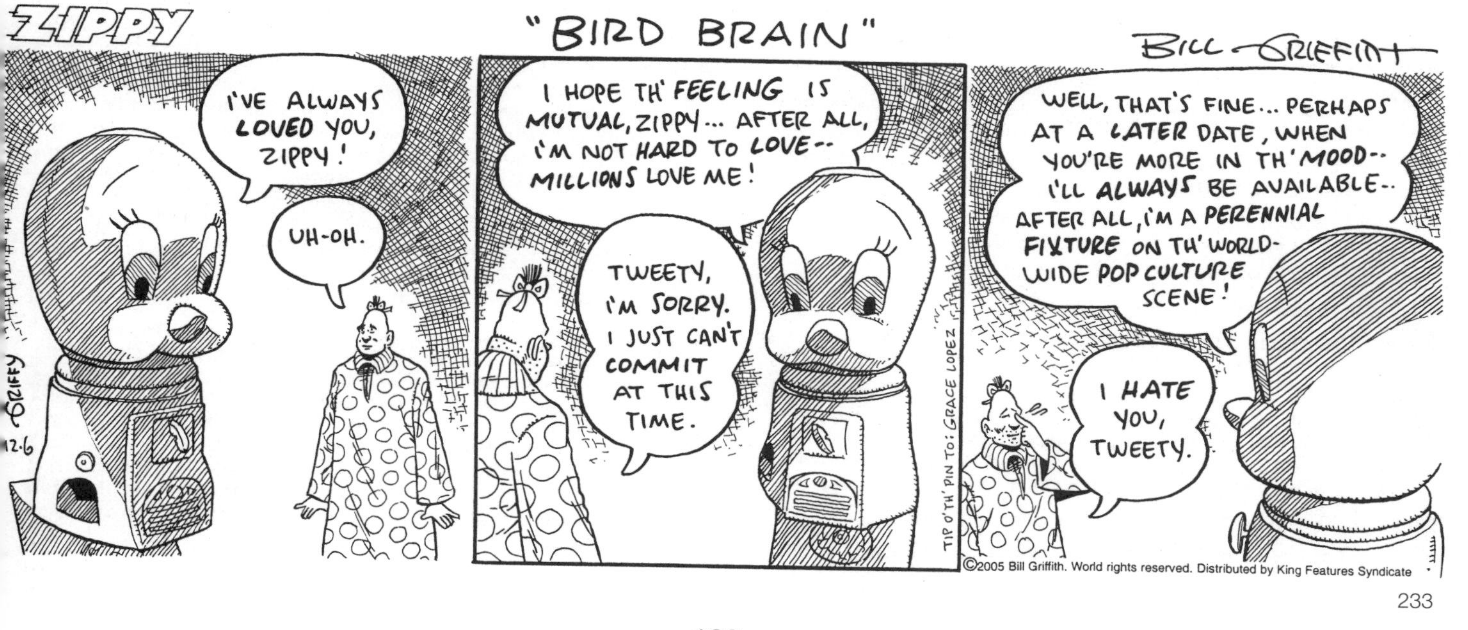
ZIPPY
"BIRD BRAIN"
BILL GRIFFITH
I'VE ALWAYS LOVED YOU, ZIPPY!
UH-OH.
GRIFFY
12-6
I HOPE TH' FEELING IS MUTUAL, ZIPPY... AFTER ALL, I'M NOT HARD TO LOVE-- MILLIONS LOVE ME!
TWEETY, I'M SORRY. I JUST CAN'T COMMIT AT THIS TIME.
TIP O' TH' PIN TO: GRACE LOPEZ
WELL, THAT'S FINE... PERHAPS AT A LATER DATE, WHEN YOU'RE MORE IN TH' MOOD-- I'LL ALWAYS BE AVAILABLE.. AFTER ALL, I'M A PERENNIAL FIXTURE ON TH' WORLD-WIDE POP CULTURE SCENE!
I HATE YOU, TWEETY.
©2005 Bill Griffith. World rights reserved. Distributed by King Features Syndicate

233

THE PINDEX

ZIPPY & GRIFFY Chapter 1

1. Pizza Town, Elmwood Park, NJ. [pg. 10]

2. Smitty's, Warrensburg, MO. [pg. 10]

3. "Clothespin" by Claes Oldenburg and Coosje Van Bruggen, Philadelphia, PA. [pg. 11]

4. "Flying Pins" by Claes Oldenburg and Coosje Van Bruggen, Eindhoven, Netherlands. [pg. 11]

5. Dean Martin (1917-1995) had a short boxing career under the name Kid Crochet. At the peak of Beatlemania in 1964, he knocked the Fab Four off the charts with his number one hit, "Everybody Loves Somebody." [pg.12]

6. Panel 1) "Rawhide" (1959-1965) TV theme song. Panel 2) "Have Gun, Will Travel" (1957-1963) TV theme song. Panel 3) "The Many Loves of Dobie Gillis" (1959-1963) TV theme song. [pg. 12]

7. Woodcarvings, Lexington, NC. [pg. 12]

8. "Guernica" dress manufactured by the Torero Company, on sale in an Abu Dhabi department store. [pg. 13]

9. James Gillray (1756-1815), English satirist and proto-cartoonist, engraved over 1500 prints, virtually defining British political caricature. He was an acknowledged influence on *Mad* magazine's creator, Harvey Kurtzman (1924-1993). [pg. 13]

10. Coney Island boardwalk, Brooklyn, NY. [pg. 14]

11. Madison Ave. and 23rd St., New York, NY. Barbara M. Jackson (1919-1998) was the author's mother. James L. Griffith (1915-1972) was his father. [pg. 14]

12. United Rubber, 54 Warren St., New York, NY. [pg. 14]

13. Museo Textil y de Indumentaria, Barcelona, Spain. [pg. 15]

14. Oakland, CA. [pg. 15]

15. Vallejo, CA. [pg. 15]

16. The Ronco Veg-O-Matic was invented by Ron Popeil (b. 1935) in 1965. He also created the Popeil Pocket Fisherman, which Zippy likes to shout three times really fast. [pg. 16]

17. The "conoid of Sturm" is described as follows: An image that falls on the retina can be thought of as being made up of many dots, just like a photo in the newspaper. If an ametropic eye (needs glasses to see well) is not optically corrected, then the image will consist of many blurred circles instead of sharp dots. The more out of focus the image is, the larger the circles are. If an astigmatic eye is not optically corrected, the blurred circles will be distorted into ellipses. [pg. 16]

18. Tucson, AZ. [pg. 17]

19. Rural Hall, NC. Shown is the "Time to re-tire" mascot of the Fiske Tire Co., c. 1920s-1930s. [pg. 17]

20. Topiary, Tavern-on-the-Green restaurant, Central Park, New York, NY. [pg. 17]

21. Clarion Hotel, Toledo, OH. Zippy recites a real spam message. [pg. 18]

22. Tell City, IN. [pg. 18]

23. Spotted in Wilmington, DE. [pg.18]

24. The "Photon Grenade Launcher" is a fictional weapon used by the crew of the original *Star Trek* TV show (1966-1969). [pg.19]

25. Columbia Diner, Hudson, NY. Farley Granger (b. 1925) starred in Alfred Hitchcock's *Rope* (1948) and *Strangers On a Train* (1951). He later played a psychiatrist and head of a family on the TV soap opera *One Life to Live*. [pg. 19]

26. "The White Room" by Ivan Albreht. [pg. 19]

27. Las Vegas, NV. Larry King was born Leibel Harvey Zelger in Brooklyn, NY in 1933. He made his on-air debut in 1957, interviewing customers who walked in to Pumpernick's Restaurant in Miami, Florida. Judith Sheindlin (Judge Judy) was also born in Brooklyn, in 1942. She is the highest paid woman in television. Among her favorite catchphrases are "You're full of baloney!" and "I'm speaking!" [pg. 20]

28. Panels 1 and 4) Winsted Diner, Winsted, CT. Panels 2 and 3) The "Woofus" by Lawrence Tenney Stevens. Made for the 1936 Texas Centennial Exposition, Dallas, TX. [pg. 20]

29. New York, New York Casino, Las Vegas, NV. Donald Trump (b. 1946) once said to an interviewer, "Do you mind if I sit back a little? Because your breath is very bad." [pg. 21]

30. Norm's Restaurant, Downey, CA (formerly a Van De Kamps windmill restaurant). [pg. 21]

31. Kingston, NY. [pg. 21]

32. Big Dog, Lane, OR. Finnish translation: Panel 2) Griffy: "I can't speak Finnish!" Panel 4) Zippy: "Do you mind if I smoke?" Dog: "Goodbye!" [pg. 22]

33. Reddy Kilowatt, created by Ashton B. Collins, was originally the mascot for the Alabama Power Company in 1926. Willie Wirehand was the mascot of the National Rural Electric Cooperative Association, 1951. [pg. 22]

34. The author visited Cape Cod as a boy from 1946 to 1960. [pg. 22]

35. Recycled tire playground, Dan's Mountain State Park, Lonaconing, MD. [pg. 23]

36. Weyburn, Saskatchewan, Canada. [pg. 23]

37. Lendy's Restaurant chain, from 1955 to the mid-1970s, VA. The newly franchised Kentucky Fried Chicken was sold inside the restaurants. [pg. 23]

38. Panels 1-4) Truncated Muffler Man, Wilson's Carpet Outlet, Jersey City, NJ. Panel 3) A&W Root Beer "Pa," Zookie's Drive-In, Glen Falls, NY. [pg. 24]

39. Panels 1 & 2) Art Museum, Milwaukee, WI. Panel 3) Kingston, NY. [pg. 24]

40. Green Brook, NJ. [pg. 25]

41. Calgary, Alberta, Canada. [pg. 25]

42. Busts of Saddam Hussein, Baghdad, Iraq. [pg. 25]

ZIPPY SOLO Chapter 2

43 A-D. Z-Man is drawn in the styles of 1950s -1960s era Superman artists Curt Swan (1920-1996) and Wayne Boring (1905-1987). Donut Dip is located in Holyoke, MA. [pg. 28-29]

44. Ernie Bushmiller (1905-1982), created the enduringly sublime daily comic strip *Nancy* in 1938. He also wrote gags for movie comedian Harold Lloyd in the early 1930s. [pg. 29]

45 A-F. Zippy's take on the traditional Japanese haiku form. Abandoning the classical 17-syllable rule, Zippy still maintains the lyricism and "shock of recognition" elements. 45A) Puerto Montt, Chile. 45B) Honolulu, HI. 45C) "Large Bear" by Tom Otterness, Broadway and 96th St., New York, NY. 45D) 1931 Studebaker Roadster, South Bend, IN (destroyed). 45E) "King/Queen" by Tom Otterness, Broadway and 103rd St., New York, NY. 45F) "Kindly Gepetto" by Tom Otterness, Broadway and 95th St., New York, NY. [pg. 30-31]

46. Frederick, MD. [pg. 32]

47. The "Amphicar" was built in Germany from 1961 to 1968. Total production was 3,878 vehicles. The Amphicar is the only civilian amphibious passenger automobile ever to be mass produced. 3,046 Amphicars were imported into the United States between 1961 and 1967. The first "Aerocar" was built in 1949 by Moulton B. Taylor. Caleb Carr (b. 1955) is an American novelist and military historian. His books include *The Alienist, The Angel of Darkness* and *Killing Time*. He currently resides in upstate New York on a farm estate called "Misery Mountain." [pg. 33]

48 A-B. Horn and Hardart "Automats" were once the world's largest restaurant chain, feeding over 800,000 people a day. They

first appeared in Philadelphia in 1902. The last Automat closed in New York City in 1991. [pg. 34]

49. 1954 Chevrolet Bel-Air. [pg. 34]

50. From Berenice Abbott photographs of New York City, 1935. [pg. 35]

51. CBGB's, 315 Bowery, New York, NY. CBGB stands for: Country BlueGrass Blues. OMFUG stands for: Other Music For Uplifting Gourmandizers. [pg. 35]

52. Prospect Park, Brooklyn, NY. [pg. 35]

53. Boardwalk, Santa Cruz, CA. [pg. 36]

54. The Hostess Twinkie was created in 1930 by James Dewar. Twinkies originally contained a banana filling, but this was replaced with a vanilla filling during the great banana shortage of World War II. [pg. 36]

55. Seven Dwarfs Family Restaurant, Wheaton, IL. [pg. 37]

56. Luna Park, Sydney, Australia. [pg. 37]

57. Petula Clark (b. 1932) is a British singer and actress. Her 1960s hits included "Downtown" and "Don't Sleep in the Subway." In 1968, she starred opposite Fred Astaire in the film *Finian's Rainbow*. [pg. 38]

58. Translation from Finnish: Panel 1) There is no toilet paper in the bathroom! Panel 2) The window won't open! Panel 3) I'm leaving tomorrow! [pg. 38]

59. Boardwalk, Wildwood, NJ. [pg. 39]

60. From a photograph by Robert Doisneau (1912-1994), Paris, 1952. [pg. 39]

61. 1952 Crown bus. [pg. 40]

62. Mr. Met was the mascot of the New York Mets baseball team, first used in 1962. He is available for Bar/Bat Mitzvahs and weddings. [pg. 40]

63. Rhyolite, NV. [pg.40]

64 A-C. Sculpture by Tom Maley (1911-2000), Field Gallery, W. Tisbury, MA (Martha's Vineyard). [pg.41]

65. Delaware, OH. [pg. 42]

66. Noah's Ark Water Park, Dells, WI. [pg. 42]

67. Negro Leagues Baseball Museum, Kansas City, MO. Lyrics from the song, "Kansas City," by Lieber and Stoller, 1959. The tune was a number one hit for Wilbert Harrison in 1959. [pg. 42]

68. DK's Donuts, Manhattan, KS. [pg. 43]

69. The Pipe King, W. Sacramento, CA. [pg. 43]

ZIPPY & CO. Chapter 3

70. The Relay Club, Mare Island, CA. The "Jaws of Life" tool was invented in 1972 as an excavation tool for the race car industry. [pg. 48]

71. Zippy, Zerbina and the kids are shown riding the Steeple-chase mechanical horses at Coney Island, c. 1940. Kid's TV star Captain Kangaroo, Bob Keeshan, (1927-2004), hosted his famous series from 1955 to 1985. Keeshan had earlier played Clarabell the Clown on the popular Howdy Doody TV show from 1947 to 1952, when he was fired in a salary dispute. [pg. 49]

72. Dole Pineapple Canning plant, Honolulu, HI. [pg. 50]

73. Alamo Motel, Ocean City, MD. In 2003, a North Carolina-based company called Magnet America began selling its first batch of 1,000 patriotic "stickies" — yellow ribbon magnets with a "Support Our Troops" message in black. All profits went to Iraq-related charities. Today, Nesun Promotions, based in Changzhou, China, is one of the largest manufacturers of the common ribbon. All profits go to Nesun Promotions. [pg. 50]

74. Hawk Bowl, Rt. 122, Wisconsin. Blue Jay and Ebb Tide Motels, Wildwood, NJ. [pg. 50]

75. Kline's Freeze, Manassas, VA. [pg. 51]

76. Capitol Bowl, W. Sacramento, CA. [pg. 51]

77. Panels 1 and 2) Lebanon, TN. Panels 3 and 4) Gadsden, AL. La Toya Jackson (b. 1956) had a 1980 hit with "If You Feel The Funk." In 2004, she released "Free The World," her response to the 9/11 attacks. Other releases include "You Blew" 1988, and "Hot Potatoe" (sic), 1989. [pg. 52]

78. Top O' The Town Laundry, Dallas, TX. Martinizing Dry Cleaning centers are found all over the United States.They use the mysterious dry cleaning techniques developed by founder Henry Martin in 1949. [pg. 52]

79. Yummy Buffet, Madison, WI. [pg. 53]

80. Frog statue spotted in the lobby of the Campus Inn, Ann Arbor, MI. [pg. 54]

81. Firelite Shopping Center, Orange, CT. Band leader, composer and arranger Ray Conniff (1916-2002) was the easy-listening king of "supermarket music" in the 1950s-1960s. Just before his death in 2002, Conniff performed his 1966 hit "Somewhere My Love" at the wedding of David Gest and Liza Minnelli. Zippy is reciting song titles by The Ramones. [pg. 54]

82. Superdawg restaurant, Niles, IL (outside Chicago). Wolverine, introduced in 1974, is a member of Marvel Comics' X-Men team. He sports three-foot-long claws on each hand that retract into his forearms, and is anti-social. [pg. 55]

83. Boardwalk, Wildwood, NJ. [pg. 55]

84. August Strindberg (1849-1912), Swedish playwright, author of "Miss Julie" and "The Dance of Death." Phyllis Diller (b. 1917), comedienne, starred in a doomed 1966 TV sitcom titled *The Pruitts of Southhampton*. [pg. 55]

85. *The Devil Doll* (1936) is a film directed by Tod Browning (*Freaks*), starring Lionel Barrymore as a madman who shrinks people and animals to doll size to seek revenge on his business partners. [pg. 56]

86. The modern Quonset hut was first manufactured at the Davisville, RI, Naval Construction Battalion Center in 1941. The classic military model is made of corrugated steel sheets, formed in a semi-circle. [pg. 56]

87. Manga can trace their propensity for big, Keane-like eyes to the first hugely successful Japanese comic series, *Astroboy*, originated in 1952 by Osamu Tezuka (1928-1989). Astroboy is the American title for *Tetsuwan Atomu*, literally "Iron-arm atom," first broadcast on Japanese television from 1963 to 1966. [pg. 57]

SUNDAY COLOR Chapter 4

88. Colorado Springs, CO. [pg. 64]

89. Munson's Diner, 9th St. and 11th Ave. New York, NY. [pg. 64]

90. Studio Diner, San Diego, CA. [pg. 64]

91. The Donut Shop, Russells Point, OH. [pg. 65]

92. Happy Donuts, Palo Alto, CA. [pg. 65]

93. Shawmut Diner, New Bedford, MA. [pg. 65]

94. Castroville, CA. [pg. 66]

95. Sculptures by Philip Grausman. [pg. 66]

96. "Matter Contemplates Spirit" by Stephen Kaltenbach, Sacramento, CA. [pg. 66]

97. "Smile," 1936. Lyrics by John Turner & Geoffrey Parsons with music by Charlie Chaplin. The tune was a Billboard #10 hit for "Nat" King Cole in 1954. The song was originally from the film *Modern Times*, Charlie Chaplin, 1936. [pg. 67]

98. 1) Seattle Public Library/ Rem Koolhaas. 2) Tu Tower, Beijing, China/Rem Koolhaas. 3) Guggenheim Museum, Bilbao, Spain/ Frank Gehry. 4) Residence, Barcelona, Spain/ Frank Gehry 5) Denver Art Museum /Rem Koolhaas. [pg. 67]

99. E. Haddam, CT. The 1/4 scale train line was built by actor William Gillette (1853-1937) and was called the Seventh Sister Short Line. [pg. 67]

100. "Yoo-Hoo" chocolate beverages began production in the early 1920s. One of its original slogans was "Me-Hee for Yoo-Hoo," popularized by New York Yankees catcher and philosopher Yogi Berra. [pg. 68]

101. Barboursville, WV. [pg. 68]

102. Amador County, CA. [pg. 69]

103. Roanoke, VA. [pg. 69]

104. Keoki's Surfin' Ass, Kona, HI. [pg. 70]

105. "Natural Hawaiian Island Stone," near Honolulu Airport, HI. [pg. 70]

106. "Gertie the Goldfish," c. 1955, Marathon, FL. [pg. 71]

107. "Blondie" was created by Murat Bernard "Chic" Young in 1930. It is now continued by his son, Dean Young. Before she married Dagwood Bumstead in 1933, Blondie's name was Blondie Boopadoop. [pg. 71]

108. Einstein statue, Byron Bay, Australia. The "Wonderbra" was introduced to the U.S. in 1994 and was called the "Ferrari of push-up bras." [pg. 72]

109. Panels 1 & 4) Einstein Statue, Washington D.C. Panels 2 & 3) Coke Man, Sabrevois, Quebec, Canada. [pg.72]

110. Mermaid Sports Bar, Mounds View, MN. [pg. 73]

111. Parody of the paintings of the big-eyed art of Walter Keane (1915-2000), most of which were actually painted by his wife Margaret Keane (proven by her at a "Paint-Off" in San Francisco in 1970). As a child in Lincoln, Nebraska, Walter sold shoes door-to-door. [pg. 73]

112. "#24" by Stuart Padnos, Grand Rapids, MI. [pg. 74]

113. McLean High School, Terre Haute, IN. [pg. 75]

114. Zippy is singing "Dawn" by the Four Seasons, 1964 (Frankie Valli, original lead singer). Wildwood, NJ. [pg. 76]

115. "Crying Giant" by Tom Otterness, 117th St. and Broadway, New York, NY. [pg. 77]

DINERAMA Chapter 5

116. Club Diner, Belmawr, NJ. [pg. 80]

117. The New Floridian Diner, Brooklyn, NY. In Ronald Reagan's autobiography, "Where's the Rest of Me?" (1965), he never mentioned his first wife, Jane Wyman. [pg. 80]

118. Café Dining Cars, Buellton, CA, now abandoned. The "café" consisted of two Los Angeles streetcars from 1914 and 1916. *Sideways* (2004) starred Paul Giamatti and Thomas Hayden Church. [pg. 80]

119. Truckee Diner, Truckee, CA. [pg. 81]

120. Panels 1 & 3) Rosebud Diner, Somerville, MA. Panel 2) United Gas Station (abandoned), somewhere in Indiana. [pg. 81]

121. Flames Coffee Shop, San Jose, CA. [pg. 81]

122. Joe's Diner, Reno, NV. [pg. 82]

123. 54 Diner, Buena, NJ. Diner slang translated: Panel 1) Oysters rolled in bacon on toast with pea soup, topped with ice cream. Panel 2) Jell-o with syrup and butter and toasted English muffin. Panel 3) Glass of water, add chocolate syrup, ketchup and hash. [pg. 82]

124. Littleton Diner, Littleton, NH. [pg. 82]

125. Sunny Day Diner, Lincoln, NH. [pg. 83]

126A-B. Shawmut Diner, New Bedford, MA. [pg. 83]

127. Texas Tavern, Roanoke, VA. [pg. 84]

128. Frank's Diner, Jessup, MD. [pg. 84]

129. Famous Lunch, Troy, NY. Their Zippy Sauce has been described as containing paprika with discernible chunks of onion and herbs, possibly thyme and oregano. The complete recipe is awaiting a Congressional investigation. [pg. 84]

130. Abandoned diner in a field, Westport, MA. Zippy parodies Walt Whitman's "O Captain! My Captain!," written as a dirge for Abraham Lincoln in 1865. [pg. 85]

131. Farina Family Diner (formerly Yankee Diner), Quechee, VT. The ingredients of a French Dip sandwich include: thinly sliced Italian roast beef doused in beef broth with oregano, garlic, basil, crushed red pepper and bay leaf on a French roll, Cheez Whiz optional. [pg. 85]

132. The Middle Of Nowhere Diner, Exeter, RI. [pg. 85]

133. O'Rourke's Diner, Middletown, CT. Justin Davisson's unmailed letter to the author is quoted. It appears in the book *Found: The Best Lost, Tossed, and Forgotten Items from Around the World* by Davy Rothbart. [pg. 86]

134. Donut Castle, Winchester, VA. [pg. 86]

135. Skee's Diner, Torrington, CT. [pg. 87]

136. Boston Trolley Diner, Hudson, MA. [pg. 87]

137. Schuyler Diner, Lyndhurst, NJ. [pg. 87]

138. Truck Stop Diner, Kearney, NJ. [pg. 88]

139. Truck Stop Diner, Winchester, VA. [pg. 88]

140. Tommy's Diner, Middletown, RI. [pg. 88]

141. John's Plain and Fancy Diner, Quakertown, PA. [pg. 89]

142. Mollie's Diner, Snowville, UT. [pg. 89]

143. The Roost, Baltimore, MD. [pg. 89]

ROADSIDE ATTRACTIONS Chapter 6

144. Kittanning, PA. [pg. 92]

145. Panel 1) Livermore, CA. Panel 2) San Jose, CA. Panel 3) Russian River area, CA. Panel 4) Willits, CA. [pg. 92]

146. Longmont, CO. [pg. 93]

147. Panel 1) Oshkosh, WI. Panel 2) Muncie, IN. Panels 3 & 4) Amador County, CA. Latin translation: This is the declension of the irregular demonstrative pronoun *hic* (this). [pg. 93]

148. Wisconsin Dells, WI. [pg. 94]

149. Metairie, LA. [pg. 94]

150. Werbany Tire Town, Gloucester Township, NJ. [pg. 94]

151. Farmington, NM. [pg. 95]

152. Cowboy Henk topiary by Peter Van Heirseele, Kortrijk, Netherlands. Belgian artist James Ensor (1860-1949) painted grotesque clowns, skeletons and expressionistic masked figures. His work presaged Surrealism and Dadaism. Ed "Big Daddy" Roth (1932-2001) was a Southern California custom car builder and creator of the Rat Fink character. [pg. 95]

153. Shopping center, Melbourne, Australia. There are no Guernica bedsheets (yet), but see "DOOMED TO REPEAT IT," pg. 13, for the Guernica dress. [pg. 95]

154. Philip Grausman sculptures, Newburgh, NY. [pg. 96]

155. Philip Grausman sculptures, campus of Pratt Institute, Brooklyn, NY. Quote in panel 3 is from Walt Whitman's poem, "Crossing Brooklyn Ferry." [pg. 96]

156. "Artist," metal sculpture by Louise Stanley, Emeryville, CA. [pg. 96]

157. Madison, WI. [pg. 97]

158. "Crying Giant" by Tom Otterness, Broadway and 117th Street, New York, NY. See also pg. 115. [pg. 97]

159. Panels 1 & 3) Robin Hood, Princeton, IN. Panel 2) Uniroyal Woman, Peoria, IL. [pg. 97]

160. Bedford County, PA. [pg. 98]

161. Pizza John, Essex, MD. [pg. 98]

162. The Golden Driller, Tulsa, OK. [pg. 98]

163. Sculptures by Gary Greff, Regent, ND. [pg. 99]

164. Phoenix, AZ. [pg. 99]

165. San Jose, CA. Hopalong Cassidy was the wild west hero of dozens of books by Clarence E. Mulford (1883-1956). "Hoppy" was portrayed in film and on TV by actor William Boyd. As Hoppy, Boyd endorsed over 2,400 products in the 1950s. [pg. 99]

166. Boardwalk, Atlantic City, NJ. [pg. 100]

167. Sacramento, CA. Among other things, physicist Richard Feynman (1918-1988) also helped develop the atomic bomb. A teaspoonful of white dwarf material would weigh about as much as 100 elephants. [pg. 100]

168. "Big Louie," Barnum, MN. [pg. 100]

169. New Virginia, IA. [pg. 101]

170. Civic Center, Duluth, GA. [pg. 101]

171A-C. Big John statue, Highway 61, south of Memphis, TN. 95A) Lyric: "Crossroad Blues" by Robert Johnson (1911-1938). 95B) Mentos (breath mints) commercial lyrics. 95C) Theme song lyrics from *The Patty Duke Show* (1963-1966), alternating with the lyrics to "Woke Up This Morning" by Alabama 3, the theme song of the *Sopranos* TV show (1999-present). [pgs. 101-102]

172. Clown head haunted house, Fremont, OH. For sale on ebay 1/7/05. Asking price, $35,000. [pg. 102]

173. Happy Harry's Drugstore, Hockessin, DE. [pg. 103]

174. Former brewery (now condos), Baltimore, MD. Face is of Mr. Boh, mascot of Natty Boh beer. Esky, was the monocled, horny little mascot of *Esquire* magazine. He was created in 1933 by cartoonist E. Simms Campbell (1908-1971). [pg. 103]

175. Warren, RI. [pg. 103]

176. Mannequins, Sydney and Darwin Australia department stores. [pg. 104]

177. 90 West St., New York, NY. The head really is of Peter Levenson, one of the building's owners. Made by Boston Valley Terra Cotta Co. [pg. 104]

178. Goofy Golf, Panama City Beach, FL. [pg. 105]

179. Sydney, Australia. [pg. 105]

180. Kakadu National Park, Northern Territories, Australia. [pg. 105]

181. Bryson, TN. The Strawberry Alarm Clock recorded their big hit, "Incense and Peppermints," in 1967. The record's B side was "Birdman of Alkatrash." [pg. 106]

182. Den Haag, Netherlands. c. 1915. [pg. 106]

183. E. Windsor, CT. [pg. 106]

184. Sanrio store, 42nd St., New York, NY. [pg. 107]

185. Australia. 1 & 3) Sydney. 2) Gosford. [pg. 107]

186. Denver, CO. Sculpture by Lawrence Argent. [pg. 107]

187. New Haven, CT. [pg. 108]

188. Darwin, Australia. [pg. 108]

189. Whale painted by Jon Buller as part of the "Whale Trail," a charity event in Lyme, CT. [pg. 108]

190. MGM Grand Hotel, Las Vegas, NV. [pg. 109]

191. Ohakune, New Zealand. [pg. 109]

192. Van Nuys, CA. [pg. 109]

193. Boardwalk, Wildwood, NJ. [pg. 110]

194. Boardwalk, Wildwood, NJ. [pg. 110]

195. The Pickle Barrel House, Grand Marais, MI. Built in 1926, this was the summer home of William Donahey (1883-1970), who created the comic feature, *The Teenie Weenies* (1912-1970). The home was a gift to Donahey from Reid, Murdock Co., manufacturer of "Teenie Weenie Sweet Pickles." [pg. 110]

196. Asbury Park, NJ. The Goo Goo Dolls, an "adult alternative rock band" from Buffalo, NY, was founded in 1985. Their original name was the Sex Maggots. [pg. 111]

197. The Modernaire Motel, York, PA. When The Modernaires vocal group (formed in 1935) worked with the Ozzie Nelson Band, they were known as The Three Wizards of Ozzie. [pg. 111]

198. 7th Ave. and 39th St., New York, NY. [pg. 111]

199. Sandusky, OH. [pg. 112]

200. Butch's Drive-In, Dos Pasos, CA. [pg. 112]

201. Somewhere in India. [pg. 112]

202. Boardwalk, Santa Cruz, CA. [pg. 113]

203. Vets Liquor, College Park, MD. [pg. 113]

204. "House" by Roy Lichtenstein (1923-1997), National Gallery Sculpture Garden, Wash. DC. [pg. 113]

205. Typewriter Eraser by Claes Oldenburg and Coosje Van Bruggen, National Gallery Sculpture Garden, Wash. DC. [pg. 114]

206. Roadside Attraction artists Christo Javacheff (b. 1935) and Jeanne Claude Denat de Guillebon (b. 1935) installed 7,500 nylon-draped "gates" in New York's Central Park in February 2004. Of their previous Key Biscayne Florida project, Christo said, "Most journalists do not understand the difference between wrapping and surrounding even though they should know that the United Kingdom is surrounded by water, it is not wrapped in water." Each year, over 100,000 New Yorkers experience homelessness. [pg. 114]

207. Santa Cruz, CA. [pg. 114]

208. Cereality really is a chain of breakfast cereal restaurants in the U.S., but it does not serve Valvoline. [pg. 115]

209. Hilo, HI. [pg. 115]

210. Oslo, Norway. Norwegian translation: "Tusen takk" is "Thank you very much." [pg. 115]

211. Milan, NY. New York Yankees catcher Yogi Berra (b. 1925) once said, "When you come to a fork in the road, take it." [pg. 116]

212. Minneapolis, MN. Sculpture by Claes Oldenburg and Coosje Van Bruggen. [pg. 116]

213. "Brushstroke" by Roy Lichtenstein (1923-1997), National Gallery Sculpture Garden, Wash. DC. [pg. 116]

214. Betty Boop was created for the Fleischer Brothers Studios in 1930 by animator Grim Natwick (1890-1990). For almost all of her screen career, she was voiced by Mae Questel (1908-1998). The Fleischer brothers always insisted, oddly, that Betty was only 16 years old. [pg. 117]

215. Brown Shoe Co., St. Louis, MO. Sculpture by Victoria Fuller. [pg. 117]

216. Mama Burger, A&W Root Beer Family member, Joshua Trees, CA. [pg. 117]

217. Hugh Mongous, Ocean Breeze Water Park, Virginia Beach, VA. Hugh and Zippy quote the lyrics to Muddy Waters' "I'm Ready," 1954. [pg. 118]

218. Manhattan, KS. [pg. 118]

219. Madison, WI. Physicist and author Brian Greene (b. 1963) is a prominent string theorist and college professor. He also contributed scientific dialogue to the John Lithgow character in the TV show, *Third Rock From the Sun*. [pg. 118]

220. Bourne, MA. [pg. 119]

221. Bus stop, Ishaya City, Japan. [pg. 119]

222. Chauncey St. subway station, Brooklyn, NY. In the *Honeymooners* TV show (1955-1956), Ralph and Alice Kramden lived on Chauncey Street. Trixie and Ed Norton were their upstairs neighbors. [pg. 119]

223. Panels 1 & 2) Amtowers Hilltop Collision Center, Keyser, WV. Panel 3) Hugo's Skating, Morrisville, VA. [pg. 120]

224. City Hall Park, New York, NY. [pg. 120]

225. Scottish Rite Temple, Mobile, AL. The sphinx is referring to 2005's Hurricane Katrina. [pg. 121]

226. Santa Rosa, CA (home of *Peanuts* creator Charles Schulz [1922-2000]). [pg. 121]

227. Sculpture by Tom Otterness, Hudson River Park, New York, NY. [pg. 121]

228. Burbank, CA. [pg. 122]

229. Shillington, PA. [pg. 122]

230. "Gigante" figures, Las Ramblas, Barcelona, Spain. Spanish translation: "Hello, Zippy! I am a Gigante! Ask me anything." [pg. 122]

231. Calgary, Alberta, Canada. [pg. 123]

232. Cadet Restaurant, Kittanning, PA. [pg. 123]

233. Sorrento, Italy. [pg. 123]

ALSO AVAILABLE FROM FANTAGRAPHICS

ANNUAL
ZIPPY
No. 1

ZIPPY ANNUAL NO. 1 (2000)
160 pages, color + black and white, softcover
$22.00 postpaid

ANNUAL
ZIPPY
2001

ZIPPY ANNUAL 2001
144 pages, color + black and white, softcover
$22.00 postpaid

ANNUAL
ZIPPY
by Bill Griffith
2002

ZIPPY ANNUAL 2002
128 pages, color + black and white, softcover
$22.00 postpaid

ANNUAL
ZIPPY
2003

ZIPPY ANNUAL 2003
128 pages, color + black and white, softcover
$22.00 postpaid

ZIPPY
From here to absurdity
Bill Griffith

ZIPPY: FROM HERE TO ABSURDITY (2005)
128 pages, color + black and white, softcover
$22.00 postpaid

Are We Having Fun Yet?
Zippy the Pinhead's
29 Day Guide To Random Activities and Arbitrary Donuts

ARE WE HAVING FUN YET?
128 pages, black and white, softcover / $15.00 postpaid

ZIPPY'S HOUSE OF FUN
FULL COLOR!!
54 MONTHS OF SUNDAYS
FANTAGRAPHICS BOOKS

ZIPPY'S HOUSE OF FUN
152 pages, full color, hardcover / $40.00 postpaid

Griffith Observatory
The Classic Strips from 1977-1980 with 16 previously uncollected pages by Bill Griffith
FANTAGRAPHICS BOOKS
Stupidity Patrol
The Doomsters
Religious Nuts
Media Addicts
Street Crazies

GRIFFITH OBSERVATORY
48 pages, black and white, magazine / $6.00 postpaid

"Get me a table without flies, Harry."
Travel Sketches by BILL GRIFFITH

"GET ME A TABLE WITHOUT FLIES, HARRY." TRAVEL SKETCHES
160 pages, black and white, softcover / $17.00 postpaid

Zippy
Zippy
No. 17
ZIPPY'S FAVORITE!
FANTAGRAPHICS BOOKS

ZIPPY QUARTERLY
15 available issues (#'s 10,13 & 18 out of print), 32-48 pages, black and white, magazines / $4.50 each postpaid
Special: All available issues PLUS *Griffith Observatory* $49.95 postpaid

TO ORDER CALL 1-800-657-1100, WRITE FANTAGRAPHICS AT 7563 LAKE CITY WAY N.E. SEATTLE, WA 98115, OR CHECK OUR WEBSITE AT WWW.FANTAGRAPHICS.COM

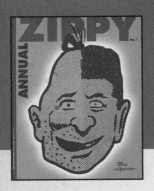

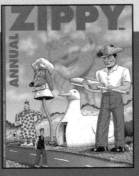

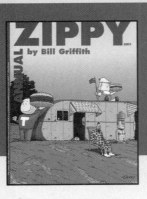

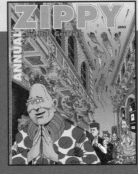

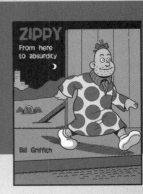

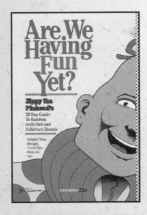

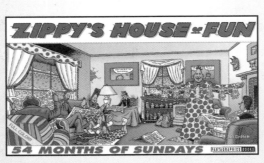

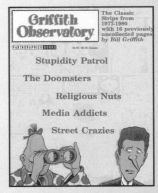

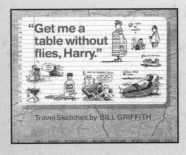

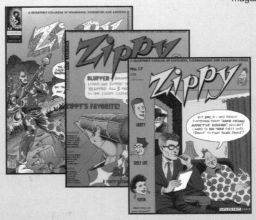